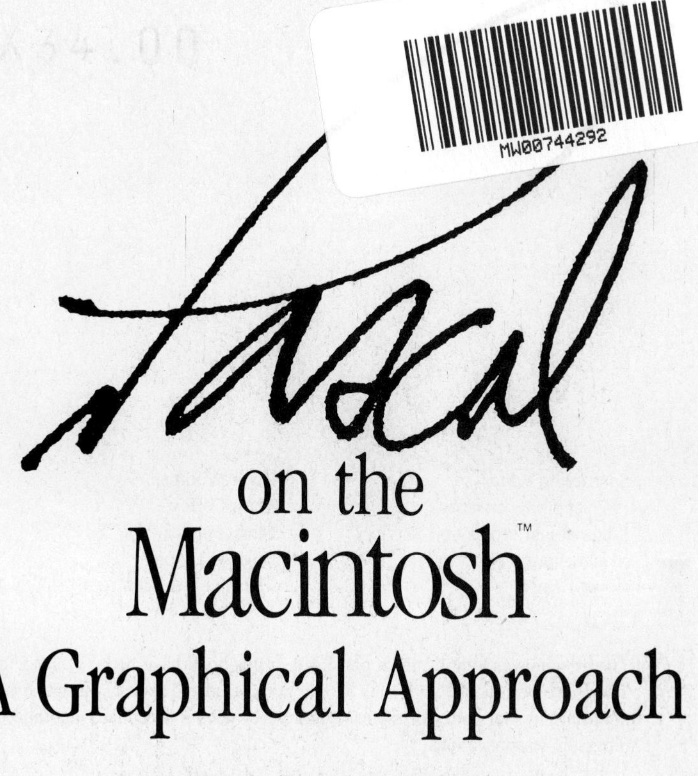

on the Macintosh™ A Graphical Approach

David A. Niguidula • Andries van Dam

Brown University

Addison-Wesley Publishing Company

Reading, Massachusetts • Menlo Park, California
Don Mills, Ontario • Wokingham, England • Amsterdam
Sydney • Singapore • Tokyo • Madrid • Bogotá • Santiago • San Juan

Sponsoring Editor Keith Wollman
Production Supervisor Mary Coffey
Editorial and Production Services Nancy Wirtes
Manufacturing Supervisor Hugh Crawford
Cover Design Marshall Henrichs

The programs and applications presented in this book have been included for their instructional value. They have been tested with care but are not guaranteed for any particular purpose. The publisher does not offer any warranties or representations, nor does it accept any liabilities with respect to the programs or applications

Library of Congress Cataloging-in-Publication Data
Niguidula, David A.
Pascal on the Macintosh.

On t.p. the registered trademark symbol "TM" is superscript following "Macintosh" in the title.
Includes index.
1. Macintosh (Computer) — Programming. 2. PASCAL (Computer program language) I. van Dam, Andries, 1938- . II. Title.
QA76.8.M3N54 1987 005.265 86-20668
ISBN 0-201-16588-0

Macintosh is a trademark licensed to Apple Computer, Inc. Many of the designations used by manufacturers and sellers to designate thier products are claimed as trademarks. Where those designations appear in this book and Addison-Wesley was aware of a trademark claim, the designations have been printed in caps or initial caps.

Reprinted with corrections May, 1988

7 8 9 10 HA 9594939291

Preface

If you look around, you'll find dozens of other books with "Pascal" in the title. A smaller, but still sizable, number of titles also include the word "Macintosh." So what's so special about the book you're holding? We believe it's a unique combination of features — some tried and true, some brand new — that sets us apart.

Pascal on the Macintosh: A Graphical Approach is an introductory textbook on programming, problem solving, and applications in Pascal for Macintosh users. The book covers the topics listed in the ACM's recommended curriculum for the introductory course for computer science majors (CS1) and in the Educational Testing Service's guidelines for the Advanced Placement Course in Computer Science. To provide the option of covering some advanced topics, this book covers more material than would normally be completed in one semester.

The book is based on Macintosh Pascal and Lightspeed Pascal software, but readers who complete it will be able to use Pascal on any machine. We take full advantage of these software packages' debugging and formatting facilities and designate which features are standard and which are specific to Macs. (Throughout the book, the term "MacPascal" refers to both Macintosh Pascal and Lightspeed Pascal unless noted otherwise.)

Readers are not expected to have any background with computers. They also need no more of a mathematical background than high school algebra and geometry. Readers are, however, expected to be comfortable using Cartesian coordinates and working with simple equations.

The subtitle, *A Graphical Approach*, implies two things that make our book special. First, the book has an interactive graphics orientation. The emphasis in the book is on using graphics to introduce students to programming in Pascal, rather than on the technical aspects of graphics programming. In our experience, we have found that using graphics in programming assignments is a more effective teaching tool than the traditional technique of assigning number- and character-crunching programs. Graphics programs are easier to debug, provide more satisfying results, and are simply more fun, but can be as technically sophisticated as more traditional assignments. By the end of the book, students should have enough of a background in graphics to write graphical programs such as simple educational and recreational video games.

Second, computer science instructors have noted that students learn by seeing concepts illustrated graphically and by hand simulating code in addition to reading text. We have taken this advice to heart. Among the 300-plus illustrations are sequences of snapshots illustrating concepts that are difficult to explain and understand, such as loops, linked lists, and binary trees. Over 50 pages of code examples give students an opportunity to see complete, well-documented programs. In addition, the book contains close to 500 exercises.

We believe our book has broad appeal. Humanities students who want only one semester of computer science should find the book as relevant and as easy to use as hardcore computer addicts who plan on spending the rest of their college careers in CS courses. In either case, students who finish the book will be able to solve problems through decomposition, read Pascal code and understand what it is doing, and, of course, write applications with approved programming style and user-interface techniques.

Concept Format

We have attempted to use a consistent approach when presenting concepts, and throughout, we have used problem solving as a central theme. First, we open each chapter with a transition/motivation section. Typically, we state a problem and show how the material covered thus far either does not solve or inefficiently solves the problem. We then introduce the concept that satisfactorily solves the problem (e.g., we could declare hundreds of separate real variables, but it would be better to use an array).

Second, we introduce the syntax and semantics of new statements or data structures and show examples that solve the problem stated in the transition/motivation section. The book contains nearly 100 *syntax boxes*, which are stylized guides to each of the Pascal and graphics statements. These standardized boxes are incorporated directly into the text.

Third, we present a complete discussion of the concept, including:

- Use of the concept in the design/pseudocode process; preventive maintenance
- Problems in using the statement or data structure; how to debug such problems using MacPascal and Lightspeed facilities
- Use of the concept to make programs more user friendly (e.g., what sort of graphics make a good interface)
- Documentation and clean methods of coding the concept to make the program easily readable by other programmers

Fourth, almost every chapter contains an example program where theory is put into practice. We take the reader through problems, step by step, as we proceed from stated question to programmed solution. A problem is stated and broken down; levels of pseudocode are shown along with the entire program as it appears on the Mac. Each program reinforces concepts that have been seen earlier, and shows an example of how the new concept is used. We also thoroughly document these example programs.

Finally, each chapter concludes with a summary, exercises, and programming problems. There are three types of exercises: **Understanding Concepts**, which test comprehension of material with short-answer questions; **Coding Exercises**, which test specific programming concepts with "write a procedure" or "modify this code" questions; and **Programming Problems**, which test overall programming ability with open-ended "write a program" questions.

Our Background

Every few years, the introductory computer science course taught by Andy van Dam at Brown undergoes major surgery. In 1983, Brown's new "electronic classroom" containing 55 Apollo DN/300 workstations was opened. Three undergraduate teaching assistants started developing a new version of the course, using the machines and the Brown Algorithm Simulator and Animator (BALSA), an innovative software system for the Apollos developed by Professor Bob Sedgewick and Marc Brown. The group developed a number of graphical simulations that allow students to learn from animated examples in conjunction with the standard lecture. In addition, students learned how to incorporate the rudiments of interactive computer graphics into their own assignments.

To accompany the lectures and the simulations, an early draft of this book was created by a student group, coordinated by David Niguidula, during the summer of 1983. The first group of students to have both the book and the BALSA simulations as resources responded positively to the entire course in general and to the book in particular, encouraging us to continue revising and refining.

While our experience in developing the book for the Apollos was helpful, the book was started fresh for the Macintosh. The primary writing took place during the fall and winter of 1985, and the book was extensively revised throughout 1986 to respond to feedback from class testing of the manuscript and to suggestions provided by academic reviewers.

Acknowledgments

Brown's Computer Science Department enjoys a reputation for being experimental and innovative, and for allowing undergraduates to take an active role in the design and implementation of introductory courses. This book, as well as the course for which it is used, exists because of the dedicated involvement of many people, almost all of whom were undergraduates at the time of their participation in the project. We wish to show our gratitude for their efforts by acknowledging their work.

The original idea for the book came from Dave Nanian and Susie Galvin, and an early version was first used in a summer course taught by Perry Busalacchi, Karen Smith, and Liz Waymire (who also implemented the first BALSA demos). Felicia Gershberg, Bill Petty, Jenny Richlin, and Mason Woo contributed to outlining, developing, editing, and proofreading the book's early drafts.

Two other individuals were of great assistance in the development of the book for the Apollos. Janine "J9" Roeth spent hundreds of hours creating and checking dozens of diagrams and code examples, many of which have been adapted for use here. The first drafts probably would not have been possible without Karen Seiler's writing and moral support; we are particularly indebted to her work on what is now Chapter 14.

The Macintosh version of the book had its first test run in a section of the introductory course led by David Block and Leslie McCall; they turned into practice the theory of a graphical approach tuned for the Macintosh. We also greatly appreciate the reviews we received from the students in that section and from academic reviewers: Steven Eisenbarth (Baylor University), Morris W. Firebaugh (University of Wisconsin, Parkside), Douglas Harms (The Ohio State University), Michael S. Hennessy (University of Oregon), William J. Keane (Boston College), Jeffrey L. Popyack (Drexel University), and Robert E. Reynolds (Reed College). We have taken to heart all the points raised in these reviews, and think that the result is considerably improved because of the students' and professors' comments.

Throughout the project, Keith Wollman of Addison-Wesley has been extremely supportive and has patiently kept us up to date and listened to our ideas. In the later drafts of the manuscript, Trina Avery graced this work with her typically superb editing and proofreading skills and provided the needed sanity checks. Members of the staff at THINK Technologies helped to point us in the proper directions when we had questions about the software. The Addison-Wesley production crew, including Mary Coffey, Nancy Wirtes, Prentice Hastings, and the folks at Graphic Typesetting Service have done a terrific job of creating a complete volume from its hundreds of parts.

Many other individuals have contributed in signficant ways. A special thanks to Eric Wolf, Jeff Vroom, Debbie Scott, James Rinzler, Debbie Lewart, Beth

Grossman, and the hundreds of undergraduate teaching assistants and students who have worked with the book in its previous incarnations. Our families and friends have had to put up with our "writing moods"; we thank them for their patience and encouragement.

Finally, we want to acknowledge one other, special individual. Amy Elizabeth Tozer has been an integral part of the project since its inception. For four years, she has done whatever needed doing from filling in missing paragraphs to showing how the book can best be used in teaching; in the Macintosh version, she has checked exercises, made backup copies, provided artwork, written and tested programs, and performed uncountable other tasks. For her willingness to take on jobs above and beyond the call, and for her persistent belief that some good was coming of all this, we are extraordinarily grateful.

How to Use This Book

We have examined what we think separates our book from the competition, taking the instructor's point of view. What also sets us apart is the combination of assumptions and expectations we have about you, the reader. We assume that you own, or have access to, an Apple Macintosh computer and Pascal software that you want to learn to use effectively. We do not, however, assume you have any programming experience. For that matter, we don't assume you have touched a Macintosh or any other computer before. (The Primer provides an introduction to the machine: you can skip it if you are already familiar with Macintosh software.)

We do not assume you are mathematically inclined. If you remember the basics of high school algebra and geometry — e.g., using variables in equations and dealing with Cartesian $(x - y)$ coordinates — you have all the math you need to know. In our analogies and examples, we show how programming concepts are similar to ideas that span the curricular spectrum.

We expect you are using this book in conjunction with a college or secondary-school course. However, it could also be used as a tutorial or for independent study.

Above all, we expect you don't want to memorize a set of program-creation "formulas" by rote; we assume you want to learn to use the computer as a flexible tool for solving problems. It is not enough to create a working program; to use our approach effectively, you must think about the requirements of the problem, the way in which it can be broken down and structured, the purpose of a program's pieces, and then determine how to write the Pascal instructions that implement those pieces. We provide an intellectual framework for problem solving, and we hope our analogies, examples, figures, and reference materials will assist you in visualizing the process. It is still ultimately your responsibility to think about problem solving, to design a strategy for your own use, and to fully comprehend the concepts we present. In short, this book — like the computer, the software and even your instructor — is merely an educational tool. It is up to you to do the learning.

Formatting and Notation

A number of notations are used throughout this text. ***Bold italics*** indicate segments of Pascal code and options on the various Macintosh menus. **Boldface** designates various items on the Mac display, such as menu options, and "reserved words" or "word symbols" (listed in Appendix A), which are the words MacPascal's "pretty printing" (the feature that displays your program) automatically puts in boldface. *Italics* introduce new terms and phrases, emphasize certain points, and denote certain algebraic expressions. The `Courier` font indicates data files and other particular inputs and outputs.

Many of the figures in this book are pictures of windows that come from runs of various programs using Macintosh Pascal, version 2.0, or Lightspeed Pascal, version 1.0.

A unique characteristic of this book is the use of syntax boxes. Syntax boxes summarize Pascal statements, declarations, and definitions. The following is an example of a syntax box:

Syntax Box Example **case**

Purpose To execute one of any number of mutually exclusive statements, depending on the value of an expression.

Syntax

```
case < selector > of
     < value 1 >:
          < statement 1 >;
     < value 2 >:
          < statement 2 >;
     ...
     < value n >:
          < statement n >[;]
[    otherwise
          < statement n+1 >]
end; {case}
```

where < selector > is an expression of type ***integer*** or ***char***, or an enumerated type.* < value 1 >, < value 2 >,...,< value *n* > are single integers or characters, or groups of integers or characters separated by commas.

< statement 1 >, < statement 2 >,...,< statement *n* >, < statement *n*+1 > are legal Pascal statements. If more than one statement is used, then the statement block must be surrounded by **begin/end** brackets.

Usage The < selector > is evaluated to a single value. If one of the values < value 1 >, < value 2 >,..., < value *n* > matches < selector >, then the corresponding < statement > is executed. If < selector > does not match any of the listed values, < statement *n*+1 > (following the **otherwise**) is executed.

Only one of the statements in the **case** construct will be performed.

Note that the **end**; of the **case** construct does not have a corresponding **begin**.

The **otherwise** clause is optional.

---

* Characters are examined in Chapter 8, enumerated types in Chapter 13.

The parts of the syntax box are summarized in the following "generic syntax box." Because the syntax boxes are reference tools, they may refer to constructs or data types that have not yet been explained. When a box is introduced, however, you will have learned enough to use the construct in your own programs. Some syntax boxes do not follow this format; they explain in more detail a Pascal concept or syntax.

Generic Syntax Box
Title

Purpose	To describe how the instruction is generally used
Syntax	Tells exactly how the statement is typed into the computer.
where	Items in **bold** are typed in literally. Items in angle brackets (< >) are replaced with your program's variables, constants, or expressions, as explained here. Items in square brackets ([ ]) are optional. Unless they appear in **bold**, the brackets are not a part of the instruction and should not be typed into the program.
Returns	(Not shown in the example) Some Pascal instructions, called functions, perform an operation and give a result. The **Returns** section indicates what type of result the function will yield.
Usage	Summarizes how Pascal interprets the instruction, when you may want to use it, and any special conditions that it may have. Items in angle brackets refer to the same items in the **Syntax** section.

D.A.N.
A.v.D.
Providence, Rhode Island

Contents

Primer: A Painless Introduction to the Macintosh

Caution: Read This Introduction!

To start you on the road to Macintosh proficiency, we have included several hands-on exercises here, in Chapter 1, and in Appendix E. These hands-on sections are designed to help you get acquainted with the Macintosh computer (Mac for short) and the Macintosh Pascal and Lightspeed Pascal software. We could tell you that everything you could ever want to know about these software packages is contained in these pages, but that wouldn't be realistic. Unfortunately, we cannot cover every possibility that you may encounter. We want to emphasize that you'll be able to follow our instructions far more often than not, but we have to warn you about the places where differences may exist. (Note that to get you started, we have to use a lot of terminology. For now, we will tell you enough to begin using your Macintosh; we will provide more complete definitions in Chapter 1.)

Hardware. When we tested our hands-on sections, we used the simplest configuration of hardware: Macintoshes with 128 or 512 kilobytes of memory and keyboards and mice. We also ran additional tests with external, single-sided floppy disk drives. If you are using a system connected to a network, that runs with a hard disk, that uses double-sided disk drives or other peripheral equipment, you will find a few minor differences between our explanation and what you can do with your equipment. To determine how to make the best use of your peripheral hardware, you should consult your manuals or your instructor before starting our hands-on exercises. (By the way, these peripherals will undoubtedly make your life easier when you begin programming.)

Pascal software. In this book, we discuss both Macintosh Pascal (also known as MacPascal) and Lightspeed Pascal. Lightspeed contains all of the features of MacPascal plus many more. Thus, unless we specifically say so, you should assume that anything that can be done in MacPascal can also be done in Lightspeed. The major difference between the two is the amount of time required to get started: Lightspeed requires quite a bit more effort, but is more powerful, particularly for larger programs. Thus, while you will see a number of differences in the early stages of this book, you will see fewer differences later.

Other software. When you work with a computer, you don't just work with one piece of software. For example, you work with an operating system called the Finder, various menu options, and other facilities. These software tools are useful for most Macintosh applications. The good news about Macintosh software tools is that they are flexible and are easily improved and updated. The bad news is that when things are improved, they don't always work the way they used to. What does this mean to you? Well, depending on the versions of the tools your system is using, you may find that our figures aren't identical to what you see on the screen. Specifically, the menus and dialog boxes may look different, although they convey the same information as what we show in our figures.

The unexpected. Suppose you have completed half of one of our hands-on exercises when suddenly the power goes out. You may not be able to start over again from the very beginning. If you find yourself bewitched, bothered, and bewildered, don't worry; just keep two things in mind. First, you cannot do any damage to your machine by pressing keys or moving the mouse. Second, there is always someone around — a resident "guru" at your school, office, or local dealership — who can get you back on the right track.

If you have previous Mac experience, you will find many similarities between the use of Pascal and the use of other software packages. However, if you are just getting started with Macs (or computers, for that matter), you may find the information in the hands-on exercises overwhelming. Relax and take your time. Soon, much of this detail will become second nature.

One final note. The vast majority of topics in this book are not software- or hardware-specific. The principles of Pascal, programming, and problem solving are applicable to most situations.

The rest of this primer is intended for those of you who have never used a Macintosh computer. If you have used any application on the Mac (such as MacPaint or MacWrite), skip the rest of the primer. Here, we will discuss the basic manipulation of the Mac; we'll leave the specifics of Pascal for Chapter 1 and beyond.

What You Should Have

We assume you have access to a Macintosh with a keyboard and a mouse. If you are planning on using Lightspeed Pascal, make sure that you are using a Macintosh with at least 512 kilobytes (512K) of memory. MacPascal will work on Macs with at least 128 kilobytes (128K) of memory.

We also assume you have Macintosh Pascal or Lightspeed Pascal disks. MacPascal is packaged on two disks: a system disk and a utilities disk. Lightspeed Pascal is packaged on three disks: a system disk, a libraries disk and a utilities disk (labeled LP1.System, LP2.Libraries, and LP3.Utilities). For now, all you need from the package is the system disk. When we refer to "the Pascal disk," we mean either the MacPascal System disk or the LP1.System disk. You should also have your own blank disk.

Your machine may be equipped with any number of accessories. Your Mac may be connected to an external floppy disk drive, a hard disk drive, a printer, a numeric keypad, and/or a modem. We will explain how to use the external floppy disk drive, but you do not need it to use Pascal. (The 3-1/2" disks that you use are called *floppy disks* even though they are encased in hard plastic. The "floppy" part is the magnetic component you view if you gently slide the shutter. In this context, the term *hard disk* refers to any external device that stores information on a hard surface, such as a steel platter.) Your Macintosh need be connected to a printer only when you want to print something. The other accessories will not be discussed in this book.

Figure 1 Macintosh with accessories

From Elliot B. Koffman, *Turbo Pascal*, 1986, Addison-Wesley Publishing Company

At this point, we assume that your Macintosh has been assembled, that the peripheral equipment (the keyboard, the mouse, and other stuff attached to your Mac) has been connected, and that the machine has been plugged in. If you are using your own Mac, follow the instructions for installing your machine. If you are using your school's or business's facilities, contact someone in charge to find out about any special instructions.

Time to Get Started

Sit down in front of your Macintosh and get comfortable. Make sure that the keyboard and your chair are at reasonable heights and that your mouse has plenty of free space in which to roam. Ready? Here we go...

• Turn on your Macintosh.

The power switch is located on the back of the machine along the left side (right side if you are facing the back). The 1 at the top of the switch means "on"; the 0 at the bottom of the switch means "off." When you flip the switch, your Mac will sound a single beep.

On the screen, you will see a picture of a disk containing a question mark. This picture is called an *icon*. You've seen plenty of icons in real life — for example, a red circle with a diagonal slash is an icon meaning "no." Macintosh uses a language of (mostly) self-explanatory icons to tell you what to do next. The disk with the question mark is an icon that means the Mac is waiting for you to insert a disk to start up the machine.

• Insert the Pascal disk into the machine's disk drive.

You can't use just any disk to start up the machine. Certain disks contain information necessary for initializing the machine; these disks are known, appropriately enough, as *start-up disks*. Your Pascal disk, for example, is a start-up disk. Your blank disk, however, is not. We will discuss the difference later in this chapter.

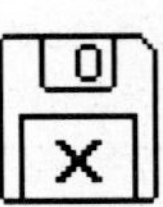

If your disk is not accepted by the machine, you will see a disk with an X on the screen. Make sure that you are loading a Pascal disk and that it is in the proper position: the side of the disk with the sliding metal segment goes into the drive first. The label of the disk should be facing up. Unless you have a defective disk, your Mac should be happy with your Pascal disk. You can tell that your disk has been accepted by the Happy Mac icon. Your contented machine will now load information from the disk into the computer's internal memory. While this is occurring, you will hear a whirring noise from the disk drive. A sign welcoming you to the Macintosh appears, followed by a blank screen and a wristwatch icon. The wristwatch means that you should wait patiently for the Mac to finish its current task — in this case, setting up the machine.

When the wristwatch turns into an arrow, you will see the Macintosh Desktop. Think of the screen as if it were the top of your desk. Each icon on the desktop represents a collection of information. Since we've just started, there is very little on the desk. On the right side, you should see two icons. In the top right is an icon representing the Pascal disk you just inserted. In the bottom right corner is the Macintosh's trash can. Both of these icons are also labeled. (If you are using MacPascal, the disk will be labeled **Pascal**; if you are using Lightspeed, the disk will be labeled **LP1.System**.)

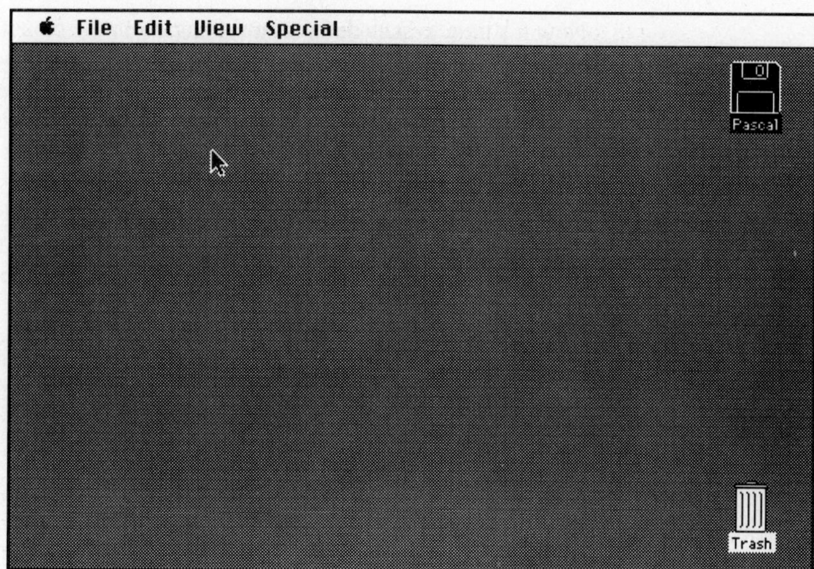

Figure 2
Initial desktop

Across the top of the screen is a white banner that contains an apple icon and the words **File**, **Edit**, **View,** and **Special**. This area is called the *menu bar*. You may also see a large rectangular region (called a *window*) containing some smaller icons. Ignore this window for the moment.

Mouse Actions

The last item on the screen is a pointer, called the *cursor*. The position of the cursor is controlled by the mouse. If you look at the bottom of the mouse, you will see that it is little more than a small ball in a protective case. To move the mouse, place it on a flat surface. Make sure the area is clean; while a peanut butter sandwich does supply a flat surface, getting food stuck on the roof of your mouse is not fun.

• Without touching its button, move the mouse around the tabletop.

As you move the mouse, keep it flat on the desk or table. When the Mac detects the mouse's movement, it moves the cursor in the same direction. The cursor cannot, however, be moved off the screen.

• Lift the mouse off the surface and place it on another part of your tabletop.

You will see that the arrow did not move while the mouse was airborne; the Macintosh moves the arrow only while the ball is rolling. Thus, if you want to move the arrow to a side of the screen but run out of tabletop before you get where you want to go, you can lift the mouse and give it a larger runway. Get comfortable with the mouse by moving the arrow around the perimeter of the screen. You can move the arrow faster across large distances by using a few short move-lift sequences than by one long move. Such a move-lift action is known as *stroking* the mouse.

Now it's time to start doing useful things with the mouse. You can perform four basic actions with your mouse: pointing, clicking, dragging, and pressing. These actions serve various purposes, depending on how you are using your Macintosh and what piece of the "computer onion" you are using (the computer onion will be discussed in Chapter 1). We shall see later how combinations of these actions, such as double-clicking, are interpreted by the Mac.

Pointing is the easiest of the mouse actions. The cursor is always pointing at something: to point at an icon, you need only move the arrow tip over the icon. In Chapter 1, you will see the cursor change from an arrow to other icons, such as a hand or a stop sign. (You have already seen the cursor change from an arrow to a wristwatch.) In those cases, make sure that the cursor is completely over the icon you want to point to.

To *click* on the trash can:

- Move the mouse so it is pointing at the trash can.
- Press the mouse button once and quickly release it.

The quick press and release of the mouse button is called *clicking* and is typically used for *selecting* objects for further manipulation. Clicking the mouse while the cursor is over an icon will reverse the icon's color. Notice that the trash can was mostly white before; now it is mostly black. This reversal of color is called *highlighting*.

- Select the Pascal or LP1.System disk icon by clicking on it.

The disk icon is now highlighted, and the trash can is back to its original state. To *drag* the trash can:

- Point to the trash can.
- Press the mouse button but DON'T LET GO.
- While still holding down the mouse button, move the arrow to another part of the desk top.
- Release the mouse button.

You have just *dragged* the trash can to a new location. Notice that when you move the mouse, the outline of the icon moves with the cursor. You can arrange the icons in any way you please by dragging them around. The Macintosh always begins a session by placing the trash can in the lower right corner, but it doesn't matter where the icon appears on the screen.

The final action you can perform with the mouse is called *pressing*, which is simply holding down the button while pointing. We shall see an example of pressing in the next section.

Passing by the Open Windows

At this point, your screen should consist of a menu bar, a Pascal disk icon, a trash can icon, and the cursor. You may have a window on the screen as well.

We said earlier that every item on the Mac Desktop represents a collection of information. To get at this information, you need to *open* an icon. This is accomplished by *double-clicking* on the icon.

If a window is not already on the screen, open the Pascal disk's window:

- Point at the Pascal disk icon.
- Double-click (i.e., click twice in quick succession) on the icon.

The information on the Pascal disk is shown in a window. (If the window does not open, your double-click may not have worked. Make sure the arrow tip is on the disk icon and try double-clicking again. If there is too little or too much time between the two clicks, the Mac may interpret them as one or two separate clicks rather than one double-click.)

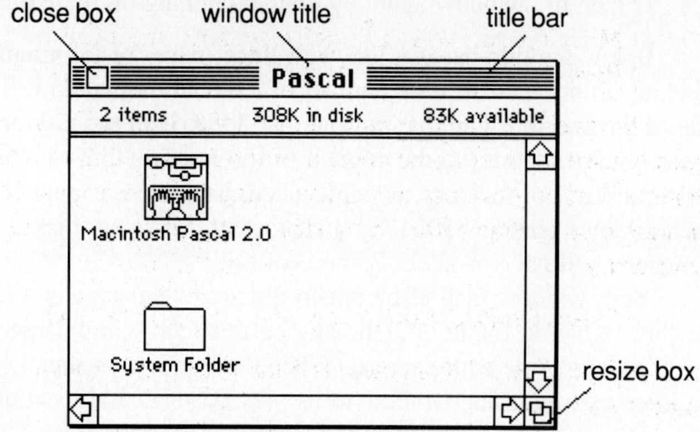

Figure 3
a. Macintosh Pascal window

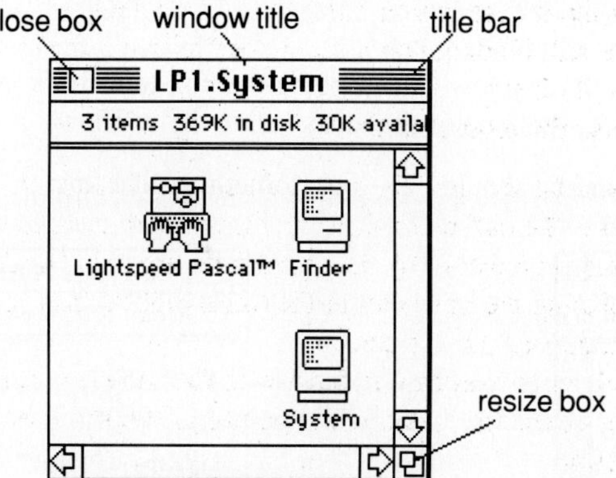

b. Lightspeed Pascal window

The window you have just opened contains icons representing the information on the Pascal disk. (Your Pascal window may contain icons other than those shown in Figure 3.) Before we look at that information, though, let's look at the structure of the window. The top of the window contains the window's name, which matches the name of the icon. The area with the stripes is called the *title bar*. The entire window can be moved by using the title bar.

To reposition the window on the screen:

- Point to the title bar.
- Drag the window to another part of the screen.

A window can be dragged only when the cursor is in the title bar. Dragging on different parts of the screen produces quite different results. For example, the icons within the window can be rearranged by dragging them to new locations.

A small square is in the window's upper left corner. This square is called the *close box* because clicking on it closes the window.

- Close the window by clicking on the close box.
- Open the window again by double-clicking on the Pascal disk icon.

Below the title bar is a line with three pieces of information. The left side of this line simply indicates the number of icons in the window. The center and right side of the line in Figure 3a indicate that 308K is in the disk and 83K is available. These comments refer to the amount of information that can be stored on the disk. A K is a kilobyte of memory; a single-sided disk contains approximately 400 kilobytes. Each kilobyte contains 1024 (2^{10}) characters. Since our disk is using 308 kilobytes of memory, the disk is about 75 percent full.

Your window may also contain a window enlarger on the right side of the title bar (not shown in Figure 3). Clicking on this icon will enlarge the window so it occupies nearly the entire screen. When the window is already full-size, clicking on the icon will return the window to its previous size and location.

The lower right corner of the window contains a *resize box*, which allows you to change the size of the window.

- Point to the resize box.
- Resize the window (by dragging the box toward the top left corner) so that the border covers one of the icons inside the window.

Your window should now look something like this:

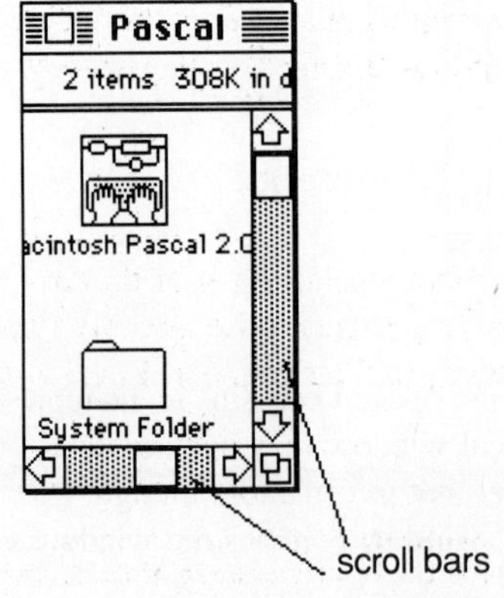

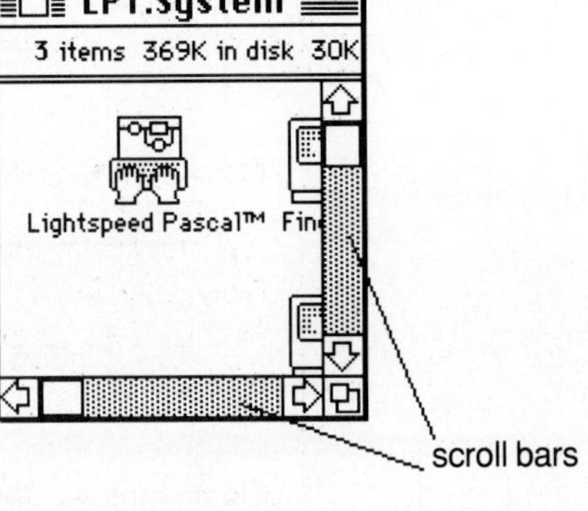

Figure 4
a. Resized MacPascal window
b. Resized Lightspeed window

Notice that the upper left corner stays in place as you drag the resize box. When you resize the window, the upper left corner is "nailed" to the desktop. You can move the upper left corner only by dragging the title bar. Also, notice that when you move the resize box, the outline of the window moves with the cursor.

In our example, some of the icons are partially or totally hidden. All of the information is still in the disk; you just can't see it all right now. This is similar to looking at a laboratory slide through a microscope. When you look through the eyepiece, you can see only a part of the entire specimen mounted on the slide. When you move the slide, another part of the specimen comes into view. In an action similar to moving the slide, you *scroll* in the window to expose the hidden icons.

- Scroll to a different part in the window by pressing on the right arrow or the bottom arrow.

The bottom and right sides of the window contain *scroll bars.* These gray scroll bars contain a single white square, the *scroll box,* which indicates the current position of the window over the entire group of icons within the Pascal disk. By pressing or clicking on the *scroll arrows*, you can move up, down, left, or right inside the window. If you hold down the mouse button over any scroll arrow, the scroll box will move in that direction. If you can't move the scroll box any farther in the scroll bar, you cannot move any farther in the window. For example, if the scroll box is immediately below the up arrow, you are at the top of the window and can't move up any more. Experiment with the scroll arrows by moving around the window.

Using the scroll arrows is sometimes too slow. The Macintosh provides another way to move around the window.

- Scroll to the top of the window by pressing on the up arrow.
- Point to the scroll box in the vertical scroll bar.
- Scroll to the bottom of the window by dragging the scroll box to the bottom of the scroll bar.

The window now shows the bottom part of the window. The Mac waited for you to stop dragging the square before scrolling the window. Because the Mac redrew the icons in the window only once, it was able to move to the bottom faster than if you had pressed on the down arrow. You can drag the square to any place within the scroll bars, and the Mac will redraw the icons in the window accordingly.

What's on the Menu?

Let's return to the menu bar. The apple and each of the four words (**File**, **Edit**, **View**, **Special**) in the menu bar represent a different set of options.* The Desktop lists the titles of all current menus in the menu bar. In this section we'll show how these menus can be used.

*The menu options described in this section are available in most versions of the Desktop; however, the options available to you depend on the contents of the disk you used to start up the Mac.

Suppose you've been working for a while and the icons in your window have become disorganized. You can imitate this condition by dragging the icons to various places within the Pascal window.

- Resize the window so all the icons can be seen.
- Rearrange the icons in the Pascal window so they overlap (see Figure 5).

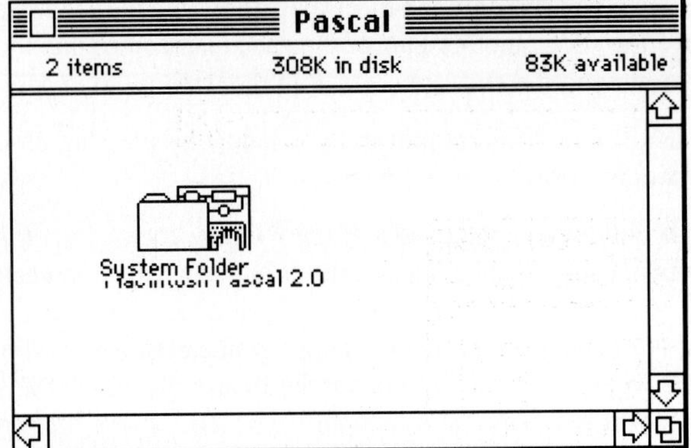

Figure 5
a. Rearranged icons in MacPascal window

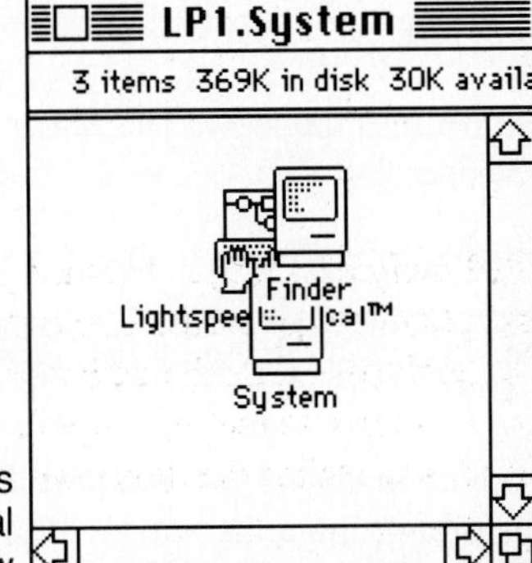

b. Rearranged icons in Lightspeed Pascal window

Special
Clean Up
Empty Trash
Erase Disk
Set Startup
Use MiniFinder...
Shut Down

It's easier to look at icons if they are arranged in straight rows and columns. Macintosh can do some rearranging by itself with the **Clean Up** command, which is located in the **Special** menu.

- Point to the word **Special** on the menu bar.
- Press on the word **Special**, but don't release the button.
- A menu appears on the screen. Without releasing the button, move down the menu until the option **Clean Up** is highlighted.
- Release the mouse button.

The icons in the window will align themselves to some extent. (**Clean Up** will arrange the icons differently, depending on the situation; the result of your selection of **Clean Up** may look different from ours.)

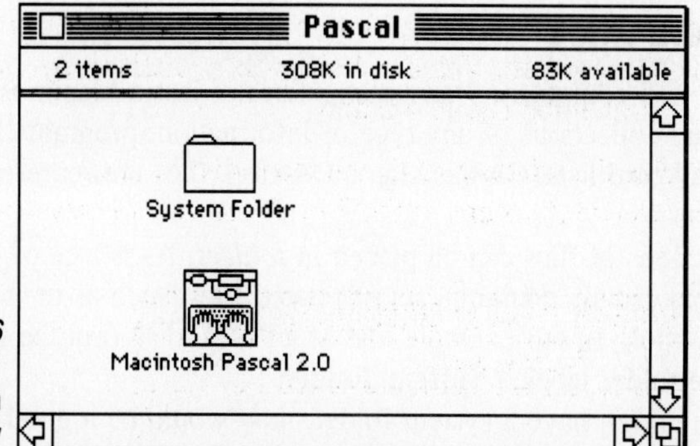

Figure 6
a. Result of **Clean Up** in MacPascal window

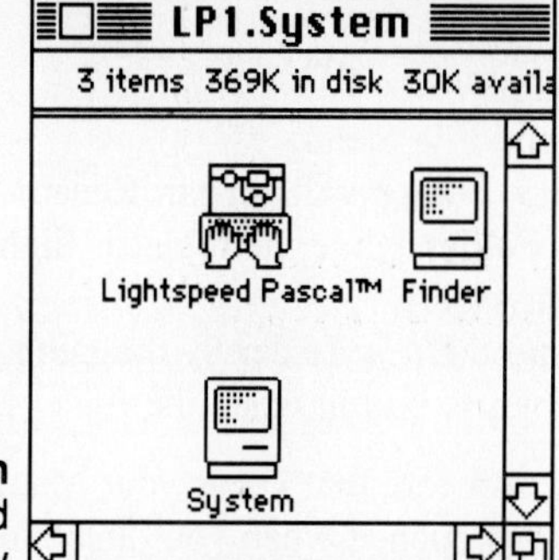

b. Result of **Clean Up** in Lightspeed Pascal window

Macintosh's menus are called *pull-down* menus because you have to choose the menu, pull it down, and select an option. As your cursor rolls over the options in the menu, each one is successively highlighted. When the option you wish to select has been highlighted, release the mouse button and that option will be executed.

There are times, though, when you realize that you don't want to choose any of the options on the menu.

- Pull down the **Special** menu.
- Move the arrow so that it is nowhere on the menu.
- Release the mouse button.

The result? There is none. If you move the arrow off the menu and release the mouse button, no action is performed.

You may have noticed that some options, such as **Empty Trash,** are gray instead of black. When you roll the cursor over gray options, they are not highlighted. Options that are gray cannot be chosen at the moment because choosing them would not make any sense. In the case of **Empty Trash**, for example, the Mac knows the trash can is already empty.

Folders and Files

Information in a computer — any computer, not just a Macintosh — is stored in *files*. Files are collections of any type of information: programs, pictures, personnel data, birthday card lists. On the Mac's Desktop, files are represented by different icons.

Collections of files can be placed in *folders*. As is true of folders in a typical office, folders usually contain a set of related files, such as the text and pictures for a chapter in a book. In our example, the MacPascal disk (not the Lightspeed disk) contains one folder labeled **System Folder**.

If you do not have a system folder, now would be a good time to create one. To do this, you will need to create a new folder using a menu option. Then, giving the folder a name, you can place the system files (denoted by the Macintosh icon) into the new folder.

To create a system folder:

- Select **New Folder** from the **File** menu.
- A new folder called **Empty Folder** will appear. Rename this folder by typing the words **System Folder** while the folder is highlighted. Backspace and retype to correct typing errors.
- Move any system icons into the new folder by dragging the icon to **System Folder** and releasing the mouse button when the folder is highlighted.

System Folder now contains the software that keeps your Mac running.

Just as the Pascal window was opened when you double-clicked on the Pascal disk icon, a window opens when you double-click on a folder. This second window can be manipulated in the same way as the Pascal disk window.

- Open **System Folder**.

The new window appears to emerge from the folder icon. If it is still visible, the **System Folder** icon in the Pascal disk window will now be dotted.

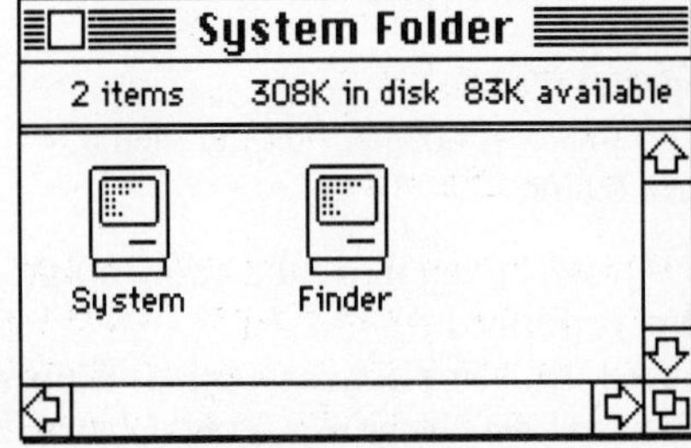

Figure 7
System Folder window

Whenever multiple windows appear on the screen, only one window contains the striped title bar. This window is called the *active* window. Only the active window can be resized or closed.

Let's return to the desktop analogy. When you have a number of papers on a real desk, they often overlap. You can see the entire page that you are currently working on, but the other pages remain partially hidden. On your Macintosh, the windows may overlap in the same way. What you need is some way of designating which window you want to work with — that is, which window you want to be active. Any window becomes active when you click on it.

- Rearrange the windows so the Pascal window is visible but is obscured by the **System Folder** window.
- Activate the Pascal window by clicking on it.

The active window is always completely visible. All of the overlapped windows are obscured as if they were separate pieces of paper. Even if the windows do not overlap, only one window is active. The active window comes to the top of the pile, and any overlapping windows are obscured.

- Activate the **System Folder** window.

Remember when we mentioned start-up disks? The programs in **System Folder** are what differentiate start-up from non-start-up disks. That is, those programs initialize the Macintosh and control the Desktop. Since you don't need to concern yourself with what these programs look like, close the folder.

- Close the **System Folder** window.

Now you should have only the Pascal window on the Desktop. The **System Folder** is no longer dotted; it is still highlighted because no other icon has been selected.

Other Menu Options

The menu immediately to the right of the apple is labeled **File**. The **Open** and **Close** options on this menu do the same thing as double-clicking on an icon and clicking on the close box. These options always refer to the active window or icon. If you click on the trash can, for example, and choose **Open**, you will be able to examine the contents of the trash can.

- If it isn't already, open the Pascal disk window.
- Choose **New Folder** from the **File** menu.
- Activate (do not open) the **Empty Folder**.
- Select **Duplicate** from the **File** menu.

The **Duplicate** option makes a copy of whatever has been highlighted. In this case, a second empty folder (called **Copy of Empty Folder**) is now available. However, since you have no current use for a second empty folder, you can throw it away, using a process similar to the one used for placing icons in folders.

To throw away the **Copy of Empty Folder**:

- Drag the **Copy of Empty Folder** to the trash can.
- Release the mouse button when the trash can is highlighted.

The **Copy of Empty Folder** is now in the trash can. As in real life, anything can be retrieved from the trash as long as the trash has not been emptied. To empty the trash can, select the **Empty Trash** option from the **Special** menu. To retrieve files from the trash, perform the following steps:

- Open the trash can.
- Drag the **Copy of Empty Folder** from the trash can back into the Pascal window.
- Release the mouse button.

Any file or folder can be copied from one disk to another simply by dragging the icon between the appropriate windows. Files can also be moved between folders on the same disk and to and from the trash can in the same way.

- Drag **Empty Folder** and **Copy of Empty Folder** to the **Trash** window.
- Close the **Trash** window.
- Choose **Empty Trash** from the **Special** menu.

View
by Small Icon
✓by Icon
by Name
by Date
by Size
by Kind

The Desktop's **Edit** menu works as it does in the Pascal editor, so let's wait until Chapter 1 to work with that particular item.

The **View** menu allows you to examine the contents of a window in different formats.

- If it isn't already, activate the Pascal window.
- Choose **by Name** from the **View** menu.

The icons disappear and are replaced by a list of files.

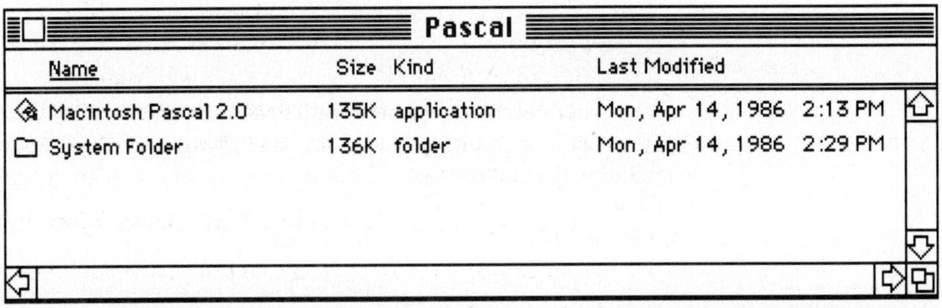

Pascal

Name	Size	Kind	Last Modified
Macintosh Pascal 2.0	135K	application	Mon, Apr 14, 1986 2:13 PM
System Folder	136K	folder	Mon, Apr 14, 1986 2:29 PM

Figure 8
a. Listing files by name in MacPascal window

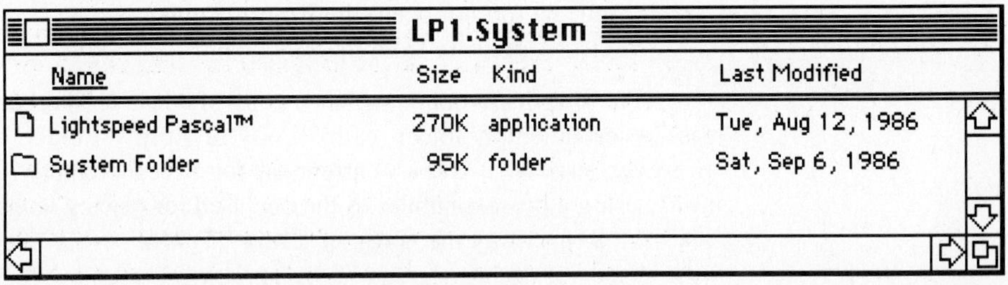

LP1.System

Name	Size	Kind	Last Modified
Lightspeed Pascal™	270K	application	Tue, Aug 12, 1986
System Folder	95K	folder	Sat, Sep 6, 1986

b. Listing files by name in Lightspeed window

Each line of the list gives information about a different file or folder. (You may have to resize the window if you don't see all four columns.) The first column lists the name of the file or folder. The second column shows its size in kilobytes. The third column describes the kind of file; each kind is designated by a different icon when you view the window by icon. The final column gives the date when each folder or file was last modified. Notice that the column heading **Name** is underlined. This means that the file list is in alphabetical order by name. By choosing the other options on the **View** menu (**by Date**, **by Size**, **by Kind**), you can rearrange the order in which the files are listed. You can also open a file that is represented textually by double-clicking on the small icon to the left of the name.

If you want to go back to iconic representations, choose **by Icon** from the **View** menu. Whenever you pull down the **View** menu, the view of the current window is designated by a checkmark. The **by Small Icon** is the same as **by Icon** except that the icons are much smaller.

The menu on the far left (denoted by the apple) contains a number of "desk accessories" that are available at all times. Depending on the contents of the start-up disk, these accessories may include a calculator, an alarm clock, and a puzzle. You can open any of these accessories by choosing that option from the menu. Each accessory contains a close box in its upper left. All of these accessories are operated with the mouse. (For more mouse practice, choose one of the options on the apple menu, and click on various things — don't worry, you can't do any damage to the machine.)

Using the Second Disk

There will come a time when you will want to save files on a blank disk. Suppose you decide to make your blank disk into a start-up disk. To do this, you have to copy the **System** folder from the Pascal disk to your disk.

If you do not have an external disk drive, your machine can hold only one disk at a time. This is a problem since you need to transfer information from the Pascal disk to your blank disk.

- If you do not have an external drive, choose **Eject** from the **File** menu.

Eject causes your Macintosh to release the Pascal disk. On the screen, the icons in the Pascal window will turn gray.

Important: NEVER FORCIBLY REMOVE A DISK FROM THE DISK DRIVE. If a disk becomes stuck, try ejecting the disk using the keyboard: press the Shift, clover, and 1 keys all at the same time. The disk in the Macintosh's internal drive should be released. To release the disk in the external drive, press Shift, clover, and 2 simultaneously.

If that doesn't work, turn the machine off. Then turn it back on *with the mouse button pressed*. This should release both disks. Finally, if you have reached the desperation point, insert a paper clip into the small hole to the right of the disk drive (this should almost *never* be necessary). Do *not* remove the disk by reaching into the drive and pulling. A forcible removal of a disk can cause untold damage to your machine and/or disk.

- Insert your blank disk into either the external or the main drive.

We assume that your disk has never been used. If this is true, you will see the following message on the screen:

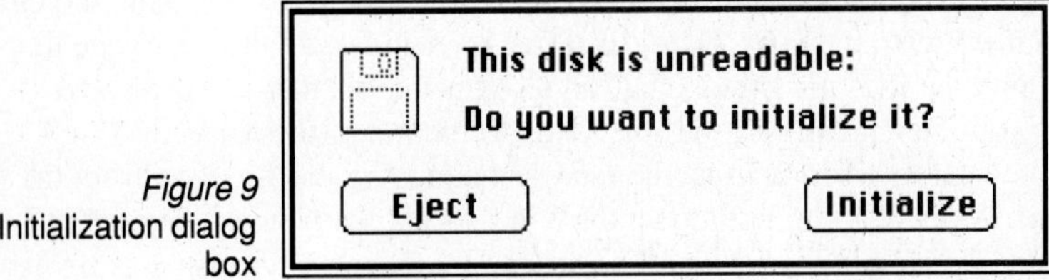

Figure 9
Initialization dialog box

The window in Figure 9 is called a *dialog box.* Macintosh uses dialog boxes when it has a question that only you can answer. You respond by choosing one of the options in the rounded rectangles. These rounded rectangles are often called *buttons.*

Macintosh cannot use a completely blank disk. To store and retrieve information on the disk, the Mac needs to set up magnetic markers. These markers use up very little space but are necessary for storing files. The process of setting up these markers is called *initializing* the disk. The dialog box informs you that the Mac is ready to initialize your disk; all it needs is your approval.

• Initialize the disk by clicking on the **Initialize** button.

Another dialog box soon appears on the screen. Macintosh wants to give a name to each disk, and so it asks you for a name:

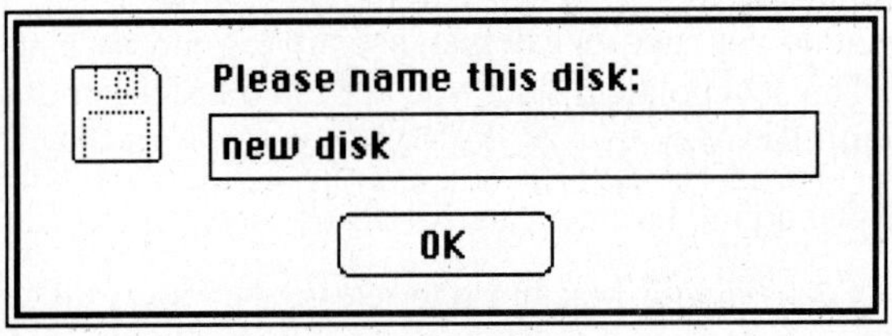

Please name this disk:
new disk
OK

Figure 10
Dialog box for naming disks

Naming the disk is a very simple operation.

• Name the disk by typing the name at the keyboard.
• If you misspell the name, backspace to erase characters.
• When the name is typed correctly, choose the **OK** button.

When the new disk has been initialized, you will see another disk icon on the right side of the Desktop. The two disk icons look identical but can be distinguished by their names.

• Open the **new disk** icon.

Double-clicking should open an empty window on the Desktop. You are now ready to copy the **System Folder** from the Pascal disk.

- Make the Pascal window active.
- Resize the Pascal and new disk windows so that both are completely visible.
- Make sure that the **System Folder** icon is visible in the Pascal window.
- Activate the **System Folder**.
- Drag the **System Folder** to the new disk window.

The files in the **System Folder** are being copied now to the blank disk. A box that says **Files remaining to copy** appears on the screen. This box indicates that the copying is still going on.

If you have an external disk drive, the copying operation will be done automatically. When the wristwatch turns back into an arrow, the transfer is complete.

If you have a single disk drive, Macintosh will ask you to swap disks by drawing a dialog box. Your blank disk will be ejected. Reinsert the Pascal disk that was previously in the drive. You may be asked to swap disks a few times, since the Macintosh can copy only one part of the file at a time.

Time to Go Home

You've had a good session. You've learned how to work with the Macintosh; now it's time to relax and savor your accomplishments. We just have to do some final cleaning up.

- Choose **Shut Down** from the **Special** menu.
- If **Shut Down** is not in the **Special** menu, activate each disk icon and choose **Eject** from the **File** menu.
- Remove each disk from its drive.
- Turn off your Macintosh.

We haven't covered everything there is to know about moving files, working with the menus, and so on. The Macintosh manuals explain the various options in more detail. Because of the consistency of Macintosh features (e.g., all windows have close boxes in the upper left), you should have little problem determining what the different menu options and accessories do. Experiment! The best way to become comfortable with the machine is to use it.

1

Programming and Problem Solving

Let's begin at the most natural place to begin: the end. You've just completed the last assignment of the final chapter. You lean back in your chair, a satisfied grin across your face. After all, you have accomplished a major feat. You have learned how to program.

Back when you first opened this book, you thought that learning how to program simply meant learning how to operate a Macintosh computer and how to use the programming language Pascal. You now know that programming is more than that.

Since you know how to program, you understand the fundamental concepts of program structure that are available in all programming languages. Your practice with programming problems has shown you how to divide large problems into their smaller components. You have learned how to manipulate text and pictures to make your programs easier to use. Your programming skills allow you to take a problem stated in English, break it into smaller components, write a solution in Pascal, and develop a program that even the most inexperienced user can operate.

The programming/problem-solving process that you have used in your assignments is the same one used to create computer applications you encounter every day. You have seen automatic bank teller machines and supermarket checkout scanners process data (monetary transactions and universal price codes, respectively). Each time you make a phone call, computer programs solve complex systems of equations to efficiently direct your call to its proper destination. You also know that computers control city traffic lights, airplanes in flight, and orbiting satellites. These applications are all the results of programmers' problem-solving skills. Although you have not yet written programs on the scale of these examples, you understand the same fundamental problem-solving and programming techniques used by real-world programmers. You can now look at the everyday uses of computers with a much clearer comprehension than you had when you began this book.

Now that we have looked at where you will be at the end, let us return to where you are now. In this chapter, we will begin by discussing terminology and examining how a computer processes information. Then to introduce you to the overall structure of a Pascal program, you will enter and run a simple program. We will then examine each part of the program in more detail. Finally, we will show how a problem can be translated from English to Pascal.

Learning to use a computer is much like learning your way around a new city. At first, all the new sights may seem overwhelming, but after a while things become familiar. Once you learn how to get where you need to go, you can explore new areas. Similarly, even though we are throwing a great deal of material at you in this chapter, it will soon become second nature.

1.1 Computer Terminology

Let's start by briefly defining the major components of the computer. The physical parts of the machine are collectively referred to as its *hardware*. This includes the internals of your Macintosh (an electronic circuit board with its integrated circuit "chips") and the parts of the computer that you can touch (the disks, screen, keyboard, and mouse). One particular part of the hardware — the microprocessor chip — interprets and executes your instructions.

The operative words here are "your instructions." By itself, a computer is useless. The hardware can do nothing unless you provide a set of explicit instructions, called a *program*. When you create a program, you create a specific, ordered list of instructions for the computer to execute. By following the instructions listed in a program, the computer can perform the task presented to it.

Programs, also known collectively as *software,* are the focus of this book. We will be looking at how you can control the machine with the instructions of the *programming language* Pascal. A language, in computer science terms, is based on a particular *grammar*. The rules of a programming language's grammar tells us how we can construct instructions that the computer can execute.

A number of computer languages are available for writing programs. We are using Pascal because it is a *high-level language*; that is, Pascal is more like English than like computerese. Pascal is also a powerful language; single instructions in Pascal can perform the same task as several lines of other languages. Perhaps the most important reason that we use Pascal, though, is that the language is designed to help programmers write software with clarity and structure. As we will see, Pascal encourages the use of structure even when your program is in its initial design phase.

Instructions in Pascal can be divided into two categories. *Declarations* and *definitions* are used to tell the computer how we want to use its memory and how we want to refer to particular locations. For example, we use declarations to tell the computer to reserve a part of memory to hold fifteen zip codes or that we want to refer to a program by the name ***FirstExample***. *Statements* are descriptions of actions that we want the computer to perform, such as adding two numbers, printing a line of text, or repeating the actions described by a particular group of statements. Together, declarations, definitions, and statements make up a program. Before we delve into writing programs, though, let's look at how a computer performs tasks.

1.2 The Processing of Information

In general, a computer follows three steps when it is given a program. It accepts as *input* a programmer's data and set of instructions. The computer then executes the instructions in the specified order to *process* the data and gives the results as *output*. The sequence is illustrated in Figure 1.1.

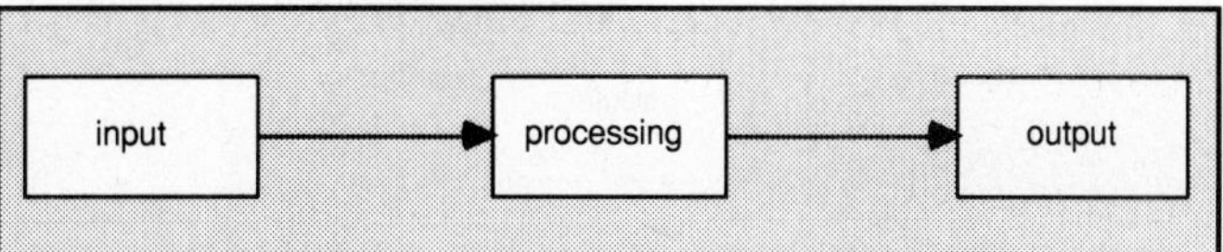

Figure 1.1
The computer processes input to produce output

This high-level model of how computers work resembles the way that many people perform their jobs. For example, let's look at an accountant filling out a federal tax form. First, a client gives the accountant the information she needs for the job: W-2 forms, receipts, and cancelled checks. With these items and other equipment such as a tax manual and a calculator, the accountant begins preparing the tax forms. When the instructions ask for calculations, the accountant presses buttons on the calculator and writes down the answers on a legal pad for future reference. As the various calculations are performed, the accountant fills in the appropriate lines on the tax form. When all the numbers have been entered, the accountant hands the completed form back to the client. The client finishes the process by signing the form and mailing it to the IRS. Figure 1.2 illustrates the accountant's method of working.

The processing box from Figure 1.1 has been expanded. During the processing stage, our accountant had help in handling two types of operations: performing calculations and storing information. She used a calculator to do all of the arithmetic. She also used the tax manual and the legal pad for "storage." This storage allowed the accountant to keep the instructions, the temporary calculations, and the partial results within reach. Because she could refer to any of the information on paper, she did not have to keep that information in her head.

The computer's method of processing is similar to the accountant's method of processing, as shown in Figure 1.3.

Your Macintosh receives input from the keyboard, the mouse, or disks. Much larger computers receive their input from magnetic tapes and large disks as well. Once input is received, it is processed by the *central processing unit* (CPU). Just as the accountant relies on a calculator and a tax manual, the CPU's control circuitry relies on two major items. First, an *arithmetic-logic unit* (ALU)* handles the arithmetic and logical calculations (such as adding and comparing numbers). Second, the computer uses *memory* to store data that is received as input or results that come from the ALU's calculations. The computer's memory also contains the list of instructions to be performed.

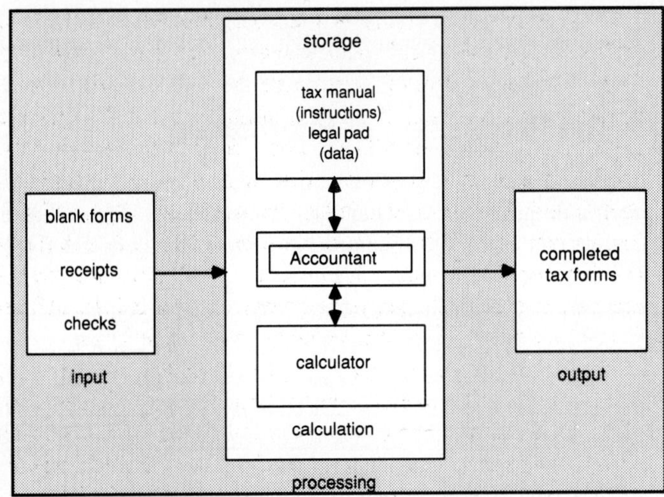

Figure 1.2 How an accountant prepares a tax return

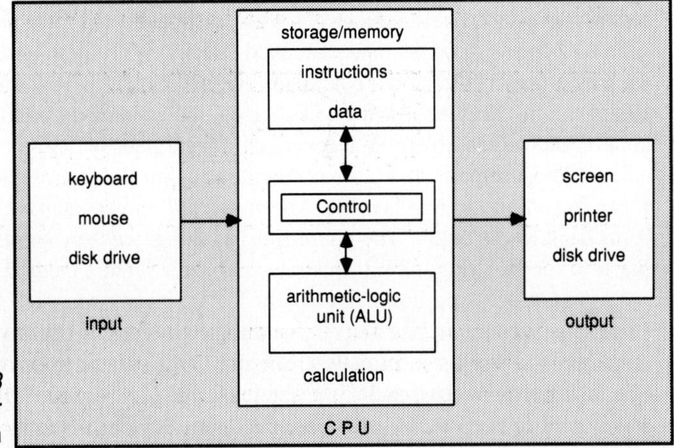

Figure 1.3 How a computer processes a program

During processing, the computer may encounter an instruction to print information. When such an instruction is found, the Mac's CPU can send the output to a screen, a printer, or a disk. Other machines may have additional output devices, such

* In your Mac, the CPU and its ALU are contained in the microprocessor chip. The specific microprocessor used in the Macintosh, Macintosh Plus, and Macintosh SE is known as the Motorola 68000®. The Macintosh II uses another microprocessor known as the Motorola 68020®.

as a magnetic tape drive. (Printing information gives you a *hard copy* of the output on paper instead of on the screen.)

You may wonder exactly how it is that a machine can "understand" your instructions. Think back to the days of the Old West. To communicate between towns that were hundreds of miles apart, telegraph companies connected wires across the plains. Operators sent messages back and forth using Morse code—a system of electrical "dots" and "dashes" representing letters, numbers, and punctuation.

A computer also runs on electrical impulses. The CPU consists of nearly 100,000 simple electronic devices, each of which is in one of two states: on or off. The CPU's equivalent of Morse code is called *machine code*. Machine code represents simple instructions and data to the computer using the equivalent of dots and dashes: zeros (CPU devices are off) and ones (devices are on). Because only two symbols are needed to represent all of the codes, machine code is also known as a *binary* code, and each individual one or zero is known as a binary digit, or *bit*. The machine code instructions that tell the CPU to retrieve and store data in memory and manipulate numbers are thus no more than a sequence of zeros and ones. A single character in the machine is stored as a sequence of eight bits, or a *byte*, and instructions and data are typically stored in two, four, or eight consecutive bytes.

So that programmers do not have to think in the low-level terms of binary machine code, let alone in terms of turning electronic devices on and off, your Pascal disk contains a program called a *translator*. MacPascal's translator is called an *interpreter*; Lightspeed's is called a *compiler*. The Pascal translator is analogous to a human interpreter or telegraph operator. A customer who wants to send a message gives it to a telegraph operator in English. The operator then translates the message into Morse code and sends the message through the wires. Likewise, you provide the

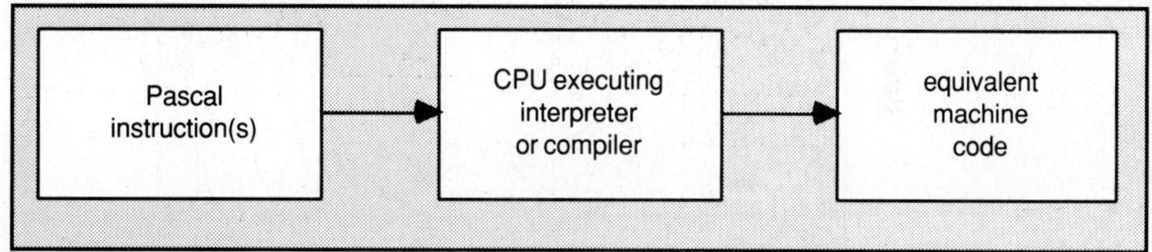

Figure 1.4
Translating a program

Pascal interpreter or compiler with a program in Pascal, and the program is then translated into the language the CPU can work with (that is, machine code) (Figure 1.4).

In an interpreter, each Pascal instruction is translated, and then the equivalent machine code is immediately executed. In a compiler, all of the instructions within a file are translated at once, and then the machine code is executed. In either case, the CPU processes the machine code using your input data as needed. (The relative advantages and disadvantages of interpreters and compilers are not relevant here.)

At some point, the user needs to see output. Just as the operator at the receiving end of a message translates Morse code into English, the Pascal translator reads machine-coded output instructions and releases a final result as human-readable output, as shown in Figure 1.5.

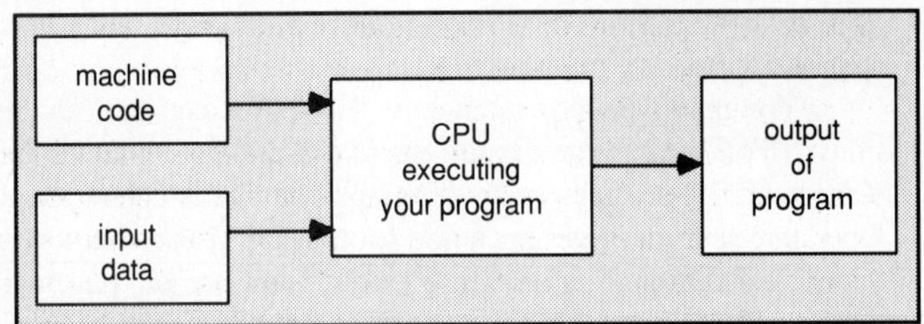

Figure 1.5
Executing a program

1.3 The Computer System as a Whole

The bare machine, which can only store and calculate, is not enough for us to do what we want to do. We also need to know how to put the program into the computer in the first place, how to store and retrieve programs from memory, and how to fix or enhance versions of existing programs. A special collection of *utilities* is provided with the Macintosh to perform these common functions. This collection of utilities is called an *operating system*, because it helps the user operate the computer.

Think of the hardware as being surrounded by levels of software in the same way that the core of an onion is surrounded by layers.

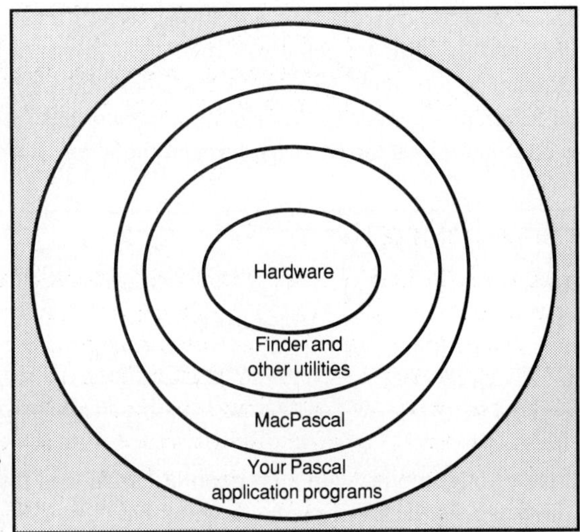

Figure 1.6
The Macintosh computer onion

The level immediately above the hardware is the Macintosh operating system, which contains a utility called the *Finder*. The Finder lets you control any number of other utilities. For example, you will often want to locate various pieces of software and data stored in the machine. To perform this location function, the Finder calls upon the Macintosh's *File System*, which tells the machine where the various pieces of software and data reside in memory. A *file* is a set of sequential lines of text that you can store and modify. Files hold arbitrary lines of text, including the instructions of a computer program. All information that you store on your disks or load into the

Macintosh is kept in files. You use the filing system any time you create folders or save files. You also use the filing system to organize your files in folders or to move folders from one disk to another.

The Finder also communicates with the other utilities that control the standard operation of the machine. For example, the Finder calls upon one utility to move windows around the screen and another to respond to choices from the pull-down menus. In short, the operating system utilities handle a number of operations that are not specific to any software but work the same way in all Mac applications.

When you insert a start-up disk into your Macintosh, the Finder program begins executing and takes control of the screen. From that point, you move into the next level of the onion by opening a file. For example, when you double-click on the MacPascal icon, the Macintosh Pascal software takes over the screen.

Each level of software has its own specific functions. This means that when MacPascal has control of the screen, you can perform only the functions allowed by MacPascal. You can create, change, or execute programs, but you cannot, for example, create a new folder on your disk. To create a new folder, you must leave MacPascal and return to the Finder.

The Finder and MacPascal levels of the onion are no more than stepping stones. These levels of software exist for the sole purpose of helping you write your own programs. When the MacPascal software is open, you can enter your own Pascal application programs. When you run such programs, you add another level of software to the system. Your program depends on the MacPascal interpreter, which in turn depends on the Finder and the other utilities that ultimately control the hardware. Your programs are thus the outermost and the most visible level of the computer onion.

1.4 Your First Program

We mentioned in the Primer that MacPascal and Lightspeed Pascal have more similarities than differences. However, MacPascal was developed with the introductory programmer in mind; Lightspeed was developed for the more advanced software developer. This means that there are important differences between the two environments, and these are most noticeable when you first start using the software. Make sure you follow the correct instructions for your software as you attack this hands-on section. (The section headings indicate which software is being discussed.)

Let's look now at how you can use your Pascal software to enter, run, and save a program that prints a two-line message. If you have never used the Mac before, please read the primer first. This section is designed as a **hands-on** tutorial, which means you will find it easier to understand if you sit in front of a machine and follow the instructions, which are preceded by bullets (•).

Getting Started: MacPascal Only

- Insert the MacPascal disk into the drive and turn on your machine.
- If a Pascal window does not appear on the screen, open it by double-clicking on the Pascal disk icon.

- Look inside the window for the Macintosh Pascal icon and open it by double-clicking.

A screen with three windows appears (see Figure 1.10 on page 12).

Getting Started: Lightspeed Pascal Only

In Lightspeed Pascal, a program is compiled in several parts. The various parts, when taken together, make up a *project*. What you will do now is build an incomplete, skeleton project called **Generic Project**. When you are writing programs, you will combine your Pascal statements with a copy of the **Generic Project** skeleton to create a complete entity. You will not need to do this again; you can make copies of **Generic Project** whenever you want to start a new project. Still, to get started, you have to create the **Generic Project** in the first place.

You will need three disks: the LP1.System and LP2.Libraries disks that came in your Lightspeed Pascal packet and your own blank disk.

- Insert the LP1.System disk in the internal drive.
- If an LP1.System window does not appear on the screen, open it by double-clicking on the LP1.System disk icon.
- Look inside the window for the Lightspeed Pascal icon and open it by double-clicking.

The windows will disappear, and a new menu bar will appear at the top of the screen.

- Choose **New Project...** from the **Project** menu.

When you do this, a dialog box will appear asking you to name the new project, as shown in Figure 1.7.

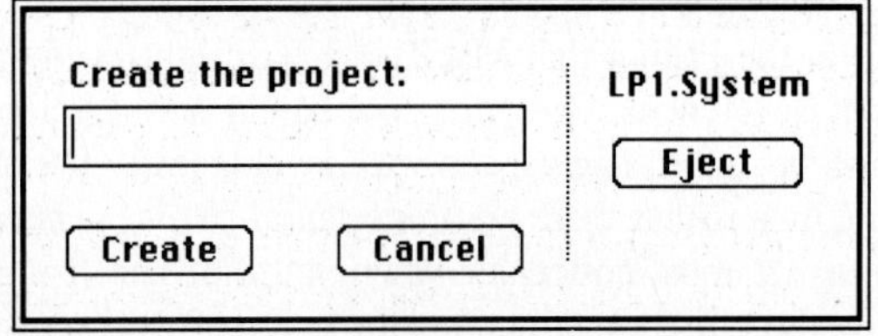

Figure 1.7 **New Project...** dialog box

Now, tell Lightspeed that you are going to create a new project called **Generic Project** and place it on the blank disk. On the right side of the dialog box is where you indicate which disk will hold the new project. The label on the right side (currently LP1.System) indicates which disk Lightspeed intends to use; the button or buttons below the label allow you to switch disks.

- If you have an external drive, load the other disk as follows:

- Insert the blank disk there into the external drive.
- If necessary, initialize and name the disk.
- If the name of the new disk does not appear on the right side of the **New Project...** dialog box, choose the **Drive** button on the right side of the **New Project...** dialog box.

- If you do not have an external drive, load the other disk as follows:

  - Choose the **Eject** button on the right side of the **New Project...** dialog box.
  - Insert the blank disk into the internal drive.
  - If necessary, initialize and name the disk.

At this point, the name of your new disk should appear on the right side of the dialog box over the **Eject** button. Now, you need to name the project you are creating.

- Type **Generic Project** in the left side of the dialog box.
- Choose the **Create** button.
- If you do not have an external drive, swap disks as indicated.

Now that you've given the new project a name, the dialog box will disappear and a single window labeled **Generic Project** appears on the right of the screen.

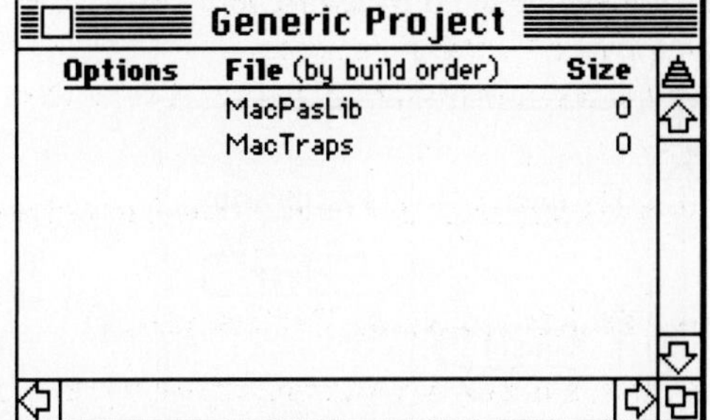

Figure 1.8
Project window

This window lists the files that make up the project. Other information (such as compile options and object size) will also appear; you need not worry about them. In fact, we will rarely refer to this project window. At the moment, however, you should notice that there are two files automatically listed in the **Generic Project**: **MacPasLib** and **MacTraps.** These two files are a part of every project. What you should do now is compile these two files and store the compiled code. The result of the compilation will be the incomplete project that will be the basis of all of your Lightspeed Pascal programs.

- Choose **Build** from the **Run** menu.

This option begins the compilation. In order to build the project, Lightspeed has to find the files to compile. The files **MacPasLib** and **MacTraps**, however, are on the LP2.Libraries disk — which is not in the machine. Lightspeed will put a dialog box on the screen indicating that it cannot find **MacPasLib** and asking if you would like to look for it.

- Choose the **OK** button in the dialog box.

A second dialog box now appears, asking you to indicate where **MacPasLib** resides. The left side of the box contains a list of files; the right side indicates the active disk.

- If you have an external drive, indicate **MacPasLib's** location as follows:

  - If the right side does not have your disk's name, choose the **Drive** button.
  - Eject your disk by choosing **Eject**.
  - Insert the LP2.Libraries disk in the empty drive.

- If you do not have an external drive, indicate **MacPasLib's** location as follows:

  - Eject the disk in the internal drive by choosing **Eject**.
  - Insert the LP2.Libraries disk into the drive.
  - Swap disks as instructed.

- To open **MacPasLib**:

  - either click on the word **MacPasLib** and choose the **Open** button
  - or double-click on the word **MacPasLib**.

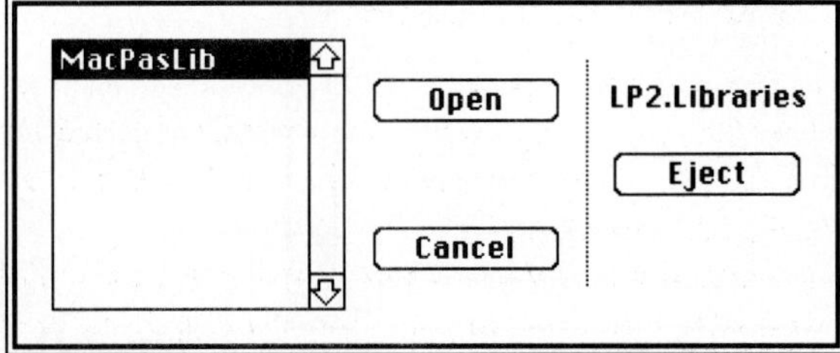

Figure 1.9
Finding **MacPasLib**

When **MacPasLib** is found, Lightspeed will ask you: **Change "LP1.System" to "LP2.Libraries" in all SUBSEQUENT (by build order) Project entries also?**

- Choose the **Yes** button; swap disks if instructed to do so.
- If Lightspeed cannot find **MacTraps**, repeat the above instructions.

The completion of the compilation means you have created **Generic Project**. You won't have to go through this process again; from now on, all you have to do is make a copy of the **Generic Project** skeleton. To do this for the first program, you have to temporarily leave Lightspeed because projects can be copied and renamed only in the Finder.

- Choose **Close Project** from the **Project** menu.
- Choose **Quit** from the **File** menu.

What you should do now is get the icon for your disk on the screen, if it isn't there already.

- If you do not have an external drive, load the other disk as follows:

• Highlight the LP1.System disk icon.
• Eject the disk by choosing **Eject** from the **File** menu.
• Insert your disk in the empty drive, swapping if needed.

- Make the new project as follows:

• Select **Generic Project** on your disk's window.
• Create a copy of **Generic Project** by choosing **Duplicate** from the **File** menu.
• Rename the **Copy of Generic Project** by typing **First Project** while the icon is highlighted.

You should now have two icons on your disk: **Generic Project** and **First Project**. At this point, the two projects are identical. To complete the **First Project**, we have to re-enter Lightspeed.

• Open **First Project** by double-clicking.
• Close the **First Project** window. (This simply hides the file list; it does not close the entire project.)
• Choose **New** from the **File** menu.

By choosing **New**, you have created a new file to hold some or all of your program statements. This is represented by a window labeled **Untitled 1**, which now appears on the left side of the screen. This window should also contain a flashing vertical bar called an *insertion point.*

The Untitled window is where you will enter and edit your Pascal statements. Editing works the same way in both MacPascal and Lightspeed Pascal. To follow our sample MacPascal editing session, set up the screen so it looks like the initial MacPascal screen.

• If it isn't there already, move the insertion point to the top line of the Untitled window by clicking below the title bar.
• At the insertion point, type the following lines:

```
program Untitled;
        { Your declarations }
begin
        { Your program statements }
end.
```

Type in the words and punctuation exactly as you see them here. If you make a mistake, press the backspace key. When you want to move to the next line, press the Return key. Don't worry about the boldfacing; Lightspeed will automatically bold the words **program**, **begin**, and **end** when you press either the Return or semicolon key.

When you have finished entering the program, you need to do only three more things to make your screen look like the initial MacPascal setup:

- Choose **Text** from the **Windows** menu.
- Choose **Drawing** from the **Windows** menu.
- Select and resize the Untitled window so it doesn't overlap the Text or Drawing window.

Each of these menu selections will bring a new window on to the screen. The purpose of these two new windows and the program skeleton you have just entered will be explained in the next section.

Editing: MacPascal and Lightspeed Pascal

At this point, your screen should look something like this:

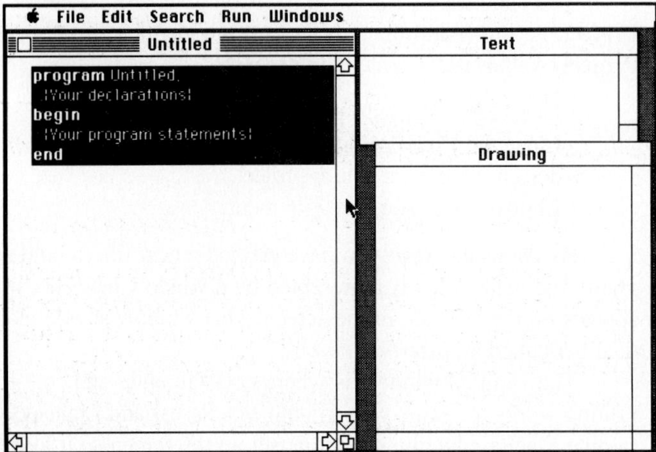

Figure 1.10
Screen setup

(Note that Figure 1.10 is the setup for MacPascal; if you are using Lightspeed, the menus across the top will be different.)

The window on the left of the screen (labeled Untitled) contains the program. You will enter your programs and edit them in this window. The Text and Drawing windows handle the program's input and output. The Text window accepts input from the keyboard and shows the textual output. The Drawing window accepts input from the mouse and shows the graphical output. We will discuss input and graphical output in more detail in Chapters 2 and 3.

As in the Finder, only one window can be active at a time. When you start up MacPascal, the program window is the active window. This window works just like the windows in the Finder: moving the scroll boxes, choosing the size box, clicking on the close box, and dragging the title bar all have the same effect on a MacPascal window as they do in the Finder.

The Untitled window currently holds a highlighted skeleton of a program. On the first line is the **program** declaration, which designates the title of the program. You can also see two *comments* in braces. Although these comments do not affect the execution of the program, they serve a vital function in programming. We'll examine comments in more detail later. Finally, the skeleton contains a **begin** and an **end**, which delimit, or designate the boundaries of, the program. The **begin** and **end** are not statements themselves but are used as brackets in the same way that { and } delimit the comments.

The Pascal *editor* allows you to enter and change programs. Before you can begin editing, make sure that the program window is active.

If you have accidentally made the Text or Drawing window active, reactivate the Untitled window by:

- Clicking anywhere in the program window or
- Pulling down the **Windows** menu and:
  - In MacPascal, choosing the top item.
  - In Lightspeed, choosing the option immediately below **Clipboard**.

This item in the **Windows** menu always matches the name in the program window's title bar. In this case, the menu contains the name **Untitled**.

- Move the mouse into the program window.

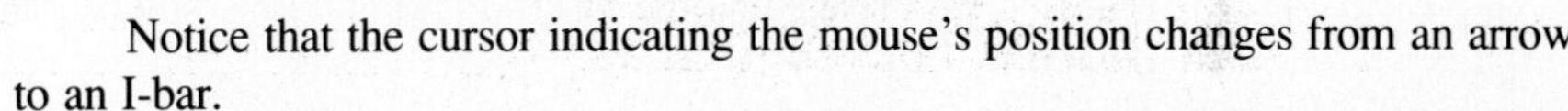

Notice that the cursor indicating the mouse's position changes from an arrow to an I-bar.

- Move the cursor to some point in the skeleton and click the mouse button.

If you are using MacPascal, the skeleton is no longer highlighted. A flashing vertical line now appears where you clicked the I-bar. This flashing line designates the *insertion point*. If you begin typing, characters will appear at the insertion point. The insertion point's position can be changed by clicking on any place in the program window. Note that just moving the I-bar does not change the insertion point — you also have to click the mouse button. (If you forget to click, the insertion point will not move, and your text will appear at the old insertion point.)

You are now ready to enter a simple program called ***First***. The program contains two statements between its **begin** and **end** brackets. Each of these statements, known appropriately as ***Writeln*** (pronounced "write-line") statements, writes a line of output in the Text window. These particular statements tell the computer to print the text "I have control" on one line and "of the machine." on the next.

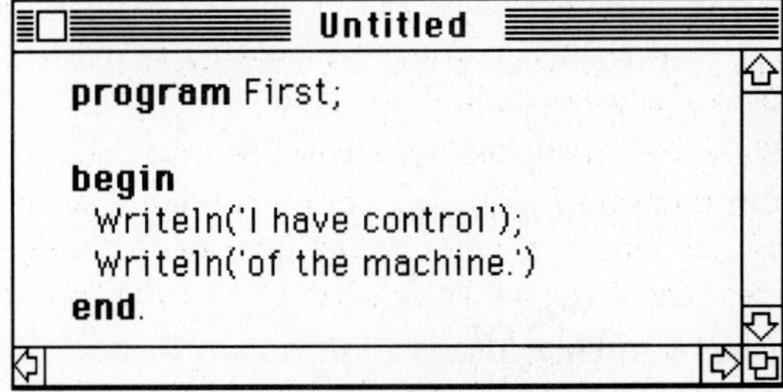

Figure 1.11
Program to enter

To edit the program skeleton so that it precisely matches the program shown in Figure 1.11, you have to take the following steps:

1. Change the program name from ***Untitled*** to ***First***.
2. Delete the comment lines
   { Your declarations } and ***{ Your program statements }***.
3. Add the lines
   Writeln('I have control'); and ***Writeln('of the machine.')***
   between the **begin** and **end** brackets. Let's take each of these steps in turn.

Changing Text: MacPascal and Lightspeed Pascal

First, you need to change the program name, which you can do in one of two ways:

- Move the insertion point between the ***d*** of ***Untitled*** and the semicolon by moving the I-bar to that location and clicking.
- Press the backspace key repeatedly until the old program name is erased.

After the word ***Untitled*** is erased, the first line contains the word **program** followed by a space and the insertion point. Now, you can enter the new name of the program.

- Type the word ***First***.

As each character is typed, it appears on the screen at the insertion point. The first line of the program should now read **program *First;***. If you make a typing mistake, backspace and retype the correct characters.

You can also change text using *selection*. Selecting an area of text enables you to treat it as a single unit. Suppose you decide to change the program name from ***First*** back to ***Untitled***.

- Select the word ***First*** as follows:
  - Move the insertion point to one end of the desired text.
  - Press the mouse button and hold it down.
  - Move the locator to the other end of the text and release the mouse
- Type ***Untitled***.

As you move the mouse, notice that the text is being highlighted — that is, the white space becomes black and vice versa. The text that you selected can be treated as a single unit. Thus, if you press Backspace, you will delete all of the characters in the selected section. If you type while the text is highlighted, whatever you enter will replace the highlighted characters.

- Now change ***Untitled*** back to ***First***.

Deleting Lines: MacPascal and Lightspeed Pascal

- Next, delete the comments ***{ Your declarations }*** and ***{ Your program statements }***.
- Select the comment ***{ Your declarations }***.

Notice that when you let go of the mouse button, the I-bar disappears. The I-bar reappears when the Macintosh senses that you have moved the mouse.

- Delete the selected text by pressing Backspace.

The insertion point is now on the left side of the line between the **program** declaration and the **begin** bracket.

- Press Backspace again to eliminate the blank line.

The insertion point now follows the last character of the previous line, in this case, the semicolon of the **program** declaration. Blank lines, like comments, do not affect the execution of the program, but they are helpful in making a program more readable.

- Reinsert the blank line by pressing Return.
- Delete the comment ***{ Your program statements }***.

After the second deletion, the skeleton should look like this:

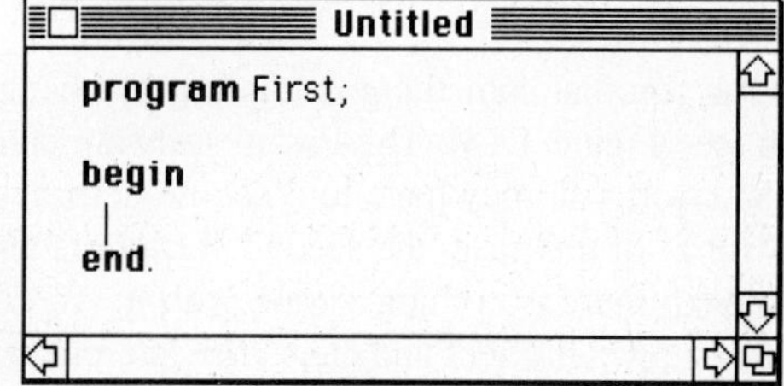

Figure 1.12 Skeleton after comments have been deleted

The I-bar may appear at a different part of the line, depending on where you started and ended your selection.

Inserting Lines: MacPascal and Lightspeed Pascal

Now enter the ***Writeln*** statements.

- At the insertion point, type the following lines (including punctuation marks) exactly as they appear below:

```
Writeln('I have control');
Writeln('of the machine.')
```

The *syntax* of the statement (the punctuation, spelling, order of symbols, etc.) is important. Pascal cannot translate your program into machine code unless each instruction follows Pascal's strict rules of syntax. For example, apostrophes (not quotation marks) are used to surround the text that you want to print. Statements, unless they immediately precede an **end** bracket, are separated by semicolons. (Sometimes the rules of syntax are confusing; you can remember what instruction you want to use, but you forget its punctuation. Later in the chapter, we will examine how the MacPascal editor can help you identify syntax errors as you type a program.)

When you enter the semicolon at the end of the first ***Writeln*** statement, MacPascal automatically indents the statement between the **begin** and **end**. The ***Writeln*** statement is always indented at the same position no matter where you begin typing. This automatic formatting feature of MacPascal is called *pretty printing*.

Pretty printing formats your program according to a number of stylistic conventions used by most Pascal programmers. For example, many *reserved words* (words that have special meaning in Pascal; see Appendix A) appear in bold on the screen. You can tell if you have accidentally misspelled a reserved word (e.g., ***profram*** for **program**) because MacPascal will not display incorrectly spelled reserved words in bold. The stylistic conventions, such as boldfacing reserved words and indenting statements between **begin** and **end**, have no effect on the program's execution. They do, however, make your programs easier to read.

Pretty printing also helps you check your program's syntax as you go along.

- Make an error by retyping the first ***Writeln*** statement without the second apostrophe:

```
Writeln('I have control );
```

MacPascal warns you that something is missing by changing the character style to outline form (see Figure 1.13). The Pascal software can give you only the general location of an error; you may have to do some detective work to figure out exactly what went wrong. In this case, the second ***Writeln*** is also displayed in outline form, even though there is nothing wrong with it. An error such as a missing apostrophe can have a snowball effect and cause the interpreter to assume that there are errors in succeeding lines.

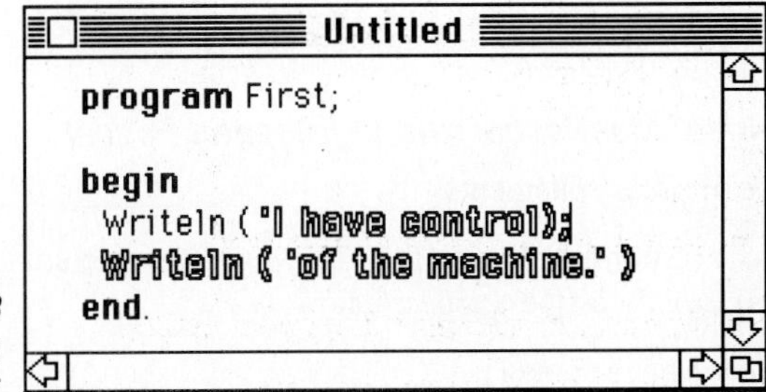

Figure 1.13 Warning of syntax error

- Correct the error by inserting the missing apostrophe.

The letter styles changes back to solid when you move the insertion point to the end of the program. Similarly, if you accidentally mangle a previously correct statement, the error will be signaled when you next press Return, move the insertion point, or enter a semicolon. When you complete the program, your result should match Figure 1.11 (page 13).

Adding Files to the Project: Lightspeed Pascal only

In Lightspeed Pascal, a program's statements can be divided into any number of files. (On the screen, each of these files appears in a separate window.) Most of the programs you write here will appear in a single file.

As we mentioned earlier, a program's statements must be translated into machine code. In Lightspeed Pascal, the statemens and machine code are stored in separate places. The program file will contain the lines of Pascal (also known as *source code*). The project contains other information about the program — specifically, it contains a list of the files which contain the Pascal source code statements, and it also contains the machine code that results from compiling those statements. When you want to work with a program, you open the project — not the program files. From the project, you can open and edit any program file, compile source code and run the machine code.

You have a program file on the screen. You also have a currently active project. However, Lightspeed does not know that you want the file to be a part of the project. The easiest way to tell Lightspeed to make the connection is as follows:

• Choose **Add Window** from the **Project** menu.

Whatever is currently in the program window will become a part of the project, and will be added to the previously compiled **MacPasLib** and **MacTraps**. Lightspeed will also need a way of referring to this new addition. Since the file is not named, a dialog box will appear on the screen, much like the dialog box for **New Project...** that we saw when creating **Generic Project**.

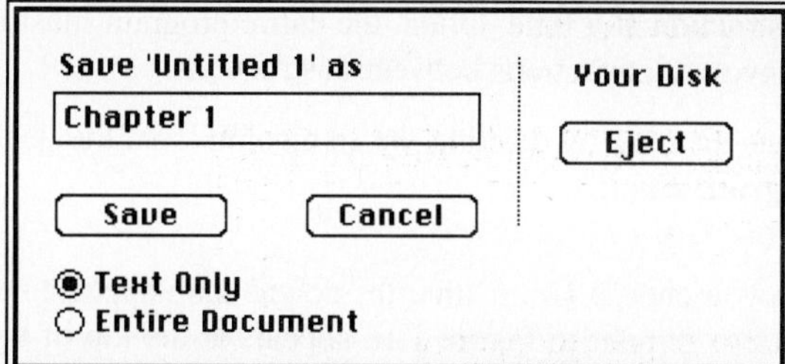

Figure 1.14 **Add Window** dialog box

To save **Untitled 1** as **Chapter 1** on your disk:

• Type **Chapter 1** as the name of the file.
• Select your disk by using the **Eject** and **Drive** buttons on the right side of the dialog box.

The dialog that appears here will ask if you want to save the program as **Text Only** or **Entire Document**. The **Text Only** option will suffice; you don't need to save (or worry about) the extra information stored when you choose **Entire Document**.

• Choose the **Save** button at the bottom of the dialog box.

Now the file has been saved, and the title bar in the program window has changed from **Untitled 1** to the new name, **Chapter 1**. The project is now complete and can be executed.

Executing the Program: MacPascal and Lightspeed Pascal

Now that you have typed the program into the machine, tell the interpreter or compiler to translate and execute it.

- Choose **Go** from the **Run** menu.

The **Go** option executes the program. (If you are using Lightspeed, you see boxes indicating the status of the execution. These boxes indicate that the program is being loaded and compiled, and then that the entire project is being updated.) The output of the program appears in the Text window.

```
Text
I have control
of the machine.
```

Figure 1.15 Output of program *First*

If you follow the messages indicated by the pretty printing, most of the code you enter will be syntactically correct. Some errors will be caught only when you run the program. Pretty printing does not catch all syntax errors because it works on only one instruction at a time. Often, the entire program must be run to catch syntax errors that involve interactions between instructions.

- Create an error by deleting the semicolon from the declaration **program** ***First;***.
- Choose **Go**.

When you choose **Go**, a "thumbs-down" icon appears next to the **begin**, and a syntax error box similar to Figure 1.16 appears at the top of the screen.

A semicolon (;) is required on this line or above but one has not been found.

Figure 1.16 Syntax error box

Because errors in computer programs are known as *bugs*, the ladybug icon appears in the box. The bug box also contains a description of the error discovered by MacPascal.

- Remove the bug box by clicking on it.
- Reinsert the semicolon and choose **Go**.
- If you are using Lightspeed, a dialog box will ask if you want to save the changes before execution. Choose the **Save** button.

The correct output should now be in the Text window.

(At this point, we should note a particular feature of Lightspeed. The **Run** menu contains three options at the bottom of its list: **Auto-Save**, **Confirm Saves**, and **Don't Save**. One of these options is always in effect; the active option is denoted by a bullet or a checkmark. These saving options determine whether a program will be saved before each execution of the program. The **Auto-Save** option will automatically save any changes you make to the file before you run it; the **Don't Save** option will not save changes when you decide to run the program. The **Confirm Saves** option allows you to do either. **Confirm Saves** is the default option, which is why the dialog box appeared when you last selected **Go**. When the dialog box appears asking if you want to save the changes, the **Save** button will make the saves and execute the program; the **Discard** button will not make the saves but will still execute the program; the **Cancel** button cancels the entire operation and stops the execution.)

Experiment with finding syntax errors by purposely changing the instructions to incorrect forms. Keep in mind that by moving the insertion point, you can determine if pretty printing is "happy" and by selecting **Go** you can catch any remaining syntax errors. Remember that the thumbs-down icon may appear after the line where an error actually exists.

Saving Your Program: MacPascal Only

(A note to Lightspeed users: the **Save As...** option is available in both MacPascal and Lightspeed. Because you have other opportunities to save your program files, particularly when you choose the **Add Window** option or when you save changes prior to execution, **Save As...** is not used as often in Lightspeed as in MacPascal. If you ever want to use **Save As...** in Lightspeed, you will see the same dialog box that you saw when you chose **Add Window**. The difference between **Add Window** and **Save As...** is that the first option adds the contents of the program window to the project; the second does not.)

Suppose you now want to save your work.

• Choose **Save As...** from the **File** menu.

The **Save As...** option puts up a dialog box similar to the one shown in Figure 1.17.

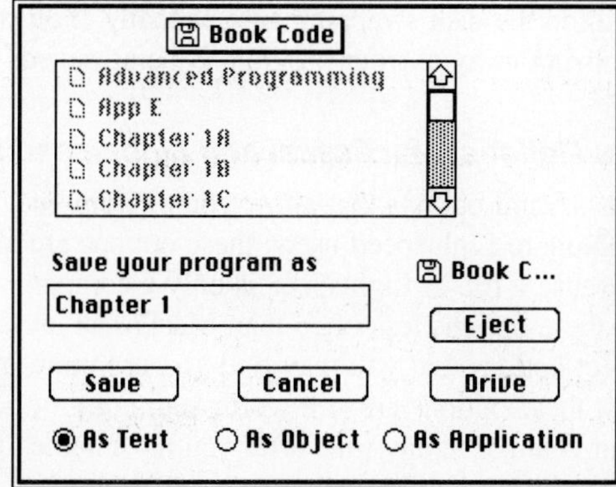

Figure 1.17 MacPascal **Save As...** dialog box

At the top of the box is the name of the current disk and a list of files on the disk. Since two files on the same disk cannot have the same name, check the names of the other files so you can avoid duplication. In a moment, you will see how to change the current disk.

The bottom of the box has three options: **As Text**, **As Object**, and **As Application**. One of these options will have a filled circle, indicating how the program will be saved. For now, use the **As Text** option. (You will use the other two options when you write large programs, larger probably than any you will write in conjunction with this book. **As Application** is used when you want to save a program that can be run without going through MacPascal. **As Object** is used to save part of a program's internal structure, that is, it saves part of the machine code generated by the interpreter. A program saved **As Object** will start up faster but occupies more space on the disk. The differences in speed and space, however, are not significant for the programs you will write here.)

The box under the heading **Save your program as** is where you name the program. Call it **Chapter 1** by typing **Chapter 1**. (Note: the insertion point is already in the box.)

Now you can save the program on your blank disk. The name at the top of the box and directly above the **Eject** button indicates the disk on which the program will be saved.

- If you do not have an external drive, save the file as follows:
  - Choose the **Eject** button to pop the Pascal disk out of the drive.
  - Insert your own disk.
  - Choose the **Save** button.

You will be asked to swap disks a few times. When the swapping is over, you will have saved the file on one disk, and the Pascal disk will be in the drive.

- If you have an external drive, save the file as follows:
  - Insert the blank disk in the external drive.
  - Choose the **Drive** button to designate that you want to use the other disk. The name above the **Eject** button should change to the other disk.
  - Choose the **Save** button.

The Mac will do the disk swapping automatically. You will hear first one, then the other drive whirring away as your program is being saved.

Other File Menu Options: MacPascal and Lightspeed Pascal

The **File** menu has several options that allow you to store your program and manipulate files. (Note to Lightspeed users: these options are also available on your **File** menu, but because a file in Lightspeed is only a component of a project, you will probably use these options less often than MacPascal users. The next section will describe project options that you may find you use more often than the options described here, but these options are still worth learning.)

To save your changes at any time after you have named the program, use the **Save** option. **Save** replaces the old copy of your program with the current version.

As a routine precaution, save your program every twenty minutes or so to guard against losing it because of unexpected machine or software failure.

When you are finished with the program file, you can choose the **Close** option. When you choose this option after making changes to a file, a dialog box asks if you want to save the changes.

Choosing the **Save** button saves the changes before closing; choosing the **Discard** button does not save changes but closes the file. (On some versions, the dialog box may ask if you want to save changes and give you **Yes** and **No** buttons instead of **Save** and **Discard**.) The third button, **Cancel**, means that you don't want to close the file after all. The **Close** option makes the program window disappear but does not exit MacPascal.

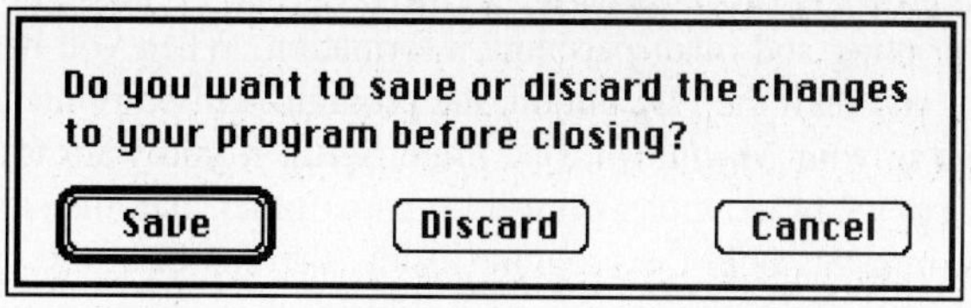

Do you want to save or discard the changes
to your program before closing?

Save Discard Cancel

Figure 1.18
Dialog box for **Close**

Unlike its function in the Finder, the close box in the top left does not do the same thing as the **Close** option. When you click on the close box, the window disappears but the file is not sent back to the disk. In other words, MacPascal still thinks the file is open, even though the window is not on the screen. If you accidentally click on the close box, you can get the window back by choosing the name of the program file from the **Windows** menu.

You can reopen a file by choosing the **Open...** option from the **File** menu. (Lightspeed users: opening a file is not the same as opening a project. When you use this option — particularly when you have several Pascal files on the same disk — make sure that you are in the correct project. The name of the current project is the first option listed in the **Windows** menu. If you are not in the correct project, use the **Open Project...** option explained in the next section.) The dialog box for **Open...** is similar to the one you see when you choose **Save As...**. The name of the current disk and the files on that disk appear on the far left of the box. Use the scroll box to view the other file names on the current disk. When you find the file

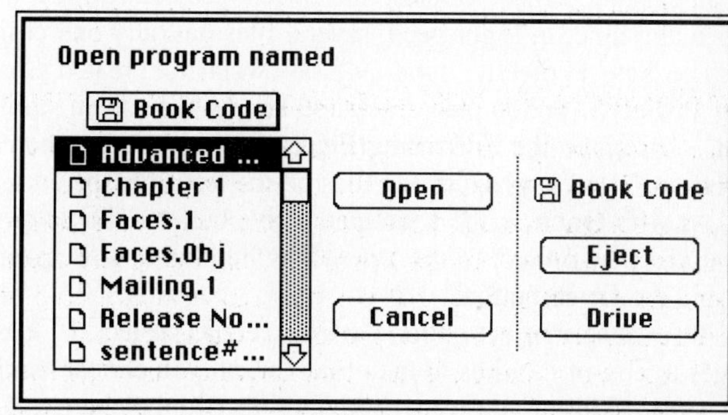

Figure 1.19
Dialog box for **Open...**

you want, you can open it one of two ways. You can double-click on the file name, or you can click on the file name once and then choose the **Open** button.

The **Eject** and **Drive** buttons in the **Open...** dialog box, as in the **Save As...** dialog box, allow you to change the current disk. Use the **Cancel** button if you decide that you don't want to open any file.

To create another file, choose **New**, which will give you a program window labeled **Untitled**.

Back to the **File** menu. Suppose you open a program that you just wanted to look at, but you accidentally entered some changes. Select the **Revert** option to go back to the last version of the program that was saved. The **Revert** option puts up a dialog box; if you agree to revert, it removes all changes and loads the latest saved version of the program into the program window.

To print the file, choose the **Print...** option. A dialog box asks about the style of printing and other pertinent information. When you have selected the options you want and then the **OK** button, the program will be printed on whatever printer is connected to your Macintosh. Use **Page Setup** if you want to do special things to the hard copy (for example, print it on paper other than the standard 8-1/2" x 11"). This option prints only the program listing; the output of the program (that is, the contents of the Text window) can be printed when the program is running. Details on how to do this are explained in Appendix E.

Additional Menu Options: Lightspeed Pascal Only

Lightspeed's **File** and **Project** menus contain some additional options that you will probably find helpful in your daily work. First, the **File** menu contains yet another save option: **Save a Copy As...**. This option allows you to make a backup copy of your current program file under another name. When you choose this option, a dialog box will appear asking you to indicate the name of the backup copy; as usual, the **Drive** and **Eject** buttons allow you to indicate the disk where the copy should be saved.

The **Delete...** option is the equivalent of throwing files in the trash can in the Finder. When you choose this option, a dialog box will appear asking you if you really want to discard the entire file currently being edited. This option should be used with caution.

The top three options on the **Project** menu allow you to create a new project, open an existing project, or close the current project. In MacPascal, only one file can be open at a time; in Lightspeed, several files but only one project can be open at a time. The **New Project...** option we saw when we created **Generic Project**. The **Open Project...** option places a dialog box on the screen similar to the box for the **Open...** option on the **File** menu (Figure 1.19, page 21). The names of the projects are listed in place of the files on the left side; the current disk appears on the right. As with **Open...**, the **Eject** and **Drive** buttons allow you to change the current disk; the project can be opened by highlighting the name of the project and choosing the **Open** button.

The **Close Project** option closes an entire project. If there have been any changes to any of the files in the project when you choose this option, a dialog box will appear asking if you want to save or discard the changes.

The **Add Window**, **Add File…** , and **Remove** options on the **Project** menu all deal with the list of files inside the project. **Add File…** is similar to **Add Window** in that it adds a program file to the project. The difference is that **Add File…** can add any Pascal file currently on the disk. When you choose this option, a dialog box appears. This box is identical to the **Open…** dialog box (Figure 1.19, page 21) except that the **Open** button is replaced by an **Add** button. You choose a file to add in the same way that you choose a file to open: highlight the file on the left side of the box and choose the **Add** button. The dialog box disappears while the file is added. Then, it will reappear, asking you to choose another file to add. You may add any number of files, but for the programs you will write in the near future, you probably will stick to projects with just one Pascal file. When the dialog box reappears, then, choose the **Cancel** button to indicate that you do not want to add any more files to the project.

The **Remove** option takes files out of the project. The easiest way to use this option is to bring up the project window (you do this by choosing the top option in the **Windows** menu). When the list of files appears, click on the name of the file you wish to remove. The **Remove** option removes the highlighted file from the project. Note that this option does not remove the file from the disk; to recover a removed file, you can use **Add File…**.

Leaving MacPascal and Lightspeed Pascal

The **Quit** option on the **File** menu sends you back into the Finder. As with **Close** (and **Close Project** in Lightspeed), if you have made any changes since your last save, you will be asked if you want to save them before quitting. In MacPascal, **Quit** is the only way that you can return to the operating system. When you return to the Finder, you should notice a new icon for your file called **Chapter 1**.

Both MacPascal and Lightspeed offer a number of other features to help you enter, edit, run, and save programs. Appendix E includes a number of time-saving operations, similar to those found in word-processing programs, that allow you to move and copy sections of your program and search and replace segments of text. The half hour you spend learning the operations in Appendix E will be repaid many times as you work on longer projects. However, you certainly have enough tools now to get started. When you are comfortable with the fundamentals, follow the hands-on exercise in Appendix E.

1.5 Problem Solving

To get you started as quickly as possible, we have taken a whirlwind tour of the inner layers of the computer onion. We have thrown many terms at you in not much space, but we certainly don't expect you to retain everything immediately. With practice, things that now appear mysterious and confusing will become second nature. Spend time using your Mac; soon you will be familiar with the Macintosh utilities and the functions of the various pieces of hardware. With these preliminaries out of the way, we can now begin our main topic of discussion: the use of programs to solve problems.

Our first example program was not very realistic. Most programs contain more than two statements. More important, writing programs of any substantial length requires the use of problem-solving techniques. When you are programming, you are using the computer to solve a large problem; therefore, it isn't practical to look at the problem and immediately begin writing Pascal instructions. The best way to solve large problems is to break them down into smaller subproblems. If the smaller problems are still too large to be translated directly into Pascal instructions, we continue to *divide and conquer* those subproblems. Eventually the problems are small enough to be represented by one, or maybe a few, instructions in Pascal. At that point, and only at that point, are we ready to write Pascal code.

The problem-decomposition method is similar to the way a bureaucracy handles complex tasks. Take a typical corporation. The person in charge of the corporation is the president. Let's suppose she wants to put a new product on the market. She can meet with her vice-presidents and delegate authority—the VP in charge of advertising will create commercials, the VP in charge of marketing will determine how to package the product, and so on. Thus, the president has broken the task into smaller subtasks.

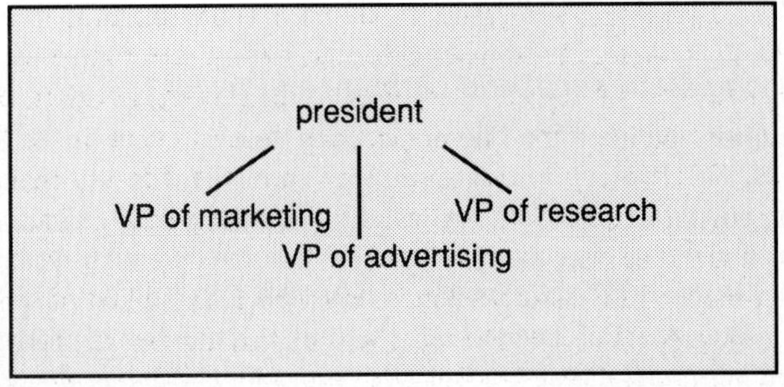

Figure 1.20
First division of tasks in a corporation

Each vice-president, however, has been left with a large task. Creating a commercial is not particularly simple. The advertising VP calls his subordinates and gives them various tasks, such as contacting commercial producers, hiring writers, and estimating the advertising budget.

In turn, the person in charge of hiring writers has to organize the list of tasks she must perform. She needs to find writers, so she tells her secretary to call the newspaper and run a classified ad. The president knows nothing about the secretary phoning the *Daily Herald*, but the secretary's act is a small subtask of the president's large-scale task.

You probably use this divide-and-conquer scheme when you write reports. You begin by thinking about the topic and making some notes or designing an outline. Then you expand each point by adding more details and supporting evidence; you also rearrange the order of the ideas to make the paper more coherent. As you write, you keep the overall structure in mind, but your advance work allows you to consider one point at a time.

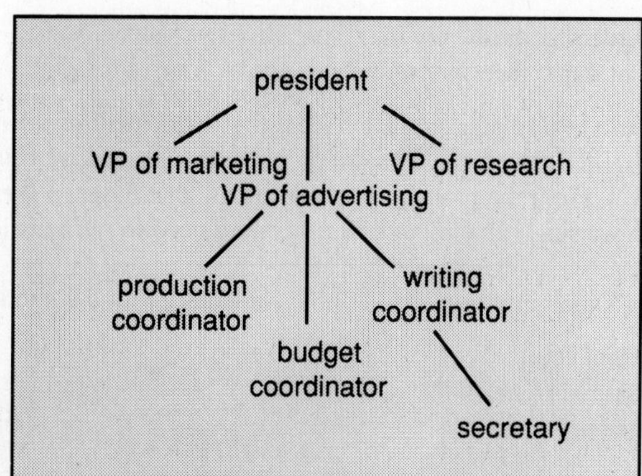

Figure 1.21
Further division of tasks in a corporation

1.6 Pseudocode

Solving a problem for a computer involves the same divide-and-conquer strategy. We begin with a problem defined in a natural language (like English). We then make a list of major tasks to be done. If the subtasks are too large to be specified easily, we break them down into smaller subtasks; they in turn can be divided into even smaller subtasks. As with reports, there may be rearrangements after the initial outline is completed, but the first outline provides the basic structure of the program.

(This strategy is also used for programs far beyond the scope of this book: programs in the "real world" are usually written by teams of people, who divide the task into separate parts.)

A programmer translates the *algorithm*, or method of solving a problem, step by step from English to Pascal. The intermediate steps, which are lists of tasks, are written in abbreviated English sentences that look more and more like Pascal instructions as the problem is broken down further. These task lists, written before the Pascal code, are known as *pseudocode*. The method of reducing a problem from a natural language to computer code is formally called *stepwise refinement* or, informally, *pseudocoding*.

Pseudocoding may sound quite simple: it seems that all you have to do is identify large problems and then list their subtasks. But a realistically complex problem often does not have an obvious breakdown. No one has yet developed a foolproof scheme for breaking down problems or a problem-solving technique that works for all people. Still, we can offer suggestions for methods of breaking down problems that work for many programmers. As you gain practice in problem decomposition, you will discover which techniques work best for you.

Let's make the pseudocoding process more concrete with an example. Suppose an amateur dramatics group wants a program that prints out the classical comedy and tragedy masks. For purposes of this simple example, the faces are identical except for the mouths. We need to break this task down into separate parts. The highest-level, or most general, task list would look like this:

Print comic face
Print tragic face

These two smaller problems are a first refinement of the main problem. Of course, we need to break down the problem enough that we can translate the pieces into Pascal. From the program ***First***, we know that Pascal's ***Writeln*** instruction prints only a single line of text. We therefore need to refine at least another level of detail.

Let's look in more detail at how we would print the comic face:

{ Print comic face}
Print top of head
Print smile

This group of statements refines, i.e., breaks down, the statement "Print comic face" from the first level of pseudocode. The statement that is being refined is put in *comment brackets*. To complete this second level of pseudocoding, let's look at how we would draw the tragic face:

{ Print tragic face }
Print top of head
Print frown

Figure 1.22 shows the complete stepwise refinement as a hierarchy.

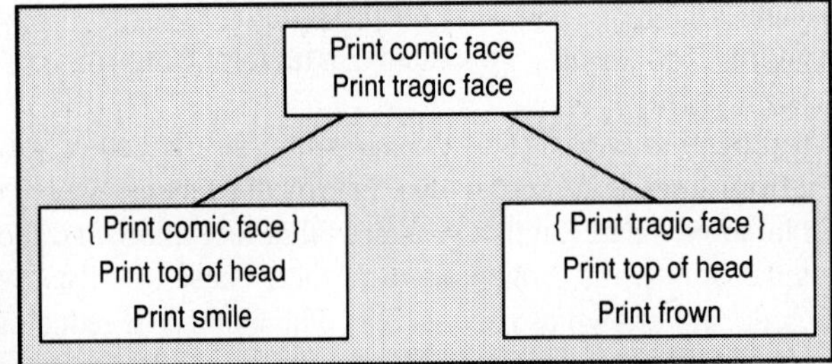

Figure 1.22 Pseudocode hierarchy

We still need to break down each of these steps into the printing of single lines. Let's determine how we might draw the top of the head using only characters that the computer can represent:

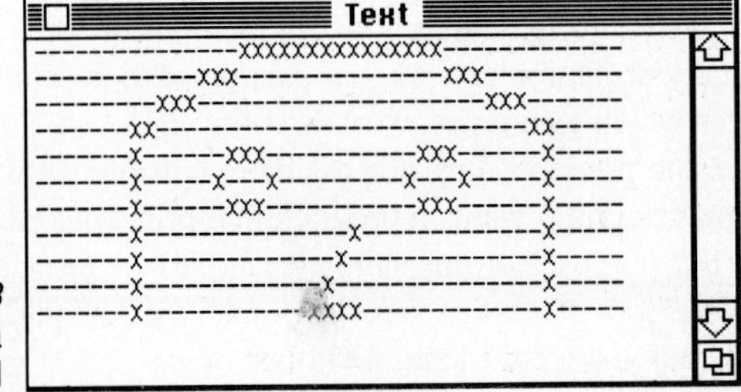

Figure 1.23 Printing the top of a head

Since a ***Writeln*** statement prints out a single line of characters, we next refine "Print top of head" into a series of ***Writeln*** statements, in which each statement will draw a single line of the top of the head. Since the entire segment "Print top of head" can be translated into code, this segment of the pseudocode is complete. We can use the same technique to complete the breakdown of the pseudocode "Print smile" and "Print frown." Now writing the program becomes a simple exercise of converting from pseudocode into *syntactically correct* Pascal code, that is, code that is correct according to the rules of Pascal's grammar. Let's look at the ***Writeln*** statement's syntax in a bit more detail.

1.7 The *Writeln* Statement

The ***Writeln*** statement provides a method of printing a sequence of characters, known as a *literal character string*. (The term *string* refers to any sequence of characters.) We have to tell the ***Writeln*** statement exactly what string to print. For example,

```
Writeln ('This is sentence #1 of the output.');
```

produces the output:

```
This is sentence #1 of the output.
```

Similarly, the following statements print out the top of the head.

```
Writeln('---------------xxxxxxxxxxxxxxx-------------');
Writeln('------------xxx---------------xxx----------');
Writeln('---------xxx---------------------xxx-------');
Writeln('-------xx---------------------------xx-----');
Writeln('-------x------xxx-----------xxx------x-----');
Writeln('-------x-----x---x---------x---x-----x-----');
Writeln('-------x------xxx-----------xxx------x-----');
Writeln('-------x---------------x-------------x-----');
Writeln('-------x--------------x--------------x-----');
Writeln('-------x-------------x---------------x-----');
Writeln('-------x------------xxxx-------------x-----');
```

After the ***Writeln*** statement outputs the literal string, it "prints" a carriage return in the output. The result is that Pascal prints subsequent output on the following line. A variant of the ***Writeln*** statement, the ***Write*** statement, does the same thing as a ***Writeln*** except print a carriage return. The syntax of the ***Writeln*** and ***Write*** statements is identical. For example, the sequence

```
Write ('This is sentence #1');
Writeln(' of the output.');
```

produces the same result as

```
Writeln('This is sentence #1 of the output.');
```

Notice that the statements consist of four parts: the word ***Write*** or ***Writeln***, the left parenthesis, the literal string within apostrophes, and the right parenthesis. A semicolon separates the end of one statement from the beginning of the next. There can be any number of spaces between the various parts. For example, MacPascal will do the same thing whether or not there is a space between ***Write*** and the left parenthesis. Spaces within apostrophes, however, are very important; each space between the apostrophes translates to a space in the output.

To print a blank line, omit the parentheses, the literal text, and, of course, the apostrophes that surround the text. This *special case* of the ***Writeln*** statement looks like this:

```
Writeln;
```

Syntax Box 1.1
Write/Writeln

Purpose To print out a sequence of characters, known as a *literal string*.

Syntax

```
Write('&lt; text &gt; ');
Writeln('&lt; text &gt; ');
```

where < text > is the sequence of letters, numbers, symbols, or spaces to be printed out.

Usage ***Writeln*** usually prints out the characters literally in the text string, followed by a carriage return. The one exception is the apostrophe.

Use two apostrophes (not a double quote) to print out a single apostrophe. To produce a blank line in the output, type the statement

```
Writeln;
```

Write performs the same function as ***Writeln*** but does not produce a carriage return in the output. The output of a ***Write/Writeln*** statement appears in the Text window.

1.8 Declaring Procedures and Programs

The division of tasks in a program is much like the division of tasks in a bureaucracy. Pascal allows us to group instructions into a logical block that performs a task. This block of declarations and statements is known as a *procedure* and typically corresponds to some subtask in the pseudocode. The procedure "in charge" of the program is called the *mainline*. Just as each person in a bureaucracy can delegate tasks to subordinates, each procedure—including the mainline—can delegate tasks to subordinate procedures. Figure 1.24 compares a corporate bureaucracy with a Pascal program.

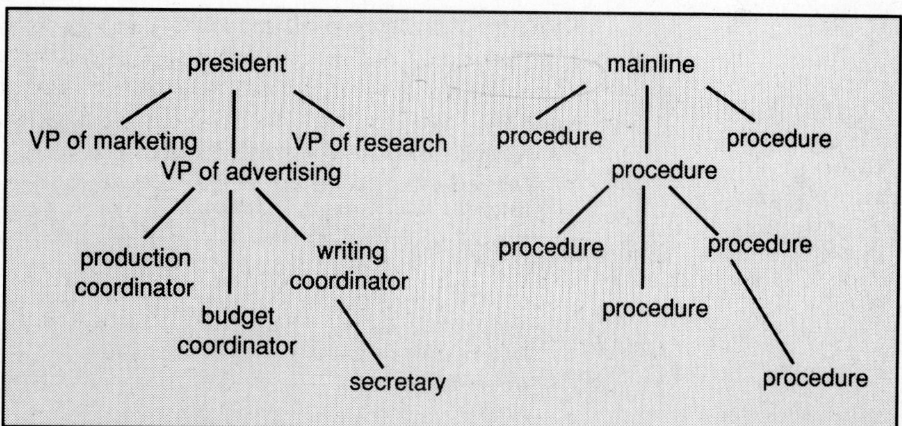

Figure 1.24
Division of tasks in a bureaucracy and in Pascal

To use procedures, you have to tell Pascal what to call the procedure and what instructions to include in it. Pascal allows you to name the procedures with the **procedure** declaration. Once a procedure is declared, Pascal has to be told where the procedure begins and ends. To do this, type the word **begin** on the line before the first line of the procedure and the word **end** after the last line of the procedure. In effect, the **begin/end** brackets convert several statements into a single compound statement, called a *block*. A semicolon typed after **end** indicates the end of the compound statement. You can think of **begin/end** as a pair of brackets or parentheses that surround blocks of statements.

In our theatrical mask example, printing the top of the head can be made into a procedure. This procedure can be called both when we are printing the comic face and when we are printing the tragic face.

We can designate procedures in our pseudocode as follows:

{ Print comic face }
Call procedure to print top of head
Call procedure to print smile

{ Print tragic face }
Call procedure to print top of head
Call procedure to print frown

Because we call procedures often, we can abbreviate the phrase "Call procedure to" to the notation "CALL:"

{ Print comic face }
CALL: Print top of head
CALL: Print smile

{ Print tragic face }
CALL: Print top of head
CALL: Print frown

The code for the procedure to print the top of the head is as follows:

```
procedure TopHead;

begin
    Writeln('---------------XXXXXXXXXXXXXXX-------------');
    Writeln('------------xxx---------------xxx----------');
    Writeln('---------xxx---------------------xxx-------');
    Writeln('-------xx---------------------------xx-----');
    Writeln('-------x------xxx-----------xxx------x-----');
    Writeln('-------x-----x---x---------x---x-----x-----');
    Writeln('-------x------xxx-----------xxx------x-----');
    Writeln('-------x---------------x-------------x-----');
    Writeln('-------x--------------x--------------x-----');
    Writeln('-------x-------------x---------------x-----');
    Writeln('-------x------------xxxx-------------x-----')
end; { TopHead }
```

In the programs in this book, we capitalize the first letter of each word of procedure names. This is only a matter of style; it has no effect on the execution of the program. You may separate words with underscores (e.g., ***Top_Head***), but no spaces or other punctuation may appear in the program's or procedure's name.

Syntax Box 1.2
procedure

Purpose To declare a block of statements as a single procedure.

Syntax

```
procedure < name > ;
begin
  < statement >s;
  < statement >
end;
```

where < name > is a sequence of letters, or letters and digits, but must begin with a letter.

< statement >s are one or more legal Pascal statements, separated by semicolons. (Note no semicolon follows the statement preceding the **end**.)

Usage The < name > cannot be one of the words that Pascal reserves for other functions. MacPascal's reserved words are in Appendix A.

Duplicate procedure names are not allowed in the same program.

Note that **begin** is not followed by a semicolon, but **end** is. This final semicolon denotes the end of a compound statement. No semicolon follows the statement preceding **end**.

Procedures must always have **begin** and **end** surrounding all the statements in the *procedure body*.

In the same way that you developed the ***TopHead*** procedure, you can create a procedure to draw the smile. The procedure named ***Smile*** appears below:

```
procedure Smile;
begin
    Writeln('-------x------x---------------x------x-----');
    Writeln('-------x-------xx-----------xx-------x-----');
    Writeln('-------x--------xx---------xx--------x-----');
    Writeln('-------x-----------xxxxxxx-----------x-----');
    Writeln('--------xx-------------------------xx------');
    Writeln('----------xxx-------------------xxx--------');
    Writeln('--------------xxx-----------xxx------------');
    Writeln('------------------xxxxxxxxx----------------');
    Writeln('-------------------------------------------')
end; { Smile }
```

The same method of breaking down pseudocode into Pascal is used to draw the frown. We will see this code shortly.

Assuming that you have now declared the procedures ***Frown***, ***Smile***, and ***TopHead***, you must guarantee that the procedures will be executed in the correct order. What you want to do is call, or *invoke*, the procedures. To invoke a procedure and thus execute it, simply type the name of the procedure followed by a semicolon.

Procedures can call any other procedures that have been previously declared. Let's move away, for the moment, from the theatrical mask example. Suppose you have another program with three procedures. The first procedure in a file is called ***Top***, followed by the procedures ***Middle*** and ***Bottom***.

```
procedure Top;
begin
    ...
end;
procedure Middle;
begin
    ...
end;
procedure Bottom;
begin
    ...
end;
```

Because ***Middle*** and ***Bottom*** are physically below ***Top*** in the file, ***Middle*** and ***Bottom*** can call procedure ***Top*** by including the line

```
Top;
```

within their procedure bodies. However, ***Top*** cannot call ***Middle*** or ***Bottom***. In the same manner, ***Bottom*** can call ***Middle***, but ***Middle*** can't call ***Bottom***.

As we mentioned earlier, every program contains a special procedure called the mainline. Although the mainline is always executed first, it appears at the end of the program. Because Pascal knows that every program will have a mainline at the bottom of the file, the mainline does not need a procedure declaration. This means that the declaration **procedure *Mainline*** does not appear before the mainline's **begin**. The mainline's **end** has a period instead of a semicolon, to designate the end of the program.

Let's go back briefly to the corporation analogy. The mainline is comparable to the corporate president, in that it can call on any of the underlings in the program. You can remember the syntactic difference between the mainline's **end** and other procedures by remembering that the president has the last word—period.

The mainline must be the last part in the program. Because of its position in the file, it is able to call any other procedure declared in the program. Except for the minor syntactic difference and its position in the program, however, the mainline is like any other procedure. The mainline can contain regular Pascal statements along with procedure calls, just like any other procedure. Thus, the mainline for drawing two faces with three blank lines between them follows the declarations of procedures ***TopHead***, ***Frown***, and ***Smile***, and looks like this:

```
begin
    TopHead;          { draw comic face }
    Smile;

    Writeln;
    Writeln;          { draw three lines between faces }
    Writeln;

    TopHead;
    Frown
end. { Faces }
```

With one more instruction (that we have already seen), we can finish the program. Just as we refer to entire procedures by single names, we need a way to refer to the entire program. Since the **procedure** declaration is used to declare a procedure, it makes sense to name a program by using the **program** declaration.

Pascal will recognize **program** and **procedure** declarations only if they are in a particular, standard order. The **program** declaration begins the program. This is

Syntax Box 1.3
program

Purpose	Denotes beginning of program.
Syntax	**program** < name > ;
where	< name > is the name of the program.
Usage	< name > may contain digits, but must begin with a letter. < name > also cannot be one of the words that Pascal reserves for other functions. MacPascal's reserved words are in Appendix A.

followed by any number of procedures. Finally, the mainline appears at the bottom of the file.

```
program < program name > ;
procedure < procedure name 1 >;
begin
   ...
end;
procedure < procedure name 2 >;
begin
   ...
end;
   ...
procedure < procedure name n >;
begin
   ...
end;
begin
   < mainline >
end.
```

1.9 Documentation

You are now ready to write the complete program. Before you do, however, we must discuss one important point: making the program understandable to the human reader. A "good" program is one that is easily used, read, or modified by other people —not just the programmer.

The process of commenting a program is called *documentation.* As we noted in the hands-on section, comments do not affect the program's execution but are used to explain the code. Programs are documented to aid the programmer in fixing errors (a process known as *debugging*) and to help others who might want to modify the program later. The goal of documentation is to make the program understandable to any reader. The aesthetics, formatting, and documentation make the Pascal code much easier to understand.

The programs in this chapter are straightforward, and detailed explanation may seem unnecessary. We are introducing conventions of commenting and pretty printing at this point, though, because it is essential to develop habits that will save considerable time later when you are writing much more complex programs. Good programmers enter their comments before the code so they can remember what each procedure is supposed to do. When a procedure seems not to work, the comments serve as useful reminders of why a section of code is in the program in the first place. Also, most programs are written by more than one person; comments are an important communication link between individuals working on the same program.

As we have seen, lines of documentation are enclosed in braces. In MacPascal, you can use the Tab key to line up your comments.

Syntax Box 1.4
Commenting

Purpose To indicate what the code is doing in natural-language terms.

Syntax { < text of comment > }

Usage Anything that appears between the comment brackets is ignored by the Pascal interpreter.

Programmers often create unexpected problems by forgetting to close the comment before typing in Pascal code. In MacPascal and in Lightspeed, the left and right comment bracket must appear on the same line.

The contents of comments are shown in Syntax Box 1.5.

Comments are of two sorts: *block comments* and *inline comments*. Block comments are used as headings for blocks of instructions in procedures and programs and should contain all the information a programmer needs to know about the procedure or program. Never assume that the person reading the documentation knows anything about the problem your program solves.

The text of a block comment should describe a specific task, be it the purpose of the program as a whole, the mainline, or another procedure. You should not mention specific Pascal syntax in a comment. For example, you should not say, "This procedure prints out three lines of text using three Writeln statements." Instead, your comments should answer the following question as completely as possible: what exactly is this procedure/program supposed to do?

Syntax Box 1.5
Block comment checklist

Block comments for each procedure should include:

1. The procedure name
2. The purpose of the procedure
3. The format of input and output used by the procedure (e.g., "This procedure asks for the user's age in years.")*
4. Error conditions and how the procedure handles them*
5. Special cases that may or may not be handled by the procedure (e.g., "This procedure calculates the date but assumes that the data does not contain any leap years.")*
6. A list of procedures that call the procedure
7. A list of procedures that are called by the procedure
8. Other complex or interesting points about the procedure

Block comments at the top of a program should include:

1. The program name
2. Your name
3. The date of last revision
4. Description of program: its major structure and breakdown, and input and output

* Items 3, 4, and 5 will be explained in later chapters.

Syntax Box 1.5 lists items that you should include in your block comments. The block comment at the top of your program, called the *header comment*, should describe the program as a whole.

While block comments give general descriptions, inline comments document any complicated, involved, or tricky piece of code. Inline comments also denote ends: in the theatrical masks program, the name of each procedure is typed in an inline comment on the same line as the procedure's end. This convention is useful when you are using many begins and ends in the same program. You will see more examples of this type of commenting, along with more complete block comments, in later chapters as the code examples become more complex.

You now have all you need to write the program. The complete program, called ***Faces***, appears on the next pages.

Code 1.1
Program *Faces*

```
{ David Niguidula       Program: Faces        July 15          }
{                                                              }
{    The Faces program prints out faces representing the two   }
{ theatrical masks: comedy and tragedy.  The two faces have    }
{ identical foreheads, eyes, and noses, but different mouths.  }
{ The program will first print the comic face and then the tra- }
{ gic face.  No input is required for the program's execution. }

program Faces;

{ Procedure: TopHead                                           }
{ This procedure prints out a face's forehead, eyes, and nose. }
{ Called by: Mainline                         Calls: none      }

  procedure TopHead;
  begin
    Writeln('---------------xxxxxxxxxxxxxxx-------------');
    Writeln('------------xxx---------------xxx----------');
    Writeln('---------xxx---------------------xxx-------');
    Writeln('-------xx---------------------------xx-----');
    Writeln('-------x------xxx-----------xxx------x-----');
    Writeln('-------x-----x---x---------x---x-----x-----');
    Writeln('-------x------xxx-----------xxx------x-----');
    Writeln('-------x---------------x-------------x-----');
    Writeln('-------x--------------x--------------x-----');
    Writeln('-------x-------------x---------------x-----');
    Writeln('-------x------------xxxx-------------x-----')
  end;  { TopHead }

{ Procedure: Smile                                             }
{ This procedure prints out the smile and chin of a comic face. }
{ Called by: Mainline                            Calls: none   }
```

Code 1.1 (continued)

```
procedure Smile;

begin
   Writeln('-------x------x----------------x------x-----');
   Writeln('-------x-------xx------------xx-------x-----');
   Writeln('-------x--------xx----------xx--------x-----');
   Writeln('-------x-----------xxxxxxx------------x-----');
   Writeln('--------xx--------------------------xx------');
   Writeln('----------xxx--------------------xxx--------');
   Writeln('--------------xxx------------xxx------------');
   Writeln('------------------xxxxxxxxx-----------------');
   Writeln('--------------------------------------------')
end; { Smile }

{ Procedure: Frown                                          }
{ This procedure prints out the frown and chin of a tragic face. }
{ Called by: Mainline      Calls: none                       }

procedure Frown;

begin
   Writeln('-------x------------------------------x-----');
   Writeln('-------x-----------xxxxxxx------------x-----');
   Writeln('-------x---------xx--------xx---------x-----');
   Writeln('-------x-------xx------------xx-------x-----');
   Writeln('-------x------x----------------x------x-----');
   Writeln('--------xx--------------------------xx------');
   Writeln('----------xxx--------------------xxx--------');
   Writeln('--------------xxx------------xxx------------');
   Writeln('------------------xxxxxxxxx-----------------');
   Writeln('--------------------------------------------')
end; { Frown }

{ Mainline                                                  }
{    The Mainline first prints out the comic face by calling the }
{ TopHead procedure and the Smile procedure.  Since the      }
{ tragic face is identical to the comic face except for the mouth }
{ Mainline calls the same procedure to print the top of the  }
{ head. To finish the tragic face, the procedure Frown is    }
{ called.                                                   }
{ Calls: TopHead, Smile, Frown                              }

begin

   TopHead;             { draw comic face }
   Smile;

   Writeln;
   Writeln;             { draw three lines between faces }
   Writeln;

   TopHead;             { draw tragic face }
   Frown

end.  { Faces }
```

1.10 Pseudocode Advice

Now that you've seen a complete example of a program's development, let's go back to some of the general principles of pseudocode. Since everyone thinks differently, there is no single way to break down a problem. Beginning programmers often wonder how they are going to create pseudocode that corresponds to lines of Pascal without writing the Pascal first. Certainly, translating a problem from human stream-of-consciousness to the computer's structured language is not a simple task. Thus, in our examples, we provide sample pseudocode to help you make the transition from English-language problems to Pascal-language code. You will probably develop your own style of pseudocoding as you gain programming experience, but for now you should start by imitating our pseudocode.

One of the nice things about computers is that they can easily repeat the same thing over and over and over again. A programmer can define a procedure once and have the computer execute the same block of statements multiple times. All the programmer needs to do is tell the computer how many times to execute the statements. As you write pseudocode, notice when you are duplicating groups of statements; then regroup the code into procedures and determine how you can best eliminate the duplication. (In the ***Faces*** example, we decided right away that we could execute the same group of statements to print the top of the head for each face. We then created a procedure to perform this task.) In Chapter 5, you will see more sophisticated ways of handling repeated code, but for now remember to make good use of procedures.

Beginning programmers often try to move from English to Pascal too quickly. You will find pseudocoding easier if you continually think of your problem in natural-language terms. In general, you should have very little Pascal syntax in your pseudocode. You may want to include certain *reserved words* that appear in Pascal, such as **begin/end**. With those key words, you can determine exactly what is included in each section of the code. You are also less likely to omit those words when you type in the program.

Write your pseudocode BEFORE you write any Pascal code. 

Underline the above sentence. Memorize it. Highlight it in bright orange marker. Draw stars in the margins. Fold down the corner of this page. Read it over before you go to bed at night (well, maybe that's going a little far...). *Designing* a program properly is more important than the actual Pascal *coding* of the program. Certain programs may appear so trivial that pseudocode seems unnecessary. You may even be able to get such a program to work. A working program, however, is not the same as a well-designed program. Essentially, you are learning problem solving and happen to be using the computer as a tool. A careful design is essential. The time you put into a program before you start coding diminishes the time spent in front of a Mac. The up-front investments in "doing it right" will pay off handsomely when you write all but the simplest programs.

Finally, we emphasize the difference between code and pseudocode. Code must be written in the language the computer understands. Pseudocode is not bound by those same restrictions. The only hard and fast rule of pseudocode is that when you break down a task, the resulting list of subtasks must correctly perform the same function as the original task.

1.11 Chapter Summary

In this chapter you have been introduced to some of the concepts and terminology that lets you talk about computers and some of the Pascal language that lets you control the machine. A computer executes a program in three steps: first, it receives input; second, it processes information using calculations and storage space as needed; third, it produces output. The processing of information requires the use of the hardware's memory and central processing unit assisted by a number of software utilities included in the computer's operating system. You will use manufacturer-provided software to help you write and run your own programs.

Programs are the computer-language solution to problems that are usually first stated in human language. Stepwise refinement (employing levels of pseudocode) means taking the problem stated in human language (for our purpose, English), breaking its large tasks into smaller components, and creating a properly ordered sequence of instructions, known as a program, for the computer to execute. Such refinement usually requires the writing of several levels of pseudocode before anything is written as Pascal declarations, definitions, and statements.

Fortunately, Pascal lends itself well to problems defined as tasks and subtasks. You do not have to create one long list of instructions for the computer to perform; instead, you can group Pascal statements into procedures. Each procedure represents a logically related group of instructions that, collectively, have a single purpose. A special procedure called the mainline, which is the first and highest-level procedure invoked by Pascal, must be placed at the end of every program.

Any number of instructions may appear inside a program. So far, we have looked at only a few: the ***Write*** and ***Writeln*** statements and the **procedure** and **program** declarations. Each of these instructions has a particular syntax that must be followed. Computers can only understand instructions that are stated in a uniform manner.

Because Pascal instructions are not natural English, we rely on documentation to explain the purpose of programs, procedures, and complex sections of Pascal code. Documentation, or comments, can appear anywhere in a program and should be used extensively during each stage of program development. Comments help us to remember the intention of each section of code; they also allow others to understand the purpose of the instructions. Comments do not affect the way computers execute programs, but they do affect the way people understand code.

Besides these general concepts about programming in Pascal, we looked at how one particular machine — the Macintosh — can be used to enter Pascal programs. Using the mouse and the keyboard, you can enter your programs in MacPascal's or Lightspeed's program window. Entering the code is done interactively; that is, the machine communicates with you as you type the code. The pretty printing feature indicates potential syntax errors and formats your program into a readable form.

Once a program is entered, it can be translated via an interpreter or compiler, and then executed. Syntax error boxes, which appear with a bug icon, let you know if an instruction's syntax is incorrect. A thumbs-down icon indicates the general location of the bug.

In Lightspeed, you have to keep track of projects as well as program files. When you open a project, you can gain entry to its component program files; typically, each of your projects will contain one file of Pascal source code and two files (**MacPasLib** and **MacTraps**) that hold other information needed to run your source code. Thus, each time you want to edit a file in Lightspeed, you should open the entire project from the Finder; when the project takes over the screen, you can then open the source code file.

1.12 Exercises

There are three types of exercises in this book. The **Understanding Concepts** problems are designed to test your comprehension of the material in the chapter. Usually these questions require a short answer in prose. The **Coding Exercises** test a specific concept or concepts in programming. Usually you are asked to write or modify a procedure, or some other part of a program. The **Programming Problems** are larger problems that use concepts from the current chapter but also rely on your mastery of knowledge from previous chapters. These problems ask you to write entire programs.

We have deliberately left open ends in a number of the exercises; for example, we rarely specify the exact format of the output. We want you to consider the problem and determine how the information should be presented to a user. We also want to discourage the idea that there is one right answer to a programming problem. If we haven't specified exactly how something should be done, do whatever makes the most sense and is the most efficient use of the programming tools at your disposal, but make sure to document your decisions.

Understanding Concepts

1. Compare the input-processing-output process with the way you prepare a laboratory experiment.

2. Which of the following are hardware and which are software?

a. mouse	e. interpreter	i. screen
b. disk drive	f. operating system	j. window manager
c. diskette	g. memory chips	
d. MacPascal	h. machine code	

3. What is the difference between a high-level and a low-level language?

4. What are two ways MacPascal tells you that your code contains a syntax error?

5. What does it mean to "divide and conquer" a problem?

6. What's the difference between ***Write*** and ***Writeln***?

7. Explain what each of the following mean to MacPascal:

   a. { } c. ;
   b. ' ' (apostrophes) d. **boldface** words

8. Semicolons separate statements from each other. Why isn't a semicolon needed between a statement and a procedure's **end**?

9. Which of the following are legal procedure names?

   a. ***Third*** b. ***3rd*** c. ***Procedure3***

10. If comments do not affect a program's execution, why do we include them?

11. Imagine that you have a robot that understands only four commands: "turn left," "turn right," "turn around," and "go forward < distance >" where < distance > is any measure of distance (e.g., 3 miles, 10 steps, 50 meters). Tell your robot how to get from where you live to where your programming class meets.

12. Imagine that you aren't feeling well and a friend offers to make breakfast for you. The problem is that your friend doesn't know a saucepan from a spatula. Describe, in pseudocode terms, how your friend should prepare scrambled eggs, toast, and orange juice. (Assume you've attached labels to all the utensils in the kitchen. Your pseudocode should describe the actions involved in making the breakfast.)

13. Given the following code:

```
procedure First;
begin
    Third;
    Writeln('Number 1')
end; { First }

{ Mainline }
begin
    Second;
    First
end. { Mainline }
```

```
procedure Second;
begin
    First;
    Third;
    Writeln('Number 2')
end; { Second }
procedure Third;
begin
    Writeln('Number 3')
end; { Third }
```

   a. In what order must these procedures appear in the file?
   b. What is the output of this program?

14. In each of the following situations, explain the first thing you would check to correct the program:

   a. MacPascal reprints a statement in outline form.
   b. You receive the error message **A semicolon (;) is required on this line or above but one has not been found.**

c. You try to call the procedure **ChangeCredit** but receive the error message **The name "ChangeCredit" has not been defined yet.**

Coding Exercises and Programming Problems

1. Write a procedure that produces the output:

   Happy birthday to you,
   Happy birthday to you,
   Happy birthday, dear < your name >,
   Happy birthday to you.

2. Write a program that prints a song's lyrics. If the song's chorus repeats, it should be printed at each repetition in the output.

3. Write a program that prints your first name in block letters that appear vertically. For example, if your name is Al, the program should print:

```
  *
 * *
*   *
*****
*   *
*   *

*
*
*
*
*
*****
```

4. Write a program that prints a list, by semester, of all of the courses you have taken over the last two years.

5. Write a program that draws a building using text (much like the text we used in the ***Faces*** program). The building should be five stories tall. The building's middle floors (all the floors except the top and the ground floor) should be identical. The top floor should include a roof; the ground floor should have at least one door.

2

Numbers, Input, and Output

Even though you have completed only one chapter, you should be comfortable with the general process of programming. You've seen that large problems can be broken down with the divide-and-conquer method. Such decompositions are easily translated to Pascal by using procedures within a program. You've also learned about the different levels of computer software, and you've seen how you can use MacPascal's features to edit and execute programs.

Your first programs, however, are very much like the first mass-produced automobiles. Henry Ford once said that you could order a Model T in any color — as long as it was black. The programs we developed in Chapter 1 have a similar limitation: they can solve any problem as long as it has to output only text.

In this chapter, we will explore the original purpose of computers — to compute numbers. In the 1960s and '70s, most people connected the word "computer" with "mathematics." For the most part, the applications that most people had contact with were numerically oriented, usually in the form of a phone bill or bank statement. Now, even though computers are used as much for textual and graphical manipulations, *number crunching* is still at the heart of computing. In fact, numbers are even used to create simple drawings. The focus of this chapter is how numbers are represented and manipulated in Pascal. We will also begin our discussion of graphics: our first program involving numbers will show how to create a simple line graph.

To solve numeric problems, we need to examine how Pascal handles input and output. Numbers (as well as text) are output with the ***Write*** and ***Writeln*** statements and input is received by the ***Read*** and ***Readln*** statements. Because these statements make programs more complex, we will add more detail to our discussion of program development. By using the line-graph example, we will expand our discussion of pseudocoding, introduce MacPascal features that help you observe what your program is doing, and show techniques for debugging programs.

2.1 Integers

Let's start with the simplest calculations Pascal can perform: arithmetic operations involving whole numbers. Whole numbers, when used in a statement, are called *literal integer constants* and are identical to the integers found in algebra. In Pascal, an *integer* is defined as any number in the set of negative and positive natural numbers and zero, i.e., {...–3, –2, –1, 0, 1, 2, 3...}.

Pascal uses a set of *integer operators* similar to those used in arithmetic. For example, addition in Pascal is represented by a + sign. Not all the Pascal operators, however, are written exactly like their algebraic counterparts: the multiplication sign is an asterisk (*) rather than an x. Examples of Pascal *expressions* consisting of integer *operands* (e.g., the 2 and 3 in 2 + 3) and operators are shown below:

2 + 3
4 * 10
5 - 2 + 7

As in algebraic expressions, certain operators take precedence over others: they have higher *priority* and are performed first. The priorities are summarized in Syntax Box 2.1.

Syntax Box 2.1
Integer operators

The three high-priority operators are:

*	Multiplication, written as < operand 1 > * < operand 2 >, computes the product of two operands.
div	Division, written as < operand 1 > **div** < operand 2 >, computes the integer quotient of < operand 1 > divided by < operand 2 >, ignoring the remainder. Thus, **div** computes how many times < operand 2 > "goes into" < operand 1 >. For instance, 6 **div** 4 = 1 and –11 **div** 3 = –3.
mod	Modulo, written as< operand 1 > **mod** < operand 2 >, finds the integer remainder of < operand 1 > divided by < operand 2 >. For example, 6 **mod** 4 = 2 and –11 **mod** 3 = 1.

The two low-priority operators are:

+	Addition, written as < operand 1 > + < operand 2 >, adds two operands.
–	Subtraction, written as < operand 1 > – < operand 2 >, subtracts the second operand from the first.

As in algebra, you can alter these priorities by using parentheses:

$$2 + 4 * 5 = 22$$
$$(2 + 4) * 5 = 30$$

The first equation is an example of normal operator priorities, whereas the second performs the addition within the parentheses before the multiplication. If no parentheses are present, a chain of operations of the same priority is evaluated from left to right.

2.2 Variables and Arithmetic Expressions

In algebra, you learned to write equations with *constants*, whose values do not change, and with *variables*, whose values can change during successive calculations. For example, suppose you wanted to find the values of x that solve the quadratic equation

$$ax^2 + bx + c = 0$$

where a, b, and c are coefficients. This equation can be solved by using the quadratic formula

$$x_1, x_2 = \frac{-b \pm \sqrt{(b^2 - 4ac)}}{2a}$$

where the variables x_1 and x_2 represent the roots that solve the equation.

If $a = 1$, $b = 3$, and $c = 2$, then the quadratic formula can be evaluated as

$$\frac{-3 \pm \sqrt{(3^2 - 4 \cdot 1 \cdot 2)}}{2 \cdot 1}$$

This equation gives the values for the root variables

$$x_1 = -1, x_2 = -2$$

Variables in Pascal are used the same way as the variables a, b, and c in the above equation. First, a variable is assigned a value. Then, whenever you refer to the variable by name, you are actually referring to the variable's value. For example, if you have a variable called ***facilities*** in a Pascal program and want to double its value, you use the expression

```
2 * facilities
```

An *arithmetic expression* is defined as a sequence of constants, variables, and operators that can be evaluated to a single value. An example is

```
bonus + hourlyRate * (numDaysWorked – daysOff) * 8
```

As you did in high school algebra, Pascal evaluates an expression by combining operands with their operators. There are three rules for evaluation:

1. Evaluation takes place from left to right, except

2. Expressions in parentheses are evaluated first, starting at the innermost level, and
3. Higher-priority operators take precedence over lower ones.

The expression above is thus evaluated as follows. First, Pascal computes the difference within the parentheses, ***(numDaysWorked – daysOff)***. Then multiplication, which has a higher priority than addition, is performed. Because evaluation goes from left to right, Pascal first multiplies ***hourlyRate*** by the result of ***(numDaysWorked – daysOff)***, then multiplies that product by 8. Finally, the value of ***bonus*** is added.

Technically, a variable is the name of a unit of computer memory used in your program. Computer memory is analogous to a large set of individually numbered post office boxes. Some of these boxes contain data values; others contain machine code instructions. Pascal reserves the necessary locations in memory to store a program's variables in the same way that the postmaster can reserve a post office box to store your mail. Unlike a post office box, however, each memory location can hold only one item. In Figure 2.1 below, the variable ***facilities*** has the value 37:

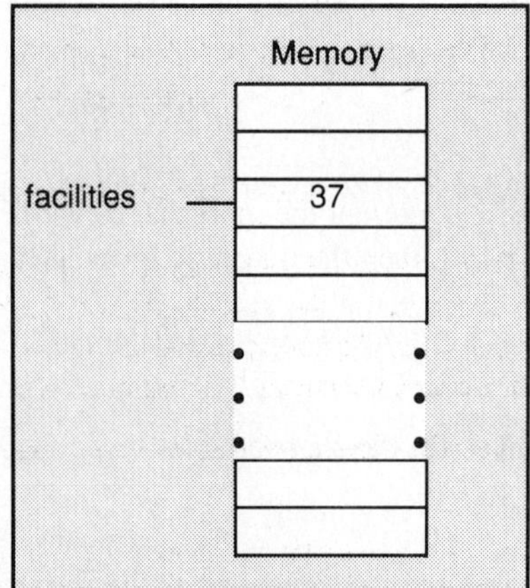

Figure 2.1
The variable ***facilities*** stored in memory

The computer can look at the contents of any individual memory location without changing those contents. It can also change the contents of a memory location by writing new information over the old information. These two operations are similar to playing back and recording over the contents of a cassette tape.

2.3 Declarations

Every variable name used in a program must be *declared,* or defined, to the Pascal interpreter or compiler, so that it can reserve an appropriate memory location. The reserved word **var** heads the list of **var**iable declarations. A variable name, called an *identifier*, may have up to 255 characters (typically, though, variable names have fewer than 10 characters). The first character of the identifier must be a letter, not a number. A variable declaration has two parts, the variable name and the variable's *data type,* which are separated by a colon (:). For example, the integer variable called ***root1*** is declared as follows:

```
var
    root1 : integer;
```

Pascal defines data types such as ***integer*** and ***real.*** (Other data types will be examined in later chapters.) Because we want ***root1*** to hold an integer, we use the data type ***integer***. The *range of representation*, which is the range of numbers that MacPascal can handle for integers, is 2 raised to the 16th power. This

Syntax Box 2.2
Declaration of variables

Purpose To define variable identifiers.

Syntax

```
var
    < variable identifier > : < data type >;
```

where < variable identifier > is a seequence of letters and numbers. The variable name may contain up to 255 characters but must begin with a letter.

< data type > is a type of data, such as ***integer***, ***longint***, or ***real.***

Usage To declare variables, mark the beginning of variable definitions with a **var** heading. The *name* of the variable goes on the left side of a colon (:) while the *type* of data (for example, ***integer***) goes on the right side of the colon. A semicolon (;) follows each declaration.

Duplicate variable identifiers cannot be declared in the same procedure.

Each procedure can have its own set of variables. Variable declarations for declared procedures are placed after the **procedure** statement and before the procedure's **begin**. The mainline's variables appear at the top of the program (between the **program** declaration and the first procedure declaration).* You may declare any number of variables.

Although it is technically possible to do so, variables should never be used outside the procedure in which they are declared. Such usage is a mark of *unstructured programming,* a practice that we are dedicated to eliminating.

*Alternatively, in MacPascal, you can place the mainline's variables immediately before the mainline's **begin.** In many other versions of Pascal, however, this is not legal.

range includes the numbers between $-2^{15}+1$, or –32,767, and $2^{15}-1$, or 32,767. To work with numbers outside this range, substitute ***longint*** for ***integer*** in the variable declarations. Variables of type ***longint*** have a range from $2^{31}-1$, or 2,147,483,647, to $-2^{31}+1$.

The following example illustrates variable declarations:

```
var
    years : integer;
    vacation : integer;
    sickDays : integer;
```

The variable declarations appear between the procedure name and the procedure's **begin**. (The mainline's variables are an exception; they appear after the **program** declaration and before the first procedure's declaration.) The variables are *local* to the procedure, which means that they can be accessed only when the procedure is active (i.e., when the procedure is being executed).

To make variables understandable, you must state their functions by documenting each variable declaration. For each declaration, we state what role the variable will play in the program. The list of definitions for a procedure's variables is called a *glossary*.

```
var
    years : integer;            { years employee has been working    }
    vacation : integer;         { number of vacation days taken      }
    sickDays : integer;         { number of days called in sick      }
```

When you are defining more than one variable of the same type, you need not repeat the type for each variable; you can separate the variable names by commas. The next example also declares three variables of type ***integer***.

```
var
    years,                      { years employee has been working    }
    vacation,                   { number of vacation days taken      }
    sickDays : integer;         { number of days called in sick      }
```

If you do not enter the glossary when you first enter the variables, pretty printing will place everything on the same line until it reaches a semicolon. For example, if we didn't include the glossary, pretty printing would format the above declaration as follows:

```
var
    years, vacation, sickDays: integer;
```

You can name variables however you want. For example, you could use the variable names ***x***, ***y***, and ***z***, or ***linguini***, ***macaroni***, and ***spaghetti*** instead of ***years***, ***vacation***, and ***sickDays***. With any of these names, Pascal would still reserve three locations in memory for the integer variables. Unclear naming of the variables, however, makes the program harder to read. In the worst case, an inappropriately named variable could totally mislead the program's reader. Because programs are often used and read by other people, programmers have developed a number of conventions for naming variables.

First, variables are given mnemonic names rather than single-letter names. Mnemonic names help you remember what they stand for (for example, the variable representing the height of a box should be named ***height*** instead of just ***h***). Mnemonic names are preferable to single letters for the same reason that people are given full names instead of just initials. After all, would *you* like to be named X?

Second, making variable names descriptive often requires the use of more than one word. Pascal, however, does not allow spaces in identifiers. In this book, we begin all identifiers with lowercase letters, but capitalize the initial letters of other words in the same identifer (e.g., ***totalProfit***, ***twoByFour***). Other programmers use underscores instead of capitalization to separate words (e.g., ***total_ profit***, ***two_by_ four***). Underscores in variable names are permitted in MacPascal but are not available in all versions of Pascal.

2.4 Assignment

You now have some variables declared as integer types, but these variables do not yet hold the values you want. Remember, a declaration simply reserves a space in memory for a variable; the declaration itself does not affect the contents of that memory location. Previous programs may have used the same places in memory that Pascal has reserved for your declarations. The values in these locations are leftover, or *garbage* values, and the program should replace them with ones you want. You can give a new value to a variable in two ways: *assignment* and *input*. We will examine input later in this chapter.

An assignment gives the value of an expression to a variable. This is accomplished with the assignment operator (:=), often pronounced as "gets."

Pascal assigns values to variables in two steps. First, the expression on the right of the assignment operator is evaluated. Then that single result is placed in the variable on the left of the assignment operator. Let's look at some examples:

```
(1) sumVehicles := 0;
(2) sumVehicles := numberCars + numberBuses;
(3) totalPeople := numInSection * 2 + teachingAssts;
```

In (1), ***sumVehicles*** is assigned the value 0. In (2), if ***numberCars*** = 5 and ***numberBuses*** = 4, then the expression on the right evaluates to 9. ***sumVehicles*** will then be assigned the single value 9. In (3), if ***numInSection*** = 125 and ***teachingAssts*** = 34, then the right side is evaluated to 125 * 2 + 34, or 250 + 34. The result 284 is assigned to ***totalPeople***.

Pascal variables can be used in the same way as algebraic variables — with one exception. You may want to give a variable a new value that is dependent on its old value. For example, to decrease ***workDays*** by the number of ***sickDays*** and store the result in ***workDays***, you would type:

```
workDays := workDays – sickDays;
```

In algebra, the *equation* ***workDays = workDays – sickDays*** makes absolutely no sense. But because of the way Pascal evaluates assignments, the *statement* ***workDays := workDays – sickDays;*** makes sense and is legal.

Syntax Box 2.3
Assignment of variables

Purpose	To assign a value to a variable.
Syntax	< variable name > := < expression > ;
where	< variable name > is a single variable identifier.
	< expression > is any combination of operands (constants, variables and parenthesized expressions) and operators that evaluates to the same *type* as the variable.
Usage	The assignment symbol (:=) is not the "equals" sign of an algebraic equation but a symbol that assigns the value of the right side (the expression) to the left (the variable).

Figure 2.2 shows Pascal's two-step evaluation of the above statement. The expression on the right is evaluated first. Thus, if ***workDays*** is 250 and ***sickDays*** is 6, the expression on the right evaluates to 244. The evaluated expression is then assigned to the variable on the left and replaces the variable's old value. Thus, ***workDays*** is assigned 244, replacing the old value of 250.

workDays := workDays – sickDays

workDays	sickDays
250	6

Before assignment

workDays	sickDays
~~250~~ 244	6

After assignment

Figure 2.2
Evaluating an assignment

The fundamental difference between the *imperative* assignment symbol of a Pascal statement and the *declarative* equals sign of an algebraic equation is that the := operator of Pascal is an *operation* that "assigns," while the = sign of algebra declares that one side "is equal to" the other and *performs no action*.

2.5 Real Numbers

The set of integers is not sufficient for all of our numeric needs. We need a way to represent numbers with fractional parts, or *real numbers*, in Pascal. Real numbers, also called *reals*, are often represented in exponential or scientific notation, meaning that the number is written as a base value (the *mantissa*) multiplied by an integer power of 10 (the *exponent*). For example:

372.4	is written as	3.724e+02
2,345,200	is written as	2.3452e+06
.053	is written as	5.3e–02

In scientific notation, the e signifies exponentiation; the sign and the two digits in the final three positions indicate a power of 10. e+02 means 10 raised to the second power. e–02 means 10 raised to the negative second power (i.e., the mantissa divided by 100). Thus, 3.724e+02 is the same as 3.724×10^2.

All the arithmetic operators used for integers can be used for reals, except for the division and modulo operators. The **div** operator used with integers is replaced by the / operator. This operator signifies division in the conventional sense. The quotient of a division problem using the / operation must be stored in a real number variable. Even if the division comes out even (e.g., 6/3), a real is needed. The computer represents the result of any / operation not as an integer but as a real (e.g., 6/3 is stored as the real 2.0e0, not as the integer 2). In addition, because memory is finite, infinitely repeating decimals are cut off after 8 digits. For example, the result of 5/3 is stored as 1.66666667. The **mod** function, which returns the integer remainder of a division of two integers, has no meaning for reals.

Syntax Box 2.4
Operators for reals in priority order

1. Multiplication (*) and division (/)
2. Addition (+) and subtraction (–)

Note: The integer operators **div** and **mod** do not work for real data.

Real numbers are represented in Pascal with the data type ***real***. MacPascal has a much larger range of representation for real data than for integer data, extending from approximately -10^{38} to 10^{38}. The smallest positive number that can be represented by a real expression is approximately 10^{-45}.

The structure of the declarations for real numbers is the same as for integers. For example, in the next declaration, ***numInApt*** is declared as an integer, and ***netIncome*** and ***deduction*** are declared as real variables.

```
var
    numInApt : integer;         { num of renters in apt. this month   }
    netIncome,                  { income left after taxes             }
    deduction : real;           { percentage of income taxed          }
```

The order of the declarations is irrelevant. The following example

```
var
    netIncome: real;            { income left after taxes             }
    numInApt : integer;         { num of renters in apt. this month   }
    deduction : real;           { percentage of income taxed          }
```

tells the interpreter exactly the same thing as the previous example.

2.6 Mixing Reals and Integers

At times you may want to use reals and integers in the same expression. Suppose you want to calculate the circumference of a circle. The radius has been measured to the closest millimeter and can therefore be represented as an integer. The formula for finding the circumference of a circle is

$$C = 2\pi r$$

where C is the circumference and r is the radius. If you use 3.14159 as an approximation of π, you have to represent π as a real. The expression for finding the circumference thus combines the integers 2 and ***radius*** and the real number 3.14159. The result of this calculation must be stored in a variable of type ***real***, since the result may have a fractional portion. To represent this equation in Pascal, you could use the assignment statement

```
circum := 2 * 3.14159 * radius;
```

assuming that you first used the variable declarations

```
var
    circum : real;              { circumference of circle             }
    radius : integer;           { radius of circle in millimeters     }
```

Variables of type ***real*** and ***integer*** do not always mix. You can assign an ***integer*** to a ***real***, but you cannot assign a ***real*** to an ***integer***, because of the difference in the range of representation. You can, however, use Pascal to store a truncated or rounded version of a ***real*** variable in the integer range as an ***integer***. To do this, you use one of Pascal's *predefined functions*. The predefined functions are blocks of code that occur often in programming, and as a convenience, Pascal allows you to refer to them using a single word. Pascal's predefined functions are much like the procedures introduced in Chapter 1 in that you can refer to an entire block of statements with a single word.

Functions in Pascal are similar to those found in mathematics. Just as you can write the equation $y = \sin(x)$, you can write the Pascal assignment statement ***answer := Sin(angle);***. Again, the difference between algebra and Pascal is that the algebraic equals sign equates, while Pascal's := symbol assigns. We say that

Pascal evaluates the ***Sin*** function and *returns* a value. This value then replaces the function in the statement in the same way that an entire expression is evaluated to return a single value that replaces the expression.

Two functions useful in manipulating variables of type ***real*** are shown in Syntax Box 2.5. The ***Trunc*** and ***Round*** functions offer two methods of eliminating the fractional portion of a real number.

Syntax Box 2.5
Trunc, Round

Purpose To truncate or round the fractional part of a real number.

Syntax

```
Trunc( < expression > )          { truncates < expression >  }
Round( < expression > )          { rounds < expression >     }
```

where < expression > evaluates to a number of type ***real.***

Returns an integer.

Usage ***Trunc*** clips off the digits to the right of the decimal point and returns the remaining integer. For example, ***Trunc***(35.3) returns 35, ***Trunc***(382.83) returns 382, ***Trunc***(32.3 + 33.1) returns 65, ***Trunc***(0.7) returns 0, ***Trunc***(–0.4) returns 0, and ***Trunc***(–2.6) returns –2.

Round returns the integer value that is closest to the real expression in parentheses. For example, ***Round***(35.3) returns 35, ***Round***(382.83) returns 383, ***Round***(32.3 + 33.1) returns 65, ***Round***(0.5) returns 1, ***Round***(–0.4) returns 0, and ***Round***(–2.6) returns –3.

Whenever a function or expression returns a value, you need to store the value somewhere. Thus, the line:

```
Trunc (month1 * month2);
```

will produce a syntax error, since no variable has been provided to store the result. You can, for example, place the returned value in a variable using an assignment statement. In this way, you are using functions such as ***Trunc*** and ***Round*** as integer expressions:

```
dollarAmount := Round (taxPrice);
leastValue := Trunc (total);
```

In summary, expressions on the right hand side of an assignment statement can contain a literal constant (***cardsReceived := 5;***), a variable (***cardsReceived := numberKids;***), a predefined function (***cardsReceived := Round(avgKids);***), or a combination of any of these (***cardsReceived := spouse + 2 * marriedKids + singleKids + numKids * Trunc(avgNumGrandKids);***).

2.7 The Drawing Window

So far in this chapter, you have been using the Macintosh essentially as an oversized calculator. While such calculations are useful, typically they are not ends in themselves. You are now ready to look at how calculations can be used in graphical applications programs.

The Macintosh is specifically designed to support graphics applications. Look closely at the Mac's screen; you will notice that it is a rectangular grid of tiny dots. The grid is known as a *raster*, and the Macintosh screen is thus a type of *raster display*. The entire Mac screen is a 512-point x 342-point rectangle, and each point can be lit individually. A user can make pictures by selectively turning points on or off. Each point on the raster is known as a *picture element*, or *pixel* for short.

With MacPascal, you can draw pictures in the area contained by the Drawing window by referring to individual pixels. Each pixel has a horizontal and vertical position. The upper left corner is always at horizontal position 0 and vertical position 0. When you start up MacPascal, or initially choose the **Drawing** option from the **Windows** menu in Lightspeed, the bottom right corner has a horizontal position of 200 and a vertical position of 200.

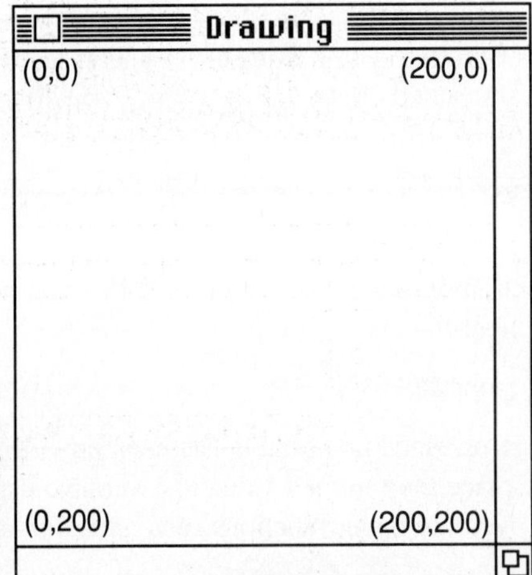

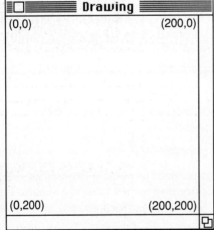

Figure 2.3 Coordinate system of initial Drawing window

This coordinate system is not quite the same as the *x-y* coordinate system used in algebra. The Drawing window's horizontal coordinate is the same as the *x* coordinate in that the pixels are numbered in increasing order from left to right. However, the pixels are numbered in increasing order from top to bottom, which is the opposite of how positive *y* coordinates are conventionally numbered in algebra. For convenience, we will refer to a pixel with the notation (< horizontal >, < vertical >).

For example, starting clockwise from the top left, the corners of the initial Drawing window are (0, 0), (200, 0), (200, 200), and (0, 200). Remember that the y axis is numbered from top to bottom; otherwise, you may wonder why your pictures are coming out upside down.

Like any other Mac window, the Drawing window can be moved or resized. No matter where the window is moved, though, the upper left corner is always (0,0). The size of a pixel always stays the same; when you increase or decrease the size of the window, you increase or decrease the number of pixels in the window. Thus, the coordinates of the upper right, lower right, and lower left corners may change.

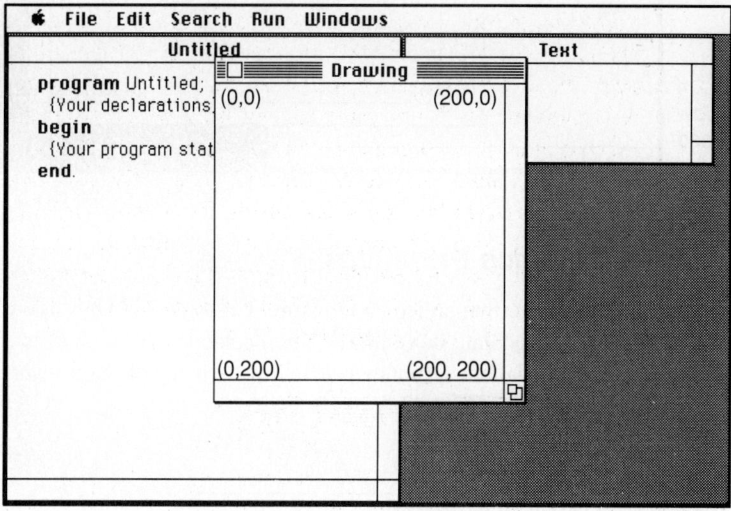

Figure 2.4
a. Drawing window moved but not resized

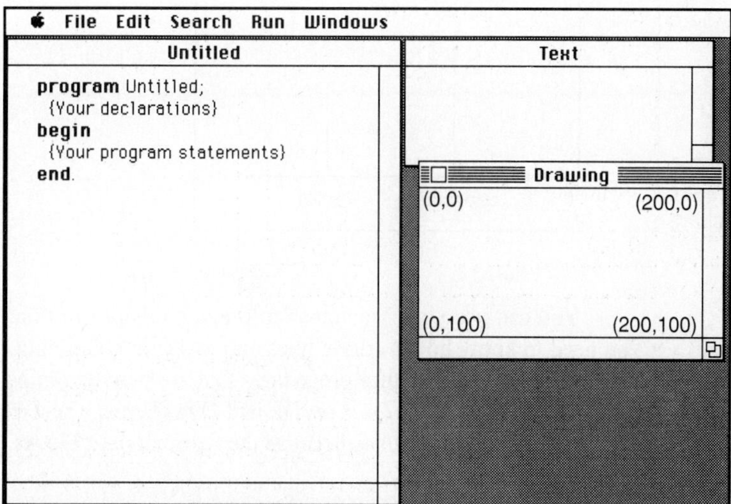

b. Drawing window not moved but cut in half vertically

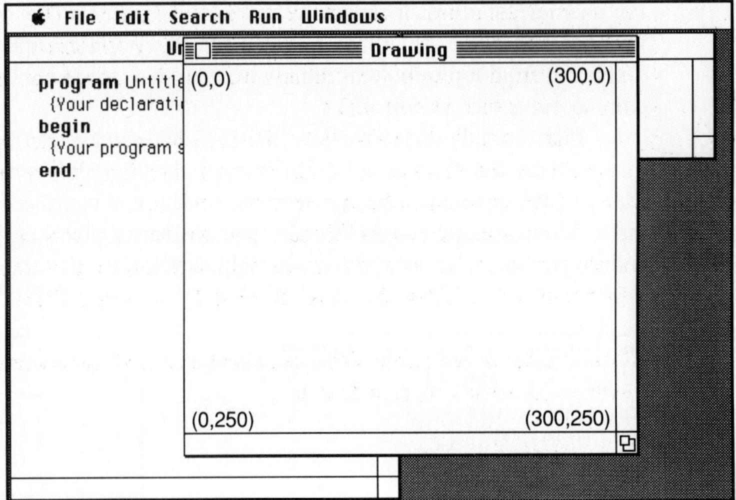

Figure 2.4
c. Drawing window moved and increased in size

2.8 Graphics Primitives

Suppose you own an ice cream store. Customers always ask you, "Which do you sell more of: chocolate or vanilla?" You decide to post a chart in your store that indicates how many gallons a month you sell of each flavor. You want your chart to look something like Figure 2.5.

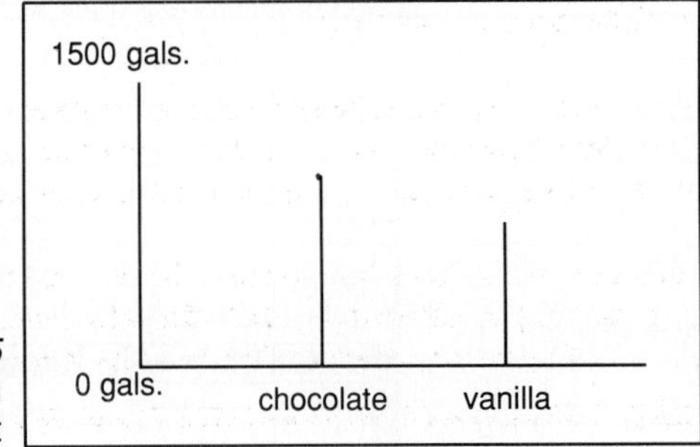

Figure 2.5
Sketch of ice cream chart

You can use your Macintosh to prepare this illustration. To do this, though, you need to know how to draw lines and text in the Drawing window. We will now look at three graphic output procedures that are included in Macintosh's QuickDraw software package: ***MoveTo***, ***LineTo***, and ***WriteDraw***. These procedures are known as graphic *primitives* because they are building blocks for more complex drawing procedures.

MacPascal uses a conceptual device called a *pen*. The pen is always positioned over a single pixel called the current position (CP for short). The current position is like a declared variable: it is initially undefined. To fix a current position for the pen, you use the procedure ***MoveTo***.

For example, ***MoveTo (50, 75)*** tells MacPascal to pick up the pen and move it over the pixel at (50, 75). However, nothing appears on the screen yet because MacPascal hasn't been told to use the pen.

The constants 50 and 75 are called *parameters*, or *arguments*. A parameter is a value supplied to a procedure. In Pascal, parameters are enclosed in parentheses. Indeed, in our first Pascal statement, ***Writeln***, we sent a literal string constant as a parameter.

Variables and expressions can also be used as parameters to the ***MoveTo*** procedure. The sequence of statements

```
newHoriz := 35;
newVert := 123;
MoveTo (newHoriz, newVert);
```

moves the current position to the location indicated by the variables, in this case, (35, 123).

Syntax Box 2.6
MoveTo

Purpose	To change the current position of the pen.
Syntax	**MoveTo(** < horiz >, < vert > **);**
where	< horiz > and < vert > are the horizontal and vertical coordinates of the new current position. These coordinates must be integer constants, integer variables, or expressions that evaluate to integers.
Usage	***MoveTo*** tells MacPascal where to move the pen, and thus where the next drawing should start. By itself, ***MoveTo*** performs no drawing; that is, the procedure produces no visible result.

Simply moving the pen's current position isn't very useful. We want to see some type of output on the screen. To draw a line, use the ***LineTo*** routine, which draws a line from the CP to any pixel that is designated. Like the ***MoveTo*** statement, ***LineTo*** takes two parameters: the horizontal and vertical coordinates of the new endpoint. For example, the two statements in Figure 2.6 draw a diagonal line in the center of the Drawing window.

```
MoveTo(50, 50);
LineTo(150, 150);
```

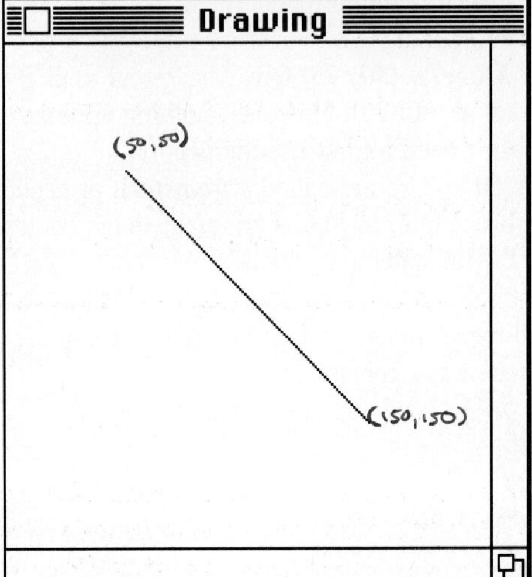

Figure 2.6
Drawing a line

After executing the two statements in Figure 2.6, the current position is at the second (in this case, the lower right) endpoint of the line. Make another call to ***LineTo*** (see Figure 2.7), and MacPascal starts at the CP and draws a line to the new endpoint.

```
MoveTo(50, 50);
LineTo(150, 150);
LineTo(170, 40);
```

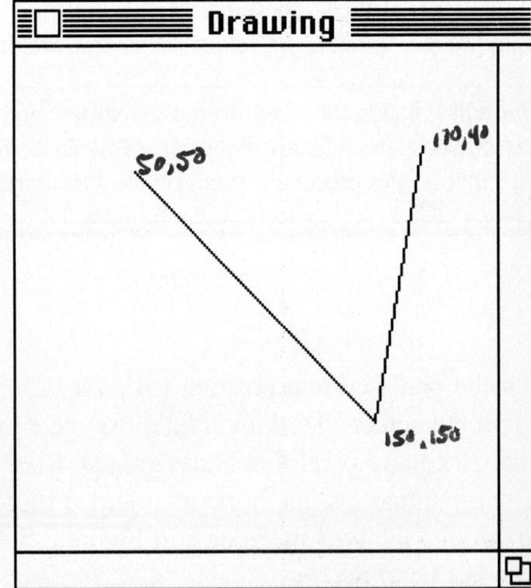

Figure 2.7
Drawing consecutive lines

Syntax Box 2.7
LineTo

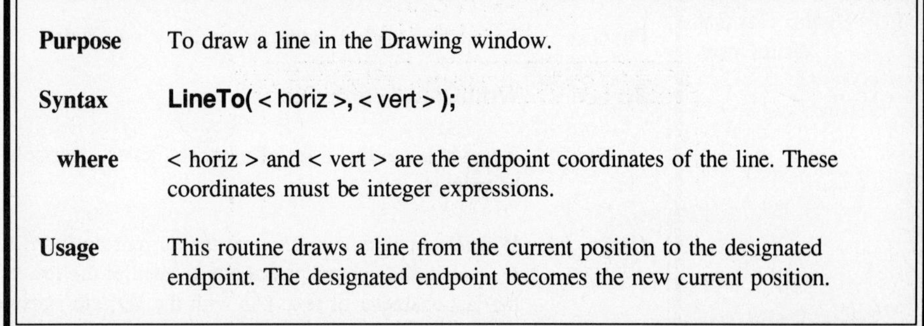

Purpose	To draw a line in the Drawing window.
Syntax	**LineTo(** < horiz >, < vert > **);**
where	< horiz > and < vert > are the endpoint coordinates of the line. These coordinates must be integer expressions.
Usage	This routine draws a line from the current position to the designated endpoint. The designated endpoint becomes the new current position.

You can now draw lines for the ice cream graph. What you need next is a way of labeling the graph. MacPascal provides a variation of the ***Writeln*** statement that prints textual output in the Drawing window. The ***WriteDraw*** statement prints text starting at the CP. The syntax of ***WriteDraw*** and ***Writeln*** statements are nearly identical; only the names of the statements are different.

Our example from Chapter 1, ***Writeln ('I have control');*** can be written in the Drawing window as follows:

```
MoveTo(10, 100);
WriteDraw('I have control');
```

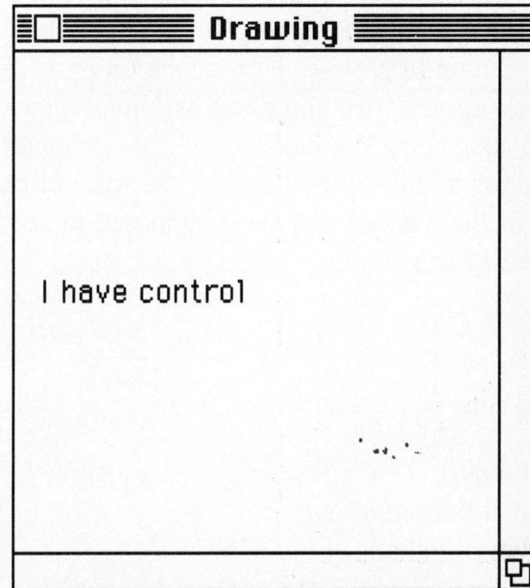

Figure 2.8
Printing text in the Drawing window

Syntax Box 2.8
WriteDraw

Purpose	To produce textual output in the Drawing window.
Syntax	**WriteDraw('< text >');**
where	< text > is the literal set of numbers, letters, symbols, or spaces to be printed.
Usage	***WriteDraw*** outputs < text > at the current position. After the text is printed, the current position is located at the lower right corner of the last character of text. (As with the ***Writeln*** statement, two apostrophes in < text > prints one apostrophe.) The ***WriteDraw*** statement can be used to output variables in the Drawing window in the same way that the ***Writeln*** statement outputs variables in the Text window.

2.9 Pseudocoding the Ice Cream Program

You now have all the tools necessary to draw the ice cream graph. To begin developing the program, you can list the tasks involved in creating the graph:

```
{ Plot ice cream consumption graph }
Draw axes for graph
Label vertical axis
Draw and label line for chocolate
Draw and label line for vanilla
```

When a level of pseudocode is broken down, think about how the individual tasks are performed. You may not be used to thinking at this level of small detail, but remember that the computer cannot improvise. If someone told you "Draw axes for [a] graph," you would pick up your pen and draw two lines. The computer, however, cannot understand such a statement. You need to tell the computer exactly how to draw the axes and how to draw and label the lines for the sales of chocolate and vanilla. To remember what each of these detailed steps is supposed to accomplish, use statements from the previous level as comments:

```
{ Draw axes }
Draw vertical line
Draw horizontal line

{ Label vertical axis }
Print '0 gallons' at bottom of axis
Print total number of gallons at top of axis
```

{Draw and label line for chocolate }
Move 1/3 distance from left along horizontal axis
Write label 'chocolate' below line
Calculate upper endpoint's vertical position
Draw line from axis to upper endpoint

{Draw and label line for vanilla }
Move another 1/3 of way along horizontal axis
Write label 'vanilla' below line
Calculate upper endpoint's vertical position
Draw line from axis to upper endpoint

Many of these tasks can be translated to Pascal statements or graphic calls. Some of the lines of pseudocode, though, need more refinement. If we assume that each pixel represents 1%, we can continue to refine as follows:

{ Calculate upper endpoint's vertical position }
Determine height of line by finding percentage of total
Draw line of length equal to number of percentage points

Knowing that the ice cream store sells a total of 1500 gallons per month, of which 800 are chocolate, 450 are vanilla, and 250 are other flavors, the program can be coded as follows:

Code 2.1
Program
IceCream

```
{ Amy Elizabeth Tozer         IceCream                   July 31    }
{ The IceCream program shows the consumption of chocolate          }
{ and vanilla ice cream at Big Steve's Ice Cream Shoppe. The       }
{ program draws a bar graph showing the percentages of             }
{ chocolate and vanilla sold in the past month. Each pixel on      }
{ the graph represents 1% of the month's total sales.              }

program IceCream1;

  var
    chocGal : integer;     { num of gallons of chocolate sold      }
    vanGal : integer;      { num of gallons of vanilla sold        }
    total : integer;       { total num of gallons sold             }
    chocPct : real;        { percentage of chocolate sold          }
    vanPct : real;         { percentage of vanilla sold            }
    curHoriz : real;       { current horizontal position           }
    lenLine : integer;     { length of vertical line               }

begin

{Draw axes}
  MoveTo(200, 150);
  LineTo(50, 150);
  LineTo(50, 50);
```

Code 2.1 (continued)

```
{Label vertical axis}
    MoveTo(10, 150);
    WriteDraw('0 gals.');
    MoveTo(10, 50);
    WriteDraw('1500 gals. ');

{Calculate percentages}
    chocGal := 800;
    vanGal := 450;
    total := 1500;
    chocPct := chocGal / total * 100;
    vanPct := vanGal / total * 100;

{Draw chocolate bar}
    curHoriz := (200 - 50) / 3 + 50;              { move 1/3 way down horiz axis  }
    MoveTo(Trunc(curHoriz) - 20, 160);
    WriteDraw('chocolate');                        { label chocolate bar           }
    MoveTo(Trunc(curHoriz), 150);
    lenLine := 150 - Round(chocPct);               { calculate upper endpoint      }
    LineTo(Trunc(curHoriz), lenLine);              { draw line for chocolate bar   }

{Draw vanilla bar}
    curHoriz := curHoriz + (200 - 50) / 3;         { move another 1/3 down axis    }
    MoveTo(Trunc(curHoriz) - 8, 160);
    WriteDraw('vanilla');                          { label vanilla bar             }
    MoveTo(Trunc(curHoriz), 150);                  { draw line for vanilla bar     }
    LineTo(Trunc(curHoriz), 150 - Round(vanPct))
end. { IceCream }
```

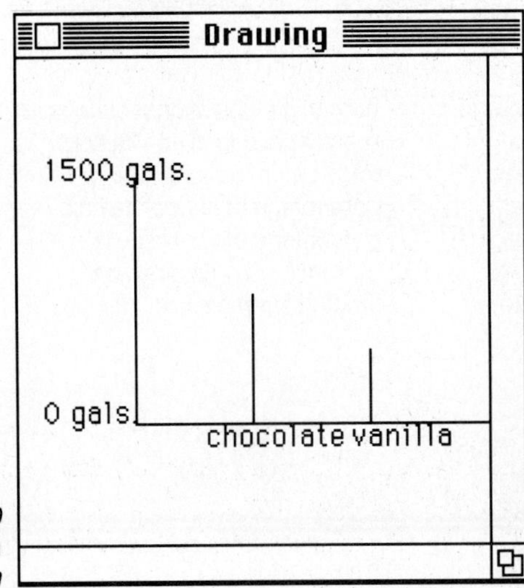

Figure 2.9
Output of program *IceCream*

2.10 Output of Variables

The ice cream program graphs only a single set of data. To use the same programs with different data sets, you need to know how to input and output variables.

The ***Writeln*** statement discussed in Chapter 1 could print out only a literal string of characters. The ***Writeln*** statement is actually more powerful than that. A list of variables and literal strings placed inside the ***Writeln***'s parentheses form a *parameter list*. Each item in the list is separated by commas, and any number of variables and literal strings may appear in the ***Writeln*** statement.

When Pascal executes a ***Writeln*** statement, it reads the arguments, one at a time, from left to right. If an argument is in apostrophes, it is printed literally. If it is a variable, and therefore not in apostrophes, the current value of the variable is printed. If it is an expression, the argument is evaluated and the result printed.

For example, if the integer variable ***partNum*** is assigned the value 12345, the statement

```
Writeln ('Part number',partNum, 'passed inspection.');
```

produces the output:

```
Part number    12345 passed inspection.
```

Notice that a number of spaces separate the text "Part number" and the value "12345". When MacPascal outputs a variable or an expression, it formats the value in a *field*. A field is the number of spaces in the textual output used to print something. One field is used for each parameter, and each field begins where the last one ended. Thus, the field for printing the value of ***partNum*** begins immediately after the text "Part number" in the output. Whenever MacPascal outputs an integer, however, the interpreter assumes that it needs a field of eight spaces. In other words, MacPascal prints an integer value so that the ones digit appears in the eighth position in the field. Figure 2.10 shows the formatting of ***partNum***'s value.

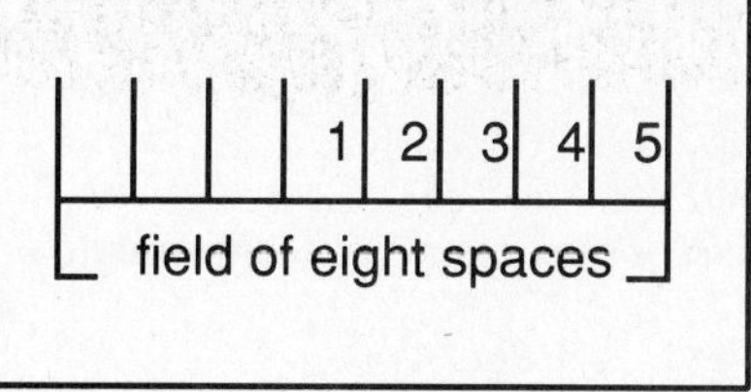

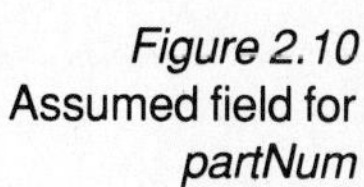
Figure 2.10
Assumed field for *partNum*

Formatting allows you to specify the width of a field. For example, you can change the field width from eight to six spaces. You specify the field width in a ***Writeln*** statement by following the parameter with a *field specification*, which is a colon followed by an integer field width.

```
Writeln ('Part number ', partNum:6, 'passed inspection.');
```

In the output, Pascal *right-justifies* the value of ***partNum*** in a field of 6 spaces. This means that the last digit of the variable appears in the rightmost position of the field. In this example, Pascal precedes the five-digit figure 12345 with one blank so that it is justified in the six-space field.

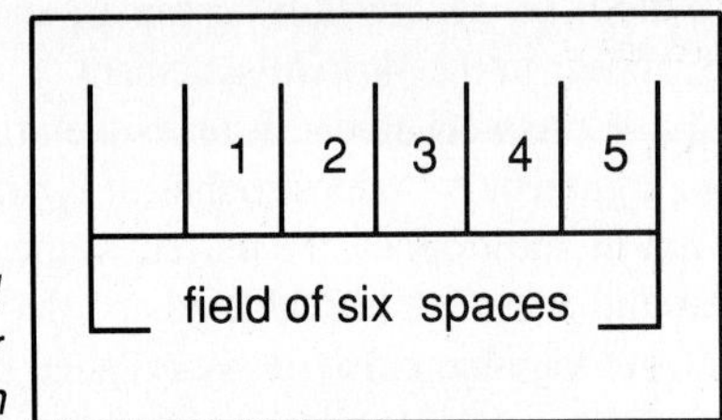

Figure 2.11
Six-space field for *partNum*

We've been talking about a "space" as if it were a constant unit of measurement. The size of a space, however, depends on the font used in the Text window. Even within a given font, the size of a blank space is usually different from the size of an "i" or an "m." The point is this: you may have to adjust the formatting to line up lines of text in the output.

If the field width is smaller than the item to be output, the item will be printed in as many spaces as necessary to accommodate it. For example,

```
Writeln ('Part number ', partNum:2, ' passed inspection.');
```

produces

```
Part number 12345 passed inspection.
```

Two other quick notes about formatting integers. First, the field width must be an integer between 1 and 255. Second, in MacPascal it is not possible to left-justify values in fields.

Real numbers can be output in one of two ways. Without a field specification, Pascal assumes that real numbers should be printed in scientific, or exponential, notation. For example:

```
normalTemp := 98.6;
Writeln (normalTemp,' is the normal body temperature');
```

produces

```
9.9e+1   is the normal body temperature
```

in the input. Also, when it formatted the value 98.6, MacPascal inserted three blanks after the exponent.

To print a real number in decimal notation, you need to specify a field width and a precision. The precision is the number of digits to the right of the decimal point. Just as a colon separates a literal string, a variable, or an expression from the field width, a second colon separates the field width and the precision. For example:

```
Writeln (normalTemp:6:2,' is the normal body temperature');
```

prints the value as shown in Figure 2.12.

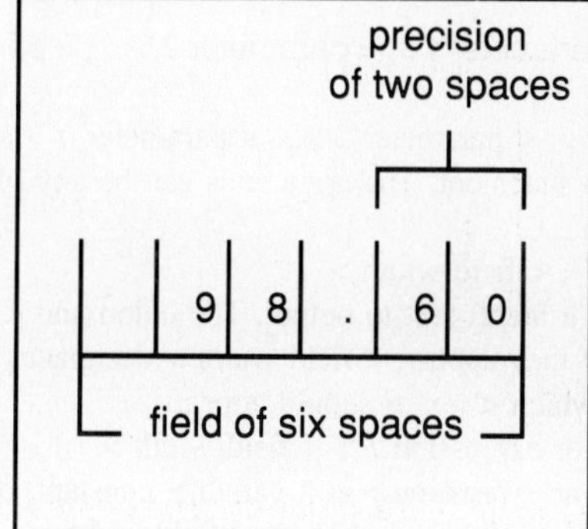

Figure 2.12 Field for *normalTemp:6:2*

The field width in this case is the total number of spaces occupied by the real number, including the digits to the right of the decimal point and the decimal point itself. In the above example, the total field width is 6, with two digits to the right of the decimal point.

```
Text
intNum =      12345
realNum = 12.345

Writeln('intNum*', intNum, '*');
intNum*    12345*

Writeln('intNum*', intNum : 10, '*');
intNum*      12345*

Writeln('intNum*', intNum : 2, '*');
intNum*12345*

Writeln('realNum*', realNum, '*');
realNum* 1.2e+1   *

Writeln('realNum*', realNum : 12 : 5, '*');
realNum*    12.34500*

Writeln('realNum*', realNum : 20, '*');
realNum* 1.23450002670e+1    *

Writeln('realNum*', realNum : 2, '*');
realNum* 1.2e+1   *

Writeln('realNum*', realNum : 10 : 2, '*');
realNum*     12.35*
```

Figure 2.13 Formatting examples

Examples of formatting for ***integer***s and ***real***s appear in Figure 2.13. To show the boundaries of each field, an asterisk (*) is printed before and after the variable's field.

Syntax Box 2.9
Writeln with variables

Purpose To output text and data in the Text window.

Syntax **Writeln (< parameter 1 >, < parameter 2 >,..., < parameter *n* >);**

where < parameter 1 >, < parameter 2 >,...,< parameter *n* > are the parameters of the ***Writeln*** statement. The arguments can be any of three different varieties:

1. ' < text > ' **:** < field width >
   < text > is a literal text to output. The colon and < field width > are optional. If they appear, < field width > designates the number of spaces in which < text > should appear.
2. < variable or expression > **:** < field width >
   < variable or expression > is a variable, constant, or expression of any type. As with the literal text, < field width > is optional.
3. < real value > **:** < field width > **:** < precision>
   < real value > is a variable, constant, or expression that evaluates to a real. < precision > indicates the number of digits to appear on the right of the decimal point. < field width > includes the spaces used by < precision > and the decimal point.

Usage Each argument can have its own field width and, if it is real, precision. Any number of arguments can be printed.

Examples of formatting appear in Figure 2.13.

If the Text window is not big enough to hold a line of output, MacPascal performs word *wraparound*. That is, it places extra carriage returns in the output so that the line is broken and all the text appears in the window. If you resize the window, the extra carriage returns disappear.

Write and ***WriteDraw*** take the same parameters as ***Writeln***. ***Write*** does not perform a carriage return at the end of a line. ***WriteDraw*** prints the output at the current position in the Drawing window.

2.11 Input

Let's go back to the ice cream store example. When coding the program, you assigned the chocolate and vanilla consumptions directly to the program's variables. To make the program more useful, though, the user should be able to input information into variables while the program is running.

Input is received by Pascal via the ***Readln*** statement, which takes one or more variables as arguments. When MacPascal encounters a ***Readln*** statement, it stops executing and waits for the user to enter values at the keyboard. The values that the user types are then stored in the designated variables.

Syntax Box 2.10
Readln

Purpose	To read data into the program variables.
Syntax	**Readln(** < var 1 >, < var 2 >, ... < var *n* >**);**
where	< var 1 >, < var 2 >, ...,< var *n* > are variables of any scalar* type (e.g., ***integer***, ***real***, ***char***, ***string***).
Usage	***Readln*** stops execution of the program and waits for input from the keyboard. If ***Readln*** contains more than one parameter, the variables are assigned values in order of appearance. That is, the first item entered goes into < var 1 >, the second item into < var 2 >, and so on. The user should enter spaces to separate multiple inputs; when the space bar is pressed, the value that has just been typed in is immediately assigned to a variable. When the user presses the Return key, MacPascal knows that the user has completed entering input and assigns the final value to the next variable in ***Readln***'s argument list. ***Read*** performs the same function as ***Readln***, except that ***Readln*** waits until the user presses Return before accepting the input; ***Read*** accepts input when the space bar, Tab key, or Return key is pressed. The differences between ***Read*** and ***Readln*** are explored in more detail in Chapter 9.

*A scalar type is a single, or atomic, data type. We will discuss non-scalar data types beginning in Chapter 9.

For example, if we declare the variable ***age*** as an integer and ***pay*** as a real, then the statement

```
Readln (age, pay);
```

stops execution and waits for the user to enter an integer value followed by a real. Of course, the user may not know this is why the program has stopped executing. To tell the user what is going on, most ***Readln*** statements are preceded by ***Write*** statements.

```
Write ('Please enter your age and hourly wages: ');
Readln (age, pay);
```

This type of request is known as a *prompt*. When these lines are executed, the user will see the window shown in Figure 2.14.

```
Text
Please enter your age and wages:
```

Figure 2.14
Prompt for input

Pascal expects the user to enter an integer, followed by one or more blank spaces, followed by a real. The user can backspace to correct a mistake, but pressing the space bar or the Return key immediately assigns the input value to the current variable in ***Readln***'s argument list. In Figure 2.15, ***age*** receives the value 22 when the space bar is pressed and ***pay*** receives the value 7.75 when the Return key is pressed.

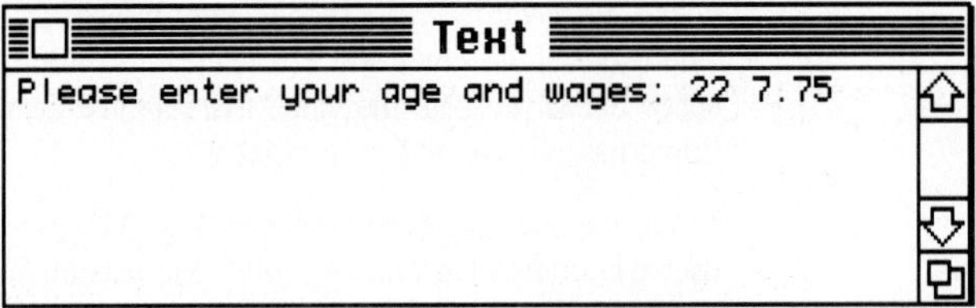

Figure 2.15
Prompt and input values in Text window

Any ***Readln*** statement that accepts more than one variable can be changed to a series of ***Readln*** statements, each of which accepts one variable. Although separate ***Readln*** statements make a program longer, the extra input statements allow for extra prompts, thus providing more clarity for the user. For example, the above prompt and ***Readln*** statements can be rewritten as follows:

```
Writeln ('Please enter your age: ');
Readln (age);
Writeln ('Please enter your hourly wages: ');
Readln (pay);
```

Because MacPascal prints prompts and other output in the Text window, make sure the Text window is visible before you run a program.

2.12 Constants

Variables are used when values are assigned or changed in a program. Suppose, though, that you know a certain value, say the speed of light, will be used frequently but will not change during the course of the program. By giving that value a name, like a variable, you avoid having to write it literally each time. You also want to keep the value constant throughout the program, i.e., make it impossible for the value to be changed by assignment or input. Pascal allows you to name a *symbolic constant*, or *constant* for short, which holds an unchangeable value. Constants are declared using syntax similar to that for variables. The declarations are listed under the heading **const**. The constant identifier is followed by an equals sign (not a colon) and the constant value.

```
const
   lightSpeed = 186281;                    { speed of light in miles/second        }
```

Constant declarations usually appear immediately after the program statement so that they can be used in the mainline or any other procedure. Unlike variables, which are local to any given procedure, constants are *global*. In this case, we can use the identifier ***lightSpeed*** wherever we need the value 186281.

In the following excerpts from a program, variables are used in the procedures where they are declared, but the constant ***lightSpeed*** can be used in both the procedure ***Einstein*** and in the mainline.

```
program Physics;

const
   lightSpeed = 186281;                    { speed of light in miles/second        }

{ Mainline Variables}
var
   earthDist: longint;                     { current distance from sun -> earth  }
   travelTime: real;                       { time for light to travel sun -> earth  }
...
procedure Einstein;

var
   energy: real;                           { energy released            }
   mass: real;                             { mass of molecule           }

begin
   ...
   { mass gets value somewhere in here }
   ...
   energy := mass * lightSpeed * lightSpeed;
   ...
end; { Einstein }
...
{Mainline}
begin
   ...
   { earthDist gets value somewhere in here }
   travelTime := earthDist / lightSpeed; { calculate time in seconds }
   ...
end. { Physics }
```

Several predefined constants exist in both MacPascal and Lightspeed Pascal. The constant ***pi*** is the value of the irrational number π taken to 19 decimal places.

The constants ***maxInt*** and ***maxLongint*** are, respectively, the largest values in the ***integer*** and ***longint*** range of representation. Because they have been previously defined in the software, you can use the identifiers ***pi***, ***maxInt*** and ***maxLongint*** in numeric expressions without declaring them.

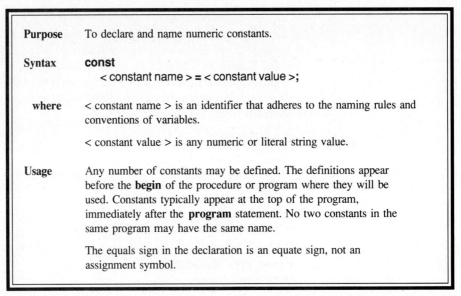

Syntax Box 2.11
const

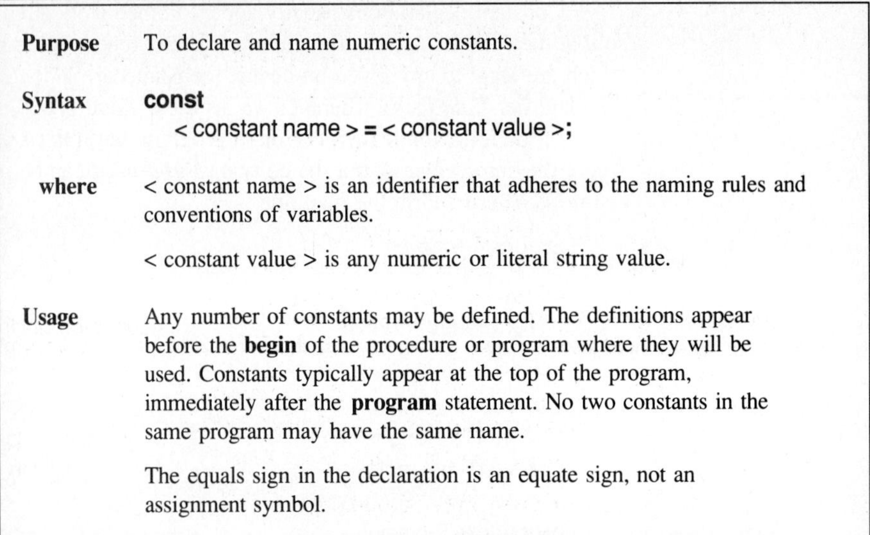

Purpose To declare and name numeric constants.

Syntax

```
const
   < constant name > = < constant value >;
```

where < constant name > is an identifier that adheres to the naming rules and conventions of variables.

< constant value > is any numeric or literal string value.

Usage Any number of constants may be defined. The definitions appear before the **begin** of the procedure or program where they will be used. Constants typically appear at the top of the program, immediately after the **program** statement. No two constants in the same program may have the same name.

The equals sign in the declaration is an equate sign, not an assignment symbol.

Constants can also be used for values that will not be changed for many runs of the program, even though they represent a value that in real life is updated occasionally. Suppose a college adminstrator wants to run a program to monitor the use of the college's Macintosh room. Throughout the program, she needs to refer to the number of Macintoshes. She can declare the following constant:

```
const
   numMacs = 35;                    { number of Macs in lab          }
```

The number of Macintoshes is not likely to change more than once a semester, so it is useful to declare it as a constant. Constants, like variables, should be documented with a glossary entry.

Graphics programs often lend themselves to the use of constants. For example, in the ice cream program, the *offsets* of the graph can be declared as constants. The offset is the distance from (0,0) to the origin of the graph's axes. If you want the graph's origin at the pixel (50, 150), you can declare the following two constants:

```
const
   horizOffset = 50;                { horizontal and                 }
   vertOffset = 150;                { vertical coords of origin      }
```

Declaring constants for the offsets has the advantage of making the individual statements more mnemonic and therefore less error prone.

2.13 Making the Ice Cream Program Interactive

You can use the concepts from the last few sections to make the ice cream program more complete. Using Pascal's input facilities, you can ask the user to enter the amount of chocolate and vanilla sold. You can also label the bars on the graph with the percentages they represent. To reflect these changes, the first level of pseudocode now looks like this:

```
Enter amounts of each flavor sold
Draw axes of graph
Label vertical axis
Calculate percentages
Draw and label chocolate bar
Draw and label vanilla bar
```

The refinement is similar to the refinement of the previous version.

```
{ Enter amounts of each flavor sold }
Input number of gallons of chocolate
Input number of gallons of vanilla

{ Draw axes of graph }
Draw vertical line
Draw horizontal line

{ Label vertical axis }
Print '0 gallons' at bottom of axis
Print total gallons at top of axis

{ Calculate percentages }
Find percentage of chocolate sold
Find percentage of vanilla sold

{ Draw and label chocolate bar }
Move 1/3 distance to left along horizontal axis
Write label 'chocolate' below line
Use percentage to calculate upper endpoint
Draw bar
Write percentage above bar

{ Draw and label vanilla bar }
Move another 1/3 distance to left along horizontal axis
Write label 'vanilla' below line
Use percentage to calculate upper endpoint
Draw bar
Write percentage above bar
```

2.14 Hand Simulating Pseudocode

Before going any further with the stepwise refinement, you should check the algorithm (solution) to see if the current solution to the problem will be performed correctly by the computer. This is done by simulating and checking the actions of the computer by hand — a process known, appropriately enough, as *hand simulation.* The key to successful hand simulation is following literally the steps you have listed. Since the computer cannot think on its own and you are going to imitate the computer, you need to forget everything you know about your program. Programming bugs are often missed because the programmer has read the code and believed that it does what it is supposed to do rather than checking each step naively and examining what actions the program actually performs.

At this point, you may be wondering, "Why don't we translate the program to code first and let MacPascal tell us if the program is correct?" MacPascal's pretty printing and bug boxes will catch your syntax errors. It cannot, however, detect *semantic* errors — logical flaws in your program that produce unwanted or incorrect results. In short, MacPascal cannot judge the intent of your program. Thorough hand simulation of pseudocode helps to prevent errors and provides the ounce of prevention that will save you endless hours of debugging later. Hand simulation of both pseudocode and code also makes you thoroughly familiar with your program. This familiarity puts you in a much better position to understand error messages and unexpected behavior than if you simply "throw" a program at the machine.

Think back to the proofs you did in high school geometry. When you proved a theorem formally, you had to check that each assertion was "legal": that is, the assertion had to follow logically from the previous assertions; the assertion itself had to be logical; and the assertion had to provide information that future assertions could use. When you hand simulate pseudocode, you are doing the same thing with each line of the code. Not only do you have to check the line itself to ensure that the computer can perform what you want it to do, you must also check the logical connections to the previous and following lines of pseudocode. Finally, the hand simulation should convince you that your algorithm works in its entirety. Each individual statement may appear to be correct, but you have to ask yourself, "Does the overall algorithm produce the correct result?"

The process of hand simulation starts at the first line of the pseudocode. One line at a time, you should go through the pseudocode as if you were the computer. At each line, make sure you have all the information needed to perform the algorithm. If a line of pseudocode says "Draw bar," make sure you know the horizontal and vertical coordinates of both endpoints. (For the purposes of hand simulation, you can pretend the computer understands pseudocode, not just Pascal.)

An easy way to keep track of variables is with a variable checklist. When the pseudocode tells you to input or assign a value to a variable, write the variable's name on the list and denote with a check that the variable now contains a value. You don't have to include the numeric values — you should simply be able to look over the list and verify that any variable you need to use has already been given a value.

For example, when you encounter the line "Input number of gallons of chocolate," add the variable "gallons of chocolate" to your list and mark that the variable has received a value. When you come to the line that asks you to compute "percentage of chocolate," note on the checklist that "percentage of chocolate" has received a value. By this method, when you come to the line "Use percentage to calculate upper endpoint," you can tell by looking over the checklist that all the necessary variables have values.

To summarize, hand simulation of your pseudocode should answer the following questions:

1. For each line of pseudocode, is all of the necessary information available?
2. Does each line of pseudocode logically follow what has come before? Does it logically lead into the succeeding lines? Is the current line itself logically correct?
3. Does the complete pseudocode yield the correct result?

2.15 Coding the Ice Cream Program

When the hand simulation convinces you that you can take each of the lines of pseudocode and write equivalent Pascal statements, you can start entering code into the Mac. The first translation of the ice cream pseudocode appears on the next pages. We shall debug the program in the next section.

Code 2.2
Interactive program
IceCream

```
{ Amy Elizabeth Tozer        IceCream                  July 31  }
{ The IceCream program shows the consumption of chocolate       }
{ and vanilla ice cream at Big Steve's Ice Cream Shoppe. The    }
{ program draws a bar graph showing the percentages of          }
{ chocolate and vanilla sold in the past month. Each pixel on   }
{ the graph represents 1% of the month's total sales.           }

program IceCream2;

  const
    total = 1500;           { total num of gallons sold per month    }
    horOffset = 20;         { horizontal position where axes meet    }
    vertOffset = 150;       { vertical position where axes meet      }
    height = 100;           { height of vertical axis in pixels      }
    width = 180;            { length of horizontal axis in pixels    }

  var
    chocGal,                { num of gallons of chocolate sold }
    vanGal : integer;       { num of gallons of vanilla sold   }
    chocPct,                { percentage of chocolate sold     }
    vanPct : real;          { percentage of vanilla sold       }
    curHoriz : real;        { horizontal position for bar      }
    upBar : integer;        { upper endpoint of bar            }
```

Code 2.2
(continued)

```
begin

{ Enter amounts of each flavor sold }
    Write('Please enter number of gallons of chocolate sold: ');
    Readln(chocGal);
    Write('Please enter number of gallons of vanilla sold: ');
    Readln(vanGal);

{ Draw axes }
    MoveTo(horOffset, vertOffset);
    LineTo(horOffset + width, vertOffset);
    MoveTo(horOffset, vertOffset);
    LineTo(horOffset, vertOffset - height);

{ Label vertical axis }
    MoveTo(horOffset - 10, vertOffset + 10);
    WriteDraw('0 gals.');
    MoveTo(horOffset - 15, vertOffset - height);
    WriteDraw(total : 4, ' gals.');

{ Calculate percentages }
    chocPct := (chocGal / total) * 100;
    vanPct := (vanGal / total) * 100;

{Draw and label chocolate bar}
    curHoriz := width / 3 + horOffset;    { move 1/3 way down horiz axis}
    MoveTo(Trunc(curHoriz) - 25, vertOffset + 15);
    WriteDraw('chocolate');    { label chocolate bar }
    MoveTo(Trunc(curHoriz), vertOffset);
    upBar := vertOffset - Round(chocPct);
    LineTo(Trunc(curHoriz), upBar);
    WriteDraw(chocPct : 5 : 1, ' % ');

{Draw and label vanilla bar}
    curHoriz := curHoriz + width / 3;
    MoveTo(Trunc(curHoriz) - 20, vertOffset + 15);
    WriteDraw('vanilla');
    MoveTo(Trunc(curHoriz), vertOffset);{ move to axis }
    LineTo(Trunc(curHoriz), vertOffset - Round(vanPct));
    WriteDraw(vanPct : 5 : 1, ' % ')

end. { IceCream }
```

2.16 Debugging with the Observe Window

Finding bugs in a program can frustrate even the best programmers, but even the best programmers write imperfect code. So it shouldn't alarm you if the program you have entered doesn't perform exactly as you intended. Somewhere in the transition from your idea of what the program should do to the computer's execution of the program, something was incorrectly translated. The best way to find bugs is to check, line by line, how the computer executes the program. Allow us to show you how to do this effectively.

We begin at the top of the program. The first things we encounter are the program statement and the declarations for the constants and the mainline's variables. To represent these declarations, we create a list of variables and constants. The list of constants, shown in Figure 2.16, serves as a reference guide; we'll use it whenever a constant is used in an expression.

const

total	1500
horOffset	20
vertOffset	150
height	100
width	175

Figure 2.16
Table of constants

The variable list keeps track of each variable's contents. While we can do this with pencil and paper, we can also let MacPascal maintain the variable list. MacPascal's Observe window allows us to look at the value of variables or expressions at any given point in the program. To use this feature, we choose the option **Observe** from the **Windows** menu. The window shown in Figure 2.17 appears on the screen.

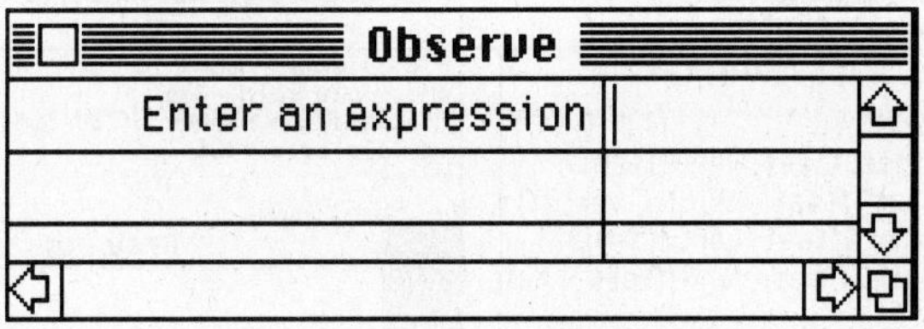

Figure 2.17
The Observe window

The Observe window contains two columns. In the right column we enter the variables and expressions we want to track; the left column shows the current value of each expression. When you first open the window, the insertion point appears in the right column of the first row, and the prompt **Enter an expression** appears in the left column of the same row. Enter an expression or variable at the insertion point. When you press Return, the prompt moves down, and the next line is highlighted. Figure 2.18 shows the Observe window after we have entered the program's variable names.

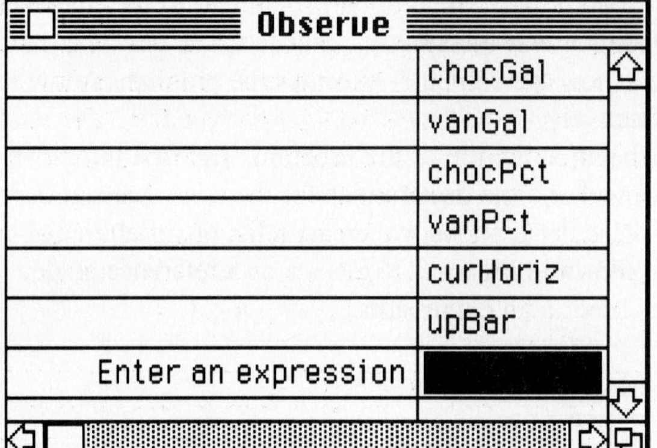

Figure 2.18
Observe window with variable names

The Observe window updates the values of its expressions each time execution pauses or halts. For example, if you choose **Step** from the **Run** menu, MacPascal executes one line of code and pauses. At the pause, all of the Observe window's values are updated. (We will examine how the Observe window is used with other **Run** menu options later in this section.)

Now that we've prepared the Observe window, we can begin stepping through the program. (If you want to follow along on your Mac, enter the program from the last section into the program window and resize the windows so they look like Figure 2.19.) The first line of the program prints a prompt. The next line asks the user to enter an integer to go into the variable ***chocGal***. We respond by entering the value 835. Similarly, we can follow the next two lines of code and enter the value 385 for ***vanGal***. The Observe window now shows the value of both these variables.

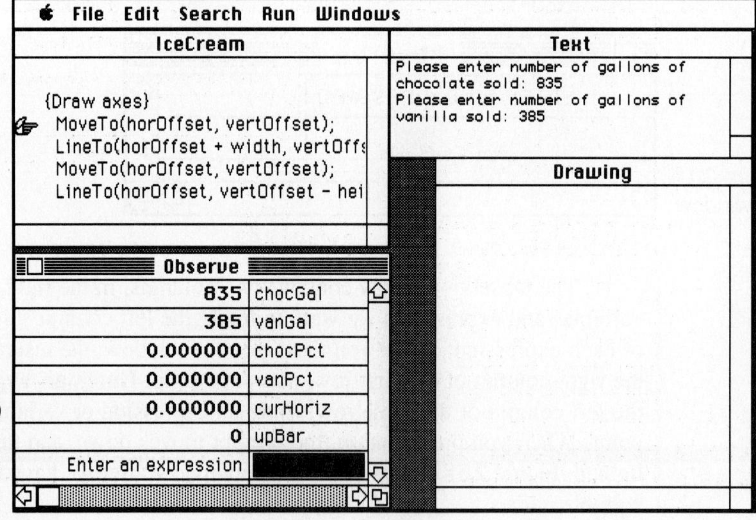

Figure 2.19
Hand simulation after *chocGal* and *vanGal* are input

The next section of code draws the axes. The next line of code moves the CP to ***(horOffset, vertOffset)***. By examining the table of constants, we see that this represents the pixel (20, 150). Make a note of this translation, since we cannot keep track of the current position in the Observe window. The next line, ***LineTo (horOffset + width, vertOffset);***, contains an expression to be evaluated. By adding ***horOffset*** (20) to ***width*** (180), we get the horizontal coordinate of the new endpoint (200). This line of code tells the computer to move from the current position (20, 150) to the new endpoint (200, 150). We update the CP's value while MacPascal draws the horizontal line (Figure 2.20).

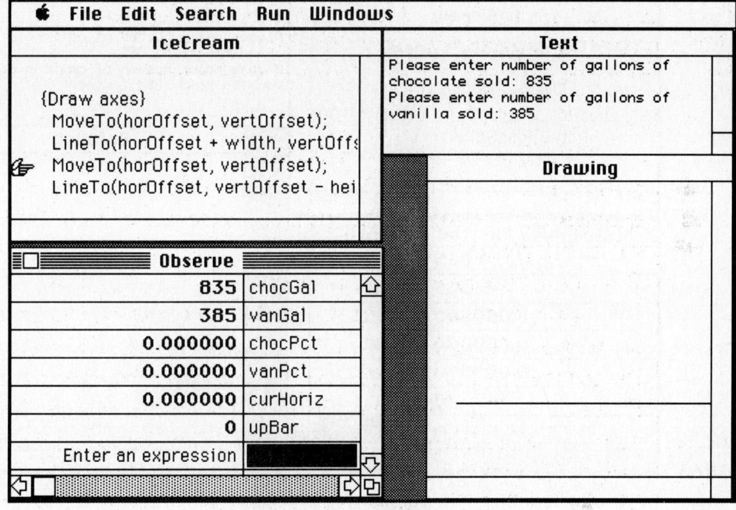

Figure 2.20
Drawing horizontal line

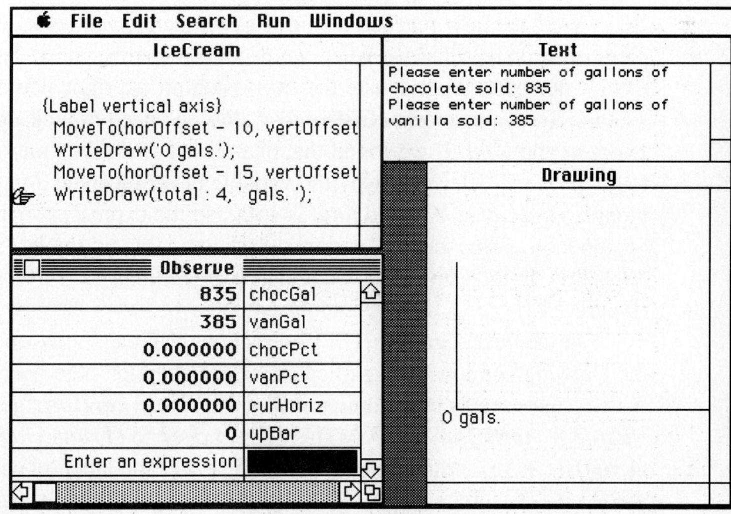

Figure 2.21
Hand simulation to second *MoveTo*

As we step through the next lines of code, the current position changes a number of times. Figure 2.21 shows the screen after we have stepped to the line ***MoveTo(horOffset – 15, vertOffset – height);***.

At this point we need to label the top of the vertical axis. The statement ***WriteDraw (total:4, ' gals. ');*** prints a label at the current position and uses the value of ***total***. Referring back to the table of constants, we know that the label '1500 gals.' should appear in the Drawing window. We choose **Step** again and verify our prediction.

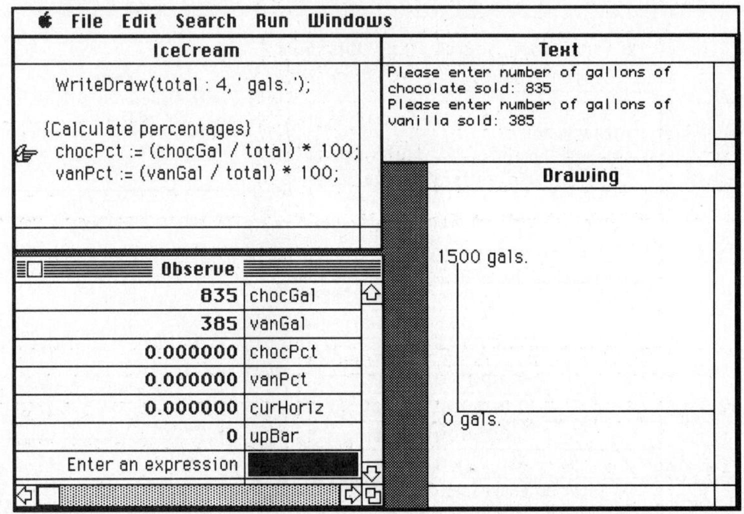

Figure 2.22
Labeling top of axis

We have now reached a pair of assignment statements. To make sure that the program is doing what we want, we need to remember how Pascal executes assignment statements. We evaluate the expression on the right side of the assignment symbol. To evaluate ***(chocGal/total) * 100***, we need to look up the values of ***chocGal*** and ***total***. If we found that one of these values is missing, we would have to go back and determine why the variable never received a value. In this case, though, ***chocGal*** is 835 and ***total*** is 1500, so the expression evaluates to 55.66666667. This value is assigned to the variable on the left side of the statement (***chocPct***). In the same way, we assign ***(vanGal/total) * 100*** to ***vanPct*** (Figure 2.23).

In the next segments, our observations alternate between the variable table and the Drawing window. Pay particularly close attention here because, as you shall see, the chocolate bar is being drawn incorrectly. First, ***curHoriz*** gets the value ***width/3 + horOffset***, or 80.0. The CP is moved to ***(Trunc(curHoriz) – 25, vertOffset + 15)***, which evaluates to (55, 165). The label 'chocolate' is then written on the screen. (The –25 and the +15 are used in the expression to position the first letter of the label in the correct location.) So far, so good (Figure 2.24).

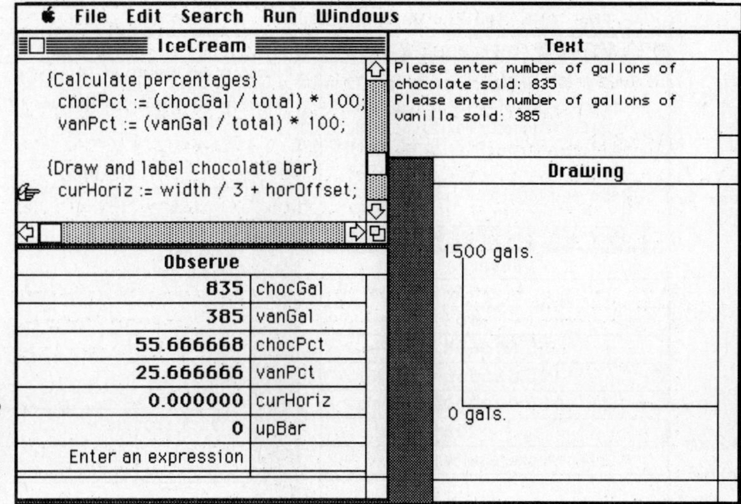

Figure 2.23
Stepping through assignment statements

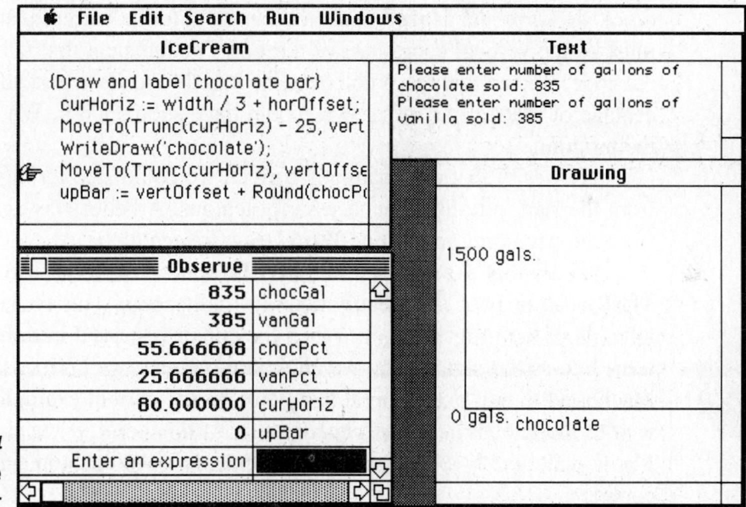

Figure 2.24
Labeling chocolate bar

Now we are ready to draw the line representing sales of chocolate. First, we move to ***(Trunc(curHoriz), vertOffset)***, which, according to the Observe window, is (80, 150). As the inline comment notes, we have moved to the horizontal axis. Next, calculate the value of ***upBar***. ***vertOffset + Round(chocPct)*** evaluates to 150 + 56, or 206. The next statement, ***LineTo(Trunc(curHoriz), upBar)***, draws a line to (80, 206), which goes off the bottom of the screen.

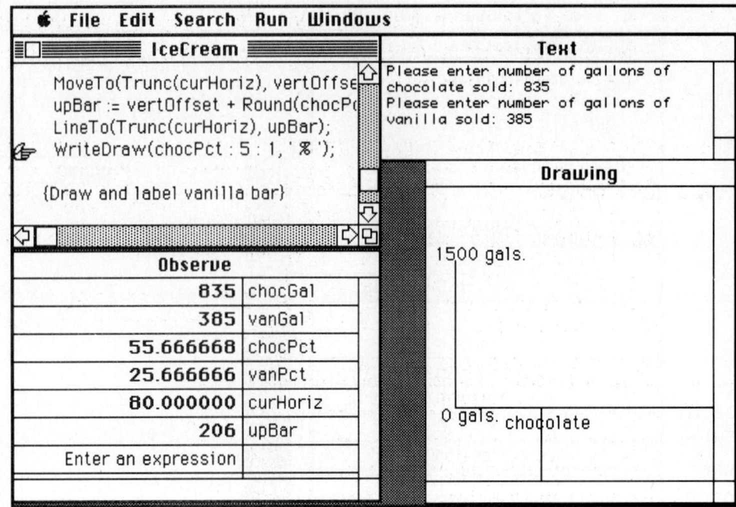

Figure 2.25
Drawing chocolate bar

We have found a bug. Now we have to figure out why it exists. We can see that the horizontal position is correct, but the vertical position of the line is not. Since we know the ***MoveTo*** statement moved to the correct place on the axis, it must be the vertical coordinate of the ***LineTo*** statement that is incorrect. Looking at the code, we see that the problem is the variable ***upBar***. Instead of adding the percentage of sales to the offset, we should have subtracted it. We make the change in the program.

To verify that our change is correct, we could step through the program again from the start, but this is unnecessarily tedious. A better way is to rerun the program from the beginning to the line ***WriteDraw('chocolate');***.

To do this, we choose the **Stops In** option (from the **Run** menu in MacPascal, or from the **Debug** menu in Lightspeed). This creates a gutter along the left side of the program code. When the cursor is moved into the gutter, the I-bar turns into a stop sign. When we click in the gutter, we insert a stop sign, which tells MacPascal to halt execution at this point. In the current example, enter a stop sign next to the line ***WriteDraw('chocolate');***. At this point, if we choose **Go**, MacPascal quickly executes all the statements up to the stop sign, and we can continue.

We can use the stops in conjunction with two other **Run** menu options. The **Step-Step** option in MacPascal and the **Trace** option in Lightspeed both perform the same operation. **Step-Step/Trace** executes the first statement, then updates the Observe window, then executes the second statement, then updates the Observe window, and so on, until the first stop sign is reached. The **Go-Go** option is similar to **Step-Step/Trace**, except that **Go-Go** takes larger steps: it executes all the statements up to a stop sign and then updates the Observe window. **Go-Go** repeats the pattern until the end of the program is reached. In short, **Step-Step/Trace** and **Go-Go** are similar to choosing **Step** and **Go** repeatedly.

Back to the problem at hand. After stopping execution at the stop sign, we choose **Step** four more times. As the result in Figure 2.26 shows, the change is correct, and we can move on.

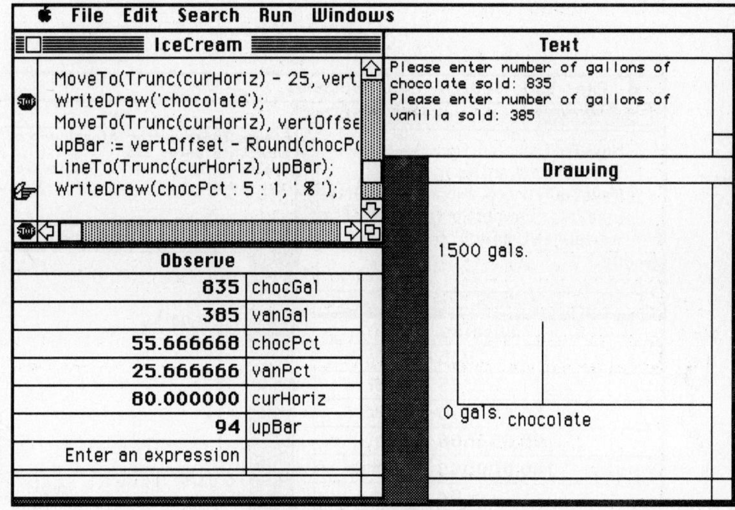

Figure 2.26
Stepping through corrected code

With the line ***curHoriz := curHoriz + width/3;***, we begin drawing and labeling the vanilla bar. Since this is an assignment statement, we evaluate the expression on the right. Since ***curHoriz*** is 80.0 and ***width*** is 180, the result is 80.0 + (180/3), or 140.0. Because each variable can hold only one value, the old value of ***curHoriz*** disappears.

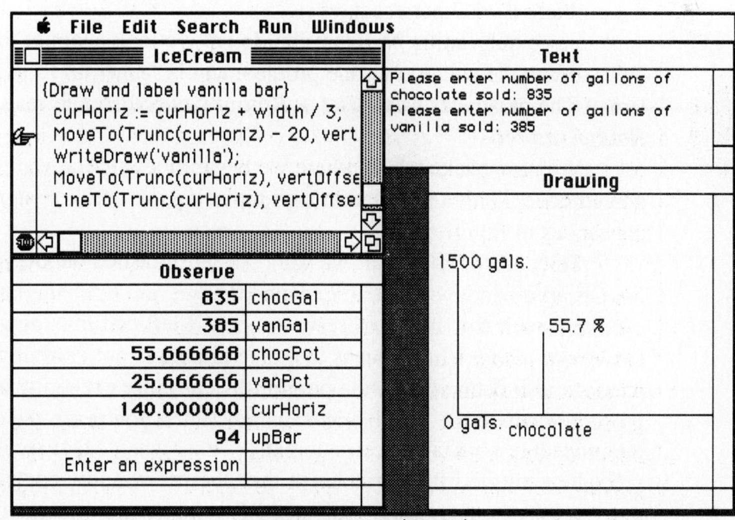

Figure 2.27
Beginning of drawing vanilla bar

When the next line refers to ***curHoriz***, we use the current value of that variable. Thus, the line ***MoveTo (Trunc(curHoriz) – 20, vertOffset + 15);*** moves the current position to (120, 165). We can simulate the last statements in the program and produce the final result.

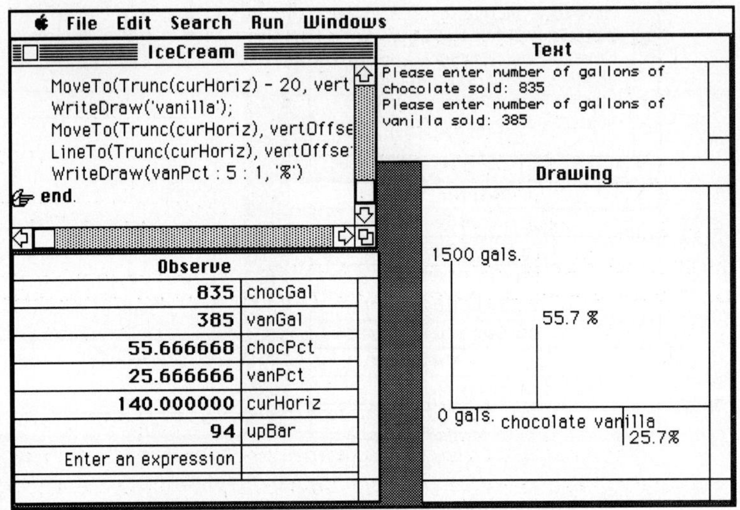

Figure 2.28
Hand simulation at end of program

When the final line has been executed, you can look at the total result and decide if it's what you want. If so, you are finished. If not, you have to find out where the problem is, and correct it.

Since our vanilla bar is upside-down, we look again at the vertical coordinates. (Very often, the solution to one problem can be generalized to solve similar problems.) The parameter ***vertOffset + Round(vanPct)*** should read ***vertOffset – Round(vanPct)***.

We now backtrack to where we began drawing the vanilla line and test the altered code. With a subtraction sign replacing the addition sign, the final result appears as in Figure 2.29.

Since this is the result we want, we are finished debugging. Something else in the Observe window needs to explained, however. After the last statement is executed, each row in the Observe window's left column contains the message *Undefined name,* which means that the variable is not currently available. This message also occurs when the program is currently executing a statement outside the procedure where the variable is declared. When you reach the end of a procedure, all the procedure's variables cease to exist. Thus, when MacPascal steps out of a procedure, all the local variables in the Observe window contain the undefined message. At the end of the program, all variables are undefined.

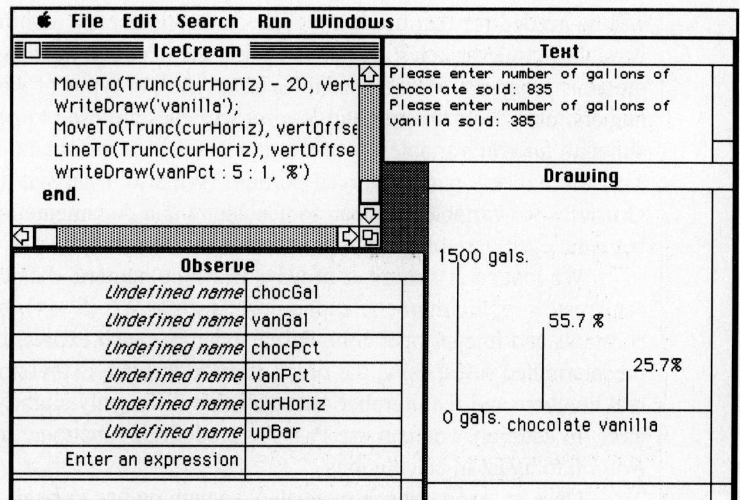

Figure 2.29
Hand simulation of final corrections

A final note on stop signs. The **Stops In** option is known as a *toggle* because it acts as an on/off switch. When the stop signs are present in MacPascal, the **Stops In** option becomes **Stops Out**; in Lightspeed, a checkmark appears next to the **Stops In** option. To remove the stop sign gutter in MacPascal, you choose **Stops Out**; in Lightspeed, you choose **Stops In** again. To remove an individual stop sign, you can click on the sign, and it will disappear. In Lightspeed, you can also remove all the stop signs without removing the gutter with the **Pull Stops** option on the **Debug** menu.

The debugging techniques described in this section rely on MacPascal features. At some point, however, you may have to debug without the benefit of an Observe window. If you do not have such debugging features at your disposal, hand simulate your code the way we hand simulated the pseudocode in Section 2.14. When you hand simulate, mimic the computer's actions, line by line and without anticipation. As you read code, don't assume that you know what should happen next; the odds are, that is where your mistake lies. Playing computer will help you understand your program more thoroughly.

2.17 Chapter Summary

Chapter 1 discussed the input-processing-output sequence used by a computer. In this chapter, you have seen how this sequence can be coded in Pascal.

To make the input-processing-output sequence do what you want, you must be able to use variables correctly. First, variables must be declared before they can be used. The **var** section of each procedure tells Pascal how many locations in memory will be needed for that procedure. The declarations only reserve the locations for variables; until variables are given values, they contain "garbage" values left over by previous programs. Pascal uses three data types, or types of variables, to handle numeric data. Both ***integer*** and ***longint*** variables are used to handle whole numbers, although ***longint*** variables have a larger range of representation. ***real*** variables are used for numbers with fractional portions. We also discussed naming conventions and glossaries for variables. Proper nomenclature and documentation help you to remember what each variable is supposed to do.

We looked at a number of ways in which numeric data can be processed. You can create simple arithmetic expressions, such as 2 * (5 + 4), by combining literal constants and integer operators. Pascal evaluates such expressions according to a set of predetermined rules, using the order of priority. Such expressions can be created using real numbers and real-number operators that differ only slightly from integer operators. In addition, you can use Pascal's predefined functions, such as ***Trunc*** and ***Round***, to assist in calculations.

Once an expression is evaluated, something has to be done with the result. Typically, the result is placed in a variable using an assignment statement. When Pascal encounters an assignment statement, it evaluates the expression on the right side of the := symbol and then places the result in the variable to the left of the :=. Because of this two-step operation, statements such as ***total := total – amtLost;*** are perfectly acceptable.

The ***Readln*** statement accepts input from the keyboard. Because the ***Readln*** statement does not tell the user what to do, input statements are preceded by prompts. These prompts, which tell the user what to enter, are usually coded with ***Write*** statements.

The values of variables can be output in the Text window with either the ***Writeln*** or ***Write*** statement. Field specifications make output more readable. Pascal allows you to specify the field width of any variable and the precision (the number of digits after the decimal point) of any ***real*** variable or expression.

When you work with numbers, it is often convenient to use constants. Constants are declared at the top of the program. Unlike variables, which are local to a single procedure, constants are global, which means that they can be used in any place in the program. Constants make the program more readable and easier to modify.

This chapter also introduced you to graphics programming. Like a number of other modern graphics machines, the Macintosh uses a raster display for graphical output. In MacPascal, graphical output goes to the Drawing window. The Macintosh uses a conceptual pen to draw on that window; the pixel where the pen is located at any moment is called the current position. Three commands manipulate the pen: the ***MoveTo*** command moves the pen to a new CP; the ***LineTo*** command draws a line from the CP to a designated pixel; and the ***WriteDraw*** command prints text starting at the CP.

Finally, we discussed hand simulation. By "playing computer," you can verify that a program actually does what you intended. Hand simulation can be performed on pseudocode or code. In either case, you should naively follow your list of instructions *exactly as they are written*. By using a variable table, you can determine if a value is incorrect and pinpoint bugs in your program. When you have entered the program into the computer, you can use MacPascal's Observe window and stop signs to monitor the change of variables throughout the program. By carefully hand simulating each stage of pseudocode, you can largely avoid the even more tedious hand simulation of the Pascal code.

2.18 Exercises

Understanding Concepts

1. What is the result when Pascal evaluates each of the following expressions?

   a. 4 + 6 * 8 c. 16 **div** 3 e. ***pi*** * 15
   b. 74 **mod** 6 d. 4.5 / 3 + 12

2. What is the difference between the algebraic expression i = i + 1 and the assignment statement ***i : = i + 1;*** ?

3. If the variable on the left of an assignment statement is of type ***integer***, do all of the variables on the right side also have to be of type ***integer***? Is this also true for ***real***s?

4. In the statement ***area : = pi * radius * radius;*** (assuming it is legal), which identifiers are variables, which are constants, and which can't you tell?

5. What does the following procedure output? Where is the CP at the end?

```
procedure DrawLines;
var
   bottom, right: integer; { coordinates for first endpoint }
begin
   bottom := 200;
   right := 200;
   MoveTo(0, 0);
   LineTo(right, bottom);
   LineTo(right div 2, bottom);
   LineTo(right, bottom div 2);
   LineTo(bottom div 2, right div 2)
end; { DrawLines }
```

6. Suppose you have the following declarations at the top of a program:

```
const
   halfChicken = 4.95;
   taxRate =.05;
var
   totalBill,
   onePersonPart: real;
   numPeople: integer;
```

What are the contents of the variables after each of the following assignment statements (assume the statements are performed in the order shown) ?

```
a. numPeople := 5;
b. totalBill := numPeople * halfChicken;
c. totalBill := totalBill + (totalBill * taxRate);
d. onePersonPart := totalBill / numPeople;
```

7. Which of the following are legitimate inputs for the statement ***Readln(maximumHours, desiredHours);*** where ***maximumHours*** and ***desiredHours*** are integer variables?

a. 18, 15
b. 18 15
c. 18< Return > 15
d. 18   15
e. 1815

8. Given the statements:

```
Write('Enter the number of chocolates in a package: ');
Readln(numChocs);
Write('Enter the cost of the package: ');
Readln(price);
```

and assuming that ***price*** has been delcared as a ***real*** and ***numChocs*** as an ***integer***, write a statement that prints the cost of a single chocolate. The cost should be output in dollar notation ($0.07). (For formatting purposes, assume that each chocolate costs less than $10.00.)

Coding Exercises

1. Write a procedure that asks the user to input a temperature in degrees Fahrenheit and outputs the equivalent temperature in Celsius. (The formula is C = 5/9(F–32).)

2. Write a procedure that adds time. The user enters two sets of minutes and seconds; your procedure outputs the result in minutes and seconds. For example, if the user wants to add 2 minutes 37 seconds to 3 minutes 41 seconds, the result should be 6 minutes 18 seconds.

3. Write a procedure that asks a user to enter a five-digit integer and prints the same number in expanded "place-value" notation. For example, if the user enters 23051, the procedure should produce the output:

(2 * 10000) + (3 * 1000) + (0 * 100) + (5 * 10) + 1

Variation: Ask the user to input the base of a number. Your procedure should output the expanded notation and the decimal equivalent. For example, if the user enters the number 23051 and indicates that the number is in base 8, the procedure should output (2 * 4096) + (3 * 512) + (0 * 64) +(5 * 8) + 1 and the decimal equivalent (9769). (Hint: consider the following pattern in the output: 4096 is 8^4, 512 is 8^3, 64 is 8^2, and so on.)

4. Write a procedure that draws a specified angle. First, the procedure should draw a vertical line from (100, 50) to (100, 100). When the user enters a number of degrees, the code should produce another line, completing the angle. In the first figure below, the user has specified an angle of 45°; in the second figure, the user has specified an angle of 90°. (You will need to use the predefined functions ***Sin*** and ***Cos***).

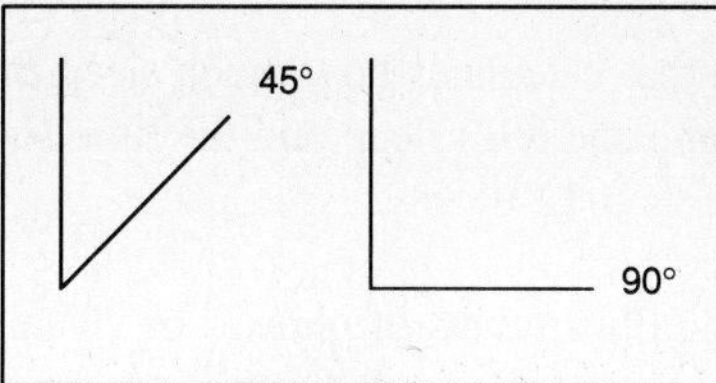

5. Write a procedure to help determine which is faster: a mile run in 3 minutes and 47.33 seconds or 1500 meters run in 3 minutes and 30.77 seconds. (A mile is equivalent to 1609 meters.)

6. Write a procedure to draw the following figure:

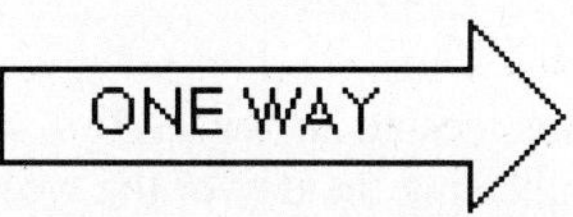

7. Write a procedure that draws a picture of a baseball diamond and the positions, as shown below:

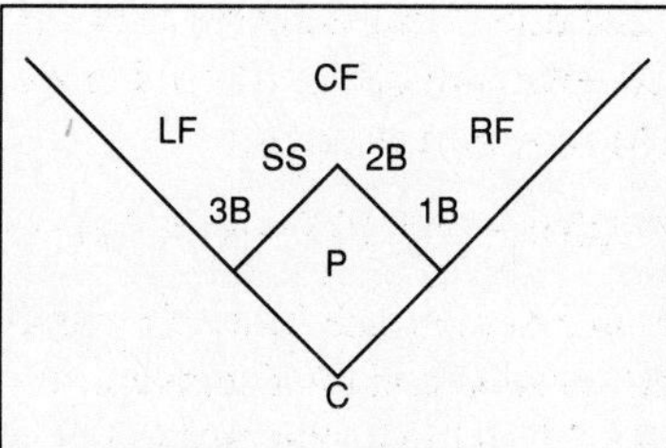

8. Write two different procedures that draw five-pointed stars, as shown below. Each procedure should have only one ***MoveTo*** command. One procedure should use as few ***LineTo*** commands as possible; the other should use 15 calls to ***LineTo***.

9. Write a procedure that calculates how much sleep the user got last night. The user should enter the time she fell asleep and the time she awoke. Assume the user did not sleep for more than 12 hours.

10. Rebuses are graphic illustrations of phrases or visual puns. For example, the picture

```
stand
  I
```

illustrates the phrase "I understand." Write code to draw rebuses in the Drawing window for the following phrases:

a. That's beneath me!
b. Philosophy's over my head.
c. A world divided
d. A position on the fence
e. A life in the balance

Programming Problems

1. Write a program that prints a calendar for the first week of January. The user should input a number indicating the day of the week for January 1 (1=Sunday, 2=Monday, and so on).

2. Write a program that shows a clock face at a specified time. We mean an "analog" clock with an hour and a second hand — a digital clock is a little too easy, no? For example, if the user indicates that it is quarter past seven (specified as 7 hours and 15 minutes), the program should output the following (without the circle):

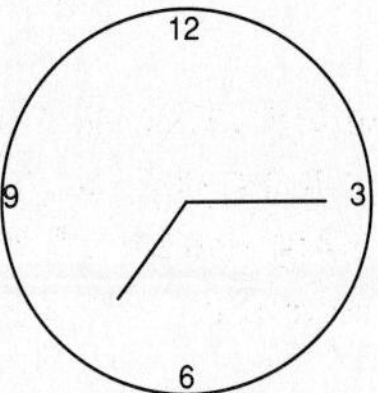

3. SAT results are calculated by comparing "raw" scores to the mean score. If the raw score matches the mean score, the SAT result is 500. A difference of 100 points on the SAT scale represents what statisticians call a standard deviation. For example, suppose the mean score is 60 and the standard deviation is 20. Then a raw score one standard deviation over the mean (60 + 20, or 80) translates to a SAT score 100 points over the mean SAT score (500 + 100, or 600). (This is a simplified version of how the Educational Testing Service calculates SAT scores.)

   Assume the SAT has 100 questions. The mean score is 60 and the standard deviation is 20 points. Write a program that calculates a user's SAT-scale score. First, determine the user's raw score by awarding one point for each correct answer, subtracting 1/4 point for each incorrect answer, and ignoring all answers left blank. Your program should ask the user for the number of questions answered correctly and incorrectly. The output should be the raw score and the equivalent SAT score.

4. Rewrite the ***Faces*** program from Chapter 1 using ***WriteDraw*** instead of ***Write*** and ***Writeln*** statements.

5. Write a program that shows where a baseball team positions its players. Start by drawing the diamond from Coding Exercise 7. Then add a procedure that allows the user to enter the uniform number of the player at each position and then prints that number near the position symbol. For example, if the user indicates that number 32 is pitching, a 32 should appear near the P in the center of the diamond.

6. A survey at Finite State University showed that 93% of the student body felt that "they were on top of their classes" in September. In October, 74% felt that way. The decline continued into November, when 57% felt they were on top of their classes and fell to a low of 38% in December. Show the results of this survey in a table in the Text window and as a line graph or bar graph in the Drawing window.

7. In Algebra I, you learned that any line can be defined as $y = mx + b$, where m is the slope of the line and b is the y-intercept. Write a program that asks the user to input a slope and a y-intercept and produces the corresponding line on a set of axes.

8. Rewrite the building program in Chapter 1, Programming Problem 5, by drawing lines in the Drawing window.

9. Write a program that shows the multiplication of a three-digit number by a two-digit number. The user should enter the numbers; your program should produce the output in long form in the Drawing window. For example, if the user enters 315 and 43, the result should look like this:

```
   315
    43
   945
 1260
 13545
```

10. Suppose you have a part-time job that pays $4.75 an hour. You want to find out how much money you will have after expenses. Write a program that will calculate this figure for a given month. Your share of the rent is fixed at $200/month. Since you live in an apartment with two other people, you pay a third of the monthly utility and grocery bills, but you pay the whole amount for your own phone and miscellaneous expenses. Also, 12% of your income is deducted as tax. Your program should allow you to enter the number of hours you have worked as well as your current expenses for utilities, groceries, phone, and miscellaneous. The program should output your total income, your expenses, and what money you have left.

3

Introduction to Graphics

As the title of this book implies, computer graphics can be a significant part of programming. But you may be asking yourself, "What's the big deal with all this graphics stuff, anyway?" The big deal is that graphics can improve a program's *user interface* (the part of the program that the user sees and interacts with). When you write a program, you are usually writing something that someone else will use. You want the program to be as easy to use as possible. You also want to present your output as clearly as possible. Graphics can complement the textual and numeric information in a program, just as illustrations can help present information in a book. Besides, designing graphics can be more fun than crunching numbers.

This chapter looks at the Macintosh's graphics capabilities. First, we will see how MacPascal programs can draw simple shapes. Then, we will examine how to draw variations on these shapes. Finally, we will look at how to enter information using the mouse instead of the keyboard and how to move and resize objects on the screen.

3.1 About Graphics

Chapter 2 introduced the graphics commands ***LineTo***, ***MoveTo***, and ***WriteDraw***. The Macintosh contains an entire set of procedures to handle graphics in a *graphics package* utility called *QuickDraw*. This software is on the same level in the computer onion as the Finder.

The QuickDraw graphics package is specific to the Macintosh. Unlike Pascal, QuickDraw does not exist on other machines. However, other machines support packages similar to QuickDraw. For example, the ***LineTo*** and ***WriteDraw*** commands may not exist in all graphics packages, but all graphics packages have some procedure to draw a line or a string of text. While here we discuss only the QuickDraw package, keep in mind that a general understanding of one graphics package will help you understand how any such package works.

Let's return to the Drawing window. As we mentioned in the last chapter, the Macintosh has a raster display, which means any pixel in the Drawing window can be manipulated at any time. While ***Writeln*** statements always print from left to right and from top to bottom, QuickDraw procedures can produce output in any direction. We can draw horizontal lines at the bottom of the Drawing window, then move the pen to a position near the top of the window and write text. The coordinate system in the Drawing window uses integers. That is, the coordinates of any pixel can be designated by integer variables, constants, or expressions. All QuickDraw procedures use integers to specify coordinates.

If you have ever worked on a newspaper or yearbook, you know that pictures are often trimmed so that they fit in a particular area: part of the original picture is trimmed and discarded. A similar process occurs in MacPascal when you try to draw outside the Drawing window. Suppose the following code exists in your program:

```
MoveTo(155, 100);
WriteDraw('This label is too long');
```

If you have not resized the initial Drawing window, you will get the following output:

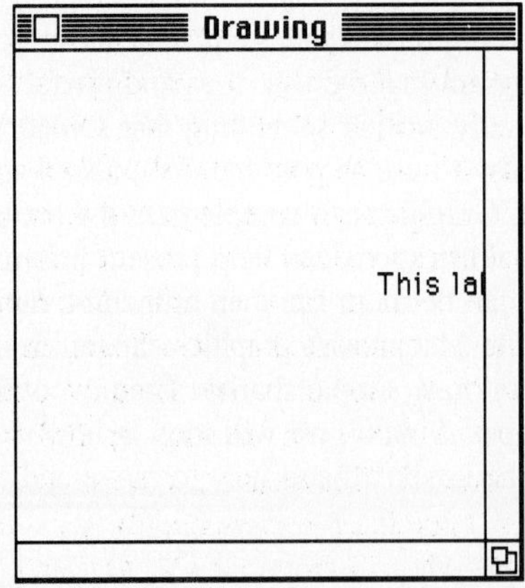

Figure 3.1
Clipped output

The text does not fit in the Drawing window. QuickDraw placed as much as it could in the window and discarded what remained. The text has been *clipped* to the window boundary.

The text appears to continue to the right of the window. It might seem that if we make the window larger, all the text would become visible. This is not the case. When we resize the window, the text is still clipped.

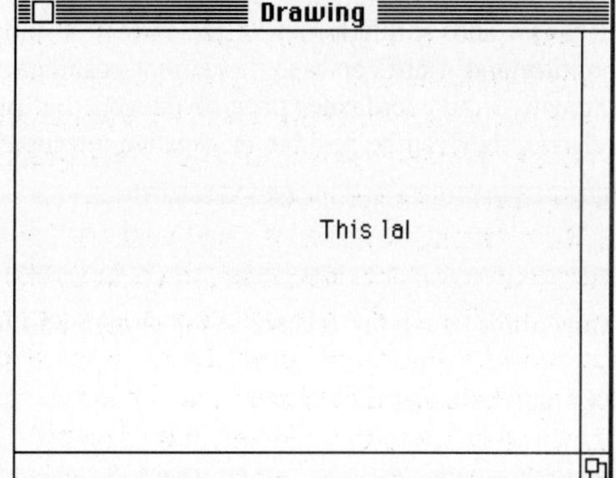

Figure 3.2
Resized window: output still clipped

QuickDraw discarded the portion that did not fit in the window during execution; this clipped portion is not restored when the window is resized. If we run the program when the window is suitably larger, however, the output is not clipped.

To quickly summarize these rules of graphics on the Macintosh:

1. All coordinates must be specified as integers.
2. All graphic output appears in the Drawing window.
3. Output is clipped to the size of the current Drawing window; if you want to use a larger Drawing window, resize it *before* you run the program.

3.2 More About Lines

In Chapter 2, we examined how to move the current position of the pen and draw lines with the ***MoveTo*** and ***LineTo*** statements. These statements require the use of *absolute coordinates.* That is, the horizontal and vertical coordinates specified as arguments are the exact location at which the command should take place. QuickDraw also allows us to move the pen or draw a line using *relative coordinates*, which means that we can move a distance relative to the current position.

For example, suppose you want to draw a vertical line from the current position. If the current position is represented by (***curHoriz***, ***curVert***), you could use the statement ***LineTo(curHoriz, curVert – 100)*** to draw a line 100 pixels up. But, since you simply want to draw a line moving up 100 pixels, you can use the statement ***Line(0, – 100)*** instead. This means that a line will be drawn from the current position to a point 0 pixels away horizontally and –100 pixels away vertically. Similarly, ***Move(– 20, 0)*** will move the CP 20 pixels to the left.

Syntax Box 3.1
Move

Purpose To move the current position.

Syntax **Move(** < diffHoriz >**,** < diffVert > **)**

where < diffHoriz > and < diffVert > are relative changes in the current position's horizontal and vertical coordinates.

Usage QuickDraw adds < diffHoriz > to the current position's horizontal coordinate and < diffVert > to the current position's vertical coordinate. Both coordinates must be integers, but since the change is relative, they can be positive or negative integers.

Syntax Box 3.2
Line

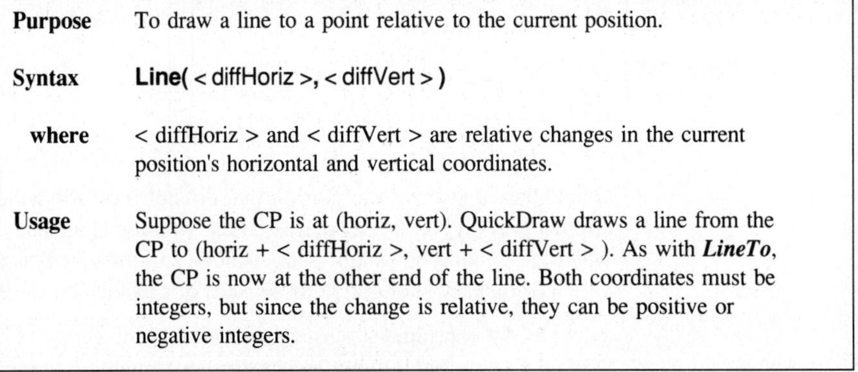

Purpose To draw a line to a point relative to the current position.

Syntax **Line(** < diffHoriz >**,** < diffVert > **)**

where < diffHoriz > and < diffVert > are relative changes in the current position's horizontal and vertical coordinates.

Usage Suppose the CP is at (horiz, vert). QuickDraw draws a line from the CP to (horiz + < diffHoriz >, vert + < diffVert >). As with ***LineTo***, the CP is now at the other end of the line. Both coordinates must be integers, but since the change is relative, they can be positive or negative integers.

Relative coordinates are useful when you want to create a procedure to draw a shape. For example, the procedure

```
procedure Square;
begin
   Line(50, 0);
   Line(0, -50);
   Line(-50, 0);
   Line(0, 50)
end; { Square }
```

draws a square above and to the right of the current position. If we have the following code in another procedure:

```
MoveTo(100, 100);
Square;
MoveTo(50, 150);
Square;
```

the output will be as shown in Figure 3.3.

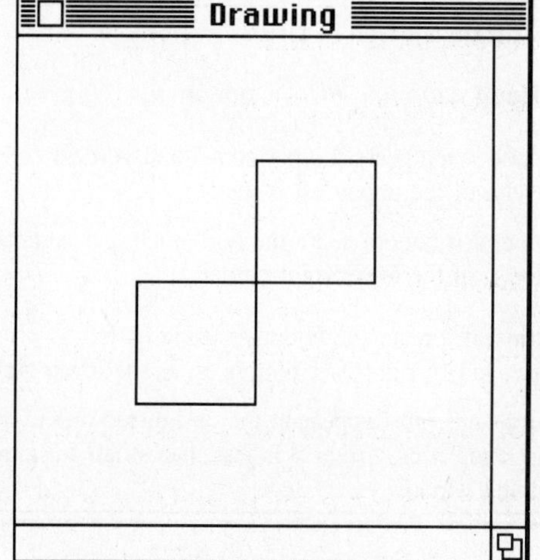

Figure 3.3
Drawing two squares with one procedure

3.3 Other Primitives

QuickDraw works with four basic shapes: rectangles, ovals, rounded rectangles, and pieces of circles (arcs and wedges). These shapes are the basis of more complex objects and, along with lines, are known as *primitive objects.*

By far the most important shape in QuickDraw is the rectangle. A rectangular region is designated by the upper left and lower right endpoints. We can draw the outline of a rectangle by using the ***FrameRect*** command. This statement takes four parameters specifying the location of the outline. We send ***FrameRect*** (in order) the top vertical, left horizontal, bottom vertical, and right horizontal coordinates. Thus, the call

```
FrameRect(35, 150, 125, 180);
```

draws a rectangular outline with a top left corner of (150, 35) and a bottom right corner of (180, 125).

QuickDraw is not always consistent in the way in which coordinates are specified. In the ***Move*** and ***Line*** commands, the horizontal coordinate is specified before the vertical. In ***FrameRect***, the order of the coordinates is vertical, horizontal, vertical, horizontal. Also, note that the top and left coordinates must be less than the bottom and right coordinates, respectively. If the first two coordinates are greater than the corresponding coordinates in the second pair, nothing appears on the screen. Thus, ***FrameRect(35, 150, 125, 180);*** produces a rectangle, but ***FrameRect (125, 180, 35, 150);*** does not.

We can draw ovals and circles using the command ***FrameOval***. In determining the coordinates for an oval, we imagine a rectangle that snugly surrounds the oval. Then, we specify the upper left and lower right coordinates of the rectangle in the ***FrameOval*** statement.

Syntax Box 3.3
FrameRect

Purpose	To draw the outline of a rectangle.
Syntax	**FrameRect(** < top >**,** < left >**,** < bottom >**,** < right > **);**
where	< left > and < top > are the horizontal and vertical coordinates, respectively, of the upper left corner. < right > and < bottom > are the horizontal and vertical coordinates, respectively, of the lower right corner.
Usage	The outline of a rectangle is drawn using (< left >, < top >) as the upper left corner and (< right >, < bottom >) as the lower right corner. The coordinates must appear in the designated order. If < bottom > is less than < top > or < right > is less than < left >, nothing appears in the Drawing window.

The syntax of ***FrameOval*** is essentially identical to that of ***FrameRect***: we specify, in order, the top, left, bottom, and right coordinates of the rectangle that surrounds the oval. For example, when QuickDraw sees the statement

```
FrameOval(50, 75, 150, 125);
```

it first creates an invisible rectangle at those coordinates; an oval is then drawn inside that rectangle.

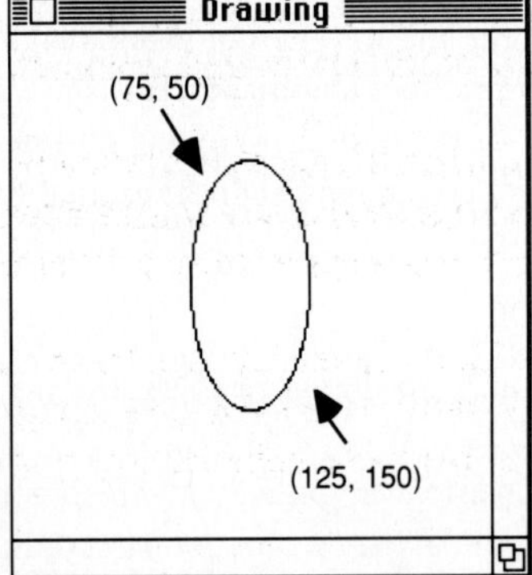

Figure 3.4
Result of
FrameOval

Syntax Box 3.4
FrameOval

Purpose	To draw the outline of an oval or a circle.
Syntax	**FrameOval(** < top >**,** < left >**,** < bottom >**,** < right > **);**
where	(< left > , < top >) and (< right > , < bottom >) specify a rectangle that circumscribes the oval.
Usage	QuickDraw fits an oval in the area specified by the rectangle. The rectangle specified by the coordinates does not appear on the screen.

A circle is drawn if the specified rectangle is a square. For example, ***FrameOval(10, 10, 90, 90)*** produces:

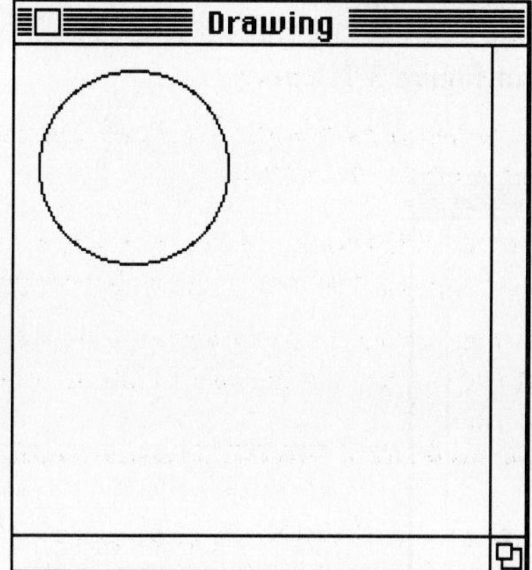

Figure 3.5
Circle drawn with *FrameOval*

Often, we want to deal with parts of shapes. If we want to draw part of a rectangle, we can use lines. If we want to draw part of an oval, however, we need to specify an arc.

We need to know three things to build an arc. First, we need to know how many animals to bring on board; next, we have to know how long a cubit is. Oops. Wrong problem. First, we need to designate the entire oval that we are dealing with. Then we need to know where on the shape the arc should start. Finally, we need to know how big the arc should be.

Suppose we want to draw the lower left quarter of the circle in Figure 3.5. Specifying the circle is no problem—we know it is surrounded by the rectangle (10, 10, 90, 90). We now need to specify the starting point and the size of the arc. These arguments are designated by degrees.

In QuickDraw, every oval has 360°. A vertical line drawn straight up from the center of the oval crosses it at the 0° mark. A line that goes straight down from the midpoint crosses the oval at the 180° mark, the point halfway around the oval. Other examples are labeled in Figure 3.6.

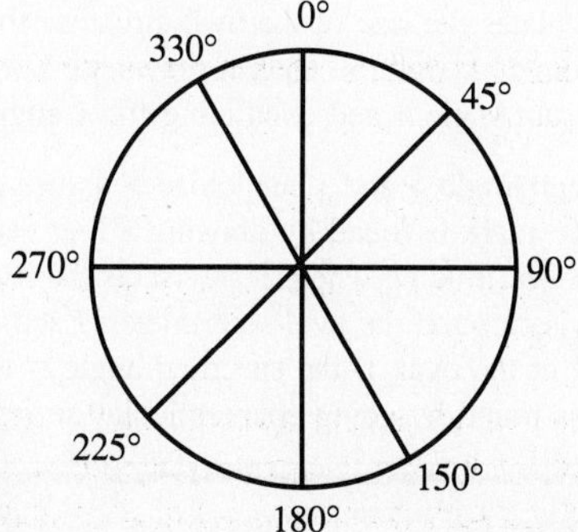

Figure 3.6
Anatomy of an oval

To draw the lower left quarter, we start at the position at the bottom of the circle, i.e., the 180° mark. The size of the arc is one quarter the size of the entire circle, or 90°. Thus, the statement

```
FrameArc(10, 10, 90, 90, 180, 90);
```

produces the result shown in Figure 3.7.

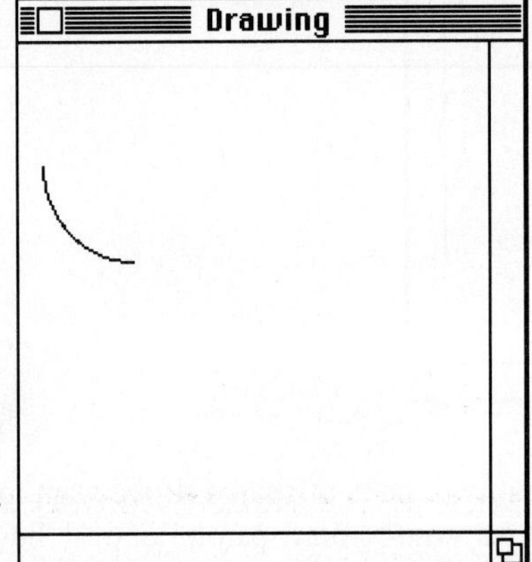

Figure 3.7
Output of *FrameArc*

Syntax Box 3.5
FrameArc

Purpose To draw a section of an oval.

Syntax **FrameArc(< top >, < left >, < bottom >, < right >, < startAngle >, < angleSize >);**

where (< left >, < top >) and (< right >, < bottom >) are the coordinates that specify an oval.

< startAngle > is the degree mark that designates the beginning of the arc.

<angleSize> is the magnitude of the angle in degrees.

Usage QuickDraw calculates the size of the oval circumscribed by < top >, < left >, < bottom >, < right >. Then it draws the border of the oval, beginning at < startAngle > and continuing for < angleSize > degrees.

Usually the < startAngle > and < angleSize > values are between –360° and 360°. The 0° mark is found by drawing a line vertically up from the oval's center and finding where it intersects the oval; degree marks increase clockwise around the oval's perimeter. Each degree represents another 1/360th of the oval. If the specified angle is less than 0°, the resulting point is found by going counterclockwise from 0°.

The final primitive is the rounded rectangle. The rounded rectangle is the shape of the buttons in the Macintosh's dialog boxes. The corners of the rounded rectangle are one quarter of an oval. The dimensions of that oval can be specified in the ***FrameRoundRect*** statement and indicate the roundness of the corners.

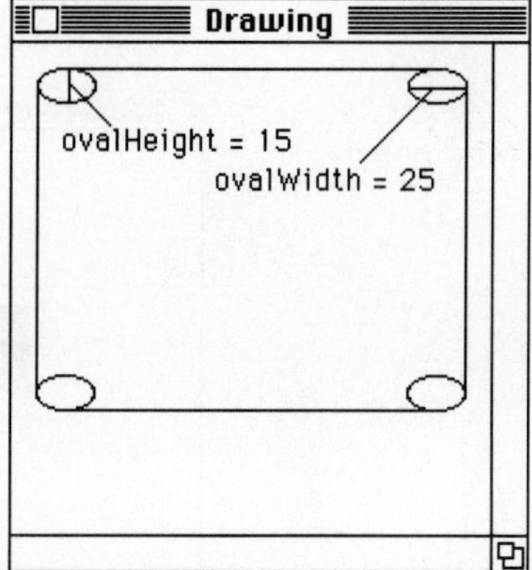

Figure 3.8
Rounded rectangle

Syntax Box 3.6
FrameRoundRect

Purpose To draw rounded rectangles.

Syntax **FrameRoundRect(** < top >**,** < left >**,** < bottom >**,** < right >**,** < ovalWidth >**,** < ovalHeight > **);**

where < left > and < top > are the horizontal and vertical coordinates of the rectangle's upper left corner.

< right > and < bottom > are the horizontal and vertical coordinates of the rectangle's lower right corner.

< ovalWidth > and < ovalHeight > are integers specifying the dimensions of the ovals used to form the corners.

Usage The oval dimensions must be positive. If the oval dimensions are negative, QuickDraw displays a regular rectangle.

If the dimensions define an oval that is too large, the rounded rectangle defaults to an oval whose size is determined by the < top >, < left >, < bottom >, and < right > coordinates.

3.4 Attributes

So far we have looked at how different shapes can be drawn. QuickDraw, like most graphics packages, also contains a set of procedures that affect the shapes' *attributes*, or appearance. We will see how a pen attribute can be changed.

In the previous section, we learned how to outline different shapes. Often, though, we want to work with shapes that are filled in. In QuickDraw terms, this means that we want to *paint* rather than *frame* a shape. To do this, QuickDraw has Paint commands that parallel the Frame commands. Figure 3.9 shows the difference between ***FrameRect*** and ***PaintRect***.

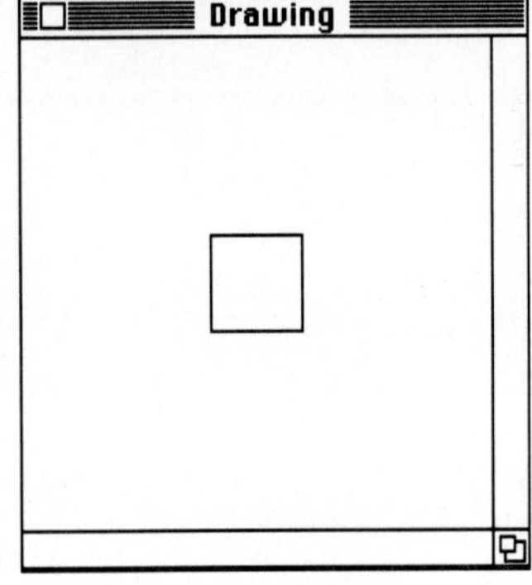

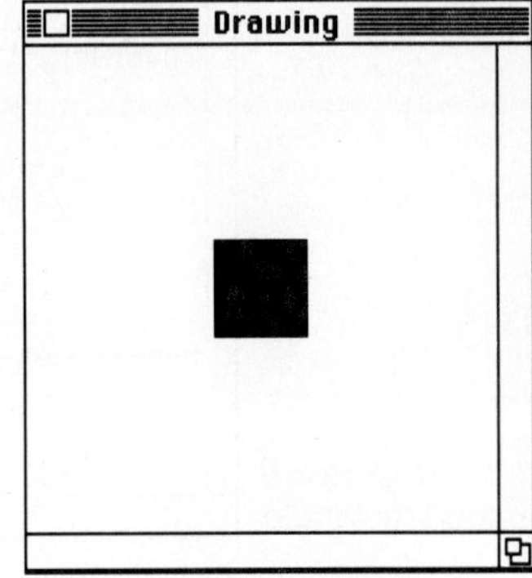

Figure 3.9

a. Framed rectangle

b. Painted rectangle in same location

Frame and Paint commands take the same arguments. In fact, the commands are identical except that Paint commands color the shape when it is drawn. The color of the paint is the current pen color (which is determined by the pen pattern). Initially, that color is black, but you can change the color.

Syntax Box 3.7
Paint commands

Purpose To draw painted shapes.

Syntax

PaintRect(< top >, < left >, < bottom >, < right >);
PaintOval(< top >, < left >, < bottom >, < right >);
PaintArc(< top >, < left >, < bottom >, < right >, < startAngle>, < angleSize>);
PaintRoundRect(< top >, < left >, < bottom >, < right >, < ovalWidth >, < ovalHeight >);

where the arguments have the same function as in the equivalent Frame statements.

Usage Paint commands print the outline of the shape on the Drawing window and fill the shape with the current pen pattern. The default pen pattern is black.

The ***PaintArc*** command does more than paint an arc. Just as ***FrameArc*** draws part of the outline drawn by ***FrameOval***, ***PaintArc*** paints part of the shape painted by ***PaintOval***. In other words, ***PaintArc*** paints a wedge.

PaintArc is useful when you want to draw a pie chart. Suppose you want to show that 40% of your salary goes to taxes. The following code draws such a picture.

```
procedure DrawWedge;

begin
   ...
   { show outline of entire salary }
   FrameOval(10, 10, 90, 90);

   { shade 40% of circle }
   PaintArc(10, 10, 90, 90, 0, 144);

   { label shaded area }
   MoveTo(70, 40);
   LineTo(100, 30);
   WriteDraw('Taxes: 40%');
   ...
end; { DrawWedge }
```

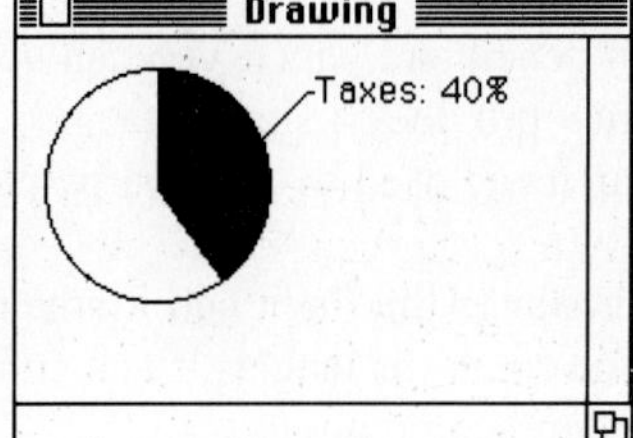

Figure 3.10 Output of *DrawWedge*

Shapes are painted using the current paint color, or pen pattern. QuickDraw allows you to change the color of the pen by using the ***PenPat*** command. On a black and white screen, the "colors" are really shades of gray—specifically, the colors we have

Syntax Box 3.8 **PenPat**

Purpose To set the pattern used by the pen.

Syntax **PenPat(** < pattern > **);**

where < pattern > is one of the available pen patterns; on a black and white screen, it is one of {***black***, ***dkGray***, ***gray***, ***ltGray***, ***white***}

Usage This command changes the pen pattern to the specified color. The initial pen pattern is black. The pen patterns are shown in Figure 3.11.

Figure 3.11
Available pen patterns

to choose from are white, light gray, gray, dark gray, and black. To change the pen's color, we call ***PenPat*** with one of the available colors (***black***, ***dkGray***, ***gray***, ***ltGray***, or ***white*** on the black-and-white screen) as an argument.
For example, to color a space inside an oval, we can use the code:

```
{ initial pen color is black }
PaintOval(20, 20, 50, 150);
PenPat(ltGray);
PaintRect(25, 70, 45, 100);
```

This produces the result shown in Figure 3.12.

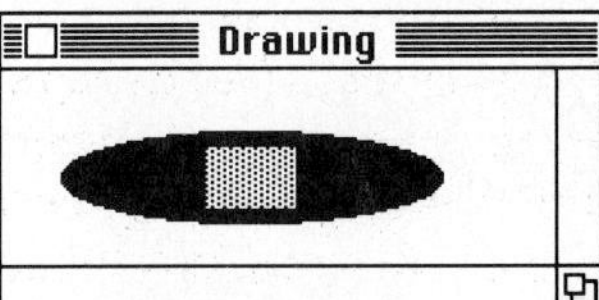

Figure 3.12
Using *PenPat* to color a rectangle inside an oval

When you are drawing with pencil and paper, you can get rid of unnecessary lines by using an eraser. QuickDraw provides a similar facility with its Erase attributes. Erase commands clear an area enclosed by a shape by painting the area in the background color—i.e., white.

The Erase commands are similar to the Paint and Frame commands. You can erase rectangles, ovals, wedges, and round rectangles. Each command takes the same arguments as the corresponding Frame command.

Syntax Box 3.9
Erase commands

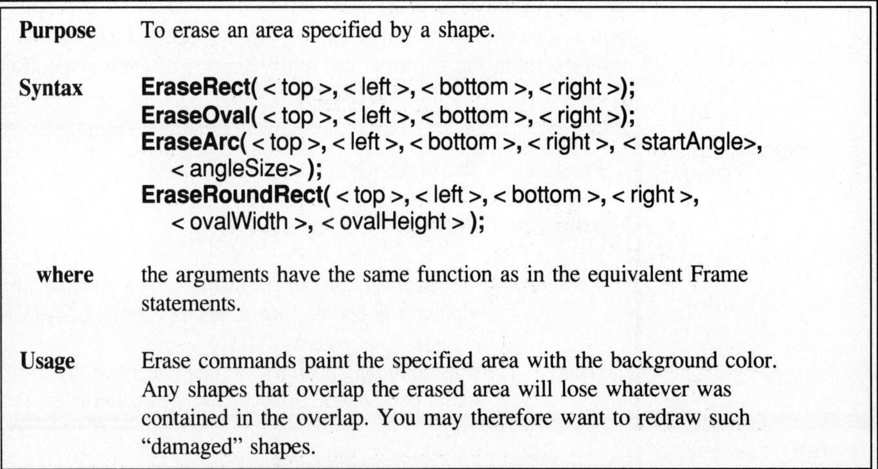

Purpose To erase an area specified by a shape.

Syntax
EraseRect(< top >, < left >, < bottom >, < right >**);**
EraseOval(< top >, < left >, < bottom >, < right >**);**
EraseArc(< top >, < left >, < bottom >, < right >, < startAngle>, < angleSize> **);**
EraseRoundRect(< top >, < left >, < bottom >, < right >, < ovalWidth >, < ovalHeight > **);**

where the arguments have the same function as in the equivalent Frame statements.

Usage Erase commands paint the specified area with the background color. Any shapes that overlap the erased area will lose whatever was contained in the overlap. You may therefore want to redraw such "damaged" shapes.

We can use ***EraseRect*** to erase the same part of the figure that we colored with the change of pen pattern earlier. We could use a ***PenPat(white);*** and ***PaintRect*** combination to color the area in white. Instead, though, we will use a single ***EraseRect*** statement:

```
PaintOval(20, 20, 50, 150);
EraseRect(25, 70, 45, 100);
```

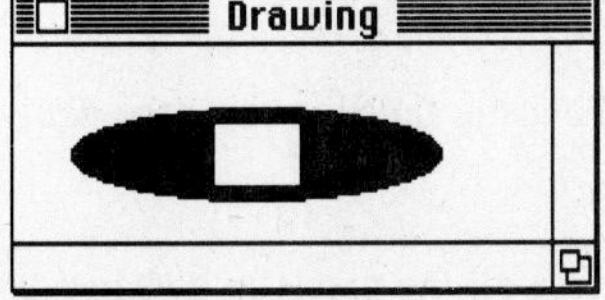

Figure 3.13
Oval with erased rectangle

The final attribute we will examine is inversion. Recall our discussion of highlighted text in Appendix E. (If you haven't read this appendix yet, now would be a good time to do so.) Highlighted text is an area in the program that has been selected for some purpose, say, cutting or copying. While the rest of the program text is black on white, highlighted text is white on black. Each pixel in the selected area is inverted.

The same thing can be done with shapes. When a shape is inverted, every pixel that is black is set to white, and vice versa. As with the Erase and Paint commands, the Invert commands take the same parameters as the Frame commands.

Figure 3.14 shows what happens when we use the following code to draw three overlapping rectangles and invert the overlapping areas.

```
PaintRect(50, 30, 80, 60);
PaintRect(65, 45, 95, 75);
PaintRect(80, 60, 110, 90);
InvertRect(65, 45, 80, 60);
InvertRect(80, 60, 95, 75);
```

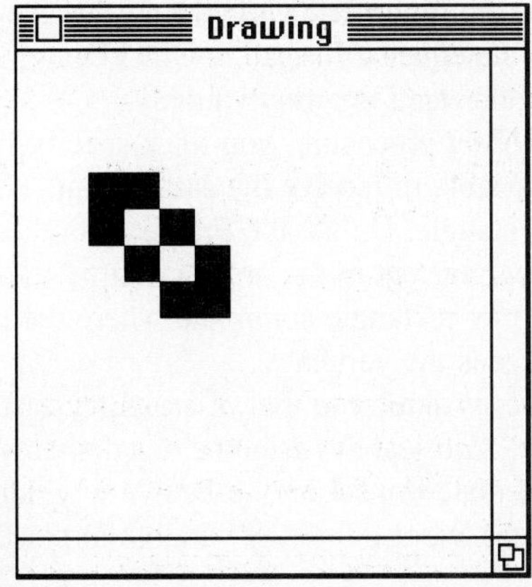

Figure 3.14
Inverted overlapping areas

Syntax Box 3.10
Invert commands

Purpose To reverse the color of a shape.

Syntax **InvertRect(** < top >, < left >, < bottom >, < right >**);**
InvertOval(< top >, < left >, < bottom >, < right >**);**
InvertArc(< top >, < left >, < bottom >, < right >, < startAngle>, < angleSize> **);**
InvertRoundRect(< top >, < left >, < bottom >, < right >, < ovalWidth >, < ovalHeight > **);**

where the arguments have the same function as in the equivalent Frame statements.

Usage Invert commands reverse all the pixels in a shape: if the pixel is white, it will be set to black, and vice versa.

3.5 Graphic Data Types

We have now looked at sixteen different commands that rely on rectangles. Each time we have drawn a shape, we have had to specify the coordinates of two corners of a rectangle. The developers of QuickDraw realized that typing the four coordinates of the same rectangle over and over again could become quite tedious. To avoid this repetitive typing, QuickDraw contains a method of referring to rectangles, and other graphic entities, such as points, by a single name.

QuickDraw provides a data type called ***rect***. This data type, like the types ***integer*** and ***real***, can be used in variable declarations.

```
var
   pieChart,                    { area for pie chart              }
   entireWindow : rect;         { area for whole Drawing window   }
```

Unlike numeric data types, however, graphic data types are specific to QuickDraw. Graphic variables also differ from numeric variables in that they do not receive values from ***Readln*** or assignment statements. Instead, a QuickDraw routine, the ***SetRect*** procedure, assigns a rectangular area to a ***rect*** variable.

When you call the ***SetRect*** procedure, you must specify five parameters. The first parameter is the ***rect*** variable to receive the assignment. The other parameters are the coordinates of the rectangle. Unlike the Frame and other output commands, however, ***SetRect*** receives parameters in the order < left >, < top >, < right >, < bottom >. ***SetRect*** is the only rectangle command where the horizontal coordinate in each pair precedes the vertical.

The purpose of ***SetRect*** is similar to that of assignment statements: to give a value to a specified variable. And just as assignment statements do not produce output, ***SetRect*** has no immediate impact on the Drawing window. To see the result of a ***SetRect*** assignment, we use the ***rect*** variable in place of the < top >,

< left >, < bottom >, < right > sequence in the graphic output statements. For example,

```
SetRect(ovalSurround, 10, 40, 50, 80);
FrameOval(ovalSurround);
PaintArc(ovalSurround, 0, 100);
```

produces the same output as

```
FrameOval(10, 40, 50, 80);
PaintArc(10, 40, 50, 80, 0, 100);
```

Syntax Box 3.11
SetRect

Purpose	To assign a rectangular region to a ***rect*** variable.
Syntax	**SetRect(< newRect >, < left >, < top >, < right >, < bottom >);**
where	< newRect > is your variable of type ***rect***. This is the variable that will get the specific rectangular area. < left > and < top > are the horizontal and vertical coordinates of the upper left corner. < right > and < bottom > are the horizontal and vertical coordinates of the lower right corner.
Usage	After a ***SetRect*** call, the ***rect*** variable < newRect > can be used in place of < left >, < top >, < right >, < bottom > in any other call. ***SetRect*** does *not* produce any output.

Let's go back to the pie chart example. Suppose you called 100 college students at midnight and asked what they were doing. You decide to show the results with a pie chart. The results are as follows:

sleeping	4%
studying	11%
no comment	18%
procrastinating	24%
working on a computer program	43%

You decide to use a different pen color for each area of the chart. To paint the arcs for each topic, you need to convert the percentages to degrees. You can do this by evaluating the expression ***Round(percentage * 360)*** if ***percentage*** is represented as a decimal. For example, to paint 50% of the circle, evaluate ***Round(.50 * 360)*** to produce the result, 180.

Each of the five calls to ***PaintArc*** requires a reference to the rectangle enclosing the pie chart. To eliminate retyping the coordinates, you can use ***SetRect***. The pseudocode for drawing the chart might look like this:

Set rectangle for pie chart
Paint arc for computer programing in black
Paint arc for procrastinating in gray
Paint arc for no comment in white
Paint arc for studying in light gray
Paint arc for sleeping in dark gray

Each "Paint arc" line of pseudocode requires two steps: changing the pen pattern and coloring the arc. The code for this procedure follows (note that this is just one procedure; other procedures in this program should label the graph or draw a legend).

Code 3.1 Procedure *GraphResults*

```
{ This procedure graphs the results of a poll of college       }
{ students' activities. The results of the poll are shown      }
{ in a pie chart, and each response is designated by a         }
{ different color.                                             }

procedure GraphResults;

   var
      pieChart : rect;        { area where chart is drawn             }
      startAngle,             { position where each arc starts        }
      angleSize : integer;    { size of arc                           }

   begin
      { Establish area for chart - note no rectangle is drawn }
      SetRect(pieChart, 50, 50, 150, 150);

      { Establish position for first arc }
      startAngle := 0;
      angleSize := Round((0.43) * 360);

      { Draw arc for 43% working on program                    }
      PenPat(black);
      { Note that the pen pattern is set to the default        }
      { color because another procedure may have               }
      { altered it.                                            }
      PaintArc(pieChart, startAngle, angleSize);

      { Draw 24% procrastinating in gray }
      PenPat(gray);    { change color }
      { old end point is new start point}
      startAngle := angleSize;
      angleSize := Round((0.24) * 360);   {move end pt}
      PaintArc(pieChart, startAngle, angleSize);

      { Draw 18% no comment }
      PenPat(white);
      startAngle := startAngle + angleSize;
      angleSize := Round((0.18) * 360);  {move end pt}
      PaintArc(pieChart, startAngle, angleSize);
```

Code 3.1
(continued)

```
    { Draw 11% studying }
    PenPat(ltGray);
    startAngle := startAngle + angleSize;
    angleSize := Round((0.11) * 360); {move end pt}
    PaintArc(pieChart, startAngle, angleSize);

    { Draw 4% sleeping }
    PenPat(dkGray);
    startAngle := startAngle + angleSize;
    angleSize := Round((0.04) * 360);
    PaintArc(pieChart, startAngle, angleSize);

    { Show outline of chart }
    PenPat(black);
    FrameOval(pieChart)
end;   { GraphResults }
```

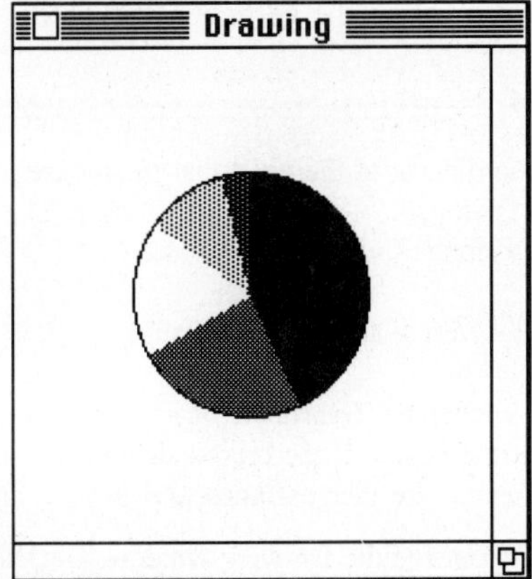

Figure 3.15
Output of procedure *GraphResults*

Syntax Box 3.12
SetPt

Purpose To assign a value to a point variable.

Syntax **SetPt(** < newPoint >**,** < horiz >**,** < vert > **);**

where < newPoint > is a variable of type ***point***.

< horiz > and < vert > are the horizontal and vertical coordinates of the desired point.

Usage ***SetPt*** associates the point variable with the pixel designated by (< horiz >, < vert >). This procedure does *not* produce any output.

QuickDraw also allows you to declare Pascal variables of type ***point***, which represent a single pixel on the screen. Point variables get values in the same way that ***rect*** variables get values. The ***SetPt*** procedure parallels the ***SetRect*** procedure: to use it, specify a ***point*** variable, followed by a horizontal and vertical coordinate. We will see in Chapter 4 how this can be useful.

3.6 Input

As we noted earlier, the focus of the examples in this book is *interactive* programming: that is, writing programs that can accept input from the user. Chapter 2 discussed how the ***Readln*** statement handles input from the keyboard. We will now look at how input can be received from the mouse.

Macintosh Pascal and Lightspeed Pascal (not QuickDraw) both supply a command called ***GetMouse***. When you move the cursor into the Drawing window, it changes into a cross-hair. When the interpreter encounters a ***GetMouse*** statement, it looks at the position of the cross-hair locator. The horizontal and vertical coordinates of the cross-hair are then returned to ***GetMouse***, which means that ***GetMouse*** always uses two integer variables as parameters. The first variable receives the horizontal coordinate; the second receives the vertical coordinate.

Syntax Box 3.13
GetMouse

Purpose	To retrieve coordinates of the pixel that the mouse is pointing to.
Syntax	**GetMouse(** < horiz >**,** < vert > **);**
where	< horiz > and < vert > are integer variables.
Usage	When Pascal encounters ***GetMouse***, it immediately determines the coordinates of the center of the cross-hair pointer. The horizontal and vertical coordinates are then assigned to < horiz > and < vert >. If the mouse is outside the Drawing window, ***GetMouse*** still returns coordinates relative to the origin, or (0, 0) point. For example, if ***GetMouse*** returns the value –20 to < horiz > and –50 to < vert >, the mouse is 20 pixels to the left and 50 pixels above the Drawing window's (0, 0) point.

The problem with ***GetMouse*** is that it assigns values immediately. The user is not given time to move the pointer to the desired location. A better method would be to let the user move the mouse and indicate when the proper point is selected by clicking the mouse button.

To handle such specifications, we can enclose the ***GetMouse*** statement in something known as a **repeat-until** loop. (Loops are explained in more detail in Chapter 5.) Type the following code fragment whenever you want to get mouse input:

```
repeat
    GetMouse(<horiz>, <vert>);
until Button;
```

The **repeat** and **until *Button;*** lines designate the boundaries of a *loop*: a block of statements that is repeated until a particular condition is true. In this case, the loop tells MacPascal to call ***GetMouse*** repeatedly and assign values to < horiz > and < vert > until the mouse button is pressed. Then, the interpreter will move to the statement following the **until *Button;*** line.

3.7 Moving Objects

Sometimes you want to change the way an object first appears on the screen. On the Desktop, for example, the Finder allows you to move the disk and trash icons and to resize the various windows. In drawing programs such as MacDraw, the user can move and resize all of the figures repeatedly until they are just right. In MacPascal, you can implement the same features for QuickDraw shapes.

First, let's look at how to move a rectangle. The ***OffsetRect*** procedure takes three parameters: the ***rect*** variable, the horizontal difference, and the vertical difference. Think back a moment to the ***Move*** command. The command ***Move(30, – 40)*** moved the pen's current position: the first coordinate (30) designates the horizontal move, and the second coordinate (– 40) designates the vertical move. Thus, if the CP was at (100, 100), the statement ***Move(30, – 40)*** would move the CP to (130, 60).

OffsetRect accomplishes the same task as ***Move*** but moves an entire rectangle instead of just the CP. Suppose we have a rectangle called ***grayRect***, formed by the following code.

```
PenPat(gray);
SetRect(grayRect, 30, 45, 80, 95);
PaintRect(grayRect);
```

Say we want to move the rectangle toward the top right of the screen. Specifically, we want to move its center 20 pixels toward the top and 40 pixels toward the right. To do this, we use the call

```
OffsetRect(grayRect, 40, -20);
```

This command changes the way QuickDraw stores the rectangle. In QuickDraw, rectangles (and ovals, arcs, and rounded rectangles) are designated by their boundaries. A ***rect*** variable is stored as four integers representing the top left and bottom right corners. As is true of ***SetRect***, the ***OffsetRect*** procedure does not affect what appears on the screen. Instead, ***OffsetRect*** changes the internal representation of the object. Thus, in the example, the left and right coordinates are increased by 40 (from 45 and 95 to 85 and 135, respectively), and the top and bottom coordinates are decreased by 20 (from 30 and 80 to 10 and 60, respectively).

Now, to move an object, you have to take three steps. First, erase the old figure. Then, use a call to the ***Offset*** procedure to specify the new location. Finally, draw the new figure at its new location. For example, the following code moves the ***grayRect*** rectangle:

```
PenPat(gray);
SetRect(grayRect, 30, 45, 80, 95);
PaintRect(grayRect);
...
EraseRect(grayRect);
OffsetRect(grayRect, 40, –20);
PaintRect(grayRect);
```

The result of this fragment is shown in Figure 3.16.

Figure 3.16 Moving a rectangle

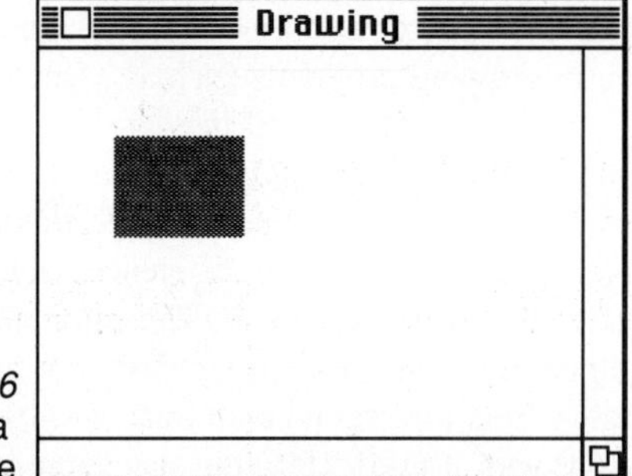

a. Before OffsetRect

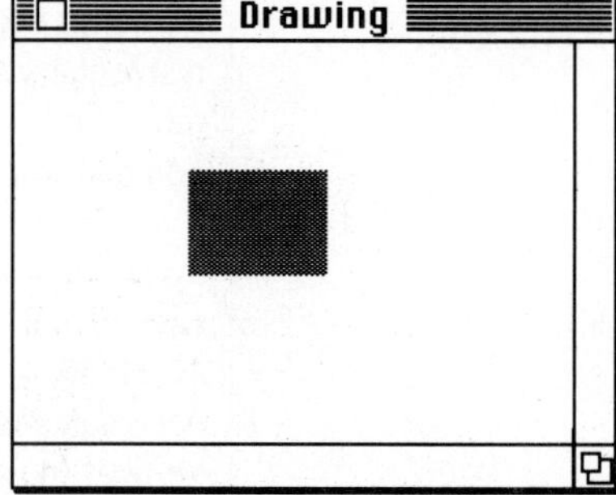

b. After OffsetRect

Syntax Box 3.14 **OffsetRect**

Purpose To move an object to a different position.

Syntax **OffsetRect(** < rect >**,** < diffHoriz >**,** < diffVert > **);**

where < rect > is of type ***rect***

Usage The < diffHoriz > and < diffVert > produce movements in the horizontal and vertical directions. Each pixel in the designated rectangle is moved < diffHoriz > and < diffVert >. If < diffHoriz > is positive, the rectangle is moved to the right; if < diffHoriz > is negative, the rectangle is moved to the left. Similarly, if < diffVert > is positive, the object is moved toward the bottom, and if < diffVert > is negative, the object is moved toward the top.

OffsetRect changes only the internal representation of the object inside QuickDraw. You must redraw the rectangle to see the effect of the command on the screen.

QuickDraw does not have ***OffsetOval***, ***OffsetRoundRect*** or ***OffsetArc*** commands, because these functions are covered by the ***OffsetRect*** command. Remember that ovals, rounded rectangles, and arcs can be defined using ***rect*** variables. For example, in the following code fragment, the ***rect*** variable ***pie*** defines an arc and the rectangle that surrounds it:

```
SetRect(pie, 10, 10, 100, 100);
PaintArc(pie, 0, 180);
FrameRect(pie);
```

Now, if we want to move this semicircle (and its frame) on the screen, we move the ***rect*** area defined by ***pie*** with the statements

```
EraseArc(pie, 0, 180);
OffsetRect(pie, 40, 40);
PaintArc(pie, 0, 180);
FrameRect(pie);
```

The arc, since it was defined using ***pie***, is moved.

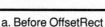

Figure 3.17
Moving a semicircle and its frame

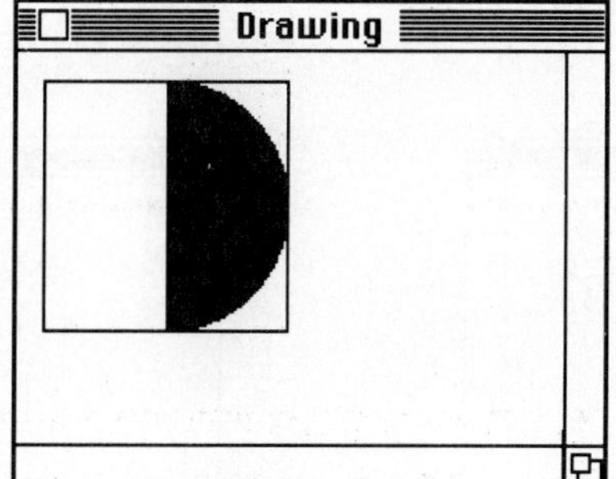

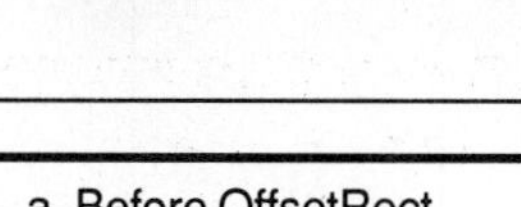

a. Before OffsetRect

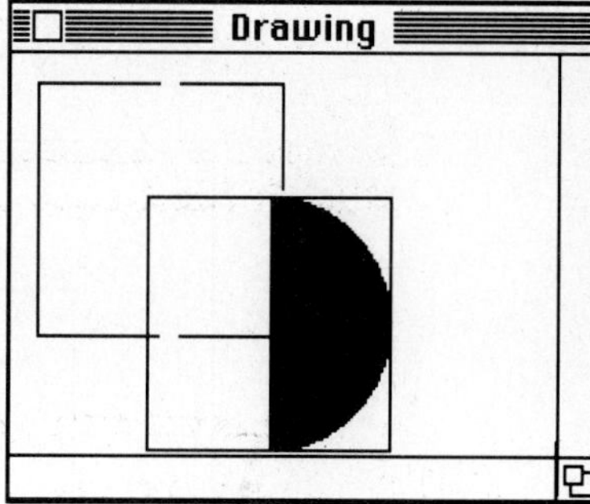

b. After OffsetRect

3.8 Resizing Objects

When creating illustrations, we frequently change the size of a figure until it is properly proportioned. What we are doing is resizing, or *scaling*, the object. This operation is also useful when we want to represent three-dimensional objects on a two-dimensional screen. To represent objects, we make *projections* of three-dimensional scenes, in which the size of each object relates not only to its intrinsic size but also to how far it is from the viewer. Think about what happens when you look in your rearview mirror. You can tell which objects are gaining on you and which you are leaving behind by watching the objects get larger or smaller. Still, your mirror shows only a two-dimensional projection of a three-dimensional object. By analogy, we can create the illusion of movement in a third dimension on the Mac by resizing two-dimensional objects.

QuickDraw changes the size of a rectangle by changing all the points in the object's internal representation, that is, the four corners of the rectangle. The change in the size of the shape is designated by two integers. Remember that in ***OffsetRect***, each point in the rectangle is moved in a designated direction. The < diffHoriz > and < diffVert > of the Offset procedures tell whether each point should move closer to or farther from the (0, 0) point. In the scaling procedure, called ***InsetRect***, we also designate a < diffHoriz > and < diffVert >. Instead of moving in relation to (0, 0), however, < diffHoriz > and < diffVert > designate movement in relation to the object's center. A positive < diffHoriz > or < diffVert > moves the point toward the center; negative differences move the point away from the center.

Let's look at an example. Consider the rectangle created and drawn as follows (shown in Figure 3.18a):

```
SetRect(middle, 50, 50, 150, 150);
FrameRect(middle);
```

This rectangle is centered at (100, 100). Now, let's see what happens when we use the following calls (shown in Figure 3.18b).

```
EraseRect(middle);
InsetRect(middle, 20, 35);
FrameRect(middle);
```

Figure 3.18
Before and after scaling rectangle

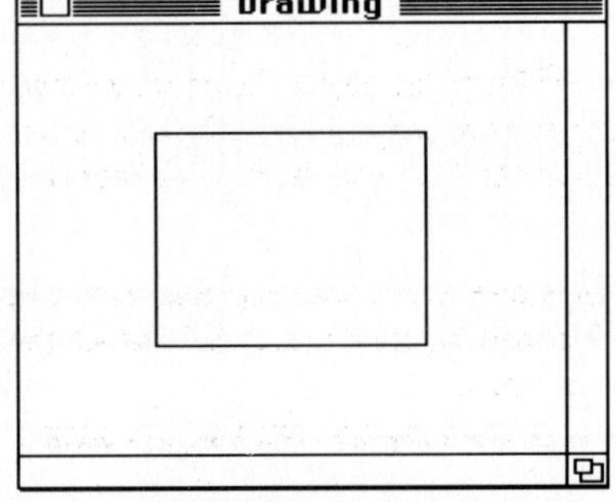

a. Before scaling rectangle

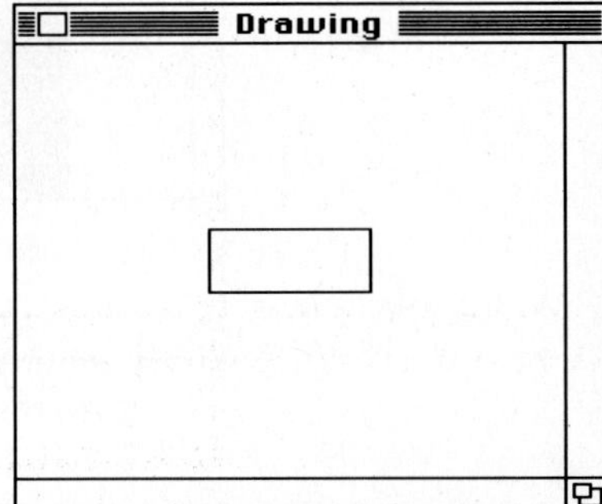

b. After scaling and redrawing rectangle

Like ***OffsetRect***, ***InsetRect*** merely changes the way QuickDraw stores an object. A call to ***InsetRect*** by itself has no effect on the screen's current display.

QuickDraw scales the stored shape by calculating the new corners for the shape and then connecting the new endpoints. To do this, it looks at each of the original corners and the center. Let's start at the top left. The original corner is at (50, 50). We want to move 20 pixels horizontally and 35 pixels vertically and to move toward the center. Since the center (100, 100) is below and to the right of the corner (50, 50), we move the point 35 pixels down and 20 pixels to the right. The new corner is thus (50+20, 50+35), or (70, 85).

Now, let's consider the bottom right. The center is above and to the left of the corner (150, 150). We thus need to scale the point 20 pixels to the left and 35 pixels toward the top. The new corner is (150 – 20, 150 – 35), or (130, 115).

The result is an object that has changed size. If the horizontal and vertical differences are positive, the object shrinks, since ***InsetRect*** moves the points toward the center. If the horizontal and vertical differences are negative, the object expands.

Syntax Box 3.15
InsetRect

Purpose	To resize rectangles.
Syntax	**InsetRect(< rect >, < diffHoriz >, < diffVert >);**
where	< rect > is a variable of type ***rect***. < diffHoriz > and < diffVert > are integers.
Usage	***InsetRect*** moves each corner of the rectangle in relation to the object's center. < diffHoriz > represents the number of pixels by which each corner is moved horizontally; < diffVert > represents the size of the vertical movement. Positive values of < diffHoriz > and < diffVert > indicate movement toward the center; negative values indicate movement away from the center. If the height or width of the object becomes less than one, the ***rect*** is assigned the empty rectangle, i.e., each point in the object's representation is set to (0,0) and the object disappears from the screen. ***InsetRect*** changes only the internal representation of the object in QuickDraw. You must redraw the rectangle to see the effect of the command on the screen.

3.9 Sample Program

To illustrate some of the concepts examined so far, let's write a program that "explodes" a piece of a pie chart. In this program, the user can enter a percentage (an integer between 0 and 100). Unlike the ***GraphResults*** procedure, however, we will not draw the pie chart in one complete circle; instead, we will separate the user-specified portion from the rest of the chart, as shown in Figure 3.19.

The first level of pseudocode follows:

```
Ask user to specify wedge to explode
Draw pie chart without wedge
Draw wedge away from pie chart
```

We begin the program by allowing the user to specify the position of the pie chart on the screen and then the percentage of the circle to be exploded.

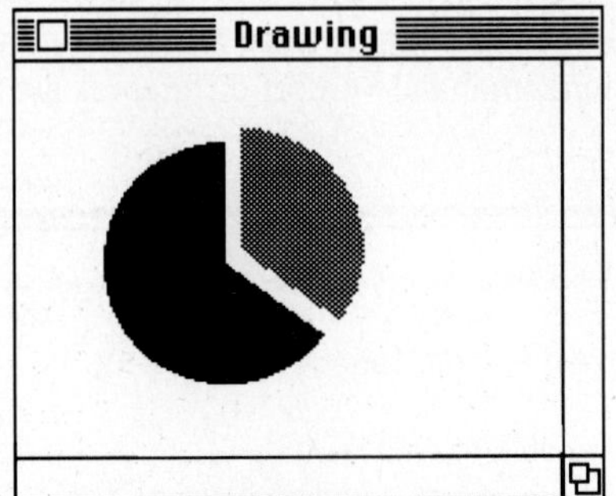

Figure 3.19
Exploded pie chart

To draw the pie chart without the wedge, we divide the work into two parts. First, we draw the entire pie chart. Then, after figuring out the size of the wedge, we erase the area to explode. To make things easier, we set one end of the exploded wedge at the 0° mark. Thus, the erased area will begin in the upper right portion of the chart. The exploded wedge should then be drawn above and to the right of the pie chart. The second level of pseudocode follows.

{ Ask user to specify wedge to explode }
Ask user to enter percentage of chart
Ask user to specify location of pie chart

{ Draw pie chart without wedge }
Draw entire pie chart
Calculate exploded wedge area in degrees
Erase wedge

{ Draw wedge away from pie chart }
Redraw same wedge above and to right of pie chart

At this stage, most of the pseudocode can be translated into Pascal. The first two lines can be translated to a ***Readln*** and **repeat-*GetMouse*-until *Button*** sequence. Then, we use a ***PaintOval*** command to draw the pie chart and an assignment statement to calculate the part of the circle to explode. After this calculation, we use an ***EraseArc*** to remove the wedge. Since the ***PaintOval*** and ***EraseArc*** commands refer to the same rectangular area, we use a ***SetRect*** statement so we can use the same ***rect*** variable in both statements.

Now, we want to redraw the exploded wedge. The wedge we want to draw is identical to the wedge we just erased. So, we move the *internal representation* of the pie chart's rectangle 5 pixels up and to the right. Then, using this altered ***rect*** variable, we call ***PaintArc*** to draw the wedge.

Code 3.2
Program
ExplodeWedge

```
{D. Niguidula        Explode Wedge          Jan. 19              }
{ This program explodes a wedge from a pie chart.                }
{ The user specifies the percentage of the chart to              }
{ explode and the location of the chart. Then, the               }
{ specified area is drawn up and to the left of the              }
{ remainder of the chart.                                        }

program ExplodeWedge;

  var
    pct : integer;               { percentage of chart to explode       }
    top, left,                   { top left boundary of pie chart       }
    bottom, right : integer;     { bottom right boundary of chart       }
    pieChart : rect;             { area where chart will be drawn       }
    areaDegrees : integer;       { area of exploded wedge in degrees    }

begin
  { specify area to explode }
  Write('Enter percentage of chart to explode: ');
  Readln(pct);

  { specify location of chart }
  Writeln('Please choose the top left corner of the chart.');
  repeat
    GetMouse(left, top);
  until Button;
  Writeln('Please choose the bottom right corner of the chart.');
  repeat
    GetMouse(right, bottom);
  until Button;

  { Draw pie chart without wedge }
  SetRect(pieChart, top, left, bottom, right);
  PaintOval(pieChart);
  areaDegrees := Trunc(pct / 100 * 360);
  EraseArc(pieChart, 0, areaDegrees);

  { Draw wedge away from pie chart }
  OffsetRect(pieChart, 5, -5);
  PenPat(gray);
  PaintArc(pieChart, 0, areaDegrees)

end. { ExplodeWedge }
```

3.10 Shortcut Commands

MacPascal and Lightspeed both provide three other graphics commands, which are special cases of commands we have seen earlier. We will not use them in this book, but you may find them useful in your own programming. We will present brief summaries of these commands and skip their syntax boxes.

The ***DrawLine*** command allows you to specify both ends of a line in one statement. For example, ***DrawLine(15, 35, 150, 140);*** draws a line from (15, 35) to (150, 140). The arguments are specified in the order horizontal, vertical, horizontal, vertical. In general, the statement

```
DrawLine(< horiz1 >, < vert1 >, < horiz2 >, < vert2 >);
```

has the same effect as:

```
MoveTo(< horiz1 >, < vert1 >);
LineTo(< horiz2 >, < vert2 >);
```

MacPascal and Lightspeed also provide two commands to draw circles. Unlike the Oval commands, the commands ***PaintCircle*** and ***InvertCircle*** ask you to specify a circle by its center and radius (in pixels). The command

```
PaintCircle(30, 50, 15);
```

paints a circle with its center at (30, 50) and a radius of 15 pixels. The syntax of these commands are as follows:

```
PaintCircle(< centerHoriz >, < centerVert >, < radius >);
InvertCircle(< centerHoriz >, < centerVert >, < radius >);
```

Note that there are no ***FrameCircle*** or ***EraseCircle*** commands. ***PaintCircle*** paints the designated circle in the current pen pattern; ***InvertCircle*** reverses the color of the pixels in the designated circle.

3.11 Chapter Summary

In this chapter we covered the fundamentals of the QuickDraw package. As we saw in Chapter 2, the graphics on the Macintosh are displayed on the rectangular grid called a raster. Each pixel on the raster is designated by a pair of integer coordinates. The graphical output appears in MacPascal's Drawing window.

We looked at nearly three dozen graphics calls that can be used in QuickDraw. These calls can be categorized into pen manipulations, primitives, attributes, graphic data type manipulations, and input.

We first looked at the pen in Chapter 2 with the ***LineTo*** and ***MoveTo*** statements. We can move the CP or draw a line using the relative coordinates of ***Move*** and ***Line*** as well as the absolute coordinates of ***LineTo*** and ***MoveTo***. We can also affect the pen's "ink." The ***PenPat*** command changes the pen pattern, or the color used by the pen.

Primitives are the building blocks for drawing complex objects. QuickDraw has four two-dimensional primitives: rectangles, rounded rectangles, ovals, and arcs. All of these primitives are based on rectangles or objects circumscribed by rectangles. A rectangle is defined by its upper left and bottom right coordinates.

Once we have decided where to draw a shape, we have to decide how to draw it. Each object can be drawn using one of four statements (Frame, Paint, Erase, Invert), which gives the shape a different attribute. Framing an object draws its outline. Painting an object fills the interior area with the current pen pattern. Erasing an object paints the object in the color of the Drawing window (i.e., white). Inverting an object changes each of the pixels in the interior to its inverse, that is, if a pixel is black, it becomes white; if it is white, it becomes black.

Because rectangles are the basis of so many graphics calls in QuickDraw, a graphic data type called ***rect*** was created to shorten code. Declaring a variable of type ***rect*** and giving it a value with the ***SetRect*** statement eliminates retyping the same coordinates over and over again. QuickDraw also defines the data type ***point*** to designate single pixels.

Interactive graphics programs depend on receiving input as well as producing output. Graphical input is handled by the ***GetMouse*** command. This procedure determines the location of the mouse at any time and stores the mouse's horizontal and vertical coordinates in variables provided by the programmer. By using the construct

```
repeat
   GetMouse( < horiz >, < vert > );
until Button;
```

you can ask the user to click on the mouse button and store the pixel under the mouse at the time of the click.

Two other commands rearrange shapes on the screen. ***OffsetRect*** relocates a rectangular area in the Drawing window. ***InsetRect*** shrinks or expands a rectangle relative to its center, thereby scaling the overall shape.

QuickDraw's graphics package is not unusual. Graphics packages always have primitives, attributes, and some method of graphical input. Some method of moving and scaling shapes is usually contained in the package as well. Memorizing QuickDraw constructs will help you write graphical programs with MacPascal; understanding QuickDraw will help you understand the fundamentals of any graphics program on any machine.

3.12 Exercises

Understanding Concepts

1. After the code that draws Figure 3.3 is executed, where is the CP?

2. What does the following code produce?

```
SetRect(circle, 50, 50, 150, 150);
PaintOval(circle);
EraseArc(circle, 90, 180);
```

3. How could you produce the same output as in Exercise 2 with one call?

4. What does the following code produce?

```
Writeln('Please choose a point.');
repeat
    GetMouse(userHoriz, userVert)
until Button;
FrameOval(–userHoriz, –userVert, userHoriz, userVert);
```

5. Suppose you make the call ***PaintRect(0, 0, 200, 200);*** to paint the entire Drawing window black (assuming the Drawing window has not been resized). What are two ways you can create a white 100x100-pixel rectangle in the center of the black area?

6. What does the following code produce?

```
SetRect(shadedArea, 75, 75, 125, 125);
PenPat(ltGray);
PaintRect(shadedArea);
PenPat(black);
PaintArc(shadedArea, 45, 180);
InvertRect(shadedArea);
```

7. What happens when the oval height specified in a call to a ***RoundRect*** command is greater than the height of the rectangle, for example, ***FrameRoundRect (60, 60, 70, 70, 12, 12);*** ?

8. What happens when you invert an area of the screen that has been painted gray?

9. What does the following code do?

```
MoveTo(100, 100);
Writeln('Please pick the other endpoint');
repeat
    GetMouse(horiz, vert);
until Button;
LineTo(horiz, vert);
```

10. What does the following code produce?

```
SetRect(middle, 50, 50, 150, 150);
PaintRect(middle);
OffsetRect(middle, 50, 50);
EraseRect(middle);
InsetRect(middle, 25, 25);
InvertRect(middle);
```

Coding Exercises

1. Modify the pie chart fragment of Section 3.4 by allowing the user to enter the percentage of her salary that goes to taxes.

2. Write a procedure to draw the following diagram.

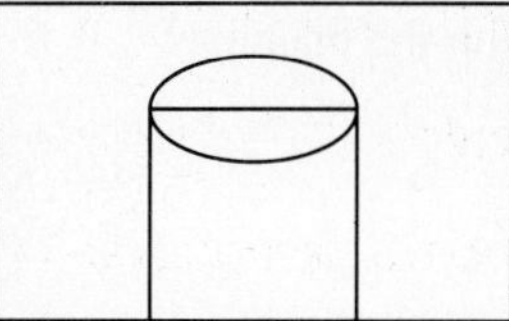

3. Write a procedure that allows the user to choose two points in the Drawing window and then uses those points as the top left and bottom right of a rounded rectangle.

4. "Do you want your pizza divided into six or eight pieces ?"
"Better make it six. I don't think I could eat eight."

   Draw two pizzas, one divided into six pieces, one into eight.

5. Write a procedure that draws a "No Right Turn" sign. Note that the arrow is curved (i.e., it is not two straight lines).

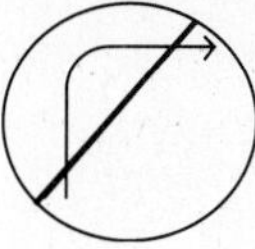

6. Write a procedure that allows the user to paint an arc using radians instead of degrees to indicate the beginning and length of the angle.

7. Write a procedure to draw the following figure:

8. Write a procedure that allows a user to specify a length, width, and height and then draws a rectangular prism of those dimensions, as shown below.

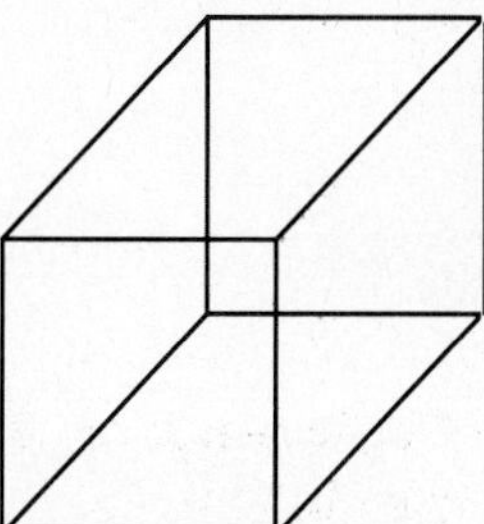

9. Show some simple animation of a stick figure jumping: define the procedures ***Standing*** and ***Jumping*** that draw the standing and jumping figures below. Then, call the procedures with the mainline:

```
begin
   Standing;
   Jumping;
   Standing;
   Jumping
end. { Animation }
```

The Drawing window should be cleared before each figure is drawn.

Programming Problems

1. Write a program that draws a musical staff. A user should be able to specify a point on the staff and see a note appear at that point.

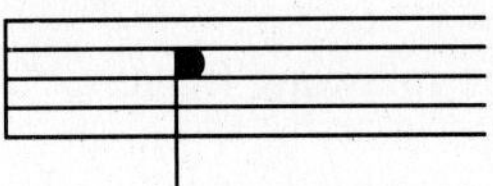

2. In a newspaper layout, a box containing two diagonal lines designates a picture. Write a program that draws a blank layout sheet (i.e., a framed rectangle, with the middle marked as shown below) in the Drawing window and allows the user to designate where three photographs belong.

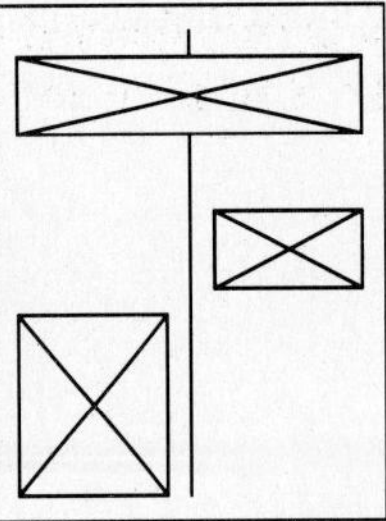

3. Write a program that begins by dividing the Drawing window into nine areas as shown below. The program should ask the user to pick a place on the Drawing window and should then invert the area the user has selected.

1	2	3
4	5	6
7	8	9

4. Number the squares in Programming Problem 3. Have the user select two squares from this board; add the two numbers together and print the sum.

5. Modify the ***GraphResults*** procedure in Section 3.5 so that the user enters the percentages at the keyboard. As a further modification, label each section of the pie chart.

6. Write a program that asks the user to draw two framed squares. Then make one square appear to be on top of the other by erasing the portion of one square that is inside the other.

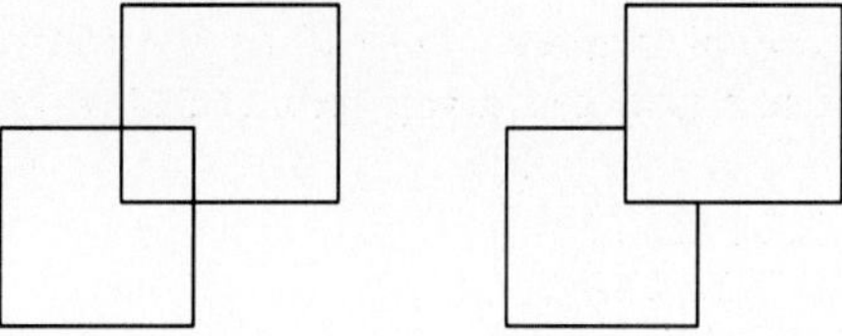

7. Write a program that draws reverse images. First, color half the screen black. Imagine that the border between the black and white parts of the screen is a mirror. Allow the user to choose an oval in the black area; draw both the oval and its mirror image.

8. Create a shadow effect. Ask the user to draw an oval. Your program should draw a framed oval at the location the user specifies and should also paint a shadow extending 3 pixels above and to the right of the oval.

9. Draw a 5x5 rectangular grid. Imagine a chess king placed in the center square; denote this by drawing an oval in the center. The king can move one square in any direction. Denote the squares that are one move away from the center by coloring them dark gray. Denote the squares that are two moves away by coloring them light gray.

10. Write a program that shows a sun rising on the horizon. The user should click on the mouse three times; with each click, the sun should be higher on the horizon.

4

Making Choices

The typical college student faces hundreds of decisions each day. As alarm clocks ring each morning, students mutter, "Should I go to class or sleep till noon?" As they arrive in their rooms after dinner, they say, "Should I study or turn on the television?" And every few paragraphs or so, they wonder, "Should I keep reading this Pascal book or find something worthwhile to do?" Situations such as these, with exactly two options, provide *binary choices*.

Binary choices are an integral part of computer science. You have seen that a computer's basic circuits are turned on or off to represent one or zero. You have learned how to set a series of pixels to black or white. In this chapter, you will see that Pascal "understands" the concept of true and false.

Typically, we use binary choices when we want Pascal to determine if a numeric or graphical comparison is true or false. If ***balance*** is a variable, is ***balance = 0*** a true or false statement? If we ask the user to pick a particular point on the screen, is it true or false that the user's point is in one of our rectangles?

Once we have a true/false answer, we can use it in one of two ways. Pascal provides a data type called ***boolean*** to store answers to true/false questions. In addition, a program's *flow of control* can be altered, depending on the binary result of a comparison.

First, we need to define the term "flow of control." A program's flow of control is the order in which a program's statements are executed. A program with no procedures is called a *straight-line* program. That is, all the statements in the mainline are executed sequentially from top to bottom (or more precisely, from **begin** to **end**). When we introduce procedures, we alter the flow of control. When a procedure is called, the flow of control moves, or *branches,* to the **begin** of the designated procedure and branches back upon completion. This chapter looks at how we can *conditionally branch* to a different part of a program. That is, we will see that Pascal can perform one task if a condition is true, another if the condition is false. But first, let's look at simple comparisons.

4.1 Evaluating Conditions

The simplest true/false decision that Pascal can make is the comparison of two numbers. From Chapter 2, you know that numbers can be represented as constants, variables, or expressions. The expressions ***2+2***, ***3* div *sides***, and ***((maxLen + 8.3) * size) + 9*** are all legal expressions, assuming that ***sides***, ***maxLen***, and ***size*** are all declared appropriately as variables or constants and that ***sides*** is an integer.

Comparisons are often used as parts of statements in Pascal; later in this chapter, we will discuss how to use them in decision-making code. For now, we need to look at how Pascal evaluates conditions—that is, how Pascal decides if a comparison is true or false. Let's look at a typical comparison.

```
(totalMarbles – marblesLost) > 50
```

This comparison is a logical condition that is either true or false—***(totalMarbles – marblesLost)*** either is or is not greater than 50. To evaluate the condition, Pascal works from left to right. First, it finds the value of ***totalMarbles*** and subtracts the value of ***marblesLost***. The result of the subtraction is then compared to 50. For example, if ***totalMarbles*** equals 60 and ***marblesLost*** equals 16, the result is 44. The comparison can then be rewritten as ***44 > 50***. Since 44 is not greater than 50, the condition ***(totalMarbles – marblesLost) > 50*** evaluates to the condition FALSE.

Pascal determines if a statement is TRUE or FALSE in the same way that you would calculate such statements. Examples:

3 > 4	evaluates to FALSE
Trunc(10.4 + 1.5) < 13.0	evaluates to TRUE
0 >= 100	evaluates to FALSE
100 <= 100	evaluates to TRUE
6.7 < > 20/3	evaluates to TRUE
3 + 8 = 33 **div** 3	evaluates to TRUE

Syntax Box 4.1
Comparisons

Purpose To determine a relationship between two expressions.

Syntax < expression 1 > < operator > < expression 2 >

where < expression 1 > and < expression 2 > are represented by constants, variables, or any combination of subexpressions.

< operator > is a legal Pascal comparison operator (listed below).

Usage The expressions can be any data type, but the expressions on each side of the operator must be compatible (e.g., both must be numeric).

Comparisons are not complete statements in Pascal. A comparison gives a result TRUE or FALSE, which must be used in the context of a complete Pascal statement.

The legal comparison operators follow.

Symbol	**Meaning**
=	equal to*
< >	not equal to
>	greater than
<	less than
<=	less than or equal to
>=	greater than or equal to

* Note the difference between the = equals operator (used in logical comparisons and in defining constants) and the := assignment operator (used for assigning values to variables).

Each side of the above comparisons reduces to a single integer or real. At times, we may want to use both integers and reals in the same comparison. If we have the following variable declaration:

```
var
    answer : integer;                    { number used in comparison }
```

then the comparison

```
    10.4 + 2.6 = answer
```

evaluates the left side to a value of type ***real*** and the right side to a value of type ***integer.*** This comparison will be true if ***answer*** is 13. MacPascal can compare integers and reals because both are treated as numbers. Integers and reals are thus known as *compatible types*. Although expressions of type ***real*** and of type ***integer*** are represented differently in memory, Pascal's comparison operators can take the difference into account and perform the comparison successfully.

4.2 if-then

We often state that we will or will not do something depending on some condition. If the light is green, then we can go. If there is nothing in the refrigerator, then it's time to go shopping. If you've been working on a program for too long, then you should do something else for a while. Each of these sentences takes the form "If < condition >, then < thing to do >." Pascal has an **if-then** statement that works in the same way.

Suppose that if the number stored in a variable is even, then we want to print it out. The following statement implements this condition. (The **mod** function, remember, returns the remainder from an integer division.)

```
if (checkNum mod 2) = 0 then
   Writeln('The number', checkNum, ' is even');
```

The **if** statement alters the flow of control. The statement's construct consists of four parts: the word **if**, a condition, the word **then**, and a statement or block of statements. The **if** < condition > **then** construct cannot exist on its own; the statement or block of statements after the **then** is a part of the **if** statement. Thus, no semicolon appears after the **then**.

Syntax Box 4.2
if-then

Purpose To execute a certain statement (or block of statements) if a particular condition is true.

Syntax

```
if < condition > then
   < statement >;
```

where < condition > is any expression that evaluates to TRUE or FALSE.

< statement > is any legal Pascal statement. If more than one statement is to follow, then **begin/end** brackets must surround the conditional code as shown below. As usual, no semicolon is needed before the **end**.

```
if < condition > then
   begin
      < statement >s ;          { conditional code          }
      < statement >             { no semicolon before end }
   end; { if }
```

Usage First, < condition > is evaluated. When < condition > evaluates to TRUE, < statement > is executed. When < condition > evaluates to FALSE, execution continues with the statement after the conditional code.

Note that the entire conditional block is treated as a single statement, since there is no semicolon after the **then**.

Pretty printing indents the < statement > or block of statements included in the **if** statement to show that they are subordinate to the **if**.

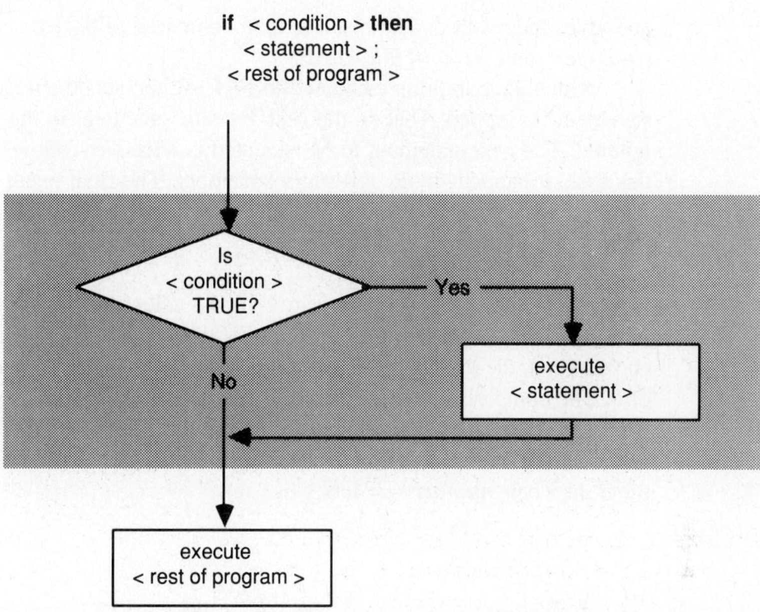

Figure 4.1
Flow of control of an **if** statement

When Pascal encounters an **if** statement, it evaluates the condition between the **if** and the **then**. If the condition evaluates to TRUE, the corresponding statement (in the above example, the ***Writeln***) is executed. Otherwise Pascal skips the corresponding statement and moves on to the next statement in the program. This sequence is illustrated in Figure 4.1. In the flow of control diagrams in this chapter and the next, the diamond-shaped boxes represent decisions (as such, the boxes have more than one exit), and the shaded areas surround a single flow-of-control construct. Notice that there is exactly one entrance and one exit for each flow of control construct.

The following short program shows a use of the first **if** statement in the chapter. The program asks the user to type in a number and prints a message if that number is even.

```
program EvenCheck;
var
   number: integer;                    { even or odd number }
begin
   Write('Please enter an integer');
   Readln(number);
   if (number mod 2) = 0 then
      Writeln('Your number,', number:3, ', is even.');
   Writeln'The program is finished.')
end. { Mainline }
```

To show the effect of the **if** statement, let's hand simulate the above program. First, the program asks the user to type in a number. Suppose the user types in 27. The next statement to be executed is the **if** statement. Pascal calculates 27 **mod** 2 and gives the result 1. The result is then compared to 0. Because 1 = 0 is FALSE, *((number* **mod** *2) = 0)* is FALSE.

Since the condition evaluated to FALSE, the statement associated with the **if** statement is skipped. That is, the first ***Writeln*** statement in the fragment is ignored. The next statement to be executed is whatever follows the **if** statement; in this case, it happens to be a ***Writeln*** statement. The final result looks like this:

```
Please type in an integer: 27
The program is finished.
```

Now, let's try this again using 4 as the value of ***number***. The user types in 4 when the first statement of the program is performed. When the **if** statement is encountered, the expression ***number*** **mod** 2 is calculated: 4 **mod** 2 yields a result of 0. The comparison is now TRUE, because ***number*** **mod** 2 = 0. Since the condition is TRUE, the statement following the **then** (the ***Writeln*** statement) is performed. The second ***Writeln*** statement is then executed. The output of the program when ***number*** = 4 looks like this:

```
Please type in an integer: 4
Your number,   4, is even.
The program is finished.
```

Any statement can be part of the **if** block, including another **if-then** statement. If we want our code to tell us when the user types in a number that is a multiple of both 2 and 3, then we could place another **if** statement inside the first **if** statement, as follows:

```
program Two3;

var
   number: integer; { even or odd number }

begin
   Write('Please enter an integer');
   Readln(number);
   if (number mod 2) = 0 then
      begin
         Writeln('Your number,', number:3, ', is even.');
         if (number mod 3) = 0 then
            Writeln(number:3, ' is also divisible by 3 and 6.')
      end; { if }
   Writeln('The program is finished.')
end. { Mainline }
```

Placing one conditional statement inside another conditional statement is called *nesting*. There is no limit to how much nesting can be done; you could revise this program to check if a number is simultaneously divisible by 2, 3, 5, and 7 by adding two more levels of nesting.

MacPascal's pretty printing feature uses indentation to show levels of nesting. When you enter the line **if** *(number* **mod** *2)* = 0 **then**, MacPascal places the cursor for the next line approximately under the "n" of ***number***. This indicates that the next line is subordinate to the **if-then**.

MacPascal automatically indents statements that are subordinate to any flow of control statement or that are part of any block of code. This feature helps to keep the program legible. Such indentation is not absolutely necessary to run your program; the interpreter or compiler just skips over the extra blanks. Still, this feature can be extremely helpful when you debug your programs. In the above example, the nested **if** statement will be executed only if the outer **if** statement (**if** ***(number* mod *2)*** **= 0 then**) is TRUE. Suppose we forgot the **begin/end** brackets. MacPascal would format the program as follows:

```
program Two3;

var
   number: integer;                              { even or odd number }

begin
   Write('Please enter an integer');
   Readln(number);
   if (number mod 2) = 0 then
      Writeln('Your number,', number:3, ', is even.');
   if (number mod 3) = 0 then
      Writeln(number:3, ' is also divisible by 3 and 6.');
   Writeln('The program is finished.')
end. { Mainline}
```

If we run the second version and enter the number 3, we will get the output:

```
3 is also divisible by 3 and 6.
```

This error results from not nesting the second **if**. By looking at the indentation of the second version, you can see that the two **if** statements are at the same level, since they are indented with the same number of spaces. Thus, the second **if** condition will be checked regardless of whether ***number*** is even. In the correct version, because the second **if** is printed to the right of the first **if**, you know the program is properly nested.

4.3 if-then-else

Sometimes you may want to do one thing if a condition is TRUE and something else if that condition is FALSE. Pascal again borrows the syntax from the English language with the **if** < condition > **then** < statement > **else** < statement > construct.

The **if-then-else** statement allows one of two mutually exclusive blocks of statements—either the **then** block or the **else** block — to be executed. As with the normal **if-then** statement, a boolean condition is evaluated. Again, if the condition is TRUE, the statement block following the **then** is executed, and flow of control goes on to the rest of the program. If the condition is FALSE, however, the flow of

Syntax Box 4.3
if-then-else

Purpose	To perform one of two blocks of code, depending on a particular condition.

Syntax	**if** < condition > **then**
	    < statement > {Note: no semicolon before else }
	else
	    < statement >;

where	< condition > is any expression that evaluates to TRUE or FALSE. < statement > is any legal Pascal statement. If more than one statement is used, then the statement block must be surrounded by **begin/end** brackets.
Usage	The < condition > after the word **if** is evaluated. When the condition evaluates to TRUE, the clause following the **if** is executed. When the condition evaluates to FALSE the clause following the **else** is executed. The **if-then-else** statement is treated by Pascal as a single statement. Thus, semicolons appear only at the end of the entire construct and not after the **then** or the **else**.

control does not move immediately to the rest of the program, but goes instead to the statement following the **else**. After the **else** block is executed, flow of control goes to the first statement outside the **if-then-else** block. Figure 4.2 illustrates this process. Since the condition can be only TRUE or FALSE, the **then** block and the **else** block cannot both be executed.

As an example, let's hand simulate the following code:

```
program EvenCheck;

var
   number: integer;                                  { even or odd number }

begin
   Write('Please enter an integer');
   Readln(number);
   if (number mod 2) = 0 then
      Writeln('Your number, ', number:3, ', is even.')
   else
      Writeln('Your number, ', number:3, ', is odd.');
   Writeln('The program is finished.')
end. { Mainline }
```

As with the example in section 4.2, the code begins by asking the user for an integer. Suppose the user types in 7. The next statement is an **if** statement. Pascal evaluates the condition after the word **if**. Since 7 **mod** 2 is not equal to 0, the condition is FALSE. Because the condition is FALSE, the statement after the **if** is not executed.

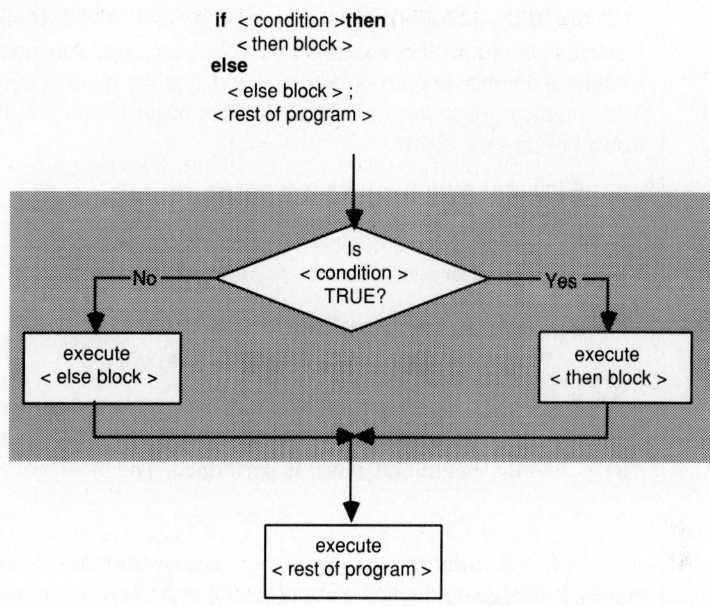

Figure 4.2
Flow of control of an **if-then-else** construct

However, this **if** statement also has an **else** clause. The statement after the **else** clause is performed when the condition in the **if** statement is FALSE. Since (***number*** **mod** *2* = 0) is FALSE, the **else** clause is executed, producing the line of output

```
Your number,    7, is odd.
```

To end the procedure, the final ***Writeln*** statement is executed. The result of the program follows:

```
Please type in an integer: 7
Your number,    7, is odd.
The program is finished.
```

Now, look at the same code when the user types in 8. When the **if** statement is encountered, the condition is TRUE, and the ***Writeln*** statement prints out the following line:

```
Your number,    8, is even.
```

Remember that the **if** and **else** clauses are actually part of one large statement. Having executed the **if** block, Pascal ignores the **else** clause and goes to the final ***Writeln*** statement. The result of this hand simulation is:

```
Please type in an integer: 8
Your number,    8, is even.
The program is finished.
```

An **if-then-else** statement is *not* the same as two **if-then** statements with opposing conditions. For example, the following code fragment was intended to print whether a number is even or odd, and add 1 to the number if it is even to make it odd. This fragment illustrates a problem that can occur if you use disjoint **if** statements instead of an **else** clause.

```
if (number mod 2) = 0 then
   begin
      Writeln('Your number, ', number:3, ', is even.');
      number := number +1
   end; { if }
if (number mod 2) < > 0 then
   Writeln('Your number, ', number: 3, ', is odd.');
```

Suppose ***number*** = 4. In this case, the program starts by calculating (***number*** **mod 2**) and gets a result of 0. Therefore, (***number*** **mod** ***2 = 0***) is TRUE, and the **begin/end** block is performed. The message

```
Your number,   4, is even.
```

is printed, and ***number*** is assigned the value of (***number*** + *1*). Since ***number*** equals 4, it is given the new value (4 + 1), or 5. Pascal continues to the next statement and recalculates (***number*** **mod 2**): 5/2 =2 with a remainder of 1; thus (***number*** **mod** ***2 < > 0***) is TRUE, and the message

```
Your number,   5, is odd.
```

is printed. The output then looks like this:

```
Your number,   4, is even.
Your number,   5, is odd.
```

Clearly, this output is not what was intended. On the other hand, the following code fragment produces the desired output.

```
if (number mod 2) = 0 then
   begin
      Writeln('Your number,', number:3, ', is even.');
      number := number +1
   end { no semicolon before else}
else
   Writeln('Your number, ', number:3, ', is odd.');
```

If we suppose ***number*** is 4, then the first **begin/end** block is performed as above. However, the **else** clause is not performed because the **if** clause has already been executed. The output for the second block of code looks like this:

```
Your number,   4, is even.
```

Thus, **if-then-else** and opposing **if-then**s are not necessarily identical. When you use **if** statements, make sure that the construct you use will give you the desired result. To check, hand simulate your code carefully and test each possible condition.

4.4 Using Booleans

In the mid-1800s, Mary Everest married an author. People who knew Mary would not have been surprised had she been attracted to a man who wrote romantic or adventure tales—after all, Sir George Everest, the man who named a mountain, was her uncle. Mary's choice of a husband, however, disappointed those adventure lovers. His works included "The Mathematical Analysis of Logic, Being an Essay Towards a Calculus of Deductive Reasoning" and the ever popular "An Investigation of the Laws of Thought, on Which are Founded the Mathematical Theories of Logic and Probability." His name was George Boole (1815-1864), and while his wife's name is attached to a mountain, Boole's name lives on in introductory philosophy and logic courses and in the boolean variables and boolean conditions of Pascal. Whose name is connected with the greater achievement? We'll leave that comparison to the reader.

As we have seen, Pascal can evaluate a condition, test whether it is TRUE or FALSE, and act upon that result in an **if-then-else** statement. Every condition that can be evaluated to either TRUE or FALSE is called a *boolean* condition. Pascal can also store a TRUE or FALSE condition in a variable called (appropriately enough) a boolean variable, and then at our convenience test it with an **if**. Declaring boolean variables is analogous to declaring a variable of type ***integer*** or ***real***. The following declaration creates a boolean variable called ***negative***:

```
var
    negative: boolean;        { indicates if a number is negative }
```

Boolean variables are much more restrictive than the other types of variables we have seen; they can have only one of the two values TRUE or FALSE. To give ***negative*** a value, we could assign a boolean constant to it:

```
negative := TRUE;
```

or we could give it the value of a boolean expression:

```
negative := Sin(theta) < 0.5;
```

While you may not have encountered boolean logic before, the above statement shouldn't appear foreign to you. You know that an assignment statement begins by evaluating the expression on the right. In this case, the expression is evaluated by finding the result of ***Sin(theta)*** (assuming ***theta*** is some constant or variable), comparing the result to 0.5, and assigning the result of the comparison to ***negative***. If ***Sin(theta)*** returns 0.13, then the assignment simplifies to ***negative := 0.13 < 0.5***. Since this comparison evaluates to TRUE, ***negative*** is assigned the value TRUE.

Boolean variables are often used in place of the condition in **if** statements. The following code fragment shows this usage of a boolean variable:

```
Write('Please enter an integer: ');
Readln(number);
negative := (number < 0);
if negative then
    Writeln('Your number is less than zero.');
```

This code fragment simply breaks the line **if *(number < 0)* then** into two parts. First the condition is evaluated and stored in ***negative***, and then the result of the comparison is checked by the **if** statement. This way of using a boolean variable is convenient when the variable is checked more than once. Let's look at a program that plays a game for either one or two players. Certain parts of the code are needed for the solitaire version of the game; others are needed for the two-player game. The following code fragment shows how some of the comparisons can be used more than once.

```
...
Write('Please enter the number of players(1 or 2):');
Readln(numPlayers);
solitaire := (numPlayers=1)
if solitaire=TRUE then
    Writeln('Welcome to the solitaire game.')
else
    Writeln('Good luck to both of you.')
...
if solitaire=TRUE then
    Writeln('Not a legal move in the solitaire game.')
...
```

solitaire is being used here as a *flag*. A flag is a boolean variable that is given a value once and is tested in several places in a program or repeatedly in the same place. In the above code, solitaire receives its value at the beginning. However, the value of ***solitaire*** is tested whenever the rules for one- and two-player games differ. Flags will be shown to be very useful when we discuss sentinels and loops in later chapters.

One final point. Consider the **if** statement

```
if solitaire= TRUE then
```

Pascal allows us to write this condition more compactly as

```
if solitaire then
```

The block following this condition is executed only if ***solitaire*** evaluates to TRUE. In other words, the two conditions are equivalent. The second form is preferred because it is terser, but either one will work.

4.5 Graphical Comparisons and Pick Correlation

One of the particularly nice features of the Macintosh is its consistency. In most Macintosh software, you can choose a menu by moving to the menu bar and picking one of the options. This section examines how to use menus in Pascal programs. Menus make a program easier to use since the user can easily examine all the possible options. In a moment, you will see how a menu option is chosen. Before a user can choose a menu option, however, the menu must be created.

The Finder's pull-down menus are rather sophisticated. By the end of the book, you will be able to make certain options unavailable and highlight an available option as the mouse passes over it. For now, though, let's concentrate on the simplest forms of menus.

Suppose you are a doghouse designer. When displaying a model, you want to show the front view and the side view. Because the views fill the entire window (and you don't want the user to resize the views), you can show only one view at a time. You can use a menu to allow the user to choose a view.

Menus usually are shown on the screen as a set of contiguous rectangles. Thus, for this doghouse example, you could use the menu shown in Figure 4.3.

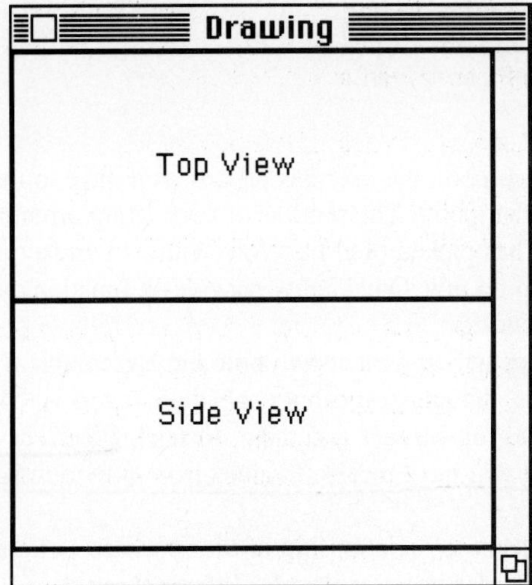

Figure 4.3
Menu for doghouse

You can draw this menu by using the graphics primitives from Chapter 3. (Usually menus do not occupy the entire screen. We will see later in the chapter how to create smaller menus.)

```
var
    front,                          { menu button for front view        }
    side : rect;                    { menu button for side view         }
begin
    SetRect (front, 0, 0, 100, 200);        { Draw menu }
    SetRect (side, 100, 0, 200, 200);
    FrameRect (front);
    MoveTo (50, 70);
    WriteDraw ('Top View');
    FrameRect (side);
    MoveTo (150, 70);
    WriteDraw ('Side View');
    ...
```

Once the menu is created, you need to be able to decode the user's choice. As we mentioned in Chapter 3, you can use the ***GetMouse*** command to determine where the user has placed the mouse.

```
var
   ...
   horiz, vert : integer;   { coordinates of user's point        }
   userPt : point;          { point chosen by user               }
begin
   ...
   Writeln ('Please choose an option'); { prompt user }
   repeat
      GetMouse (horiz, vert);
   until Button;
   SetPt (userPt, horiz, vert);
   ...
```

Once you know what point the user has picked, you have to determine which rectangle contains that point. The process of correlating a point on the screen with the button the user has picked (and therefore with its corresponding action) is called *pick correlation.* To do this, QuickDraw provides a function called ***PtInRect*** (pronounced "point-in-rect").

PtInRect takes two arguments: a point and a rectangle. Unlike the graphics primitive statements, though, you cannot substitute < top >, < left >, < bottom >, < right > coordinates for the ***rect*** argument. Instead, ***PtInRect*** expects variables of type ***point*** and ***rect*** that have received values from previous ***SetPt*** and ***SetRect*** statements.

PtInRect looks at the relationship of the specified point and rect. If the point is inside or on the border of the rectangle, ***PtInRect*** returns TRUE. Otherwise, it returns FALSE. This boolean function can be used within any boolean expression, just as predefined arithmetic expressions can be used within any arithmetic expression.

To complete the doghouse example, you can use ***PtInRect*** to determine whether the user wants to see the front or side view. First, the user's point is stored in a ***point*** variable. Then, MacPascal determines if the ***point*** is in the rectangle ***top***. If so, the top view is shown. If ***PtInRect (userPt, top)*** returns FALSE, the side view is shown.

```
...
    if PtInRect (userPt, top) then
        TopView              { call procedure to draw top view }
    else
        SideView             { call procedure to draw side view }
end; { Procedure }
```

Syntax Box 4.4
PtInRect

Purpose	To determine whether a point resides inside or outside a rectangle.
Syntax	**PtInRect (< point >, < rect >);**
where	< point > is a variable of type ***point*** and < rect > is a variable of type ***rect***.
Returns	TRUE if < point > is in < rect >, FALSE if < point > is not in < rect >.
Usage	You *must* use arguments of type ***point*** and ***rect***. (You may *not* use < top >, < left >, < bottom >, < right > to define the rectangle.) < point > and < rect > must be defined before they are used here. The value returned by ***PtInRect*** must be placed in a boolean variable or expression.

4.6 Logical Operators

You now know how to establish and evaluate conditions and how to use them to determine flow of control. Up to this point, the complexity of these conditions has been fairly limited. For greater flexibility, Pascal also allows the programmer to test for multiple or opposing conditions. Pascal uses three logical operators — **not**, **or**, and **and** — to operate on boolean expressions. Each of these logical operators is similar to its English equivalent.

not

not specifies the opposite of a given boolean condition. This concept is best shown by example:

```
var
   overdrawn : boolean;        { indicates if balance goes below 0    }
   balance,                    { amount of money in checking acct     }
   withdrawal : real;          { amount taken out of account          }
begin
   ...
   balance := balance - withdrawal;
   overdrawn := (balance < 0);
```

```
if not overdrawn then
    Writeln('You have $', balance:6:2, 'left in your account.');
  ...
end; { Procedure }
```

The line **if not *overdrawn* then** is the equivalent of **if *overdrawn* = *FALSE* then**. The version in the above fragment is easier to understand, however; **if not *overdrawn* then** is closer to everyday English than **if *overdrawn* = *FALSE* then**.

Syntax Box 4.5
Effect of **not**

< expression >	**not** < expression >
TRUE	FALSE
FALSE	TRUE

or

Next we look at the operators that combine two or more boolean expressions and return a single boolean result: **and** and **or**. These operators work on booleans the same way that mathematical operators work on numbers.

Suppose a bank charges a customer $3.00 if she has less than $400.00 in her account during the month or if she writes more than 12 checks in that month. The code fragment to determine whether to apply this charge might look like this:

```
...
if (balance < 400.00) or (numChecks >= 12) then
    balance := balance - 3.00; { deduct service charge }
...
```

The statement ***balance := balance – 3.00*** is executed only if at least one of the conditions ***(balance < 400.00)*** and ***(numChecks >= 12)*** is TRUE. In other words, if either or both of the boolean conditions are TRUE, then the entire expression evaluates to TRUE. If both conditions are FALSE, the entire expression evaluates to FALSE.

For example, suppose ***balance*** = 500.00 and ***numChecks*** = 14. The expression ***(balance < 400.00)*** is FALSE, since 500.00 < 400.00 is FALSE. On the other hand, ***(numChecks >= 12)*** is TRUE in this case, since 14 > = 12 is TRUE. Thus, the entire boolean condition evaluates to (FALSE) **or** (TRUE). Since at least one of the expressions evaluated with the **or** operator is TRUE, the entire expression evaluates to TRUE and the assignment statement is executed.

The next table lists all the possible combinations of two boolean expressions and the value that results from combining them with a boolean operator. This type of table, known as a *truth table*, is used often in logic theory.

Syntax Box 4.6
Effect of **or**

< expression 1 >	< expression 2 >	< exp. 1 > **or** < exp. 2 >
FALSE	FALSE	FALSE
FALSE	TRUE	TRUE
TRUE	FALSE	TRUE
TRUE	TRUE	TRUE

and

Suppose the same bank sends toasters to new customers who deposit more than $250.00. If the bank checks its accounts once a month, then a new customer is one who has had an account for 31 days or fewer. The code fragment for such a problem follows:

```
if (numDays <= 31) and (balance > 250.00) then
    SendToaster;
```

and evaluates to TRUE only when both expressions are TRUE; otherwise, **and** evaluates to FALSE. Thus, the procedure ***SendToaster*** is called only if both ***numDays <= 31*** and ***balance > 250.00*** evaluate to TRUE. The truth table for **and** follows.

Syntax Box 4.7
Effect of **and**

< expression 1 >	< expression 2 >	< exp. 1 > **and** < exp. 2 >
FALSE	FALSE	FALSE
FALSE	TRUE	FALSE
TRUE	FALSE	FALSE
TRUE	TRUE	TRUE

The results of boolean operations can be stored in boolean variables, just as the results of mathematical operations are stored in numerical variables. The last example can be rewritten using a flag as:

```
var
    numDays: integer;          { num of days account has been open      }
    balance: real;             { amount of money in account             }
    awardWinner: boolean;      { indicates if customer wins toaster     }
begin
    ...
    awardWinner := (numDays <=31) and (balance > 250.00);
    if awardWinner then
        SendToaster;
    ...
end; { procedure }
```

In the same way that multiplication takes priority over addition, boolean operators have different priorities, as listed below.

Syntax Box 4.8
Priority of boolean operators

1. **not** (highest)
2. **and**
3. **or** (lowest)

Use parentheses to change the order of evaluation.

The logical operators can be chained together, just as arithmetic expressions can contain more than one arithmetic operator.

```
if draw and ((horiz = vert) or (not (vert <= 0) ) ) then
   LineTo (horiz, vert);
```

This expression looks fairly complicated, but you can evaluate it without much difficulty as long as you start with the innermost expression and work outward.

Say that both ***horiz*** and ***vert*** equal 10. You begin evaluating the large expression with the innermost expression: ***vert <= 0***. Since ***vert*** = 10, ***vert <= 0*** is FALSE. **not** ***(vert <=0)*** is then TRUE. Using substitution, you can rewrite the expression like this:

```
if draw and ((horiz = vert) or (TRUE)) then...
```

Now you can evaluate ***((horiz = vert)*** **or** ***(TRUE))***. Since both ***horiz*** and ***vert*** equal 10, ***horiz = vert*** is TRUE. ***(TRUE*** **or** ***TRUE)*** evaluates to TRUE. Now the expression looks like this:

```
if draw and TRUE then...
```

If ***draw*** is TRUE, then the expression becomes ***TRUE*** **and** ***TRUE*** and evaluates to TRUE. This in turn makes the entire expression TRUE, and the ***LineTo*** statement is executed. If ***draw*** is FALSE, the entire expression is FALSE, and the statement is not executed.

When you use the **and** and **or** operators, *both* conditions are evaluated, even though it isn't always necessary. You must consider how MacPascal evaluates the condition to ensure that the evaluation does not cause an error under any circumstances. For instance, a statement might read:

```
if (num <> 0) and (total / num > 1.0) then
   ...
```

This causes a problem when ***num*** = 0. In this case, the first condition is FALSE; thus, the whole boolean expression is FALSE, no matter what value is held by ***total***. Still, Pascal always evaluates both sides of an **and** operator. When ***total/num*** is evaluated, MacPascal tries to divide the value of ***total*** by the value of

num, which is 0. Since the interpreter cannot divide by 0, a run-time error (an error that arises while the program is running) occurs. Run-time errors usually cause the program to *bomb* or *crash*, meaning that execution stops abruptly. In contrast, the following code avoids the error situation.

```
if (num <> 0) then
   if (total/num > 1.0) then
      ...
```

4.7 case

There are two groups of people in the world: those who divide the world into two groups and those who don't. For those who use only binary choices, **if-then-else** statements are sufficient for all their decision-making needs. The rest of us, though, who don't see the world as all TRUE and FALSE, need to have multiple choices. The **case** construct allows us to choose from more than two mutually exclusive choices.

The **case** statement is something like a vending machine. Inside a coin-operated machine, a simple mechanism figures out how many of each coin have been inserted. Figure 4.4 illustrates how this works. A deposited coin falls onto a ramp that has a hole for each different type of coin.

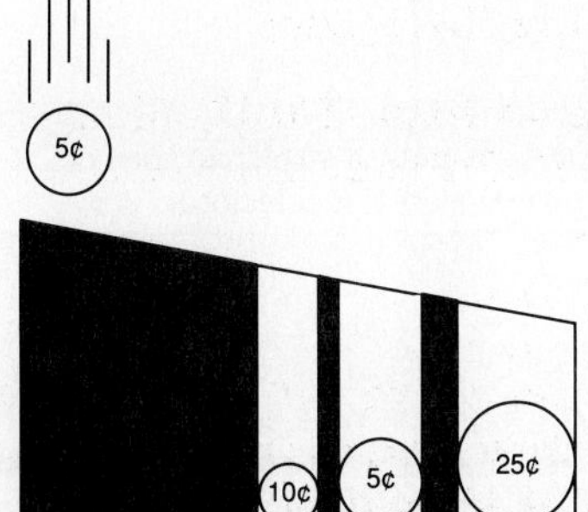

Figure 4.4 Vending machine operation

Suppose the machine accepts dimes, nickels, and quarters. When the coin hits the ramp, it rolls down until it finds a hole in which it fits. The coin then falls in that hole. Since the holes are arranged from smallest to largest, the first hole holds dimes, the second, nickels, and the third, quarters. When you deposit a nickel, it rolls down the ramp until it finds the second hole, and the machine registers that you have entered five cents. If you deposit a dime, the coin falls into a different hole, and a different amount is registered by the machine.

A **case** statement contains a variable or expression called a *selector*. The selector is a variable or expression that evaluates to an ordinal data type — that is, a data type where all possible values can be counted. Integers and (as we will see later) characters are ordinal types; reals, because all possible values cannot be counted, are not. The selector is followed by the word **of** and a list of possible values.

The coin is like the **case** statement's selector. Depending on the value of the selector, the flow of control moves to a different part of the program. Pascal matches the value in the selector to one of the values in the **case** statement's list. Each value is associated with a statement or block of statements. The flow of control moves to the statement or block that is associated with the selector's value. Just as the coin can fall in only one hole of the vending machine, only one value in the list can be matched by the selector. When the appropriate list of statements has been executed, the flow of control moves to the **case** statement's **end**. Pascal then executes the next line of code. This process is illustrated in Figure 4.5.

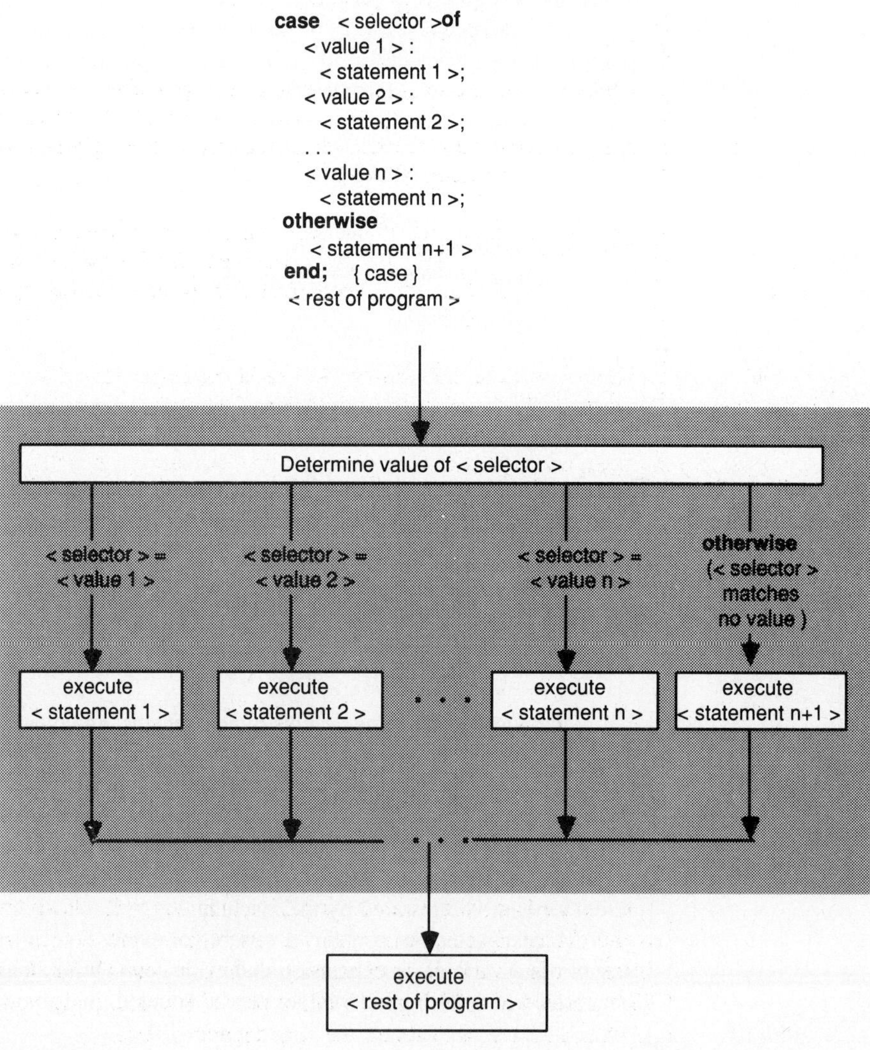

Figure 4.5
Flow of control for **case** statement

Syntax Box 4.9
case

Purpose To execute one of any number of mutually exclusive blocks of statements, depending on the value of an expression.

Syntax

```
case < selector > of
     < value 1 >:
          < statement 1 >;
     < value 2 >:
          < statement 2 >;
     ...
     < value n >:
          < statement n >[;]
[    otherwise
          < statement n+1 >]
end; {case}
```

where < selector > is an expression of type ***integer*** or ***char***, or an enumerated type* < value 1 >, < value 2 >,...,< value *n* > are single integers or characters, or groups of integers or characters separated by commas.

< statement 1 >, < statement 2 >,...,< statement *n* >, < statement *n*+1 > are legal Pascal statements. If more than one statement is used, then the statement block must be surrounded by **begin/end** brackets.

Usage The < selector > is evaluated to a single value. If one of the values < value 1 >, < value 2 >,..., < value *n* > matches < selector >, then the corresponding < statement > is executed. If < selector > does not match any of the listed values, < statement *n*+1 > (following the **otherwise**) is executed.

Only one of the statements in the **case** construct will be performed.

Note that the **end**; of the **case** construct does not have a corresponding **begin**.

The **otherwise** clause is optional.

---

* Characters are examined in Chapter 8; enumerated types; in Chapter 13.

Let's look at an example. Imagine that you are a new chef at a restaurant. When the waiters hand you orders, you notice that they write down only the number of the menu choice. Since you haven't yet memorized what all these numbers mean, you have to refer to the menu constantly to remind yourself that #3 is the Hunan Crispy Fish. Instead of referring back to the printed menu, though, you can program the kitchen's Macintosh to print the corresponding item.

```
var
   orderNum : integer; { item ordered by customer }
begin
   Write ('Please enter the order number: ');
   Readln (orderNum);

   case orderNum of
      1 :
         Writeln ('Hot and Sour Soup');
      2 :
         Writeln ('Peking Dumplings');
      3 :
         Writeln ('Hunan Crispy Fish');
      4 :
         Writeln ('Little Chopsticks Special')
   end
end; { Procedure }
```

When MacPascal runs this procedure, it first prints the prompt and accepts the input. Then it executes exactly one of the options in the **case** statement. For example, if you type 3, "Hunan Crispy Fish" appears in the Text window. All the ***Writeln*** statements in the other cases are ignored, and the procedure ends.

A problem arises with the **case** construct if the value of the variable does not match any of the available options. Unlike the **if** statement, which simply continues execution on the first line after the statement, an "unmatched" **case** statement causes a run-time error. To avoid this situation, MacPascal provides the **otherwise*** option as a "none of the above" case.

Let's return to the restaurant example. If the user does not enter an integer between 1 and 4, nothing is printed. This is not particularly user-friendly, so let's add an error message to be printed if the user enters an incorrect order number:

```
case orderNum of
   1 :
      Writeln ('Hot and Sour Soup');
   2 :
      Writeln ('Peking Dumplings');
   3 :
      Writeln ('Hunan Crispy Fish');
   4 :
      Writeln ('Little Chopsticks Special');
   otherwise
      Writeln ('We''re all out of that tonight.')
end;
```

Again, only one ***Writeln*** statement is executed. However, the **otherwise** guarantees that one statement is *always* executed. The **otherwise** clause handles every possible value of ***orderNum*** not listed.

*Although **otherwise** is not strictly a part of standard Pascal, it is found in many versions of the language.

Let's consider a slightly more complex **case** statement. In the game of blackjack, the dealer can take three actions, depending on the total of her cards. If she has 21, the house wins. If her total is between 17 and 20, she must stay, i.e., take no more cards. If her total is less than 17, she must take another card.

We can use multiple values of the expression in the **case** statement to produce the same actions. In the blackjack example, we want the same result if the dealer has 17, 18, 19, or 20. In the code, we show that these multiple values yield the same result by separating the values with commas.

```
case total of
    21 :
        Writeln ('Blackjack. House wins.');
    17, 18, 19, 20 :
        Writeln ('Dealer stays.');
    otherwise
        Writeln ('Dealer must take another card.')
end; { case }
```

4.8 if-then-else if

Suppose you want to expand the doghouse example. Instead of allowing the user to see just the front or side view, you want to add a top view. You also want to draw a smaller menu across the top of the screen that does not have to be erased. Because the new menu does not occupy the entire screen, however, you must check if the user's indicated point lies in any button's rectangle at all. To do so, you can use an extended sequence of **if-then-else** statements.

In a **case** statement, Pascal's flow of control moves directly to the value that matches the selector. In an **if-then-else if** construct, each multiple condition has to be checked in turn. Figure 4.6 shows how the flow of control works in the **if-then-else if**; compare this with Figure 4.5.

When Pascal encounters an **if-then-else if** construct, it evalutes the boolean condition after the first **if**. If this condition evaluates to TRUE, the corresponding code is executed and the flow of control moves to the next statement after the **if-then-else if** construct. If the first condition is FALSE, Pascal looks at the next boolean condition. Again, if this condition evaluates to TRUE, the appropriate code is interpreted and executed; otherwise, the next boolean condition is evaluated. The conditions are checked, one at a time and from top to bottom, until one evaluates to TRUE. Thus, for < conditional code 3 > to be executed, boolean conditions 1 and 2 must have been FALSE and boolean condition 3 must be TRUE.

The **if-then-else if** construct can contain a final **else**, which performs the same purpose as the **otherwise** in the **case** statement. If none of the other conditional code blocks is executed, the final **else**'s block is performed.

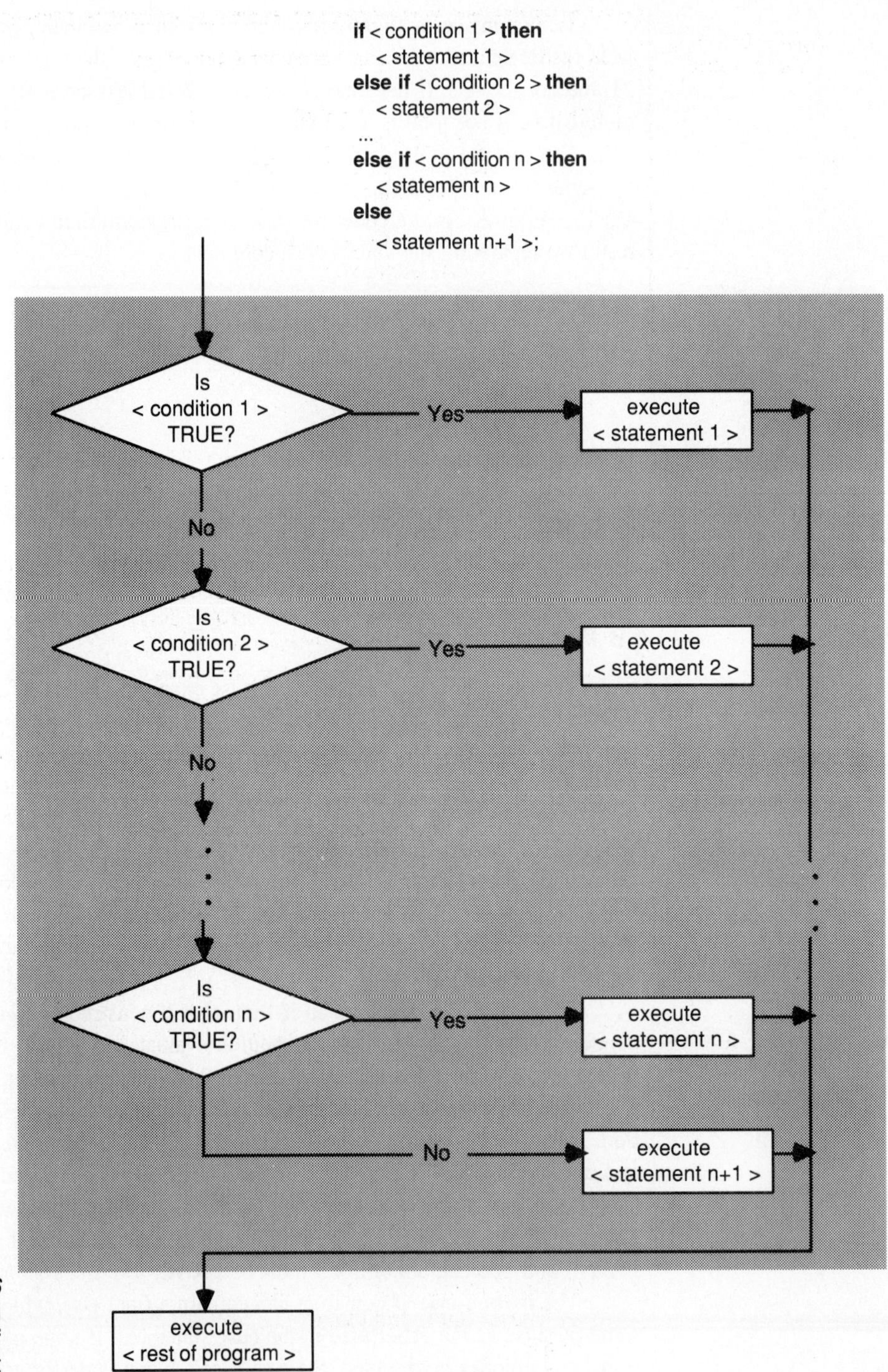

if < condition 1 > **then**
< statement 1 >
else if < condition 2 > **then**
< statement 2 >
...
else if < condition n > **then**
< statement n >
else
< statement n+1 >;
Is < condition 1 > TRUE?
Yes
execute < statement 1 >
No
Is < condition 2 > TRUE?
Yes
execute < statement 2 >
No
Is < condition n > TRUE?
Yes
execute < statement n >
No
execute < statement n+1 >
execute < rest of program >

Figure 4.6
Flow of control of an **if-then-else if** statement

Syntax Box 4.10
if-then-else if

Purpose To allow for multiconditional branching.

Syntax:

if < condition 1 > **then**
    < statement 1 >
else if < condition 2 > **then**
    < statement 2 >
...
else if < condition *n* > **then**
    < statement *n* >
[**else**
    < statement >] ;

where < condition 1 >, < condition 2 >,..., < condition *n* > are expressions that evaluate to TRUE or FALSE.

< statement > is any legal Pascal statement. If more than one statement is used, then the statement block must be surrounded by **begin/end** brackets.

Usage < condition 1 > is evaluated first. If it evaluates to TRUE, then < statement 1 > is executed. The rest of the **if-then-else if** construct is ignored. If < condition 1 > is FALSE, then < condition 2 > is checked; if < condition 2 > is FALSE, < condition 3 > is checked. This process continues until a condition evaluates to TRUE. At this point, the statement following the associated **if** or **else if** is executed. If none of the conditions evaluates to TRUE, the statement following the final **else** is executed.

The **if-then-else if** statement is treated by the interpreter as a single statement. Semicolons must be used only at the end of the entire construct, not after the **then** or the **else**.

The final **else** and its associated < statement > are optional.

Let's return to the doghouse. The pseudocode for the doghouse program now looks like this:

```
Draw menu on top of screen
Ask user to pick button
IF user chooses top view
   CALL: Show top view
ELSE IF user chooses side view
   CALL: Show side view
ELSE IF user chooses front view
   CALL: Show front view
ELSE
   User didn't pick in menu — print error message
```

From this pseudocode we can create the following mainline:

Code 4.1
Program *Doghouse*

```
program Doghouse;

  var
    side,                          { menu box for side view         }
    front,                         { menu box for front view        }
    top : rect;                    { menu box for top view          }
    userPt : point;                { pt chosen by user              }
    horiz, vert : integer;         { coords of user's point         }

{ Procedures SetTopView, SetSideView, SetFrontView defined here.    }

{ The mainline draws the menu and then asks the user to choose a    }
{ button. When it has determined which button has been selected,    }
{ the mainline prints a message and then calls a procedure to print }
{ the appropriate view of the doghouse.                             }

begin
  { Draw menu }
  SetRect(top, 0, 0, 60, 15);
  SetRect(side, 60, 0, 120, 15);
  SetRect(front, 120, 0, 180, 15);
  FrameRect(top);
  FrameRect(side);
  FrameRect(front);

  { Label menu }
  MoveTo(6, 10);
  WriteDraw('Top');
  MoveTo(70, 10);
  WriteDraw('Side');
  MoveTo(130, 10);
  WriteDraw('Front');

  { Prompt user }
  Writeln('Please choose an option from the menu.');
  repeat
    GetMouse(horiz, vert);
  until Button;
  SetPt(userPt, horiz, vert);

  { Draw appropriate view }
  if PtInRect(userPt, top) then
    begin
      Writeln('This is the top view.');
      DrawTopView
    end
  else if PtInRect(userPt, side) then
    begin
      Writeln('This is the side view.');
      DrawSideView
    end
```

Code 4.1
(continued)

```
    else if PtInRect(userPt, front) then
      begin
        Writeln('This is the front view.');
        DrawFrontView
      end
    else
      Writeln('You did not pick a point on the menu')
  end. { Mainline }
```

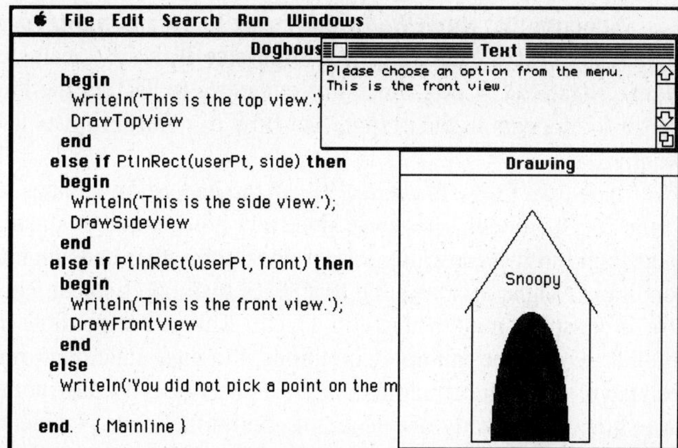

Figure 4.7
Output of program
Doghouse

The **if-then-else if** construct means that MacPascal sequentially checks each condition and executes the first statement associated with a TRUE condition. Suppose the user chooses the point (170, 5). MacPascal first checks if this point is in the rectangle designated by ***top***. Since this is FALSE, MacPascal skips to the next **else if** and evaluates the condition ***PtInRect (userPt, side)***. Since this is also FALSE, MacPascal moves to the third **else if**. When it determines that ***PtInRect (userPt, front)*** is TRUE, it calls on the procedure ***DrawFrontView***. Now that one condition has been found to be TRUE, all future conditions can be ignored, and MacPascal can skip to the statement following the final **else** or **else if**'s statement.

The **if-then-else if** construct is preferable to a **case** statement in two situations. In the above example, we could not list the multiple possibilities in integer form. Since the values of the **case** statement's selector must be of an ordinal type, we must use **if-then-else if** whenever the decision is to be based on a real or graphic data type.

The **case** statement also falls short when the multiple possibilities are not mutually exclusive. For example, suppose we ask the user how many programs he has written and how many chapters he has read. We can print a message using an **if-then-else if** as follows:

```
...
if (numChapsRead = 17) then
   Writeln('You''ve finished the book.')
else if (numProgsFinished > 7) then
   begin
      Writeln('Your asssignments are complete');
      Writeln('but please read the rest of the book anyway.')
   end { else if }
else
   Writeln('You have more work to do.')
end. { program }
```

Suppose that ***numChapsRead*** is set to 16 and ***numProgsFinished*** is set to 8. When Pascal evaluates the **if-then-else if**, it first evaluates the condition ***(numChapsRead = 16)***. Since this evaluates to TRUE, the line "You've finished the book" appears in the output, and flow of control moves to the end of the program.

Now, we know that ***numProgsFinished > 7*** evaluates to TRUE since 8 > 7 is a true statement. However, since a condition that evaluates to TRUE has already been found in the construct, Pascal does not bother checking any of the remaining conditions. Thus, it is possible that more than one boolean condition in an **if-then-else if** construct may evaluate to TRUE. This is not possible in a **case** statement. In other words, the multiple conditions in a **case** statement must be mutually exclusive, while the conditions in an **if-then-else if** construct need not. In either case, however, exactly one block of conditional code is executed.

4.9 Chapter Summary

You saw in Chapter 2 how Pascal "understands" and manipulates numbers. In this chapter you have seen how Pascal works with the concept of TRUE or FALSE. For example, you can ask Pascal to tell us if ***number < 0*** is a true statement. You can use any of six operators (<, >, =, <=, >=, <>) to compare two expressions.

Once you know whether a comparison is TRUE or FALSE, you can use this information to alter a program's flow of control. You can designate a block of statements and tell Pascal that the block should be executed only if a particular condition is TRUE. The **if-then** statement tests the condition and tells Pascal whether the block should be executed. The more general **if-then-else** statement tells Pascal to perform one block if a condition is TRUE and another block if the condition is FALSE.

The results of comparisons can be stored in boolean variables. Booleans may contain only the values TRUE or FALSE. A boolean variable is declared in the same manner as a numeric or graphic variable is declared. Booleans can also receive values in assignment statements.

Pascal provides three logical operators for creating more complex boolean expressions. The **not** operator flips the value of a boolean expression. The **and** operator looks at two boolean expressions and returns TRUE if and only if both conditions are TRUE. The **or** operator also looks at two boolean expressions but returns TRUE if either or both expressions are TRUE.

You are not limited to using only TRUE or FALSE tests; you can also have multiple choices. The **case** statement executes one block of code, depending on the value of a selector. The selector must be an ordinal type (the only ordinal type discussed thus far is the data type ***integer***). To use the **case** statement, you have to know all the possible values of the selector and tell Pascal what code is associated with each value. If the selector's value is not associated with any code, MacPascal puts up a bug box and halts the program's execution. Adding a "none of the above" case with the **otherwise** clause avoids this problem.

case statements are insufficient when you are not dealing with ordinal types, or when the different conditions are not mutually exclusive. These situations require the use of the most general **if-then-else if** construct. Essentially, this construct is a series of **if** statements nested inside **else** statements. Pascal checks the condition following the **if** and each **else if** until it finds a condition in the construct that evaluates to TRUE. The code associated with that condition is executed and the flow of control then moves to the rest of the program.

4.10 Exercises

Understanding Concepts

1. In the following code, assume that ***year*** is an integer variable. Which values of ***year*** will cause the statement

   ```
   Writeln(year, ' is not a leap year');
   ```

   to be executed?

   ```
   if year mod 100 = 0 then
      if year mod 400 <> 0 then
         Writeln(year, ' is a leap year')
   else if year mod 4 = 0 then
      Writeln(year, 'is a leap year')
   else
      Writeln(year, 'is not a leap year');
   ```

2. What is the output of the following if ***balance*** is 20? 0? –15? How can the code be changed so that each input does not yield conflicting messages?

   ```
   if balance < 0 then
      begin
         Writeln('You owe money');
         Writeln('Balance has been reset to 0.');
         balance := 0
      end;
   if balance >= 0 then
      Writeln('You have a surplus of cash');
   ```

3. In the game of fizz-fuzz, players count off the numbers from 1 to 100. When a player's number contains a 7 *or* is divisible by 7, the player should not count the number but instead should say "fizz." If the player's number contains a 7 *and* is divisible by 7, the player should say "fizz-fuzz." Write a conditional statement that prints the appropriate message, depending on the contents of the variable ***playerNum***.

4. Assume that ***place*** is an integer variable and contains a value from 1 to 5. Write a **case** statement that prints one of the following, depending on the value of ***place***: 1st, 2nd, 3rd, 4th, 5th.

5. What's wrong with the following code? How can you fix it?

```
Write('How much is your coin worth?');
Readln(coin);
Write('The face on your coin is ');
case coin of
   1.00:
      Writeln('Susan B. Anthony.');
   0.50:
      Writeln('John F. Kennedy.');
   0.25:
      Writeln('George Washington.');
   0.10:
      Writeln('F.D. Roosevelt.');
   0.05:
      Writeln('Thomas Jefferson.');
   0.01:
      Writeln('Abraham Lincoln.');
   otherwise
      Writeln('You''ve got a bad coin there.')
end; { case }
```

6. Rewrite the following code, using as few statements as possible:

```
var
   redPrice, bluePrice,       { price of colas }
   redSize, blueSize: real;   { size of cola containers, in ounces }
begin
   Write('Enter the price and size of Red Cola');
   Readln(redPrice, redSize);
   Write('Enter the price and size of Blue Cola');
   Readln(bluePrice, blueSize);
   if redPrice/redSize > bluePrice/blueSize then
      begin
         Writeln('Red Cola costs ', redPrice/redSize:3:1, 'cents per ounce');
         Writeln('Blue Cola costs ', bluePrice/blueSize:3:1,'cents per ounce');
         Writeln('Red Cola is the better buy.')
      end { if }
```

```
    else if redPrice/redSize < bluePrice/blueSize then
      begin
        Writeln('Red Cola costs ', redPrice/redSize:3:1, 'cents per ounce');
        Writeln('Blue Cola costs ', bluePrice/blueSize:3:1, 'cents per ounce');
        Writeln('Blue Cola is the better buy.')
      end { else if }
    else if redPrice/redSize = bluePrice/blueSize then
      begin
        Writeln('Red Cola costs ', redPrice/redSize:3:1, 'cents per ounce');
        Writeln('Blue Cola costs ', bluePrice/blueSize:3:1, 'cents per ounce');
        Writeln('Neither cola is a better buy.')
      end { else }
end; { procedure }
```

7. Write a conditional statement that prints the absolute value of the number stored in the ***real*** variable ***distance***.

8. What is the bug in the following code? How can it be corrected?

```
Readln(numHours, hourlyWage);
{ Calculate weekly pay }
wages := numHours * hourlyWage;
if numHours > 40 then
   { calculate overtime pay—1 1/2 times normal pay }
   overtimeHours := numHours - 40;
   wages := wages + (overtimeHours * hourlyWage * 3/2);
Writeln('You have earned $', wages:5:2);
```

9. Suppose you have two boolean variables called ***geneLikes*** and ***rogerLikes***, and both have received values. Write code that will print the message "Two thumbs up" if both variables are TRUE, "Split decision" if exactly one is TRUE, and "Two thumbs down" if both are FALSE.

10. A store that normally sells cassettes for $2.95 each gives discounts for large orders. The store gives a 10% discount if you buy 10-19 tapes, a 25% discount if you buy 20-29 tapes, and a 33% discount if you buy 30 or more tapes. The following code is supposed to ask the user to enter the number of cassettes she wants to buy and then output the cost. What is wrong with the code? How can it be debugged?

```
program Tapes;

const
   price = 2.95;                 { full cost of one cassette          }

var
   numToBuy: integer;            { # of cassettes the user will buy   }
   cost,                         { total cost                         }
   discount: real;               { % off for large order              }
```

```
begin
  Write('How many cassettes do you want to buy?');
  Readln(numToBuy);

  { Calculate discount }
  if numToBuy > 10 then
    discount :=.10
  else if numToBuy > 20 then
    discount :=.25
  else if numToBuy > 30 then
    discount :=.33
  else
    discount := 0.0 { no discount }

  { Calculate total cost }
  cost := price * numToBuy;
  cost := cost - (discount * cost);
  Writeln('The purchase price is $', cost:5:2)
end. { Tapes }
```

Coding Exercises

1. Write a procedure that allows a user to choose two points to define a rectangle. Your procedure should allow the user to pick any two opposing corners in any order.

2. Telephone area codes are three-digit numbers in which the middle digit is either 0 or 1 and the first digit is any number except 0 or 1. Write a procedure that asks the user to enter a three-digit number and prints a message indicating whether the number is a legitimate area code.

3. All the composite (i.e., non-prime) numbers between 2 and 100 are multiples of 2, 3, 5, or 7 (except, of course, 2, 3, 5, and 7). Write a procedure that, when the user enters a number between 2 and 100, determines if the number is prime or composite.

4. Revise the ***Faces*** program from Chapter 1. The new version should ask the user to enter a number. If the user enters 1, the comic face should be drawn; if the user enters 2, the tragic face should be drawn.

5. Write a procedure that asks the user to enter a year since 1950 and then prints the name of the U.S. president in that year. (When more than one president served in the same year, print the name of the individual who served longer.)

6. Write a procedure that asks the user to input a channel number and then outputs the call letters of the corresponding TV station.

7. Write a program to demonstrate addition. Ask the user to enter two three-digit numbers. Then show the result in vertical form, with the carries indicated when appropriate. For example, the addition of 358 and 447 is shown as:

```
  11
  358
+ 447
  805
```

8. A basketball player's uniform number must be made up of digits from 0 to 5. Write a procedure that determines if a given one- or two-digit number can be used as a uniform number.

9. Ask the user to enter the current win-loss records of two teams. Your procedure should tell whether the team that currently has the poorer record has a chance of finishing with the better record. Assume that both teams will play 162 games. For example, if Cleveland has a 93-57 record and Detroit has an 84-68 record, Detroit still has a chance to finish with a better record than Cleveland. However, if Detroit has an 80-71 record, it has no chance of beating Cleveland. (Hint: calculate the leading team's *magic number,* which is the number of games that the leading team needs to win or the trailing team needs to lose to make the lead secure for 162 games.)

10. Write code that, when given the direction, distance, and departure time of a flight, outputs the arrival time. Assume that the plane flies at 600 miles per hour. The user should be asked to indicate if the flight is east/west or north/south; each 1000 miles in an east/west direction indicates a change in time zone.

11. In a certain figure skating competition, three judges rate performances on a scale of 1.0 to 6.0. Higher scores are better, and scores are given to the nearest tenth of a point. The lowest of the three scores is ignored, and a skater's final score is the average of the other two judges' ratings. Write a procedure that accepts three judges' scores and outputs the skater's final score.

Programming Problems

1. Write a program that, when given a number from 1 to 1000, prints the equivalent in Roman numerals.

2. For dinner, you are preparing chicken (which takes 45 minutes), potatoes (which take an hour), and cauliflower (which takes 20 minutes). Write a program that asks the user to enter the time when dinner will be served and prints (in order) the time when he should start preparing each item.

3. A survey asked doctors what cold remedies were best. Twenty-six percent recommended aspirin; 23% recommended a non-aspirin reliever, and the rest recommended chicken soup.

Write a program that draws these results as either a bar graph or a pie chart, depending on a choice made by the user.

4. Write a program that asks the user to enter a number from 1 to 6, then outputs the way in which that number is represented on a die:

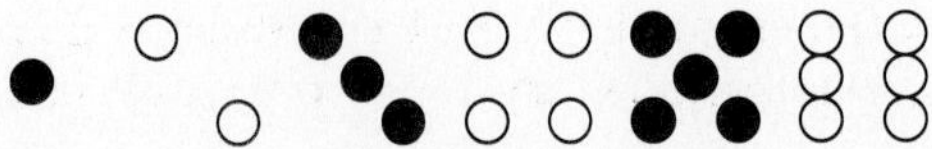

5. Create a menu-driven program that allows the user to choose to draw a rectangle, a circle, or a triangle. The user should be able to choose the shape to draw and select the endpoints (or center and radius) of the shape. This is called a *layout* program.

6. (This is an extension of the previous problem.) If the user chooses to draw a rectangle or circle, allow her to choose the color of the shape. The two menus (the color menu and the shape menu) should appear at separate times; that is, the user should first choose a color and then choose a shape.

7. Write a program that allows a user to enter a digit from 0 to 9 and see the input value in the Drawing window, using one of the following formats:

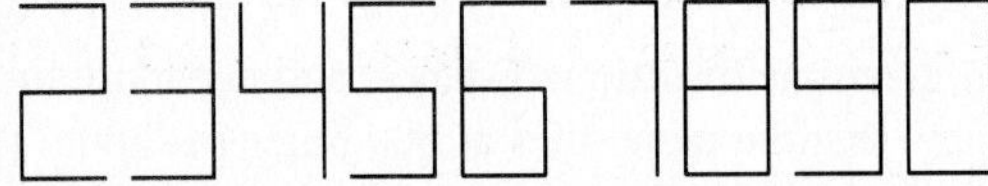

8. Write a program that clips lines outside a certain area. First, ask the user to specify a rectangular area as the clipping area. Then ask the user to choose two endpoints of a line. Your program should draw only the part of the line that is in the clipping area. (Hint: divide the possibilities into 0 endpoints inside the area, 1 endpoint inside the area, and 2 endpoints inside the area. You will also need to consider how lines intersect.)

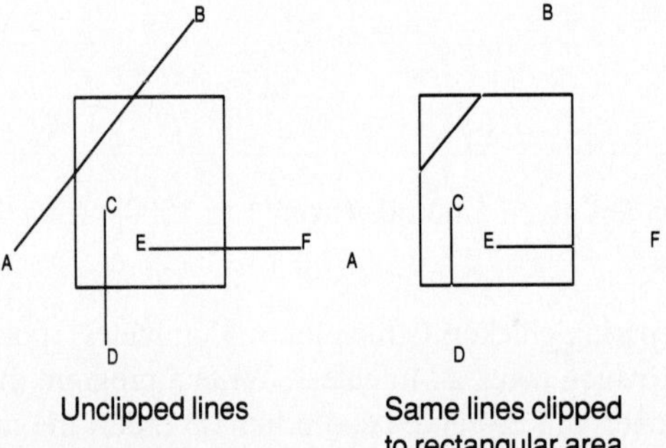

Unclipped lines

Same lines clipped to rectangular area

9. Write a program that calculates biorhythms. Biorhythms are cycles of a person's life. Each person has three cycles which begin at birth: a physical cycle of 23 days, an emotional cycle of 28 days, and an intellectual cycle of 33 days. An attribute is strong in the first half of its cycle; otherwise, that attribute is weak. For example, days 1 through 13 are the

strong days in the emotional cycle; days 15 through 27 are the weak days. The halfway and end points of a cycle (for example, days 14 and 28 of the emotional cycle) are known as critical days. To calculate a biorhythm, your program should first ask for the user's birthdate and the current date. This information will tell you the person's age in days. (To deal with leap years, just add 1 day for each four years of age.) Your program should then determine whether the user is in the strong or weak half of each cycle. As an extension, you may also want to tell the user when the next critical day in each cycle will occur.

10. Write a program that asks the user to enter a number of beats in 4/4 (musical) time. The user may enter 0.5, 1.0, 1.5, 2.0, 2.5, 3.0, 3.5, or 4.0 beats; the program's response should use some combination of whole, half, quarter, eighth, and dotted notes. The figure below indicates the number of beats for each type of note.

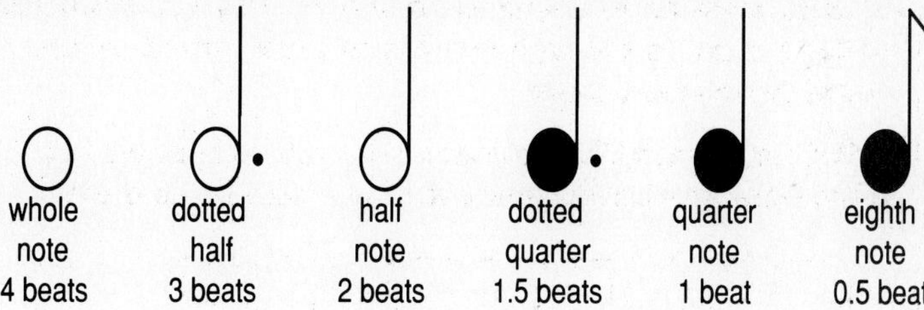

Loops

By now, you've probably realized that a computer cannot do anything that a person can't do by hand. Ironically, the advantage of the computer is that it *can't* think—it doesn't "mind" doing the repetitive jobs that people *could* do but would rather avoid. Among the most mundane tasks known to humankind are those that have to be performed over and over again. This chapter discusses *loops*—programming constructs that repeat blocks of statements.

We will look at three new statements, **for**, **repeat-until**, and **while**, that allow us to repeat blocks of code. Like the **if-then** and **case** statements, loops affect a program's flow of control, that is, the order in which statements are executed. This chapter completes our discussion of flow of control. In addition, we will look at how to use loops to create an all-purpose menu package and how to use sentinels to terminate input loops.

5.1 Definite Loops

In Chapter 3, you used QuickDraw to draw lines and rectangles. Now, let's take a closer look at how the QuickDraw package creates these shapes.

Drawing a line in QuickDraw is a matter of connecting a series of pixels, which are illuminated individually. For the purposes of this example, we'll simplify the technical details and assume that QuickDraw has a local procedure, ***ColorPixel(horiz, vert);***, which illuminates a single pixel at ***(horiz, vert)***. Thus, lighting one pixel is equivalent to executing one ***ColorPixel*** call.

To draw the line, QuickDraw takes the endpoints specified by the current position and the ***LineTo*** call and illuminates all the pixels between the endpoints. To keep the example simple, let's draw a horizontal line from (0, 10) to (100, 10). In this case, QuickDraw would need to illuminate 101 pixels. With no repetition constructs, QuickDraw would need 101 separate statements to draw the 101 pixels.

```
ColorPixel(0, 10);
ColorPixel(1, 10);
ColorPixel(2, 10);
...
ColorPixel(99, 10);
ColorPixel(100, 10);
```

Such repetition is unnecessarily tedious, even for a computer.

Let's see how to make use of a loop construct to eliminate the repetition. First, note that whenever QuickDraw draws a horizontal line, the vertical coordinate doesn't change. To figure out how many pixels have to be drawn, QuickDraw starts at the current position's horizontal coordinate and illuminates pixels, one at a time, until it reaches the horizontal coordinate designated in the ***LineTo*** statement. QuickDraw does this by calling the procedure ***ColorPixel*** repeatedly. Because QuickDraw can determine exactly how many pixels must be drawn on the line, we can use a construct known as a *definite* loop. In Pascal, the statement used for definite loops is called a **for** statement.

The **for** loop consists of four parts: an *upper and a lower limit*, which are integer expressions that indicate how many times the loop should be executed; a *loop counter*, which is an integer variable that keeps track of which execution of the loop is currently in progress; and a *loop body,* which is the block of statements to be repeated. Figure 5.1 illustrates how these parts work.

The first thing a **for** loop does is give the loop counter an initial value. Then the loop counter is compared to the loop's upper limit. When the loop counter's value exceeds the upper limit, the loop exits. Before then, however, the statements that make up the loop body are executed. After each execution of the loop body, the loop counter is incremented (increased by 1), and the loop's *exit condition* (in this case, whether the loop counter's value exceeds the upper limit) is tested again.

Going back to the QuickDraw example, you can see how a horizontal line is drawn with a **for** statement.

```
for curHoriz := leftHoriz to rightHoriz do
    ColorPixel(curHoriz, lineVert);
```

The first time through the loop, the loop counter ***curHoriz*** receives the value ***leftHoriz***. Then, ***ColorPixel*** is called to color the pixel at

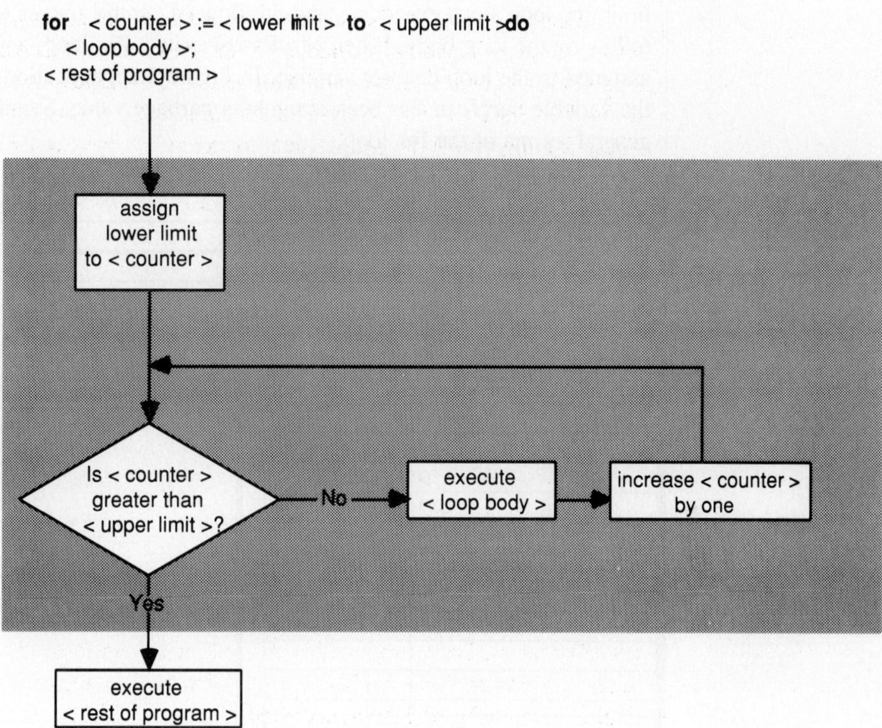

Figure 5.1
The **for** loop process

(***curHoriz***, ***lineVert***). After the loop body (in this case, the single call to ***ColorPixel***), the flow of control returns to the top of the loop, and ***curHoriz*** is incremented. Each pass through the loop increments ***curHoriz*** by one until it reaches the value of ***rightHoriz***. Remember that ***lineVert*** stays the same throughout the execution of the loop.

Assume that the line is being drawn from (0, 10) to (100, 10). This means that, in a code fragment preceding the loop (not shown here), ***lineVert*** is set to 10, ***leftHoriz*** is set to 0, and ***rightHoriz*** is set to 100. When the loop is encountered, ***curHoriz*** is initialized to the same value as ***leftHoriz*** (0). Then, since ***curHoriz*** (0) is less than ***rightHoriz*** (100), the body of the loop is executed. The point (***curHoriz***, ***lineVert***), or (0, 10), is illuminated.

Now that the bottom of the loop has been reached, the flow of control returns to the top of the loop. ***curHoriz*** is incremented by one and now has the value 1. ***curHoriz*** is still less than ***rightHoriz***, and thus the point (1, 10) is illuminated. In this fashion, each point on the line is illuminated. Figure 5.2a shows the loop just before the pixel (5, 10) is painted.

The loop continues, and eventually ***curHoriz*** is set to 100. Because ***curHoriz*** is still not greater than ***rightHoriz***, the loop is executed (see Figure 5.2b). After (100, 10) is illuminated, the flow returns to the top of the loop, and ***curHoriz*** increases to 101. Now that the loop counter is greater than the upper limit, the loop stops executing, and the flow of control moves to the first statement following the loop body. When MacPascal exits a **for** loop, a garbage value is assigned to the loop counter variable. In Figure 5.2c, execution has left the loop, and the variable ***curHoriz*** has been assigned a garbage value. Syntax Box 5.1 shows the general format of the **for** loop.

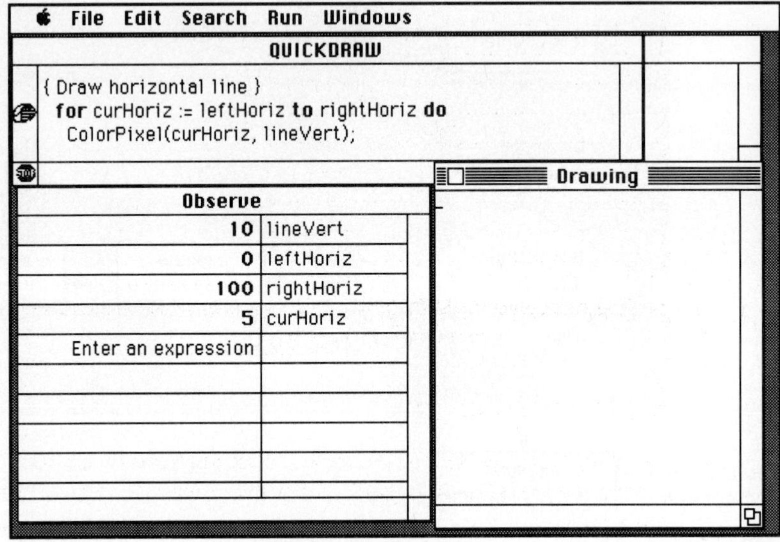

a. Fifth time through loop

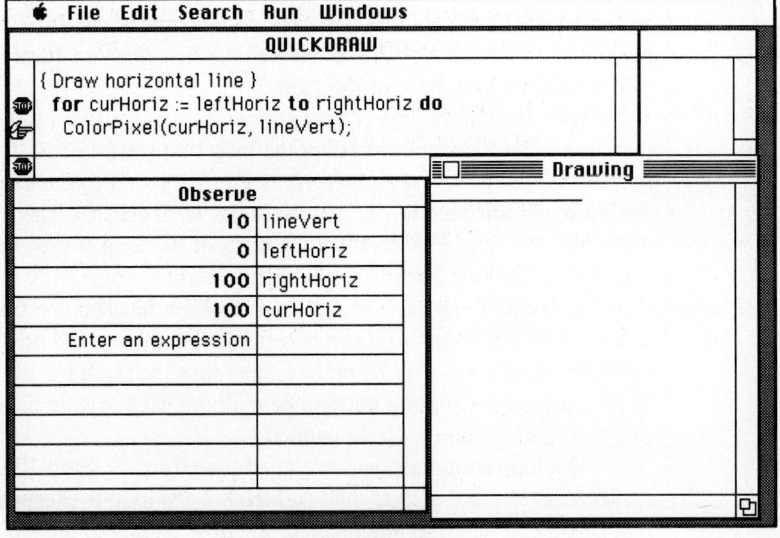

b. Final iteration of loop

Figure 5.2
Hand simulation of horizontal line code

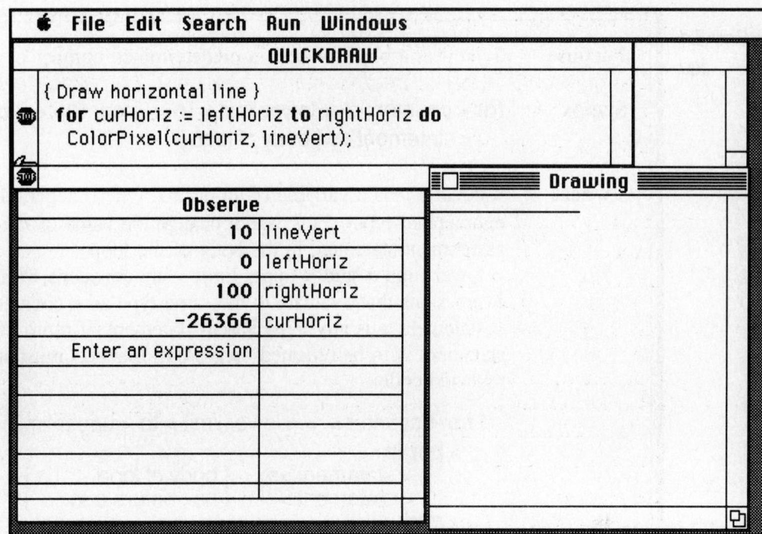

Figure 5.2 (continued)

c. Variable values after loop is complete

5.2 Nested Loops

Any legal Pascal statement can be placed in the body of a loop. This includes other loops. Putting flow-of-control statements inside other flow-of-control statements is relatively common in programming and is another example of *nesting*. We first saw an example of nesting in Chapter 4 with the nested **if-then** statement.

QuickDraw has an element that draws an object in zero dimensions (a pixel); by using one **for** loop, QuickDraw can draw an object in one dimension (a line). An object in two dimensions can be drawn by nesting two loops. Assume for the moment that we are writing the code for ***PaintRect*** from scratch. First, we think about what it is we want—to draw a filled rectangular area—and then we figure out how to get the machine to do it.

The box drawn by ***PaintRect*** is filled in by drawing a sequence of closely spaced horizontal lines. This differs from drawing a single straight line, because neither the horizontal nor the vertical coordinate is held constant. What we want to do is temporarily put the vertical coordinate at its lowest value, draw a horizontal line, increase the vertical coordinate by one, draw another horizontal line, and continue until the vertical coordinate reaches its upper limit. By definition, this is the process performed by a **for** loop. From this description, we can create the following pseudocode:

```
FOR each vertical coordinate DO
    Draw a horizontal line
```

We said previously that pseudocode should contain very little Pascal, yet here we use the notation *FOR each... DO*. Flow-of-control constructs are the major exception to our "no Pascal in the pseudocode" rule. Using the reserved words FOR, DO,

Syntax Box 5.1
for

Purpose To repeat a block of code a predetermined number of times

Syntax

```
for < counter >:= < lower limit > to < upper limit > do
    < statement >; { body of loop }
```

where < counter > is a variable of an ordinal type (integer, character, or enumerated type). You cannot change the value of < counter > with an assignment statement in the body of the loop.
< lower limit > and < upper limit > are constants, variables, or expressions that evaluate to the same type as < counter >.
< statement > is any legal Pascal statement. If more than one statement is to be repeated, **begin/end** brackets must surround the repeated code:

```
for < counter > := < lower limit > to < upper limit > do
   begin
      < statement >s;    { body of loop       }
      < statement >      { no ; before end    }
   end;
```

Usage The **for** loop executes the statements in the body of the loop as many times as specified by the upper and lower limits.
When the **for** statement is first encountered, < counter > is assigned the value of < lower limit >. That value then is compared to < upper limit >. As long as < counter > is less than or equal to < upper limit >, the statements in the body of the loop are executed. When the last statement in the body of the loop is performed, the flow of control returns to the **for** line. Then < counter > is increased by one and again compared to < upper limit >. When < counter > is greater than < upper limit >, the flow of control exits the loop and moves to the statement immediately following the last statement in the body of the loop.

If < lower limit > is greater than < upper limit >, the loop body is not executed.

As with other flow-of-control statements, the entire block of a **for** loop is actually one statement. No semicolon appears after the **do** on the top line. This implies that the loop body is part of the **for** statement; the **for** line cannot stand alone.

See also Syntax Box 5.4, backward **for** loops.

IF, THEN, ELSE, CASE (and, as we shall see, WHILE, REPEAT, and UNTIL) in the pseudocode forces us to group blocks of tasks into loops or conditional branches. In our pseudocode examples, reserved words are in upper case. Our discussion of program development is made more complete in Chapter 7.

For now, we need to expand the line of pseudocode that says, "Draw a horizontal line." From the last section, we know that the code

```
for curHoriz := leftHoriz to rightHoriz do
    ColorPixel(curHoriz, lineVert);
```

draws a horizontal line at a vertical value of ***lineVert***.

At this point, to code the line "FOR each vertical coordinate DO," we need to use three variables: a counter, the loop's lower limit, and the loop's upper limit. All of these variables must be of type ***integer***. If we create the variables ***curVert***, ***topVert***, and ***bottomVert***, the pseudocode can be translated into the Pascal line:

```
for curVert := topVert to bottomVert do
```

Thus, the finished code fragment looks like this:*

```
for curVert := topVert to bottomVert do
    begin
        for curHoriz := leftHoriz to rightHoriz do
            ColorPixel(curHoriz, curVert);
    end; { for curVert }
```

Let's hand simulate this segment when QuickDraw receives the call

```
PaintRect(10, 10, 100, 100);
```

We'll assume that some earlier part of the code (not shown here) set ***topVert*** to 10, ***bottomVert*** to 100, ***leftHoriz*** to 10, and ***rightHoriz*** to 100. In this fragment, ***curVert*** begins at ***topVert*** (10).

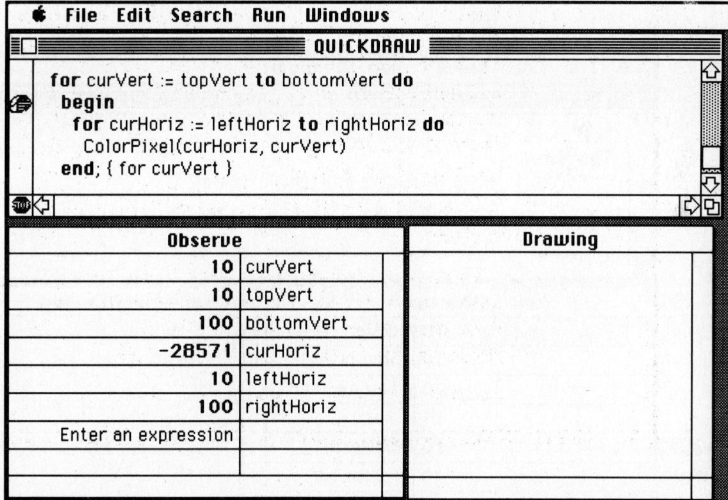

Figure 5.3
Beginning of hand simulation of *PaintRect*

The flow of control moves to the next statement, which is the *inner* **for** loop. Here ***curHoriz*** is assigned the value of ***leftHoriz*** (10). At this point, the pixel at (***curHoriz***, ***curVert***) [(10, 10)] is illuminated.

* The **begin/end** brackets are actually not needed in this fragment because the inner **for** loop is one statement. The brackets are included here for clarity.

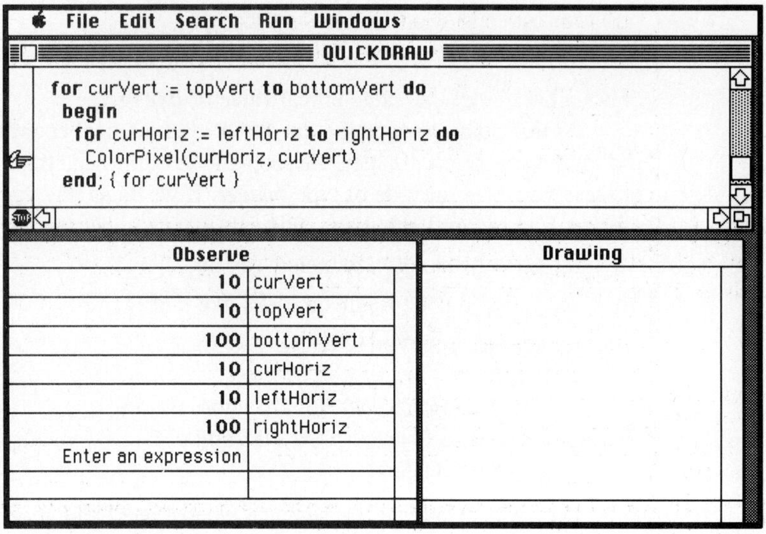

File Edit Search Run Windows

QUICKDRAW

```
for curVert := topVert to bottomVert do
  begin
    for curHoriz := leftHoriz to rightHoriz do
      ColorPixel(curHoriz, curVert)
  end; { for curVert }
```

Observe	
10	curVert
10	topVert
100	bottomVert
10	curHoriz
10	leftHoriz
100	rightHoriz
Enter an expression	

Drawing

Figure 5.4
Hand simulation of ***PaintRect:*** ***curHoriz*** = 10; ***curVert*** = 10

The flow of control then goes back to the top of the inner loop; ***curVert*** keeps the same value, but ***curHoriz*** is incremented to 11. For the moment, ***curVert***'s value is frozen at 10.

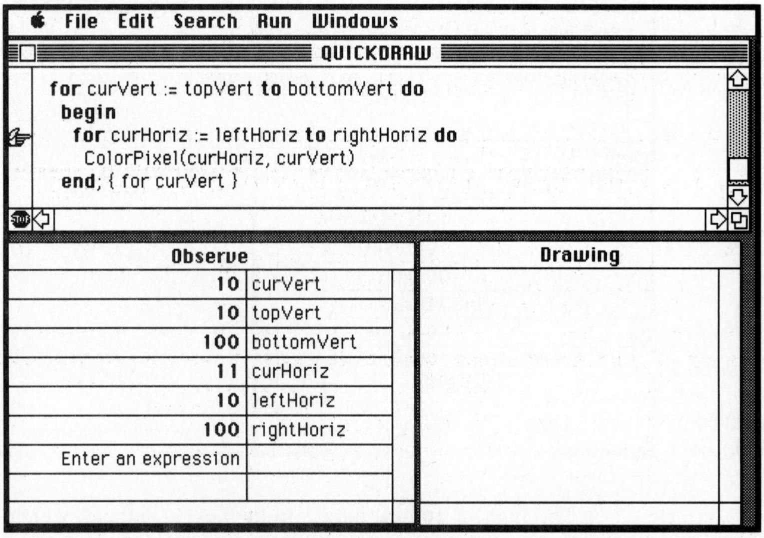

File Edit Search Run Windows

QUICKDRAW

```
for curVert := topVert to bottomVert do
  begin
    for curHoriz := leftHoriz to rightHoriz do
      ColorPixel(curHoriz, curVert)
  end; { for curVert }
```

Observe	
10	curVert
10	topVert
100	bottomVert
11	curHoriz
10	leftHoriz
100	rightHoriz
Enter an expression	

Drawing

Figure 5.5
Hand simulation of ***PaintRect:*** ***curHoriz*** =11; ***curVert*** = 10

The inner loop continues execution (***curHoriz*** continues to increase by 1), and a horizontal line is drawn where ***curVert*** = 10.

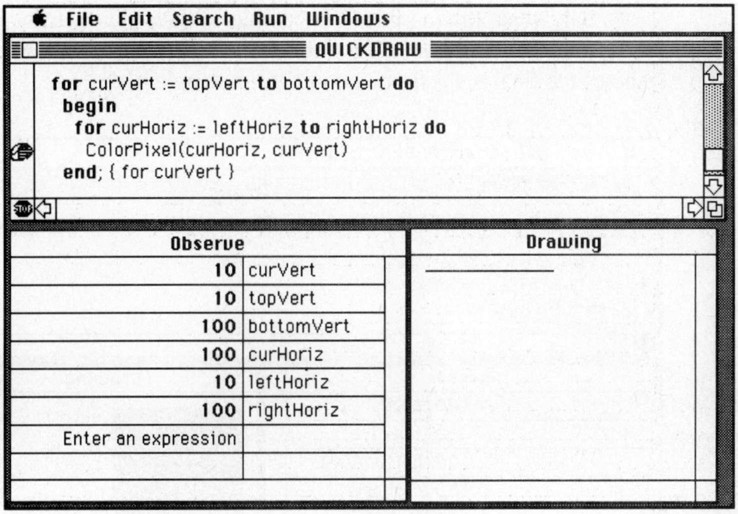

```
for curVert := topVert to bottomVert do
  begin
    for curHoriz := leftHoriz to rightHoriz do
      ColorPixel(curHoriz, curVert)
  end; { for curVert }
```

Observe	
10	curVert
10	topVert
100	bottomVert
100	curHoriz
10	leftHoriz
100	rightHoriz
Enter an expression	

Figure 5.6
Hand simulation of ***PaintRect:*** ***curHoriz*** = 100; ***curVert*** = 10

Now ***curHoriz*** is incremented and has the value 101. Since this is greater than ***rightHoriz***, the flow of control exits the loop and goes to the statement immediately following the end of the current loop. In other words, the call to ***ColorPixel*** is skipped, and the flow of control moves to the **end**; bracket. This signals the end of the outer loop body's execution, and the flow of control moves to the top of the outer, or ***curVert***, loop statement.

curVert is now increased by one, and the inner **for** loop starts from the beginning again, drawing a line where ***curVert*** = 11. Again, ***curHoriz*** starts at ***leftHoriz*** (10) and goes to ***rightHoriz*** (100).

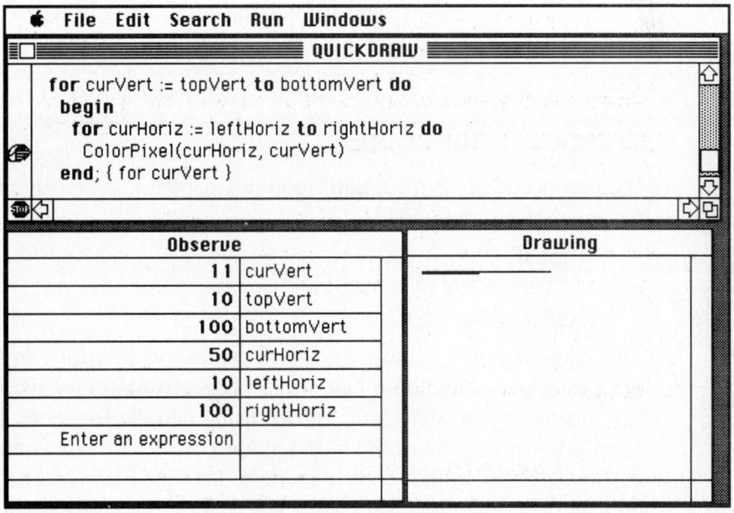

```
for curVert := topVert to bottomVert do
  begin
    for curHoriz := leftHoriz to rightHoriz do
      ColorPixel(curHoriz, curVert)
  end; { for curVert }
```

Observe	
11	curVert
10	topVert
100	bottomVert
50	curHoriz
10	leftHoriz
100	rightHoriz
Enter an expression	

Figure 5.7
Hand simulation of ***PaintRect:*** ***curHoriz*** = 50; ***curVert*** = 11

Only when the inner loop is completed does the outer loop counter increase. The outer loop stops after a horizontal line is drawn where ***curVert*** = 100. Figure 5.8 shows the final hand simulation of the rectangle code.

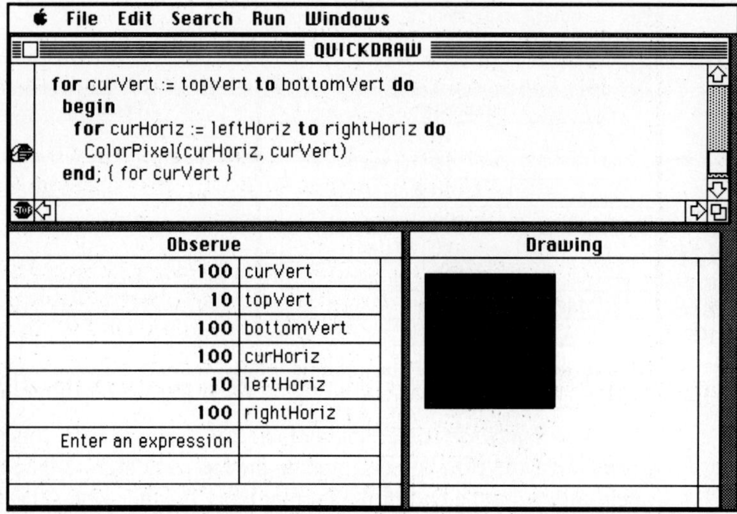

Figure 5.8
Completed hand simulation of ***PaintRect*** code: last pixel of rectangle is being drawn

The important idea is that all the statements inside a loop body, including nested loops, must be executed completely before the counter of the outer loop is incremented.

In practice, it would be prohibitively time consuming to simulate 100 iterations of a **for** loop, let alone two nested loops. Usually, you can restrict your tests to the first and last time through the loop (called the *boundary conditions*) and a typical "in between" case. If your simulations of all three tests provide correct results, you can be fairly confident that the loop will work correctly under all conditions.

5.3 repeat-until Loops

We introduced the **repeat-until** loop in Chapter 3. To receive a user's pick from the mouse, we used the code

```
repeat
    GetMouse(horiz, vert);
until Button;
```

This code fragment continues to store the mouse's position in ***horiz*** and ***vert*** until the user presses the mouse button. The **repeat-until** construct is one of Pascal's two *indefinite loop* statements. When using definite **for** loops, you need to state exactly how many times the loop will execute before you enter the loop. The upper and lower limits of the loop counter are determined before the **for** loop begins execution. With an indefinite loop, however, you do not know when you are going to exit

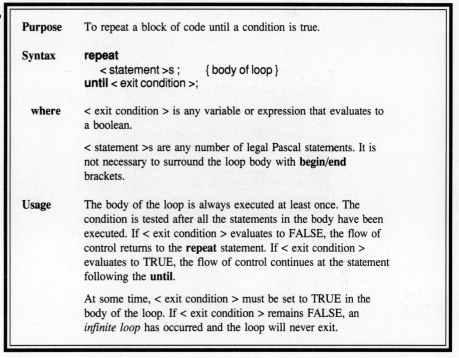

Syntax Box 5.2
repeat-until

Purpose To repeat a block of code until a condition is true.

Syntax

```
repeat
     < statement >s ;          { body of loop }
until < exit condition >;
```

where < exit condition > is any variable or expression that evaluates to a boolean.

< statement >s are any number of legal Pascal statements. It is not necessary to surround the loop body with **begin/end** brackets.

Usage The body of the loop is always executed at least once. The condition is tested after all the statements in the body have been executed. If < exit condition > evaluates to FALSE, the flow of control returns to the **repeat** statement. If < exit condition > evaluates to TRUE, the flow of control continues at the statement following the **until**.

At some time, < exit condition > must be set to TRUE in the body of the loop. If < exit condition > remains FALSE, an *infinite loop* has occurred and the loop will never exit.

the loop until the loop has already been entered. Some action or assignment inside the loop causes the loop to stop executing.

When Pascal encounters the repeat-until code fragment, it determines what coordinates are under the cursor. Then, after ***GetMouse*** assigns values to ***horiz*** and ***vert***, Pascal tests the condition following the **until**. If the condition is TRUE, the loop is exited, and the flow of control moves to the statement following the **until**. If the condition is FALSE, the flow of control returns to the top of the loop. Figure 5.9 shows how this flow of control works.

In the mouse input loop, the exit condition is the boolean function ***Button***, which monitors the mouse button. ***Button*** returns the value TRUE when the button is down and FALSE when it is up. If the user is moving the mouse instead of pressing the button, the function ***Button*** is FALSE, so the flow of control moves back to the top of the loop. ***horiz*** and ***vert*** are then given new values by ***GetMouse***, and the flow again moves to the **until** condition. ***horiz*** and ***vert*** thus are updated continually until the button is pressed. You can't predict how many times ***GetMouse*** will update ***horiz*** and ***vert***, but the indefinite loop will wait as long as necessary for the user's response.

Let's look once again at the doghouse program in Chapter 4. To make the program more useful, we can enclose the menu picking in a **repeat** loop. At the pseudocode level, the menu segment of the algorithm is expressed this way:

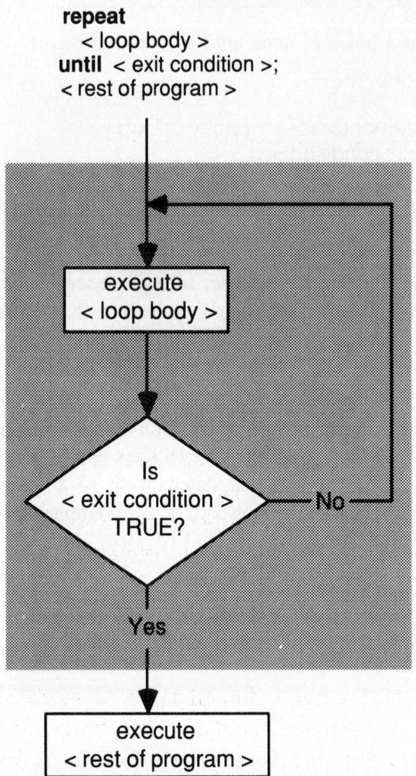

Figure 5.9
Flow of control for **repeat-until** loop

```
REPEAT
   IF user chooses top view THEN
      Show top view
   ELSE IF user chooses side view THEN
      Show side view
   ELSE IF user chooses front view THEN
      Show front view
   ELSE
      Print message telling user that she didn't pick on menu
UNTIL user asks program to stop
```

This algorithm is incomplete, however, because the user has no way of telling the program to halt. To solve this problem, we can add a *stop* button to the menu. The stop button indicates that the exit condition of the **until** is true. The simplest way of handling this is to add a boolean variable, or flag, to the program. The flag is initially set to FALSE and is changed only when the stop button is picked. The following pseudocode example shows the menu fragment after the stop button has been added and a flag called ***done*** has been created.

```
Set done to FALSE
REPEAT
    IF user chooses top view THEN
        Show top view
    ELSE IF user chooses side view THEN
        Show side view
    ELSE IF user chooses front view THEN
        Show front view
    ELSE IF user chooses stop THEN
        Set done to TRUE
    ELSE
        Print message telling user that she didn't pick on menu
UNTIL done
```

By hand simulating, you can see that the loop in the pseudocode has only one exit. The exit condition specified in the **until** line occurs in one place in the loop: when the user picks the stop button. With any other choice, the condition ***done*** remains FALSE and the **until** condition is not met. The flow of control then returns to the **repeat** line and the loop continues executing.

5.4 The Generic Menu

You now have all the tools needed to build a general menu package. Using the primitives provided by QuickDraw, you can draw menu buttons; with the ***GetMouse*** call, the user can communicate with the program by choosing a particular button. By using a boolean variable, you can allow users to stop a section of the program at their own discretion; by using a loop, you can use the same menu continually.

Let's combine these features to write the following pseudocode for a generic menu:

```
Draw n menu buttons plus stop button
Set exit condition to FALSE
REPEAT
    Ask user to pick a button from 1 to n, or stop
    IF user picks button 1 THEN
        Action 1
    ELSE IF user picks button 2 THEN
        Action 2
    ...
    ELSE IF user picks button n THEN
        Action n
    ELSE IF user picks stop THEN
        Set exit condition to TRUE
    ELSE
        User didn't pick on the menu
UNTIL exit condition
```

Each time the loop is executed, three things happen. First, the user is asked to pick a button. The IF-THEN-ELSE IF construct then determines which button was chosen. Finally, the action associated with the menu button is performed.

In later chapters, you will see a number of menu examples, some of which may be more complex. The framework described in the above pseudocode, however, can serve as the backbone of any menu you may want to use.

5.5 while Loops

Pascal offers another type of indefinite loop construct, a **while** loop. For the most part, **while** loops can be used in the same situations as **repeat** loops. The main difference between the **while** and the **repeat** loop is that the exit condition for a **while** loop is checked at the top of the loop and the **repeat**'s exit condition is checked at the bottom. This means that the body of a **repeat** loop is *always* executed at least once, whereas the body of a **while** loop may be bypassed altogether.

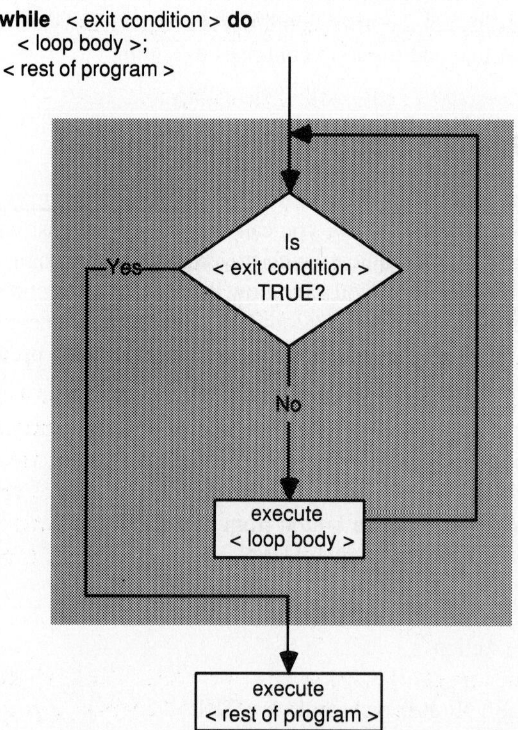

Figure 5.10
Flow of control for **while** loop

Programmers often confuse the use of the boolean condition in the **while** and **repeat** loops. A **while** loop exits when the condition is FALSE; an **until** loop exits when the condition is TRUE. Thus, the **while** loop's condition can be restated as "continue to loop if TRUE," as opposed to the **repeat**'s "exit loop if TRUE" condition. Still, in the jargon of computer scientists, both conditions are referred to as "exit conditions."

while loops, like **repeat** loops, are used when the programmer doesn't know how many times the loop will be executed, as is often the case when a program is dealing with large numbers. Suppose a mathematician wants you to write a program to input an integer and then raise it to successive powers. You want to find all the powers of the integer factor less than a given maximum. Your pseudocode might look like this:

```
Input factor to be raised to successive powers
Input maximum number
Initialize product to factor
WHILE product < maximum DO
   BEGIN
      Print out product
      product := factor * product
   END { WHILE }
```

This pseudocode can be translated into the following code:

```
Write('Please input integer to be raised to powers: ');
Readln(factor);
Write('Please input the maximum number: ');
Readln(maximum);
product := factor;
while product < maximum do
   begin
      Writeln(product : 1, ' is a power of ', factor : 1);
      product := factor * product
   end; { while }
```

Suppose the mathematician inputs 5 for ***factor*** and 500 for ***maximum***. ***product*** is first given the value of ***factor*** (5). A value must be given to ***product*** before the loop begins so that the condition ***product < maximum*** can be checked the first time the **while** loop is encountered. This is an example of *priming the pump*: a variable used inside the loop body is given a value before the loop begins.

When the **while** loop is first encountered, the condition ***product < maximum*** is tested. Since (5 < 500) is true, the loop body is executed and the message

```
5 is a power of 5
```

appears in the output. ***product*** is then multiplied by ***factor*** and assigned the value 25. The flow of control returns to the top of the **while** loop, and the condition is retested. 25 < 500 is true, so the message

```
25 is a power of 5
```

also appears in the output. ***product*** is again multiplied by 5 and is assigned the value 625. When the condition at the top of the **while** loop is tested the next time (625 < 500), it evaluates to FALSE. The flow of control then goes to the statement immediately following the end of the loop.

Syntax Box 5.3
while

Purpose To repeat blocks of code **while** a condition is true.

Syntax

```
while < exit condition > do
    < statement >;          { body of loop }
```

where < exit condition > is a variable or expression that evaluates to a boolean.

< statement > is any legal Pascal statement. If more than one statement is to be repeated, **begin/end** brackets must surround the repeated code.

Usage < exit condition > is tested before the body of the loop is executed. If < exit condition > is TRUE, the body is executed. (Thus, the "exit" condition is really a "continue looping" condition.) When the entire loop body has been executed, the flow of control returns to the top of the **while** loop. < exit condition > is then checked again. When < exit condition > is FALSE, the flow of control continues at the statement after the end of the loop.

Note that < exit condition > must be set to FALSE in the body of the loop. If < exit condition > always remains TRUE, an infinite loop has occurred and the **while** loop will never exit.

5.6 Loops and Input

repeat and **while** loops are similar and may even appear interchangeable. At times it may not be obvious which loop should be used in a particular situation. To show the difference, let's look at how indefinite loops are used to control input.

As we said in Section 5.4, a generic menu uses a **repeat** loop. With a little editing, we can change a menu's loop from a **repeat** to a **while**. If the code for a **repeat** loop with a menu looks like this:

```
done := FALSE;
repeat
   repeat
      GetMouse(horiz, vert);
   until Button;
   SetPt(userPt, horiz, vert);
   if PtInRect(userPt, button1) then
      ...
   else if PtInRect(userPt, stop) then
      done := TRUE;
until done;  { repeat }
```

then we can use a **while** loop with the following changes:

```
done := FALSE;
while not done do
   begin
      { Get user's point }
      repeat
         GetMouse(horiz, vert);
      until Button;
      SetPt(userPt, horiz, vert);

      { do a pick correlation }
      if PtInRect(userPt, button1) then
         ...
      else if PtInRect(userPt, stop) then
         done := TRUE
   end; { while }
```

When we changed the loop from a **repeat** to a **while**, we had to make two other changes. The exit condition was changed from ***done*** to **not** ***done***. Also, a **begin/end** bracket was added to the **while** loop, and pretty printing changed the indentation appropriately.

repeat loops are preferable to **while** loops for accepting input from a menu. In the **while** loop in the above example, the boolean condition is checked immediately after it is set. The program hasn't had a chance to set the condition to FALSE, and therefore the check is not necessary. In the **repeat** loop, the status of ***done*** is not checked until the body of the loop has been performed once. Thus, the unnecessary check at the top of the **while** loop is eliminated.

On the other hand, **while** loops are preferable to **repeat** loops in some situations when the input is coming from the keyboard. You can use a particular piece of typed-in data to allow the user to indicate when he wants to stop (in the same way you used a particular button on a menu). This data value, called a *sentinel*, marks the end of data.

Suppose you want to write a program to draw a line graph that shows the average speed of traffic over the George Washington Bridge (or your hometown equivalent) every hour. You will be using data that somebody else gathered: you know that a speed check was done every hour, starting at noon, but you don't know how long the information was gathered.

The input for the program is a list of the average speeds, rounded to the closest mile per hour. In other words, the data are of a list of positive integers. To code the program, you know that you need an indefinite loop, since you don't know how much data was collected. However, you do need a way to exit the program.

To solve this problem, you can ask the person collecting the data to enter a negative integer as a sentinel. The sentinel can't be confused with an average speed; traffic may grind to a standstill, but you assume it isn't going backward. The researcher's list of data might look like this:

```
48
23
46
44
47
-2
```

Let's look at the pseudocode for this problem:

```
Set horiz and vert coordinates to lower left corner of graph
Get first speed
WHILE speed > 0 DO
   BEGIN
      Set new point
      Draw line from old point to new point
      Draw asterisk at new point
      Make the new point into the old point
      Get next speed
   END { WHILE }
```

In this graph, the horizontal coordinate represents minutes elapsed, and the vertical axis represents miles per hour. Since the smaller vertical coordinates are toward the top of the Drawing window, showing an increase in speed means decreasing the vertical coordinate. Thus, you can plot the vertical coordinate of the graph by subtracting the speed from the vertical offset. For example, suppose you set the graph's origin at (50, 150). The vertical offset is 150. A speed of 50 mph is graphed at a vertical coordinate of 150 – 50, or 100; a speed of 45 mph is plotted at the vertical coordinate of 150 – 45, or 105. With this in mind, you can refine the line "Set new point" to the next level:

```
{ Set new point }
Add 60 to horizontal coordinate
Set vertical coordinate to (vertical offset – speed)
```

Now the problem can be coded:

Code 5.1 Procedure *DrawGraph* with **while** loop

```
procedure DrawGraph;

const
   vertOffset = 150;            { vertical coord of origin        }
   horOffset = 50;              { horizontal coord of origin      }

var
   oldMins,                     { horiz coordinate of old point   }
   oldSpeed,                    { vert coordinate of old point    }
   newMins,                     { number of minutes elapsed       }
   newSpeed: integer;           { avg speed during this hour      }
```

Code 5.1 (continued)

```
begin
    { set initial positions to origin }
    oldMins := horOffset;
    oldSpeed := vertOffset;
    MoveTo(oldMins, oldSpeed);

    { prime the pump }
    Write('Please enter the average mph for the first hour: ');
    Readln(newSpeed);

    while newSpeed > 0 do
        begin
            newMins := oldMins + 60;
            LineTo(newMins, vertOffset- newSpeed);
            WriteDraw('*');

            { store point that has just been created }
            oldMins := newMins;
            oldSpeed := newSpeed;
            Write('Please type in the next speed');
            Write(' or a negative number to stop: ');
            Readln(newSpeed)
        end { while }
end; { DrawGraph }
```

Notice that the pump was primed with the ***Readln*** statement before the **while** loop. Given the data 48, 23, 46, 44, 47, –2, the procedure outputs the result shown in Figure 5.11.

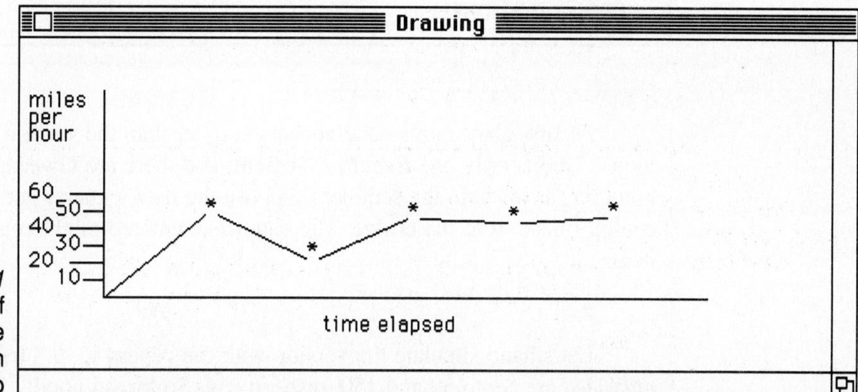

Figure 5.11 Output of procedure *DrawGraph* with **while** loop

Changing the above code to use a **repeat** instead of a **while** is a simple operation. With a few changes, the code looks like this:

Code 5.2
Procedure *DrawGraph* with **repeat** loop

```
procedure DrawGraph;

const
   vertOffset = 150;        { vertical coord of origin      }
   horOffset = 50;          { horizontal coord of origin    }

var
   oldMins,                 { x coordinate of old point     }
   oldSpeed,                { y coordinate of old point     }
   newMins,                 { number of minutes elapsed     }
   newSpeed: integer;       { avg speed during this hour    }

begin
   { set initial positions to origin }
   oldMins := horOffset;
   oldSpeed := vertOffset;
   MoveTo(oldMins, oldSpeed);

   repeat
      Write('Please enter the speed for this hour ');
      Write('or a negative number to stop:');
      Readln(newSpeed);
      newMins := oldMins + 60;
      LineTo(newMins, vertOffset– newSpeed);
      WriteDraw("*");

      { store point that has just been created }
      oldMins := newMins;
      oldSpeed := newSpeed;
   until newSpeed <= 0

end; { DrawGraph }
```

At first glance, this code appears simpler than the version with the **while** loop. There is only one ***Readln*** statement, and there are fewer lines. The problem, however, arises with the sentinel. Suppose the data gatherer got caught in traffic and couldn't make it to the bridge. The data to be entered might consist of this solitary item:

```
-2
```

Let's hand simulate the version with the **repeat** loop. First, ***oldMins*** and ***oldSpeed*** are set to 50 and 150, respectively. So far, so good.

Now, the program accepts the first datum: the –2. After ***newMins*** is set to ***oldMins*** + 60, or 60, you have the following call:

LineTo(60, –2);

This draws a line below the vertical axis. As Figure 5.12 shows, this isn't what we want.

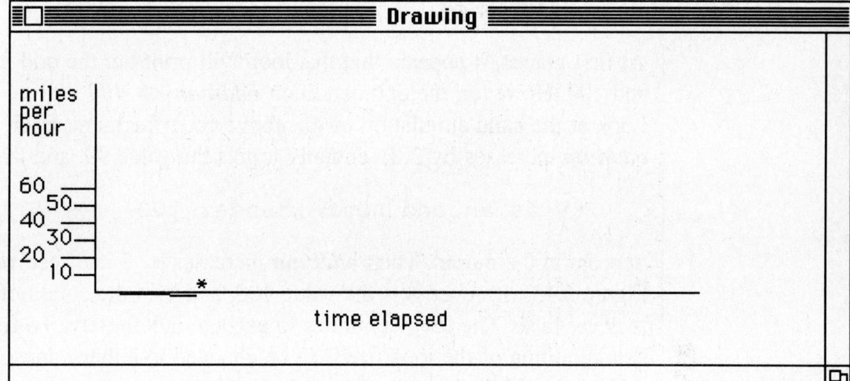

Figure 5.12 Output of procedure *DrawGraph* with **repeat** loop

But will the version with the **while** loop work? Let's try hand simulation. Again, ***oldMins*** and ***oldSpeed*** are set to 50 and 150, respectively. Then the ***Readln*** statement primes the pump by reading the –2. Note that the loop hasn't been entered yet. The next statement is **while *newSpeed* < *0* do**. Since ***newSpeed*** = –2, the condition is FALSE. Therefore, the loop is not entered.

When you write programs with indefinite loops, you need to ask one question: is there a case where the body of the loop should be skipped altogether? If such a case exists, you need a **while** loop; if the body of the loop should be executed at least once in all instances, you need a **repeat** loop.

5.7 Common Errors

Regardless of which loop you use, you should always carefully hand simulate to see that the loop behaves correctly at the boundary conditions (the entrance and the exit of the loop) and in a typical situation in between. You should also hand simulate naively to make sure that the loop iterates the correct number of times. Although this eliminates a good many mistakes, some loop errors still occur frequently. This section looks at common problems associated with loops and how to avoid them.

Infinite Loops

We previously touched on one common loop problem: the *infinite loop*. This bug occurs when the loop's exit condition is not satisfied: the condition on a **repeat** loop is never changed to TRUE, or the condition on a **while** loop is never changed to FALSE. For example, the following loop will never exit:

```
oddnum := 1;
while oddnum <> 100 do
  begin
    Writeln(oddnum:3, ' is an odd number under 100');
    oddnum := oddnum + 2
  end; { while }
```

At first glance, it appears that this loop will print out the odd numbers between 1 and 100. However, the exit condition ***oddnum* <> *100*** will never become FALSE. Look at the hand simulation of the above code fragment. Each time through the loop, ***oddnum*** increases by 2. Eventually it gets the value 99, and the line

```
99 is an odd number under 100
```

appears in the output. Then ***oddnum*** increases by 2 and receives the value 101 (see Figure 5.13). It never gets the value 100, and thus the condition of the **while** loop is never false. The loop continues to execute indefinitely. To fix the program, the exit condition of the loop needs to be changed to either ***oddnum* <= *100*** or ***oddnum* < *101*.**

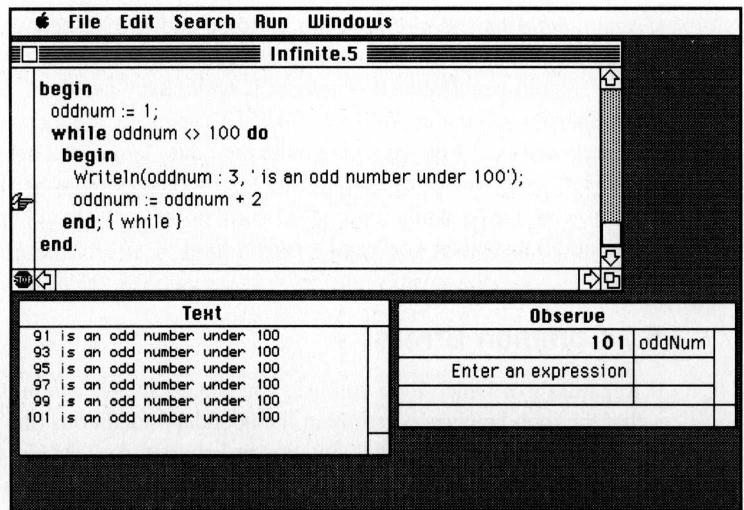

Figure 5.13
Hand simulation of infinite loop; ***oddnum*** = 101

Infinite loops are particularly dangerous. If the loop never ends, the program's execution will never end. Should you get caught in this situation, you will need to stop the program by some other method. In MacPascal, you can always halt execution of a program by choosing **Halt** from the **Pause** menu; in Lightspeed, you can do the same thing by clicking on the "bug spray can" icon that appears in the menu bar when the program is running. Careful hand simulation, however, should catch infinite loops before they occur at the computer.

Loops That Don't Start

Loops that are entered incorrectly can be as serious as loops that never exit. When you hand simulate pseudocode, make sure that your entering condition is correct. A **while** loop exit condition that is set to FALSE before the **while** is encountered prevents execution of the loop.

The following example is intended to print out all odd numbers less than 2, followed by all odd numbers less than 3, and so on up to all odd numbers less than 100.

```
continue := TRUE;
for current := 2 to 100 do
   begin
     oddnum := 1;
      while continue do
        begin
           Writeln(oddnum:1, ' is an odd number less than', current: 1);
           oddnum := oddnum + 2;
           if oddnum > current then
              continue := FALSE

        end  { while }
   end; { for }
```

The first time through the loop, ***current*** starts at 2 and ***oddnum*** is set to 1. The **while** condition is true, and the inner loop is entered. The message

```
1 is an odd number under 2
```

is printed. ***oddnum*** is then increased by 2 and assigned the value 3. Because the **if** condition is true (3 > 2), ***continue*** is set to FALSE. When the **while** condition is checked, the condition is FALSE, and the loop body is skipped. The flow of control goes to the **end**; of the **for** loop and then back to the **for** line, where ***current*** is increased to 3. ***oddnum*** is reset to 1, but ***continue*** is still FALSE. Therefore, the inner **while** loop will not be entered again.

To fix this loop, move the line that initializes ***continue***—i.e., ***continue := TRUE;***—between the lines ***oddnum :=1;*** and **while *continue* do**.

Forgetting to include **begin/end** brackets can also cause problems. The following code will output just one number:

```
oddnum := 1;
while oddnum <= 100 do
   Writeln(oddnum : 1, ' is an odd number under 100');
oddnum := oddnum + 2;
```

This program will also be caught in an infinite loop since the body of the loop consists of one statement (the ***Writeln***). Remember, if no **begin/end** brackets are found in a **for** or **while** loop, Pascal assumes that the loop body is one line long. In this case, ***oddnum*** is never incremented, and the line

```
1 is an odd number under 100
```

will be printed an infinite number of times.

Off-By-One Errors

Another problem is an *off-by-one* error, which occurs when a loop executes one too many or one too few times. The following code fragment, which is intended to add the odd integers from 1 to ***number***, demonstrates this problem.

```
Write('Please type in the maximum integer: ');
Readln(number);
sum := 0;
count := 1;
while (count < number) do
   begin
      sum := sum + count;
      count := count + 2
   end; { while }
```

This loop will produce an incorrect result if ***number*** is odd. In that case, the loop is actually computing the sum of the odd integers from 1 to (***number*** – 2), instead of from 1 to ***number***. The **while** condition should have been written as:

```
while (count <= number) do
```

Conditions similar to off-by-one errors can occur with **for** loops. Look at the code fragment:

```
limit := 0;
for distance := 1 to limit do
   { body of loop }
```

The body of this loop will not be executed because the first value of ***distance*** (1) is not less than or equal to the value of ***limit*** (0).

For the same reason, the loop body in the following example will be executed only once:

```
limit := 1;
for distance := 1 to limit do
   { body of loop }
```

The nasty thing about off-by-one errors is that they usually do not generate error messages—they just generate wrong answers. To make things worse, you may not even recognize that the results are incorrect. An error of this kind can be difficult to detect once a program has proceeded to the testing stage.

How can you avoid off-by-one errors? Obviously, a good set of test cases with known answers is a tremendous help. You may not always have such test cases handy, however. As soon as you write a loop, you should make three tests (two of which we have already seen). First, be sure that the loop will not be entered when you don't want it to be (say, in special cases such as when the input is different from expected). Second, test the exit conditions to see that the loop will be exited when it should be and not until then. And third, examine the conditions for the first and last cycles of the loop (the boundary conditions) to be certain they are executed properly. This final test often eliminates off-by-one errors. Make these assessments for every loop in every program—developing this habit will save you an untold amount of grief.

5.8 Special Loop Conditions

The loops discussed thus far are the simplest ones provided by Pascal. While these basic loops are the ones most commonly used, two variations—backward **for** loops and indefinite loops with multiple exits—can be used in special cases.

Backward for Loops

Pascal allows **for** loops to count backward via the use of the key word **downto**. The syntax for such loops is almost identical to the regular **for** loop: the difference is that < lower limit > **to** < upper limit > is replaced by < upper limit > **downto** < lower limit >. When the loop is first encountered, the loop counter is initialized to < upper limit >. Then, each time flow of control returns to the top of the loop, the counter decreases by 1. The loop exits when the counter is less than < lower limit >. (See Syntax Box 5.4).

Syntax Box 5.4
Backward **for** Loops

Purpose To repeat a statement or a block of statements a definite number of times

Syntax

```
for < counter > := < upper limit > downto < lower limit > do
    < statement > ;
```

If more than one statement is to be repeated, the entire block of code must be surrounded by **begin/end** brackets.

```
for < counter > := < upper limit > downto < lower limit > do
    begin
        < statement >s;
        < statement > { no ; before end }
    end;
```

where < counter >, < upper limit >, and < lower limit > must all be integers. < counter > is initially given the value of < upper limit >. Each time the loop body is executed, the flow of control returns to the **for** line, and < counter > is decreased by one. The loop continues to execute as long as < counter > is greater than or equal to < lower limit >.

Usage The backward **for** loop is identical to the forward **for** loop except for the counting.

Both the incrementing and the decrementing loops terminate when < counter > passes the limit value after the **to** or **downto**.

Indefinite Loops with More Than One Exit

When we discussed **if** statements, we introduced the logical operators **and**, **or**, and **not**. Since the exit conditions on **repeat** and **while** loops are merely boolean conditions, we can use any boolean expression after the **until** or between the **while** and the **do**. These include using logical operators; thus, indefinite loops can have multiple exit conditions.

To end our discussion on loops, let's look at a loop with a *double exit* condition. Consider a program that helps a user balance a checkbook. The program can let the user know if the account is overdrawn. If the balance in the checking account goes below zero, execution of the program should halt and a message should be printed out. The program should also stop executing when the user picks the stop button.

These features can be added to the program with some revisions in **procedure** ***Calculate***. Changing the exit condition on the loop from

```
until done;
```

to

```
until done or (balance < 0);
```

provides two exits for the loop: (1) when the stop button is picked (setting ***done*** to TRUE) and (2) when the balance dips below zero. In either case, the flow of control continues to the line immediately following the end of the loop. However, if the loop exits when the user picks the stop button, a message that the account is overdrawn should not be printed. You need to place an **if-then** statement immediately after the end of the loop.

```
repeat
  ...
until done or (balance < 0);
if balance < 0 then
  Writeln('Your account is overdrawn.');
```

Whenever a loop has more than one exit condition, the code immediately following the loop should include an **if-then** or a **case** statement to determine which exit condition is true.

5.9 Chapter Summary

In this chapter, we looked at different types of loops. Loops are either definite or indefinite and are used to repeat blocks of code.

The definite loop in Pascal is known as a **for** loop and allows code to be executed a known number of times. Pascal provides two forms of indefinite loops: the **repeat-until** loop and the **while** loop. Both of these use a boolean (exit) condition to signal the end of the loop's execution. While the two loops are similar, they are not interchangeable; the body of a **repeat** loop is always executed at least once, but the body of a **while** loop need not be executed at all.

Loops are powerful programming tools, but they are often the cause of serious programming bugs. Infinite loops, off-by-one errors, and incorrectly entered or exited loops can occur if the pseudocode for the program is not done carefully. The best way to catch such bugs is to hand simulate the pseudocode and Pascal code naively, especially for the entry and exit boundary conditions.

To enclose a menu in a loop, we usually add a stop button to the main menu. When the stop button is picked, a boolean condition is set to the exit condition of the loop. Menus are enclosed in **repeat-until** loops.

5.10 Exercises

Understanding Concepts

1. What does the following code produce?

```
side := 5;
for row := 1 to side do
   begin
      for col := 1 to row do
         Write('*');
      Writeln
   end; { for }
```

2. A loop consists of three parts: an initialization of the loop counter, a method of changing the counter, and an exit condition. How are these things indicated in a **for** loop?

3. What does the following code produce? How can it be rewritten with an indefinite loop?

```
border := 5;
top := 0 ;
bottom := 200;
for currentRect := 1 to (100 div border) do
   begin
      case currentRect mod 4 of
         0:
            PenPat(black);
         1:
            PenPat(dkGray);
         2:
            PenPat(ltGray);
         3:
            PenPat(white)
      end; { case }
```

```
        PaintRect(top, top, bottom, bottom);
        top := top + border;
        bottom := bottom - border
    end; { for }
```

4. What is the difference between the following two fragments?

a.
```
counter := 2;
while counter < 100 do
    begin
        counter := counter + 2;
        Writeln(counter, ' is an even number')
    end; { while }
```

b.
```
repeat
    counter := 2;
    Writeln(counter, ' is an even number');
    counter := counter + 2
until counter >= 100;
```

5. What's wrong with the following code?

```
Write('Please enter the cost of the first item or 0 to exit: ');
Readln(cost);
while cost <> 0 do
    total := total + cost;
Writeln('Please enter the cost of the next item or 0 to exit: ');
Readln(cost);
```

6. This code is supposed to calculate ***base*** to the ***exponent*** power. What is wrong here? How can it be fixed?

```
Write('Enter the base number and exponent');
Readln(base, exponent);
result := base;
for curPower := 1 to exponent do
    result := result * base;
Writeln(base:2, ' to the ', exponent:2, ' power = ', result);
```

7. What will cause the following loop to exit?

```
repeat
    ...
    if playerWins then
        begin
            winnings := winnings + 100;
```

```
            if winnings > 5000 then
                done := TRUE
        end
    else
        begin
            losses := losses - 100;
            if winnings < losses then
                done := TRUE
        end
    until done;
```

8. What does the following code do?

```
repeat
    GetMouse(horiz, vert);
until Button;
Writeln('rubber-banding');
newHoriz := horiz;
newVert := vert;
repeat
    MoveTo(horiz, vert);
    PenPat(white);
    LineTo(newHoriz, newVert);
    PenPat(black);
    MoveTo(horiz, vert);
    GetMouse(newHoriz, newVert);
    LineTo(newHoriz, newVert);
until Button;
```

9. Rewrite Exercise 8 with **while** instead of **repeat** loops.

10. In the following code, how many times will the ***Write*** and ***Writeln*** statements in the inner loop be executed?

```
Write('Enter number of players in tournament: ');
Readln(numPlayers);
matchNum := 1;
for opponent1 := 1 to numPlayers do
    for opponent2 := opponent1 to numPlayers do
     begin
        Write('Match number ', matchNum:2, ': ');
        Writeln('Player ', opponent1:2, 'vs. ', opponent2:2);
        matchNum := matchNum + 1
     end; { for }
```

Coding Exercises

1. Write a procedure that tells how to distribute change. Given an amount under $1.00, your procedure should indicate how many quarters, dimes, nickels, and pennies are needed. (Use the largest coins you can—you could give someone 41¢ in pennies, but you probably wouldn't be too popular with the customers.)

2. Write a procedure that draws a chessboard (an 8 x 8 grid, with alternating black and white squares).

3. Draw a circle with a 50-pixel diameter in the center of the Drawing window. Write a procedure to make 200 movements of the circle as follows:

   a. Each move should move the circle 4 pixels vertically and 3 pixels horizontally.
   b. Initially, the vertical move should be toward the top of the screen and the horizontal move toward the left of the Drawing window.
   c. Assume that the Drawing window has not been resized, that is, it is a grid of 200 x 200 pixels.
   d. When the circle's outline hits a border of the window, it should "bounce off the wall." For example, if it hits the top wall, it should start moving toward the bottom; if it hits the left wall, it should start moving toward the right.

4. Write a procedure that allows the user to enter any number of positive real values (a sentinel should indicate the end of input). The procedure should print the smallest number among those entered by the user.

5. Suppose the Drawing window represents a still pond. Ask the user to pick a point to represent a stone being thrown into the water. Write a procedure to simulate the ripples of water that surround the stone. When the stone hits the water, circular waves start appearing, centered where the stone hit. In your procedure, a new wave begins every 1/5 of a second. Each wave's radius increases by 3 pixels each 1/10 of a second. Simulate the wave movements for 30 seconds (assume that each iteration of the procedure's loop takes 1/10 of a second to execute).

6. Write a procedure that asks the user to enter a number of sides. Your procedure should respond by drawing an equilateral polygon with the specified number of sides.

7. In the Continental Basketball Assocation, a game is divided into quarters. A team gets 1 game point for winning a quarter and 3 game points for winning the game. Write a procedure that asks for the score of each team in each quarter and prints both the total score and the total game points for each team.

8. You win the game of blackjack if your hand scores exactly 21 or less than 21 but more than the dealer. Initially, a player is dealt two cards. An ace can be worth either 1 or 11, the face cards are all worth 10, and the other cards are worth their face value. A player can ask for additional cards until he decides to stop or he

"busts" (his score goes over 21). Write a procedure that deals a hand to a player. After the first two cards (and each additional card) is dealt, your code should ask the user whether he wants to hit (get another card) or stick (stop). The procedure should print the player's running total and indicate if the user busts.

To "deal cards," use the ***Random*** function. ***Random*** is a function that returns an integer in the integer range of representation. By using the statement

```
newCard := Abs(Random mod 13) + 1;
```

you assign a random value between 1 and 13 to ***newCard***. If ***newCard*** is 1, 11, 12, or 13, this means that an ace, jack, queen, or king, respectively, has been dealt.

9. Write a procedure that allows a student to enter an arbitrary number of numeric grades. When the user enters a negative number, the procedure should print the average.

10. Write a procedure that prints all the prime numbers between 1 and 100.

Programming Problems

1. Modify the music layout program from Programming Problem 10 in Chapter 4. The user should be able to enter three measures of notes. In this example, measures are 4 beats long; the ends of measures are denoted by vertical bars. For the sake of simplicity, your program should allow the user to enter only complete measures. For example, if a measure begins with a dotted half note (3 beats), the user should not be allowed to make the next note a half note (2 beats), since the total number of beats in the measure would be more than 4.

2. Write a program that draws the pattern of stars on the American flag. The pattern consists of five rows of 6 stars alternating with four rows of 5 stars.

3. Modify the shape layout program in Programming Problems 3 and 4 of Chapter 4 by exiting when the user chooses a stop button. Extension: when the user chooses a shape button, the program should ask the user how many of that shape to draw.

4. In the atomic shell model, the nucleus of an atom is surrounded by orbits, or shells, of electrons. The shells fill starting at the shell closest to the nucleus; one shell must be filled before an electron can reside in the next shell. The innermost

shell holds 2 electrons; the next shells (in order, going away from the nucleus) hold 8, 8, and 18 electrons. Write a program that asks the user to enter an atomic number from 1 to 36 (the atomic number is equal to the number of electrons) and draws a model of the shells.

5. Draw a thermometer that has markings in Fahrenheit from –20°F to 100°F on one side and Celsius on the other. Have the thermometer indicate a temperature specified by the user.

6. In volleyball, six players initially line up as follows:

```
1 2 3
4 5 6
```

The player at the bottom right (number 6) is the first server. Each time a team regains the serve, the players rotate. The server moves to the top left, and the player on the top right moves to the bottom left. The other players each move one position toward the right:

```
6 1 2
3 4 5
```

Write a program that shows all the possible rotations from the initial position.

7. Write a program that asks the user to input two integers (one with two digits and one with four digits) and shows the long division of the smaller into the larger in the Drawing window. For example, if the user enters 64 and 8195, the Drawing window should contain:

```
     128
 64/8195
   64
   179
   128
    515
    512
      3
```

8. Write a program that draws a clock with an hour, a minute, and a second hand. Your program should ask the user for and then display the current time. After the time is shown, your program should execute a loop that moves the hands. Each iteration of the loop should correspond to a movement of one second (even though the loop will take less than one second to execute). Show the clock movements for an hour (i.e., 3600 iterations of the loop).

9. Write a program that successively divides the Drawing window in half. First, paint half of the window black. Then, paint half of the black area white. Then, paint half of the last white area black again. Keep dividing until either the length or the width of the area to paint is less than 1 pixel.

Parameters and Functions

In Chapter 1, we compared a program to a corporation. The mainline is the "president" and delegates tasks to the procedures. The procedures, in turn, complete these tasks independently, calling on lower-level procedures when necessary. In this way, the program is run efficiently without overexertion on the part of the "president."

But how effective can a corporation president be without passing information back and forth with subordinates? Like all efficient managers, the mainline and other procedures need this two-way communication ability. In this chapter, we will look at how procedures communicate with each other through *parameters* and special versions of procedures called *functions*.

Let's quickly review variables. When a procedure is invoked, the first thing Pascal does is reserve space for the variables listed in the **var** declarations. Pascal then executes the procedure, using the variables you have specified. When the procedure ends, the variables disappear and are no longer available. Since the variables exist only within the context of a procedure, they are said to be local to that procedure.

Suppose you have two procedures called ***DinnerBill*** and ***FoodExpenses***. Both procedures have a number of local variables. Also, ***FoodExpenses*** calls ***DinnerBill***.

```
procedure DinnerBill;

var
   { DinnerBill variables }

begin
   ...
end; { DinnerBill }

procedure FoodExpenses;

var
   { FoodExpenses variables }

begin
   ...
   DinnerBill;
   ...
end; { FoodExpenses }
```

When ***FoodExpenses*** is called, its local variables come into existence and are available. Then, when ***DinnerBill*** is called, the variables local to ***FoodExpenses*** are frozen. Since only one procedure, and thus one set of local variables, is available at any time, the variables local to ***FoodExpenses*** cannot be used by ***DinnerBill.*** When ***DinnerBill*** finishes, however, the values of ***FoodExpenses***'s local variables are no longer frozen.

Parameters can be used like variables. Like variables, their purpose is to store data. Unlike variables, though, parameters exist beyond the scope of a single procedure. They are *passed* from one procedure to another and form communication links between two procedures. Parameters allow you to control the flow of data from one procedure to another in a structured manner.

6.1 One-Way Communication

Imagine that you are having an intimate dinner for two. You decide to pull out all the stops and prepare your grandfather's secret family recipe for shish kabobs. Granddad told you that the success of the recipe depends on marinating the meat properly. Knowing that the meat should soak in the marinade all day, you rush to the kitchen the moment you wake up. You look at the recipe and see that the marinade consists of five parts soy sauce and two parts Worcestershire sauce. Since the dinner is for only two people, you measure five tablespoons of soy sauce and two tablespoons of Worcestershire sauce and pour the combination in a bowl.

The dinner, of course, is terrific. The next day, your dinner partner raves about your cooking ability to everyone within earshot. Eventually, word reaches all of your friends, and they insist that you prepare this succulent dish for the party you have been planning.

You know that fifteen of your friends will be descending on your house for dinner. Again, you get up early on the morning of the party and prepare the marinade.

The recipe hasn't changed; you still need five parts soy sauce and two parts Worcestershire sauce. However, because you are marinating much more meat, you use 2-1/2 cups of soy sauce and 1 cup of Worcestershire sauce. You are maintaining the proportions of the ingredients, but the actual amount of marinade has changed. Because you have stuck to Granddad's recipe your large dinner is just as tasty as your small one.

In your two preparations of the marinade, you used the same recipe but got different results (i.e., enough food for two as opposed to enough food for fifteen). The only difference in the preparation was how you defined the term "part." In the first case, a part was a tablespoon; in the second, a part was half a cup. In theory, the recipe works with any definition of "part," as long as you stick to the ratio of five parts soy sauce to two parts Worcestershire sauce.

In Pascal, we can treat procedures like recipes. Just as Granddad's recipe always produces shish kabobs, we can write procedures that always perform the same action. In addition, we can create a procedure that has to receive some information from its caller to perform its customized job. You had to define the term "part" before preparing the marinade; in Pascal, we can give some value to a *parameter* (a.k.a. an *argument*) before executing the body of the procedure. By *passing parameters*, we can repeat a procedure with different data and get different results.

Many of the statements we examined in earlier chapters are calls to one of Pascal's or QuickDraw's predefined procedures. For example, the ***PenPat*** statement is a call to a procedure that takes one parameter: the new color of the pen (in reality, the colors ***white***, ***ltGray***, ***gray***, ***dkGray***, and ***black*** are constants declared by QuickDraw). ***PenPat*** performs the same task every time it is called. The only difference from one usage to the next is the value of the parameter.

A more complex example of parameters is the ***FrameRect*** procedure. ***FrameRect*** takes four parameters: top, left, bottom, and right. Each time you call ***FrameRect***, you must pass a value for each parameter. In addition, each value you pass must be an integer. There is a *one-to-one correspondence* between the values you pass, or *send*, to the procedure and the values that the procedure *receives*. In other words, the first parameter must represent the top, the second must be the left, and so on. ***FrameRect*** always draws the outline of a rectangle; the size and the position of the rectangle depend on the parameters that it receives.

Even more complex are the ***Read*** and ***Write*** procedures and their relatives (***Readln***, ***Writeln***, ***WriteDraw***), because they take any number of parameters. These procedures are special cases; all other Pascal procedures always take the same number of parameters.

We've discussed parameters without explaining how they are specified in Pascal. Now, we will examine how to declare procedures with parameters. Suppose you want to write a program to draw concentric circles on the screen. That is, you want to center one circle on a specific point and then draw more circles that share this same center. To do this, you would create a procedure that draws a single framed circle. (Even though MacPascal and Lightspeed both have commands to draw painted and inverted circles, there is nothing to draw a framed circle.) A circle is geometrically defined by its center and its radius. The command that QuickDraw uses to draw framed round shapes draws an oval defined by the rectangle that circumscribes it.

Suppose you decide to draw a circle at the point (50, 50) with a radius of 20. To use ***FrameOval***, you have to calculate the top, left, bottom, and right of the surrounding rectangle.

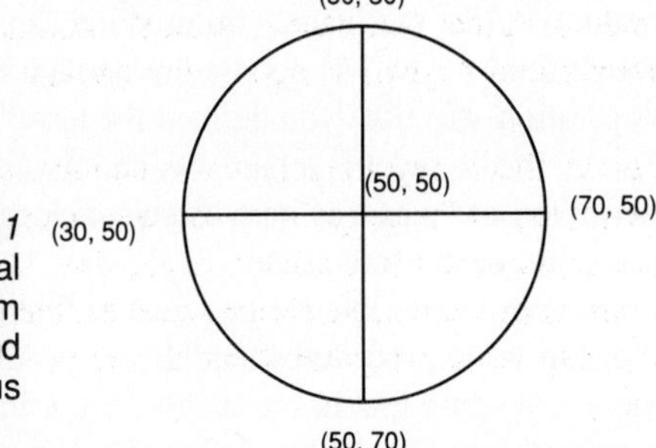

Figure 6.1 Calculating oval coordinates from the center and the radius

The top of the surrounding rectangle is found by subtracting the radius (20) from the center's vertical coordinate (50 – 20, or 30). The bottom is found by adding the radius to the center's vertical coordinate (50 + 20, or 70). The left and right coordinates of the rectangle are found in the same way: subtracting the radius from the center's horizontal coordinate gives the left coordinate of the rectangle; adding the radius to the center's horizontal coordinate gives the rectangle's right coordinate. From this information, you can code the procedure to draw this circle as follows:

```
procedure DrawCircle;

var
    centerHoriz, centerVert: integer;      { coordinates of circle's center        }
    radius: integer;                       { length from center to border          }
    top, left,                             { upper left of surrounding rect        }
    bottom, right: integer;                { lower right of surrounding rect       }

begin
    centerHoriz := 50;
    centerVert := 50;
    radius := 20;                          { set values for center and radius      }

    top := centerVert – radius;            { calculate vertical borders of rect    }
    bottom := centerVert + radius;

    left := centerHoriz – radius;          { calculate horiz borders of rect       }
    right := centerHoriz + radius;

    FrameOval(top, left, bottom, right)
end; { DrawCircle }
```

This procedure draws the same circle in the same place at all times. By using the parameters, we can generalize this procedure to draw a circle of any size and at any position.

What you want to do is draw a circle, given its center and its radius. Thus, the procedure should work on the assumption that the center point and the radius of the circle have been set elsewhere. Remember that the variables declared in a procedure's **var** section are local to that procedure. That is, local variables cannot receive values or be used in expressions outside the procedure. Since the center and the radius are to receive their values outside the procedure ***DrawCircle***, the variables representing them (***centerHoriz***, ***centerVert***, and ***radius***) must be parameters instead of local variables.

To declare a procedure that accepts parameters, you must formally declare the parameters as part of the procedure heading. The procedure needs to know the names and the data types of the parameters it is receiving. Since this is the same information that a procedure needs to know to declare a variable, the parameters in the procedure heading look much like a list of variable declarations. The change of ***DrawCircle*** looks like this:

```
{ Procedure DrawCircle                                                  }
{                                                                       }
{ This procedure draws a framed circle, given the center point and      }
{ the radius of the circle. The upper left and bottom right corners     }
{ of the rectangle that circumscribes the circle are calculated and     }
{ sent to a QuickDraw routine.                                          }

procedure DrawCircle(centerHoriz: integer;    { center's horiz coord     }
                     centerVert: integer;     { center's vertical coord  }
                     radius: integer);        { length from ctr to border }

var
  top, left,                                 { upper left of surrounding rect  }
  bottom, right: integer;                    { lower right of surrounding rect }

begin
  top := centerVert – radius;                { calculate vertical borders of rect }
  bottom := centerVert + radius;

  left := centerHoriz – radius;              { calculate horiz borders of rect    }
  right := centerHoriz + radius;

  FrameOval(top, left, bottom, right)
end; { DrawCircle }
```

The syntax of a procedure declaration with parameters is similar, but not identical, to a variable declaration list. The name of the parameter is followed by its data type. The parameters are separated by semicolons and enclosed in parentheses. A semicolon follows the closing parenthesis and separates the procedure declaration from the rest of the procedure; this final semicolon also means that you do not need a semicolon after the final parameter's data type. (In this case, ***radius: integer*** is not followed by a semicolon because it is the last parameter.) Like variables, parameters with the same data type can be separated by commas. The procedure heading

```
procedure DrawCircle(centerHoriz,     { center's horizontal coord    }
                     centerVert,      { center's vertical coord      }
                     radius: integer); { length from ctr to border   }
```

declares the same three parameters of type ***integer*** as the earlier example.

Once the parameters are declared, they can be treated as local variables. The same calculations can be used to determine the values of ***top***, ***left***, ***bottom***, and ***right*** whether ***centerHoriz***, ***centerVert***, and ***radius*** are declared as parameters or variables. Changing the local variables into parameters, though, generalized the procedure. ***DrawCircle*** can now draw a circle of any size and any shape—all it needs are the coordinates of the center and the length of the radius.

Syntax Box 6.1
Procedure declaration with value parameters

Purpose To declare the procedure name and receive parameters as local variables.

Syntax **procedure** < name > (< parameter list >);

where < name > is any legal procedure name.

< parameter list > is the list of parameters received by the procedure and has the following structure:

< parameter sublist 1 > : < parameter type 1 >;
< parameter sublist 2 > : < parameter type 2 >;
...
< parameter sublist *n* > : < parameter type *n* >

where < parameter sublist 1 >, < parameter sublist 2 >,..., < parameter sublist *n* > are sublists of one or more parameter names (called formal parameters). Individual parameters in each sublist are separated by commas. < parameter type 1 >, < parameter type 2 >,..., < parameter type *n* > are the corresponding data types of each parameter sublist.

Usage The parameters received by the called procedure must have the same types as the parameters sent by the calling procedure. That is, if the first parameter sent is an ***integer***, then the first parameter received must also be declared an ***integer***.

Semicolons are used to separate parameter lists. The last parameter is an exception; a right parenthesis is placed before the semicolon. There is no semicolon after the procedure < name >.

The procedure treats the parameters as if they were local variables, i.e., as if they were declared in the procedure's **var** section. Parameters, having been declared in the parameter list, should not be declared again in the **var** section of the procedure.

There need not be a parameter list for every procedure declaration. If the procedure takes no parameters, no parameter list is necessary.

What you need to know now is how to send the values of the center and the length to ***DrawCircle***. You have seen how to extend a procedure declaration to include a list of parameters to receive. The method of invoking a procedure can be similarly modified to include a list of parameters to send.

Up to this point, you have been invoking procedures simply by typing the procedure name. To send parameters, you need to type the name and list the parameters in parentheses. For example, you can draw a circle with a radius of 20 and a center of (50, 50) by using the following call:

```
DrawCircle(50, 50, 20);
```

The order of the parameters is crucial. The first parameter in the call is received by the first parameter listed in the procedure heading. The parameters passed by the calling procedure are *actual* parameters; the parameters received by the called procedure are *formal* parameters. Note that the caller of a procedure never needs to know the names of the formal parameters declared with the procedure; the caller needs to know only the type of each parameter and the order in which they are declared. In the example, the actual parameter 50 is received by the formal parameter ***centerHoriz***, the second parameter 50 is received by ***centerVert***, and the actual parameter 20 is received by ***radius***.

Entire expressions can also be used as actual parameters because they are evaluated prior to being passed. The following code fragment uses variables and an expression as actual parameters:

```
const
   numCircles = 30;                { total number of concentric circles   }
   circleWidth = 3;                { difference in each circle's radius   }
   ...

procedure Concentric;

var
   userHoriz, userVert: integer;   { coords of point picked by user       }
   counter: integer;               { loop counter                         }

begin
   Writeln('Please pick the center of the circles');
   repeat
      GetMouse(userHoriz, userVert);
   until Button;
   for counter := numCircles downto 1 do
      DrawCircle(userHoriz, userVert, circleWidth * counter)
end; { Concentric }
```

Let's look at what happens when ***DrawCircle*** is called. Before, when a procedure was called, the flow of control was simply turned over to the new procedure. Now there is an intermediate step to pass parameters prior to activating the procedure.

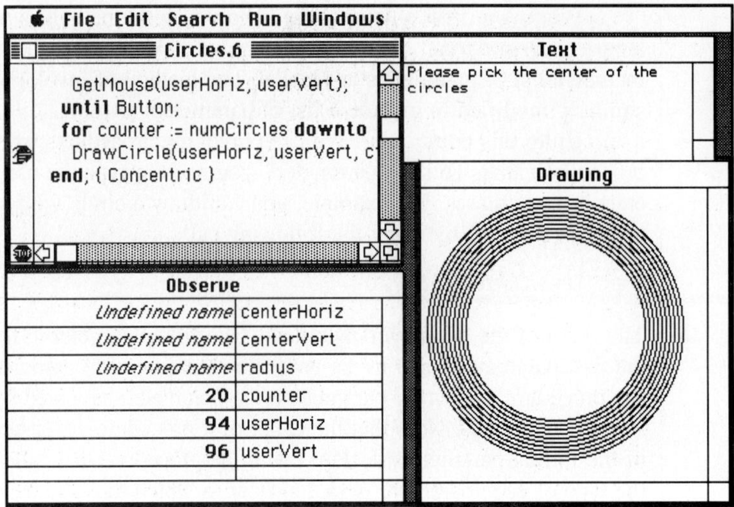

a. Just before sending control to ***DrawCircle***

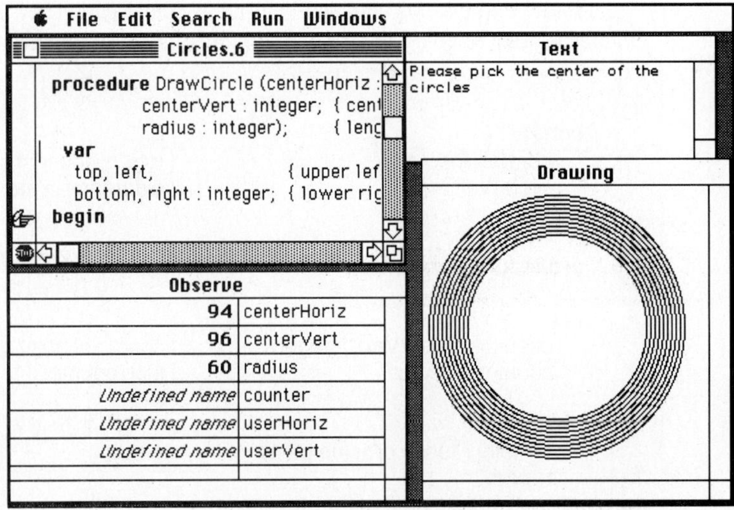

Figure 6.2
Call to ***DrawCircle*** when ***counter***=20

b. At **begin** of ***DrawCircle***

Figure 6.2a shows a typical call to ***DrawCircle***. Suppose the user has picked the point (94, 96). When Pascal encounters the call to ***DrawCircle***, it *copies* the values of the actual parameters into the formal parameters. First, Pascal gets the value of the first parameter in ***Concentric***'s actual parameter list (***userHoriz***, which has been set to 94 by ***GetMouse***). Pascal then copies the value into the first parameter in ***DrawCircle***'s formal parameter list (***centerHoriz***). Pascal next copies the value of ***userVert*** into the corresponding parameter in ***DrawCircle***'s list; thus, ***centerVert*** is assigned the value of ***userVert*** (96).

The third parameter in ***Concentric***'s list is an expression. To copy the value into the formal parameter, Pascal has to evaluate the expression. At this point, ***counter*** has the value of 20. This value is multiplied by the constant ***circleWidth*** to yield 60. This final result is then copied into ***radius***.

When the right parenthesis at the end of the **procedure** statement is encountered, Pascal knows that no more parameters have to be sent, and flow of control goes immediately to the procedure ***DrawCircle***. Figure 6.2b shows that ***Concentric***'s variables are no longer defined, since ***DrawCircle*** is now in control.

When ***DrawCircle*** has finished executing, the values of the parameters are *not* sent back. Thus, there is a one-way communication link between the two procedures. Formal parameters that provide a one-way link between any two procedures are called *value* parameters.

Figure 6.3 illustrates graphically how the one-to-one mapping of value parameters works for the ***DrawCircle*** procedure. Note that information flows in one direction only, from the calling procedure to the called procedure.

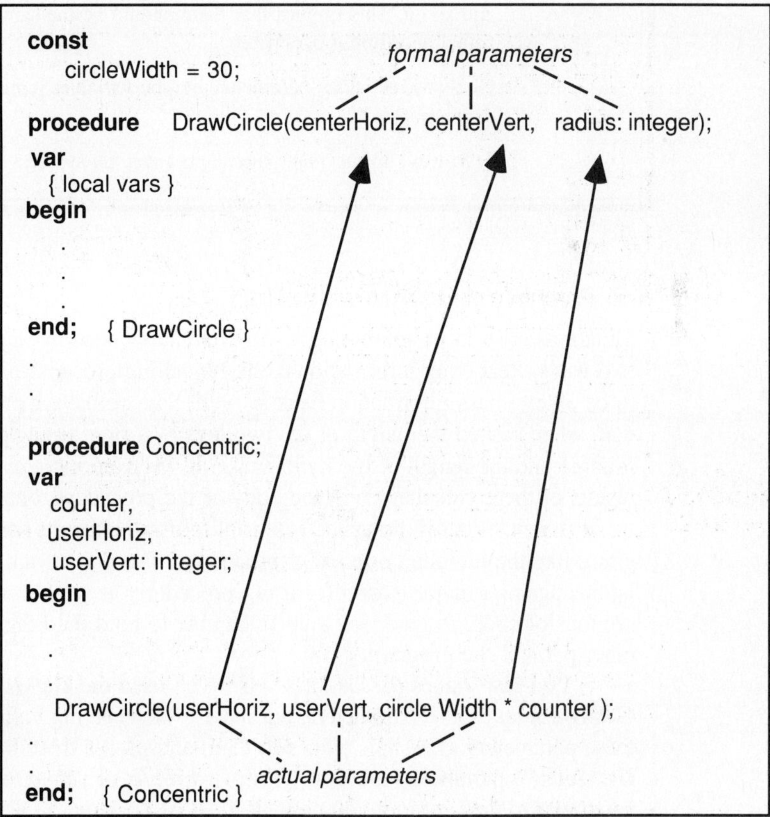

Figure 6.3
One-to-one mapping of value parameters

Syntax Box 6.2
Procedure call with parameters

Purpose To call a procedure and send parameters.

Syntax < procedure name > (< parameter 1 >, < parameter 2 >,...,
< parameter *n* >);

where < procedure name > is the name of the procedure being called.

< parameter 1 >, < parameter 2 >,..., < parameter *n* > are the actual parameters being sent.

Usage The actual parameters sent by this procedure must have the same data types as the formal parameters declared in the called procedure. That is, if the first parameter received by the called procedure is a ***real***, < parameter 1 > must also be a ***real***.

The parameters are separated by commas.

There is a one-to-one correspondence between the actual and the formal parameters. The first parameter sent in a procedure call is received by the first parameter listed in the procedure heading, and so on. This implies that there should be the same number of actual and formal parameters.

One-way, or *value,* parameters can be variables, constants, or expressions.

Two-way, or *variable,* parameters must always be variables.

6.2 Two-Way Communication

Situations arise in programming when procedures need to be able to communicate two ways. Receiving information from the calling procedure is not enough; we have to be able to pass information back as well. Say we have a procedure in a program that, when passed the length of the two legs of a right triangle, finds the area of the triangle and the length of the hypotenuse. If we were just going to print out the results of these calculations in the body of the procedure, one-way parameters would be sufficient. What if, however, we want to use the results somewhere else in the program, like the mainline or another procedure? We don't want to go through the calculations again; a major reason for using procedures is so that we don't have to repeat sections of code. Instead, we want to be able to hold onto the results and use them in other parts of the program.

You saw values passed back when you used the ***GetMouse*** procedure call. ***GetMouse*** takes two parameters, but instead of receiving values from a caller for these parameters, it assigns values to them and passes them back to the caller. ***GetMouse***'s parameters are examples of *variable*, or *var, parameters*. For a formal parameter to pass information back, it must be declared a variable parameter by placing the keyword **var** in front of its declaration in the procedure heading. Variable parameters thus allow a two-way "dialogue" between procedures. We say these parameters *return* values, in much the same way that predefined functions, such as ***Trunc,*** return values. (Functions will be examined in more depth later in this chapter.)

A procedure can use both types of parameters, as do ***SetPt*** and ***SetRect***. Both of those procedures have a single *variable* parameter (the first parameter) of a graphical data type followed by two or four *value* parameters of type ***integer***.

Calling a procedure with variable parameters looks no different from calling a procedure with value parameters. The only restriction is that a variable—not a constant or an expression—must be listed in the procedure call. This is because a variable parameter can send back a new value. The calling procedure must be able to receive the new value when the called procedure finishes executing. A new value can be received only by a variable. This is why, for example, only variables can be listed as parameters to ***Readln***—a user cannot input a value into a constant or an expression.

The position of the **var** and the semicolons in a parameter list determine which parameters are two-way and which are one-way. In the procedure heading, the **var** indicator is in effect until a semicolon is found. Syntax Box 6.3 shows four different parameter lists, each having a different meaning.

Syntax Box 6.3
Value and variable parameters

(parm1, parm2 : integer);	Both ***parm1*** and ***parm2*** are value parameters.
(parm1 : integer; **var** parm2 : integer);	***parm1*** is a value parameter.; ***parm2*** is a variable parameter.
(**var** parm1 : integer; parm2 : integer);	***parm1*** is a variable parameter.; ***parm2*** is a value parameter.
(**var** parm1, parm2 : integer);	Both ***parm1*** and ***parm2*** are variable parameters.

Whether received as values or variables, parameters can be used within a procedure as if they were local variables. The only difference between the two types of parameters is that changes made to variable parameters, unlike those made to value parameters, are passed back to the calling procedure. In other words, when the procedure ends, a variable parameter is no longer like a local variable: while local variables cease to exist, a variable parameter transfers information back to the caller.

We usually think of a variable parameter as a two-way parameter: the caller passes an initial value to the callee, and when the flow of control returns to the caller, the final value of the parameter is passed back. In fact, you do not have to initialize an actual variable parameter by assigning a value to it in the caller procedure. Even if you send a procedure a variable with a garbage value (a variable that has yet to receive a value from an assignment or ***Readln*** statement), the called procedure can assign some value to it and send that new value back.

Syntax Box 6.4
Procedure declaration with value and variable parameters

Purpose To declare the procedure name, establish value parameters as local variables, and establish variable parameters as aliases for the variables passed to them

Syntax **procedure** < name > (< parameter list >);

where < name > is any legal procedure name.

< parameter list > is the list of parameters received by the procedure and has the following structure:

[**var**] < parameter sublist 1 > : < parameter type 1 >;
[**var**] < parameter sublist 2 > : < parameter type 2 >;
...
[**var**] < parameter sublist *n* > : < parameter type *n* >

where [**var**] indicates a variable (two-way) parameter sublist. The reserved word **var** is not used for value (one-way) parameters.

< parameter sublist 1 >, < parameter sublist 2 >,..., < parameter sublist *n* > are sublists of one or more parameter names (called formal parameters). Individual parameters in each sublist are separated by commas.

< parameter type 1 >, < parameter type 2 >,..., < parameter type *n* > are the corresponding data types of each parameter sublist.

Usage The format used to call a procedure with variable parameters is the same as that for a procedure with value parameters (see Syntax Box 6.2).

var is in effect until Pascal finds a semicolon. For example, in

```
procedure Add(var total,
              final : integer;
              subtotal : integer);
```

total and ***final*** are both set as variable parameters, but ***subtotal*** is not (because the **var** is no longer in effect).

The last parameter is followed by a right parenthesis and a semicolon.

We have been talking about parameters in general and discussing concepts in the abstract. Let's look at a concrete example of how parameters can be used.

Suppose you want a procedure that allows the user to create a polygon with a given number of endpoints. The user can pick the location of each of the endpoints with the mouse. While the user is creating the shape, the procedure calculates the perimeter of the polygon and returns it to the caller. The first level of pseudocode for the procedure looks like this:

```
Ask user to pick first point
FOR each line DO
   BEGIN
      Ask user to pick point
      Draw line to new point
      Calculate length of perimeter to this point
   END {FOR}
```

Picking points and drawing lines are tasks you have seen before. Let's concentrate, then, on the line "Calculate length of perimeter to this point." Calculating the perimeter of the polygon can be done as each point is added to the shape. The polygon's total perimeter is equal to the total length of each line. As you draw each line, you can calculate its length using the algebraic distance formula. If you have the line from ***(oldHoriz, oldVert)*** to ***(newHoriz, newVert)***, the length of the line is represented by

$$distance = \sqrt{((newHoriz - oldHoriz)^2 + (newVert - oldVert)^2)}$$

You can perform this function with the help of two functions that are predefined in MacPascal. The ***Sqrt*** function takes one argument, which may be an expression of either type ***integer*** or ***real***, and returns the *positive* square root of the number. The ***Sqr*** function also takes a single argument of type ***integer*** or ***real*** and returns the square of the number. ***Sqrt*** will always return a ***real*** value; ***Sqr*** will return an ***integer*** if the argument is an ***integer***, and a ***real*** if the argument is a ***real***. For example, ***Sqr(4)*** returns the integer 16, but ***Sqr(4.0)*** returns the real 16.0.

To determine the perimeter, you need to know the endpoints of each line. Therefore, you need to keep track of both the point the user selects and the most recent point the user has selected. That is, if the points are numbered starting at 1, you first need to keep track of points 1 and 2. When the user picks point 3, you need to look at the line between points 2 and 3. You keep track of each pair of points until the user picks the final point. Then you have to calculate the length of the line between the last point and the first point. Thus, for all lines except the last the destination point of each line is the point the user has picked. This destination point becomes the origin point of the next line. When you reach the last line, the destination point of the last line is the first point picked by the user. The second level of pseudocode reflects these changes:

```
Ask user to pick origin of first line
FOR each line
   BEGIN
      IF this is not last line in polygon
         Ask user to pick destination point
      ELSE
         Set destination point to first point
      Draw line from origin point to destination point

      { Calculate length of perimeter to this point }
      Determine length of current line
      Add length to running total
```

Set origin point to current destination point
END { FOR }

At this point, you can make a list of parameters. You know that the number of points in the polygon is a given: that is, the number of points is defined somewhere else and passed to the procedure. This value will not be changed during the procedure, and thus the number of points should be a value parameter.

The procedure is supposed to communicate information back to its caller. Specifically, the caller needs to know the total perimeter, which can be represented by a real. Since two-way communication is needed, the perimeter has to be a variable parameter.

The code for drawing the polygon and a sample run of the program follows.

Code 6.1 Procedure *DrawPolygon*

```
program PolyDraw;
   var
      totalPerim : real;

{ Procedure DrawPolygon                                              }
{ This procedure draws a polygon using a set of connected lines.     }
{ The user is asked to pick each vertex of the polygon. When the     }
{ user has picked the given number of points, the procedure          }
{ closes the shape.  DrawPolygon also calculates the perimeter       }
{ of the shape by adding the length of each line to the running total. }

procedure DrawPolygon (numPoints : integer;       { num of pts in polygon      }
   var perim : real);                              { perimeter of polygon       }

var
   curPoint,                                       { loop counter               }
   origHoriz, origVert,                            { coords of origin of a line }
   destHoriz, destVert,                            { coords of destination of a line }
   firstHoriz, firstVert : integer;                { coords of pt chosen by user }
   lenLine : real;                                 { length of current line     }

begin
   perim := 0.0;

   Writeln('Please pick first point of polygon');
   repeat
      GetMouse(firstHoriz, firstVert);
   until Button;

{ prepare to draw first line }
   MoveTo(firstHoriz, firstVert);
   origHoriz := firstHoriz;
   origVert := firstVert;
```

Code 6.1 (continued)

```
    for curPoint := 1 to numPoints do
       begin
         if (curPoint < numPoints) then
            begin
               Writeln('Please pick point number', (curPoint + 1) : 3,
                                                   ' on the  polygon');
               repeat        { get next point from user }
                  GetMouse(destHoriz, destVert);
               until Button;
            end { if }
         else
            begin
               destHoriz := firstHoriz; {destination is first point }
               destVert := firstVert
            end; { else }
         LineTo(destHoriz, destVert);
         { calculate  perimeter to this point }
         lenLine := Sqrt(Sqr(destHoriz - origHoriz) + Sqr(destVert - origVert));
         perim := perim + lenLine;

         origHoriz := destHoriz;
         origVert := destVert { destination of one is origin of next }
      end { for }
end; { Draw Polygon }

{ mainline }
begin
   DrawPolygon(6, totalPerim);
   Writeln('perimeter = ', totalPerim : 8 : 2, ' pixels')
end.
```

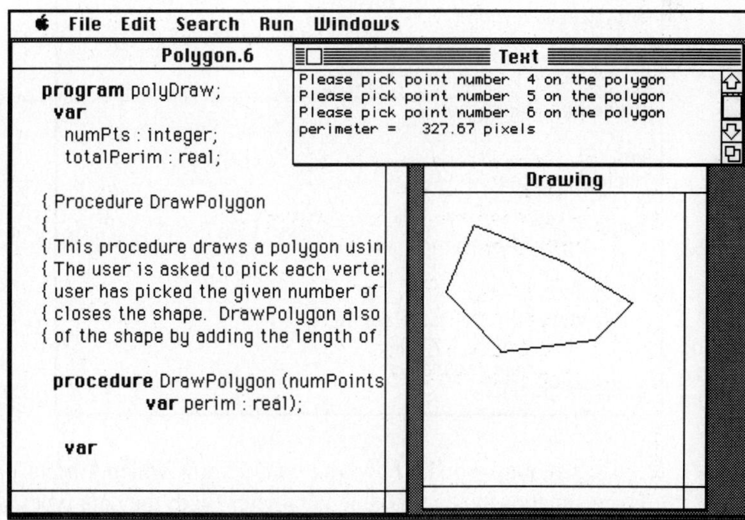

Figure 6.4 Output of *DrawPolygon*

Suppose the call to ***DrawPolygon*** was the following line:

```
DrawPolygon(6, totalPerim);
```

Assume that ***totalPerim*** has been declared a ***real*** in the calling procedure. When ***DrawPolygon*** has completed execution, the value of ***perim*** is passed back to the caller. Therefore, ***totalPerim*** receives the value held in ***perim***. Any value ***totalPerim*** may have had before the procedure call is now overwritten.

In effect, the procedure ***DrawPolygon*** used the variable formal parameter ***perim*** as a different name for the actual parameter ***totalPerim***. You can think of the formal variable parameters as *aliases* for the variables in the calling procedure. When ***DrawPolygon*** assigned a value to ***perim***, it was effectively assigning the same value to ***totalPerim*** in the calling procedure.

If you visualize main memory as a series of boxes, each box holding a value, then think of ***perim*** and ***totalPerim*** as different names for the same box. Since the actual and formal parameters refer to the same place in memory, the use of a variable parameter is known as a *call by reference*. The use of a value parameter is known as a *call by value*.

Figure 6.5 shows the communication link between the formal and the actual parameters, when both variable and value parameters are used.

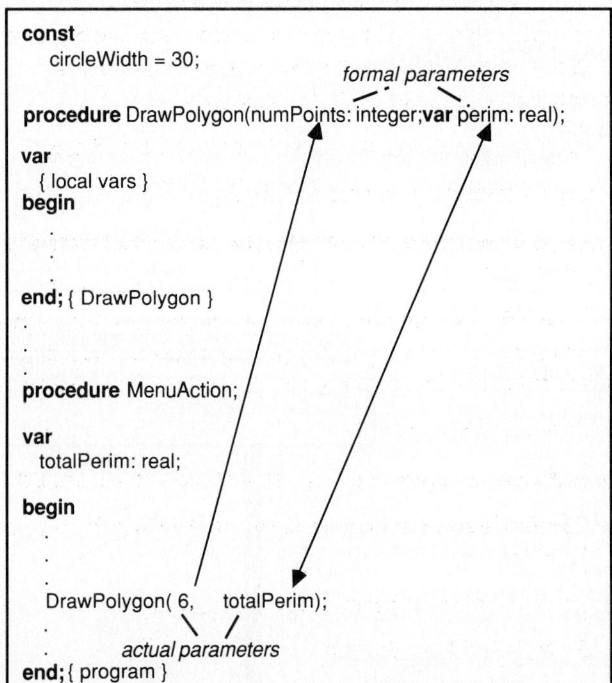

Figure 6.5
One-to-one mapping of value and variable parameters

You may wonder how you would know which kind of parameter to use in any given situation. Use a variable parameter (with the data types we have seen thus far) *only* when the caller needs the new value that the parameter holds. To decide, look at the procedure that receives the parameter and see whether the value of the parameter is changed. If the value is *never* changed, use a value parameter. If the value does change, look at the caller and ask yourself whether the calling procedure needs the new value. If not, you should once again use a value parameter.

Value parameters make it impossible to change accidentally the value of a variable. Variable parameters, on the other hand, provide no such protection, since any change in the variable parameter's value is reflected in the actual parameter's value when the procedure ends. Be careful to use the appropriate kind of parameter. Unless forced to do otherwise, always use value parameters. (In Chapter 11, when we discuss large data structures, we will see an exception to this rule.)

6.3 Parameter Problems

Let's go back to the ***DrawCircle*** procedure with its three value parameters. When you call this procedure from within your program, you must pass it three values. Each of these actual parameters can be a variable, a constant, or an expression that evaluates to the correct type, in this case ***integer***. If the value you pass to a value parameter is a variable, it must be assigned a value before it is sent. In any procedure call, the types of the actual parameters must match the types of the formal parameters. When MacPascal tries to send an ***integer*** to a ***real***, for example, the interpreter produces a bug box with the error message

An incompatibility between types has been found.

Lightspeed's compiler produces the message

Type incompatibility between an actual and formal value/VAR parameter.

There are two other common types of "mismatching" mistakes. The first of these is passing the wrong number of parameters to a procedure. If you include the following statement in your program

```
DrawCircle(30, 40);
```

you will receive a message telling you that too few parameters were passed, such as

Too few parameters have been used in a call to a procedure or function.

Passing too many actual parameters, as in the call

```
DrawCircle(30, 40, 25, 90);
```

results in a corresponding message, such as

Too many parameters have been used in a call to a procedure or function.

The final mismatching error often produces no message but still causes incorrect results. A common error with ***FrameArc*** is to pass the degree mark of the wedge's ending point instead of the size of the wedge. For example, if you have a circle circumscribed by the rectangle (10, 10, 80, 80) and you want to draw a 40-degree angle starting at the bottom of the circle, as in Figure 6.6a, you *should* type the call

```
FrameArc(10, 10, 80, 80, 180, 40);
```

Very often, though, programmers enter the ending degree of the angle instead of the size. The result

```
FrameArc(10, 10, 80, 80, 180, 220);
```

(Figure 6.6b) is quite different from the previous wedge. Always make sure your procedure calls provide the correct information in the correct order.

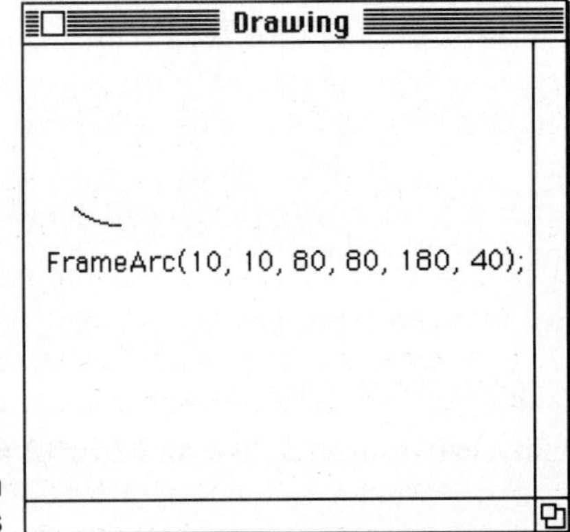

a.

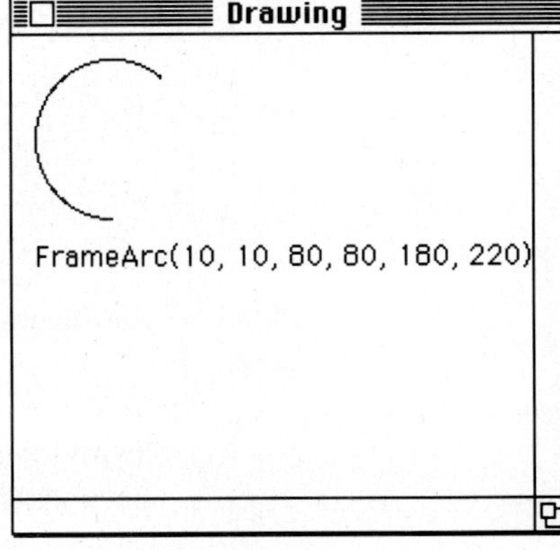

b.

Figure 6.6
Semantic error in sending parameters

When you use variable parameters as well as value parameters, there are two more points to double-check. First, you must check the actual parameters that you are passing. If you pass a constant to a variable parameter, the Pascal translator will respond with a message similar to:

A constant, expression, or invalid packed array element has been passed as an argument to a VAR parameter.

Second, you must check to make sure your parameters are declared correctly, with variable parameters where necessary and value parameters everywhere else. A complete list of all five checkpoints follows.

Checking the five points in Syntax Box 6.5 *before* you type in your code will save a lot of debugging time.

Syntax Box 6.5
Five-point checklist for parameter passing

1. Are there the same number of actual and formal parameters?

2. Does the type of each formal parameter match the declared type of its corresponding actual parameter?

3. Are the values passed as parameters in the correct order?

4. Are only variables passed to variable parameters?

5. Is each parameter of the correct kind? Are there variable parameters whenever a value must be returned to the caller? Are there value parameters everywhere else?

6.4 Functions

The final method of interprocedural communication is through the use of *functions*. Functions are used whenever a set of statements results in a single value. We have discussed functions in previous chapters, for instance, ***Trunc***, ***Round***, and ***PtInRect***. These functions are predefined in MacPascal and QuickDraw, as are many mathematical and trigonometric functions. A list of predefined functions appears in Appendix B.

Functions are similar to procedures. Perhaps the easiest way to think about them is as a special type of procedure. Like other procedures, functions must be declared within the program before they are referenced. (Functions predefined by MacPascal or QuickDraw need not be declared in your program.) Functions can also take parameters. ***Trunc*** and ***Round***, for example, take one parameter each, a ***real***. The body of a function, like any other procedure, has its own declaration section with local variables and constants and a section containing code.

How do functions differ from ordinary procedures? We have said that functions are used when a set of statements results in a single value. This value can be assigned to a variable or used wherever a constant or expression can be used. Now, since a function can return a value, we have to specify the type of value returned by the function; the type of ***PtInRect***, for example, is ***boolean***. Because functions have types, their declaration statements (headings) are different from procedure headings.

As an example, let's write a function to compute the absolute value of the difference between two integers.

```
function AbsDiff(num1,   { first number              }
   num2: integer):       { second number             }
   integer;              { Returns: absolute value of }
                         { the difference             }
```

```
begin
  if (num1 - num2 >= 0) then
    AbsDiff := num1 - num2
  else
    AbsDiff := (num1 - num2) * (-1)
end; { AbsDiff }
```

There are two obvious syntactic differences between the function heading and the procedure heading. First, the word **procedure** is replaced by the word **function**. Second, the parameter list is followed by a colon and a data type. The final data type is the type of the single value returned by the function. In the above example, the function returns an integer.

Notice also that the name of the function appears on the left side of an assignment statement. In the assignment statements we have seen thus far, a variable gets the value of the expression on the right of the := symbol. In this case, the assignment to the function name ***AbsDiff*** is the final result of the statements' calculations.

Look at what happens when you call the function ***AbsDiff***. To call the function and assign the result to a variable, you would type something like this:

```
change := AbsDiff(firstNum, secondNum);
```

where ***change*** is a variable of type ***integer***.

The call to the function must place the name of the function in a position where the returned value can be used appropriately. In other words, the value must either be assigned to a variable (as in the above example) or be passed as a value parameter to a procedure or another function (as in the following two statements):

```
Writeln('The difference between nums 1 and 2 is',
   AbsDiff(firstNum, secondNum));
InvertRect(0, 0, AbsDiff(firstNum, secondNum),
   AbsDiff(firstNum, secondNum));
```

or be part of a more complex expression, such as:

```
totalDistance := AbsDiff(origin, destination)*tripsPerMonth*12;
```

If this seems a little too abstract, think about how you used the function ***PtInRect*** to choose buttons from a menu. When MacPascal encounters the line **if *PtInRect(userPt, stopButton)* then**, it calls the function ***PtInRect*** to determine if the point ***userPt*** is in the rectangular area defined by ***stopButton***. The function returns TRUE or FALSE to the **if-then**, and the flow of control is altered appropriately.

Because functions are similar to procedures, you must make sure that the type, number, and order of parameters in the function call and the function declaration match. The similarity of functions and procedures creates a few new problems as well. For example, suppose the following line was sitting alone in a program:

```
AbsDiff(firstNum, secondNum);
```

Syntax Box 6.6
Function

Purpose To declare the function name and its parameters.

Syntax **function** < name > (< parameter list >) : < type >;
or
function < name > : < type >;

where < name > is any legal procedure name.

< type > is any data type (e.g., ***integer***, ***real***, ***boolean***) and represents the type returned by the function.

< parameter list > is the list of parameters received by the procedure and has the following structure:

< parameter sublist 1 > : < parameter type 1 >;
< parameter sublist 2 > : < parameter type 2 >;
...
< parameter sublist *n* > : < parameter type *n* >

where < parameter sublist 1 >, < parameter sublist 2 >,..., < parameter sublist *n* > are sublists of one or more parameter names (called formal parameters). Individual parameters in each sublist are separated by commas.

< parameter type 1 >, < parameter type 2 >,..., < parameter type *n* > are the corresponding data types of each parameter sublist.

Usage Since functions are used to return a single value, only value parameters are sent to them. *In most cases, if you need to return more than one value, you should be be using a procedure.*

Note that if the function takes no parameters, the parameter list is omitted.

Function calls, unlike procedure calls, are not statements in themselves; they are used in place of any expression of data type < type >.

To return a value, the body of the function must include a statement that assigns the value to the function name:

< function name > := < expression >

where < function name > is the name of the function.

< expression > is any expression that evaluates to the same type as the function.

By convention, this statement is usually the last one in the body of the function.

If ***AbsDiff*** were a procedure, this statement would be fine. However, since ***AbsDiff*** is a function, the returned value has nowhere to go. Thus, MacPascal produces the message

The name "AbsDiff" doesn't make sense here.

and Lightspeed generates the message

"AbsDiff" looks like it's being used as a procedure, but it isn't a procedure name.

You must also remember to assign a type to every function in its declaration. For example, if you used the following line as a function declaration:

```
function AbsDiff(num1, num2 : integer);
```

the interpreter or compiler would tell you that a type specification is required with a message similar to:

A colon(:) is required on this line or above but one has not been found.

Finally, you must be careful to use the name of the function only on the *left* side of an assignment statement within the body of the function declarations. If you mistakenly place the function name on the right side of the assignment statement, it will be interpreted as another call to the function. The function will keep calling itself when it gets to the statement in question, and your program will go into an infinite loop.

To avoid misplacing the function name, many programmers use it only once within the body of the function: at the end when assigning the value to the function. If the function can take on different values within the body, a temporary variable is used to compute these values, and its value is assigned to the function in the last statement of the body. We have rewritten the ***AbsDiff*** function to use this convention. The modified code appears below.

```
function AbsDiff(num1,                    { first number                          }
        num2: integer):                   { second number                         }
        integer;                          { Returns: absolute value of            }
                                          {     the difference                    }

var
        diff : integer;                   { temporary value of absolute diff      }

begin
        diff := num1 - num2;

        if (diff < 0) then
            diff := diff * (-1);          { reverse sign if difference is negative }
        AbsDiff := diff
end; { AbsDiff }
```

The second function body is considered cleaner because the value of the function is assigned only once, and the difference between the two numbers appears once instead of twice. However, when you use a temporary value, you must remember to assign a value to the function at some point. If we had omitted the final line

```
AbsDiff := diff
```

the program would have run, but no value would have been returned from this function. The value we wanted would have been placed in the local variable ***diff***—which disappeared when the function ended.

6.5 Documenting Parameters/Functions

The addition of parameters to programs makes them more complex. Because there are more possible points of confusion, you must include more documentation to clarify them. Parameters are special variables, and therefore require glossaries just like ordinary variables. There are two common places for these glossaries; which of these you use is a matter of style. One place for parameter glossaries is next to the formal parameter declarations; this is the method we have used throughout this book. The second place where the glossary may appear is in the block comment for the procedure below "Called by" and "Calls." This method is often used so that all the information corresponding to a procedure is contained within the block comment. Some people enjoy typing so much that they put the glossaries in both places. You, and the people reading your programs, might find this a bit excessive.

Functions require the addition of yet another piece of information to the block comment: "Returns," which describes what the function returns. You should also include a glossary definition next to the function's type, as we did for the ***AbsDiff*** function. Examples of this type of documentation are in the next section.

6.6 An Extended Example

Let's use the procedures and functions we have written so far in a larger program. This example will produce a graphical layout program, which is used to build pictures from a number of predefined shapes. Many layout programs exist for graphics machines; MacPaint and MacDraw are two such programs that are available on the Macintosh.

In a typical layout program, the screen is divided into two sections. One part contains a menu that lists the options available to the user. The remainder of the screen is the drawing area, where the user can create the shapes. This layout program will allow the user to draw circles, rectangles, and polygons. For the purpose of this example, assume that the user is a rancher who wants to fence off her land. Each shape that she draws represents a length of fence. At the end of the program, the rancher wants to know how much fence to buy.

Since this is a menu-based program, the first level of pseudocode is modeled on the generic menu introduced in Chapter 5.

```
CALL: Draw menu
Set done to FALSE
REPEAT
   Pick menu button
   IF button picked is Rectangle THEN
      CALL: Draw Rectangle
   ELSE IF button picked is Circle THEN
      CALL: Draw Circle
   ELSE IF button picked is Polygon THEN
      CALL: Draw Polygon
   ELSE IF button picked is Stop THEN
      Set done to TRUE
   ELSE
      Tell user that pick was not on menu
UNTIL done = TRUE
Print total perimeter of fences
```

You have seen how to draw a menu. Even though the line of pseudocode "Draw menu" does not translate to a few lines of Pascal, you do not need to refine it further because you can use the previous solution to the problem of drawing menus.

Let's look at how each shape can be drawn. The rectangle is the easiest shape to draw. We can ask the user to pick the upper left and bottom right corners of the rectangle and use ***FrameRect*** to draw the shape's outline. The perimeter of the rectangle is the length of the sides. If we hark back to fifth-grade arithmetic, we can recall that the formula

rectangle perimeter = 2 * *width* + 2 * *length*

calculates the perimeter. The width is found by calculating the difference between the left and right coordinates, the length by finding the difference between the top and bottom coordinates.

It is possible that the user could pick the bottom right corner before picking the top left corner. In that case, subtracting the bottom coordinate from the top coordinate yields a negative number. This will cause an error when the perimeter is calculated; after all, how can the rancher buy a negative amount of fencing? We can use the ***AbsDiff*** function defined in the last section to find the absolute difference between the horizontal and vertical coordinates.

Drawing a circle is only slightly more complicated. Again, the user can pick two points: the center and a point on the circle's border. Using the distance formula, we can calculate the radius of the circle. Once we have the center and the radius, we can call the ***DrawCircle*** procedure from Section 6.1. We also need to know the radius to calculate the circle's circumference. The pseudocode for these two procedures follows:

```
{ Draw Rectangle }
Ask user to pick top left point
```

```
Ask user to pick bottom right point
Draw framed rectangle between top left and bottom right
Calculate perimeter
Add perimeter to total fencing

{ Draw Circle }
Ask user to pick center
Ask user to pick point on circle's border
Use distance formula to calculate radius
Draw circle
Calculate circumference
Add perimeter to total fencing
```

Finally, we need to decide how to draw polygons. We can ask the user to enter the number of points for the polygon, but most layout systems close a polygon when the user picks the original point for a second time. We will adopt this strategy here. Thus, if the user starts the polygon at (50, 50), we will stop when the user picks on or near that point.

Because a pixel is so small, it isn't realistic to expect a user to pick on the precise pixel where she started. We close the polygon when the user picks near the first point. Now what we need to do is define "near." Usually, the user can be within a few pixels in any direction of the original point. The exact number of pixels is known as the *tolerance*. Suppose we decide that the polygon should close if the user picks any point within three pixels of the original point. If the user started at (50, 50), this means that the final point can be anywhere in the rectangle defined by (47, 47) and (53, 53).

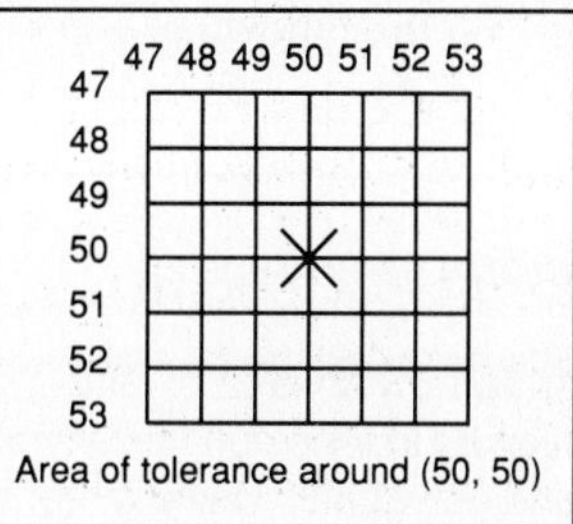

Area of tolerance around (50, 50)

Figure 6.7
Tolerance area

The pseudocode for drawing the polygon follows.

```
Initialize perimeter to 0
Ask user to pick origin of first line

REPEAT
    Ask user to pick destination point
    IF user has picked in tolerance area THEN
        Set destination point to first point
    Draw line from origin point to destination point
```

{ Calculate length of perimeter to this point }
Determine length of current line
Add length to running total of perimeter

Set origin point to current destination point
UNTIL user has picked in tolerance area
Add polygon perimeter to total fencing area

We can use the ***AbsDiff*** function here to determine whether the user's point is in the tolerance area. If the absolute difference between the horizontal coordinates and the vertical coordinates is less than the tolerance, then the user has picked near the first point.

In this program, the mainline can do only three things: call a procedure to draw the menu, call a procedure to draw the shapes, and print the total fencing area. Notice that the only variable parameters are those that need to be sent back to the caller. Also, parameters received by one procedure can be sent as parameters to another procedure.

Finally, parameters in different procedures have the same name, since each parameter is treated as a variable local to that procedure. (This feature is particularly useful when more than one person is working on a program; each person can write procedures and create identifiers without worrying about the identifiers created by others.)

The following program is a little longer than others we have seen thus far, but it is certainly worth your while to hand simulate the code. As you do so, remember that when you are executing a procedure, you can treat parameters as if they were locally declared variables. It is only when you enter and exit the procedure that you need to pass information to and from other procedures.

The complete program appears on the following pages.

Code 6.2
Program ***Fence***

```
{ Program: Fence            D. Niguidula        Sept. 23        }
{                                                               }
{ This program allows a user to show how an area of land        }
{ should be fenced. The user is allowed to fence off three types }
{ of areas: circular, rectangular, and polygonal. Using a menu,  }
{ the user can choose an area to fence or to stop putting up    }
{ fences. When the user chooses stop, the program tells the user }
{ how many feet of fence she will need. (The scale of the dia-  }
{ gram is one pixel per foot.)                                  }

program Fence;

  const
    tolerance = 3;         { space defined to be "near" a pixel    }
```

Code 6.2 (continued)

```
var
    circBtn,              { button for drawing circular areas       }
    rctBtn,               { button for drawing rectangular areas    }
    polyBtn,              { button for drawing polygonal areas      }
    stopBtn : rect;       { button for indicating end of fencing    }
    totalFence : real;    { total amount of fencing needed          }

{ Function AbsDiff                                                  }
{                                                                   }
{ This function calculates the absolute difference between two     }
{ integers.                                                         }
{                                                                   }
{ Called By: GetCirclePts, DrawPolygon, DrawRect                    }

  function AbsDiff (num1,{ first number                             }
      num2 : integer) :  { second number                            }
    integer;             { Returns: absolute value of difference    }

    var
      diff : integer;    { temporary value of absolute diff         }

  begin
    diff := num1 - num2;
    if (diff < 0) then
      diff := diff * (-1);
    AbsDiff := diff
  end; { AbsDiff }

{ Procedure PickPoint                                               }
{                                                                   }
{ This procedure allows the user to choose a point and returns the  }
{ coordinates to the calling procedure.                             }
{                                                                   }
{ Called by: GetCirclePts, DrawRect, DrawPolygon, FenceArea         }
{ Calls : none                                                      }

  procedure PickPoint (var horiz, vert : integer); { coords of user's point }

  begin
    repeat
      GetMouse(horiz, vert)
    until Button
  end; { PickPoint }

{ Procedure DrawCircle                                              }
{                                                                   }
{ This procedure draws a framed circle, given the center point and  }
{ the radius of the circle. The upper left and bottom right corners }
```

Code 6.2
(continued)

```
{ of the rectangle that circumscribes the circle are calculated           }
{ and are sent to a QuickDraw routine.                                    }
{                                                                         }
{ Called by: GetCirclePts        Calls: none                              }

   procedure DrawCircle (centerHoriz : integer;{ center's horiz coord       }
        centerVert : integer;              { center's vert coord           }
        radius : integer);                 { length from ctr to border     }

      var
         top, left,                        { upper left of surrounding rectangle   }
         bottom, right : integer;          { bottom right of surrounding rectangle }

   begin

      top := centerVert - radius;          { calculate vertical borders of rect }
      bottom := centerVert + radius;
      left := centerHoriz - radius;
      right := centerHoriz + radius;       { calculate horiz borders of rect }

      FrameOval(top, left, bottom, right)
   end; { DrawCircle }

{ Procedure GetCirclePts                                                  }
{                                                                         }
{ This procedure asks the user to define a circle by picking two points.  }
{ The user is first asked to pick the center of the circle; then the user }
{ is asked to pick a point on the circle's border. Using these points, the }
{ procedure determines the circle's radius. The center point and radius   }
{ are used to draw the circle and calculate the circumference.   The      }
{ circumference is added to the total amount of fencing.                  }
{                                                                         }
{ Called by: FenceAreas      Calls: DrawCircle, AbsDiff, PickPoint        }

   procedure GetCirclePts (var fencing : real);  { total amt of fencing }

      var
         centerHoriz, centerVert,           { coordinates of circle's center   }
         borderHoriz, borderVert : integer; { coords of pt on circle's border  }
         radius : real;                     { dist from center to border       }
         horizDiff, vertDiff : integer;     { difference between coords        }

   begin
   { Get center point }
      Writeln('Please pick the center point');
      PickPoint(centerHoriz, centerVert);

   { Get point on border }
      Writeln('Please pick the point on the border');
      PickPoint(borderHoriz, borderVert);
```

Code 6.2 (continued)

```
    {Calculate length of radius }
      horizDiff := AbsDiff(centerHoriz, borderHoriz);
      vertDiff := AbsDiff(centerVert, borderVert);
      radius := Sqrt(Sqr(horizDiff) + Sqr(vertDiff));

      DrawCircle(centerHoriz, centerVert, Round(radius));
    { add circumference to total fencing }
      fencing := fencing + (2 * pi * radius)
    end; { GetCirclePts }

  { Procedure DrawRect                                          }
  {                                                             }
  { This procedure draws a rectangle at a location indicated    }
  { by the user. The user chooses the top left and bottom       }
  { right points of the rectangle. The area is framed on the    }
  { screen, and the perimeter is added to the running total.    }
  {                                                             }
  {Called by: FenceAreas  Calls: PickPoint                      }

    procedure DrawRect (var fencing : real);     { total amt of fencing       }

      var
        top, left,                               { upper left of  rectangle   }
        bottom, right : integer;                 { bottom right of rectangle  }

    begin
      Writeln('Please pick the top left corner');
      PickPoint(left, top);

      Writeln('Please pick the bottom right corner');
      PickPoint(right, bottom);

      FrameRect(top, left, bottom, right);

      fencing := fencing + (2 * AbsDiff(top, left) + 2 * AbsDiff(bottom, right))
    end; { DrawRect }
  { Procedure DrawPolygon                                            }
  {                                                                  }
  { This procedure fences a region using a set of connected lines.   }
  { The user is asked to pick each vertex of the polygon. When the   }
  { user has picked a point that is on or near the first point, the  }
  { procedure closes the shape. As the procedure executes, the       }
  { perimeter is calculated.  The total perimeter of the shape is    }
  { then added to the running total.                                 }
  {                                                                  }
  { Called by: FenceAreas           Calls: AbsDiff, PickPoint        }
```

Code 6.2
(continued)

```
procedure DrawPolygon (var fencing : real);
                                        { total amt of fencing              }

    var
        polyPerim : real;               { perimeter of current polygon      }
        origHoriz, origVert,            { coords of origin of a line        }
        destHoriz, destVert,            { coords of destination of a line   }
        firstHoriz, firstVert : integer; { coords of pt chosen by user      }
        polyDone : boolean;             { indicates if user has finished    }
        lenLine : real;                 { length of current line            }

begin
    polyPerim := 0.0;
    polyDone := FALSE;
    Writeln('Please pick first point of polygon');
    PickPoint(firstHoriz, firstVert);

{ prepare to draw first line }
    MoveTo(firstHoriz, firstVert);
    origHoriz := firstHoriz;
    origVert := firstVert;

    repeat
        Writeln('Please pick the next point on the polygon');
        PickPoint(destHoriz, destVert);

        if (AbsDiff(destHoriz, firstHoriz) < tolerance) and
            (AbsDiff(destVert,  firstVert) < tolerance) then
                begin

                    polyDone := TRUE;
                    destHoriz := firstHoriz;
                    destVert := firstVert
                end; { if }

        LineTo(destHoriz, destVert);

    { calculate length of perimeter to this point }
        lenLine := Sqrt(Sqr(destHoriz - origHoriz) + Sqr(destVert - origVert));
        polyPerim := polyPerim + lenLine;

        origHoriz := destHoriz;
        origVert := destVert;  { destination of one is origin of next }

    until polyDone;

    fencing := fencing + polyPerim
end; { Draw Polygon }
```

Code 6.2 (continued)

```
{ Procedure DrawMenu                                                   }
{                                                                      }
{ This procedure draws the menu on the screen. The menu area           }
{ is designed to be small so the drawing area is as                    }
{ large as possible.                                                   }
{                                                                      }
{ Called by: Mainline          Calls: none                             }

  procedure DrawMenu (var circ,            { button for circular areas     }
          rct,                             { button for rectangular areas  }
          poly,                            { button for polygonal areas    }
          stop : rect);                    { button for indicating end     }

  begin

     SetRect(circ, 0, 0, 50, 15);
     SetRect(rct, 50, 0, 100, 15);
     SetRect(poly, 100, 0, 160, 15);
     SetRect(stop, 160, 0, 200, 15);
     FrameRect(circ);
     FrameRect(rct);
     FrameRect(poly);
     FrameRect(stop);

  {Label menu }
     MoveTo(10, 10);
     WriteDraw('Circle');
     MoveTo(65, 10);
     WriteDraw('Rect');
     MoveTo(102, 10);
     WriteDraw('Polygon');
     MoveTo(165, 10);
     WriteDraw('Stop')
  end; { DrawMenu }

{ Procedure FenceAreas                                                 }
{                                                                      }
{ FenceAreas allows the user to pick a button from the menu.           }
{ If the user does not pick on the menu, an error message is           }
{ printed. If the user chooses the stop button, the procedure          }
{ halts execution. If the user chooses a shape button, another         }
{ procedure is invoked to allow the user to fence the appro-           }
{ priate area.                                                         }
{                                                                      }
{ Called by: Mainline                                                  }
{ Calls: DrawCircle, DrawRect, DrawPolygon, PickPoint                  }
```

Code 6.2
(continued)

```
procedure FenceAreas (circFence,       { button for drawing circles          }
      rectFence,                        { button for drawing rectangles       }
      polyFence,                        { button for drawing polygons         }
      stop : rect;                      { button for stopping fences          }
      var fencing : real);              { amount of fencing that is needed    }

   var
      done : boolean;                   { indicates end of drawing            }
      userHoriz, userVert : integer;    { coords of user's point              }
      userPt : point;                   { point chosen by user                }

begin
   fencing := 0.0;                      { initialize amount of area    }
   done := FALSE;

   repeat
      Writeln('Please pick a button on the menu.');
      PickPoint(userHoriz, userVert);
      SetPt(userPt, userHoriz, userVert);

   { invoke action depending on button chosen }
      if PtInRect(userPt, circFence) then
         GetCirclePts(fencing)
      else if PtInRect(userPt, rectFence) then
         DrawRect(fencing)
      else if PtInRect(userPt, polyFence) then
         DrawPolygon(fencing)
      else if PtInRect(userPt, stop) then
         done := TRUE
      else
         Writeln('You did not pick on the menu.');

   until done = TRUE
end; { FenceAreas }


{ Mainline                                                              }
{ The Mainline calls one procedure to draw the menu. The values          }
{ passed back to the Mainline are then sent on to a procedure that       }
{ draws the fences. Finally, the total amount of fencing is printed.     }
{ Called by: System    Calls: DrawMenu, FenceAreas                       }

begin

   DrawMenu(circBtn, rctBtn, polyBtn, stopBtn);
   FenceAreas(circBtn, rctBtn, polyBtn, stopBtn, totalFence);
   Writeln('You have drawn ', totalFence : 8 : 2, ' feet of fence.')

end. { Fence }
```

Figure 6.8 shows a sample run of the ***Fence*** program. We chose to draw, in order, a circle, a rectangle, and a triangle (polygon).

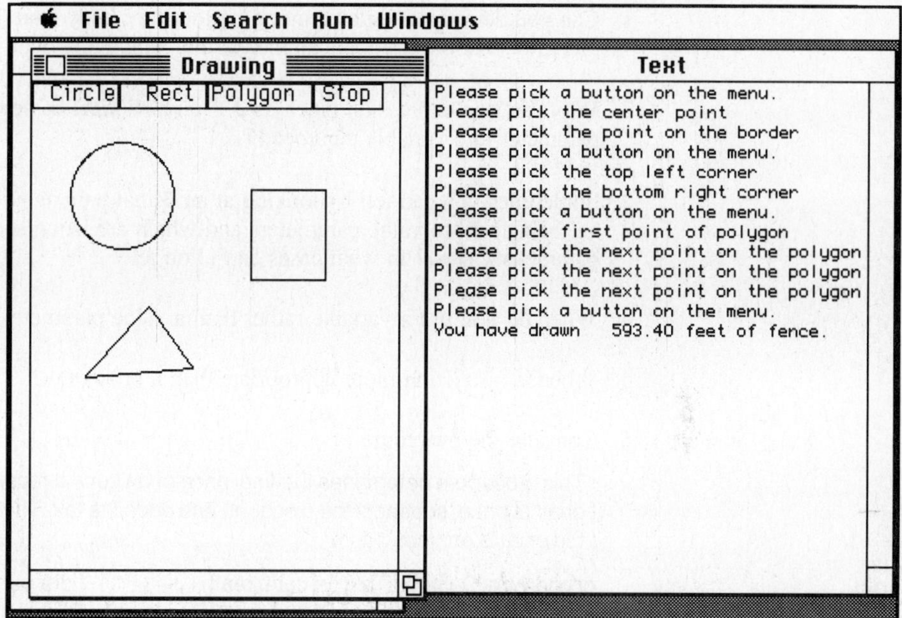

Figure 6.8
Output of program ***Fence***

6.8 Chapter Summary

Value parameters provide a one-way communication link from the calling procedure to the procedure called. Use them when you want to perform the same subtask repeatedly with different information.

var, or variable, parameters allow the called procedure to pass information back as well as receive it. Use them when you want to set a value in a procedure and send it back to the caller.

Take care that the calling routine passes the correct number of parameters (the same number as in the declaration of the called procedure), of the proper type, and in the proper order. Use variable parameters only when the calling procedure needs a value from the procedure called.

Functions are a special kind of procedure. They are used when a set of statements results in a single value. This value is the return value of the function and must be set somewhere within the body of the function. A function's type is the type of the returned value and must be declared in the function heading.

Parameters and functions are special kinds of variables; like all variables, they should have glossary definitions.

Parameters received by one procedure can be passed to another. Also, formal and actual parameters can have the same names.

6.9 Exercises

Understanding Concepts

1. Can you determine, by examining a procedure body from **begin** to **end**, which identifiers are declared as parameters and which are local variables?

2. Why can't an expression (such as ***2 * circleWidth***) be sent as an actual parameter to a variable parameter?

3. Sometimes you can tell by looking at an actual parameter list which parameters are being sent to value parameters and which are being sent to variable parameters. How? In what cases can't you tell?

4. When do you use a variable rather than a value parameter?

5. When is a function more appropriate than a procedure?

6. Consider the procedure

```
{ This procedure determines the final price of an item. It receives the       }
{ original price, subtracts the discount, and adds the tax. The discoun-      }
{ ted price is printed.                                                       }

procedure ComputeTax(percent: real;                { discount on the item      }
   var price: real);                               { original price of the item }

   var
      taxes: real;                                 { tax on an item            }

begin
   price := price - (price * percent / 100);
   Writeln('The sale price is $', price:5:2);
   taxes := 0.06 * price; { add 6% sales tax }
   price := price + taxes
end; { ComputeTax }
```

Given the mainline code

```
   ...
   discount := 10.0;
   price := 35.0;
   ComputeTax(discount, price);
   Writeln('The sale price is ', discount:8:2, '% off the normal price');
   Writeln('With tax, the total price is ', price:5:2);
   ...
```

a. What are the values of ***percent*** and ***price*** at the **begin** of ***ComputeTax***?

b. What are the values of ***percent*** and ***price*** at the **end** of ***ComputeTax***?

c. What are the values of ***discount*** and ***price*** before ***ComputeTax*** is called?

d. What does the code fragment output?

7. In each of the following, identify which are value parameters and which are variable parameters.

a.
```
function Accept(tolerance: real;
                datum: real):
                boolean;
```

b.
```
procedure First( var num1,
                 num2: integer;
                 num3: real);
```

c.
```
procedure Second(var num1 :integer;
                 num2: real;
                 num3: integer);
```

d.
```
procedure Third( num1: integer;
                 var num2: real;
                 var num3: integer);
```

e.
```
procedure Fourth(var num1: real;
                 num2: integer;
                 var num3,
                     num4: integer;
                 num5: real);
```

8. Here is a rewrite of the procedure in exercise 6:

```
procedure SalePrice( );

begin
    percent := percent / 100;
    price := price - (price * percent);
    Writeln('The sale price is $', price:5:2)
end; { SalePrice }

procedure ComputeTax(percent: real;
    var price: real);

begin
    SalePrice( );
    price := 1.06 * price
end; { ComputeTax }
```

Fill in the formal and the actual parameters for ***SalePrice***.

9. Document the following function:

```
function PickPoint: point;

var
    horiz, vert: integer;
    userPoint: point;
```

```
begin
    Writeln('Please choose a point on the screen.');
    repeat
        GetMouse(horiz, vert);
    until Button;
    SetPt(userPoint, horiz, vert);
    PickPoint := userPoint
end; { PickPoint }
```

10. Fill in the parameters in the following program:

```
program Exercise10;

const
    sentinel = 0;          { marks end of input }

var
    total,                 { total of nums entered by user        }
    number,                { current number entered by user       }
    count: integer;        { count of numbers entered thus far    }
    average: real;         { average of the numbers               }

{ The Init procedure initializes the variables used to keep track of    }
{ the average.                                                          }
{ Called by: Mainline  Calls: none                                      }

procedure Init ( );

begin
    count := 0;
    total := 0;
    average := 0.0
end; { Init }

{ The Update procedure begins by incrementing the count of num-         }
{ bers. Then, the new value is added to the running total. Finally,     }
{ the new average is computed and output.                               }
{                                                                       }
{ Called by: Mainline  Calls: none                                      }

procedure Update( );

begin
    count := count + 1;
    total := total + newValue;
    curAverage := total/count;
    Writeln('The new average is ', curAverage:8:2 )
end; { Update }

{ The mainline begins by calling a procedure to initialize the varia-   }
{ bles. Then, the user is prompted to input integer values. As each     }
{ integer is entered, the Update procedure computes and prints          }
{ the average of the numbers entered thus far. The program ends         }
```

```
{ when the user enters the sentinel value.                    }
{ Calls: Init, Update                                         }

begin
   Init(    );

   Write('Enter an integer, or zero to stop: '); { prime pump }
   Readln(number);

 while number <> sentinel do
   begin
      Update(    );

         Write('Enter an integer, or zero to stop: ');
         Readln(number)
      end; { while }

   Writeln('The final average is ', average:8:2)

end.
```

Coding Exercises

1. Write a function called ***Large3*** that is sent three integers and returns the value of the largest. Then write a procedure that accepts the input of five integers and calls ***Large3*** (multiple times if necessary) to find the largest of the five.

2. Write an "exclusive or" (also known as "xor") function. The function should receive two booleans as parameters and should return a boolean. The function should return TRUE if and only if exactly one of the parameters is TRUE.

3. Write a procedure that moves a paddle according to how the user moves the mouse. Start with a rectangular paddle with the corners at (30, 85) and (40, 115). As the user moves the mouse, the paddle should move in the same direction. The procedure should receive the old coordinates of the paddle as parameters. Then it should determine the mouse's current position and reset the paddle so the point selected by the mouse is over the paddle's center. Finally, the paddle's new coordinates should be returned to the caller.

4. The predefined function ***Random*** returns an integer between –32768 and 32767. Write a function called ***RandomRange*** that translates a random number returned from ***Random*** to an integer within a range specified by the parameters of ***RandomRange***. For example, to generate random integers between 1 and 3, ***RandomRange*** should begin by calling ***Random***, and then translate the result so ***RandomRange*** will return any result one-third of the time.

5. Write a program with a mainline and two other procedures. In one procedure, the user should enter the dates of the month when the full moon and the new moon occur. Assume that the visible portion of the moon changes on a constant basis. In the second procedure, ask the user to enter the current date, then show the area of the moon that is visible that day.

6. Write a function that, when given two points, draws a rectangle and returns the area in square pixels.

7. Write a function called ***Collinear*** that receives six integer parameters and returns a boolean. The first four parameters designate a line (they appear in the order < horizontal >, < vertical >, < horizontal >, < vertical >). The fifth and sixth parameters designate, respectively, the horizontal and vertical coordinates of another point. The function should return TRUE if this final point is on the same line designated by the first four parameters. Otherwise, the function should return FALSE.

8. Write a procedure that, when given horizontal and vertical coordinates, draws and labels a point. The position of the label depends on where the point resides in the window. The label should be between the point and the nearest corner of the screen.

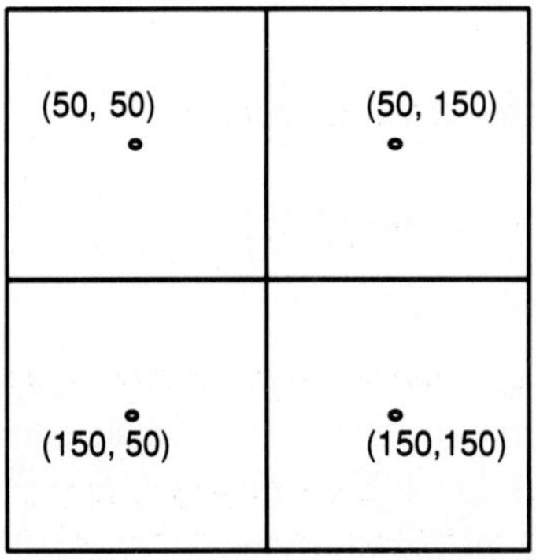

(50, 50)
(50, 150)
(150, 50)
(150,150)

9. Given the following mainline, write the procedures ***DrawMenu***, ***DrawCircle***, and ***FinalMessage***. (***PickPoint*** is defined in "Understanding Concepts," Exercise 9.) Also, document the mainline and its variables as needed.

```
var { mainline variables }
    fillCircle,
    frameCircle,
    stop: rect;
    paintTotal,
    frameTotal: real;
    done: boolean;
    userPt: point;

{Mainline                                                        }
{ The Mainline first calls a procedure to draw the menu buttons  }
{ and then initializes the total areas. Then, the user is asked to }
{ choose a menu button. If the user chooses to draw a framed     }
{ circle or a filled circle, a procedure is called that allows the }
{ user to draw the shape, and calculates the new shape's area.   }
```

```
{ When the user chooses the stop button, a final message is printed      }
{ that tells the user how many pixels were enclosed by painted           }
{ circles and how many by framed circles.                                }

begin
   { Initialize menu and totals }
   DrawMenu(fillCircle, frameCircle, stop);
   paintTotal := 0.0;
   frameTotal := 0.0;
   done := False;
   repeat
      userPt := PickPoint;
      if PtInRect(userPt, fillCircle) then
         DrawCircle(TRUE, paintTotal)
      else if PtInRect(userPt, frameCircle) then
         DrawCircle(FALSE, frameTotal)
      else if PtInRect(userPt, stop) then
         done := TRUE
      else
         Writeln('You missed the menu.')
   until done;

   FinalMessage(frameTotal, paintTotal)
end. { Program }
```

10. Given the following mainline, fill in the procedures ***BillChange*** and ***CoinChange***.

```
{ This procedure asks the user for the amount of the                        }
{ current purchase and determines the change to be returned.                }
{ Two other procedures, BillChange and CoinChange, indicate                 }
{ how the change is to be distributed, respectively, in $20, $10,           }
{ $5, and $1 bills and in 25¢, 10¢, 5¢, and 1¢ coins. These procedures      }
{ also deduct the appropriate number of bills and coins from the            }
{ total in the cash register.                                               }

procedure MakeChange(var numBills,             { total num of bills         }
                         numCoins: integer);   { total num of coins         }

var
    cost,                                      { total cost of item         }
    amtReceived,                               { amount of cash received    }
    change: real;                              { amount to give back        }

begin
    Write('How much is the total purchase?');
    Readln(cost);
    Write('Enter amount received: ');
    Readln(amtReceived);
    change := amtReceived - cost;
    Writeln('Your change is $', change:5:2);
```

```
    { Determine distribution of change }
    BillChange( );
    CoinChange( );

    Write('Your change consists of ', numBills:3, 'bills');
    Writeln('and ', numCoins:3, 'coins')

end; { MakeChange }
```

Programming Problems

1. Imagine that you work for a television station and are in charge of illustrating results on election night. Assume there are three candidates running for one office. As reporters call in, they tell you how many votes a candidate has received in a particular district. Each reporter gives you the name of a candidate and the number of votes. You input this data into your program. The program should then show a bar graph indicating the *total* number of votes for each candidate. The program should end when all of the reporters have called in or when one candidate has reached 100,000 votes.

2. A sociologist has completed a survey of a population and wants to graph the results. The population has been divided into five categories. Write a program that allows the user to enter the percentage that fits into each category (i.e., the prompt should be something like "What percentage said 'No comment'?"). Draw a pie graph where each slice represents one of the five categories. (Your program should contain one procedure or function whose sole purpose is to paint a section of the pie chart.)

3. Write a program that allows a user to specify a circle by choosing three points on its circumference.

4. Write a program to determine which size of floor wax is the best bargain. The user should enter the prices and sizes of each container; a negative number can be used as a sentinel. The program should determine which size container has the best price per ounce.

5. Write a program that charts the three television networks' ratings for a season. A rating of 25.7 means that 25.7% of the televisions in an area were tuned to a particular program. For each week in the 13-week season, input the ratings for each network. Then chart the progress of the networks during the season on a line graph:

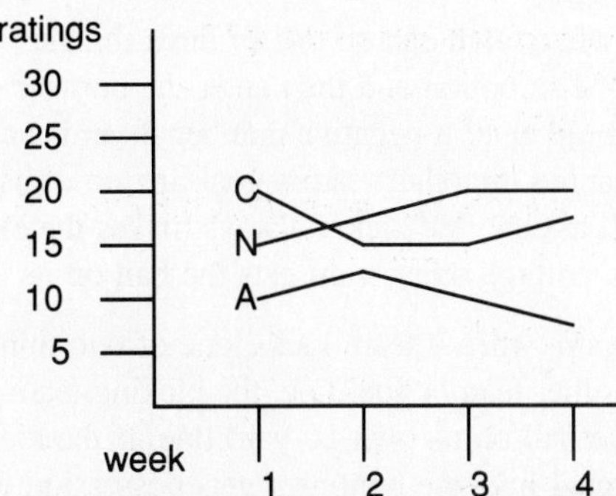

6. Modify the music layout program (Chapter 5, programming problem 1) so that the user can enter an indefinite number of measures. As a further modification, allow the user to enter changes in the number of beats per measure.

7. Write a program that allows an elementary school student to check her multiplication skills. The program should provide the user with ten multiplication problems, one at a time. Both factors should be between 0 and 12 (you can use the ***RandomRange*** function from coding exercise 4). The user should get three chances to answer each question. At the end of the quiz, the user should be told how many questions she got right on the first try, on the second, and on the third. Keep in mind that this program would probably be used by third- and fourth-graders.

8. Write a program that keeps track of the line of scrimmage and possession in a football game. A football field is 100 yards long, as diagrammed below:

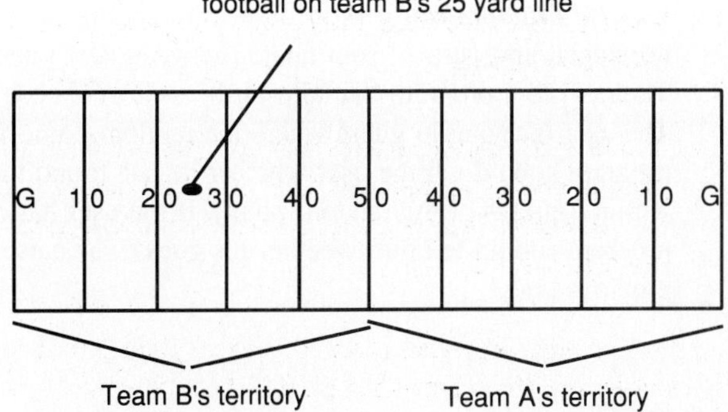

The game begins with one team possessing the ball on its own 20-yard line. Using passes and rushes, the team with the ball has four plays (known as downs) to gain 10 yards. If the team does not gain 10 yards in four plays, the ball changes hands.

On each down, a team can do one of three things: pass, rush, or kick. The user should choose an option and then enter the number of yards gained on the play (the user should enter a negative number if yards are lost on the play).
If a team reaches the other team's goal line on a rush or a pass, the team scores 7 points (we'll assume the kicker always makes the extra point after the touchdown), and the other team gets the ball on its own 20-yard line.

In this program, when a team kicks, one of two things can happen. If the kick reaches the other team's goal line, the kicking team gets 3 points, and the other team gets the ball on its own 20-yard line. If the kick doesn't reach the opponent's goal line, the opponent gets possession wherever the kick is retrieved.

Your program should indicate, after each down, who has the ball, where the next play will begin, and whether the next play is the 1st, 2nd, 3rd, or 4th down. When necessary, the score should also be updated.

9. Modify the ***Fence*** program in Section 6.6 by allowing several users to fence areas. Each user's area should be denoted by a different color (i.e., pen pattern) on the screen.

10. Write a program that balances a checkbook. First, the user should be asked to enter an initial balance. Then, the user can choose from three menu items: write a check, make a deposit, or stop. If the user makes a financial transaction, ask the user for the amount of the check or deposit. After each transaction, the program should print the current balance. When the user picks stop, the program should output the totals of the deposits and the checks along with the final balance.

11. Use the ***RandomRange*** procedure from coding exercise 4 to assign a random horizontal and vertical coordinate [between (0, 0) and (200, 200)] to a point. Then, write a program that allows the user to choose points with the mouse. The user is trying to guess where the random point resides. With each guess, the program should tell the user whether he has found the point (i.e., picked a point within 2 pixels of the random point). If the user has not found the point, the program should tell him whether his guess was closer or farther than his previous guess.

7

Program Development

At this point, you have encountered all of Pascal's flow-of-control structures. With these decision-making and repetition constructs, you can write powerful programs. Powerful programs, of course, are more difficult to design and fix than simple programs. In Chapter 1, we gave a basic introduction to pseudocode. Now that you can write much more complex programs, we can discuss some strategies for writing pseudocode for such programs and give some general advice on debugging techniques. Our discussion will range from a general overview of problem solving (which is applicable to many disciplines beyond computer programming) to specific facilities available only with MacPascal and Lightspeed.

Pseudocoding and debugging are usually best learned by practice, not theory. The examples throughout this book represent our standard form of pseudocoding and debugging. We are deliberately avoiding giving you a precise method and syntax for pseudocode because there is no definitive way of creating a program. Just as every student outlines a paper differently, every student will pseudocode a program differently. Besides, we cannot reduce problem solving to a foolproof recipe that will work for all situations. In this chapter, we will give some hints on how to break down a programming problem from English to Pascal and how to get that final Pascal code to work. You will learn more about pseudocode, however, when you use it than when you read about it.

Although we cannot provide a definitive method for solving problems, we can discuss techniques that many programmers use. The process of breaking down a problem is not merely an academic exercise; even the most experienced programmers must decompose a problem step by step. There is no task more impossible than trying to debug some unstructured, stream-of-consciousness code; breaking down the problem on paper is an up-front investment in time and energy that saves many hours of debugging later. This chapter provides you with a frame of reference for solving programming problems. We encourage you to try our technique of program development at least once; you can then alter it or decide to use some other strategy.

The best way to discuss program development is through illustration. We will show how a particular program is developed and what thought processes are involved. Throughout this chapter, we will refer to that example, bringing the problem from English to various levels of pseudocode, translating the final version of pseudocode to Pascal, and debugging the Pascal code. **Thus, the program that you will see will contain bugs until the very end.** At times you may say to yourself, "That bug is so obvious! How did they miss that?" All the problems we illustrate are typical of what happens in the development stages of programming. Besides looking at the actual changes made to the code, you should keep track of the *strategies* used to debug the pseudocode and the code.

In Chapter 1, we briefly discussed the steps in developing a program by the method of top-down design. These steps bear repeating and are shown again in Figure 7.1. First, the problem is stated in English. Then, the first level of pseudocode is created by listing the various tasks involved in solving the problem. Hand simulation catches and corrects any errors made in the algorithm. Note that debugging takes place at all levels of pseudocode; the sooner an error is caught, the less time that will be spent debugging Pascal. After each level of pseudocode has been hand simulated, the method of *stepwise refinement* provides more details. When we believe the

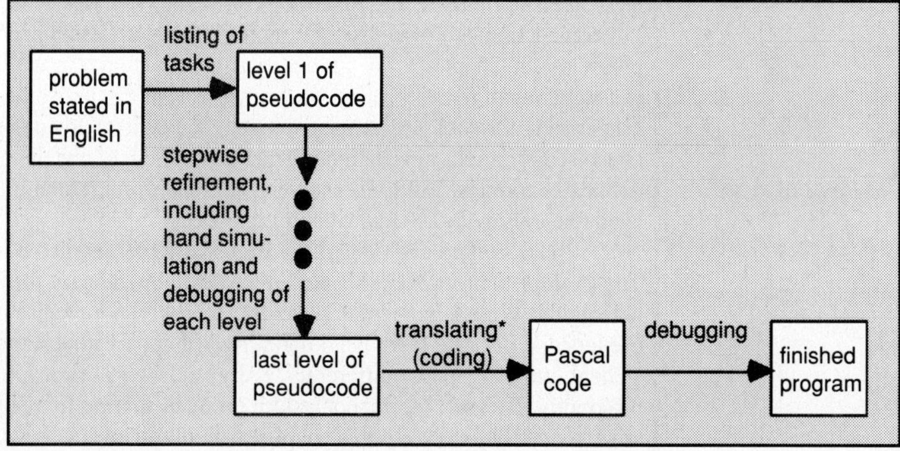

Figure 7.1 Steps in developing a program

* In this context, "translating" refers to your translating pseudocode to code; the translator in Chapter 1 referred to the MacPascal interpreter or Lightspeed compiler.

current level of pseudocode is correct, and has been refined to the point where each line of pseudocode translates easily to a few lines of Pascal, we code the entire program in Pascal. From there, we debug the code to create a finished program.

7.1 Getting Started

To begin a program, you need to define the problem you want to solve. Begin at the simplest level, such as "I want a program to write form letters to 25 people" or "I need a program that analyzes data from a student survey." A one- (or maybe two-) sentence description can be seen as the first list of tasks, and thus the first level of pseudocode.

From that starting point, gather all the relevant information about the problem. Some of the questions you may want to ask are: What information will the program have at the start? What information will be made available during the program's execution? Are there any special cases? How will the user interact with the program? What output should the program produce? Collecting this information about the problem is a skill you have probably acquired from researching term papers or preparing laboratory experiments. You need to understand *what* you want to accomplish before you tackle the problem of *how* to accomplish it.

After you have gathered most of the details about the problem, you can begin the process of stepwise refinement. The pseudocode begins with the one-sentence definition of the problem. You can then take the pieces of information you have collected and sort them into the order you would use in solving the problem by hand. In other words, before you can tell the computer how to solve a problem, you have to decide how you would solve it manually.

Let's begin our example by stating the problem: we want to create an online calculator. The calculator will perform four functions—addition, subtraction, multiplication, and division—and will perform all operations on integers. However, instead of pressing buttons as on a hand calculator, the user will click the mouse button.

The calculator contains a small keypad with a set of eighteen square buttons, as shown in Figure 7.2. To use a calculator, you press the buttons, and the result appears in an area known as the display. The display shows either the number you are currently entering or the result of an operation.

A calculator deals with arithmetic expressions. Each number in an expression is called an entry; the entries are separated by one of the four operators. The process of connecting more than one operator in an expression is called *chaining*. When operations are chained together, the result of one operation is used as the first entry of the next. This means that the calculator needs to maintain a running total, which is shown in the display after each operation is performed.

Let's look at an example of chaining. Suppose the user wants to find the answer to 4 + 7 – 16 * 3. First the user enters the entry 4, the operator +, and the entry 7. When the calculator knows that the entry is finished (something we'll have to figure out later), the calculator displays the running total of 11. This total (11) is used as the first entry of the next operation; thus, the next part of the expression

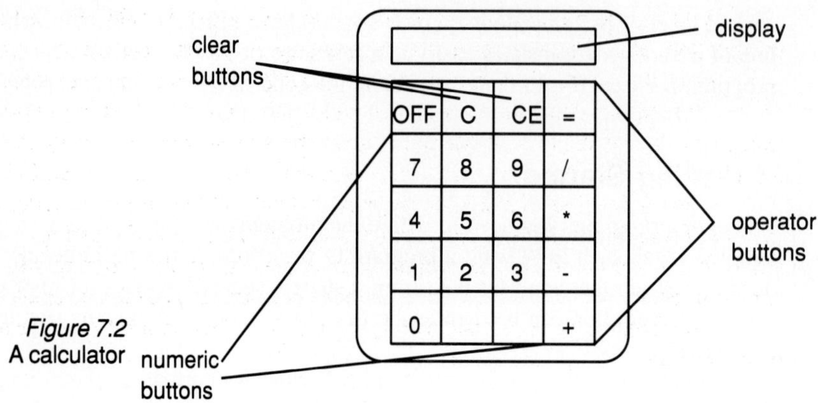

Figure 7.2
A calculator

evaluates to 11 – 16, or –5. This result is then used as the entry in the last operation. Multiplying –5 by 3 yields the product –15 as the final result.

The calculator's eighteen buttons are allocated as follows. Ten buttons represent the digits 0 through 9. These buttons are the numeric buttons.The five buttons in the right column are the operator buttons; the +, –, *, / buttons indicate the operations of addition, subtraction, multiplication, and division; the equals sign is used to end an expression. Pressing this last operator button simply means that the current running total should be shown, including the result of the last operation. The OFF button indicates that the user is finished with the calculator.

The two buttons in the center of the top row of the calculator's keypad are marked "C" and "CE." These buttons are used for clearing, or setting something to 0. The "C" button is the clear button. This resets the entire expression and sets the running total to 0; thus, a 0 should appear on the display. The CE button is the "clear entry" button. This button also places a 0 on the display but does not clear the running total. The CE button is used when the user enters an entry incorrectly. For example, if you press the buttons in the order shown in Figure 7.3,

Figure 7.3
Using the Clear button

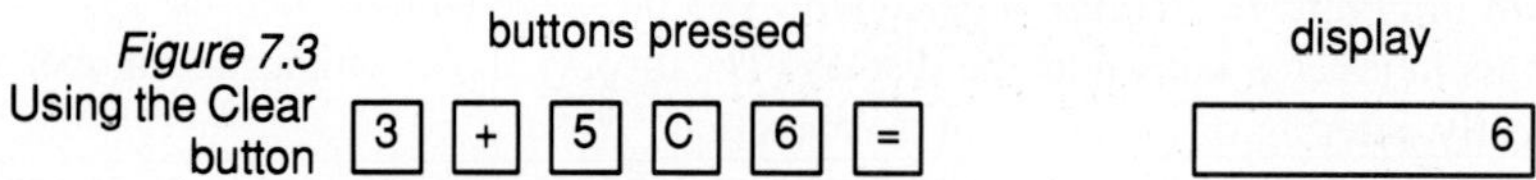

the first three button presses are wiped out, and pressing the equals sign shows a running total of 6. If, however, you press CE instead of C, as shown in Figure 7.4,

Figure 7.4
Using the Clear Entry button

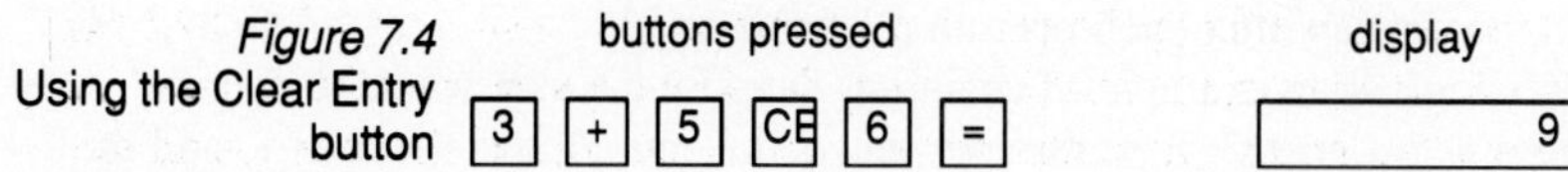

you get the result of 9. When the CE button is pressed, the entry 5 is erased, but the running total (3) remains. Thus, the calculator yields the result of 3 + 6.

With this description, we have enough to get started. Should we need more information later, we can refer to any program specifications that we may have. For purposes of this academic exercise, the only specifications that exist are those in this chapter. In real life, though, we would spend much more time creating *requirements specifications*. Teams of analysts and programmers usually create a very specific design and are sure that the goals of the program are clearly stated in sufficient detail.

We will develop a calculator program that fills all the minimum requirements (i.e., performs four arithmetic functions and allows chaining and clearing). Furthermore, we will make the program *extendible*, that is, the program will be simple to change, so we can add more buttons and functions to the calculator later. Before we actually write the calculator program, let's look in a bit more detail at the process of developing pseudocode.

7.2 Pseudocode Development

After you have made a complete outline of the problem at hand, you can begin the process of stepwise refinement. First, create a list of the tasks involved in the program. From there, you can create the first full level of pseudocode by listing the tasks and subtasks in order. The order should reflect the method you would use to solve the problem by hand.

When the first full level of pseudocode has been completed, examine it to see if any sections can be regrouped. For example, if a subtask is performed in more than one place, you may want to create a separate procedure or put the subtask in a loop. The best way of finding where your pseudocode can be consolidated or simplified is by hand simulating. As you naively step through each level of pseudocode, you should not only check that your algorithm solves the problem, but you should also notice if your algorithm is repeating or backtracking on itself. Let's look at an example of repetitive pseudocode.

```
IF home score = visitor score THEN
    Print a message noting that there was a tie
ELSE
    Print the names of all players on winning team
IF home score <> visitor score THEN
    BEGIN
        Add one win to winning team's total wins
        Add one loss to losing team's total losses
    END
```

When we hand simulate, we notice that the line "Print the names of all players on winning team" is performed only when "home score = visitor score" is FALSE. In other words, the program should print out the winning team members' names only when the home score does not equal the visitors' score. This is the same condition represented by "home score <> visitor score." Since both actions (the printing of the winning team members and the adding) are done when the game is not a tie, we can combine the two sections:

```
IF home score = visitor score THEN
    Print a message noting that there was a tie
ELSE
    BEGIN
        Print the names of all players on winning team
        Add one win to winning team's total wins
        Add one loss to losing team's total losses
    END
```

Fewer lines in the pseudocode means fewer lines in the Pascal code, thus fewer chances for bugs in the program. Shorter programs are usually more efficient programs.

When the hand simulation shows that your algorithm is correct at this level of specificity, you are ready to proceed to the next level of pseudocode. Bringing a problem from English to Pascal can be summarized this way: write a level of pseudocode, hand simulate for corrections, regroup the pseudocode if necessary, and go to the next level of pseudocode. When each line of pseudocode can be translated easily into a few lines of Pascal, your pseudocoding is complete.

We can show the process of pseudocoding in pseudocode form:

```
REPEAT
    Write the next level of pseudocode
    Hand simulate this pseudocode
    WHILE pseudocode does not solve problem OR is repetitive DO
        BEGIN
            Rewrite/regroup current level of pseudocode
            Hand simulate new version of pseudocode
        END { WHILE }
UNTIL each pseudocode line translates easily to a few lines of Pascal
```

7.3 Specific Items in Pseudocode

Compared to English, the language of Pascal is limited and follows strict rules. For example, the word **for** has only one meaning in Pascal and makes sense in only one context. In English, words have many meanings, and context can change those meanings. Thus, we cannot compile a list of the "legal" statements in pseudocode. We can, however, categorize the types of statements that pseudocode can contain. We will spend more time discussing how to incorporate procedures into pseudocode in the next section. Now, though, let's look at three items that help bring a problem from English to Pascal.

Flow-of-control constructs. In Chapters 4 and 5, we looked at the different forms of flow of control. Since most algorithms depend on having the correct parts of the code executed at the correct time, flow-of-control constructs are essential in pseudocode. Even though pseudocode is usually more English than Pascal, the reserved words IF, THEN, ELSE, CASE, OTHERWISE, FOR, DO, REPEAT, UNTIL, and WHILE (and also, as we saw in Chapter 1, BEGIN and END) are helpful in organizing pseudocode.

You should not concentrate on the exact syntax of the construct. You can write "IF datum is a legal value THEN" in your pseudocode without worrying (for the moment) about *how* you are going to determine if the datum is legal.

Placing flow-of-control structures into your pseudocode also gives you an opportunity to determine whether a particular branching or looping statement is appropriate. This is the time to ask yourself questions such as "I know I need to repeat this section — how do I know when I should stop repeating it?" or "Have I taken all possible conditions into consideration?" These questions will help you decide whether to use an indefinite or a definite loop, or an **if-then-else if** rather than a **case**.

User interface. The user interface of a program is what the user actually sees when the program is run and includes prompts, menus, and output. When you write any program, remember that you are not necessarily writing the program for yourself. You must tell a user who doesn't know what Pascal code looks like how to use the program, and you need to display results in an understandable format.

Consider what the user will need to use your program. Your prompts should tell the user what to do next; your output should present information so that the user can understand it. Chapter 10 will discuss user interface considerations at length.

Error conditions and special cases. Since your program is written for anyone to use, assume that the user is going to make mistkaes... er, mistakes. How will your program handle these errors? Chapter 4 mentioned error conditions. When the user was supposed to pick from a menu, we anticipated that she might pick somewhere that wasn't on the menu. By adding a check (in this case, a final **else** to the **if** ***PtInRect***... sequence), we handled the error so that the user would know what had happened.

Special cases are usually exceptions to the "typical" part of an algorithm. Consider an algorithm that determines the day of the week a person's birthday falls on. The same algorithm could be used for any date of the year except February 29. Since this extra day does not occur every year, an adjustment to the algorithm has to be made, say, printing the day for March 1 in non-leap years. The possibility of a February 29 birthdate is a special case; you need to determine whether to handle it differently from the normal cases.

When you are writing your pseudocode, think about the error conditions and the special cases. Often it is easier to think about the "typical" cases first and then see if the algorithm has to be modified for the special cases and error conditions. Usually it is better to have an algorithm that works for *all* cases; that is, no special cases exist. Still, you need to think of those possibilities that lurk in the darkness, just waiting to make your program bomb. Don't be afraid to be a paranoid programmer — paranoia pays.*

---

* As the saying goes, "Paranoia is merely a healthy understanding of the nature of the universe."

7.4 Specifying Procedures

One of the most important aspects of structured programming is the proper use of procedures. Programmers need a feeling for when it is appropriate to create a procedure and how to specify a procedure in pseudocode.

Procedures are usually developed in pseudocode simply by expanding some subtask into smaller parts. A single subtask in the third level of pseudocode may expand to eight sub-subtasks in the fourth level. Still, there is a single task statement in the third level that explains the entire group of subtasks in the fourth level. This suggests that the stuff in the fourth level can stand alone as a single logical unit and can thus be translated to a procedure or function.

Some programmers develop procedures in pseudocode by using lots of paper. When they complete one level of pseudocode, they write each statement in the algorithm at the top of a separate piece of paper. Then they develop the subtasks of the task listed at the top of each page. For example, a statement at the top of one page may say "print three numbers in sorted order," and the remainder of the page contains some algorithm for printing the numbers in sorted order. With this system, the programmer can concentrate on one subtask at a time.

Three things should be implicit in the pseudocode for each procedure. First, you identify the procedure's *effect*. This is usually the subtask being broken down; for example, an effect can be given as "prints three numbers in sorted order." Next, you specify what the procedure *requires*. The sorting procedure needs three numbers to perform the sort. You should be able to list the information that the procedure needs from the rest of the program before it can begin its task. Finally, you need to recognize what the procedure will *return*. When the procedure has completed its task, you need to know what changes the calling routine will expect. Thus, the rest of the program should be able to look at each procedure as a "black box." The calling routine sends some input to the box; something happens inside the box; finally, the black box produces a result or change in the input. The black box for a procedure that, given two points, draws a line and determines the length of that line, is illustrated in Figure 7.5.

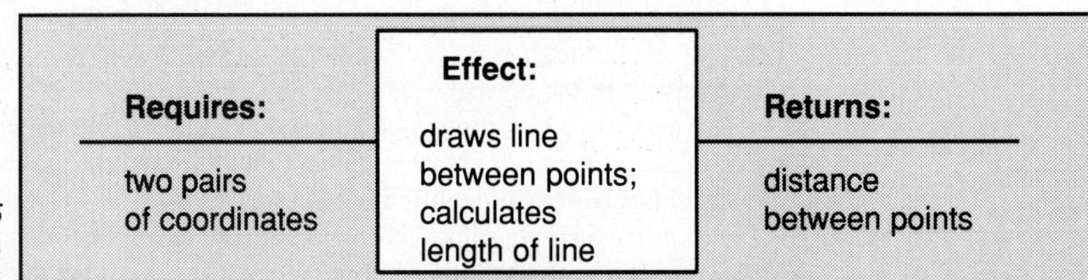

Figure 7.5 The procedure as black box

One way of measuring a procedure's power is the range of the problems it can solve: a more powerful procedure can be used in a larger number of situations. In writing pseudocode, look for situations in which two (or more) similar—if not identical—tasks are being performed, and then try to create a procedure that can execute both tasks. Let's pick up the Ice Cream program in Chapter 2 at the point where the pseudocode is as follows (from p. 61):

```
{ Draw and label chocolate bar }
Move 1/3 distance right along horizontal axis
Write label 'chocolate' below line
Use percentage to calculate upper endpoint
Draw bar
Write percentage above bar

{ Draw and label vanilla bar }
Move another 1/3 distance right along horizontal axis
Write label 'vanilla' below line
Use percentage to calculate upper endpoint
Draw bar
Write percentage above bar
```

In this refinement, the chocolate and vanilla bars are drawn in separate procedures, yet the algorithms are nearly identical. The placement of the bar on the graph is slightly different, but that information can be specified with parameters. The pseudocode can be modified as follows:

```
{ Given distance, draw chocolate or vanilla bar }
Move specified distance along horizontal axis
IF distance is 1/3 along axis THEN
   Write label 'chocolate' below line
ELSE
   Write label 'vanilla' below line
Use percentage to calculate upper endpoint
Draw bar
Write percentage above bar
```

(Chapter 8 will discuss how to send strings, such as the labels "chocolate" and "vanilla," as parameters.)

The advantages of broad-purpose procedures are that they can be incorporated more easily into other programs and they allow easier expansion of the original program. Thus, to change the Ice Cream program so that it draws a graph for 31 flavors instead of just 2, more calls are made to this procedure.

7.5 Pseudocoding the Calculator

This section will show how we pseudocoded the calculator problem. It may seem a bit tedious to follow such a long and detailed example, but stick with it — we'll show lots of useful design and debugging techniques as we do our stepwise refinement. Before you read this section, though, **break down the problem**

yourself. Don't say, "Oh, that's obvious; anyone can see that the book's method is the best breakdown to use." While it may be the best breakdown for us, that does not mean it's the way you would do it. Reading this passage is similar to reading about bicycle riding: you can get the general idea, but to really learn how to ride, you need to try it yourself.

Problem solving is more complex than riding a bicycle. While there is basically only one way to get a bicycle to move, there is no unique way to solve a problem.

We cannot stress this point enough.

Individual programmers will have any number of different ingredients in their pseudocodes. The exact algorithms, the level of refinement in each version, the syntax of the pseudocode, the number of levels of refinement (which will probably translate to the number of procedures and functions), and particularly the technique of pseudocoding — all these will vary for each programmer. What is constant is the object of pseudocoding: translating a problem from English to Pascal. Each complete level of pseudocode should provide a solution to the original problem, even if that solution needs more refinement.

We do not want you blindly to *accept* our method of designing programs; we want you to *understand* our method and then decide what parts of our methodology you can use in your own work. As you read this section, note the differences between your problem breakdown strategies and the particular top-down design described here. By comparing your notes to ours, you can determine which aspects of our method to incorporate into your own strategy. Through understanding our approach to programming, you may gain a better understanding of your own methods of solving problems.

Level 1: Refinement

Back to the calculator. From the outline of tasks described earlier in the chapter, we can create a level of pseudocode as follows:

```
Draw calculator
User selects calculator buttons
Respond to user's selections
```

This pseudocode does not contain even as much detail as the short description of the calculator program given earlier. We deal with generalities first because it is easy to get too caught up in specifics. If we progress too rapidly through the pseudocode, we are likely to implement a piece of Pascal code that may solve one aspect of the problem but is not useful when the rest of the problem is solved.

Level 2: Refinement

The above pseudocode also gives a framework into which we can fill the other specific things we know about the calculator. The line "User selects calculator buttons" can be modified simply by referring to the specifications. The buttons can be divided into five categories: the numeric buttons, the operator buttons (+, –, *, /, =), the C button, the CE button, and the OFF button. Let's consider how the program should "respond to user's selections" in each of these cases.

When a numeric button is pressed, the number appears on the far right of the display. If other numbers are entered in the current entry, previous numbers move to the left.

When an operator button is pressed, the calculator displays the current running total. An operator also signals the ending of one entry and the beginning of the next.

When either C or CE is pressed, the display shows 0. In the case of the CE button, that is all that happens. When the C is pressed, though, the running total is reset to 0 as well.

We can also consider the error condition occurring when the user presses no button whatsoever. When a user misses a button on a real calculator, nothing happens; this calculator also will not output anything if the user misses the calculator.

Finally, when the user presses the OFF button, the program should exit. With this information, we can refine the pseudocode into this first really substantive level:

```
Draw calculator
Set done to FALSE
REPEAT
    IF user presses numeric button THEN
        Show number on display
    ELSE IF user presses operator button THEN
        BEGIN
            Calculate new running total
            Show new total on display
        END { operator button }
    ELSE IF user presses C button THEN
        BEGIN
            Show 0 on display
            Set running total to 0
        END { C button }
    ELSE IF user presses CE button THEN
        Show 0 on display
    ELSE IF user presses OFF button THEN
        Set done to TRUE
    ELSE
        User has not pressed a button
UNTIL done
```

The transformation from a list of tasks to this current level of pseudocode appears to be a large leap: suddenly, the pseudocode has flow-of-control constructs and boolean conditions. On closer inspection, however, you can see that the pseudocode is no more than a specific application of the generic menu discussed in Chapter 5. You can often bring problems closer to a solution by reapplying the answers of other problems. If you are pseudocoding and notice that a series of tasks looks like a problem you have already solved, it is probably worthwhile to look at the old solution and see if it can be adapted to the current situation.

Level 2: Hand Simulation

At this point, we should hand simulate the pseudocode. Since we are still in the early stages of the program, we need to deal with it on a general level. We are "executing" the pseudocode in a manner similar to the way MacPascal interprets or Lightspeed compiles code, except that we are "executing" lines of high-level pseudocode rather than Pascal.

All we are doing when we hand simulate pseudocode is testing the current status of the algorithm. If the current level of pseudocode solves the problem, we begin the next level of refinement; if not, we fix the current list of tasks and check this level again. In the current level of the Calculator program, we are keeping track of what is on the display, what is in the running total, and what happens when any button is pressed. We do not, for the moment, concern ourselves with any lower-level details such as how the number is displayed or how to determine which button was pressed. All we are doing now is checking that the individual tasks in the algorithm, when combined, produce the desired result.

The first line says "Draw calculator." Details such as the exact size and position of the buttons have not been determined yet, so we assume that the calculator's layout looks like Figure 7.2. Should this positioning be a problem, we can always change it later.

Next, we examine the possible inputs from the keypad. Have we covered all the buttons in the IF-THEN-ELSE IF construct? We consider what happens when specific buttons are pressed. For example, when a 5 is pressed, the pseudocode says to display it on the screen. We check each category of keys similarly. Since the current pseudocode correctly solves the stated problem, we begin the next level of refinement.

Level 3: Refinement

To begin the third refinement, we break down the line "Draw calculator." We list the three parts of the calculator as follows:

```
{ Draw calculator }
Draw outer round rectangle
Draw display
Draw buttons
```

Next, we enter the loop and consider all the possible inputs from the calculator's buttons. Let's start with the numeric input. When the user enters a number, the hand simulation says that we should "show number on display." However, that is not all we have to do. We also need to keep track of the number in some variable. (A common mistake in interactive program development is to concentrate so much on the output and user interface — the *front end* of the software — that we neglect the internal representation of data — the *back end.*)

The solution seems simple enough: create an integer variable to hold the current entry. But that doesn't solve all the problems. When the user wants more than one digit in an entry, we need to do two things. First, we need to change the entry variable. "Moving the digits to the left" can be accomplished internally by multiplying the current entry by 10. Then we can add the new number. For example, if the current entry is 37, and the user presses the 8 button, we can multiply 37 by 10 and add 8 to get the new entry of 378. Once this new entry has been calculated, we can erase the old display and show the new entry. Tentatively, this development can be reflected by replacing the line "Show number on display" with the following pseudocode:

```
{ IF user presses numeric button THEN }
   BEGIN
      Multiply current entry by 10
      Add new digit to current entry
      Print current entry in display
   END { numeric button }
```

From here, we can refine the next line from level 2. The next step is to examine what happens when the user presses an operator button. According to the pseudocode, we should "calculate new running total" and "show new total on display."

We calculate the new running total by adding, subtracting, multiplying, or dividing the old running total and the current entry. Thus, to calculate the new running total, we have to know the old running total, the current entry, and *the most recent operator*. This means that when an operator button is pressed, we need to store it for later use.

The operator button also separates the numeric entries in an expression. By pressing an operator button, the user indicates that one entry is completed and the next is about to begin. We can signal this in the pseudocode by setting the current entry back to 0.

We can now refine the pseudocode for this section as follows:

```
{ ELSE IF user presses operator button THEN }
    BEGIN
       Calculate new running total using current entry, old
           total, and last operator
       Show new total on display
       Store current operator for later use
       Set current entry to 0
    END { operator button }
```

To check the refinement, let's make sure this algorithm works for all cases. We'll assume that the pseudocode for accepting entries works correctly. Let's say that we want to test the expression 7 + 12 * 5. The user makes the first entry (7), followed by the addition button. The pseudocode says to calculate a new running total using current entry, old total, and last operator. The current entry is 7, but neither the old total nor the last operator has a value. Since 7 is the first entry, we want the display to show a 7. In general, the first entry should remain on the screen and become the new running total. One way to solve this problem is to set the initial old total to 0 and the initial operator to addition. This way, the algorithm will always be able to perform some calculation, even when the user has made only one entry.* To correct the pseudocode, we need to set the initial operator and total before entering numbers in an expression. The initialization should take place before any buttons are pressed, so we place the lines "Set initial operator to +" and "Set running total to 0" before the REPEAT.

Now that the new running total (7) has been calculated and displayed, the operator (+) has to be stored for later use and the current entry reset to 0. Now the user enters a 12 and then a multiplication sign. When the multiplication sign is pressed, we follow the same algorithm: the running total (7), the last operator (+), and the current entry (12) create the new running total of 19. This result is printed in the display, the multiplication sign is stored, and the current entry is reset to 0. So far, so good.

Let's enter the last number and complete the expression. When the user enters a 5 followed by the equals sign, we calculate the new total by multiplying 5 by 19 and print the result 95 in the display. The next line of pseudocode says to store the equals sign for later use. However, we do not want to use the equals sign like the addition and multiplication signs, since it indicates the end of the expression. This means that we should reset things to their original state: put the current entry and running total back to 0 and set the last operator to addition. This is only slightly different from choosing one of the other operators, so we need not separate the equals sign from the other operators in the main part of the pseudocode. We revise the current section of pseudocode as follows:

```
{ ELSE IF user presses operator button THEN }
  BEGIN
    Calculate new running total
      using current entry, old total, and last operator
    Show new total on display
    Determine which operator was pressed
    IF operator is equals sign THEN
      BEGIN
        Set running total to 0
        Store + as last operator
      END { equals sign }
    ELSE
      Store current operator for later use
```

*Another method is to make the first entry a special case.

```
    Set current entry to 0
  END { operator button }
```

Let's now consider the clear button. When the C button is pressed, the pseudocode says to "Show 0 on display" and "Set running total to 0." Fine, but what about the operator? The C button, after all, should reset the expression, but in the example the old operator has remained. As with the equals sign, we need to set the last operator to the addition sign to reset the expression properly.

```
{ ELSE IF user presses C button }
  BEGIN
    Show 0 on display
    Set running total to 0
    Store + as last operator
  END { C button }
```

When the user presses the CE button, the pseudocode says to "Show 0 on display." This is certainly still true. We can't really break down this line further at this point.

Finally, let's look at the last two conditions. When the user misses all the buttons, the pseudocode does not indicate that anything has happened. For now, let's say that we will print an error message in the text window. (We said earlier we would do nothing if all the buttons were missed, but for testing and debugging purposes, it's a good idea that every action have some visible result.) When the user presses the OFF button, the exit condition of the loop is set to TRUE. The flow of control moves to the bottom of the loop and the program does indeed stop.

The third revision of pseudocode is complete. We now have the following:

```
{ Draw calculator }
Draw outer round rectangle
Draw display
Draw buttons
Set loop exit condition to FALSE
Set running total to 0
Set initial operator to +

REPEAT
  IF user presses numeric button THEN
    BEGIN
      Multiply current entry by 10
      Add new digit to current entry
      Print current entry in display
    END { numeric button }
  ELSE IF user presses operator button THEN
    BEGIN
      Calculate new running total
        using current entry, old total, and last operator
```

```
            Show new total on display
            IF operator is equals sign THEN
               BEGIN
                  Set running total to 0
                  Store + as last operator
               END { equals sign }
            ELSE
               Store current operator for later use
            Set current entry to 0
         END { operator button }
      ELSE IF user presses C button THEN
         BEGIN
            Show 0 on display
            Set + as last operator
            Set running total to 0
         END { C button }
      ELSE IF user presses CE button THEN
         Show 0 on display
      ELSE IF user presses OFF button THEN
         Set done to TRUE
      ELSE
         { User has not pressed a button }
         Print error message in Text window

   UNTIL done
```

Level 3: Hand Simulation

Now it is time to hand simulate the complete level of pseudocode. We want to make sure the pieces fit together properly and see if any sections of the pseudocode should be restructured or rearranged. We don't want to ignore the forest for the trees.

Hand simulation reveals two places where we have to modify the algorithm. First, when we press a numeric button, the pseudocode says to multiply the current entry by 10, add the new digit to the current entry, and print the current entry in the display. This algorithm appears to work for all of the typical cases. Let's check if it works for the first digit in the entry. To multiply the current entry by 10, there has to be a current entry. Therefore, we need to set the current entry to 0 before the first digit is entered. If the current entry is 0, the algorithm works; we multiply 0 by 10, get 0, and then add the first digit. Thus, we add the line "Set current entry to 0" to the pseudocode above the REPEAT. Notice that we are not breaking down any task here; we are simply correcting the pseudocode so it works correctly at this level.

The other modification stems from a combination of the pieces. Let's examine what happens when we use the sequence shown in Figure 7.4 (3, +, 5, CE, 6). The display will show a 3 when the 3 is pressed and retain the 3 when the addition sign is pressed. Next, the display will show a 5 when that button is pressed, and the current entry will be set to 5. Then, when the CE is pressed, the display will show 0.

Finally, when the 6 is pressed, we go to the numeric button procedure and find that the display will show 56. Even though we removed the 5 from the display, we haven't removed it from the current entry variable. Thus, we need to set the current entry to 0 for a CE press; we modify this section of the pseudocode as follows:

```
{ ELSE IF user presses CE button }
   BEGIN
      Show 0 on display
      Set current entry to 0
   END { CE button }
```

This is an example of where naive hand simulation is crucial. We easily could have missed this bug if we hadn't kept track of the contents of the current entry variable. It would have been easy to assume that the CE button performed the correct function. You cannot skim pseudocode; pay attention to *all* the details, since that is exactly what the computer will do to your program.

When the hand simulation of this level is complete, we take a moment to see if we need to clean up the pseudocode. We probably should since it has become quite unwieldy. We do not have to place all the refinements in the main REPEAT loop; we will probably not code the pseudocode as one long mainline. To designate "procedures" in the pseudocode, we list a general task in the place where the "procedure" will be called and show the refinement in another place in the pseudocode. The following is the pseudocode modified after the hand simulation. Note that we have designated "procedures" to reset the equation (thus removing some repeated pseudocode), to update an entry when a numeric button is pressed, and to complete a portion of the expression when an operator button is pressed. The calls to these procedures in the main section of pseudocode are signaled with the word "CALL."

```
CALL: Draw calculator
Set loop exit condition to FALSE
CALL: Reset expression
Set current entry to 0

REPEAT
   IF user presses numeric button THEN
      CALL: Update entry
   ELSE IF user presses operator button THEN
      CALL: Complete portion of expression
   ELSE IF user presses C button THEN
      BEGIN
         Show 0 on display
         CALL: Reset expression
      END { C button }
```

```
    ELSE IF user presses CE button THEN
      BEGIN
        Show 0 on display
        Set current entry to 0
      END { CE button }
    ELSE IF user presses OFF button THEN
      Set done to TRUE
    ELSE
      { User has not pressed a button }
      Print error message in Text window
  UNTIL done

{ Draw calculator }
Draw outer round rectangle
Draw display
Draw buttons

{ Reset expression }
Set running total to 0
Set initial operator to +

{ Update entry }
Multiply current entry by 10
Add new digit to current entry
Print current entry in display

{ Complete portion of expression }
Calculate new running total
  using current entry, old total, and last operator
Show new total on display
IF operator is equals sign THEN
  BEGIN
    Set running total to 0
    Store + as last operator
  END { equals sign }
ELSE
  Store current operator for later use
Set current entry to 0
```

Level 4: Refinement

We begin the next refinement by figuring out more details about how to draw the calculator. As we saw in Figure 7.2, the calculator consists of eighteen buttons. Simply drawing the buttons is easy; we can use the various QuickDraw primitives to create rectangles and text. The problem arises when we consider how the layout will be used. Looking at the main IF-THEN-ELSE IF in the pseudocode, we see that the buttons are divided into five categories: the numeric buttons, the operator buttons, the C button, the CE button, and the OFF button. These categories can be represented as variables of type ***rect*** in QuickDraw.

By defining the ***rect*** variables properly, we have created a way to determine which area of the screen was chosen. In the cases of the numeric and operator buttons, though, we still have no way to determine *which* button has been selected. This is not important for the mainline, but it is important in the procedures that update the entry and the total. The obvious answer is to create a ***rect*** variable for each button. If we did, though, we would be forced to pass eighteen variables as parameters.

So how else can we determine which button has been pressed? Well, we know what point has been chosen, and we know the area of the screen. We can correlate the pick with the appropriate button by thinking of the numeric and operator areas as grids. We can tell which button was picked in the operator area by taking advantage of the fact that all the operators lie in a single column. The vertical coordinate of the pick will tell us which button was chosen. We start by seeing if the vertical coordinate is between the top and bottom boundaries of the addition button. If it isn't, we see if the vertical coordinate is within the boundaries of the subtraction button, and so on.

Similarly, the coordinates of a pick in the numeric area will tell which button was picked. The vertical coordinate tells which row was selected. Then the horizontal coordinate tells which button on that row was chosen. Figure 7.6 shows the boundaries of the rows and columns.

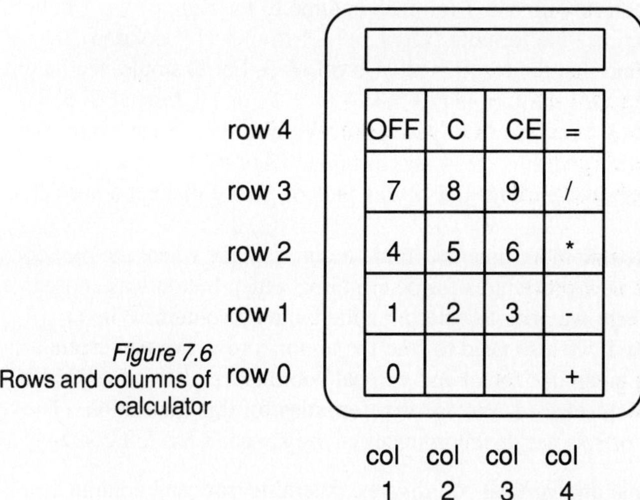

Figure 7.6
Rows and columns of calculator

The pseudocode for determining which button was picked follows:

```
{ Determine which operator button was picked }
Using vertical coordinate, determine what row was picked
```

```
CASE row OF
    0: operator is +
    1: operator is –
    2: operator is *
    3: operator is /
    4: operator is =
END { CASE }

{ Determine which numeric button was picked }
Using vertical coordinate, determine what row was picked
Using horizontal coordinate, determine what column was picked
IF user picked in row 0 and column 1 THEN
    Digit := 0
ELSE
    Digit := 3 * (row – 1) + column
```

You may be wondering how to arrive at the expression that determines what digit was selected. The expression comes from looking at how the layout of the rows and columns corresponds to the digits. For example, button 1 is in row 1, column 1; button 6 is in row 2, column 3, and button 8 is in row 3, column 2. We need some way of deriving the button from the row and column numbers. We start, say, at the 1 button. For each row we move up, we arrive at a button that is 3 larger (e.g., the 4 button is one row above and 3 greater than the 1 button). For each column that we move to the right, we move to a button that is 1 larger. This suggests that to find a button, we add 3 for each row up and 1 for each column to the right of the 1 button. From this observation comes the formula "Digit := (3 * row) + (1 * column)." Check this and you'll find that the result is always off by 3. For example, the button in row 3 and column 2 yields the formula (3 * 3) + (1 * 2), or 11, instead of 8. To correct this, we change (3 * row) to (3 * (row – 1)). We also reduce the expression (1 * column) to "column" and thus create the formula "Digit := 3 * (row – 1) + column." The 0 button, however, does not fit this pattern, so we make it a special case.

We hand simulate one more time and find one more place where the pseudocode is still repetitive. In the new procedures for determining which button was chosen, there are two places where we need to determine the button's column. When a numeric button is pressed, we also need to find the button's row. We can create a generic procedure that, given horizontal and vertical coordinates, determines which row-column pair has been selected. We use two formulas for this translation. (The horizontal and vertical offsets are the coordinates of the keypad's top left corner.)

```
{ Using horizontal and vertical coordinates, determine row and column }
column number := (user's horiz – horiz offset) DIV (size of button)
row number := (user's vert – vert offset) DIV (size of button)
row number := max number of rows – row number
```

(Yes, the derivation of these formulas is vague. Think about what each element in the formula represents, and test it a few times. You'll pick up the idea. These formulas recur in graphics programming.)

In some ways, hand simulation of pseudocode is like proofreading a draft of a paper. Writers often proofread their drafts once for style and organization (e.g., rearranging paragraphs and clarifying arguments) and once for accuracy and punctuation (e.g., checking facts, citing sources, and correcting grammar). Many programmers hand simulate once to find bugs and again to regroup or break down tasks. Here, we have checked for repetition and accuracy. Now we hand simulate once more to see if each line can be easily translated into code. At this point, when we read each line of pseudocode, we can say, "OK, I know how to code that idea in Pascal." Since we can do this for the entire pseudocode, we are finished with the refinement. (The only difference between level 3 and level 4 is the refinement of drawing the calculator. Typically, graphics calls require a little more modification than other parts of the program because more arithmetic and geometry are involved.) The current hand simulation brings no modifications, so the complete pseudocode is as follows:

```
{ BEGIN mainline }

CALL: Draw calculator
Set done to FALSE
CALL: Reset expression
Set current entry to 0

REPEAT
   IF user presses numeric button THEN
      CALL: Update entry
   ELSE IF user presses operator button THEN
      CALL: Complete portion of expression
   ELSE IF user presses C button THEN
      BEGIN
         Show 0 on display
         Reset expression
      END { C button }
   ELSE IF user presses CE button THEN
      BEGIN
         Show 0 on display
         Set current entry to 0
      END { CE button }
   ELSE IF user presses OFF button THEN
      Set done to TRUE
   ELSE
      { User has not pressed a button }
      Print error message in Text window

UNTIL done { END of mainline }
```

```
{ Reset expression }
Set initial operator to +
Set running total to 0

{ Update entry }
CALL: Determine which numeric button was picked
Multiply current entry by 10
Add new digit to current entry
Print current entry in display

{ Complete portion of expression }
CALL: Determine which operator button was picked
Calculate new running total
   using current entry, old total, and last operator
Show new total on display
IF operator is equals sign THEN
   Reset expression
ELSE
   Store current operator for later use
Set current entry to 0

{ Draw calculator }
Draw outer round rectangle
Draw display
Draw buttons
Create rect variables for C, CE, OFF, numeric, and operators

{ Determine which operator button was picked }
CALL: Using horizontal and vertical coordinates, determine row and column
CASE row OF
   0: operator is +
   1: operator is –
   2: operator is *
   3: operator is /
   4: operator is =
END { CASE }

{ Determine which numeric button was picked }
CALL: Using horizontal and vertical coordinates, determine row and column
IF user picked in row 0 and column 1 THEN
   Digit := 0
ELSE
   Digit := (row – 1) * 3 + column

{ Using horizontal and vertical coordinates, determine row and column }
column number := (user's horiz – horiz offset) DIV (size of button)
row number := (user's vert – vert offset) DIV (size of button)
row number := max number of rows – row number
```

7.6 Translating Pseudocode to Code

Writing pseudocode is an individual process. Each programmer recognizes bugs and breaks down problems in a slightly different manner. In the last section, you saw how one way to develop the calculator problem into a final version of pseudocode. Given the same problem, you probably would develop the segments in a different order.

In some respects, translating pseudocode to code should be an almost automatic process. Each task in the pseudocode should represent no more than a few lines of Pascal statements. However, the other components of writing a program — declarations of constants and variables, documentation, and dealing with Pascal syntax — may make that final mental leap from pseudocode to Pascal slightly more complicated. As you will see, the translation may also require revisions of the pseudocode.

Many programmers find it easiest to code a program in the same order in which it will be executed. In this way, they maintain the top-down style of breaking down the problem. Following this rule of thumb, we will start coding the mainline of the calculator.

We first look at the first line of pseudocode, "Draw calculator." In the last level, we designated this as a separate procedure, so the mainline doesn't have to do anything more than call a procedure. The code now looks like this:

```
{ Mainline }
begin
    DrawCalculator ( );
```

At this point, we can pursue one of two paths: finish coding the mainline or begin coding ***DrawCalculator***. We will follow the second, although the first would work as well. As each procedure is coded, we consider what information the procedure needs to receive and what it will return. Data not needed outside the procedure should be declared as local variables; other data must be defined as parameters.

The pseudocode for "Draw calculator" tells us that the procedure requires no incoming information and returns five ***rect*** variables. We thus need to send five variables of type ***rect*** as parameters to the procedure.

Variables and constants should be declared as needed; this way, we don't enter variables that serve no purpose. Speaking of purpose, it is best to write down the glossary entry for each variable *as it is created,* since that is when its purpose is still fresh in mind. The code now looks like this:

```
{ Mainline variables }
var
    num,                                    { numeric keypad       }
    clear,                                  { C button             }
    clearEntry,                             { CE button            }
    ops,                                    { operator buttons     }
    stop: rect;                             { OFF button           }
```

```
{ Procedure DrawCalculator }
procedure DrawCalculator( var num,          { numeric keypad   }
              clear,                        { C button         }
              clearEntry,                   { CE button        }
              ops,                          { operator buttons }
              stop: rect;                   { OFF button       }
begin
   ...
end; { DrawCalculator }

{ Mainline }
begin
   DrawCalculator (num, clear, clearEntry, ops, stop);
```

We can next fill in the code for the procedure to draw the calculator. We begin by drawing a sketch that shows the coordinate positions.

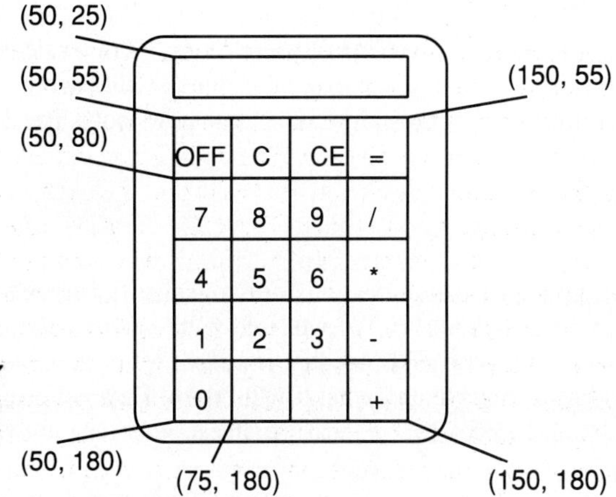

Figure 7.7 Coordinates for calculator

The lines "Draw outer round rect" and "Draw display" thus become very easy — we simply create shapes at the coordinates designated in the diagram. Sometimes, though, minor refinements of the algorithm are made in translating pseudocode to Pascal. For example, when we encounter the line "Draw buttons," we know one easy way to code it — call ***FrameRect*** eighteen times and print eighteen pieces of text, once for each button. When we start to write the code, though, we find that this process is just too long and tedious. It seems that there should be a faster way.

We go back to pseudocode. Instead of thinking about the buttons as individual rectangles, look at Figure 7.7 — we can see the keypad as a set of lines and text. When we draw a grid by hand, we drew all of the vertical lines, then all of the horizontal lines, and finally the text. We can use the same algorithm to draw the keypad.

```
{ Draw buttons }
Draw vertical lines
Draw horizontal lines
Draw text
```

To draw the vertical lines, we need to know the endpoints of each line. All the vertical lines have the same top and bottom coordinates. The diagram shows that we should draw the lines at horizontal coordinates that are 25 pixels apart. Thus, for each line, we should increase the horizontal coordinate by 25. The pseudocode for drawing vertical lines follows:

```
{ Draw vertical lines }
horizontal coordinate starts at left border
WHILE horiz coordinate is not at right border DO
   BEGIN
      Draw line from top to bottom of keypad
      Increase horizontal coordinate by 25
   END { WHILE }
```

This pseudocode easily translates into Pascal. We introduce constants to represent the borders of the keypad and the size of the buttons. The horizontal lines can be drawn using a similar algorithm. (It is not unusual to work with literal constants when you first write code. It is a good idea, however, to change these literal constants quickly to named constants. It is easy to forget, for example, that we are increasing the horizontal coordinate by 25 because 25 is the size of a button. Using the constant ***btnSize*** helps us remember why we are performing the addition and gives the program more flexibility. For the same reason, we define the constants ***padLeft*** = 50, ***padRight*** = 150, ***padTop*** = 55, and ***padBottom*** = 180.)

Finally we draw the text. When using pen and paper, we wrote the labels from left to right. We can do the same here using ***WriteDraw*** statements. For each line, we draw the appropriate labels for that row.

The procedure is now missing only one thing: documentation. Commenting programs at this stage may seem silly, because changes are almost inevitable. Still, commenting now will serve as a reminder of the original intention of the procedure. In large programs, it becomes difficult to remember the purpose of each routine. By commenting along the way, we avoid the problem of trying to remember what a routine written days, weeks, or even months ago actually does. With the block comment, we have completed the procedure to draw the calculator.

Code 7.1
Procedure
DrawCalculator

```
{ Procedure DrawCalculator                                    }
{                                                             }
{ This procedure draws the calculator on the screen. First, the }
{ outer round rectangle is drawn. Next, the display is shown.  }
{ The next part of the procedure is devoted to drawing the     }
{ pad. First, the lines are drawn; then, the text is added.    }
```

Code 7.1
(continued)

```
{ Finally, the various areas of the pad are designated as            }
{ rectangular areas in QuickDraw, for later use in picking.          }
{                                                                    }
{ Calls: none   Called by: Mainline                                  }

 procedure DrawCalculator (var num,            { numeric pad         }
    clear,                                     { C button            }
    clearEntry,                                { CE button           }
    ops,                                       { operator buttons    }
    stop : rect);
                                               { OFF button          }
 var
    lineCtr,                                   { row of text being printed }
    horizPos, vertPos : integer;               { current pos for lines     }

begin
{ Draw outer round rect and display }
    FrameRoundRect(displayTop - 5, padLeft - 5, padBottom + 5, padRight
        + 5, 5, 5);
    FrameRect(displayTop, padLeft, displayTop + btnSize, padRight);

{ Draw buttons }
{ Draw vertical lines }
    horizPos := padLeft;
    while horizPos < padRight do
        begin
            MoveTo(horizPos, padTop);
            LineTo(horizPos, padBottom);
            horizPos := horizPos + btnSize
        end; { while }

{ Draw horizontal lines }
    vertPos := padTop;
    while vertPos < padBottom do
        begin
            MoveTo(padLeft, vertPos);
            LineTo(padRight, vertPos);
            vertPos := vertPos + btnSize
        end; { while }

{ draw text }

    for lineCtr := 0 to maxRows do
        begin
{ get position for text }
            vertPos := lineCtr * btnSize + padTop;
            vertPos := vertPos + (btnSize div 2);
```

Code 7.1 (continued)

```
            case lineCtr of
               0 :
                  WriteDraw(' OFF  C  CE   = ');
               1 :
                  WriteDraw('  7   8   9   / ');
               2 :
                  WriteDraw('  4   5   6   * ');
               3 :
                  WriteDraw('  1   2   3   - ');
               4 :
                  WriteDraw('  0           + ');
            end { case }
         end; { for }

   { set rect variables }
      SetRect(num, padLeft, padTop + btnSize, padRight - btnSize, padBottom);
      SetRect(ops, padRight - btnSize, padTop, padRight, padBottom);
      SetRect(stop, padLeft, padTop, padLeft + btnSize, padTop + btnSize);
      SetRect(clear, padLeft + btnSize, padTop, padLeft + (2 * btnSize),
         padTop + btnSize);
      SetRect(clearEntry, padLeft + (2 * btnSize), padTop, padLeft + (3 *
         btnSize), padTop + btnSize)
   end;
```

We now return to the mainline pseudocode. We create a boolean variable ***done*** and set it to TRUE. Next, we hit the line "Reset expression." This problem was refined in the pseudocode to "Set initial operator to +" and "Set running total to 0." Now we have to ask the question: how do we set the operator to +? The answer: by using integer constants to represent the various operators. Since each operator is in a different row, we can correlate the operators and the rows:

```
const
   add = 0;                    { operator codes }
   sub = 1;
   mult = 2;
   divide = 3;
   equals = 4;
```

Why wait until now to decide how to represent the operators? Software engineers who work with large-scale programs often recommend waiting until late in the stages of pseudocode development to designate how data will be stored. This way, all the information is available before the decision on how to represent it is made. More on this when we discuss compound data structures.

After coding the "Reset expression" procedure, we return to the mainline and find the word "REPEAT." The flow-of-control constructs in the pseudocode often can be copied directly into Pascal. However, during translation, you may change one flow of control construct to a similar type of code. While you may decide to change a WHILE in the pseudocode to a **repeat-until** in Pascal, you are still coding an indefinite loop. Similarly, a multiway branch can be pseudocoded as an IF-THEN-ELSE IF construct and yet end up as a **case** statement.

The process of translation continues for each line of pseudocode. For the remainder of the calculator program, no other changes were made to the algorithm. Compare the pseudocode to the program and analyze how each step in the pseudocode was translated. Remember, though, that our translation still has bugs.

Code 7.2
Program *Calculator*

```
{ Program: Calculator    D. Niguidula    November 11                }
{                                                                   }
{ This program creates an online calculator in the Drawing          }
{ window. The calculator can perform four arithmetic func-          }
{ tions (addition, subtraction, multiplication, and division)       }
{ on integers.                                                      }
{   The program begins by displaying the calculator. When it        }
{ appears, the user may use the mouse to enter the numbers          }
{ and operators of an expression.  If the user wants to cor-        }
{ rect a mistake, she can use the CE (clear entry ) button.         }
{ If the user wants to reset the entire expression, she can         }
{ use the C button. When the user is done with the calculator,      }
{ she should press the OFF button.                                  }

program Calculator;

const
   add = 0;                    { operator codes                     }
   sub = 1;
   mult = 2;
   divide = 3;
   equals = 4;
   padLeft = 50;               { coordinates of corners of key pad  }
   padRight = 150;
   padTop = 55;
   padBottom = 180;
   btnSize = 25;               { width and length of each button    }
   displayTop = 20;            { top of display                     }

   maxRows = 5;                { num of rows in pad                 }
```

Code 7.2
(continued)

```
 { Mainline variables }
var
   num,                                  { numeric pad                   }
   clear,                                { C button                      }
   clearEntry,                           { CE button                     }
   ops,                                  { operator buttons              }
   stop : rect;                          { OFF button                    }
   done : boolean;                       { indicates end of program      }
   lastOp : integer;                     { saves last operator           }
   curEntry,                             { current number in expression  }
   total,                                { current running total         }
   userHor, userVert : integer;          { coord of point chosen by user }
   userPt : point;                       { point chosen by user          }

{ Procedure DrawCalculator                                          }
{ This procedure draws the calculator on the screen. First, the     }
{ outer round rectangle is drawn. Next, the display is shown.       }
{ The next part of the procedure is devoted to drawing the          }
{ pad. First, the lines are drawn; then, the text is added.         }
{ Finally, the various areas of the pad are designated as           }
{ rectangular areas in QuickDraw, for later use in picking.         }
{ Calls: none   Called by: Mainline                                 }

procedure DrawCalculator (var num,       { numeric pad          }
     clear,                              { C button             }
     clearEntry,                         { CE button            }
     ops,                                { operator buttons     }
     stop : rect);                       { OFF button           }
 var
   lineCtr,                              { row of text being printed  }
   horizPos, vertPos : integer;          { current pos for lines      }

begin
{ Draw outer round rect and display }
   FrameRoundRect(displayTop - 5, padLeft - 5, padBottom + 5, padRight + 5, 5, 5);
   FrameRect(displayTop, padLeft, displayTop + btnSize, padRight);

{ Draw buttons }
{ Draw vertical lines }
   horizPos := padLeft;
   while horizPos < padRight do
      begin
         MoveTo(horizPos, padTop);
         LineTo(horizPos, padBottom);
         horizPos := horizPos + btnSize
      end; { while }
```

Code 7.2 (continued)

```
{ Draw horizontal lines }
    vertPos := padTop;
    while vertPos < padBottom do
        begin
            MoveTo(padLeft, vertPos);
            LineTo(padRight, vertPos);
            vertPos := vertPos + btnSize
        end; { while }

{ draw text }

    for lineCtr := 0 to maxRows do
        begin
{ get position for text }
            vertPos := lineCtr * btnSize + padTop;
            vertPos := vertPos + (btnSize div 2);

            case lineCtr of
                0 :
                    WriteDraw(' OFF  C  CE   =');
                1 :
                    WriteDraw('  7   8   9    /');
                2 :
                    WriteDraw('  4   5   6    *');
                3 :
                    WriteDraw('  1   2   3    -');
                4 :
                    WriteDraw('  0            +');
            end  { case }
        end; { for }

{ set rect variables }
    SetRect(num, padLeft, padTop + btnSize, padRight - btnSize, padBottom);
    SetRect(ops, padRight - btnSize, padTop, padRight, padBottom);
    SetRect(stop, padLeft, padTop, padLeft + btnSize, padTop + btnSize);
    SetRect(clear, padLeft + btnSize, padTop, padLeft + (2 * btnSize), padTop +
        btnSize);
    SetRect(clearEntry, padLeft + (2 * btnSize), padTop, padLeft + (3 * btnSize),
        padTop + btnSize)
end;

{ Procedure Display                                                  }
{ This procedure places a number in the calculator's display.       }
{ Called by: Calculate, Update, Mainline   Calls: none               }
procedure Display (showNum : integer); { number to display          }

begin
    MoveTo(padLeft, displayTop + btnSize);
    WriteDraw(showNum : 16)
end; { Display }
```

Code 7.2
(continued)

```
{ Procedure ResetExp                                                    }
{ To reset the expression, this function resets the running             }
{ total and the operator.                                               }
{ Called by: Calculate, Mainline   Calls: none                          }

procedure ResetExp (total,             { current running total          }
    oper : integer);                   { last operator                  }
begin
  total := 0;
  oper := add
end; { ResetExp }

{ Procedure GetRowCol                                                   }
{ Given horizontal and vertical coordinates in the pad, this            }
{ procedure determines the row and column of the button that            }
{ was selected.                                                         }
{ Calls: none      Called by: GetDigit, GetOp                           }

procedure GetRowCol (horiz, vert : integer;         { user's pt         }
    var row, col : integer);                  { position of btn on pad  }

begin
  col := (horiz – padLeft) div btnSize;
  row := (vert – padTop) div btnSize;
  row := maxRows – row
end; { GetRowCol }

{ Function GetOp }
{ This function determines which operator button has been               }
{ pressed. First, the row and column of the button are deter-           }
{ mined. Then, given that information, the function returns the         }
{ turns the appropriate indicator.                                      }
{ Calls: GetRowCol     Called By: Calculate                             }

function GetOp (horiz, vert : integer) :            { user's point      }
  integer;                                  { Returns: operator button  }

 var
  row, col : integer;                       { position of button on pad }

begin
  GetRowCol(horiz, vert, row, col);
  GetOp := row
end; { GetOp }
```

Code 7.2 (continued)

```
{ Function GetDigit }
{ This function determines which numeric button has been        }
{ pressed. First, the row and column of the button are de-      }
{ termined. Then, given that information, the function re-      }
{ turns the number of the button.                               }
{ Calls: GetRowCol     Called By: Update                        }

function GetDigit (horiz, vert : integer) :          { user's point }
    integer;     { Returns: number of selected button }

    var
        row, col,                        { position of button on pad   }
        dig : integer;                   { new digit                   }

begin
    GetRowCol(horiz, vert, row, col);
    if (row = 0) and (col = 1) then
        dig := 0
    else
        dig := (row - 1) * 3 + col;

    GetDigit := dig
end; { GetDigit }


{ Procedure Calculate                                             }
{ This procedure performs a calculation when an operator but-     }
{ ton is chosen. The operator previously pressed determines the   }
{ function that is performed. Using the running total and the     }
{ current entry, the procedure calculates a new total. Then, the  }
{ current operator is stored for later use. If the current opera- }
{ tor is the equals sign, the expression is reset.                }
{ Called by: Mainline    Calls:   GetOp, Display                  }

procedure Calculate (userHoriz, userVert : integer;

                                        { point chosen by user              }
    var lastOp,                         { last operator button chosen       }
    total,                              { current running total             }
    curEntry : integer);                { value of current entry            }

var
    opBtn : integer;                    { designates current operator       }
```

Code 7.2
(continued)

```
begin
   opBtn := GetOp(userHoriz, userVert);

   case lastOp of
      add :
         total := total + curEntry;
      sub :
         total := total - curEntry;
      mult :
         total := total * curEntry;
      divide :
         total := total div curEntry
   end; { case }
   Display(total);

   if lastOp = equals then
      ResetExp(total, lastOp)
   else
      lastOp := opBtn;
   curEntry := 0
end; { Calculate }

{ Update }
{ This procedure updates the current entry. It is called when a          }
{ numeric button has been selected. First, the routine deter-            }
{ mines which button has been selected. Then, the entry's value          }
{ is changed.                                                            }
{ Calls: GetDigit, Display     Called by: Mainline                       }

procedure Update (userHor, userVert : integer;          { user's pt      }
    var curEntry : integer);                            { current entry  }

var
   numBtn : integer;       { indicates button selected }

begin
   numBtn := GetDigit(userHor, userVert);
   curEntry := curEntry * 10;
   curEntry := curEntry + numBtn;  { update entry }

   Display(curEntry)
end; { update }
```

Code 7.2
(continued)

```
{ Mainline }
{ The mainline begins by initializing the screen and the equa-      }
{ tion. It then expects the user to choose a button with the        }
{ mouse. Then, depending on the area of the pad chosen by           }
{ the user, the mainline sends flow of control to the appropri-     }
{ ate procedures. When the user presses the OFF button, the         }
{ program ends.                                                      }
{ Calls: DrawCalculator, ResetExp, Update, Calculate, Display       }

begin
   DrawCalculator(num, clear, clearEntry, ops, stop);
   done := FALSE;
   ResetExp(total, lastOp);
   curEntry := 0;

   repeat
   { get user's selection }

      repeat
         GetMouse(userHor, userVert);
      until Button;
      SetPt(userPt, userHor, userVert);

{ take appropriate action }
      if PtInRect(userPt, num) then
         Update(userHor, userVert, curEntry)
      else if PtInRect(userPt, ops) then
         Calculate(userHor, userVert, lastOp, total, curEntry)
      else if PtInRect(userPt, clear) then
         begin
            ResetExp(total, lastOp);
            Display(total)
         end { else if }

      else if PtInRect(userPt, clearEntry) then

         begin
            curEntry := 0;
            Display(curEntry)
         end { else if }

      else if PtInRect(userPt, stop) then
         done := TRUE
      else { error message if pick is off pad }
         Writeln('No button was pressed.')
   until done
end. { Calculator }
```

7.7 Debugging

Programs hardly ever work the first time, although we always strive for that satisfying event. Even the most carefully designed and hand-simulated program could have a flaw because of a miscopied variable name or a missing **var** before a parameter. We can take advantage of MacPascal's debugging facilities to help determine where the program is going wrong. These facilities help you determine the values of variables and the program's flow of control. The debugging facilities you use here will be particularly useful in finding and removing bugs from large programs.

The most obvious bugs are syntax bugs that are caught by the machine itself. The Macintosh places "bug boxes" on the screen when a syntax error is discovered. MacPascal recognizes errors at two stages. First, it checks each line to see if it can be translated into machine language. At this point, the interpreter or compiler finds errors such as mistakes in punctuation or undeclared variables. (If you choose **Check** from the **Run** menu, only this first stage of the error checking is performed.) The second stage picks up errors that occur when statements interact with each other or when MacPascal attempts to but cannot execute the code. These include syntax errors, such as mismatches in parameter passing, and semantic errors, such as division by 0.

Errors revealed by bug boxes are usually easy to fix. MacPascal indicates the line at which the error was found. The line with the thumbs-down icon does not always locate exactly where the problem exists, but it does tell you where to start looking.

Semantic errors that the Macintosh does not catch are harder to eliminate. The rest of this chapter discusses methods of removing bugs that may not cause a Pascal error but still cause incorrect results.

7.8 Test Data

Once you clear a program of syntax errors, you can test its semantics. *Testing* a program means making sure that a program handles all the possible inputs. *Test data* are the inputs that you use.

To test a program, we begin by creating a list of test data. We do this here by looking through the code for ***Readln*** and ***GetMouse*** statements. For each input statement, we consider all the possible values we could give to the program. We then choose one value for each category (e.g., if the program accepts a single integer, we may want to use a negative number, a positive number, and zero as test data).

For each piece of test data, we determine what the program should do. At first glance, this seems to defeat the purpose of the computer — if you can figure out the answer without the computer, why go to the trouble of programming? Remember, most software is developed for other people to use or for your own repeated use. You don't want someone else to find a bug that you haven't considered.

Now we test the calculator program, one part at a time. First, we look at the simplest function: does the calculator turn off correctly? Since the OFF button is the only exit from the program, we need to make sure it works; otherwise the user may be caught in an infinite loop.

Next, does the calculator distinguish among the buttons correctly? That is, when a button is pressed, does the program determine *which* button was pressed? To test this, we use an algorithm that a four-year-old would use: press all the buttons and see what happens.

Once we make sure the buttons are working, we need to ensure that they do their jobs correctly. First, we examine the numeric keys. Can we make all the numbers appear? We need to see if we can generate integers with single or multiple digits.

After we are confident that the entries work, we move to the operator keys. We start by looking at the simple cases — a sequence of an entry, an operator, an entry, and the equals sign. We check the special cases of negative results and division by 0. After testing each function individually, we end the testing by checking chain operators. Our test equations and the results they should yield follow.

sequence of buttons	expected result	testing for:
3 + 8 =	11	addition
7 – 4 =	3	subtraction
4 – 8 =	– 4	negative result
7 * 6 =	42	multiplication
8 / 4 =	2	division
13 + 18 =	31	multiple digits
6 / 0 =	undefined	division by 0
3 + 8 - 4 =	7	chaining with
6 – 2 * 5 =	20	different
3 * 6 / 2 =	9	combinations
12 / 4 + 7 =	10	

The "trick" to creating test data is to find the simplest examples that cover the largest range of possibilities. For example, when testing chaining, we listed four expressions, each of which uses a different series of operators. Each operator has to work when it is the second operator in a chain. Since the algorithm for the third operator is the same as for the second operator, we do not need to test longer chains.

Checking longer and more complex equations can give you a better feeling about your program. It helps your confidence just to see your program correctly do something complicated. As you tackle and eliminate each bug, it's helpful to the ego to be able to say, "I've really accomplished something. I can make the computer do what I want."

Notice also that there is a definite method in this testing madness. We can't very well check whether expressions work if the buttons are not working correctly. When creating test data, determine which elementary functions have to work before any other functions can work. Then, thoroughly test those first operations. By the time you get around to testing the more advanced functions, you can feel assured that any bugs you find are not in some simpler operation, and you can concentrate on the more complex code.

7.9 Using MacPascal Debugging Tools

Running the program with test data will probably tell you that the program has a bug. Now you have to figure out where you went wrong. The bugs that result from semantic errors are often hardest to fix because they are the hardest to find. MacPascal offers a number of tools that help you find these problems faster.

The Observe window can be a great help in tracking bugs. By examining the values of variables, we can find off-by-one and arithmetic errors. We can also determine whether a value is being initialized at the correct time and whether parameters are being sent in the correct order. As we have seen, the Observe window prints the values of listed variables when the program is halted. When using **Go** or **Go-Go**, the Observe window is updated at each stop sign; when using **Step** or **Step-Step/Trace**, the Observe window is updated after each statement is executed. Now, we could do a completely thorough check by listing every variable in the Observe window and stepping through every line in the program. But who wants to bother with all that? Instead, we can use some discretion to decide what variables to check and where to stop the program.

Often you can determine that the problem is in a particular procedure. If you think this is the case, try placing a stop sign at the procedure's **begin**. When you choose **Go**, the program executes all of the statements up to the beginning of the procedure. If all the preconditions required by the procedure are in place, you know that the problem has not occurred before the procedure is executed.

At this point, you may want to list all the local variables and parameters and step through the procedure. Before each statement is executed, predict what changes will occur in the Observe window. It is tempting to watch the values of the variables flash by in the Observe window with the hope that the problem will just appear. Sometimes, this technique works, but not often enough to make it a safe bet. However, by *interactively* debugging — that is, making the debugging an active rather than a passive process — you will find MacPascal's tools more useful.

Let's assume that each step in the procedure yields exactly the results you want. When you reach the end of the procedure, you may want to step one more line and see if the procedure returns what it is supposed to.

It is entirely possible that you could check every line in the procedure, check its preconditions and its returning values, and find that everything seems to be correct. Yet you just *know* that the problem is in that procedure. The next step is to scream in frustration. Go ahead. It will make you feel better. Taking a break is also a good idea; sitting in front of a computer for marathon sessions can be draining. (In fact, some folks prefer to sit in front of the computer only when absolutely necessary; they find their bugs by hand simulating a hard copy of the program. Still, they are using the same methods outlined in this chapter.)

Getting away from the screen also helps you gain a better perspective on your program. When staring at a screen, you tend to try to make minor adjustments to code you have already written. Sometimes, those minor revisions make things unnecessarily complex or even wrong. It may actually save time to go back to your pseudocode and rewrite sections from scratch. Remember the overall purposes of the procedure and program; the adjustments you are making may not be necessary if you view the problem from a slightly different angle.

In general, begin debugging by pinpointing small parts of the program to correct. Usually, you will find some particular portion of the program where things are going wrong. However, if you have no idea where to start, try putting stop signs at the **begin** and **end** of procedures and at the beginning of loops and branching statements.

7.10 The Instant Window

MacPascal has another tool for debugging: the Instant window. This facility helps to test procedures and to make minor adjustments to the code. To use the Instant window, choose the option **Instant** from the **Windows** menu. This places a small window in the middle of the left side of the screen. The window has a button labeled **Do It** and the comment ***{Any statements, any time.}***.

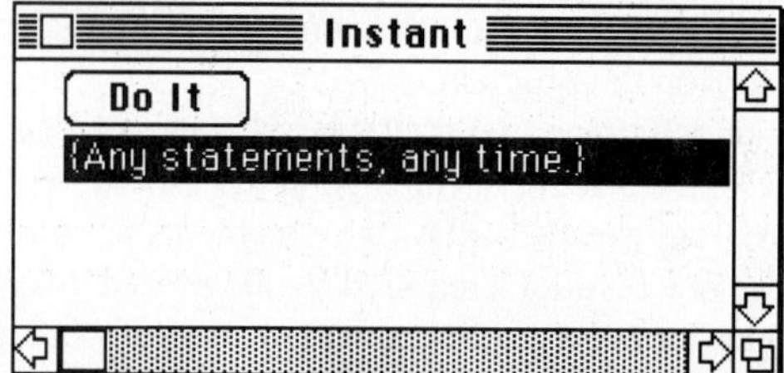

Figure 7.8
The Instant window

You can enter and edit statements in the Instant window just as if you were using the program window. When you click on the **Do It** button, MacPascal executes the statements in the Instant window.

So what statements should be in the Instant window? Well, consider what this window does. It is usually used in conjunction with stop signs. What you typically want to do is stop the program, enter statements in the Instant window, and choose the **Do It** button. This tells MacPascal to execute the statements in the Instant window as if they were the next statements in the program. In effect, you are seeing what would happen if you inserted statements into the code at the place you stopped. Thus, you can refer to any variables that are active at the stopping point, or you can call a previously declared procedure. The advantage of the Instant window is that you keep the program in suspended animation while you test various segments of code. If you constantly made small revisions in the program window and then tested them, you would spend much more time reinterpreting or recompiling the entire program. The next section shows how the Instant window can be used.

7.11 Debugging the Calculator Program

Let's return now to the Calculator program and discuss how to get the code to work. First, we run the program, and we get the result shown in Figure 7.9.*

---

* If you are testing this program using Lightspeed, use the **Source Options...** item from the **Project** menu to change the font to Geneva 12-point.

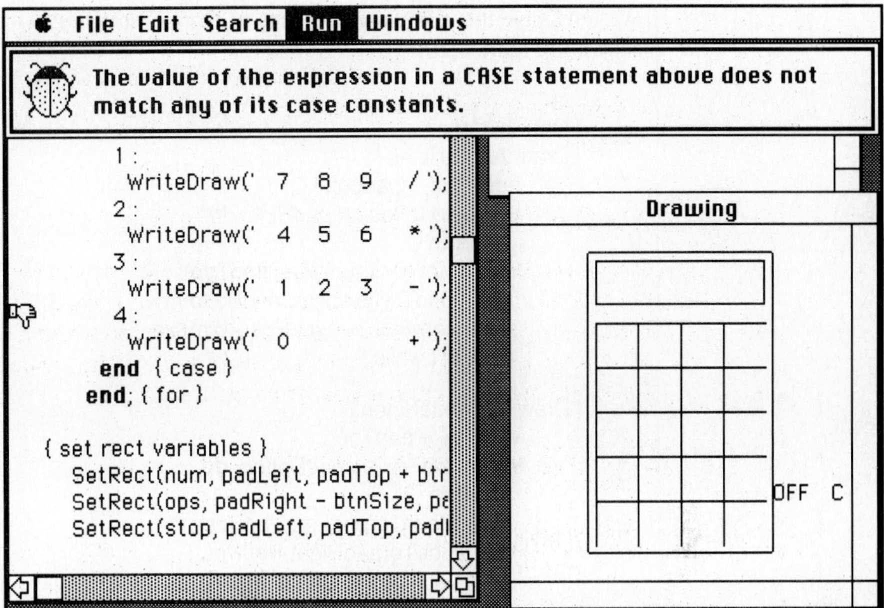

Figure 7.9
First run of *Calculator* program

Three errors are noticeable in this run. First, we fix the error that halted the program. The bug box tells us that ***lineCtr*** in procedure ***DrawCalculator*** is not receiving a value between 0 and 4 — otherwise, the **case** statement would have executed correctly. The ***lineCtr*** bug is easy to find, since the variable gets a value in only one place: the **for** loop. We note that the error occurs when the loop counter goes to 5. We adjust the upper limit from ***maxRows*** to ***maxRows – 1*** to correct the error.

Second, the keypad is missing one horizontal and one vertical line. To begin solving this problem, we place stop signs next to the **while** loops in ***DrawCalculator***. We also use the Observe window to monitor the progress of the variables ***horizPos*** and ***vertPos***. By choosing **Go-Go**, we can watch as the keypad is slowly built. We notice that when the first loop is exited, ***horizPos*** has a value of 150; when the second loop is exited, ***vertPos*** has a value of 180. According to Figure 7.7, these values are the correct coordinates of the last line in either direction. Still, the loop is exited before the last line is drawn. We look at the exit condition of the first **while** loop — the condition should be changed from ***horizPos < padRight*** to ***horizPos <= padRight*** to get one more iteration. Similarly, we change the condition of the second **while** loop by adding an equals sign after the less-than sign.

The third problem in the initial run is that the text is drawn at the wrong position. We ask, "How did it get there?" The ***WriteDraw*** command, you will recall, prints text at the current position. So what is the current position? Oops. We forgot to move the current position. We insert the statement ***MoveTo(padLeft,vertPos)*** just above the **case** statement in ***DrawCalculator***.

We now have the following revisions to ***DrawCalculator***, which yield the display shown in Figure 7.10.

```
...
{ Draw buttons }
{ Draw vertical lines }
        horizPos := padLeft;
        while horizPos <= padRight do
            begin
                MoveTo(horizPos, padTop);
                LineTo(horizPos, padBottom);
                horizPos := horizPos + btnSize
            end; { while }

{ Draw horizontal lines }
        vertPos := padTop;
        while vertPos <= padBottom do
            begin
                MoveTo(padLeft, vertPos);
                LineTo(padRight, vertPos);
                vertPos := vertPos + btnSize
            end; { while }

{ draw text }

        for lineCtr := 0 to maxRows - 1 do
            begin
            { get position for text }
                vertPos := lineCtr * btnSize + padTop;
                vertPos := vertPos + (btnSize div 2) + 3;
                MoveTo(padLeft, vertPos);
```

Now that the calculator has been drawn correctly, we can test the buttons. We begin with the OFF button. If that works, we know the program will exit correctly. We click on the OFF button — *voila!* the program stops.

Next we try a numeric button. For some reason, when we press the 7 button, 9 appears in the output. Then, when we press the 4 button, numbers overlap in the display, as shown in Figure 7.11.

We attack one problem at a time. To get rid of the overlapping, we clear the display before printing each number. This is done by modifying the ***Display*** procedure: at the beginning of the routine, we add the statement
EraseRect(displayTop, padLeft, displayTop + btnSize, padRight);
to clear the display, then redraw its outline by using a ***FrameRect*** with the same coordinates. Since the text is coming too close to the bottom of the display, we modify the ***MoveTo*** statement to ***MoveTo(padLeft, displayTop + btnSize –5);***.

To check that these changes work, we halt execution at the end of the ***Display*** procedure. We then type the commands ***Display(12);*** and ***Display(7);*** in the

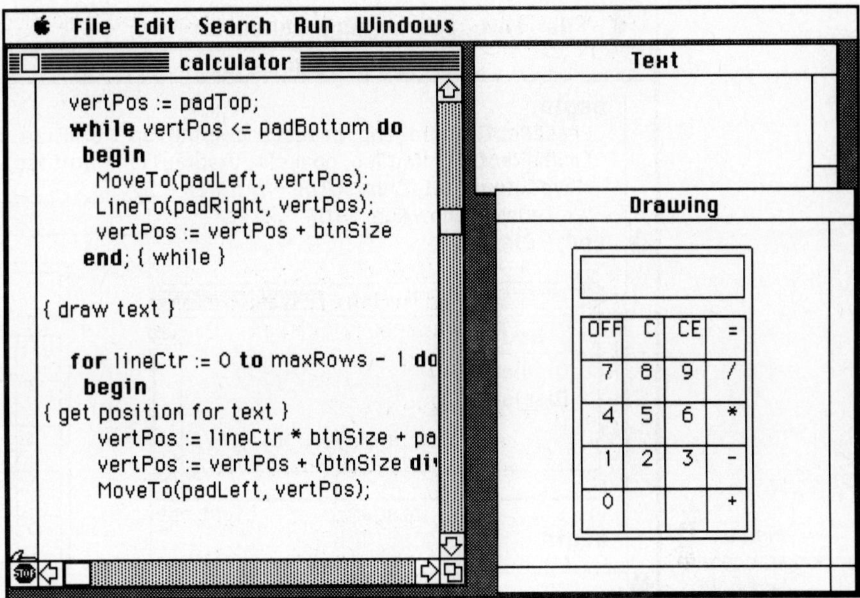

Figure 7.10 Drawing window after debugging *DrawCalculator*

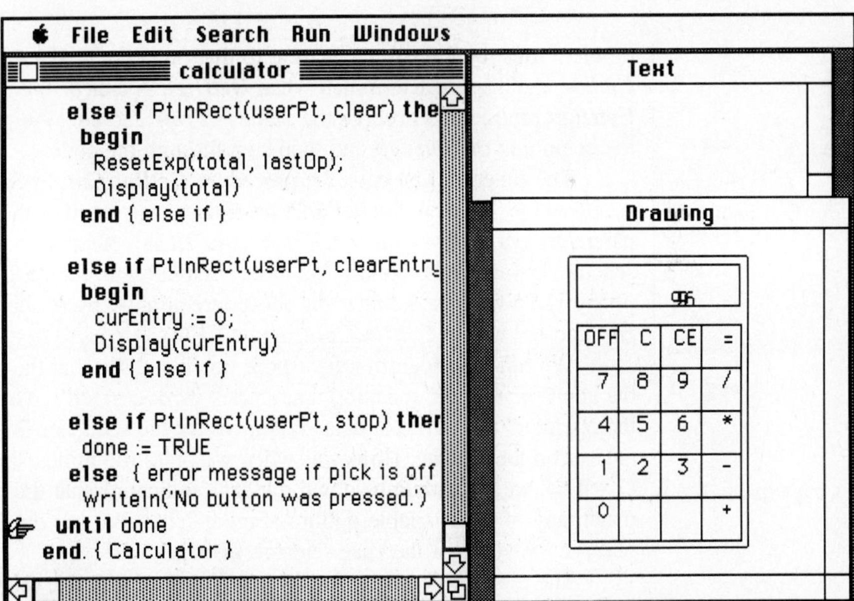

Figure 7.11 Overlapping numbers in the display

Instant window. When the code is executed, a 12, then a 7 appear in the display (Figure 7.12). Since this is the correct response, we can move on.

Now we address the problem that the wrong number is being displayed when a button is pressed. Since we just determined that ***Display*** works correctly, the

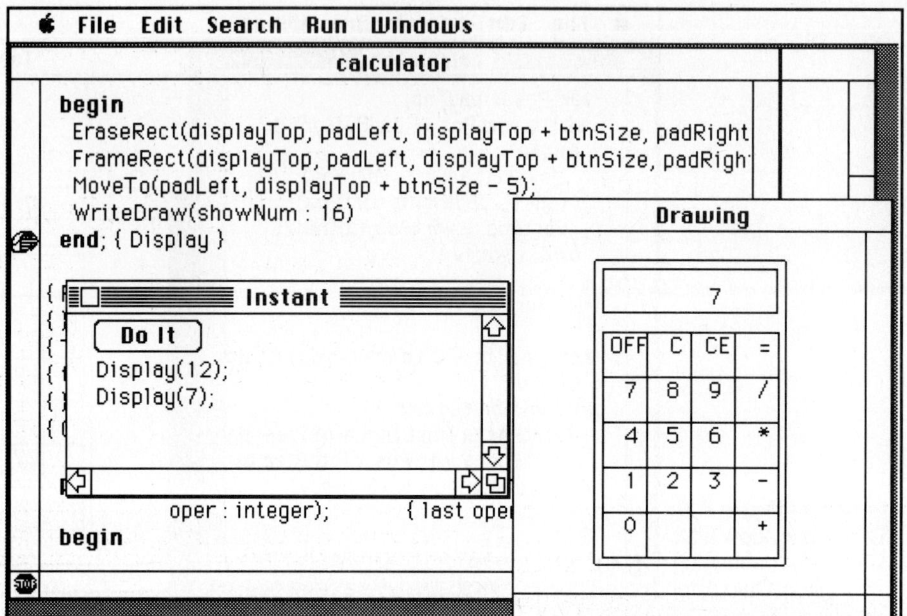

Figure 7.12
Checking procedure *Display* with Instant window

problem must be the parameter sent to that procedure. According to the code in ***Update***, the digit is determined when ***GetDigit*** is called. We step through the ***GetDigit*** routine and observe the values of ***row*** and ***col***. We place a stop sign at the beginning of ***GetDigit*** and then step through the code.

The function first calls the procedure ***GetRowCol***. In ***GetRowCol***, when we press the 7 button, the variable parameter ***row*** receives the value 4 and the parameter ***col*** receives the value 0 (Figure 7.13a). According to the numbering scheme, however, the button 7 is in the first column, the third row. Both values are off by 1. To fix this, we alter the procedure slightly by recalculating the values of ***row*** and ***col*** within ***GetRowCol*** (Figure 7.13b).

We run the program a few more times and see that the keys 1 through 9 display the appropriate digit, meaning that entries work correctly. Now, let's move to testing the operators with the test data. When we try the sequence 3 + 8 =, we get the correct answer on the display. However, when we press the minus sign in the next operation (7 – 4 =), we get a thumbs-down message indicating that the **case** selector didn't match any of the available options (Figure 7.14). We run the program again and observe the value of the **case** selector, ***lastOp***.

The mistake occurred because the value of the **case** selector was ***equals***. The minus sign generated the error because the previous equals sign did not generate a proper reset of the expression. We look at ***ResetExp*** — the procedure's parameters are value instead of variable. We add the word **var** before each parameter and go on, but we still find the same error. We try stepping through the program (Figure 7.15).

When the equals sign is pressed, the call to ***ResetExp*** at the bottom of ***Calculate*** is not executed. The condition ***lastOp = equals*** must be FALSE.

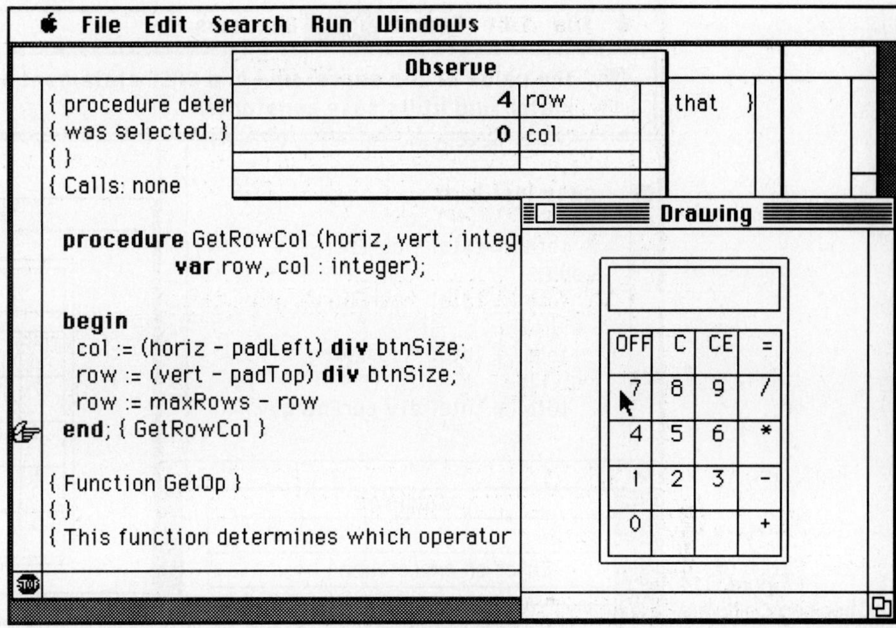

a. Off by one errors

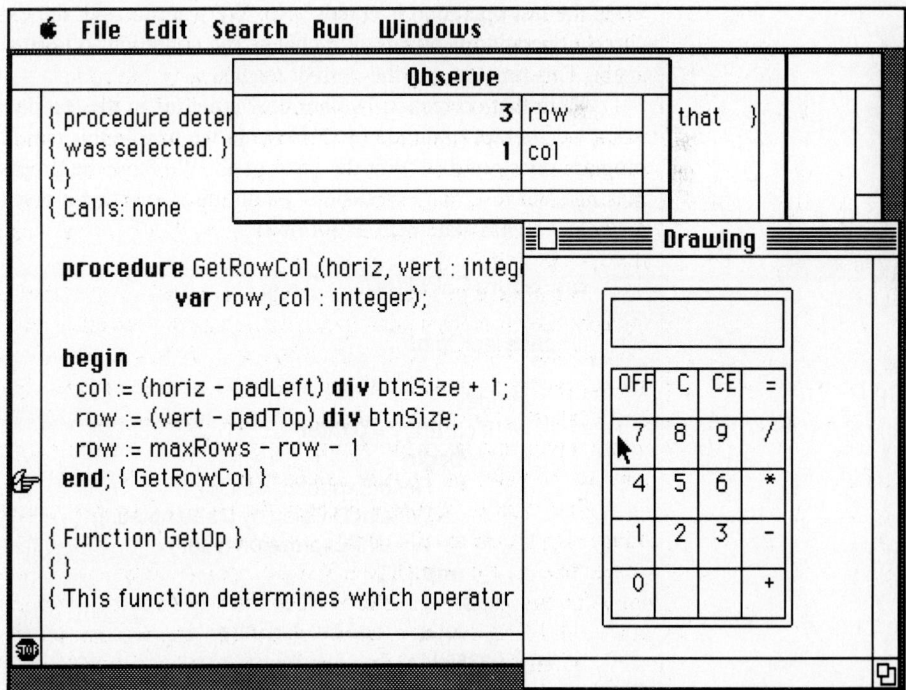

Figure 7.13
Fixing numeric display

b. Errors fixed

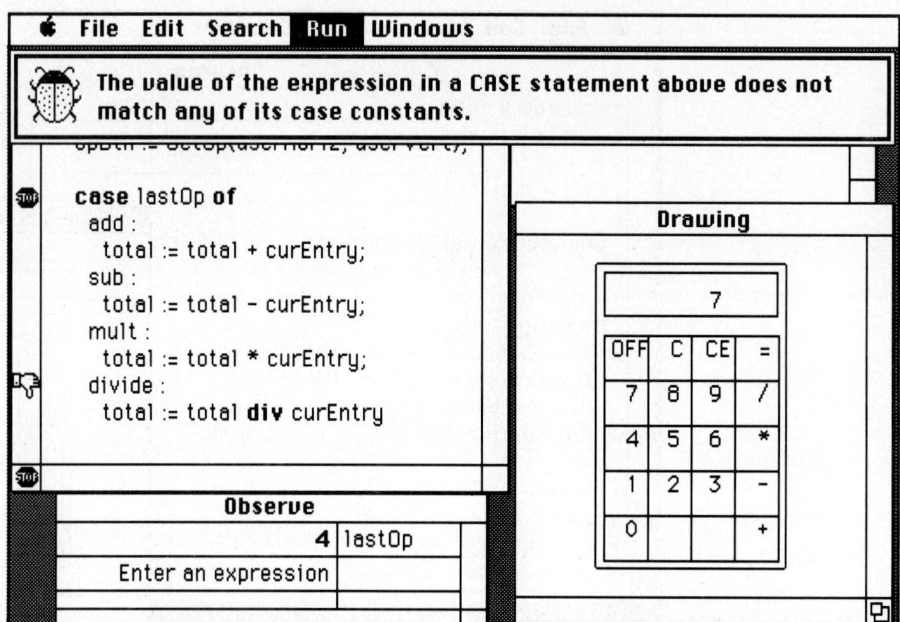

Figure 7.14
Checking *Calculate*

Then we think about what that condition means. Do we want to reset the expression when the last operation is equals? No. We want to reset the expression when the *current* operation is equals. We change the condition to ***opBtn = equals*** and try again. This time we get the correct results.

With that correction, we are now quite far in the test data. The next error occurs when we attempt to divide by 0. How do we handle this condition? Currently, the program does not deal with the error at all. We have the program print a textual error message and reset the expression. To do this, we revise a portion of procedure ***Calculate***'s **case** statement as follows:

```
procedure Calculate (...
    ...
    case lastOp of
        ...
        divide :
            if curEntry = 0 then
                begin
                    ResetExp(total, lastOp);
                    Writeln('Division by 0 attempted.');
                    Writeln('Expression reset')
                end { if }
            else
                total := total div curEntry
    end; { case }
...
```

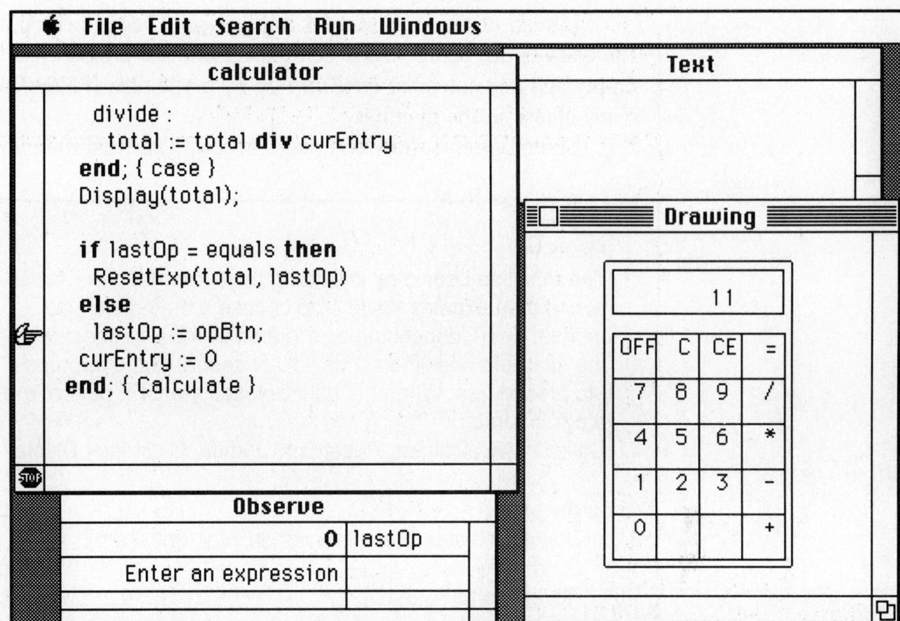

Figure 7.15
Stepping through *Calculate*

The remainder of the operations go smoothly. Now we just have to test the C and CE buttons. We try the sequences from Figures 7.3 and 7.4. The sequence 3 + 5 CE 6 = works fine; the tests yield the correct results. However, when we press the sequence 3 + 5 C 6, we see the result in Figure 7.16.

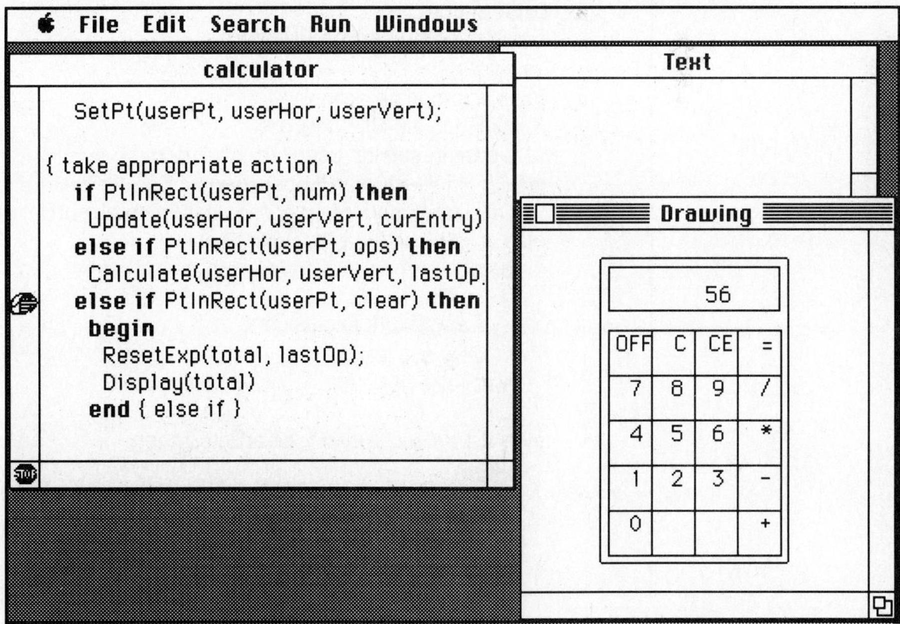

Figure 7.16
Checking Clear button

Instead of the expression and the display being cleared, the current entry is 56. The entry is not being reset when the C button is pressed. To fix this bug, we simply add the statement ***curEntry := 0;*** in the **else if *PtInRect(userPt, clear)*** clause in the mainline.

The program is now complete. Whew. The final mainline appears below.

Code 7.3
Final mainline

```
{Mainline                                                      }
{The mainline begins by initializing the screen and the equa-  }
{tion. It then expects the user to choose a button with the    }
{mouse. Then, depending on the area of the pad chosen by       }
{the user, the mainline sends flow of control to the appropri- }
{ate procedures. When the user presses the OFF button, the     }
{program ends.                                                 }
{Calls:DrawCalculator, ResetExp, Update, Calculate, Display    }

begin
  DrawCalculator(num, clear, clearEntry, ops, stop);
  done := FALSE;
  ResetExp(total, lastOp);
  curEntry := 0;

  repeat
  {get user's selection}

    repeat
      GetMouse(userHor, userVert);
    until Button;
    SetPt(userPt, userHor, userVert);

    {take appropriate action}
    if PtInRect(userPt, num)then
      Update(userHor, userVert, curEntry)
    else if PtInRect(userPt,ops) then
      Calculate(userHor, userVert, lastOp, total, curEntry)
    else if PtInRect(userPt, clear) then
      begin
        curEntry := 0;
        ResetExp(total, lastOp);
        Display(total)
      end {else if}

    else if PtInRect( userPt, clearEntry) then
      begin
        curEntry := 0;
        Display (curEntry)
      end {else If}
```

Code 7.3 (continued)

```
        else if PtInRect (userPt, stop) then
            done := TRUE
        else {error message if pick is off pad)
            Writeln('No button was pressed.')
    until done
end. (Calculator)
```

7.12 Debugging with Stubs

We have just developed an entire program from start to finish. At each step of development, we refined an entire level of pseudocode or code. Sometimes, though, it is desirable to pseudocode, translate, and debug entire sections of code before even considering how to break down another part of the problem. This method of program development is known as debugging with *stubs and drivers.*

Developing a program with stubs and drivers begins in the same way that any other program is developed: with a definition of the problem. Once the problem is defined, you can list tasks to perform and organize the list into the first level of pseudocode. Thus, when you start to pseudocode the program, you write out the first levels for the entire problem.

When the program is large, however, each task may require a number of procedures. We saw earlier that you can concentrate on one task at a time. From the first levels of pseudocode, you know which tasks will come before and which will come after the current task. Because you know the order of tasks, there is no reason that everything has to be done at once. Instead of typing the entire prepared code into the Macintosh and then trying to get the whole thing to work, you can enter parts of the program and get pieces working at a time.

A stub is a procedure that does little more than print a message that the procedure has been called. While stubs by themselves have no purpose, they can be helpful when you want to test a calling procedure. After the calling procedure has been tested thoroughly, you can replace the stub with a full procedure. For example, suppose we want to test the mainline in the calculator program. We simply want to see if the correct procedure is called when a particular button is pressed. Now, we can use the mainline that ended the last section. For the mainline to work, we need to define the procedures ***Calculate***, ***Update***, ***ResetEntry***, and so on. However, we don't want to concern ourselves with what each subroutine does; we only want to make sure that the mainline is working. Instead of typing in the code for these routines, we type in stubs. A typical stub procedure follows:

```
procedure Calculate( userHor, userVert: integer;
                     var lastOp, total, curEntry: integer);

begin
    Writeln('Calculate has been called.')
end; { Calculate }
```

The code in ***Calculate*** at this point does no calculation. Instead, when one of the operator buttons is pressed, ***Calculate*** is called and the string in the ***Writeln*** statement is printed. Flow of control returns to the mainline, and the user is expected to pick another button.

Pascal doesn't care that ***Calculate*** has no purpose at the moment. As long as the procedures in the calling routine are declared, Pascal can allow the procedure to be called. We can thus check and debug every line of the mainline, even though the subprocedures do no more than print messages. Once the mainline is debugged, ***Calculate*** and the other procedures can be modified to perform their intended functions.

We could have eliminated both the formal and actual parameters when we specified the stub procedure ***Calculate***. But as long as we have them declared, we may as well check whether the parameters are being passed correctly. For example, we know that the ***Calculate*** routine receives two value and three variable parameters. We give arbitrary values to the variable parameters as follows:

```
procedure Calculate( userHor, userVert: integer;
                     var lastOp, total, curEntry: integer);

begin
   Writeln('userHor = ', userHor: 3, 'userVert = ', userVert: 3);
   lastOp := 3;
   total := 5;
   curEntry := 8;
   Writeln('Calculate has been called.');
   Writeln('lastOp, total, curEntry have received values.')
end; { Calculate }
```

The arbitrary values are then passed back to the calling procedure, and the two messages are printed in the Text window. We can go through all the stubs and add assignment statements. At the top of each stub, we list the values of the parameters that were received. In this way, we know that garbage values are not being passed to value parameters. The method of printing parameter values in stubs lets us check the communication links between procedures. When we are sure that each procedure has the correct value and variable parameters, we can go on to filling in the rest of the statements.

7.13 Debugging with Drivers

Stubs are used to check a procedure that calls other procedures. In the above example, the mainline was fully implemented, but the procedures it called were not. Sometimes, though, we may want to implement the subprocedures and leave the calling procedures for later. We can use drivers for this purpose. Drivers are short procedures whose sole purpose is to check subprocedures. The driver assigns values to the subprocedure's parameters and prints the subprocedure's results. In short, a driver's pseudocode looks like this:

Assign values to send to subprocedure
Call subprocedure
Print results of subprocedure

The Instant window is well suited for debugging with drivers, since we can call a procedure with different parameters. We can also use the Observe window to print the results. In fact, we used drivers in debugging the Calculator. In testing the ***Display*** procedure, we stopped the program in the mainline and entered the calls ***Display(12);*** and ***Display(7);*** in the Instant window. The parameters 12 and 7 were simply test cases; we just wanted to see if the display would show two different numbers without overlapping them. This allowed us to check one particular aspect of the ***Display*** procedure.

Drivers can be more complex; you may want to check how more than one procedure interact. For example, you may take the parameters returned by one procedure and send them to another.

The point of stubs and drivers is that you do not have to run your entire code to test sections of it. These tools allow you to use either a top-down (writing the mainline and then each subprocedure) or a bottom-up (writing individual tasks and connecting them later) technique. By concentrating on one small area at a time, even the largest programs can be made manageable.

7.14 Final Suggestions

Computer programming is often thought of as a rigorous, systematic discipline. While planning, hand simulating, and meticulous debugging are certainly part of programming, creativity and intuition also are important.

Many folks are initially put off by programming because they associate it with mathematical skills: they claim, "I don't have a logical/analytical/mathematical mind." There's no denying that logical skills are useful in programming, but this does not mean that programming requires a completely rigid style of working.

Think for a moment about how you attack problems in other disciplines. Consider how you write a paper, create a sketch, compose music, design athletic strategies, or solve a word problem in math. All these endeavors require some combination of analytical and creative thought. You can write down phrases of music as they come to you and rearrange them into a complete piece later. Similarly, you can work on particular aspects or a program — say, how you want the screen to look or how you want to store the data — first and later create the whole from the parts.

In short, remember this: approach programming not as an entirely new concept but rather as a variation on a common theme. Think about how you approach other problems you face; odds are good that you can adapt this approach to solving programming problems.

7.15 Chapter Summary

This chapter introduced no new Pascal concepts. Rather, it discussed methods of making a program work. Pseudocode and debugging are two tools that make programming easier. They are both highly individualized items; that is, programmers pseudocode and debug with their own individual methods. Still, systematic techniques exist for pseudocoding and debugging.

Pseudocode can be developed by successively adding Pascal concepts to an original list of tasks. As the algorithm becomes more and more like programming language statements, you can add flow-of-control statements, consider error conditions, and think about the details of the user interface. You can also specify a procedure's requirements, effects, and return values.

The Pascals on the Macintosh provides several facilities for debugging. We have already examined the Observe window, the use of stop signs, and the four methods of running a program (**Go**, **Go-Go**, **Step**, **Step-Step/Trace**). Here we introduced the **Instant** window. When you press the Instant window's **Do It** button, MacPascal executes whatever code you have entered into the window. Usually, you will want to stop the program, because code in the Instant window can refer to any active variables or predeclared procedures. However, the Instant window can perform any statement at any time.

Stubs and drivers are inverse techniques. A stub is a dummy procedure that does little more than receive parameters and print a message indicating that the stub was called. By seeing where the stub was called, however, you can make sure that the caller is calling procedures in the correct order and with the correct parameters.

Stubs are used to implement procedures that call other procedures. You use drivers to implement a single procedure that is called by others. The driver calls the completed procedure with appropriate variables and then prints any changes that the called procedure may have made. Both techniques allow you to test your program a piece at a time.

Pinpointing bugs is crucial to debugging. Stubs, drivers, and the Mac facilities are all more useful when you concentrate on a 20-line segment, rather than trying to contemplate an entire 1500-line program.

7.16 Exercises

Understanding Concepts

1. Think about the last program you wrote. What do you look for when you are given a programming assignment? What planning strategies did you use? Do you use pseudocode (be honest!)? Do you write code on paper before entering it into the Mac? When do you debug online? When do you hand simulate? Do you use the Mac facilities, the various options on the **Run** menu, stop signs, the Observe and Instant windows? When do you add documentation to your program?

2. Find yourself a partner and choose a programming assignment from an earlier chapter. Keep a journal of how your partner proceeds. Ask her to think aloud as she outlines, codes, and debugs the problem. When she is done, trade places: your partner keeps a journal of your actions as you solve a different programming problem. Seeing a journal of your actions taken by an observer should help you understand your own programming techniques.

   Break down problems 3 through 6. You need not refine the steps to the level of code but establish a set of subtasks and decide the order in which they should be performed.

3. At a residential college, 1800 students need housing. Your job is to determine the order in which students can choose their housing. Students give you lists indicating whom they want to live with. They can live in groups of 1, 2, 3, or 4 and with students from other years (for example, seniors and juniors can live together). From the students' lists, create the order of selection. Your order should give priority to more advanced students — e.g., seniors should pick ahead of juniors — but students in the same class should all have the same priority.

4. Prepare a timetable for providing cocktails, a three-course meal (hot appetizer, cold salad, hot main course), and dessert to 200 people. Your one restriction: the oven can heat only 50 appetizers or main courses at a time.

5. A restaurant has 10 tables for 2, 20 tables for 4, 5 tables for 6, and 1 table for 10. Divide the potential customers equally among 6 waiters and waitresses.

6. Create a linoleum tile pattern. First create the pattern within a square area, then repeat it so it fills the screen.

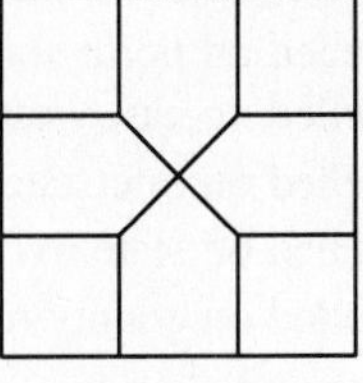

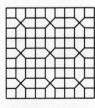

original

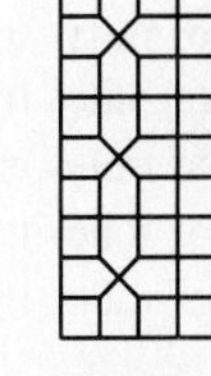

repeated pattern

Translate the pseudocode fragments in problems 7-10 to code. Some of the algorithms may have to be broken down further and/or debugged.

7.
```
FOR each zip code entered by user DO
    IF (first digit is not 0) OR (first digit is not 1) THEN
        Add 1 to count of zip codes not in the northeast
Print number of zip codes not in northeast (that do not begin with 0 or 1)
```

8.
```
Print "The movie will be shown at"
Enter showtime of first film
WHILE current showtime is before midnight DO
    BEGIN
        Print current show time
        IF show time is before 6:00 p.m. THEN
            Print "(matinee)"
        Add 2 hours 15 minutes to current show time
    END { WHILE }
```

9.
```
FOR each batter DO
    REPEAT
        Get current pitch
        CASE current pitch OF
            ball: add 1 to ball count
            strike: add 1 to strike count
            foul: IF strike count < 2 THEN
                        Add 1 to strike count
            fair: Call FairHit procedure
        END { CASE }
    UNTIL FairHit is called, ball count = 4 or strike count = 3
```

10.
```
FOR each route on trip DO
    BEGIN
        Enter route number
        Enter other information on route
        IF route number is odd THEN
            Add to total miles on north-south routes
        ELSE
            Add to total miles on east-west routes
    END

Print total number of miles travelled on north-south routes
Print total number of miles travelled on east-west routes
Print total number of miles travelled on interstates
Print total number of miles travelled on state roads
Print total number of miles travelled on county roads
```

11.-13. Hand simulate and debug the following code fragments:

11.

```
{ This procedure draws a heart shape inside a specified rectangle. }

procedure Heart(top, left,                    { top left corner of rect       }
                bottom, right: integer);      { bottom right corner of rect

begin
   horizMid := left + right div 2;
   vertMid := top + bottom div 2;
   FrameArc(top, left, vertMid, horizMid, 270,180);
   FrameArc(top, horizMid, vertMid, right, 270,180);
   MoveTo(left, top + ((bottom – top) div 4));
   LineTo(horizMid, bottom);
   LineTo(right, top + ((bottom – top) div 4))
end; { Heart }
```

12.

```
const
   sentinel = 0;   { indicates user wants to exit }

{ Process shoe orders until user asks to stop }
procedure ProcessShoeOrders(var curStock: integer);    { num of pairs of shoes left }
   var
done: boolean;   { indicates end of processing }
shoeSize: real;  { shoe size to find }

begin
   while not done do
      begin
         Write('Please enter a shoe size or ', sentinel:2, 'to exit: ');
         Readln(shoeSize);
         if not done and (shoeSize <> sentinel) then
            CheckInventory(shoeSize, curStock); { Assume call is correct }
         if curStock <= 0 then
            Writeln('No shoes left')
      end { while }
end; { ProcessShoeOrders }
```

13.

```
{ This program calculates the number of ways that a number of          }
{ people can be arranged at a table. If there are n guests, the total  )
{ number of arrangements is n!, or n * (n-1) * (n-2),.., 3 * 2 * 1.    }
{ The program asks the user to enter the number of guests, and         }
{ then responds by printing the number of arrangements.The             }
{ process repeats until the user enters the sentinel.                  }
```

```
program Seating;

const
   sentinel = -1;    { marks end of data                              }

var
   numGuests,      { number of guests to seat                         }
   guestCtr,       { current guest in loop                            }
   arrange: integer;                    { number of arrangements       }

begin
   Write('Enter the number of guests to be seated or ', sentinel:2, ' to exit: ');
   Readln(numGuests);
   arrange := 1;

   while (numGuests <> sentinel) do
      begin
         for guestCtr := 1 to numGuests do
            arrange := arrange * guestCtr;

         Write('There are ', arrange:3, ' arrangements for ');
         Writeln( numGuests: 2, ' guests');

         Write('Enter the number of guests to be seated or ');
         Write( sentinel:2, ' to exit: ');
         Readln(numGuests)

      end { while }
end. { Seating }
```

String Manipulation

For most of their history, computers have been perceived as machines that perform scientific calculations or "number crunching." Yet while a great deal can be done by manipulating numbers, completely numeric data has its limitations. Since the 1960s, computers have also been used to store and manipulate large amounts of textual data. Most large newspapers and magazines are typeset via computers. Businesses, government agencies, and schools use computers to maintain rosters of employees, taxpayers, and students. Language scholars use computers to analyze patterns in written texts. In the jargon of computer scientists, sequences of characters are known as *character strings*. This chapter shows how MacPascal allows us to store and manipulate single characters and character strings.

8.1 Character Types

So far, we have been dealing with numeric, boolean, and graphic variables. Pascal also provides a method of storing single letters, symbols, and blanks in variables. Any single character that can be typed on the keyboard can be represented in a variable declared as a ***char***, just as the set of integers can be represented in variables of type ***integer***. A partial list of the set of legal ***char*** values follows (the full list of legal ***char*** values appears in Appendix F).

'A', 'B',..., 'Y', 'Z', 'a', 'b',..., 'y', 'z', '1', '2',..., '9', '0', '!', '@', ';', '(', ')',...

Note that each character is *delimited,* or surrounded, by apostrophes. These are necessary if you are using a character as a constant value; they tell the interpreter that the symbol is to be treated as a character constant, rather than as a variable identifier, numeric constant, or punctuation symbol. Just as the delimiting apostrophes in a ***Writeln*** statement are not part of the output, the delimiting apostrophes surrounding a character are not part of the character. For example, the following **const** declaration creates a constant called ***confirm***. The constant will hold the character ***y***; it will not contain the apostrophes.

```
const
    confirm = 'y';                  { indicates that user wants to stop }
```

Characters are not often used as constants; more frequently, they are used to generate textual menus. You have seen standardized multiple choice tests, in which the characters A, B, C, D, and E denote the five different answers to a particular question. If you have ever used a spreadsheet program, you know that characters can represent different commands (for example, entering a C could mean "clear the current cell"). In either case, the user enters a character and the program executes some operation (in the case of a spreadsheet, the program manipulates the data in the rows and columns; in the case of a multiple choice test, the program indicates whether the user made the correct choice).

To create menus using characters, you need variables that can hold characters. To do this, you can use the data type ***char***. Like numeric, graphic, and boolean variables, character variables are declared in the **var** section of each procedure.

```
var
    request: char;          { user's menu response   }
    total: real;            { total of hand thus far }
```

The declared character variable, like other variables, initially holds a garbage value. As with variables of other types, the ***char*** variable can receive a value in one of two ways: through an assignment statement or through a ***Readln*** statement. If you use an assignment statement, the character must be delimited by apostrophes:

```
request := 'h';             { initial value for request   }
```

To use characters in a textual menu, you need to receive a character from the user and then tell Pascal to perform the appropriate action. Suppose you want to write a program to play the game of blackjack (first examined in Chapter 4). During the game, the player may take cards (known as "hitting") until he wants to stop (known as "staying"). Since ***char*** is an *ordinal type* (i.e., all the values for characters can be counted), you can use a ***char*** variable as the selector in a **case** statement. The following code fragment prompts the user to enter either the character 'h' or the character 's'. Depending on the user's choice, the fragment either calls another procedure or prints the user's total for the hand.

```
var
    request: char;          { user's choice                      }
    done: boolean;          { indicates that hand is finished    }
    total: integer;         { total for hand thus far            }
```

```
begin
    ...
    Write('Please enter h to hit, s to stay: ');
    Readln(request);
    case request of
        'h':
            begin
                Writeln('Picking another card...');
                HitCard(total)
            end; { 'h' }
        's':
            begin
                Writeln('Your final total is', total:4);
                done := TRUE
            end; { 's' }
        otherwise
            Writeln('You did not enter a legal option. ')
    end; { case }
    ...
end; { procedure }
```

When Pascal reads the ***Readln*** statement at the top of this fragment, it asks the user to input a character. If the user enters 'h', the line "Picking another card..." is output and the procedure ***HitCard*** is invoked. If the user enters 's', Pascal prints a message using the value of ***total*** and sets the boolean variable ***done*** to TRUE. In all other cases, the fragment prints an error message.

Pascal accepts only one character from the keyboard for each character variable in a ***Readln*** statement. Thus, if the user inputs the word 'halt' for the above code fragment, ***Readln*** accepts the first character — 'h' — and performs the ***Writeln*** statement and procedure call associated with the 'h' case. The remaining characters in the input ('a', 'l', and 't') are ignored.

Not only can you use characters as a **case** statement selector, you can also use the comparison operators (discussed in Chapter 4) to compare characters. Again, apostrophes are needed to distinguish the ***char*** variables from identifiers. The following is a list of some of the legal character comparisons in MacPascal:

```
'a' = 'a'        'a' <= 'c'
'a' < 'b'        'b' >= 'b'
'A' < 'a'        'B' > 'A'
'a' <> '+'       '3' < 'a'
'a' > ' '        '3' > '2'
```

All of the above comparisons evaluate to TRUE when used in boolean expressions.

Any character, whether it is a letter, number, symbol, or blank, can be compared to any other character. It is, therefore, meaningful for one character to be "less than" or "greater than" another character. This is possible because each character is represented in memory by a unique number in binary code. A number of different coding schemes exist for representing the characters; the specific code used by the Macintosh is based on the ASCII (American Standard Code for Information Interchange) code. The ASCII code is used by many other computers; the Macintosh character set merely defines more of the decimal values. The complete Macintosh character set appears in Appendix F.

The order of characters, known as the *collating sequence,* determines which characters are less than or greater than others. For example, the number sign (#) is stored in memory as the binary value 100011, which translates to 35 in decimal. When Pascal compares characters, it compares the characters' numeric values. Thus, the number sign is less than the dollar sign ($), because the representation of the number sign (35) is less than the representation of the dollar sign (36). Of course, this all happens internally; you do not have to concern yourself with this level of detail when you are programming in Pascal.

8.2 Literal Strings

Characters by themselves are not used very often in MacPascal because this version of the language can handle sequences of characters known as strings. We first looked at character string processing in Chapter 1. The ***Writeln*** statement allows you to print a line of text. Since the string is written literally into the program, the text found between the apostrophes is known as a *literal string.*

Some examples of literal strings are:

1. 'What is your name?'
2. 'Please input a number between 5 and 7: '
3. 'Aren''t computers fun?'
4. ''
5. ' '

Strings 1 and 2 show that a string can be any combination of letters, symbols, numbers, and blank spaces. String 3 shows a special case: the two apostrophes in ***Aren''t*** are necessary to persuade Pascal to print a single apostrophe. String 4 is the *null,* or *empty,* string. If this string is used as the parameter in a ***Writeln*** statement, no characters are printed. On the other hand, if string 5 is the parameter to a ***Writeln*** statement, a single blank space is added to the output. A blank is not the same thing as a null string, because a blank counts like any other character.

8.3 String Variables

In your daily life, you have seen many uses of computer that save time and are used to help people. In addition to these proper uses of computers, you have undoubtedly also seen some of the abuses of computers. Let's look at one example: computerized junk mail. Before the advent of computer-based text processing, everybody got the same advertising flyers. These days, though, computers are used to "personalize" a company's come-on. Instead of sending the message "YOU ARE ELIGIBLE TO

RECEIVE A SPECIAL DISCOUNT ON A BUILD-IT-YOURSELF YACHT. YOU HAVE THE CHANCE TO BECOME THE ENVY OF YOUR ENTIRE TOWN WHEN YOU BRING YOUR NEW YACHT DOWN THE STREET," mailing houses can now generate a message such as "YOU, JEFF VROOM, ARE ELIGIBLE TO RECEIVE A SPECIAL DISCOUNT ON A BUILD-IT-YOURSELF YACHT. MR. VROOM, YOU HAVE THE CHANCE TO BECOME THE ENVY OF GUILFORD, CT, WHEN YOU BRING YOUR NEW YACHT DOWN WINGATE ROAD." Such "individualized" mass mailings are possible because character string variables for items such as the name, town, and address of the recipient can be placed in the letter and replaced with specific values. To program such a mailing, we need to define and use string variables.

The data type **string** can be used to declare string variables. The following example shows two different ways in which a string can be declared:

```
var
    name: string;          { name of recipient              }
    state: string[2];      { recipient's state of residence }
```

The first declaration creates a variable called ***name***. This variable can hold a maximum of 255 characters. In this case, **string** is used in the same way that you have seen other data types used (***integer***, ***real***, ***boolean***, ***char***). The second declaration, though, creates a variable with a different size. The variable ***state*** is also a string, but it can hold a maximum of 2 characters. The maximum length of the string held by the variable is placed between square brackets, and the length must be indicated by an integer constant between 0 and 255.

We specify a length of a string variable when we know the maximum number of characters a string will need to hold. The string length alters the amount of memory MacPascal sets aside to manipulate the string. Since we rarely use strings of 255 characters, declaring a string length allows more memory to be used for other variables and calculations. Using as little memory as possible is particularly important when you are using a computer with a small amount of memory, such as the Macintosh.

String variables receive values in the same way as other variables do. For example, you can use a string in an assignment statement:

```
name :='Amy Elizabeth Tozer';
```

The above example assigns a literal string to a variable and thus uses apostrophes. The apostrophes do not count as part of the string itself but the spaces between the words do count. Thus, in this example, ***name*** receives a 19-character string.

The assumption is that ***name*** is a string variable with a length of at least 19. If ***name*** is declared to hold, say, 15 characters (i.e., if ***name:*string*[15];*** had appeared in the **var** declarations), then a run-time error message similar to **A STRING value is too long for its intended use.** will apppear in a bug box. If ***name*** is declared to have more than 19 characters, the remaining characters in ***name*** (i.e., the characters starting at the 20th position) will have undefined (garbage)

Syntax Box 8.1
Declaring string variables

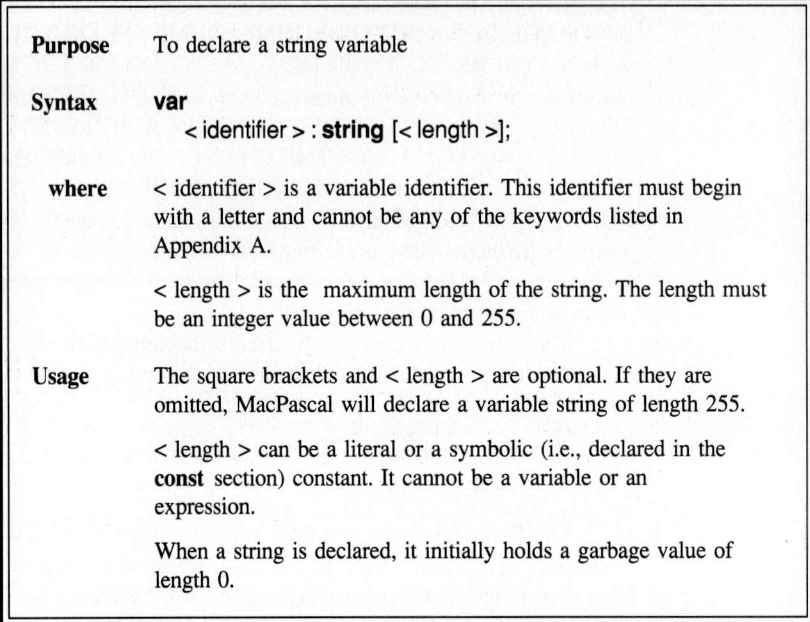

Purpose To declare a string variable

Syntax **var**
< identifier > : **string** [< length >];

where < identifier > is a variable identifier. This identifier must begin with a letter and cannot be any of the keywords listed in Appendix A.

< length > is the maximum length of the string. The length must be an integer value between 0 and 255.

Usage The square brackets and < length > are optional. If they are omitted, MacPascal will declare a variable string of length 255.

< length > can be a literal or a symbolic (i.e., declared in the **const** section) constant. It cannot be a variable or an expression.

When a string is declared, it initially holds a garbage value of length 0.

values. We shall see later why the number of characters in a string is important in comparisons.

String variables can also receive values from input statements. Again, assuming we have declared ***name*** as a string of some length, we can use the following code fragment to input a name:

```
Write('Please enter the recipient''s name:');
Readln(name);
```

When MacPascal encounters this fragment, it prints the prompt in the text window and waits for the user's input. The user may enter any string. If the user makes a mistake, she may use the backspace key to erase characters. When the user presses the Return key, MacPascal assigns the string that appears on the screen to the string variable. The user does not have to enter the delimiting apostrophes.

Thus, if we want to input the string 'Amy Elizabeth Tozer' to ***name***, using the above code fragment, the Text window will look like Figure 8.1.

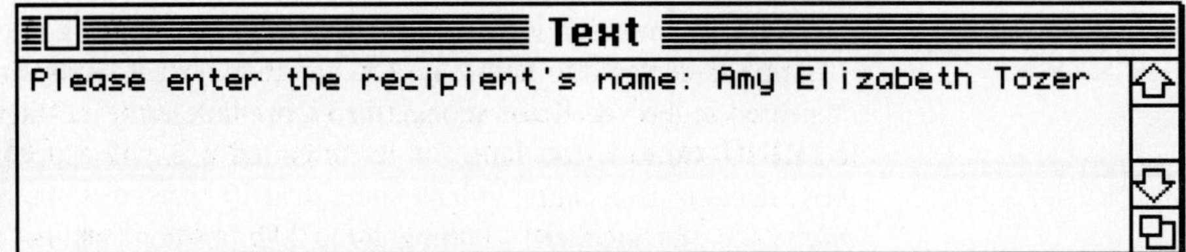

Figure 8.1
Text window when strings are input

Once we have given a value to a string variable, we can use it in comparisons. For example, the following code fragments are legal Pascal statements:

```
while name < 'M' do                    { process names up to, but not       }
    begin                              { including those starting with 'M'  }
        ...
    end; { while }

if name <> '' then                     { compare to null string             }
    begin
        ...
    end; { if }
```

In comparing two strings, Pascal begins by comparing the first characters of the strings. If the first characters are identical, Pascal then compares the second characters. Pascal searches until it finds characters in corresponding positions that are not identical. At that point, it compares the characters the same way that it would compare two variables of type ***char***.

The following are examples of TRUE string comparisons:*

1. 'able' < 'baker'
2. 'RED' >= 'BLUE'
3. 'Woo' > 'Wolf'
4. 'red' > 'RED'
5. '^number' < 'number'
6. '#$@*!' = '#$@*!'
7. 'lamp' < 'lamppost'

Examples 1, 2, and 3 are typical cases. The comparisons stop after the first character in 1 and 2 because the 'a' in 'able' is less than the 'b' in 'baker' and the 'R' in 'RED' is greater than or equal to the 'B' in 'BLUE'.

In example 3, the first two characters of each string are identical. However, MacPascal will not claim that two strings are equal until all of the characters have been compared. When MacPascal compares the third characters (the second 'o' in 'Woo' and the 'l' in 'Wolf'), it finds that the character on the left is greater than the corresponding character on the right; therefore, the string on the left is greater than the string on the right.

Examples 4 and 5 again stop after the first character, but the comparison may not seem as obvious as in 1 and 2. In both 4 and 5, Pascal checks the numeric representations of the first character. It determines that the 'r' of 'red' is greater than the 'R' of 'RED' and that the leading blank space in '^number' is less than the 'n' in 'number'.

In example 6, Pascal needed to look at all characters of both strings. Since all five characters in both strings were identical, the entire strings must be equal.

In the final comparison, the first four characters of 'lamp' and 'lamppost' are identical. When Pascal tried to compare the fifth character of both strings, it noticed

* Throughout the remainder of this chapter, the caret (^) denotes a blank space.

that the string on the left did not have a fifth character. Since nothing remained of the left string, a null character (represented in the ASCII collating sequence as a 0) was compared to the fifth character of 'lamppost'. Since the representation of the null character is less than that of any other character, the string on the left is determined to be less than the string on the right.

String variables are output using the ***Write***, ***Writeln***, and ***WriteDraw*** statements. For example, the following code fragment echo prints the user's name:

```
procedure EchoPrint;

var
    name: string[30];                    { user's name }

begin
    Write('What is your name? ');
    Readln(name);
    Writeln('Nice to meet you,' name)
end; { EchoPrint }
```

When this procedure is run, the result shown is Figure 8.2.

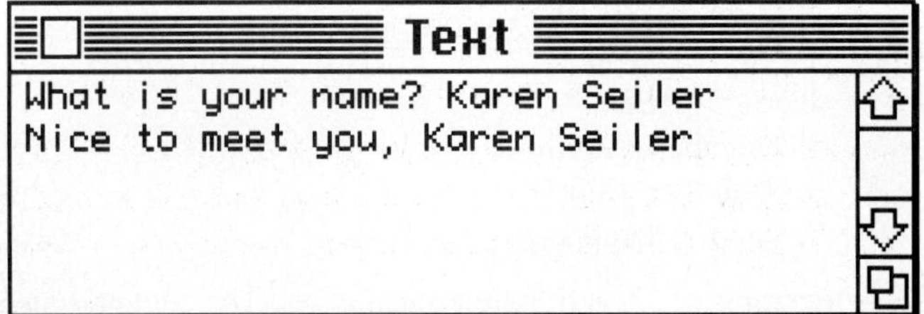

Figure 8.2
Text Window output of procedure *EchoPrint*

Strings can also be formatted in fields. As with the numeric field widths specified in Chapter 2, the width of the field determines the number of spaces that appear in the the output for the string. Below are some examples of string formatting. To show the limits of the field in the output, the ends of the fields are denoted by asterisks (*).

```
place := 'Medford Lakes';
Writeln('*', place, '*');       produces   *Medford Lakes*
Writeln('*', place:18, '*');    produces   *^^^^^Medford Lakes*
Writeln('*', place:10, '*');    produces   *Medford^La*
```

In the first line is a string output with no field width specification. MacPascal takes as much room as needed to output the entire string. The current length of the string is not the same as the maximum length of the string. The variable ***place*** can hold up to 255 characters; still, when no field width is specified, MacPascal outputs only as many characters as have been assigned to the variable. In the second line, the string has been right-justified. In the final line, the string is truncated at the length of the field width.

8.4 Using Strings

Let's look at two examples of using strings. First, we'll examine how to create the form letter mentioned in the previous section. Second, we'll see how to use string parameters to create a general procedure for making menu buttons.

The form letter uses five pieces of information: the recipient's name, street address, city, state, and sex. We can generate form letters by asking the user to enter this information and then inserting the input in the appropriate places. The recipient's sex is needed to generate the appropriate title. For simplicity, we will use the titles MR. for all males and MS. for all females. The pseudocode for this simple procedure looks like this:

```
Enter recipient's name
Enter recipient's street address
Enter recipient's city
Enter recipient's state
Enter recipient's sex
IF recipient is female THEN
    title is 'MS.'
ELSE IF recipient is male THEN
    title is 'MR.'
Print form letter using name, street, city, state, title
```

We certainly will not need strings of length 255 for this program. We can choose a shorter string length, say 80, since most names and addresses have no more than 80 characters. The code for this procedure follows:

Code 8.1 Procedure *FormLetter*

```
{ Procedure FormLetter                                          }
{                                                               }
{ This procedure generates a form letter for a contest. The user }
{ is asked to input the recipient's name, street address, city,  }
{ state, and sex.  A form letter is then printed, inserting the  }
{ user's information where needed.                              }

   procedure FormLetter;

      var
         first, last,             { recipient's name             }
         address,                 { recipient's street address   }
         city : string[80];       { recipient's home town        }
         state : string[2];       { post office abbreviation for }
                                  {     recipient's home state   }
         sex : char;              { M for male; F for female     }
         title : string[3];       { either MR. or MS.            }
```

Code 8.1 (continued)

```
begin
{ Receive information on recipient }
   Write('Please enter the recipient''s first name: ');
   Readln(first);
   Write('Please enter the recipient''s last name: ');
   Readln(last);
   Write('Please enter the recipient''s street address: ');
   Readln(address);
   Write('Please enter the recipient''s home town: ');
   Readln(city);
   Writeln('Please enter the two-letter abbreviation for');
   Write('the recipient''s state: ');
   Readln(state);
   Write('Please enter M if the recipient is male or F if female: ');
   Readln(sex);

   if sex = 'M' then
      title := 'MR.'
   else
      title := 'MS.';

{ Print form letter }
   Writeln;
   Writeln('YOU, ', first, ' ', last, ', ARE ELIGIBLE TO RECEIVE A SPECIAL');
   Writeln('DISCOUNT ON A BUILD-IT-YOURSELF YACHT. ', title, ' ', last, ',');
   Write('YOU HAVE THE CHANCE TO BECOME THE ENVY OF ');
   Writeln(city, ', ', state, ',');
   Writeln('WHEN YOU BRING YOUR NEW YACHT DOWN ', address, '.')

end; { FormLetter }
```

```
Please enter the recipient's first name: JEFF
Please enter the recipient's last name: VROOM
Please enter the recipient's street address: WINGATE ROAD
Please enter the recipient's home town: GUILFORD
Please enter the two-letter abbreviation for
the recipient's state: CT
Please enter M if the recipient is male or F if female: M

YOU, JEFF VROOM, ARE ELIGIBLE TO RECEIVE A SPECIAL
DISCOUNT ON A BUILD-IT-YOURSELF YACHT. MR. VROOM,
YOU HAVE THE CHANCE TO BECOME THE ENVY OF GUILFORD, CT,
WHEN YOU BRING YOUR NEW YACHT DOWN WINGATE ROAD.
```

Figure 8.3 Output of procedure *formLetter*

You can refer to an individual character in a string by its position number. The characters in a string are numbered from left to right, starting with 1. To refer to an individual character, use the notation < string var >[< position >]. For example, if the string variable ***name*** holds 'Amy Elizabeth Tozer', then ***name[1]*** holds the character 'A', ***name[4]*** holds a blank character, and ***name[19]*** holds the character 'r'. You can use any character within a string as if it were a variable of type ***char***.

Let's look at how we could change the ***FormLetter*** procedure. We know that the title of the recipient will be either MR. or MS. Both titles are three characters long, start with an M, and end with a period. The second character is either R or S, depending on whether the recipient is male or female. We can use a base string of 'M^.' for the title and insert either an 'R' or an 'S' when we know the recipient's gender. The following code inserts the appropriate character into the title string:

```
procedure MakeTitle;

var
    sex: char;                  { M for Male, F for female              }
    title: string[3];           { either MR. or MS.                     }
    charToInsert: char;         { either R or S depending on gender     }

begin
  { set title to base string }
  title := 'M .';

  { enter recipient's sex }
  Write('Please enter M if recipient is Male; F if Female: ');
  Readln(sex);

  { set appropriate character }
  if sex = 'F' then
    charToInsert := 'S'
  else if sex = 'M' then
    charToInsert := 'R';

  { complete title by placing char in second position }
  title[2] := charToInsert
end;
```

Notice that the final line of the procedure (***title[2] := charToInsert***) does not cause a syntax error. It is true that ***title*** is declared as a **string[3]** and ***charToInsert*** is declared as a ***char***. However, ***title[2]*** is a single character in the string ***title***. Therefore, both sides of the assignment symbol are of type ***char***, and the assignment is legal.

Finally, let's look at how to use a string parameter to create a general procedure for making menu buttons. Menu buttons are often created with plain text. The pseudocode for creating such a button should be familiar to you by now:

Set coordinates of rectangle
Frame rectangle
Place text inside rectangle

Say you want the text to appear about five pixels in from the left border and vertically centered in the button. To create a general procedure to make a menu button, you need the coordinates of the rectangle, the text with which to label the button, and the rect variable to refer to the graphic entity later in the program. You can pass this information as parameters to the procedure:

```
procedure MakeButton( buttonLabel: string;        { text to insert               }
                      left, top,                  { top left corner of btn       }
                      right, bottom: integer;     {bottom right corner of btn    }
                      var button: rect);          { hold btn in memory           }

begin
  { Set memory for rectangle }
  SetRect(button, left, top, right, bottom);

  { Show rectangle on screen }
  FrameRect(button);

  { find vertical center of button }
  centerVert := Abs(top - bottom) div 2;

  { Draw text in button }
  MoveTo(left + 5, centerVert);
  WriteDraw(buttonLabel)

end; { MakeButton }
```

In the ***MakeButton*** procedure, ***buttonLabel*** can be any string. This procedure can be used for any menu button you want to create. For example, the statement:

```
MakeButton('STOP', 0, 0, 20, 12, stopBtn);
```

creates a button in which the text STOP begins at the point (5, 6) and the coordinates are stored in the ***rect*** variable ***stopBtn***.

8.5 String Operations and Functions

So far, we have seen that string variables can be manipulated in the same way as characters in declarations, assignments, input, and output. In this section, we will look at some functions that can be performed only on strings. The string functions available in MacPascal and Lightspeed are found in many other versions of Pascal, most notably UCSD Pascal (so called because it was developed at the University of California, San Diego). While the particular syntax of MacPascal's string functions may not appear in all other versions of Pascal, functions usually exist that perform the same operation. After looking at the string functions, we will look at a sample program that uses them.

Length

A string's length is not necessarily the same as its declared maximum length. Simply because you have declared a string with the declaration ***name:* string[80];** does not mean that the name will occupy all 80 characters. The length of a string is the number of characters received by a string variable. Remember, a string variable receives a value from an assignment statement or from a ***Readln*** statement. In the case of the ***Readln*** statement, the length of the string is the number of characters on the screen when the user presses the Return key.

To determine the length of a string, we can use the ***Length*** function, which returns an integer value indicating the length of the string. The null string returns the smallest value — it has a length of 0. Since a string variable can hold up to 255 characters, the greatest value returned by ***Length*** is 255.

Syntax Box 8.2
Length

Purpose	To find the length of a string.
Syntax	**Length(** < string > **)**
where	< string > is a literal or variable string. It can also be a string expression, meaning that it can contain any function that returns a string.
Returns	an integer between 0 and 255.
Usage	***Length*** finds the number of characters in a string. For example, ***Length('Apt.^#A3')*** returns 8, ***Length('Susie^Galvin')*** returns 12, ***Length('^^^')*** returns 3, and ***Length('')*** returns 0.

Concatenation

MacPascal allows us to combine two or more strings in a single variable. Suppose we have a program to create a class list for the graduation booklet of a university. The program asks the user to input a student's name and then determines if the student is scheduled to graduate. If the student is scheduled to be in the ceremony, then the program asks what degree the student is to receive. Even though the name and the degree are entered at different times, we want to be able to print the name and the degree next to each other, separated by a comma. We want to create a string variable that contains (in order) the student's name, a comma, and the degree. In other words, we want to *concatenate,* or join, the name, the separating comma, and the degree. MacPascal provides a ***Concat*** function to concatenate strings.

The strings that are concatenated can be of any length as long as the total length of the result is no more than 255 characters. Suppose that in the graduation program we have the following variable declarations:

```
var
    name: string[30];            { name of graduate                    }
    degree: string[6];           { degree graduate will receive        }
    listing: string[40];         { a single line in the grad. program  }
```

Assume ***name*** and ***degree*** have been given values earlier in the program. We can concatenate the contents of these variables into the variable ***listing*** by using the following statement:

```
listing := Concat(name, ',', degree);
```

listing will receive the value of ***name***, followed immediately by the literal comma, followed immediately by the value of ***degree***.

Syntax Box 8.3
Concat

Purpose	To join two or more strings.
Syntax	**Concat(** < str 1 >**,** < str 2 >**,...,** < str *n* > **)**
where	< str 1 >, < str 2 >,..., < str *n* > are literal or variable strings. Each string can also be a string expression, meaning that it can contain any function that returns a string.
Returns	a string.
Usage	***Concat*** begins by finding the end of < str 1 >. The first character of < str 2 > is then attached to the end of < str 1 >. Then the first character of < str 3 > is attached to the end of < str 2 >. This joining continues until < str *n* > is attached to the end of < str *n* – 1 >. No blanks are placed between string expressions. For example, ***Concat('now', 'here')*** returns "nowhere". If the concatenated string is longer than 255 characters, a run-time error will occur.

The ***Concat*** function does not place spaces between the various components; if you want spaces, you have to specify them. For example, if ***first***, ***last***, and ***wholeName*** are **string** variables and we have the following code fragment:

```
...
first := 'David';
last := 'Nanian';
wholeName := Concat(first, last);
...
```

then the variable ***wholeName*** will receive the value 'DavidNanian'. To separate the first and last names by a space, we can concatenate a blank with the first name and alter the code as follows:

```
...
first := 'David';
first := Concat(first, ' '); { add a blank to end of first }
last := 'Nanian';
wholeName := Concat(first, last);
...
```

In this fragment, ***wholeName*** will receive the value 'David^Nanian'. We could also achieve the same result in fewer lines by concatenating the first name, the blank, and the last name in one statement:

```
...
first := 'David';
last := 'Nanian';
wholeName := Concat(first, ' ', last);
...
```

Parsing

MacPascal also provides functions to look at parts of strings. In programming problems, it is often useful to *parse* a sentence, that is, isolate single words in the sentence. For example, we could write a procedure to count how many sentences begin with the word 'The' or to determine how many people have a 'III' as part of their names. The ***Pos*** and ***Copy*** commands allow us to manipulate parts of strings.

Suppose we have a string variable called ***entireName*** that contains a person's first name, a blank, and the last name. (We are assuming that the first name does not contain a blank.) To parse the first and last names from ***entireName***, we need to find where the first blank in the string exists. The ***Pos*** function allows us to search in a string for some pattern. The function returns the position of the first occurrence of the pattern.

For example, suppose ***entireName*** contained the value 'Andy^van^Dam'. To find the first blank, we can use the function call

```
firstBlank := Pos(' ', entireName);
```

This statement will find the first occurrence of a string consisting of a single blank in ***entireName***. In this case, the first blank appears in the fifth position, so ***firstBlank*** receives the integer value 5.

Even though the source string ***entireName*** contains more than one blank, the above call to ***Pos*** always returns the value of the first blank. A second call to the function (e.g., ***secondBlank := Pos(' ', entireName);***) also returns the value 5 because the search for the pattern always begins at position 1. Later we will see how to search for further occurrences of a pattern in a string. If the pattern is not found in the source string, ***Pos*** returns the value 0.

Once we have found the blank following the first name, we can copy the first name from the source string to another string so we can work with just it. This is done by using the ***Copy*** function. ***Copy*** is to strings as ***FrameArc*** is to ovals. Recall that the ***Arc*** commands allow us to work with parts of ovals. To use any of the ***Arc*** commands, we have to specify the total oval, the degree mark at which we are starting, and the length of the arc. ***Copy*** performs an analogous function: it returns a part of a string. To use the ***Copy*** function, we have to specify the total string, the position at which we are starting, and the length of the string we want to copy.

Continuing with the above example, we can store the first and last names in separate variables using the following code. Notice that ***blank*** has been declared as a character string **const**.

```
const
   blank = ' ';                          { a string of one blank             }

var
   firstName,                            { first name of person              }
   lastName,                             { last name of person               }
   entireName: string[80];               { person's whole name               }
   firstBlank: integer;                  { place where first name ends       }

begin
   ...
   entireName := 'Andy van Dam';
   firstBlank := Pos(blank, entireName);       { find end of first name }
   firstName := Copy(entireName, 1, firstBlank);
                                         { copy first name + blank }
   lastName := Copy(entireName, firstBlank +1,
      Length(entireName)–firstBlank);
                                         { copy remainder of name }
end; { procedure }
```

In the above code, ***firstBlank*** receives the value 5 since that is where the first blank appears. Then the function ***Copy*** is used to retrieve the first name. The code tells the interpreter to use the source string ***entireName***. MacPascal begins at the first position of ***entireName*** and retrieves 5 characters, since this is the value of ***firstBlank***. Thus, ***firstName*** receives the value 'Andy^' (the string 'Andy' followed by a blank). ***Copy*** has no effect on the variable ***entireName***; the variable still holds the value 'Andy^van^Dam' even though the first name has been copied into another variable.

The second call to ***Copy*** uses a nested function. Again, ***entireName*** is used as the source string. The copying begins at the position ***firstBlank***+1, which evaluates to 6. The number of characters is found by evaluating the expression ***Length(entireName) – firstBlank***. The function ***Length(entireName)*** returns the value 12, and ***firstBlank*** has the value 5, so the expression evaluates to 12 – 5, or 7. Thus, MacPascal starts at position 6 and copies the next 7 characters, as shown in Figure 8.4.

Removing and Replacing

As we discuss in Appendix E, the **Everywhere** option on MacPascal's **Search** menu tells the editor to find every occurrence of a string, remove each occurrence, and

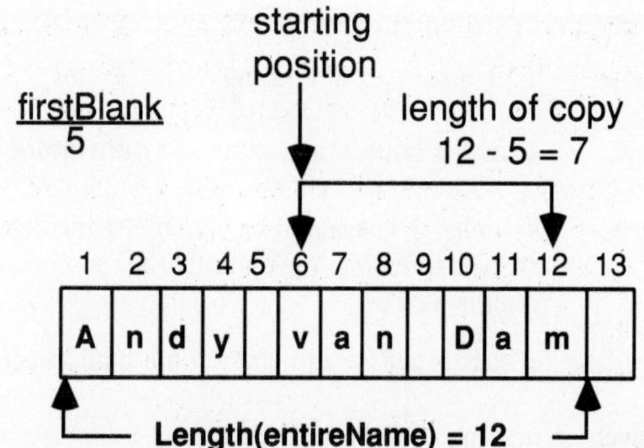

Figure 8.4
Process used by ***Copy*** function

Syntax Box 8.4
Pos

Purpose To indicate where a pattern can be found in a string

Syntax **Pos(** < pattern >, < source > **)**

where < pattern > and < source > are literal or variable strings. Each string can also be a string expression, meaning that it can contain any function that returns a string.

Returns the integer position where < pattern > first occurs in < source >

Usage ***Pos*** begins at the start of < source > and searches for the first occurrence of the < pattern > string. If the < pattern > is found, ***Pos*** returns the character position in < source > where < pattern > first occurs. If < pattern > is not found, ***Pos*** returns 0.

For example, if we have the assignment statement

```
name := 'Amy^Elizabeth^Tozer';
```

we will get the following results from ***Pos***:

Pos('my', name) returns the value 2

Pos('z', name) returns the value 8 (the first occurrence)

Pos('xyz', name) returns the value 0 (pattern not in string)

Pos('', name) returns a garbage value (cannot search for null string)

Syntax Box 8.5
Copy

Purpose To copy a part of a string

Syntax **Copy(< source >, < start >, < num chars >)**

where < source > is a literal or variable string. The string can also be a string expression, meaning that it can contain any function that returns a string.

< start > and < num chars > are both integer expressions.

Returns a string

Usage ***Copy*** copies < num chars > characters from the string < source > beginning at position < start >.

If < num chars > is less than or equal to zero, a null string is returned.

If < start > is less than 1, ***Copy*** still begins at position 1. If <start > + < num chars > is greater than the length of the string, then ***Copy*** copies only the characters up to the end of the string.

For example, if we have the assignment statement:

```
name := 'Amy^Elizabeth^Tozer';
```

we will get the following results from ***Copy***:

Copy(name, 5, 10) returns the value 'Elizabeth^'

Copy(name, 15, 2) returns ' To'

Copy(name, 4, 0) returns ' ' (the null string)

Copy(name, 12, 10) returns 'th^Tozer' (copy stops at end of source)

replace the old string with a new string. How do we implement such a capability in Pascal programs? We have already seen how to find a pattern in a string by using the function ***Pos***; let's look at the functions MacPascal provides to remove and replace parts of strings.

You can think of MacPascal's ***Omit*** function as performing the reverse of the ***Copy*** function. While ***Copy*** returns the substring specified by the < start > and < num chars > parameters, ***Omit*** returns everything *except* the part of the string specified by the < start > and < num chars > parameters.

Let's go back to the name parsing example. Instead of copying the entire last name, we simply remove the first name from the ***entireName*** string and place the result in ***lastName***.

```
const
   blank = ' ';                          { a string of one blank         }
var
   firstName,                            { first name of person          }
   lastName,                             { last name of person           }
   entireName: string[80];               { person's whole name           }
   firstBlank: integer;                  { place where first name ends   }

begin
   ...
   entireName := 'Andy van Dam';
   firstBlank := Pos(blank, entireName);   { find end of first name }
   firstName := Copy(entireName, 1, firstBlank);
                                           { copy first name + blank }
   lastName := Omit(entireName, 1, firstBlank)
                                           { copy remainder of name }
end; { procedure }
```

In this example, the variable ***lastName*** receives the value returned by the ***Omit*** function. This function starts with the source string ***entireName***. Then it starts at position 1 and goes to position ***firstBlank***, or 5. This part of the string is then ignored, and ***lastName*** receives the remainder of the original string. Thus, ***lastName*** receives the value 'van^Dam'.

For a final look at manipulating names, suppose that a first and last name are stored in a single string variable. Then, because we want the name to look official, we decide to add the middle initial. You can use MacPascal's ***Include*** function to perform this task.

Include inserts one string into another string at a specified position. In the name example, we found the end of the first name by searching for the first blank. At that position, we can include the middle initial, a period, and another space. The following code example shows how this can be done:

```
const
   blank = ' ';                          { a string of one blank   }

var
   entireName: string[80];               { person's whole name           }
   firstBlank: integer;                  { place where first name ends   }
   initial: char;                        { person's middle initial       }
   initialToInclude: string[3];          { string that will be included  }

begin
   ...
   { Ask user to enter middle initial }
   Write('Please enter the recipient''s middle initial: ');
   Readln(initial);

   { Concatenate period and space to initial }
   initialToInclude := Concat(initial, '. ');
```

```
    { find end of first name }
    entireName:= 'Eric Wolf';
    firstBlank := Pos(blank, entireName);

    { include initial }
    entireName := Include( initialToInclude, entireName,firstBlank+1);
    ...
end; { procedure }
```

In this procedure, suppose the user enters the initial 'J'. The call to the ***Concat*** function returns the string 'J.^' to the variable ***initialToInclude***. Then ***firstBlank*** receives the position of the first blank in ***entireName***, which is 5. Thus, the call to ***Include*** asks MacPascal to insert the string 'J.^' at position 5+1, or position 6. The result in ***entireName*** is ' Eric^J.^Wolf '.

Syntax Box 8.6
Omit

Purpose To copy a string except for a specified portion.

Syntax **Omit(** < source >**,** < start >**,** < num chars > **)**

where < source > is a literal or variable string. The string can also be a string expression, meaning that it can contain any function that returns a string.

< start > and < num chars > are both integer expressions.

Returns a string.

Usage ***Omit*** copies the contents of the string expression < source > except for a specified substring. That specified substring extends for < num chars > characters beginning at position < start >.

If < start > is less than 1, the substring to omit will still begin at position 1. If < start > + < num chars > is greater than the length of the string, then ***Omit*** will omit only the characters up to the end of the string.

For example, if we have the assignment statement:

```
name := 'Amy^Elizabeth^Tozer';
```

we will get the following results from ***Omit***:

Omit(name, 5, 10) returns the value 'Amy^Tozer'

Omit(name, 15, 2) returns 'Amy^Elizabeth^zer'

Omit(name, 1, 19) returns '' (the null string)

Omit(name, 1, 20) returns '' (omission stops at end of source)

Omit(name, 10, 0) returns 'Amy^Elizabeth^Tozer'

Syntax Box 8.7
Include

Purpose To insert a string inside another string at a specified position

Syntax **Include(** < str to include >**,** < original str >**,** < position > **)**

where < original str > and < str to include > are literal or variable strings. These strings can also be string expressions, meaning that they can contain any function that returns a string.

< position > is an integer expression.

Returns a string

Usage ***Include*** copies the contents of the string expression < str to include > into < original str > at the position specified by < position >.

If < position > is less than 1, then < str to include > is concatenated to < original str > beginning at position 1. If < position > is greater than the length of < original str >, then < str to include > is attached to the end of < original str >.

The resulting string must not be more than 255 characters.

In the resulting string, the first character of < str to include > occupies the position specified by < position >, and the length of the returned string is equal to ***Length(***< original str >***) +*** ***Length(***< str to include >***)***.

For example, if we have the assignment statements

```
name := 'Amy^Tozer';
newPart := 'Elizabeth';
```

we will get the following results from ***Include***:

Include(newPart, name, 0) returns 'ElizabethAmy^Tozer'

Include(newPart, name, 20)returns 'Amy^TozerElizabeth'

Include(newPart, name, 5) returns 'Amy^ElizabethTozer'

8.6 Sample Program

The following example demonstrates a number of the string functions discussed in this chapter.

A palindrome is a word or phrase that reads the same forward and backward. For example, “radar” is a palindrome because “radar” spelled backward is “radar.” We can write a program that accepts strings from the user and determines if the string is a palindrome. For purposes of this example, we assume that any trailing or leading blanks that the user types are accidental and should be eliminated. We will use a non-palindrome, STOP, as the sentinel.

The high-level pseudocode for this program follows:

```
CALL: Print instructions for user
Get first string
WHILE user hasn't entered sentinel DO
   BEGIN
      CALL: Remove excess blanks
      CALL: Reverse string
      Print string and reversed string
      IF string is palindrome THEN
         Print message indicating that string is a palindrome
      Get next string
   END { WHILE }
```

Other versions of Pascal provide built-in string functions to remove blanks. Unfortunately, MacPascal does not. This is unfortunate because accidental presses of the space bar are not immediately apparent on the screen. For example, suppose you want the user to enter the capital of Iowa. Depending on the input, you will tell the user whether the answer is right or wrong. Your code for interpreting the user's input looks like this:

```
if answer = 'DES MOINES' then
     Writeln('Yes, that is correct')
else
     Writeln('No, that is not right');
```

You have told the user to enter the input in all capital letters. However, a user who inputs the string '^DES MOINES' will be told that the answer is not correct. To solve this problem, we remove all the blanks that appear at the beginning and the end of a string. Functions that do this are often referred to as *trimming* functions. The pseudocode for these two functions is as follows:

```
{ Remove excess blanks }

{ Remove initial blanks }
Start at position 1
WHILE first position contains blank DO
     Omit first blank
Return string without initial blanks

{ Remove trailing blanks }
Set final position to end of string
WHILE last position contains blank DO
     Move final position back one space
Return string without trailing blanks
```

The only problem left in the palindrome program is to reverse the string. To accomplish this task, we build a new string by peeling one character at a time off the old string.

```
{ Reverse string }
Start new string at null
FOR each character in string DO
    BEGIN
        Find the next character from back of old string
        Concatenate character to front of new string
    END { FOR }
```

This loop should start at the end of the old string. To determine where the old string is, we can use the ***Length*** function. The ***Copy*** function can be used to find the next character. By using these string functions, we can translate each line of pseudocode into Pascal code. The full program and output appear on the following pages.

Code 8.2
Program *Palindrome*

```
{ Palindrome                          June 10            }
{                                                        }
{ This program reads in strings, reverses each           }
{ string, and prints a message when the string is a      }
{ palindrome. The user types in strings to check; the    }
{ program halts when the user enters the sentinel.       }

program Palindrome;

   const
      sentinel = 'STOP';          { string to halt execution      }

{ Mainline variables }
   var
      front,                      { string entered by user        }
      back : string;              { reverse of user's string      }

{ Procedure Instructions                                         }
{                                                                }
{ This procedure tells the user what the program does and        }
{ what is expected of him or her.  The messages tell the         }
{ user what type of input format and exit command to use.        }
{                                                                }
{ Called by: Mainline    Calls: none                             }

   procedure Instructions;

   begin

      Writeln('This program examines palindromes.');
      Writeln('You will be asked to enter a word or phrase.');
      Writeln('You should type a response and press RETURN.');
      Writeln('The program will then examine if your word or');
      Writeln('phrase is the same backward and forward -- in');
```

Code 8.2
(continued)

```
        Writeln('other words, if it is a palindrome. When you are');
        Writeln('finished, type the response ', sentinel);
        Writeln
    end; { Instructions }

{ Function Reverse                                             }
{                                                              }
{ Function Reverse is sent the string that the user entered    }
{ and returns a string containing the characters of the ori-   }
{ ginal string in reverse order. Each character, going from    }
{ the last to the first, is copied from the original string and }
{ then concatenated onto the returned string.                  }
{                                                              }
{ Called by: Mainline    Calls: none                           }

    function Reverse (front : string) :       { string entered by user          }
        string;                               { Returns: reverse of user's string }

        var
            back,                       { reversed string being built  }
            letter : string;            { single char in string        }
            charCtr : integer;          { loop counter                 }

    begin

        back := '';      { initialize reverse string to the null string }

        for charCtr := Length(front) downto 1 do
            begin
                letter := Copy(front, charCtr, 1);
                back := Concat(back, letter)
            end; { for }
        Reverse := back
    end; { Reverse }

{ Procedure PrintAndCheck                                      }
{                                                              }
{ This procedure prints out the original string and its re-    }
{ versed version. It then compares the original and reversed   }
{ strings and prints a message if the strings are identical.   }
{                                                              }
{ Called by: Mainline    Calls: none                           }

    procedure PrintAndCheck (forwd,          { string going forward        }
        backwd : string);                    { same string going back      }

    begin
        Writeln(forwd, ' <- reversed is -> ', backwd);
```

Code 8.2
(continued)

```
        if forwd = backwd then
            Writeln('*** This is a palindrome ***');

        Writeln
    end; { PrintAndCheck }

{ Function Ltrim and Function Trim                                     }
{                                                                      }
{ The following two routines remove blanks from a string.              }
{ Ltrim removes the leading blanks from a string and Trim              }
{ removes the trailing blanks.  The length of the string returned      }
{ by both functions is changed (unless no blanks were removed).        }
{                                                                      }
{ Called by: Mainline    Calls:  none                                  }

    function Ltrim (str : string) : string;         { removes leading blanks    }
    begin

        while Pos(' ', str) = 1 do
            str := Omit(str, 1, 1);
        Ltrim := str

    end; { Ltrim }

    function Trim (str : string) : string;          { removes trailing blanks   }
    begin
        if str <> '' then
            while (str[Length(str)] = ' ') and (Length(str) > 1)do
                str := Copy(str, 1, Length(str) - 1);
        if str = ' ' then
            Trim :=''
        else
            Trim := str
    end; { Trim }

{ Mainline                                                }
{                                                         }
{ The Mainline controls the processing of input to the pro-  }
{ gram. It first calls the procedure that prints the user's  }
{ instructions. Then it checks each input item against      }
{ the sentinel. If the string input is not the sentinel, the }
{ processing procedures are called. Execution terminates     }
{ when the user enters the sentinel.                        }
{                                                         }
{ Called by: Mainline    Calls:  none                      }
```

Code 8.2 (continued)

```
begin

    Instructions;
    Write('Please enter the first word or phrase: ');
    Readln(front);
    front := Ltrim(Trim(front));  { removing blanks }

    while front <> sentinel do
        begin
            back := Reverse(front);
            PrintAndCheck(front, back);
            Write('Please enter the next word or phrase: ');
            Readln(front);
            front := Ltrim(Trim(front))
        end { while }

end. { Palindrome }
```

```
This program examines palindromes.
You will be asked to enter a word or phrase.
You should type a response and press RETURN.
The program will then examine if your word or
phrase is the same backward and forward -- in
other words, if it is a palindrome. When you are
finished, type the response STOP

Please enter the first word or phrase: SLOOP LOOPS
SLOOP LOOPS <- reversed is -> SPOOL POOLS

Please enter the next word or phrase: STOP POTS
STOP POTS <- reversed is -> STOP POTS
*** This is a palindrome ***

Please enter the next word or phrase: RADAR
RADAR <- reversed is -> RADAR
*** This is a palindrome ***

Please enter the next word or phrase: 380
380 <- reversed is -> 083

Please enter the next word or phrase:      BLANKS BEFORE AND AFTER
BLANKS BEFORE AND AFTER <- reversed is -> RETFA DNA EROFEB SKNALB

Please enter the next word or phrase:  SMUG PALS SLAP GUMS
SMUG PALS SLAP GUMS <- reversed is -> SMUG PALS SLAP GUMS
*** This is a palindrome ***

Please enter the next word or phrase: EMIT PLUG
EMIT PLUG <- reversed is -> GULP TIME

Please enter the next word or phrase: ABLE WAS I ERE I SAW ELBA
ABLE WAS I ERE I SAW ELBA <- reversed is -> ABLE WAS I ERE I SAW ELBA
*** This is a palindrome ***

Please enter the next word or phrase: STOP
```

Figure 8.5 Output of program *Palindrome*

8.7 Chapter Summary

In this chapter, we looked at the last of the atomic data types (meaning that variables of these types can hold one value): ***char*** and **string**. For the most part, variables of type ***char*** and **string** are like variables of the other atomic data types. Variables of these types are declared in the **var** section of a procedure and can receive values via assignment or ***Readln*** statements. ***char***s and **string**s can be output using ***Write*** and ***Writeln*** statements and the same field-width formatting syntax used for integers. To use a ***char*** or **string** literally in your program, you must delimit the text with apostrophes. A symbolic constant can also receive a ***char*** or **string** value as long as the text appears inside apostrophes.

Comparisons can be performed on characters. This is possible because each character is stored with a unique binary representation. One character is less than another if the binary value of the first character is less than the binary value of the second. String comparisons are performed by comparing characters in corresponding positions in the two strings, one at a time. When MacPascal finds that a character in one string is not equal to the character in the corresponding position in the other string, then it can say that one string is less than or greater than the other. Because of this algorithm, MacPascal can determine if two strings are equal only by comparing all the characters in both strings and finding that each set of corresponding characters are equal.

Since MacPascal provides a **string** data type, ***char*** variables are not used very often. Rather, they are used to create textual menus. Since ***char*** is an ordinal type, ***char*** variables can be used as the selector in a **case** statement.

Strings behave slightly differently from the other atomic data types because a string is actually a sequence of multiple characters. Typically, a maximum length is declared for string variables. The string's length can vary from 0 characters (a special string known as the null string has this length) to 255 characters. The maximum length of the string is important in assignment statements; if you try to assign a string of 25 characters to a variable declared as **string[20]**, a run-time error will occur. Except for this size consideration, though, strings of any declared length can be manipulated in the same way.

You can also refer to any individual character in a string simply by giving the name of the string variable and the position of the character in the string. The leftmost character in any string is at position 1, the character immediately to its right is at position 2, and so on.

MacPascal provides a number of predefined functions and procedures for manipulating string expressions. The ***Length*** function returns the current number of characters (not the declared maximum length) of a string. The ***Concat*** function joins two or more strings together into one string. The ***Pos*** function returns the position in a string at which a pattern is first found. The ***Copy*** function returns a specified section of a string. The ***Omit*** function returns everything in a string *except for* a specified section. The ***Include*** function inserts one string in another at a specified location. All these functions can be used on string variables of any declared length.

8.8 Exercises

Note: In these exercises, a caret (^) denotes a blank.

Understanding Concepts

1. When is a ***char*** more appropriate than a **string[1]**?

2. Declare a character constant called ***pop*** that contains an apostrophe.

3. What is the difference between the assignment statements ***start := TRUE;*** and ***start := 'TRUE';***?

4. Which string functions return integers? Which return strings?

5. Which of the following comparisons return TRUE? Which return FALSE?
   a. 'a' < 'A'
   b. '*' > '^*'
   c. 'LESS' < 'GREATER'
   d. '^U^S^A^' = 'USA'
   e. 'DeStefano' >= 'Desmond'
   f. ' ' > '^'

6. If you have the declaration

```
var
    short: string[5];
```

   what does ***short*** contain after the following assignments:
   a. short := 'A';
   b. short := 'BCDEF';
   c. short := 'GHIJKLM';

7. Given the assignment statements ***alpha := 'pizza';*** and ***beta := 'zapped';***, what is returned by:
   a. Length(alpha)
   b. Length(beta[3])
   c. Cat(alpha, alpha)
   d. Copy(alpha, 3, 2)
   e. Pos(alpha, 'za')
   f. Pos('za', beta)
   g. Pos('z', alpha)
   h. Omit(beta, 3, 4)
   i. Pos(alpha, beta)
   j. Cat(Copy(alpha, 3, 2), Copy(beta, 3, 4))
   k. Cat(Copy(beta, 1, 3), Omit(beta, 1, 3))

Coding Exercises

1. Write a function that, when given a name in the form < last >, < first >, returns a name in the form < first > < last > (i.e., the function receives one string parameter and returns a string value. The incoming string contains a comma separating the last and first names.).

2. Write a function that, when given a string, returns the number of words in the string. A word is defined as one or more characters surrounded by blanks or a set of characters at the beginning or end of the string.

3. Write a function to compress blanks, that is, to receive a string and eliminate any extra blanks. Thus, whenever the function finds two or more blanks in a row in the parameter it receives, the multiple blanks are replaced by a single blank. For example, if the function is sent '^^10^^^^Downing^^^St.^^', it should return '^10^Downing^St.^'.

4. Write a program that accepts three strings in any order and outputs them in alphabetical order.

5. Sets of strings are often designated by using *regular expressions.* For example, the regular expression **a*** designates all strings that begin with a. In this notation, the asterisk is used as a wild card: it matches any string, including the null string. Thus, **a*** includes 'ab', 'aA', 'a!', 'all of these', and 'a'. Write a procedure that determines if a string is in the set designated by each of the following.
   a. **a***
   b. ***a**
   c. ***a***
   d. *

6. Write a function that calculates simple arithmetic expressions. The function heading looks like this:

```
{ This function calculates <operand1> <operator> <operand2>. The        }
{ operator may be one of four characters: + (addition), – (subtraction), }
{ * (multiplication), / (divison). The result of the calculation is re-  }
{ turned to the caller.                                                  }

function Calculate (operand1, operand2: real;    { nums in the equation  }
                     operator: char):            { one of +, –, *, /     }
                     real;                       { result of operation   }
```

7. On a telephone, letters are associated with digits as follows:

2: A B C	5: J K L	8: T U V
3: D E F	6: M N O	9: W X Y
4: G H I	7: P R S	

Write a procedure that, when given a string of any length, translates the letters to the corresponding telephone digits. Generate an error message if the string contains letters (Q and Z) that cannot be translated.

8. We know a certain professor who uses a bizarre shorthand. Whenever he's in a hurry, he writes messages by dropping all the vowels except those that appear at the beginning of a word. Thus the message 'Please buzz office phone' becomes 'Pls bzz offc phn'. Write a function that takes a string and returns the shorthand version.

9. Newspaper people use a headline count to calculate the amount of space needed for a headline. In this count, all lowercase letters take one space except f, i, j, l, and t, which can take 1/2 space, and m and w, which each take 1-1/2 spaces. All uppercase letters take 1-1/2 spaces, except M and W, which each take 2 spaces. All other symbols, spaces, and numbers take one space, except for periods, commas, and semicolons, which take 1/2 space. Write a function that receives a string and returns the headline count.

10. In Spanish, regular verbs consist of two parts: a root and a suffix. The suffix of the infinitive form is usually -ar, -er, or -ir. For example, the verb *hablar* (to speak) has the base *habl* and the suffix *ar*. The infinitive's suffix dictates how the verb is conjugated. The following chart shows the general rule for conjugating -ar verbs and the specific example of *hablar*.

	Singular	*Plural*	*Singular*	*Plural*
1st person	<base>+o	<base>+amos	*hablo* (I speak)	*hablamos* (we speak)
2nd person	<base>+as		*hablas* (you speak)	
3rd person	<base>+a	<base>+an	*habla* (he/she speaks)	*hablan* (they speak)

Note that second person plural is not typically used. Write a procedure that, when given an -ar infinitive, a person (1st, 2nd, or 3rd), and a number (singular or plural), prints the appropriate form of the verb.

11. Write a procedure that accepts Roman numerals as input and prints the decimal equivalent.

Programming Problems

1. Add a Text button to the Layout program (introduced as the ***Fence*** program in Chapter 6). When the user chooses the Text button, the user enters text in the Text window and then selects a point in the Drawing window. The text then appears in the Drawing window at the designated point.

2. Write a program that decodes messages encrypted with a letter-substitution code. A letter-substitution code is a 26-character string in which each character in the code corresponds to the letter in the same position in the alphabet. For example, in the code ZYXWVUTSRQPONMLKJIHGFEDCBA, each Z in the encrypted message corresponds to an A, each Y becomes a B, and so on. Thus, YLMW XZOO J translates to BOND CALL Q. Given coded messages, your program should print the translation. The first line of input will be the 26-character code. Each line after that corresponds to one message. The sentinel STOP designates the end of the messages.

Variations:

a. Use the numeric instead of the alphabetic code. The first line of input is still the 26-character code. The rest of the input consists of integers. The integers 1 to 26 correspond to a position in the code (1 being the first character in the code, 2 the second, and so on). Any integer over 26 corresponds to a blank. Messages are terminated with a 0; the end of data is indicated by –1. A translation should be printed only when an entire message has been entered. For example, the input sequence

```
NOPQRSTUVWXYZABCDEFGHIJKLM
22 15 18 29 16 5 18 14 26 35 14 7 7 14
16 24 0 15 8 12 45 15 2 25 2 20 1 14 0 -1
```

should produce the result:

```
ICE CREAM ATTACK
BUY BOLOGNA
```

b. Print warning messages if any of the key words PRODUCE, DELI, or SARDINES appears in the decoded message. Note that *only* the key words should signal the change. 'DELICIOUS', for example, should *not* trigger a warning.

c. Replace the key words from the preceding variation with other words. All occurrences of PRODUCE should be replaced by SALAD, DELI with LUNCHMEAT, and SARDINES with GRANOLA. Print the message after all replacements have been made.

3. Write a program that adds chemical compounds or at least their symbols. In chemistry, a compound is denoted by a series of atomic symbols (e.g., H, O, Cl, Ne, Ag) and numbers. H_2O, for example, indicates two atoms of hydrogen and one of oxygen. Your program should accept two compound names and yield a result telling how many atoms of each element would be in the combination. For example, in this program, if we input H2O (note that subscripts cannot be lowered in the Text window) and HCl, you would output that the result would have 3 atoms of H for each atom of O and each atom of Cl. (Note that element

names begin with a capital letter; if a second letter is present, it is always lowercase.)

4. Write a program that accepts a time notation, such as 9:20, and prints the time as it would be spoken, such as "twenty minutes past nine." The output should follow these conventions:

Input	*Output*
x:00	"x o'clock"
x:01–x:14, x:16–x:29	"< number > minutes past x"
x:15	"quarter past x"
x:30	"half past x"
x:31–x:44,x:46–x:59	"< number > minutes to x+1"
x:45	"quarter to x+1"

5. Write a program that parses arithmetic expressions with parentheses. Your output should indicate the order in which expressions are evaluated. For example, the input (c+((b–x) * n)) should yield:

    expression #1: (b–x)
    expression #2: (#1 * n)
    expression #3: (c+ #2)

   Assume that the expressions have balanced sets of parentheses and that they consist solely of parentheses, arithmetic operators (+,–,*, /), and single-letter variables.

6. Write a program that allows two people to play hangman. The first person inputs a single word. A number of dashes then appear on the screen, one dash for each letter in the word. Then the other person guesses letters. If the letter is in the word, then the appropriate dashes are replaced by the letter. For example, if the first user enters the word "obnoxious" and the second user guesses "o," the program displays 'o--o--o--'. If the user's letter is not in the word, the letter counts as a miss. The second user continues guessing until she gets the entire word or misses seven times. Something to think about: what happens if a user guesses a letter twice?

7. Write a program that converts numbers from base-10 to a base defined by the user. If the user asks for a base greater than 10, you should use letters as digits. For example, the first 20 numbers in base 16 are: 1, 2, 3, 4, 5, 6, 7, 8, 9, A, B, C, D, E, F, 10, 11, 12, 13, 14.

8. Write a program that generates random serial numbers for dollar bills. The serial number begins with a letter indicating one of the federal reserve banks:

A: Boston	E: Richmond	I: Minneapolis
B: New York	F: Atlanta	J: Kansas City
C: Philadelphia	G: Chicago	K: Dallas
D: Cleveland	H: St. Louis	L: San Francisco

The letter is followed by eight random digits. The sequence ends with a random letter between A and L.

9. Write a program that generates all the two-letter combinations that contain at least one vowel (a, e, i, o, u, y).

10. Write a program that capitalizes titles. The first word of a title is always capitalized. The other words are capitalized unless they contain three or fewer letters.

Files

The Macintosh has been in the vanguard of a new age of personal computers. Unlike many comparable machines, the Macintosh is used as easily by non-technical people as by experienced programmers. The machine is simple to use because it has a high-quality user interface: at any time, the user can easily understand what the computer is doing.

The Macintosh is designed to be interactive, meaning that the machine reacts to the user's commands as they are entered. Any time you perform an action with the mouse or touch the keyboard, the Mac gives an explicit response. Because most Macintosh software is designed primarily for interactive activities, the developers of MacPascal assumed that the programs you write will also be interactive. That is, when MacPascal reaches a ***Readln*** statement, it assumes that the user will input data from the keyboard. Similarly, MacPascal assumes that the user wants to see the output from ***Writeln*** and QuickDraw instructions on the screen.

For most programs, particularly those that make effective use of graphics, interactive I/O (computer shorthand for input and output) works well. There are times, though, when the user cannot be expected to enter all the input at the keyboard. In the last chapter, we discussed how to use string functions to find and replace parts of strings. Such a program could be used to correct spelling errors in a paper or an article; for instance, you could search for each occurrence of a common error (such as "teh") and replace it with the correct spelling ("the"). It isn't practical to expect the user to retype an entire paper as input to a spelling correction program. Besides wanting the output to appear in the Text window, the user would also want to keep the changed document somewhere on a disk. This chapter shows how to accommodate these types of needs by using file I/O.

9.1 About Files

The term "file" in computer science is something like the term "atom" in chemistry. We talk about different types of files, such as data files, program files, and output files, just as we talk about lithium atoms, carbon atoms, and einsteinium atoms. We also describe parts of files, just as we talk about electrons, protons, and neutrons. However, the term "file," like the term "atom," eludes simple definition. Up to this point, we have used the term "file" without having provided a complete definition. Still, through your manipulation of files on the Desktop, you probably have a vague notion of what a file is.

So, what exactly *is* a file? Let's say that a file is a collection of data that resides outside the main memory. The contents of a file appear in main memory only when needed by the CPU. Usually, the contents of a file are stored on some external storage device, that is, one outside of main memory, such as a disk. We can think of the data in a file as characters, numbers, graphic elements, or other things; internally, the data are always represented as a series of bits. Typically, the data are related in some way. For example, a file can hold a five-page paper, a program that calculates a company's budget, or next week's shopping list. As far as the computer is concerned, though, the data in a file need to be related only to the application that opens the file. On the Mac's Desktop, this relationship is designated by an icon, such as the (from top to bottom) MacPaint, MacPascal, and Lightspeed Pascal project icons you see on the left. In all cases, though, the computer sees a file as a sequence of zeroes and ones in a particular area of memory.

Files are used in a Pascal program for input and output. During a program's execution, a file can be used in one of three ways: as a *read-only* file, a *write-only* file, or a *read-write* file. The contents of a read-only file can be used only as the input to a program; a write-only file can only receive output from a program; a read-write file can be used for both purposes.

A file consists of an ordered sequence of data items known as *components*. The number of components in a file is determined by how the file is used. Suppose a file contains the data '123 456'. Depending on how it is used, we can say that this file consists of seven characters, two integers, or a single string. The components of a file are numbered consecutively beginning at 0. When you are looking at a file's contents (you will see how to do this later in the chapter), the components are numbered from left to right and from top to bottom. In the last example, if the contents of the file are being used as integers, the integer 123 is component 0 and the integer 456 is component 1.

MacPascal maintains a *current file position* for each file. The file position indicates where the next input will come from or where the next output will go to.

Components in read-only and write-only files are accessed *sequentially*. Say you have a file that is being used for input. Initially, the current file position is at component 0. After the first component is read, the current file position is set to 1. The next read from the file gets the second component and increments the current file position to 2. Similarly, the first time you write a component to a file, the current file position moves to the end of the written component. The next write action puts an element immediately after the first component. We shall see, later in this chapter, that components in read-write files can be accessed *randomly* as well as sequentially; that is, we can read or write these components in any order.

```
Write(fileBuf, 'first output ');
Write(fileBuf, 'second output');
```

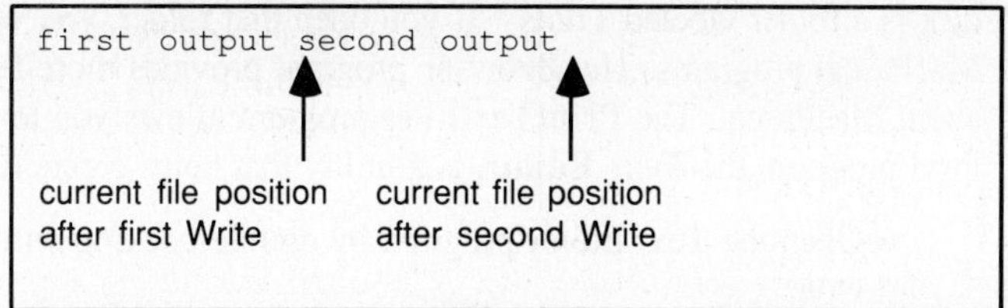

Figure 9.1
Sequential writing of components

The next section examines the most common way to use files in introductory programming: using read-only files for input. Files that contain all the input a program will receive are often called *data files*.

9.2 Creating Data Files

Suppose you are the sports editor for a school newspaper. Each day you publish a scoreboard that lists the previous day's results for each of the school's varsity teams. To keep track of what games are happening on which days, you decide to create files on your Macintosh. In each file, you want to keep a list of one day's games. For example, the file ***Oct 2 Schedule*** contains all the games scheduled for October 2.

For each game, you need to record three things: the team that is playing (e.g., women's lacrosse, men's curling), the opponent, and your school team's current record of wins and losses. The team and the opponent should be stored as strings; the record should appear as two integers. For reasons that will be explained later in the chapter, the strings should appear on separate lines. A sample data file looks like this:

```
Men's bowling
Bowling Green U.
38 16
Women's mountain climbing
Appalachian State U.
 16  7
```

This file shows that the men's bowling team currently has a win-loss record of 38-16 and is playing Bowling Green U. On the same day, the women's mountain climbing team, with a record of 16-7, faces Appalachian State U.

If you are familiar with a text processing program such as MacWrite or Microsoft Word™, you can use it to enter a data file. Just be sure to use the **As Text** option when you save the file. The MacPascal and Lightspeed Pascal packages each contain a method of creating data files that we now briefly explain.

Using MacPascal's Text Editor (MacPascal only)

(This is a **hands-on** section for MacPascal users; a similar section for Lightspeed users follows.)

The MacPascal Utilities disk contains an editor for creating data files. On that disk is a folder labeled **Tools**.* If you open that folder, you will see three handy MacPascal programs. The **Browser** program provides more technical information about MacPascal. The **PrintTextFiles** program allows you to print a data file. The third program, the **Text Editor**, is a utility that helps create data files.

- Open the Text Editor program by double-clicking on the **Text Editor** icon.

The Text Editor program's code now appears. You need to run the program to enter the editor.

- Start the program by choosing **Go** from the **Run** menu.

When the program begins to execute, a dialog box appears on the screen, showing that the program wants you to choose a file to edit. If you want to edit an old file, choose the filename either by highlighting the name and choosing the **Open** button or by double-clicking on the name. Use the vertical scroll bar to move up and down in the list of available files.

In this case, you want to create a new file. To do this, choose the **Cancel** button, which means that you do not want to edit an existing file. The dialog box disappears and a single window, which represents the new file you will be editing, appears on the screen. All the features in the text editor are features you have seen in creating MacPascal files. For example, a flashing vertical line again represents the insertion point (Figure 9.2).

- Enter the following data:

```
Men's bowling
Bowling Green U.
38 16
Women's mountain climbing
Appalachian State U.
 16 7
```

To enter this data, you can use many of the same features that you use to enter programs. The backspace key erases the character to the left of the insertion point.

---

* In version 1.0 of Macintosh Pascal, the **Tools** folder is on the MacPascal disk.

Figure 9.2
Initial Text Editor window

The mouse can be used to select portions of the file. The Return key moves the insertion point to the next line.

When you have selected text, you can use the **Edit** menu to **Cut**, **Copy**, or **Clear** the text. The cut or copied section of text is placed at the insertion point when you choose **Paste** on the **Edit** menu. The **Edit** menu also contains the option **Select All**, which allows you to select the entire file. (If you haven't used these options, see the hands-on exercise in Appendix E.)

Finally, we need to save the file.

- Choose **Save** from the **File** menu.

A dialog box asks you to name the file.

- Choose the desired disk using the **Eject** and **Drive** buttons.

On the right side of the dialog box is the name of the current disk. The **Eject** and **Drive** buttons allow you to change the current disk, as we have seen previously.

- Name the file by typing ***Oct 2 Schedule.***
- When the file name is entered, save the file by choosing the **Save** button in the dialog box.

Your file will now be saved under the name you have chosen. If you decide that you do not want to save the file after all, choose the **Cancel** button in the dialog box. This gives control back to the Text Editor. Should you choose **Save** after the file has been named, the Text Editor will again allow you to choose the name of the file. If you save a file twice under two different names, two identical files will be saved. If you save the file using the current name, the Text Editor places another dialog box on the screen, asking if you want to replace the previous version of the file.

When the data file has been created and saved, you can leave the Text Editor program.

- Exit the Text Editor by choosing **Quit** from the **File** menu.

If you have made any changes since the last save, the Text Editor asks if you want to save them before quitting.

When you leave the Text Editor, you return to MacPascal. From there, you can choose **Go** again to create another data file. You can edit a MacPascal program by choosing **Close** to get rid of the Text Editor and then choosing **Open...** or **New** to get another MacPascal program. You can also return to the Desktop by choosing **Quit**. Figure 9.3 summarizes these options.

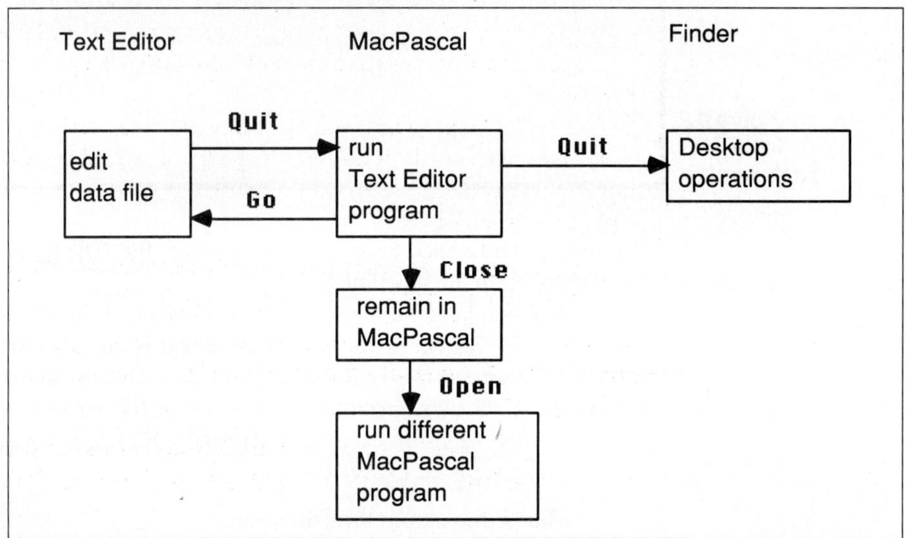

Figure 9.3
Options when exiting MacPascal text editor

Using Lightspeed's Text Editor (Lightspeed only)

Lightspeed's Text Editor is very similar to the Lightspeed Pascal editor. To begin using the editor, you first need to compile the program that runs the editor. We suggest you store the text editor on a separate disk.

- Start up your Mac with the LP1.System Disk.
- If you have an external drive, insert the LP2.Libraries disk there.
- If you do not have an external drive, eject the LP1.System disk and insert the LP2.Libraries disk in the internal drive.
- Eject the disk in the internal drive and insert (and initialize) a new blank disk.

You should now have three disk icons on the screen.

- If they are not already open, open the windows for the disks.
- Copy the **MacPasLib** and **MacTraps** files and the **Text Editor Demo** folder from the LP2.Libraries window to the new disk window, swapping disks if needed.
- To make the new disk a startup disk, copy the **System Folder** from the LP1.System disk to the new disk.

At this point, your new disk contains all the software it needs to run the text editor and to start up the Mac. You now need to build the editor application.

• Open the **Editor Project** from the **Text Editor Demo** folder.

The project window contains the names of the various files that make up the text editor program.

• Choose **Build & Save As** from the **Project** menu.

This command allows you to save the compiled code as an *application*. In Lightspeed terminology, an application is a set of compiled Pascal statements that can be run directly from the Desktop by double-clicking. We'll elaborate momentarily.

A dialog box appears, asking you to name the code you are compiling. The dialog box contains the prompt **Save 'Editor Project' as**, and three options appear at the bottom of the box. Since the compiled code should be saved as an application, you should:

• Choose **Application** from the options at the bottom of the dialog box.
• Name the compiled code **Editor Application**.

Now Lightspeed will begin building the application. The dialog boxes that appear next are identical to the boxes you saw when building the **Generic Project** in Chapter 1.

• A dialog box will tell you that Lightspeed **Cannot find the file "MacPasLib". Would you like to look for it?** Choose the **OK** button.

The **Open** dialog box appears next.

• Use the **Eject** and **Drive** buttons to choose your disk.
• When your disk is the current disk, **MacPasLib** should be highlighted in the column on the left side. If it isn't already, highlight **MacPasLib** now.
• Choose the **Open** button.

Lightspeed had assumed that MacPasLib was on the LP1.System disk; now it has been found on your disk. Lightspeed now presents a dialog box asking if the other parts of the project are also on your disk.

• When Lightspeed asks if you want to **Change "LP1.System"** to **"<your disk name>" in all SUBSEQUENT (by build order) Project entries also?**, choose the **Yes** button.

The files in the project are then loaded and compiled, and the application is built.

• Choose **Quit** from the **File** menu.

You should now be back at the Desktop. You will notice a new icon representing the Editor Application. This is the compiled code that you have just built. We no longer need the source code.

• Throw away the **MacPasLib** and **MacTraps** files and the **Text Editor Demo** folder.

All that should be left is the System folder and the Editor Application.

• Choose **Shut Down** from the **Special** menu.

Now that you have created the Editor Application disk, you won't have to go through the above process again. Let's look next at how to create a data file.

• Start up the Mac with the disk containing the Editor Application.
• Open **Editor Application.**

The Editor Application assumes you want to open an existing file; thus, the first thing you see when you open the application is the same window you see when you choose **Open...** in Lightspeed.

• Choose **Cancel** from the **Open...** dialog box.
• Choose **New** from the **File** menu.

A new window labeled **Untitled1** appears on the screen. The window represents a new data file. All the features in the text editor are features you have seen in creating Lightspeed files. For example, a flashing vertical line again represents the insertion point.

• Enter the following data:

```
Men's bowling
Bowling Green U.
38 16
Women's mountain climbing
Appalachian State U.
 16 7
```

To enter this data, you can use many of the same features that you use to enter programs. The backspace key erases the character to the left of the insertion point. The mouse can be used to select portions of the file. The Return key moves the insertion point to the next line. If you make a mistake, the **Edit** menu contains an **Undo** option.

When you have selected text, you can use the **Edit** menu to **Cut**, **Copy**, or **Clear** the text. The cut or copied section of text is placed at the insertion point when you choose **Paste** on the **Edit** menu. The **Edit** menu also contains the option **Select All**, which allows you to select the entire file. (If you haven't used these options, see the hands-on exercise in Appendix E.)

Now, let's save the file.

• Choose **Save As...** from the **File** menu.

A dialog box asks you to name the file.

• Choose the desired disk using the **Eject** and **Drive** buttons.

On the right side of the dialog box is the name of the current disk. The **Eject** and **Drive** buttons allow you to change the current disk, as we have seen previously.

- Name the file by typing ***Oct 2 Schedule.***
- When the file name is entered, save the file by choosing the **Save** button in the dialog box.

Your file will now be saved under the name you have chosen.

The remaining options on the **File** menu — **Open, Close, Save, Page Setup, Print, Transfer,** and **Quit** — serve the same purpose as their counterparts in the Lightspeed program editor. (See Appendix E for a summary of the Lightspeed Pascal menu option functions.)

The **Windows** menu allows you to make one of the windows active. The top of the menu lists up to five text files that are currently open. Choosing any of those window names, or the option **Clipboard**, will make that window active. The other option on this menu, **Font Control**, allows you to choose the font for the open windows.

As always, you should experiment with the various menu options to make sure you understand their functions. When you are done, you should leave the Text Editor.

- Choose the **Quit** option from the **File** menu.

You will return to the Desktop. The icon for the data file you have saved should be in the same window as the Editor Application.

9.3 File Variables

To use a file in a program, you need a way of referring to it. As usual, you use variable declarations to create references. The data type ***text*** is used to refer to a file. The ***text*** data type does not mean that the file can hold only textual values. Integers, reals, booleans, or any other type of data that can be stored can be in the file.

A declaration of a ***text*** variable is not exactly like declarations of other variables. An ***integer*** variable declaration reserves space in memory for an integer; a ***text*** variable declaration does *not* reserve space for a file. Instead, an area called a *file buffer* is reserved in memory. Every reference to the ***text*** variable is a reference to the buffer. This buffer is filled by Pascal with the component at the current file position. Therefore, the ***text*** variable does not refer to the entire file, but just one component. A buffer, in short, is a gateway between files and your programs.

Two file buffers called ***input*** and ***output*** are predefined in all implementations of Pascal. File buffers can be associated with devices — various pieces of hardware — as well as files. In MacPascal,* the predefined ***text*** variable ***input*** is associated with the keyboard, and ***output*** is associated with the screen (specifically, the Text window).

In MacPascal, all you need to do to create a new file buffer is declare a ***text*** variable. In most other versions of Pascal, you have to list the file variable as a *program parameter* as well as declare it as a ***text*** variable. For example, if your program receives input using a file buffer called ***source*** and sends output to a file designated by ***destination***, you could use the following declaration of your program and file variables:

* All remaining references to MacPascal in this chapter also apply to Lightspeed Pascal.

```
program WorkWithFiles(source, destination);

var
    source,              { input file buffer     }
    destination: text;   { output file buffer    }
```

Unlike parameters for procedures, the order of program parameters is irrelevant. The declarations **program *WorkWithFiles(source, destination);*** and **program *WorkWithFiles(destination, source);*** produce the same result. Most programs simply use the predefined variables ***input*** and ***output***; thus, most programs begin with the line:

```
program NoExtraFiles(input, output);
```

In the versions of Pascal we are using in this book, program parameters are never needed: it is always assumed that ***input*** is associated with the keyboard and ***output*** with the Text window. If you ever use another version of Pascal, however, you will probably need to use program parameters for all programs.

9.4 Reading from Files

It is crucial that the order of the data in your file matches the program's input specifications. For example, if a program expects two strings followed by two integers, you will cause an error if you place the integers before the strings. You also need to remember the semantics of the data. It is important, for example, that the first string is the home team and the second is the opponent. While your program will not bomb if the strings are out of order, you will get quite different results if the strings do not contain the correct data.

Each character you enter in a data file affects the input. Blank spaces are important when you are entering ***char*** or **string** type data. In addition, two special characters are also found in a data file. At the end of each line is an invisible marker called an < eoln > (*end of line*) marker, which is a character added to the data file each time you press Return. When you exit a file, an < eof > (*end of file*) character marker is placed after the final component in the file. You cannot see the < eoln > and < eof > markers, but they are a part of your data file. In the above example, the markers are placed as follows:

```
Men's bowling < eoln >
Bowling Green U.< eoln >
38 16< eoln >
Women's mountain climbing< eoln >
Appalachian State U.< eoln >
 16 7< eoln >
< eof >
```

If you left the insertion point after the 7 on the final line instead of pressing Return, the final line markers would be placed as follows:

```
...
Appalachian State U.< eoln >
 16 7< eof >
```

We'll return to markers in a moment, but let's first get back to file variables. You've declared a variable of type ***text*** to hold the file buffer. Before you can start reading from the file, though, you need to open it. Suppose you've declared the variable ***games*** as a ***text*** type, and you want to use the file ***Oct 2 Schedule*** as input. The statement ***Reset(games, 'Oct 2 Schedule');*** accomplishes this task.

A ***Reset*** statement does a number of things. Its two parameters are a text variable and a string representing the title of a file. When MacPascal executes this statement, the file ***Oct 2 Schedule*** is opened as a read-only file. The current file position for the file is set to component 0. Since you haven't read anything yet, the file buffer ***games*** is set to the top of the file and is now available as a gateway to the contents of ***Oct 2 Schedule***.

You can now begin reading from the file using the ***Read*** and ***Readln*** statements. Up to this point, these statements have been pretty much synonymous. When reading from a file, though, the differences between the two becomes more important. Remember the difference in reading from the keyboard: ***Read*** does not wait for a carriage return before accepting typed input. Thus, when you input a ***char***, ***Read*** immediately accepts the first character you type; ***Readln*** waits for the Return, so you can backspace over the entry.

Previous chapters have assumed that the input to ***Read*** and ***Readln*** statements was coming from the keyboard. This is because you did not specify any file from which these statements could get input. To read from the file ***Oct 2 Schedule***, you need to list the file buffer ***games*** as the first parameter to ***Read*** or ***Readln***.

Whenever MacPascal encounters a ***Read*** or ***Readln***, it looks at the first parameter. If the parameter is a file buffer, input is received from that file. Otherwise, MacPascal assumes that input is coming from the predefined file ***input***, that is, the keyboard. The remainder of the ***Read*** and ***Readln*** statements are syntactically the

Syntax Box 9.1
Reset

Purpose To open a file for read-only access

Syntax **Reset(< file buffer >, < filename >);**

where < file buffer > is a variable of type ***text***.
< filename > is a string expression.

Usage The file specified by < filename > is opened by this statement. After this statement, < file buffer > can be used as the first parameter in ***Read*** or ***Readln*** statements to read input from the file.

The current file position is initialized to point to component 0 (the first component of the file).

same whether input comes from a file or the keyboard. The execution of the input statements, however, is somewhat different when input comes from a file. A ***Readln*** statement reads data and then moves the current file position to the beginning of the next line in the file.

When accepting numeric data, ***Read*** skips blanks and < eoln > characters to find the next number. Suppose you have the following lines in the data file ***records***:

```
92    68
90   70
```

If you use the statements

```
Reset(recBuf, 'records');
Read(recBuf, wins);
Read(recBuf, losses);
Read(recBuf, wins2);
```

the variable ***wins*** receives the value 92 because the first ***Read*** will accept the first file component. The current file position then is set to the next component, so the result of ***Read(recBuf, losses);*** is that ***losses***, as expected, receives the value 68. When the third ***Read*** is executed, Pascal skips the < eoln > character and assigns the next value (90) to ***wins2***.

The statements:

```
Reset(recBuf, 'records');
Readln(recBuf, wins);
Read(recBuf, losses);
```

do something quite different. ***wins*** again receives the value 92. However, since you used a ***Readln*** to input the value, the current file position moves to the first component on the next line; thus, ***losses*** receives the value 90. The value 68 has been passed over because ***Readln*** moves the current file position to the next line. ***Read***, on the other hand, simply moves the current file position to the next component.

You can use ***Readln*** statements for the sole purpose of moving the current file position to the next line. For example, suppose you decide you need only the wins of each record (the first integer on each line). The following code first reads 92 into ***wins***. The ***Readln*** statement then moves the current file position to the next line. The value 68 is skipped and the value 90 is input into ***wins2***. Essentially, the primary difference between this code and the previous example is that the line ***Readln(recBuf, wins)*** is broken into two parts: one to read the value and another to move the current file position to the next line.

```
Reset(recBuf, 'records');
Read(recBuf, wins);
Readln(recBuf);
Read(recBuf, wins2);
```

Syntax Box 9.2
Read and **Readln** from files

Purpose To receive input from a data file

Syntax
Read(< file buf >**,** < var 1 >,..., < var *n* > **);**
Readln(< file buf >**,** < var 1 >,..., < var *n* > **);**

where < file buf > is a variable of type ***text***.
< var 1 >,..., < var *n* > are variables of type ***integer***, ***real***, ***char***, ***string***, or any enumerated type.

Usage ***Read*** and ***Readln*** assign values to < var 1 >,..., < var *n* > by obtaining sequential components from the file associated with < file buf >. That is, < var 1 > receives the component at the current file position, < var 2 > receives the following component, and so on.

Blanks should be used to separate numeric data in a file. When reading numeric data, ***Read*** and ***Readln*** skip all blanks and < eoln > characters in the file until a number is found.

When any of < var 1 >,..., < var *n* > is a string variable, both ***Read*** and ***Readln*** assign all characters between the current file position and the next < eoln > marker to the variable. If the string is input with a ***Read***, the current file position is then set to the < eoln > marker; if a ***Readln*** is used, the current file position moves to the beginning of the next line.

If ***Read*** or ***Readln*** attempts to assign the < eoln > marker to a character or string variable, the result can vary. You may not get an error when the input is made, but when you try to use the variable's contents (the < eoln > marker), the program may crash.

The file designated by < file buf > must have been previously opened with ***Open*** or ***Reset***.

You may previously have used either ***Read*** or ***Readln*** to input strings from the keyboard. When reading strings from a data file, you should always use ***Readln***. When a string is entered from the keyboard, MacPascal receives all the characters you type before you press the Return key. When reading a string from a data file, MacPascal receives all the characters between the current file position and the next < eoln > marker. The current file position is then at the < eoln > marker. If you use ***Read*** to input the string, the file position does not move to the next line. The next ***Read*** will then try to assign the < eoln > marker to a variable, and the result of such an action is unpredictable. ***Readln***, on the other hand, moves the file position to the next line, and the file is ready for the next input.

Typically, you want the user to choose the data file to use at run time. In the sports schedule example, the user will want to use a different file each day. Thus, it is not a good idea to place a specific file name inside a program if the same program is likely to be used with different input files. MacPascal provides a command that allows the user to choose a file on any disk for input. This command is a string function called ***OldFileName***.

OldFileName takes one parameter. This parameter is a prompt that appears in a dialog box. The dialog box allows the user to choose a file in the same way that the **Open...** command on MacPascal's **File** menu allows you to choose a program to edit. When the user chooses a file with the mouse, the name of the file is returned as a string.

Let's look at an example.

```
sched := OldFileName('Please choose the schedule');
```

When MacPascal interprets this statement, the following dialog box appears:

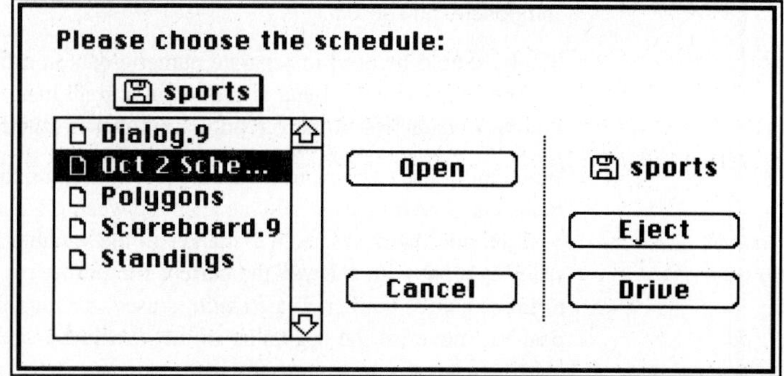

Figure 9.4
Dialog box result of OldFileName

This dialog box is identical to the box you see when you choose **Open** in MacPascal. Note that the prompt parameter appears at the top left of the box.

The files on the disk appear in the left side of the box. A vertical scroll bar allows the user to move up and down the list. The user can choose the name of the desired data file in one of three ways: she can double-click on the name, she can click on the name and then choose the **Open** button, or she can highlight the name and then hit Return. None of these actions opens the file the way we think of opening a file for editing in MacPascal; in this context, choosing the button **Open** means that the file name chosen is the returned value of the function. Choosing the **Cancel** button returns a null string.

The right side of the dialog box indicates the disk on which the data file can be found. Again, the **Eject** and **Drive** buttons can be used to change the current disk.

OldFileName can be nested inside a ***Reset*** statement. For example, the statement

```
Reset(games, OldFileName('Please choose the schedule:'));
```

puts up a dialog box with the prompt **Please choose the schedule:**. When the user chooses a file, the filename is returned to the program. Then the file is opened as a read-only file, and ***games*** becomes the file buffer for the chosen file.

You may want to ensure that the user cannot select the **Cancel** button. Since the **Cancel** button returns a null string, you can compare the returned value from the function to the value '' (the null string). If this comparison is TRUE, then the user chose the **Cancel** button, and you want the dialog box to reappear to force the user to choose an existing file. This process can be coded by putting the ***OldFileName*** command in a **repeat-until** loop:

```
repeat
   sched := OldFileName('Please choose a file to use: ');
until sched <> '' ; { repeat if user picks Cancel }
Reset(games, sched); { open file for read-only access }
```

You can also give the user the option of using either the keyboard or a file to enter data. In the following code, the user is asked to choose a file name. If the user chooses a name, the code associates the text variable ***games*** with the designated name. If the user chooses the **Cancel** button, the next ***Read*** or ***Readln*** assumes that the user wants to use the keyboard. The text variable ***input*** is assigned to ***games***, which means that ***games***, like ***input***, is now associated with the keyboard.

```
sched := OldFileName('Choose a filename, or Cancel to use the keyboard:');
if sched <> '' then                    { user wants to use file }
   Reset(games, sched)
else                                   { user wants to use keyboard }
   games := input;
Readln(games, wins, losses); { works for either file or keyboard input }
```

Syntax Box 9.3
OldFileName

Purpose	To allow a user to choose an existing file
Syntax	**OldFileName(**< prompt >)
where	< prompt > is a string expression.
Returns	a string
Usage	This function shows a dialog box using the designated < prompt >. The user can choose a file by double-clicking on the file name or by choosing the name and then the **Open** button. In either case, the file name will be returned as a string value. If the user chooses the **Cancel** button, the function returns the null string. The **Eject** and **Drive** buttons in the dialog box allow the user to remove the disk or list the files on the disk in the other drive, respectively.

9.5 Sentinels

Sentinels, as you saw in Chapter 5, indicate the end of data. A sentinel can be used in file I/O the same way as in interactive I/O. Let's look again at the schedule example from Section 9.2. The number of games varies from day to day, so you need some method to designate the end of data. Since each set of data begins with a string, you should use a string sentinel. If you use the sentinel 'STOP', then the data file will look like this:

```
Men's bowling
Bowling Green U.
38 16
Women's mountain climbing
Appalachian State U.
 16 7
STOP
```

Since you don't know how many items are in the input, you can use an indefinite loop to read the data. The pseudocode for this procedure is:

```
Set file to read-only
Read first team
WHILE sentinel has not been read DO
   BEGIN
      Read opponent
      Read wins
      Read losses
      ...
      { process data }
      ...
      Read next team
   END { WHILE }
```

Since the team and opponent names are strings, you should use ***Readln*** statements to get each of those items. We also know that the wins and losses will be on the same line, so you can use a ***Readln*** to read both pieces of data:

```
program Scoreboard;

const
   sentinel = 'STOP';              { designates end of data        }

var
   sched: text;                    { file buffer for input file    }
   inFile,                         { name of file chosen by user   }
   sport,                          { local team playing            }
   opponent: string[40];           { opposing team                 }
   wins, losses: integer;          { record of local team          }

{ Functions Ltrim and Trim are here — see page 311.}
```

```
begin
   { Ask user to choose data file }
   repeat
      inFile := OldFileName('Please choose the schedule');
   until inFile <> '';
   Reset(sched, inFile);

   Readln(sched, sport); { prime the pump }
   sport := Ltrim(Trim(sport));
   while sport <> sentinel do
      begin
         Readln(sched, opponent); { get opponent's name }
         opponent := Ltrim(Trim(opponent));
         Readln(sched, wins, losses); { get local record }
         ...
         { process data }
         ...
         Readln(sched, sport);
         sport := Ltrim(Trim(sport))
      end { while }
end. { Scoreboard }
```

Removing the blanks with ***Ltrim*** and ***Trim*** (see Chapter 8) ensures that the loop exits when the sentinel is read. Thus, the user can type '   STOP', '   STOP   ', or 'STOP   ' and achieve the same result.

The problem with string sentinels is that they are defined in the Pascal program. Usually the programmer and the data file creator are two different people. A data file creator who has no knowledge of programming may not know why the sentinel is important. The data file creator may also simply forget the sentinel at the end of the file. Suppose you tried to run the above code on a data file that did not contain the 'STOP' sentinel. When the procedure tries to receive an input value after the < eof > marker, the program will bomb, and an error similar to **An attempt**

Syntax Box 9.4
Eof

Purpose	To detect the end of file.
Syntax	**Eof(**< file buffer >**)**
where	< file buffer > is a text variable.
Returns	a boolean value.
Usage	***Eof*** returns TRUE if the current file position in the file associated with < file buffer > is at the < eof > marker. Otherwise, ***Eof*** returns FALSE. < file buffer > must have been used in a ***Open***, ***Reset***, or ***Rewrite*** statement prior to the call to ***Eof***. When the file is initially opened, the value returned by ***Eof*** is FALSE.

has been made to access data beyond the end of a file or string will appear in a bug box.

To avoid this situation, Pascal provides a function that detects every data file's built-in sentinel: the < eof > marker. The Pascal function ***Eof*** returns a boolean value. It returns TRUE when the current file position has reached the < eof > marker in the file, that is, when the file position has moved beyond the last component in the file. At all other times, ***Eof*** returns FALSE.

You can change the code for reading input from the schedule file so that the loop exits when the < eof > marker is found instead of the string sentinel. To do this, you need to change the exit condition of the loop. You can also remove the pump-priming statement because a value for ***sport*** is no longer needed to test the exit condition. Now the first line of each set of input is read at the top of the loop.

```
program Scoreboard;

var
   sched: text;                    { file buffer for input file        }
   inFile,                         { name of file chosen by user       }
   sport,                          { local team playing                }
   opponent: string[40];           { opposing team                     }
   wins, losses: integer;          { record of local team              }
{ Functions Ltrim and Trim are here — see page 311.}

begin
   { Ask user to choose data file }
   repeat
      inFile := OldFileName('Please choose the schedule');
   until inFile <> '';
   Reset(sched, inFile);

   while not Eof(sched) do
      begin
         Readln(sched, sport);
         sport := Ltrim(Trim(sport));
         Readln(sched, opponent); { get opponent's name }
         opponent := Ltrim(Trim(opponent));
         Readln(sched, wins, losses); { get local record }
         ...
         { process data }
         ...
      end { while }
end. { program }
```

When you run this program using the data file ***Oct 2 Schedule***, MacPascal first opens the file with the ***Reset*** command. Then MacPascal reaches the condition of the **while** loop. Since the current file position is at the top of the file and the file is not empty, ***Eof(sched)*** returns FALSE and the loop condition is TRUE. The loop is executed, and the information about the men's bowling match is entered. Flow of control then returns to the top of the loop. Since the current file position is still not at the < eof > marker, ***Eof(sched)*** returns FALSE, and the loop executes again. After the team, the opponent, and the record for the mountain climbing event are read, the loop condition is again tested. Now the current file position is at the < eof > marker, so the function ***Eof(sched)*** returns TRUE. The loop condition **not** ***Eof(sched)*** is FALSE, so the loop exits.

The < eoln > marker can also be used as a sentinel. Let's look at how graphics can be stored in a data file. A picture is often stored in a data file as a series of output primitives. Each line of the data file contains a character representing a primitive and a series of coordinates. For example, the following data file represents a picture with two primitives:

```
L 0 0 200 200
R 35 35 70 70
```

If 'L' represents a line and 'R' represents a rectangle, this data file can be interpreted as a line from (0,0) to (200, 200) and a rectangle with corners at (35, 35) and (70, 70). In both cases, we know that the primitives can be defined with four coordinates. But how could we specify a primitive with a varying number of coordinate pairs? A polygon, for example, can be specified by three or more coordinate pairs, but we don't want to be forced to use a separate character code for 3-sided, 4-sided, and *n*-sided polygons. If we establish the condition that each primitive must be listed on a separate line, then we can use the < eoln > marker as a sentinel. Pascal has a ***Eoln*** function that is analogous to the ***Eof*** function. ***Eoln*** returns TRUE when the current file position is at an < eoln > marker. When ***Eoln*** returns TRUE, we need to use an empty ***Readln*** statement to move the current file position to the next line.

By using the ***Eoln*** function, we can use the single code "P" at the beginning of each line to specify a polygon. The following code fragment reads and draws lines, rectangles, and polygons from a data file:

Code 9.1
procedure
ReadAndDraw

```
procedure ReadAndDraw;
   var
      graph : text;                    { file buffer for graphics data file     }
      shapeType : char;                { indicates type of primitive            }
      origHoriz, origVert,             { coords of one endpoint or corner       }
      destHoriz, destVert,             { coords of other endpt or corner        }
      horiz, vert : integer;           { coords of endpt of polygon             }
begin
   Reset(graph, OldFileName('Please choose the graphics data:'));
   while not Eof(graph) do
      begin
         Read(graph, shapeType);
         case shapeType of
            'L' :  { line }
               begin
                  Read(graph, origHoriz, origVert, destHoriz, destVert);
```

Code 9.1 (continued)

```
                MoveTo(origHoriz, origVert);
                LineTo(destHoriz, destVert)
            end; { line }

        'R' : { rectangle }
            begin
                Read(graph, origHoriz, origVert, destHoriz, destVert);
                FrameRect(origVert, origHoriz, destVert, destHoriz)
            end; { rectangle }

        'P' : { polygon }
            begin
            { get first point }
                Read(graph, origHoriz, origVert);
                MoveTo(origHoriz, origVert);

            { read rest of points }
                while not Eoln(graph) do
                    begin
                        Read(graph, horiz, vert);
                        LineTo(horiz, vert)
                    end; { while }

            { draw line back to first point }
                LineTo(origHoriz, origVert)
            end { polygon }
        end; { case }

        Readln(graph) { move to next line in file }
    end { while }
end; { ReadAndDraw }
```

Syntax Box 9.5
Eoln

Purpose	To detect the end of a line
Syntax	**Eoln(**< file buffer >**)**
where	< file buffer > is a variable of type ***text***.
Returns	a boolean value
Usage	***Eoln*** returns TRUE if the current file position in the file associated with < file buffer > is at an < eoln > marker. Otherwise, ***Eoln*** returns FALSE. < file buffer > must have been used in a ***Open***, ***Reset***, or ***Rewrite*** statement prior to the call to ***Eoln***.

9.6 Writing to Files

Let's complete the sports schedule example. For each game in the schedule, the user wants to enter the score of the game at the keyboard and have the result printed as shown:

```
Bowling Green U. 3, Men's Bowling (38-17) 1
```

The winning team is listed on the left. The local team's record is updated and printed in parentheses.

You want to send the output to a file so that the newspaper's typesetting program can print the scoreboard automatically. Now, you could choose the appropriate option (the **Preferences** option from the **Windows** menu in MacPascal, the **Run Options...** from the **Project** menu in Lightspeed), and designate that you want to send output to a file as well as to the screen (see Appendix E). While this is sufficient for many applications, our discussion of files would not be complete unless we described how to write to a file designated by a text variable.

To tell Pascal that you want to send output to a file, you first have to designate a file as write-only. This is done using the ***Rewrite*** command. Like ***Reset***, this command takes two parameters: a text variable and a string that represents the file name. The current file position is set to component 0, so that writing will begin at the top of the file.

You can use the ***OldFileName*** function in the ***Rewrite*** statement. This allows you to use an existing file as a write-only file. When you write into an existing file, you *overwrite* its contents. This means that the previous contents of the file are replaced by the new output from the program starting at the current file position.

If you want to create a new file, use MacPascal's ***NewFileName*** function. Like ***OldFileName***, this function takes one parameter as a prompt. This function puts up a dialog box similar to the **Save As...** box in MacPascal. For example, the statement ***NewFileName('Enter name of output file:')*** produces the dialog box in Figure 9.5.

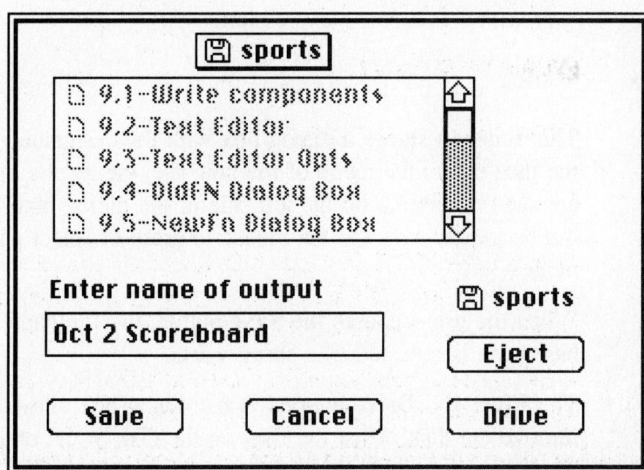

Figure 9.5
Dialog box from NewFileName

Notice that the prompt is truncated after the word ***output***. The number of characters that you can fit in the prompt varies, because the width of each letter varies. The dialog box has enough space to show 42 i's but only 14 W's. In general, about 20 characters fit in the prompt.

The user can enter the new file name in the box on the left. The area on the right side of the larger box designates the disk on which the new file will be held. The **Eject** and **Drive** buttons again allow the user to eject the current disk or use the disk in the other drive. When the user chooses the **Save** button, the name in the box on the left is returned to the program. This string value can then be used in a ***Rewrite*** command to open the file for writing. Notice that the term **Save** is a misnomer here; the file hasn't been opened yet, so there is nothing left to save.

Syntax Box 9.6
Rewrite

Purpose To open a file for write-only access

Syntax **Rewrite(**< file buffer >**,** < filename >**);**

where < file buffer > is a variable of type ***text***.
< filename > is a string expression.

Usage This statement opens the file specified by < filename >. After this statement, < file buffer > can be used as the first parameter in ***Write*** or ***Writeln*** statements to send output to the file.

The current file position is set to component 0 (the first component of the file).

Syntax Box 9.7
NewFileName

Purpose To allow a user to create a new name for a new file

Syntax **NewFileName(**< prompt >**)**

where < prompt > is a string expression.

Returns a string

Usage This function shows a dialog box with the designated < prompt >. As the user enters the name of the new file, the results of the keystrokes are seen in an area on the left side of the dialog box. The user can use the backspace key and the mouse to erase or select parts of the file name.

When the user chooses the **Save** button, the file name that the user has typed is returned as a string value.

The **Eject** and **Drive** buttons in the dialog box allow the user to remove the disk or list the files on the disk in the other drive, respectively.

Syntax Box 9.8
Write and **Writeln** to files

Purpose	To send output to a file
Syntax	**Write(** < file buf >**,** < exp 1 >**,...,** < exp *n* > **);** **Writeln(** < file buf >**,** < exp 1 >**,...,** < exp *n* > **);**
where	< file buf > is a variable of type ***text***. < exp 1 >,..., < exp *n* > are expressions of any printable type.
Usage	These statements are identical to the ***Write*** and ***Writeln*** statements introduced in Chapter 2 except that the output is sent to the file associated with < file buf > instead of to the Text window. If any < exp > evaluates to a real value, it can be formatted with a field width and precision as follows: < exp > **:** < field > **:** < precision > Any other expression can be formatted with a field width: < exp > **:** < field > If no expressions follow < file buf > in a ***Writeln*** statement, a blank line appears in the file. The current file position moves to the position immediately following the output printed by ***Write*** or ***Writeln***. ***Writeln*** adds an < eoln > marker after the output.

Syntax Box 9.9
Close

Purpose	To close a file
Syntax	**Close(**< file buffer >**);**
where	< file buffer > is a variable of type ***text***.
Usage	***Close*** closes the file associated with < file buffer >. The file is stored on the disk designated when the file was opened. < file buffer > must have been previously opened with ***Open***, ***Reset***, or ***Rewrite***.

When the file is eventually closed, however, this **Save** command takes effect and the file is saved under the given name.

Once a file has been opened with ***Rewrite***, you can write to it with the ***Write*** and ***Writeln*** statements. The only difference between writing to the file and writing to the Text window is that the first parameter to ***Write*** or ***Writeln*** must be a ***text*** variable. All of the formatting that you use with ***Write*** and ***Writeln*** (specifying field widths and precisions, interspersing literal text with variables, generating blank lines with empty ***Writeln*** statements) have the same effect when you write to a file.

When you are finished writing to a file, close the file by using the ***Close*** procedure. ***Close*** receives one parameter: a variable of type ***text***. This command stores the file associated with the designated ***text*** variable on the disk.

9.7 Example Program

We can now prepare the code for the sports schedule example. To recapitulate, the input for the program consists of a file with the sports, the opponents, and the records. For each game, the user is asked to input the score from the keyboard. The record of the school team then is updated and the score is printed in the form shown in Section 9.6.

The pseudocode for this program looks like this:

```
Open schedule file
Create file for output
WHILE still more data DO
   BEGIN
      Read sport, opponent, record from file
      Read score from keyboard
      IF local team wins THEN
         BEGIN
            Add one to team's wins
            Write output to file in form:
            < local team > (< record >) < score >, < opponent > < score >
         END { IF }
      ELSE
         BEGIN
            Add one to team's losses
            Write output to file in form:
               < opponent > < score >, < local team > (< record >) < score >

         END { ELSE }
   END { WHILE }
```

The code for this program appears below, followed by the input file and the output as seen on the screen and in the output file.

Code 9.2
Program *Scoreboard*

```
{ Scoreboard       D. Niguidula   October 7                    }
{  This program prepares a file of sports results.             }
{ The input for the program comes from a data file.            }
{ The data file consists of a series of scheduled games        }
{ for a local team. For each game, the data file con-          }
{ tains three pieces of information: the sport, the            }
{ opponent, and the record of the local team.                  }
{  The program reads the information for each game. Then,      }
{ the user is asked to enter the result of the game at the     }
{ keyboard. Using this information, the local team's record    }
{ is updated, and the result is printed in a file.             }
```

Code 9.2
(continued)

```
program Scoreboard;
   var
      sched,                      { input file; contains info on each game    }
      results : text;             { output file; result is printed on 1 line  }
      sport,                      { local team                                }
      opponent : string[80];      { opposing school                           }
      wins, losses : integer;     { local team's current record               }
      gameResult : char;          { indicates if local team has won           }
      winScore,                   { points scored by winning team             }
      loseScore : integer;        { points scored by losing team              }

{ Procedure ReadScore                                                 }
{ This procedure reads the sport, opponent, and record of the local   }
{ team from a file. Then the user is asked to enter the result of     }
{ the game at the keyboard.                                           }
{ Called by: Mainline              Calls: none                        }

   procedure ReadScore (var sched : text;  { input file               }
      var sport,                  { local team                        }
      opponent : string;          { opposing school                   }
      var wins, losses : integer; { local team's record               }
      var gameResult : char;      { indicates if local team has won   }
      var winScore,               { points scored by winning team     }
      loseScore : integer);       { points scored by losing team      }

   begin
{ get data from input file }
      Readln(sched, sport);
      Readln(sched, opponent);
      Readln(sched, wins, losses);

{ get score from keyboard }
      Writeln;
      Writeln('Game: ', sport, ' vs. ', opponent);
      Write('Please enter the winning score: ');
      Readln(winScore);
      Write('Please enter the losing score: ');
      Readln(loseScore);
      repeat
         Write('Did the local team win? (enter y for yes, n for no): ');
         Readln(gameResult);
      until (gameResult = 'y') or (gameResult = 'n');
   end; { ReadScore }

{ Procedure WriteScore                                                }
{ This procedure provides the output of the program. The local        }
{ team's record is updated, and the score is printed in the given file. }
{ Called by: Mainline                  Calls: none                    }
```

```
procedure WriteScore (var results : text;         { output file                    }
    sport,                                        { local team                     }
    opponent : string;                            { opposing school                }
    var wins, losses : integer;                   { local team's record            }
    gameResult : char;                     { indicates if local team has won       }
    winScore,                              { points scored by winning team         }
    loseScore : integer);                  { points scored by losing team          }

begin
    if gameResult = 'y' then { local team has won }
        begin
            wins := wins + 1;

{ use format <local team> (<record>) <score>, <opp.> <score> }

            Write(results, sport, ' (', wins : 2, '-', losses : 2, ') ');
            Write(results, winScore : 2, ', ');
            Writeln(results, opponent, ' ', loseScore : 2)
        end{ if }

    else { opponent has won }
        begin
            losses := losses + 1;

{ use format <opp.> <score>,  <local team> (<record>) <score> }

            Write(results, opponent, ' ', winScore : 2, ', ');
            Write(results, sport, ' (', wins : 2, '-', losses : 2, ') ');
            Writeln(results, loseScore : 2)
        end { else }

end; { WriteScore }

{ Procedure Mainline                                                      }
{  The Mainline handles much of the file manipulation. It begins          }
{ by asking the user to designate the input and output files.             }
{ It determines when all of the data has been processed by seeing         }
{ if the end of the input file has been reached. Finally, the program     }
{ ends by closing the input and output files.                             }
{ Calls: ReadScore, WriteScore                                            }

begin
{ initialize files }
    Reset(sched, OldFileName('Please choose a schedule: '));
    Rewrite(results, NewFileName('Enter results filename: '));

{ process each game in input file }
    while not Eof(sched) do
        begin
            ReadScore(sched, sport, opponent, wins, losses, gameResult,
                winScore, loseScore);
```

Code 9.2 (continued)

```
            WriteScore(results, sport, opponent, wins, losses, gameResult,
                winScore, loseScore)
        end; { while }

    { close files }
        Close(sched);
        Close(results)
    end. { Scoreboard }
```

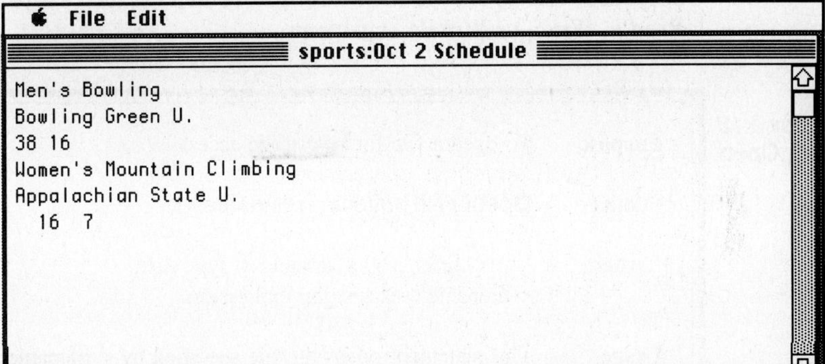

Figure 9.6 Input file to *Scoreboard* program

```
Text

Game: Men's Bowling vs. Bowling Green U.
Please enter the winning score: 3
Please enter the losing score: 1
Did the local team win? (enter y for yes, n for no): n

Game: Women's Mountain Climbing vs. Appalachian State U.
Please enter the winning score: 94
Please enter the losing score: 87
Did the local team win? (enter y for yes, n for no): y
```

Figure 9.7 Output of *Scoreboard* program in Text window

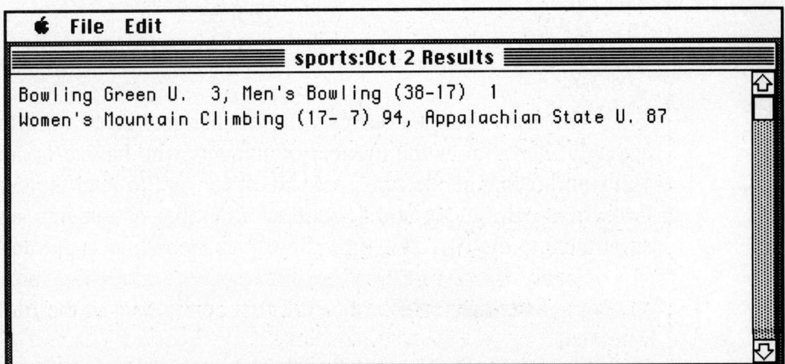

Figure 9.8 Output of *Scoreboard* program in output file

9.8 Reading and Writing

Reset and ***Rewrite*** can be used to change a file's status at any time. Be careful when switching a file's status from read-only to write-only. The ***Reset*** and ***Rewrite*** statements set the current file position back to the top of the file. Changing a data file to write-only with ***Rewrite*** overwrites the file's previous contents.

Occasionally, we want to open a file for both reading and writing. To open a read-write file, we use the ***Open*** statement. ***Open*** is syntactically identical to ***Reset*** and ***Rewrite***; it takes a ***text*** variable and a string value as parameters. When the file is opened with ***Open***, the file buffer can be used as the first parameter in ***Read***, ***Readln***, ***Write***, or ***Writeln*** statements.

Syntax Box 9.10
Open

Purpose	To open a file for read-write access
Syntax	**Open(< file buffer >, < filename >);**
where	< file buffer > is a variable of type ***text***. < filename > is a string expression.
Usage	This statement opens the file specified by < filename >. After this statement, < file buffer > can be used as the first parameter in ***Read*** or ***Readln*** statements to receive input from a file, or in ***Write*** or ***Writeln*** statements to send output to the file. The current file position is set to component 0 (the first component of the file).

Read-write files are used to update the data in a file. Say we have a file that holds the current list of classes and the enrollment in each class. The file may look something like this:

```
English 1  100
Comp Sci 11  134
History 52  325
Music 298   5
...
```

The names of the courses will not change, but the enrollment will need updating. If we know the number of students who have dropped or added a class, we will want to change the file's contents. We want to read the current contents, find out the current enrollment, add or subtract a number of students, and write the new enrollment to the file. Thus, the file serves as both an input and an output file.

Finally, the ***Seek*** procedure allows you to move the current file position to any component in the file. Since the first component in the file is numbered zero, the statement sets the current file position to the top of the file associated with the file buffer ***inData***.

If you specify a component number that is greater than the number of components in the file, the current file position moves to the < eof > marker. Thus, if we want to add data to the end of an existing file, we use the following code:

```
Open(fileBuf, OldFileName('Please choose a file to update'));
Seek(fileBuf, maxLongint);          { move to < eof > }
Write(... );                        { start writing new data at end of file }
```

The file buffer designated in ***Seek*** must be associated with a read-write file. This means that the file buffer must have been opened with ***Open***. Also, we used the predefined constant ***maxLongint***. This constant is equal to the largest number in the ***Longint*** range of representation. This number must be greater than the number of the largest component in any file; thus, any time ***maxLongint*** is used as the second parameter to ***Seek***, the current file position moves to the < eof > marker.

Syntax Box 9.11
Seek

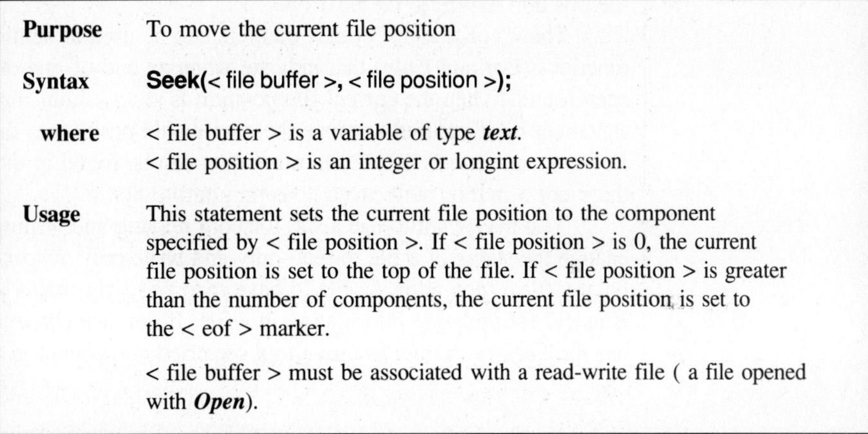

Purpose To move the current file position

Syntax **Seek(**< file buffer >**,** < file position >**);**

where < file buffer > is a variable of type ***text***.
< file position > is an integer or longint expression.

Usage This statement sets the current file position to the component specified by < file position >. If < file position > is 0, the current file position is set to the top of the file. If < file position > is greater than the number of components, the current file position is set to the < eof > marker.

< file buffer > must be associated with a read-write file (a file opened with ***Open***).

9.9 Chapter Summary

Files are used when we want to process a large amount of data. A file contains a set of related information and is stored on an external device. (In all likelihood, the only external devices you have been using are your disks. On other machines, files are stored on magnetic tapes and drums and digital disks.) Each piece of data in a file is called a component; components are numbered in a file starting at 0.

Files can be used in a program in one of three ways: read-only, write-only, and read-write. These terms designate whether the file is open for input, output, or both. Before a file can be used, it must first be opened. Pascal provides three statements for opening files: ***Reset*** for read-only files, ***Rewrite*** for write-only files, and ***Open*** for read-write files.

You must specify the file that you want to open, reset, or rewrite. The ***OldFileName*** function allows you to use any file that currently exists. The dialog box that appears when you call this function even allows you to use a file on another disk. The ***NewFileName*** function allows you to create a file when the program is executing. Again, a dialog box appears, and the new file can be stored on any disk.

A file can be created using the Text Editor program that comes with the MacPascal and Lightspeed Pascal packages. When you enter the data file, you also enter invisible < eoln > markers at the end of every line and an invisible < eof > marker at the end of the file.

Once the data file has been created, you need a way of referring to it in the program. This is done by declaring a variable of type ***text***. The ***text*** variable is a file buffer, which means it acts as a gateway between the file on the disk and the program.

Text variables, when used as the first parameter to ***Read***, ***Readln***, ***Write***, or ***Writeln*** statements, allow input to come from or output to go to a specified file. The output statements act the same as if you were writing to the Text window. When reading from a file, ***Readln*** differs from ***Read*** in that after each ***Readln***, the current file position moves to the next line.

The < eof > and < eoln > markers can be used as sentinels. Pascal provides two functions (***Eof*** and ***Eoln***) that indicate when an end-of-line or end-of-file marker has been found. When the current file position is at an < eoln > marker, a ***Readln*** statement must be used to move the current file position to the next line. When the ***Eof*** function returns TRUE, no more data can be found in the file. Reading beyond the < eof > marker will cause your program to bomb.

You may want to use a file for both reading and writing. ***Reset*** and ***Rewrite*** change the status of a file to read-only and write-only, respectively, and can be used on any file. ***Open*** allows a file to have read and write status simultaneously, which is useful for updating information in a file. If you use ***Open*** to open a file, you can use the ***Seek*** procedure to move to a specified component in the file.

9.10 Exercises

Understanding Concepts

1. How do the commands ***Open***, ***Reset***, and ***Rewrite*** differ from one another?

2. Given the file:

```
555 1212
406 0531
```

how many components are in this file if you treat them as integers? as components of type **string[8]**?

3. In the file in exercise 2, what is component number 0 if you read the contents as integers? as components of type **string[8]**?

4. What does the following code do?

```
Rewrite(excFile, 'Excuses');
Write('What''s your excuse this time?');
Readln(excuse);
while excuse <> 'NO MORE' do
   begin
      Write(excFile, excuse);
      Writeln;
      Writeln(excFile);
      Write('What''s your excuse this time?');
      Readln(excuse)
   end; { while }
```

5. What's wrong with the following code fragment (assuming ***textFile*** is a variable of type ***text***)?

```
Reset( textFile, OldFileName('Please choose a file'));
Writeln(textFile, 'This is the first line of the file');
```

6. What does the file ***Result*** contain after this fragment?

```
Rewrite(resText, 'Result');
Writeln(resText, 'The first line');
Rewrite(resText, 'Result');
Writeln(resText, 'The second line');
```

7. After the following code fragments, where is the current file position? (Assume that ***inFile*** has been declared as a ***text*** variable and ***current*** as a ***char*** variable.)

   a.
```
Reset(inFile, 'Something');
while not Eoln(inFile) do
   Read(inFile, current);
```

   b.
```
Reset(inFile, 'Something');
while not Eof(inFile) do
   begin
      while not Eoln(inFile) do
         Read(inFile, current);
      Readln
   end; { while }
```

   c.
```
Reset(inFile, 'Something');
while not Eoln(inFile) do
   Read(inFile, current);
Readln(inFile);
Rewrite(inFile);
```

8. What does the following code do? Provide a block comment and glossary for the code.

```
program Exercise8;

var
   inLine: string[40];
   file1, file2: text;

begin
   Open(file1, 'First File');
   Open(file2, 'Second File');

   while not Eof(file1) do
      begin
         Readln(file1, inLine);
         Writeln(file2, inLine)
      end { while }

end. { Exercise8 }
```

Coding Exercises

1. Write a procedure that prints the contents of a file in the Text window.

2. Write a procedure that concatenates two files. The user should specify two existing files. The contents of these files should then be printed, one after the other, in the Text window.

3. Write a procedure that deletes the contents of a file. Allow the user to confirm that she really wants to delete the contents.

4. Write a procedure that allows the user to select any number of files and stores the names of those files in a new file called ***selections***.

5. Write a procedure that, given a string and a file, prints all lines in the file that contain the specified string.

6. Write a procedure that compares two files and prints those lines that occur in both files.

7. Write a procedure that asks a user to enter his or her age, year of graduation, sex, astrological sign, the amount of cash in his or her wallet, and the number of films seen in the last month. Store the information in a file. Assume that this procedure will be called many times for many different users.

8. Modify the previous exercise so that the user also enters a unique ID number. Then write another procedure that, when given an ID number, allows the user to modify the associated information in the file.

9. Write a procedure that uses the file created in coding exercise 7 and performs some statistical analysis. What is the average amount of cash held by the people in the

file? Do seniors see more movies than sophomores? Are there an equal number of male Geminis and female Capricorns? Create your own inquiries into this data base.

10. Assume that the block letters A-Z have been stored in files called ***blockA***, ***blockB***,..., ***blockZ***. Write a procedure that accepts a string as input and outputs the same string in block letters.

Programming Problems

1. Suppose you have two files called ***College*** and ***Grad***. ***College*** is a list of all undergraduate students; ***Grad*** is a list of all graduate students. Both files contain names in the form < last name >, < first name >. Both files also contain one name per line, and both files are in alphabetical order. Write a program that creates a third file called ***University***. At the end of the program, ***University*** should contain the merged contents of ***College*** and ***Grad*** in alphabetical order (this is known as a *merge sort*). For example, if ***College*** contains:

```
Hacker, Hilary
Wood, Chip
```

   and ***Grad*** contains:

```
Degree, Phil H.
Sincere, Monroe
Teacher, Mary Ann
```

   then ***University*** should end up with:

```
Degree, Phil H.
Hacker, Hilary
Sincere, Monroe
Teacher, Mary Ann
Wood, Chip
```

2. Create a program to check spelling. This program requires the use of two files: a document and a dictionary. The dictionary consists of a number of entries. Each entry is on two lines: the first line of the entry is the misspelled word, and the second line of the entry is the correctly spelled word. For example, the dictionary could look like this:

```
TEH
THE
WNAT
WANT
TAHT
THAT
...
```

   Your program should work with one line of the document at a time. If the line contains any of the misspelled entries, replace it with the correct spelling. The final output should be a new file with all the correct spellings.

3. Add a Load Picture option to the Layout program. When 'Load Picture' is selected, the program should allow the user to choose a file. The file contains all the objects in a picture, and each line in the file contains the information about one object. Each line contains a character (representing the type of object), the position of the object, and, if necessary, the object itself. More specifically, the following formats can appear in the file:

   T < horiz > < vert > < string > — designates a Text string. When this line is encountered in the file, < string > should be placed at (< horiz >, < vert >).
   R < top > < left > < bottom > < right > — designates a Rectangle. This line should generate a framed rectangle with corners at (< left >, < top >) and (< bottom >, < right >).
   O < top > < left > < bottom > < right > — designates an Oval. This command is similar to the Rectangle command, but a framed oval is drawn instead of a framed rectangle.
   L < horiz1 > < vert1 > < horiz2 > < vert2 > — designates a Line. This command should generate a line starting at the point (< horiz1 >, < vert1 >) and ending at (< horiz2 >, < vert2 >).

   Variation: Add a Start Saving option. This option allows the user to name a file. Then each of the other drawing commands (Line, Text, Rectangle, Oval) draws a shape on the screen and store the appropriate information in a file, using the formats above.

4. Write a Mad Libs™ program. A Mad Lib is a story with certain words left out. These words are replaced by parts of speech in parentheses. For example, a Mad Lib could start like this:

   A long, long time ago in a (noun) far, far, away, there lived
   a (adjective) boy by the name of (name).

   This story is in a file. The Mad Libs program should look through the file and ask the user to fill in words at the keyboard. For example, a program using the above file as input should first ask the user to enter a noun, followed by an adjective, followed by a name. The rest of the story is not revealed to the user until all the words have been filled. The entire story — with the user's entries replacing the parenthetical expressions — should be output in a new file.

5. Write a simple noninteractive word processing program. In the input file are two types of lines: *text* and *commands*. Commands have a period at the beginning of the line; text lines begin with any other character. Your program should copy text from an input file to an output file, one word at a time. In the output file, no line should contain more than 60 characters (including blanks). Words may

not be split between lines. Along with text, the following commands can appear in the file, each command on its own line:

.B — break a line. This means that the current file position should move to the beginning of the next line in the output file.

.S — skip a line. This means that a blank line should appear in the output file at this position.

.P — start a new paragraph. The current file position moves to the beginning of the next line in the output file and then prints five spaces.

.I <spaces> — indent the next lines a number of spaces. Whenever the current file position in the output file is moved to a new line, **<spaces>** number of spaces should be printed at the beginning of the line.

6. Write a program for a multiple-choice quiz. Each question in the quiz has four possible answers, and each answer is assigned a point value. The input comes from a file that could begin as follows:

```
Where do you feel most comfortable?
10 In open areas
20 In crowded elevators
30 In open areas in crowded elevators
40 Perched atop the Empire State Building
What makes you feel the most embarrassed?
...
```

Each of the questions and possible answers should be copied from the file to the Text window. The user should choose one option. The program should then determine the number of points for the user's option. For example, if the user chooses the option "In crowded elevators" from the above file, the program should determine that the option is worth 30 points. A new question is then read from the file. The end of the questions is marked by the sentinel 'STOP'. The user's point value for all of the questions is totaled. The total is used to print the final message. The final messages correspond to a scale listed after the 'STOP' marking the end of the questions, as follows:

```
{ questions here }
STOP
0 100 You like people at a distance
110 200 You like to be intimate with people
210 300 You aren't sure what you like
310 400 You are King Kong
< eof >
```

Thus, if the user scores 250 points on the scale, he should see the message "You aren't sure what you like."

7. Write a program that tests a student's punctuation skills. The program uses two previously prepared files. One file, called ***examples***, contains one unpunctuated

sentence per line. The other file, called ***answers***, is identical to ***examples*** except that each sentence has been punctuated. The program should display one sentence at a time from ***examples***. The user responds by indicating which words should be followed by punctuation, and what mark should follow the selected word. The user should continue to add punctuation until he enters a sentinel. At that point, the program should compare the student's sentence to the correct answer. If the sentences match, an appropriate message should be printed; otherwise, the user should be shown the differences between his version and the version in ***answers***.

8. Write an electronic date book that allows a user to store and retrieve dated messages. Your program should allow the user to do two things:

   a. *Add messages.* The user should be able to enter one-line messages. These messages should be placed in a file called ***calendar***. Each message should contain a date in < month >/< day > format, as the examples illustrate:

   ```
   9/20 Happy birthday to me.
   2/1 Finish Groundhog's Day shopping.
   7/6 Fly to Frankfurt or Geneva - whatever.
   ...
   ```

   b. *Retrieve messages.* When the user enters the current date, the program should print (in the Text window) all the messages for today and for the next two days. For example, if the user indicates that today is 3/30, the program should print all messages for 3/30, 3/31, and 4/1.

9. You've learned that pictures on the Mac are really a series of pixels colored black or white. To store a picture, you may indicate which pixels are black — you can then assume the remainder are white. Reducing this further, you can store a picture as a sequence of horizontal lines, where you designate the starting and stopping points for each horizontal sequence of black pixels. This technique is known as *run length encoding*. The following is an example of such a file:

   ```
   19 5 18
   20 4 22
   21 3 27 61 82
   ...
   ```

   In this file, the first number on each line is a vertical coordinate. Then, each line contains pairs of horizontal coordinates representing starting and stopping points. These are the borders of the black areas of the picture. Thus, the above file means that lines should be colored from (5,19) to (18,19); from (4,20) to (22,20); from (3,21) to (27,21); and from (61,21) to (82,21). Write a program that draws a picture based on such a file.

10. Write a program that quizzes the user on world capitals. Create a file called ***WorldCaps*** with any number of two-line sets. In each set, the first line is a

Capital and the second is the nation:

```
Ottawa
Canada
Quezon City
Philippines
Stockholm
Sweden
...
```

The user should indicate whether she wants to see the capital and respond with the nation or vice versa. The user should get three guesses to match the answer before the program moves to the next capital-nation pair. When < eof > is reached, the program should tell the user how many times she correctly responded on the first guess, on the second guess, on the third guess, and not at all.

10

Interactive Techniques, Regions, and External Documentation

In his book *Professional Pascal,* Henry Ledgard makes a distinction among "professional" programmers.* He claims that while there are many true professionals writing software, there are many more who believe they are professionals but are really amateurs — a group Ledgard calls "P-sub-A programmers." The differences between the two groups are not clearly defined, but among other things, Ledgard says that the P-sub-A programmer:

- perpetuates the mythical user (assumes the user is just like the programmer)
- considers work reading (offering one's own work for open criticism) a nuisance
- deals with documentation later
- gets on with the job

whereas the professional programmer

- writes programs for a large class of users (does *not* assume user knowledge)
- writes programs that *anyone* can read

---

* Henry Ledgard, *Professional Pascal* (Reading, Mass.: Addison-Wesley, 1986), pp. 9-20.

- writes beautiful documentation *first*
- writes programs with concern for future and larger systems

To conclude his list of distinctions, Ledgard says the P-sub-A programmer "writes software for the computer" while the professional "writes software for the human reader."

Why do we mention this now? Because we want you to think of yourself as a professional programmer. After reading half of an introductory text on a single language, we certainly don't expect you to have all the tools that a professional needs. However, we do expect you to have the *attitude* of a professional. We want you to be able to distinguish between a "good" and a "bad" program. For example, a working program is not necessarily the same thing as a "good" program. A good program is easy for other people to use, read, and modify.

A program is easy to use if the interface is well designed for its intended audience. A program is easy to read if it is documented well and uses mnemonic identifiers for constants, variables, and procedures. A program is easy to modify if, among other things, it contains components — procedures and functions — that comprise logical units, and it uses **const** declarations in place of literal constants.

This chapter will look at two topics that are integral to good programming practice. First, it will examine how to design a good *user interface*, which is the way the user and your program interact with each other. We will look at the two important principles of a good interface — consistency and clarity. Later, we will examine how to make a program easier to read by developing *external documentation*: documentation that allows a user — and other programmers — to understand your work.

In between these two topics, we will discuss some of the more advanced graphics techniques available in QuickDraw. Graphics have been emphasized throughout this book because graphics can provide a natural and simple user interface. You have already seen that menus allow a program's user to see all the options available at a given time and that an option can be picked from the menu without using the keyboard. Chapter 3 introduced the QuickDraw primitives, which allow you to represent non-textual information graphically. Of course, text and graphics can be mixed to provide clearer output. This chapter will look at how to define collections of primitives known as regions. Before we discuss these more advanced graphics calls, we will look at how any program—whether graphical or textual—can be made more *user friendly*.

10.1 The Importance of Feedback

It's springtime again, and students at our favorite college, Finite State U., are getting ready to select their rooms for next year. FSU has a large student body and a number of housing options: apartments, suites, fraternities/sororities, coed dorms, and so on. The administrators at FSU have thoughtfully developed a computer program to ease the selection process. The program allows students to input some information, such as the desired number of roommates, their housing preferences, and their class years. The program then outputs the names of the rooms that are available—saving many hours of trudging all over campus.

One student heard about the room program in her introductory computer science class and immediately ran out to the college's central computer center to try it. She soon realized, however, that something was wrong with the program. When she ran it, all that appeared on the screen was the cryptic line:

```
WAITING FOR INPUT:
```

The student was annoyed. How was she supposed to know what to input? She tried typing "GO" but was greeted with the messages:

```
NO, THAT'S WRONG. TRY AGAIN.
WAITING FOR INPUT:
```

She tried "RUN", but the program responded:

```
NOT APPLICABLE HERE.
WAITING FOR INPUT:
```

Her frustration intensified when similar error messages kept appearing as she continued to type different instructions. Finally, she tried typing a number; at this point the screen cleared and flashed the message:

```
PROGRAM INTERRUPT 040753 OCCURRED IN NON PASCAL
  SUBPROCEDURE.
INPUT OF NON STRING TYPE.
```

At this point, the keyboard locked. Nothing the student typed appeared on the screen. Finally, she got up and left in disgust.

Unfortunately our hypothetical student's dilemma is not far removed from reality. Many programmers become so involved with coding and debugging that they forget that their work is intended for human users. In all likelihood, the programs you have written up to this point have been for yourself; that is, you expect to be the only user of your program. Most of the time, though, you will want to make your programs general enough for anyone to use. Thus, the interactive techniques used in your programming should be helpful not only to you but to any potential user as well.

The user interface is a dialogue between the user and a computer program. As a programmer, you are responsible for both ends of this dialogue: you must write the computer program's lines, but you must also consider all the user's possible responses and have your program react appropriately. The next two sections will discuss the textual feedback of your program and then look at methods of improving the graphic feedback.

The most obvious forms of textual feedback are the prompts and messages that appear in your program's Text window. A prompt tells users what sort of input should be provided. Having provided the input, users expect some sort of reaction. Your program should tell users what it is doing, so they can see how the program has responded to their requests.

Textual feedback, like other interactive techniques, is done well when it has consistency, clarity, and applicability. Consistency means that the same situation should always produce the same result or precede the same action. For example, suppose you have a layout program that allows the user to draw shapes using any of the five pen "colors." A consistent program would allow users to choose the color first, and then the points of the shape. An inconsistent program might ask users to choose the color first for circles, but the points first for rectangles.

Clarity implies two things. First, what users see when they run the program should be understandable. The messages that the computer outputs are often the only guide to your program. A user-friendly message is a concise, unambiguous statement that describes the present status of the program. For example, these messages are not friendly to most users:

```
?
>
What?
Unintelligible input has been discarded.
```

These messages do not give any direction. While users may understand that they did something wrong, they don't know what to do next or how to fix the error. On the other hand, the following messages are more user-friendly:

```
Type 'quit' to end the program.
Please input the # of rock groups to process:
Incorrect command...type HELP for legal commands.
```

These messages are clearer because they explain what the program expects next.

Clarity also implies that the output is clear, that is, easy to see and read. Blank lines in the textual output can be used to separate "dialogues" between the program and the user. Figure 10.1 shows two outputs with a single difference. The output in Figure 10.1b has a blank line after each transaction, while the output in Figure 10.1a does not. Note what an improvement in clarity these blank lines yield.

Keep your users in mind when you are programming. Who will be using your program? What assumptions can you make about them? The user interface should be appropriate to the audience you are writing for. Prompts should be different for 7-year-olds than for 15-year-olds. Your program may assume that the users have some

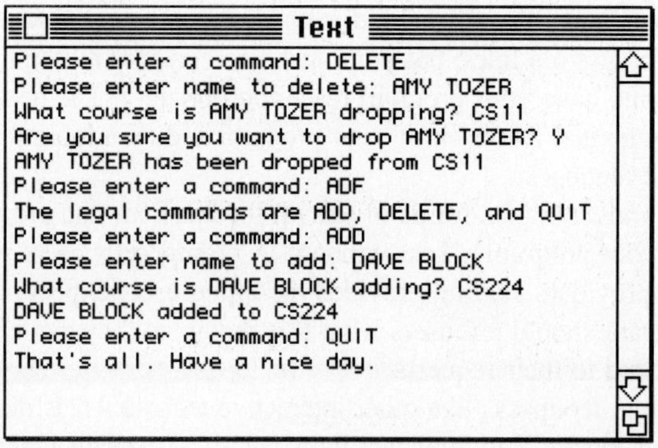

```
Text
Please enter a command: DELETE
Please enter name to delete: AMY TOZER
What course is AMY TOZER dropping? CS11
Are you sure you want to drop AMY TOZER? Y
AMY TOZER has been dropped from CS11
Please enter a command: ADF
The legal commands are ADD, DELETE, and QUIT
Please enter a command: ADD
Please enter name to add: DAVE BLOCK
What course is DAVE BLOCK adding? CS224
DAVE BLOCK added to CS224
Please enter a command: QUIT
That's all. Have a nice day.
```

Figure 10.1a
Output without extra blank lines

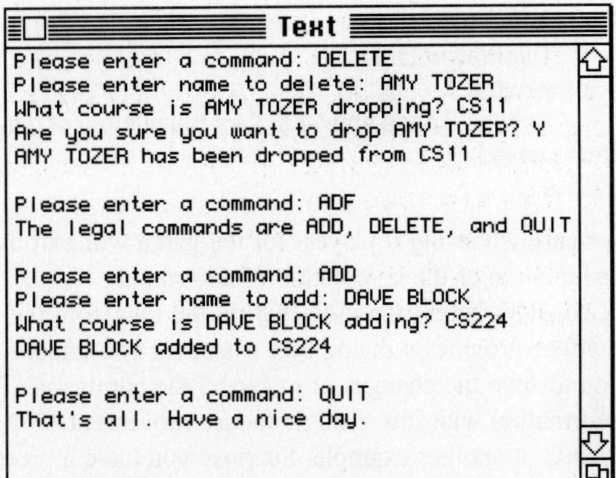

Figure 10.1b Output with extra blank lines

specific knowledge. For example, the prompt:

```
Please enter the systolic and diastolic pressures:
```

will make sense to medically trained users who know that systolic and diastolic pressures are the two numbers in a blood pressure reading.

Conversely, your program should not overestimate users' technical knowledge—even in terms of what they know about programming. For example, when you see "Please choose the corners for the rectangle," you know that you should pick the top left corner followed by the bottom right. Users who know nothing about QuickDraw may choose the bottom before the top, or may choose four corners. If you are going to use this prompt, your program should be able to handle either situation. As a general rule, whenever in doubt, expect that users have less, rather than more, specific knowledge.

10.2 User-Friendly Features

User friendliness isn't limited to the prompts and output statements included in a program. There are several features you should put into your programs to make them more friendly. For example, your program should include an *exit*, which is an easy way to stop execution (without bombing—that's *too* easy). The stop button on a menu is an example of an exit. Another example can be seen in the following code:

```
repeat
   Write('Are there 1 or 2 players in this round (0 to exit)?');
   Readln(players);
   case players of
      0 :
         done := TRUE;          { exit program }
      1 :
         PlayAgainstComputer;
```

```
        2 :
            TwoPlayerGame;
        otherwise
            Writeln('Please enter 1 or 2 for the number of players or 0 to exit')
    end; { case }
until done;
```

In the above case, choosing 0 players for the game will exit the program. Users can thus end the game after the completion of any round.

Also, consider letting the user *confirm* the exit from the program. The MacPascal editor provides a dialog box whenever you choose **Close** or **Quit**, allowing you to save the changes or to cancel the command. This way, you can't lose any information with just a single mouse movement.

Let's look at another example. Suppose you have a program driven by a menu. The menu gives the user three options: add a person to a class list, write out the list, or exit the program. A user may have typed in the entire roster for a large lecture class and want to press the "write" button to print out the entire enrollment. Instead, the user accidentally hits the button on the mouse too soon and selects the button indicating an exit. If the changes aren't saved automatically, the user will have wasted hours of typing. Asking for a confirmation lets the user undo a "dangerous" command.

For example, this code fragment includes a confirmation:

```
function GetPoint: point;                { returns point chosen by user      }

var
    userHoriz, userVert: integer;        { coords of user's point            }
    tempPt: point;                       { temporary point variable          }

begin
    repeat
        GetMouse(userHoriz, userVert);
    until Button;
    SetPt(tempPt, userHoriz, userVert);
    GetPoint := tempPt
end; { GetPoint }

...
{ Choose option from menu }
    repeat
        Writeln('Please choose an option from the menu.');
        userPt := GetPoint;
        if PtInRect(userPt, addButton) then
            AddStudent
        else if PtInRect(userPt, writeButton) then
            WriteClass
        else if PtInRect(userPt, exitButton) then
            begin
                Writeln('Are you sure you want to exit?');
                Writeln('If so, please pick EXIT again');
                userPt := GetPoint;
```

```
                done := PtInRect(userPt, exitButton)
            end {else}
        else
            Writeln('You did not pick on the menu')
    until done;
...
```

In the above code, the user has to pick the exit button twice before ***done*** is set to TRUE. Any other combination will continue the program's execution. Users of your program will appreciate the chance to stop an incorrectly specified command from executing.

Error checking is another form of user-friendly programming. Suppose you have a program that draws squares. The program prompts the user to input the size of one side of the square. The following code fragment does the input and drawing of the square:

```
Write('Please enter a side length: ');
Readln(sideLength);
PaintRect(0, 0, sideLength, sideLength);
```

If a user enters a 0 or any negative number, the program will have difficulty trying to draw the square. If the length of the side is 0, the ***PaintRect*** call simply draws a single point. If, however, the value of the side length is negative, the square will not appear on the screen. To handle the error conditions, the code could be revised in this way:

```
Writeln('Please enter a side length: ');
Readln(sideLength);
if sideLength > 0 then
   PaintRect(0, 0, sideLength, sideLength)
else
   begin
      Writeln('Side length entered must be greater than 0.');
      Writeln('Shape will not be drawn.')
   end; { else }
```

The best approach to error checking is "paranoid programming." The one rule of paranoid programming is simple: act on Murphy's law, "if anything can possibly go wrong, it will." Anticipate all the possible flawed data that an inexperienced user might input and make sure your program can handle them.

A great deal of error checking may appear to be tedious and unnecessary. You may ask yourself, "What sort of moron would make that kind of mistake?" There are two reasons why your program should be foolproof. First, even the most experienced worker can accidentally hit the wrong button on a keyboard or pick the wrong button on a menu. If your program "bombs" because of a small typo, it will be the source of great frustration. Second, the users of your program may not know anything about computers; they may just want to type in data and get output. Your programs should be as unmysterious as possible to have the greatest usefulness.

Another common feature is the *help facility,* which allows a user to find out more about the program at any moment. Typically, users can choose a "help" option from a menu. The program should respond by printing appropriate text, which may include a general overview of the program or an explanation of the current list of options. At different points of the program the help facility may print different messages. In any case, the help facility should help users understand what is going on and what to do next.

The help facility is an example of another principle of good user-interface design: your program should require as little memorization as possible. Users should be able to use your program as a tool to accomplish some ends. Users should be able to concentrate on the task they are trying to accomplish, rather than figuring out how to use your program. Users should be able to determine easily how your program works while the program is running.

Macintosh software developers keep this principle in mind. All the menus in Macintosh programs list all the available options; users do not have to remember which options are specific to MacPascal and which are common to other applications. Macintosh users do not have to worry about learning new ways of choosing options; the pull-down menu and the clicking features are common to all Mac software. This consistency promotes a level of "knowledge transfer." When users learn to do something in one program (such as choose an option from the menu or cut and paste) and find that they can use that action in another program, it makes the learning of the new program easier. Again, the idea behind good user-interface techniques is to make programs as easy to use as possible.

10.3 Setting Window Sizes

So far, we have concentrated on the effective use of text. Consistency and clarity are also issues when designing the graphic parts of your programs. The Macintosh software standards are a particularly good example of how graphics can be used effectively. All the programs that run on the Mac have a certain consistency. All programs use windows, scroll bars, and a close box. The menu options are always located in pull-down menus, which are always located at the top of the screen.

Consistency and clarity in graphics make your programs easy to look at. The graphic and textual feedback should appear in natural, consistent locations. For example, when MacPascal finds an error, the thumbs-down icon always appears to the left of the line where the error occurred. This simple feature is known as *visual continuity*. In addition, a good graphics interface uses a *structured display*. This means that the various parts of the screen are arranged so that the user knows where to look for specific information. The Mac's dialog boxes, for example, always appear in the middle of the screen.

In MacPascal and Lightspeed, we can arrange the positions of the Text and Drawing windows as the program runs. This allows us to position messages and graphic output in such a way that users can follow both easily.

All the MacPascal windows are stored as ***rect*** variables in the Mac's memory. It follows that we specify a new size for a MacPascal window by specifying a new value for its ***rect***. However, the ***rect*** variables we have seen thus far have always specified an area in the Drawing window; when moving entire windows, we need to specify a part of the screen. Thus, the coordinates for the windows must be in the *screen coordinate* system. This coordinate system is just like the one in the Drawing window. The origin, or (0, 0) point, is at the top left of the screen, and coordinates increase from left to right and from top to bottom. The bottom right corner has the coordinate (512, 342).

Typically, we want to leave the menu bar visible. The menu bar is 38 pixels tall. If we use the rectangular area of the screen bordered by (4, 40) for the top left and (508, 338) for the bottom right, we will fill the screen except for the menu bar and a thin, 4-pixel-wide border on the edges (see Figure 10.2).

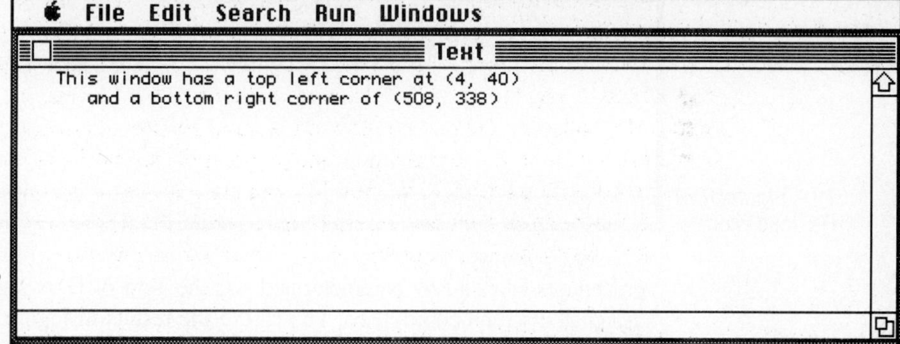

Figure 10.2
Screen coordinate system(Not to scale.)

Say we want to size the windows so that the Text window occupies the top quarter of the screen and the Drawing window occupies the rest, as in Figure 10.3. To resize these windows, we need to create two of our own ***rect*** variables. We need these because we can't get at the system's internal ***rect***s. After creating and assigning values to our ***rect*** variables, we will then copy from our variables into the Window Manager's ***rect*** locations using the procedures ***SetTextRect*** and ***SetDrawingRect***.

In our code, we will call the new ***rect*** variables ***topQuarter*** and ***remains***. After the variables are declared, we give them values using the ***SetRect*** procedure. ***SetRect*** does not care whether the ***rect*** variable receives Drawing window coordinates or screen coordinates. However, it always receives parameters in the order

< rectVar >, < left >, < top >, < right >, < bottom >

Using the coordinates from Figure 10.3, we write the code

```
SetRect(topQuarter, 4, 40, 508, 108)
SetRect(remains, 4, 138, 508, 338)
```

Remember, ***SetRect*** does not produce any output. To resize the two windows we use the procedures ***SetTextRect*** and ***SetDrawingRect***. Each of these MacPascal

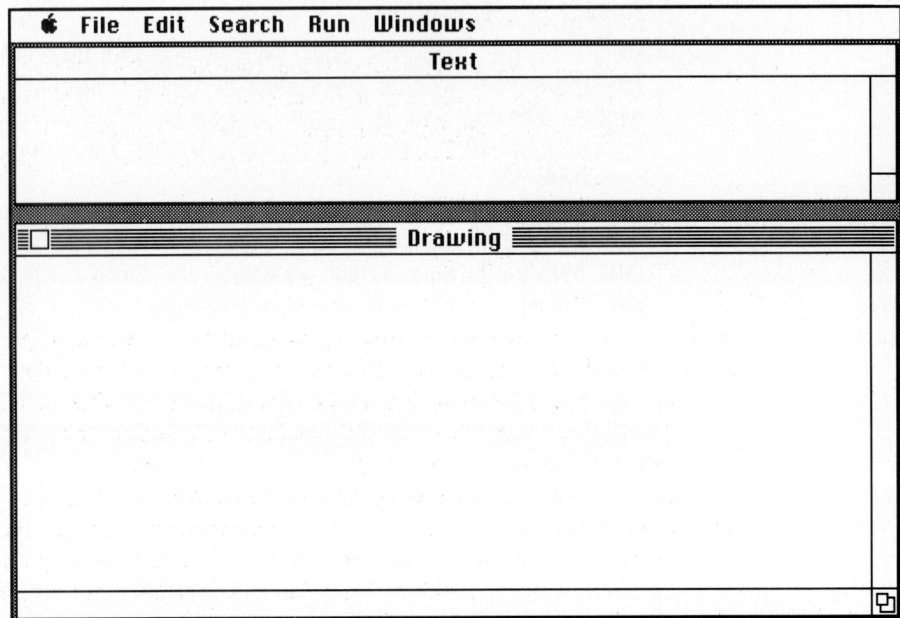

Figure 10.3
Resized window

procedures takes a ***rect*** parameter and sets the Text or Drawing window to the designated screen coordinates. To achieve the results in Figure 10.3, we use the code

```
{ Set new sizes in our temporary variables }
SetRect(topQuarter, 4, 40, 508, 108)
SetRect(remains, 4, 138, 508, 338)
{ Copy from our rects to the Window Manager's }
SetTextRect(topQuarter);
SetDrawingRect(remains);
```

Syntax Box 10.1
SetTextRect, SetDrawingRect

Purpose	To resize window during program execution
Syntax	**SetTextRect(** < rect > **);** **SetDrawingRect(** < rect > **);**
where	< rect > is a variable of type ***rect***.
Usage	These procedures set the Text or Drawing window to the designated coordinates. The < rect > variable must have previously received some value in the screen coordinate system. Unlike ***PaintRect*** and the other primitives, ***SetTextRect*** and ***SetDrawingRect*** *cannot* take the parameter list (< top >, < left >, < bottom >, < right >).

10.4 Regions

So far this chapter has discussed the front end of the program — the part the user sees. Now let's shift gears and discuss the internal parts of a program, in particular some advanced graphics techniques available in QuickDraw.

Suppose you use the following primitives to draw a triangle:

```
MoveTo(125, 25);
LineTo(150, 50);
LineTo(100, 50);
LineTo(125, 25);
```

Now suppose you want to paint this area. It would be possible to paint the area with the commands seen thus far. For example, you could draw a series of vertical lines, filling the triangle from the bottom to the top. This would mean drawing a line whose vertical coordinate was 25, 26, 27, and so on up to 50. It would be much better to be able to refer to this whole area at once.

Let's backtrack for a second. We mentioned before that lines, rectangles, ovals, and rounded rectangles are *primitives* because they form the building blocks for other shapes. QuickDraw allows you to create objects known as *regions* that are a combination of primitives. More formally, a region is a representation of a specific area of pixels.

Regions can have any type of shape. Think about the regions of land that we call states. Some states are enclosed shapes with simple borders, such as Colorado and Wyoming; others are enclosed shapes, but have more complicated borders, such as Wisconsin and Kentucky; still others consist of multiple parts, such as Michigan and Hawaii. Regions of the screen can also have unusual shapes, multiple parts, or even interior holes. Figure 10.4 illustrates regions with these particular characteristics.

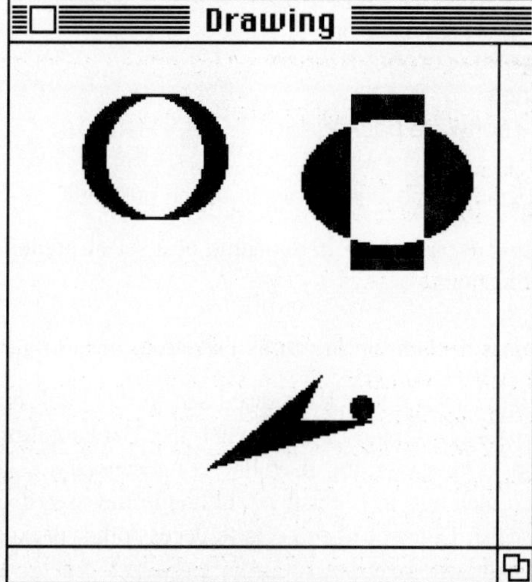

Figure 10.4
Three types of regions

You have to execute three steps to use a region. First, you initialize the region by telling QuickDraw to reserve memory. Next, you define the shape of the region. Finally, you frame, paint, erase, or invert the region, just as you drew the primitive shapes.

Preparing QuickDraw (MacPascal Only)

QuickDraw's package is stored in two parts in the Macintosh's memory. The first part, which contains the primitives, attributes, input statements, and other calls, is available every time you use MacPascal. The second part, which contains the procedures that control regions, has to be loaded into MacPascal before it can be used. (Both parts are always available in Lightspeed Pascal.)

Whenever you have a MacPascal program that uses regions, you need to add a statement after the **program** declaration. This new declaration tells MacPascal that an additional set of procedures will be needed for this program.

```
program CreateStuff;
   uses
      QuickDraw2;
```

The other part of the QuickDraw package is known to MacPascal as QuickDraw2. (Since both parts are always defined to Lightspeed, QuickDraw2 has no meaning in a project.) If you do not include the **uses** statement and then try to use a region, you will receive a syntax error message stating that the region-handling routines have not been defined. This will be the only use of the **uses** declaration in this book.

Syntax Box 10.2
uses

Purpose To make a software package available for use

Syntax

```
program < program name > ;
   uses
      < software package > ;
```

where < program name > is the name of the program.

< software package > is the name of a set of predefined procedures and functions.

Usage The **uses** declaration has to be used only once in a program.

The only software package discussed in this book is QuickDraw2. This package should be used when the MacPascal program uses regions. Otherwise, the **uses** line is unnecessary. (QuickDraw2 has no meaning in Lightspeed, although the **uses** declaration can be used in Lightspeed projects to access other packages.)

Initializing Regions

A rectangle is always defined to QuickDraw in the same way. If QuickDraw knows about the top left and bottom right coordinates, it can work with the rectangle as a whole. Any rectangle can be defined if those two points are known. Region definitions, however, can vary. A region can have any number of edges along its perimeter or can comprise any number of shapes and lines. Because of this variation, the Macintosh uses different amounts of memory for different regions. For example, a region of three lines requires less memory space than a region of four ovals. Because regions are *dynamic* (that is, the amount of memory used by the region is determined as the program is running), two steps are needed to initialize a region.

First, a variable of type ***rgnHandle*** has to be declared. (***rgnHandle*** is another graphic data type that, like ***point*** and ***rect***, is particular to QuickDraw.) The ***rgnHandle*** declaration indicates that a region will be used in the procedure. To give a ***rgnHandle*** its initial value, the ***NewRgn*** function must be used in an assignment statement. For example, to initialize a region called ***triangle***, the following code should be used:

```
var
   triangle: rgnHandle;        { region to show triangle      }
begin
   triangle := NewRgn;         { initialize region            }
   ...
end.
```

The ***NewRgn*** function can be used with any variable of type ***rgnHandle***. This assignment statement < rgnHandle variable > ***:= NewRgn;*** is *the only way* in which a region can be initialized. In the above code example, QuickDraw recognizes that ***triangle*** designates a block of memory, but the size of that block is yet to be determined.

Syntax Box 10.3
NewRgn

Purpose	To initialize a region
Syntax	< region > **:= NewRgn;**
where	< region > is a variable of type ***rgnHandle***.
Usage	The ***NewRgn*** function sets < region > to the empty region. That is, the region at this point has no shape. ***NewRgn*** must be used before < region > can be used in any other QuickDraw procedure.

Defining Regions

After the region is initialized, you need to define the area of the region. Suppose, for example, that you want to collect the following set of primitives into the region shown in Figure 10.5:

```
{ Draw arrow }
MoveTo(125, 25);                    { draw triangle     }
LineTo(150, 50);
LineTo(100, 50);
LineTo(125, 25);
FrameRect(50, 112, 100, 138);       { add rectangle     }
```

To specify where the collection begins and ends, use the procedures ***OpenRgn*** and ***CloseRgn***. These procedures are used in the same way as the reserved words **begin** and **end.** ***OpenRgn*** tells Pascal to begin collecting objects. ***CloseRgn*** marks the end of the collections and also tells the computer where the region definition should be stored. The following code sets the region ***arrow*** to the picture in the last figure.

```
var
    arrow : rgnHandle;

begin
    arrow := newRgn;
    OpenRgn;                            { start region definition   }

    { Draw arrow }
    MoveTo(125, 25);                    { draw triangle             }
    LineTo(150, 50);
    LineTo(100, 50);
    LineTo(125, 25);
    FrameRect(50, 112, 100, 138);       { add rectangle             }

    CloseRgn(arrow)                     { close region definition   }
end;
```

QuickDraw uses a region definition to determine which pixels are inside and which are outside the region. Thus, if you want to define a region, you should use a

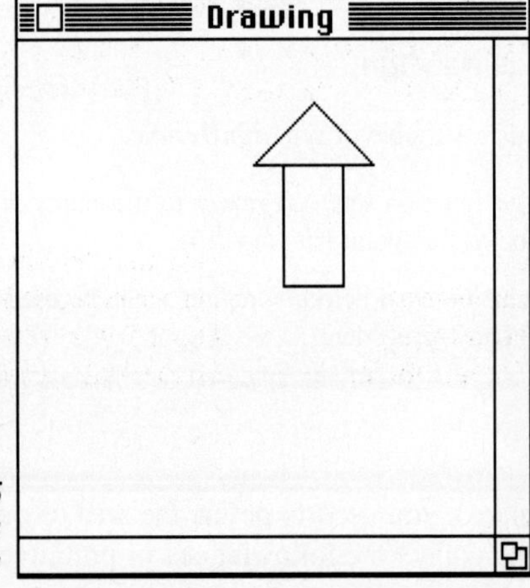

Figure 10.5
Primitives to draw arrow

combination of *closed* objects. If you can put a pen down on any point on the boundary of an object, trace the entire boundary, and end up where you started, then the object is closed.

Closed objects can be formed in one of two ways. First, a closed object can be formed from a sequence of lines, as was the triangular part of the arrow. In QuickDraw, the lines defined by calls to ***LineTo*** and ***Line*** become part of the region boundary. It is up to you, though, to make sure that the lines outline a closed object; QuickDraw will *not* check that your lines form a closed boundary. The results of using an open-ended region are unpredictable.

The other object in the arrow definition is the rectangle defined by the ***FrameRect*** call. Closed objects can also be formed in QuickDraw by calling ***FrameRect***, ***FrameOval***, and ***FrameRoundRect***. These procedure calls define closed objects by themselves. ***FrameArc*** does not define a closed object, so it does not affect the region's definition. Also, in this segment of the definition, you are defining only the region's boundaries; thus, the ***Paint***, ***Erase***, and ***Invert*** commands have no effect on the region definition.

In short, the region definition is affected by calls to ***FrameRect***, ***FrameOval***, ***FrameRoundRect***, and closed outlines formed by calls to ***Line*** and ***LineTo***.

Objects in a region definition can overlap, but the overlapping area can be treated as if it were outside the region. (More about this when we get to drawing regions.)

Important: *Defining a region does not actually draw that region.* When ***OpenRgn*** is called, QuickDraw calls a procedure called ***HidePen***. This procedure acts as if QuickDraw removes the ink from the pen: although the pen moves as the region's primitives are drawn, nothing appears on the screen.

There is one way of drawing the region as it is being defined. When ***OpenRgn*** is called, the pen on the Drawing window is hidden. If you add the statement ***ShowPen*** immediately after the ***OpenRgn***, the primitives in the definition are drawn as they are encountered. The definition of the region is the same whether the pen is hidden or revealed.

You can also include statements between the ***OpenRgn*** and ***CloseRgn*** calls that are not QuickDraw calls. For example, you can include textual output or input statements. The following code allows the user to define a triangular region:

```
procedure TriRegion;

var
    triangle: rgnHandle;                    { memory for triangle region    }
    horizOne, vertOne: integer;             { coordinates of first point    }
    horizTwo, vertTwo: integer;             { coordinates of second point   }
    horizThree, vertThree: integer;         { coordinates of third point    }

begin
{ Define Region }
    triangle := NewRgn;
    OpenRgn;
```

```
{ ask user to choose outline of triangle }
    Writeln('Please pick the first point of the triangle');
    repeat
        GetMouse(horizOne, vertOne);
    until Button;
    Writeln('Please pick the second point of the triangle');
    repeat
        GetMouse(horizTwo, vertTwo);
    until Button;
    Writeln('Please pick the third point of the triangle');
    repeat
        GetMouse(horizThree, vertThree);
    until Button;

    MoveTo(horizOne, vertOne);
    LineTo(horizTwo, vertTwo);
    LineTo(horizThree, vertThree);
    LineTo(horizOne, vertOne);
    CloseRgn(triangle);

    { note: region has not yet been drawn }

end; { TriRegion }
```

Syntax Box 10.4
OpenRgn

Purpose	To denote the beginning of a region definition
Syntax	**OpenRgn;**
Usage	***OpenRgn*** signals the beginning of the definition of a region. The outline of the region is defined by the endpoints of lines and boundaries of objects within the definition. No more than one region can be open at any time. ***OpenRgn*** hides the pen, meaning that the output from the following primitives is not seen. A call to ***ShowPen*** after a call to ***OpenRgn*** reveals the output.

Drawing Regions

Once a region is defined, it can be used as if it were a rectangle, oval, or other primitive. The commands ***FrameRgn***, ***PaintRgn***, ***EraseRgn***, and ***InvertRgn*** perform functions equivalent to ***FrameRect***, ***PaintRect***, ***EraseRect***, and ***InvertRect*** on the designated region. ***FrameRgn*** draws the outline of the region. ***PaintRgn*** paints the interior of the region with the current pen pattern. ***EraseRgn*** paints the interior of the region with the background color. ***InvertRgn*** reverses all of the pixels in the area defined by the region.

Syntax Box 10.5
CloseRgn

Purpose	To denote the ending of a region definition
Syntax	**CloseRgn(< region >);**
where	< region > is a variable of type ***rgnHandle***.
Usage	***CloseRgn*** marks the end of a region definition. The list of primitives between the last ***OpenRgn*** statement and the ***CloseRgn*** call are stored in < region >. Thus, ***CloseRgn*** should be preceded by an ***OpenRgn*** statement. ***CloseRgn*** cancels ***OpenRgn's*** hiding of the pen and causes the pen to be revealed. Thus, after a ***CloseRgn***, graphical output is seen. < region > must have been previously initialized with a ***NewRgn*** assignment.

Syntax Box 10.6
ShowPen, HidePen

Purpose	To turn graphical output on or off
Syntax	**ShowPen;** **HidePen;**
Usage	***HidePen*** removes the ink from QuickDraw's pen. That is, no graphical output appears after a ***HidePen*** statement. The pen's current position is still altered by various graphics procedures. ***ShowPen*** performs the opposite function: it causes graphical output to appear on the screen. You can hide or show the pen any number of times in the program. ***OpenRgn*** performs an automatic ***HidePen***; ***CloseRgn*** performs an automatic ***ShowPen***.

Figure 10.6 shows the result of each of these commands when they are added to the arrow region defined in the last section. (In Figures 10.6 c and d, the statements ***PenPat (dkGray);*** and ***PaintRect(0, 0, 200, 200);*** are executed first.)

Why was the line segment common to the triangle and the rectangle not drawn by ***FrameRgn(arrow)*** in Figure 10.6a? Because the overlapping *border* is considered to be inside the region. Overlapping *areas* are another matter. Consider the following region:

```
OpenRgn;
PaintOval(50, 50, 100, 100);
PaintOval(50, 80, 100, 130);
CloseRgn(twoCircles);
```

When you paint this region with the statement ***PaintRgn (twoCircles);***, the overlapping area is left uncolored, as shown in Figure 10.7. Overlapping areas are considered, for the most part, to be outside the region. (Yes, that's ambiguous, but explaining the details of how QuickDraw calculates "inside" and "outside" is beyond the scope of this book.)

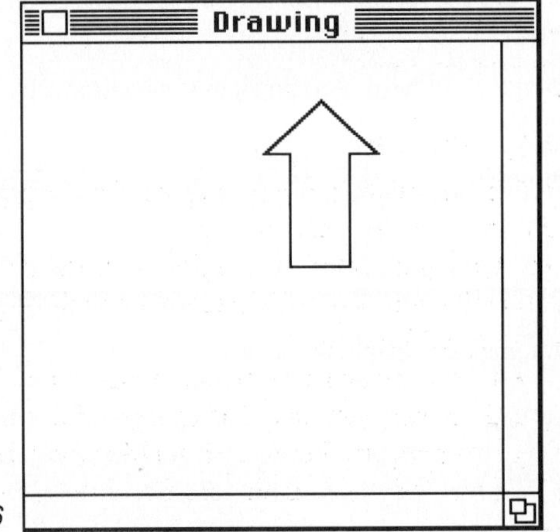

Figure 10.6

a. FrameRgn(arrow);

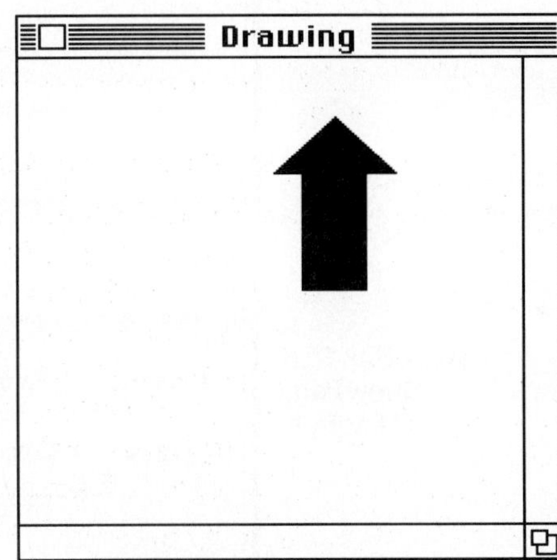

b. PaintRgn(arrow);

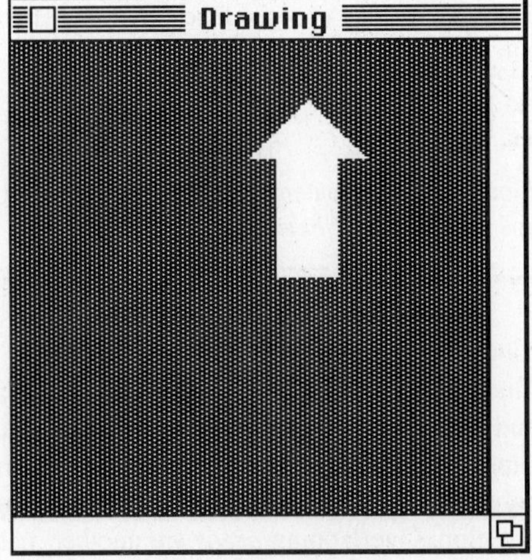

Figure 10.6

c. EraseRgn(arrow);

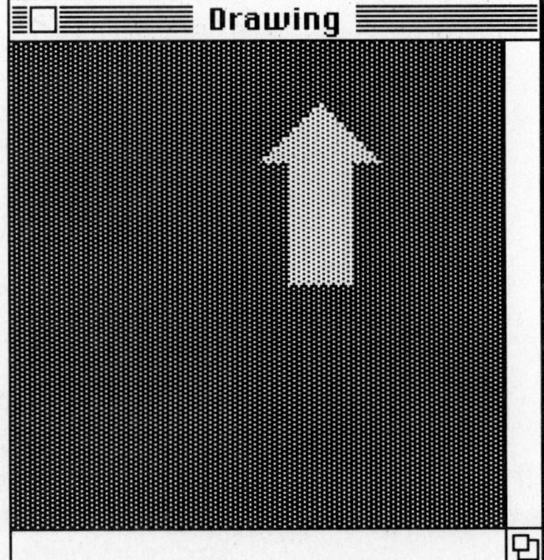

d. InvertRgn(arrow);

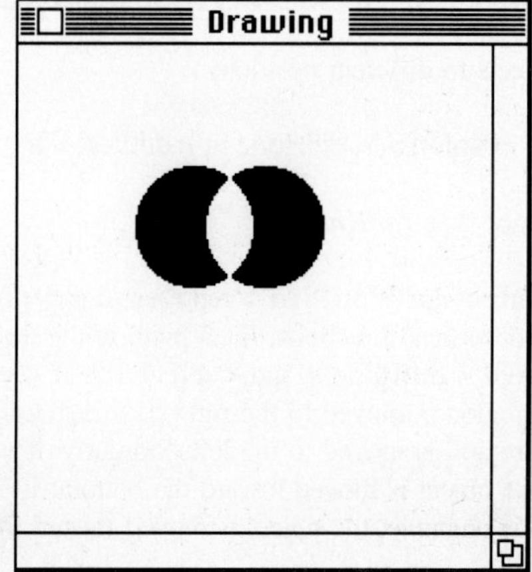

Figure 10.7
Painting region with overlapping areas

Moving and Scaling Regions

OffsetRect and ***InsetRect*** move and scale rectangles; the corresponding procedures ***OffsetRgn*** and ***InsetRgn*** move and scale regions.

OffsetRgn takes three parameters: the region to move and the distances to move the shape horizontally and vertically. Each point in the region definition is changed by the designated differences.

InsetRgn can be used to scale an object about its center. This procedure resizes the region by a designated amount. The amount of change in the size of the shape is designated by two integers. Recall that in ***OffsetRect***, each point in the rectangle is moved in some designated direction. The < diffHoriz > and < diffVert >

Syntax Box 10.7
Drawing Regions

Purpose To draw a region with a particular attribute

Syntax

```
FrameRgn( < region > );
PaintRgn( < region > );
EraseRgn( < region > );
InvertRgn( < region > );
```

where < region > is a variable of type ***rgnHandle***.

Usage ***FrameRgn*** draws the outline of each shape in the region.
PaintRgn paints the region in the current pen pattern.
EraseRgn paints the region in the background color.
InvertRgn reverses the color of the pixels in the region.

< region > must be previously initialized with a ***NewRgn*** assignment. You can use the drawing commands before defining the region with ***OpenRgn*** and ***CloseRgn***, but nothing will appear in the output.

Syntax Box 10.8
OffsetRgn

Purpose	To move objects to different positions
Syntax	**OffsetRgn(** < region >, < diffHoriz >, < diffVert > **);**
where	< region > is of type ***rgnHandle***
Usage	The < diffHoriz > and < diffVert > represent a movement in the horizontal and vertical directions. Each pixel in the designated region is moved < diffHoriz > and < diffVert >. If < diffHoriz > is positive, the region is moved to the right; if < diffHoriz > is negative the region is moved to the left. Similarly, if < diffVert > is positive, the object is moved toward the bottom; if < diffVert > is negative, the object is moved toward the top. The ***Offset*** commands change only the internal representation of the object inside QuickDraw. You must redraw the rectangle or region to see the effect of the command on the screen.

Syntax Box 10.9
InsetRgn

Purpose	To resize regions
Syntax	**InsetRgn(**< region >, < diffHoriz >, < diffVert >**);**
where	< region > is a variable of type ***rgnHandle.*** < diffHoriz > and < diffVert > are integers.
Usage	***InsetRgn*** moves each point in the region's representation in relation to the object's center. < diffHoriz > represents the number of pixels that each point is moved horizontally; < diffVert > represents the size of the vertical movement. Positive values of < diffHoriz > and < diffVert > indicate movements toward the center; negative values indicate movements away from the center. If the height or width of the object becomes less than one, the ***rgnHandle*** is assigned the empty region and the object disappears from the screen. Each point in the object's representation is set to (0,0). The ***Inset*** commands change only the internal representation of the object inside QuickDraw. You must redraw the region to see the effect of the command on the screen.

of the offset procedures tell whether each point should move closer to or further from the (0, 0) point. In ***InsetRgn***, a < diffHoriz > and < diffVert > are also designated. Instead of moving in relation to (0,0), however, < diffHoriz > and < diffVert > designate movement in relation to the object's center. A positive < diffHoriz > or < diffVert > moves each point in the region's internal representation toward the center—negative differences move the points away from the center.

Just as with the ***Offset*** commands, the ***Inset*** procedures merely change the way QuickDraw stores an object. A call to ***InsetRect*** or ***InsetRgn*** by itself has no effect on the screen's current display.

The result is an object that has changed size. If the horizontal and vertical differences are positive, the object shrinks, since ***InsetRgn*** moves the points toward the center. Likewise, if the horizontal and vertical differences are negative, the object expands.

Disposing Regions

Since regions can occupy a great deal of space in memory, you may want to dispose of a region when you no longer need it. The ***DisposeRgn*** statement frees the ***rgnHandle***'s contents in memory but does not erase the shape from the screen.

Syntax Box 10.10
DisposeRgn

Purpose	To signal that a region is no longer needed
Syntax	**DisposeRgn(** < region > **);**
where	< region > is a variable of type ***rgnHandle***.
Usage	< region > must have been initialized from a ***NewRgn*** assignment.
	This command does not affect any output on the Drawing window. When you use this command, you can no longer refer to < region > in ***CloseRgn*** or any region-drawing procedure.

10.5 External Documentation

Let's shift gears once again. We have stated repeatedly that documentation is just as important as actual Pascal code. Here we say it again: documentation is just as important as actual Pascal code. Such repetition wouldn't be necessary if programmers consistently documented their work. Unfortunately, the computing field is glutted with poorly documented and even completely undocumented programs.

Many people in the field have overlooked the usefulness of a well-written set of instructions. Besides helping the user, these written instructions, called *external documentation* (exDoc, for short), provide a helpful tool when you write any large program.

The documentation discussed so far in this book has all been internal—that is, part of the program. We have emphasized the significance of this documentation as an aid to the author of the program and any other programmer who may want to amend it. Good internal documentation allows us to determine easily what is happening in each part of the program.

You may begin to find that you are writing programs that have a usefulness far beyond the boundaries of your particular computer system. Suppose the people at your college or workplace want to adopt a program developed somewhere else. The person on the street who will use the program won't care about its internal workings but will want to know how to *use* it. The programmer who adapts the program for your system, however, will want to know about its code and its *design*. Thus, two types of documentation are needed outside the program. Together, these are known, appropriately enough, as external documentation.

Writing does not end when you leave humanities courses; in fact, in computer science, writing is nothing short of essential. An exDoc is a written description of your program and is prepared in the same way that you prepare papers for history or literature classes. A well-documented non-working program is preferable to a badly documented but working program. The first can be fixed easily; the second cannot be modified without the possibility that the entire program will be damaged. Also, most real-world programming is done by teams of people who design and code separate procedures. Communication between people is necessary, and documentation provides the most immediate form of communication.

You should prepare your external documentation as you would prepare any piece of writing. Correct grammar and spelling count, as do introductions, conclusions, word choices, organization, and logic of presentation. In short, it should be easy for potential users of your program to read and to understand.

By convention, computer programmers have set standards for external documentation. An exDoc consists of two parts, corresponding to the two types of readers mentioned above: the *user's guide* (for users) and the *program description* (for programmers). Both the user's guide and the program description should be *reader-based* prose as opposed to *writer-based* prose. That is, exDoc should be written with the reader in mind. The major difference between the two parts of the exDoc is the audience being addressed.

The User's Guide

The user's guide is written for those who want to use your program but couldn't care less about how the program is coded. You should not assume that the user knows anything about Pascal, your current operating system, or even computers in general. Readers of the user's guide want only to type in some data and get results.

The user's guide begins with a motivation of the program. The first few paragraphs should answer the question, "Why would anyone want to use this program?" Users should be able to tell right off if they should read the entire user's guide or if the program will not meet their needs.

The bulk of the user's guide is a description of how to run the program. Include the exact format of input and output and what error conditions could arise in the program (and how your program will respond). This description may repeat some of the things listed in the program's block comments, but readers of a user's guide will probably never see the internal documentation.

One important feature of a user's guide is a section containing sample input and sample output. It is usually a good idea to include some input that causes errors, so users can see how your program handles imperfect data. If your program uses graphics, you will probably want to include pictures of the displays and menus that appear during the program. In general, you should expect less, rather than more, technical ability from a user. Remember that a novice user can become easily confused by an abundance of computer science buzzwords.

The Program Description

As your programs become more complex and useful, you should also supplement them with additional external documentation. Suppose for a moment that you have just been hired by a computer company to troubleshoot and maintain other people's programs. The job involves debugging the programs and updating blocks of code wherever necessary. Most of these programs are rather large—often fifty pages or more. The thought of reading through fifty pages of code just to find out how the program works is not very appealing, no matter how well the program is documented.

A user's guide is not adequate for those who want to change a program. Although it is helpful, a user's guide contains too little technical information about how a program works to be of much use to someone who wants to modify it.

What a programmer needs is a *program description,* which acts as a technical companion to the user's guide. This document includes explanations of essential algorithms and unique problem-solving methods; a description of how the procedures relate to one another, accompanied by a diagram (called the *module interconnection diagram*); and detailed explanations of important functions, procedures, and major flow-of-control constructs. When your program stores a great deal of data, you may want to include a diagram showing how the information is stored. Complete external documentation also includes high-level pseudocode for the entire program and specifications for each module (in our case, a module is defined as a procedure or function; in larger programs, the term "module" may refer to sets of procedures and functions) of the program.

Another section sometimes included in research and industrial organizations is a description of possible modifications and extensions to the program. This type of speculation is especially useful if the project you are designing is a prototype or preliminary version of a program that someone else is likely to modify. This section usually includes suggestions on how to make the program more user friendly, more efficient, or more versatile.

Many organizations require that external documentation be written before programs are actually coded. From reading the user's guide, prospective users can provide detailed feedback on the functionality and user interface that the package will provide. By writing a detailed program description, implementors can make more accurate projections about the time and expense involved in the project. It is a good idea to get into the habit of writing a brief program description before you start coding; this practice can help you understand the usefulness of your program. Also, if you have trouble explaining how the program works, its design may be too complex.

10.6 Example Program

The following example program illustrates how to move and resize regions. The program gives the illusion that an object is moving in three dimensions.

Instead of showing the pseudocode and development, this example shows you only the code and external documentation. In real life, this is usually all that is at your disposal when you want to modify or analyze a program.

Code 10.1
Program *Boat*

```
{ Program Boat        D. Niguidula        January 26              }
{    The Boat program illustrates some of the animation           }
{ techniques available in QuickDraw. The program shows            }
{ the image of a boat in the middle of the Drawing                }
{ window. The user can move the boat around the screen            }
{ by specifying a wind direction. When the user enters            }
{ a direction, the program responds by moving the boat            }
{ a constant number of pixels. (West is "behind" the              }
{ screen; north is on the right side.)                            }
{    The program runs with a menu that gives the user             }
{ four choices. The user can continue to move the boat            }
{ in its current direction, ask for help, change the wind         }
{ direction, or quit. The program window should be closed         }
{ before choosing Go from the Run menu.                           }

program Boat;
   uses
      QuickDraw2;                    { not used in Lightspeed Pascal     }

   const
      speed = 6;                     { number of pixels for each move    }

   var
      boat : rgnHandle;              { sailboat image                    }
      northSouth, eastWest : real;   { speed in each direction           }
      done : boolean;                { indicates when program is done    }
      command : char;                { user's request                    }

{ Procedure: Help                                           }
{    This procedure prints the list of legal commands.      }
{ Called by: Mainline       Calls: none                     }
```

Code 10.1
(continued)

```
    procedure Help;

    begin
        Writeln('The following are the legal commands:');
        Writeln('    D : Direction');
        Writeln('    Q : Quit');
        Writeln('    H : Help');
        Writeln('    C : Continue in current direction');
        Writeln('When you enter the direction, you should');
        Writeln('use some combination of N, E, S, W to');
        Writeln('indicate the wind''s direction . ')
    end;  { Help }

{ Procedure: Move                                            }
{   Move relocates the boat. A movement to the left or       }
{ right indicates (respectively) a movement south or         }
{ north. If the boat shrinks, it is moving toward the west;  }
{ if it expands, it is moving toward the east.               }
{ Called by: Mainline    Calls: none                         }

    procedure Move (boat : rgnHandle;        { sailboat image         }
        northSouth,                          { longitudinal speed     }
        eastWest : real);                    { latitudinal speed      }

    begin
        EraseRgn(boat);
        OffsetRgn(boat, Round(northSouth), 0);
        InsetRgn(boat, Round(eastWest), Round(eastWest));
        PaintRgn(boat)
    end;  { Move }

{ Procedure: DrawBackground                                  }
{   This procedure creates the horizon and a sunset.         }
{ Since the sunset is in clear view, the user believes       }
{ that he is facing west.                                    }
{ Called by: Initialize      Calls: none                     }

    procedure DrawBackground;

    begin
{ draw horizon }
        MoveTo(0, 125);
        LineTo(512, 125);
        PenPat(dkGray);
        FrameArc(70, 136, 180, 376, 270, 180);

{ draw rays }
        MoveTo(256, 68);
        LineTo(256, 51);
```

Code 10.1 (continued)

```
        MoveTo(325, 83);
        LineTo(335, 65);

        MoveTo(181, 83);
        LineTo(171, 65);

        PenPat(black)
    end;   { DrawBackground }

{ Procedure: CreateBoat                                          }
{   This procedure creates the sailboat as a single region.      }
{ Initially, it draws in the center of the screen.               }
{ Called by: Initialize     Calls: none                          }

    procedure CreateBoat (var boat : rgnHandle);  {sailboat image }

    begin
        boat := NewRgn;
        OpenRgn;
{ draw mast}
        MoveTo(256, 125);
        LineTo(256, 75);
        LineTo(266, 75);

{ draw sail }
        LineTo(283, 118);
        LineTo(266, 118);
{ draw bottom }
        LineTo(266, 125);
        LineTo(286, 125);
        LineTo(278, 145);
        LineTo(244, 145);
        LineTo(236, 125);
        LineTo(256, 125);
        CloseRgn(boat);
        PaintRgn(boat)
    end;   { CreateBoat }

{ Procedure: Initialize                                          }
{   This procedure initializes the direction of movement         }
{ for the boat. It also calls routines to draw the sailboat      }
{  and the background. In addition, the screen's windows         }
{ are set properly for this program.                             }
{ Called by: Mainline      Calls: Background, CreateBoat         }

    procedure Initialize (var boat : rgnHandle;         { sailboat image           }
        var northEast, eastWest : real);                { speed in each direction  }

        var
            txt,                          { screen rect for Text window      }
            drw : rect;                   { screen rect for Drawing window   }
```

Code 10.1 (continued)

```
    begin
    { create rectangles in screen coordinates }
        SetRect(txt, 2, 40, 510, 120);
        SetRect(drw, 2, 122, 510, 340);
        SetTextRect(txt);
        SetDrawingRect(drw);

    { initialize speeds }
        northSouth := 0.0;
        eastWest := 0.0;

    { initialize image }
        CreateBoat(boat);
        DrawBackground
    end;  { Initialize }

{ Procedure: NewDirection                                    }
{   The wind changes direction in this procedure. The user   }
{ is asked to enter a string for the new direction. This     }
{ string will consist of the characters N, E, S, W--any other }
{ characters in the string will generate an error message.   }
{ Only the first three characters in the string will be used. }
{   The direction indicated is where the wind is coming      }
{ from -- therefore, the boat is moved in the OPPOSITE       }
{ direction.                                                 }
{   Each time the boat is moved, it is moved a constant      }
{ number of pixels. This movement, the boat's speed, is      }
{ divided among the directions input by the user. For        }
{ example, if the speed is 6 and the user enters SSW, the    }
{ boat will be moved 2/3 speed (4 pixels) toward the         }
{ north and 1/3 speed (2 pixels) toward the east.            }
{ Called by: Mainline     Calls: none                        }

    procedure NewDirection (var northSouth,          { longitudinal speed    }
       eastWest : real);                             { latitudinal speed     }

        var
            direction : string[80];      { direction input by user              }
            speedPart : real;            { portion of movement in one direction }
            curChar : integer;           { current portion of user's direction  }

    begin
        Write('What is the wind''s direction? ');
        Readln(direction);
        if Length(direction) > 3 then
            begin
                direction := Copy(direction, 1, 3);
                Writeln('Direction truncated to ', direction : 4)
            end; { if }
```

Code 10.1 (continued)

```
    { Re-initialize direction }
        northSouth := 0.0;
        eastWest := 0.0;

    { determine the ways to divide the speed }
        if direction <> '' then
            begin

                speedPart := speed / Length(direction);
                for curChar := 1 to Length(direction) do
                    case direction[curChar] of
                        'n', 'N' :
                            northSouth := northSouth - speedPart;
                        's', 'S' :
                            northSouth := northSouth + speedPart;

                        'e', 'E' :
                            eastWest := eastWest + speedPart;
                        'w', 'W' :
                            eastWest := eastWest - speedPart;
                        otherwise
                            if direction[curChar] <> '' then
                                Writeln(direction[curChar], ' is not one of N, E, S, W');
                    end    { case }
            end { if }
    end;  { NewDirection }

{ Mainline    }
{   The mainline handles the main menu for the program.          }
{ After the screen and variables have been initialized, the      }
{ mainline prompts the user for a command. If the user           }
{ enters 'D', the user will be asked to designate the wind       }
{ direction and the boat will be moved. If the user enters       }
{ 'H', the program will print the list of legal commands.        }
{ If the user enters 'C',  the boat will continue to move        }
{ in its current direction. If the user enters 'Q', the program  }
{ will exit.                                                     }
{ Calls: Move, Initialize, Help, NewDirection                    }

begin
    Initialize(boat, northSouth, eastWest);
    done := FALSE;

    repeat
        Write('Please enter a command (enter H for help): ');
        Readln(command);
        case command of
            'h', 'H' :
                Help;  { print help message }
```

Code 10.1
(continued)

```
            'd', 'D' :
                begin
                    NewDirection(northSouth, eastWest);
                    Move(boat, northSouth, eastWest)
                end;  { D }
            'q', 'Q' :
                done := TRUE;  { quit program }
            'c', 'C' :
                Move(boat, northSouth, eastWest); { continue in same direction }
            otherwise { error }
                Writeln(command : 1, ' is not a legal command')
        end;  { case }
    until done
end. { Boat }
```

User's Guide

This program lets you maneuver a sailboat around the screen by controlling the wind direction.

To begin the program, load the Sail and MacPascal disks.* To load the program, double-click on the icon on the Sail disk called **Boat**. Then choose the command **Go** from the **Run** menu.† When the program is entered, you will first see this screen.

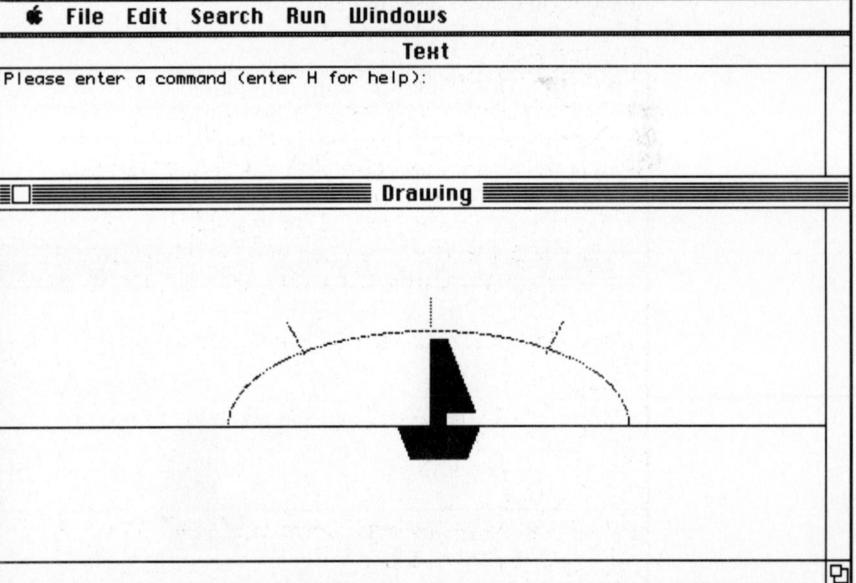

Figure 10.8
Setup for *Boat*

* We assume the user has been given a disk called **Sail**.
† We also assume that the user has a general knowledge of how to use the Mac and knows how to load disks and choose menu options.

You are looking into a sunset. Your sailboat is on the horizon. The boat will move according to directions that you provide.

You will communicate with the program by entering commands at the keyboard. In the text window, you will see a prompt to "Please enter a command" from the following list.

Command	*Action*
D	Set direction from which wind blows
H	Help
C	Continue sailing in same direction
Q	Quit sailing

Let's look at each command in turn.

D (for direction): If you want to set the wind direction, type a D and press Return. After entering the D, you will see the statement "What is the wind's direction?" in the Text window. Enter the wind direction by typing some combination of the letters N, E, S, and W (north, east, south, and west) and pressing Return. For example, if the wind is coming from the East, type an E and press Return. Up to three letters can be entered for the wind direction; for example, you can enter SSW for south southwest.

After you press Return, the boat will move in the specified direction. Note that a wind coming from the east is going toward the west. Thus, if you enter an E for the wind movement, the boat will move toward the sunset; a wind coming from the west will move the boat closer to you. Winds coming from the north or south move the boat to the left or right, respectively.

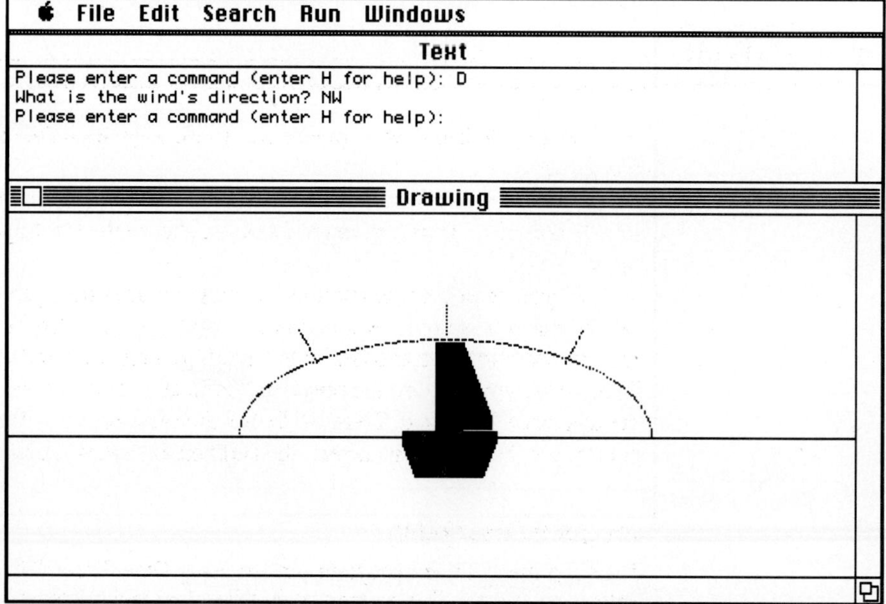

Figure 10.9
Moving boat after setting direction

When the boat has moved, you will again see the prompt "Please enter a command (enter H for Help):". You can enter a D to change wind direction or choose one of the other commands.

C (for continue): If you want the boat to continue moving in the same direction, enter the C command. The boat will be moved, and you will again be asked to enter another command. (The wind initially has no direction; thus, if you begin the program by entering C, the boat will "continue" to move in its non-existent direction — in other words, it won't move.) The wind will continue to blow from the same direction until you again enter the D command.

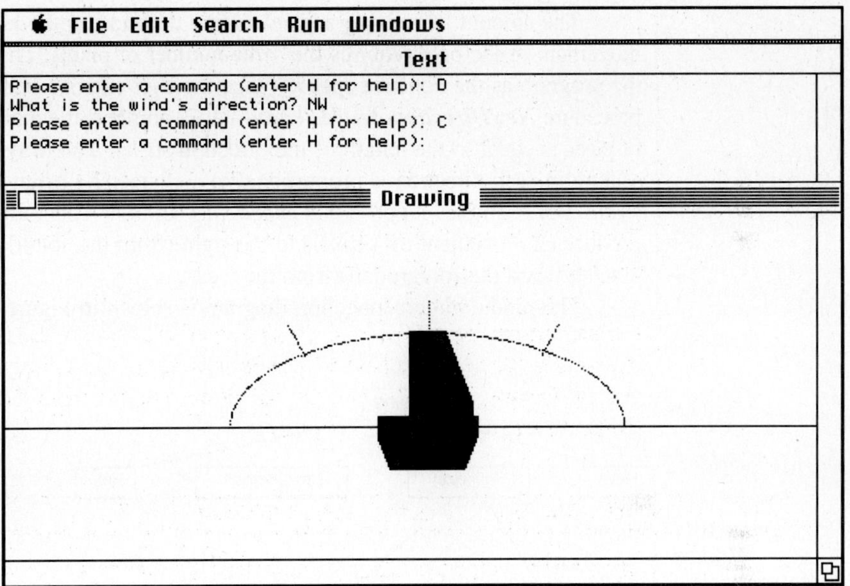

Figure 10.10 Continuing to move boat

H (for help): If you want to see a summary of all the commands, enter the H command.

Q (for quit): When you have finished sailing, end the program by entering the Q command. To return to the Desktop, choose the **Quit** option from the **File** menu.

If you enter a command that the program does not understand, the message "< command > is not a legal command " will appear in the Text window, and you will be asked to enter another command. If you enter a wind direction that is not N, E, S, or W, you will see the message "< direction > is not one of N, E, S, W," and the character is ignored. Thus, SQW has the same effect on the boat as SW. If you enter more than three characters, the additional characters are ignored.

Program Description

Boat is a menu-driven program written using QuickDraw. The user is prompted to enter a command. The program then takes the appropriate action.

Initially, the program resets the Text and Drawing windows. The sunset and horizon are drawn in the background, and the sailboat is created. The image of the boat is a region. The region is painted in the center of the screen.

The movement of the boat is accomplished by relocating and resizing the region. When the user enters a wind direction, ***Boat*** accepts it as a string. The program then looks at each character in that string. Each occurrence of 'N' in the string represents a relocation to the left; each 'S' represents a relocation to the right. Occurrences of 'E' and 'W' represent resizings. A wind movement from the east is shown by shrinking the region; a movement from the west is shown by expanding it.

The amount of resizing and relocating depends on the length of the string. Each movement of the boat requires the same number of pixels. This number is found in the program as the constant ***speed***. When the user enters a wind direction, the procedure ***NewDirection*** divides ***speed*** into a number of equal parts. The number of parts is equal to the length of the direction string. This way, the movement and scaling in each direction is proportional to a character's occurrence in the direction string. For example, suppose that ***speed*** was set to 6. Then, the string 'SSW' produces a movement of 4 pixels to the right (from the south) and a resizing of 2 pixels toward the foreground (from the west).

The module interconnection diagram is shown in Figure 10.11.

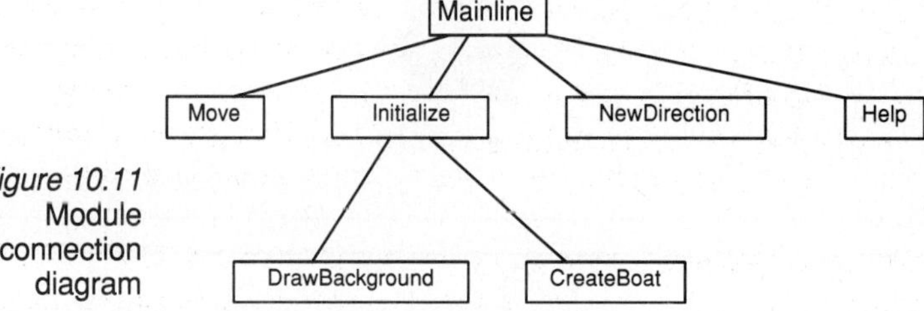

Figure 10.11 Module interconnection diagram

10.7 Chapter Summary

Throughout most of this book, we concentrate on methods of making your programs more elegant and efficient. In this chapter, we looked at three methods of making your programs easier to use.

First, we discussed the fundamentals of user interface techniques. There are many ways in which a procedure can represent the same information. No matter how your program shows the relevant data, though, your textual messages and graphic displays should be consistent and clear. The user should know what input the program expects and what result the input will yield (this is sometimes known as the law of least astonishment). The output should also be clear and readable.

A user-friendly program can also contain features that protect the user's data and tell the user what is going on. The user should always have a way to exit a program or a transaction. If an exit has potentially undesirable side effects (e.g., erasing the contents of a file), it's usually a good idea to include a confirmation. Menus are friendly because they spell out all of a user's options. Even with menus, however, a user may enter an illegal input. Your program should be able to handle such cases and should provide an error message that tells the user (nicely) about the mistake.

The program should also be easy to look at. Information should be displayed in appropriate locations; the user's eye should be drawn naturally to important messages. Without cluttering the screen unnecessarily, the program should display all the information the user needs to know. By and large, expect the user to memorize as little as possible. Help facilities also make it easier for the user to understand what the program does.

A pair of graphics commands help you utilize these interactive techniques. ***SetTextRect*** and ***SetDrawingRect*** allow you to change the size of windows during a program's execution. These commands require the use of screen coordinates as opposed to the Drawing window coordinates.

Then, we looked at regions. In MacPascal (not Lightspeed), regions are part of the QuickDraw2 package. The program declaration of any MacPascal program that uses regions must be followed by the line **uses** ***QuickDraw2;***. The other region statements we looked at are available in both MacPascal and Lightspeed. A region is first initialized by the ***NewRgn*** statement. This sets aside memory for the border of the region. Then the region is defined between ***OpenRgn*** and ***CloseRgn*** statements. Any legal Pascal statement can appear between the opening and closing of the definition, but only the border formed by certain graphics calls are stored in the ***rgnHandle*** variable. Once the region is defined, it can be drawn using the ***FrameRgn***, ***PaintRgn***, ***EraseRgn***, and ***InvertRgn*** procedures. The region definition can also be moved and scaled with the ***OffsetRgn*** and ***InsetRgn*** procedures. The ***DisposeRgn*** instruction recycles the memory used by a region's definition.

We concluded our discussion of documentation in this chapter. The external documentation, or exDoc, consists of two parts: a user's guide and a program description. Both sections describe the program, but the user's guide is geared to non-technical readers, while the program description is written for other programmers. The user's guide contains a motivation for the program, sample input/output, and a description of possible error conditions. The program description includes a module interconnection diagram, an explanation of the program's flow of control, and descriptions of important functions and procedures. Many program descriptions also include high-level pseudocode and module specifications. In writing an exDoc for a program that uses complex data structure (such as arrays, records, or the structures discussed in Chapters 13-16), you should also include a picture of the data structure in the program description.

The best writers are those who keep the readers in mind; by the same token, the best programmers are those who keep the users in mind. When you write your programs, remember that most users will not read your Pascal code to figure out how to run your program. By using meaningful messages and user-friendly interactive techniques, you can help users take proper advantage of your program.

The easiest way of helping the user is to tell him what he has to do next. Still, you need to consider the possibility that the user will do something wrong. With proper exits and error checking, you can protect the user from the consequences of doing the wrong thing.

10.8 Exercises

Understanding Concepts

1. What do the following code fragments output?

   a.
```
dome := NewRgn;
OpenRgn;
FrameArc(25, 50, 75, 100, 270, 180);
FrameRect(50, 50, 100, 100);
CloseRgn(dome);
PaintRgn(dome);
```

   b.
```
olympic := NewRgn;
OpenRgn;
FrameOval(45, 45, 75, 75);
FrameOval(45, 75, 75, 105);
FrameOval(45, 105, 75, 135);
FrameOval(60, 60, 90, 90);
FrameOval(60, 90, 90, 120);
CloseRgn(olympic);
PaintRgn(olympic);
```

   c.
```
trapezoid := NewRgn;
OpenRgn;
FrameRect(30, 30, 50, 80);
MoveTo(30, 30);
LineTo(20, 50);
Line(20, 0);
MoveTo(80, 30);
Line(0, 20);
Line(10, 0);
Line(-10, -20);
CloseRgn(trapezoid);
PaintRgn(trapezoid);
```

   d.
```
trap2 := NewRgn;
OpenRgn;
MoveTo(30, 30);
Line(50, 0);
Line(10, 20);
Line(-70, 0);
Line(10, -20);
CloseRgn(trap2);
PaintRgn(trap2);
```

2. Look over the User's Guide and Reference Manual for Macintosh Pascal or Lightspeed Pascal. What assumptions have the authors made about the readers? How do the two volumes or sections differ in approach? How would you improve the documentation?

3. Write external documentation for the last program you created.

4. What advantages are there to writing your exDoc before starting to code? Where would exDoc best fit in the way you personally develop programs?

5. Is it possible to have coordinates that are less than 0 in the screen coordinate system? in the Drawing window's coordinate system?

6. In the following code, where is the cursor in the screen coordinate system if ***GetMouse*** assigns ***horiz*** and ***vert*** the values –70 and –40 (respectively)? –100 and 60? 53 and 82? 15 and –45?

```
SetRect(bottomRight, 312, 130, 512, 330);
SetDrawingRect(bottomRight);
repeat
    GetMouse(horiz, vert)
until Button;
```

Coding Exercises

1. Write a procedure that allows a user to choose from a menu and highlights the user's choice by inverting the chosen button.

2. Modify the previous exercise by drawing a thick border around the chosen button's border.

3. Write a procedure that, after the user specifies three vertices, paints a triangular region.

4. Write a procedure that tracks the mouse movement by circling the crosshairs. That is, the mouse's current position should be denoted by the symbol shown below:

The procedure exits when the user presses the mouse button.

5. Write procedures to draw the following shapes as single regions (note: in (d), the labels are not part of the region):

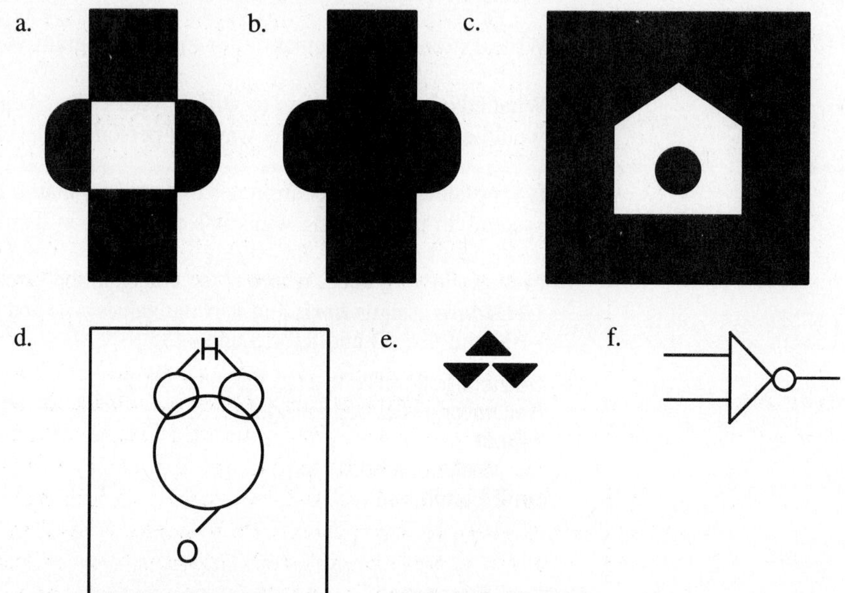

Programming Problems

1. Write a program that simulates the Desktop icons. Place four icons — one for each of four files — on the right side of the screen. If the user clicks on an icon, the contents of the file should be printed on the left side of the screen.

2. As an extension to the previous problem, allow the user to close as well as open files. Use a different icon for opened and closed files (such as opened and closed envelopes). Only one file can be open at any time.

3. Modify the Layout program (seen, in among other places, as the ***Fence*** program in Chapter 6) so that the user can create a menu option. The menu should consist of circles, lines, rectangles, and a region that the user specifies at the beginning of the session.

4. Another Layout modification: add two menu options called Start Region and Stop Region. After choosing Stop Region, the user can choose Move Region to choose a new location for the newly created shape.

5. It's late in the evening, and your restaurant is down to four pies (one each of apple, pecan, cherry, and Key lime) and three quarts of ice cream (one each of

vanilla, chocolate, and double rainbow swirl). The pies provide six servings; the quarts are enough for four servings each.

Your program should keep inventory on the desserts. The user should see pop-up menus. First, the user should see a menu with the options Pie, Ice Cream, Help, and Stop. Help and Stop should be self-explanatory. Choosing the other buttons causes a second menu to appear *in place of* the first menu. This second menu should allow the user to choose a type of pie or ice cream. After the selection is made, the program should show how much is left of each dessert and then return the main menu to the screen.

6. Write a program that checks the Pascal syntax of a procedure or function heading with parameters. The input should be a single string, such as:

```
procedure Swim(var height, depth: integer; lifeguard: string);
```

The first word should be either "procedure" or "function". Next is the routine's name and a left parenthesis. Following this are the parameter lists, which begin with either the word "var" or a variable name. The variable name (or names separated by commas) is followed by a colon, a variable type, and a semicolon, or a right parenthesis and a semicolon. Variable names can be any combination of letters and digits that begins with a letter; legal variable types (for this program) are "integer," "real," "boolean," "string," and "char." Your program should either confirm that the input string is a correct heading or print out error messages. These messages should be as specific as possible (e.g., "You messed up" is not sufficient).

7. Write a program that moves a cursor around the Drawing window. The cursor should be an 8-pixel-wide and 16-pixel-long inverted rectangle and should initially be in the window's top left corner. Its movement is controlled at the keyboard. When the user presses the 'h' key, the cursor should move 8 pixels to the left of its current position; the 'l' (letter ell) key should move it 8 pixels to the right. The 'j' and 'k' keys should move the cursor 16 pixels toward the top and bottom of the window, respectively. The 'q' key should exit the program. (Something to consider: what happens when the cursor hits the edge of the window? Document how you handle this situation.)

8. Write a program that allows the user to answer the following word problem:

Two cars are moving toward each other. At 4 p.m., the cars are 120 kilometers apart. One car is moving at 70 kilometers per hour. The cars pass each other at 4:45 p.m. Assuming it is moving at a constant speed, how fast is the other car traveling?

Illustrate the user's answer. Using the user's response, show (in the Drawing window) the positions of the cars at five-minute intervals (i.e., at 4:00, 4:05,

4:10, etc.). Allow the user to try different speeds until she correctly answers the question. (Your program should use constants, so that the numbers in the problem can be changed easily.)

9. Write a program that illustrates the f-stops on a camera. The f-stop is a measure of aperture, or the diameter of the lens opening. The f-stop sequence is 1.8, 2.8, 4, 5.6, 8, 11, 16, 22. Each number represents an opening half the size of the previous number (the openings get smaller as the f-stops get higher). Illustrate the f-stop opening with two circles, as shown below:

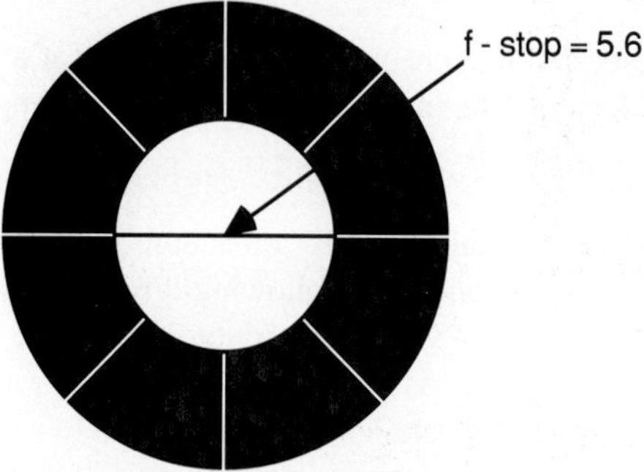

As the user changes the f-stop, redraw as little of the illustration as possible. Do not redraw the outside circle.

10. Write a program that allows the user to resize the Drawing window during the program's execution. Remember that ***GetMouse*** returns coordinates in the Drawing window's system; you will need to convert those coordinates to the screen coordinate system.

11

Arrays and Type Declarations

In previous chapters, we've dealt with programs in which a small number of simple variables are involved. Integers, reals, booleans, characters, and strings each represent a single piece of data and are therefore thought of as *atomic* data types. In contrast, files store arbitrarily large amounts of data on disks, but we read or write one component at a time. This chapter begins our study of *composite* (or *compound*) *data structures* — collections of logically related data items stored and manipulated in the program's internal storage area.

All the composite data structures that we will discuss (arrays, records, sets, linked lists, stacks, queues, and trees) have the same general purpose: they allow programmers to store more than one datum in a single variable. In some form or other, each data structure maintains a list of items. However, each structure handles the list in a different way to deal with a different situation. Each of the following chapters will discuss the organization and uses of a particular data structure. Keep in mind that several different forms of composite structures exist, each with a specific purpose. By the end of the book, you should be able to analyze a particular data storage problem and determine which data structure is most appropriate. We will start with the simplest of the compound data structures: the array.

11.1 About Arrays

Suppose we are writing a program for Turbulent Airlines. The company flies passengers on nearly 100 flights a day. In this program, the user wants to be able to refer to any flight at any time, using its unique flight number. At this point, we are not going to write the entire program; we simply need to decide how to store the data so that we can gain access to any part of the data at any time.

What we have learned thus far about variables would let us deal with this problem, but it wouldn't be a whole lot of fun. We would have to declare nearly 100 different variable names, one for each flight. Then we would need nearly 100 separate assignment statements to assign the flight numbers to these variables. As if that weren't enough, to actually use the variables, we might have to pass nearly 100 variables around as parameters. The following is just a small number of the variable declarations for the flight numbers:

```
var
    LAToBoston,                        { num for flight LAX-BOS }
    ProvToCleveland,                   { num for flight PVD-CLE }
    PhilaToSanFran,                    { num for flight PHL-SFO }
    SarasotaToNY,                      { num for flight SRQ-JFK }
    ...
    WallaWallaToNewark: integer;       { num for flight WAL-EWR }
```

(The airline industry has a three-letter code for each airport. For example, BOS is the code for Boston's Logan Airport; JFK is the code for Kennedy Airport in New York City. Sometimes the codes are not mnemonic; EWR is the code for Newark International, SRQ the code for Sarasota/Bradenton.)

One problem inherent in using these 100 individual variable names is that there is no relationship between the variables. There is nothing in the program that indicates that these 100 locations in memory together comprise all the flight numbers for a single airline. Each separate variable is an independent and unrelated piece of information. Besides, the amount of typing required to enter these variables might make you think that you would be better off with pencil and paper.

What we need is a way of grouping related variables together under a single name. We would like to declare the name with one statement and pass it easily as a parameter to other procedures. Pascal uses a convention that you will probably remember from high school math: *subscripted variables*. In math, several points on a curve might be called P_1, P_2, P_3, and so on. Similarly, mathematical notation allows us to refer to a set of flight numbers as $flight_1$, $flight_2$, $flight_3$, and so on. We can do the same thing in Pascal. But since subscripts cannot be typed into the program, we put the "subscript" in square brackets after the variable (i.e., ***flightNums[1]***, ***flightNums[2]***, ***flightNums[3]***). This is the same notation that we have used to refer to any single character in a string. Indeed, a string is implemented in MacPascal as an array of characters.

flightNums is unlike any variable we have seen before, because it stores an entire list of items, not just one. ***flightNums*** is an example of a Pascal data structure called an *array*. An array is a compound data type that stores a predetermined number of data under a single name. The data must all be of the same data type and be used for the same purpose in the program. Using arrays makes programs easier to write and easier to read, since an entire collection can be referenced by a single name instead of separate variable names.

Think of an array as a sequence of storage positions of a predetermined length. Each storage position is separate from the others, that is, the value of one location does not affect the value of any other location. Still, the storage locations all belong to an integrated group.

Before we learn how to use an array, it may be helpful to visualize the data structure. Figure 11.1 shows the array ***flightNums***. This array name applies to each of the 100 elements, or positions, in the array. Notice, though, that each element has its own subscripted name and is separate from all other elements. We can work with the contents of, say, ***flightNums[17]*** without knowing anything about any of the other elements.

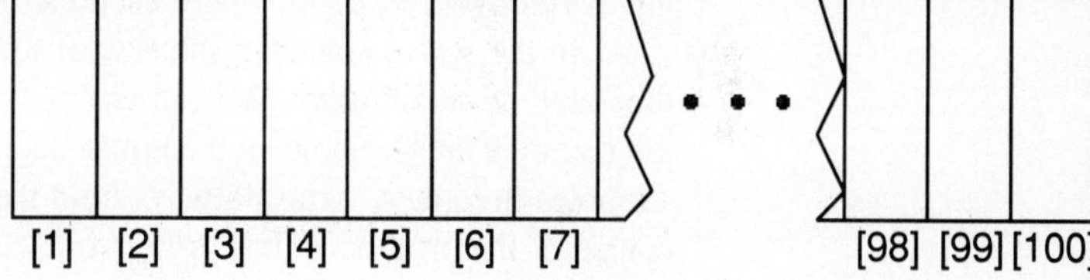

Figure 11.1 An array of 100 elements

11.2 Declaring Arrays

Using an array solves all the problems in the flight numbers example. We can store all 100 flight numbers in one data structure and pass that around as a single parameter instead of keeping track of 100 separate items. However, we have to tell Pascal that we want to use an array.

Declaring an array is not very different from declaring ordinary single variables. Because an array is a compound data structure, however, we must specify exactly how big the data structure is going to be (how many elements it will have). Each element in an array is numbered, and all the elements must be enumerated in an increasing sequence. That is, we can number the elements from 1 to 1000, from 0 to 1, or from 63 to 847. Negative numbers can also be used in the array's enumeration. For example, it is legal to number the elements from –100 to –1 or from –50 to +50. We can also use ***char*** types, such as 'a' to 'z', or enumerated types (explained in Chapter 13) to number an array's elements. We cannot, however, skip any values in specifying the array; that is, we cannot have an array whose four elements are numbered 2, 4, 6, and 8. Thus, to tell Pascal about an array, we need to specify the *upper and lower bounds* of the array's *range*. Pascal will then be able to determine the size of the array.

Specifying the range tells Pascal *how many* positions to reserve. But we cannot leave it at that. Imagine going to a supermarket and asking for "a dozen." After giving you a quizzical look, the grocer would ask, "A dozen what?" It makes a difference whether you are ordering a dozen mangoes or a dozen watermelons. Arrays can be used to collect any type of data, as long as all the elements are the same type. Thus, we need to specify the data type as well as the range of the array's elements.

Let's look at an example of an array declaration:

```
const
   maxFlights = 100;              { max number of airline's flights }

var
   flightNums : array[1..maxFlights] of integer;
```

The variable identifier ***flightNums*** appears on the left side of the colon in the **var** section. The right side of the colon begins with the keyword **array**, indicating that the variable is an array. The range is then specified in square brackets. The first and last elements are separated by two periods, which are the equivalent of ellipses (...) in English. Following the range is the keyword **of** and the data type of all elements (in this case, integer). Thus, ***flightNums*** is an array with 100 elements, numbered from 1 to 100, where each element is an integer.

In the above example, the size of the array can be easily changed by changing the value of ***maxFlights***. We can use constant identifiers in the ranges of arrays as long as they are declared in the **const** declaration section. We cannot, however, use variables in ranges. Arrays always hold the same number of elements throughout the course of the program. Thus, arrays can be used only when the amount of data to be stored is known before execution of the program. In the case where the exact size of the array is unknown when the program is written, you must plan for the worst case by setting up an array large enough to handle the maximum amount of data the program could encounter. While it is acceptable to leave part of the array unused, your program may crash if you don't leave enough room for all of your data.

11.3 Using Arrays

The array declaration gives a name to the entire list of items. When you use arrays, however, you usually want to work with only one item at a time. To do this, you have to be able to gain access to any individual item in the array. Any integer value that is in the range, including negative numbers, can be used as a subscript, or *index*, in the array. The array name ***flightNums*** in the example above is followed by an index value in square brackets. Each index value uniquely identifies a single element in the array. It is important to note that the subscripts of an array as specified by the range bear no relation to the actual information stored in the various subdivisions of the array. The index values in Pascal, like subscripts in math, merely provide a method of referring to one item when many items have the same collective name.

Suppose we want to use the third array element in the ***flightNums*** array declared above. In Pascal, all compound variables are denoted starting with the group name on the left. Thus, we begin by telling Pascal that we want to work with ***flightNums***. Then we need to specify the particular element within the array. This is done by enclosing the array index (in this case, the integer 3) in square brackets as follows:

```
flightNums[3]
```

Syntax Box 11.1
Declaring arrays

Purpose To declare a variable of an array type

Syntax

```
var
    < array var > : array[ < low bounds >..< up bounds > ] of
        < elem type > ;
```

where < array var > is any legal variable identifier.

< low bounds >..< up bounds > gives the *range* of the array. < low bounds > and < up bounds > both must be constants of an ordinal type (integers, characters, enumerated types). < up bounds > must also be greater than < low bounds >. < low bounds > and < up bounds > represent, respectively, the lower and upper bounds of the array subscripts.

< elem type > is the data type of each individual element in the array. This type may be any predefined type (see Appendix A) or any type declared in the program's **type** declarations.

Usage The range of the array (< low bounds >..< up bounds >) says two things about the array: the number of subdivisions in the array and the legal values of the subscript or index to the array.

When you use ranges, you must be careful about how many elements are in the array you are declaring. The range includes both the lower bound and the upper bound in the range. If you define an array with a range from 1 to 5, you have 5 elements. If you declare it from 0 to 5, you have 6 elements, and array position 0 is the first position in the array.

An array variable complete with a subscript number refers to a single element and therefore can be used in Pascal statements just as any other simple variable might be. The following expresion assigns the contents of an integer variable to the fourth element in the array ***flightNums***:

```
flightNums[4] := currentFlight;
```

Figure 11.2 illustrates what happens when the information from the variable ***currentFlight*** is stored in the array.

As we said in Chapter 9, we can gain access to files in one of two ways: sequentially or randomly. The same thing can be done with arrays — and it's even easier. The above assignment statement is an example of random access. We placed a value in the fourth element in an array without processing any information in array elements 1, 2, or 3. Random access simply means that we can refer to any element at any time and manipulate the elements in any order.

Sequential access means that we look at the elements in an array in order. Very often, we want to use the elements in an array from the first element to the last. The

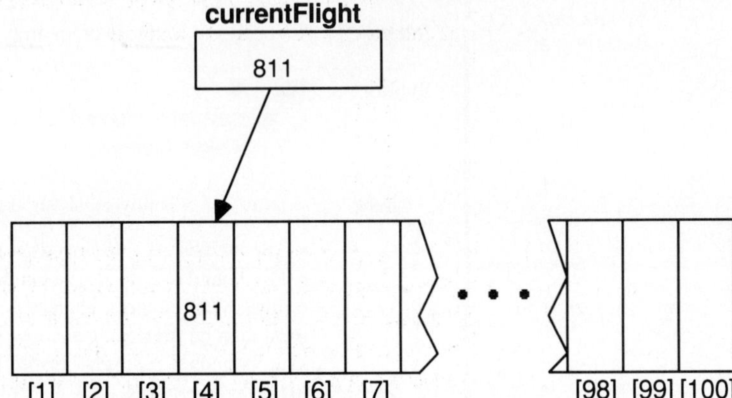

Figure 11.2 Loading information into *flightNums[4]*

upper and lower bounds of the array are ordinal types (integers, characters, enumerated types) — just like the upper and lower bounds specified in a **for** loop. When we gain sequential access to an array, we often want to repeat the same action for each element. Since we know how many elements are in the array, we can use a definite loop to initialize, read into, and print out consecutive elements.

In the following example, the elements in an array are sequentially read and printed.

```
program ReadAndPrint;

const
    arraySize = 5;                              { max number of flights      }

var
    count: integer;                             { current array index        }
    flights: array[1..arraySize] of integer;    { all flight numbers         }

begin
    { read values into array }
    for count := 1 to arraySize do
        begin
            Write('Please input the flight number: ');
            Readln(flights[count])
        end; { for }

    { print contents of array }
    for count := 1 to arraySize do
        Writeln('Array slot', count:1, ' holds flight number ', flights[count]:4)
end; { ReadAndPrint }
```

In the above code fragment, the counter for the **for** loop is used to index successive locations in the array. The index value begins at one and is incremented by one each time through the loop. After the loop has finished executing, the operations contained within the loop have been performed on every element of the array.

Take a look at what happens in the first **for** statement. Suppose that five flight numbers that you want to load are:

```
882
166
200
701
190
```

As the loop is entered for the first time, ***count*** is set to 1. First, the prompt appears on the screen. Then, the ***Readln*** statement is executed and the number 882 is read into ***flights[1]***. Flow of control returns to the top of the loop and ***count*** is incremented to 2. When MacPascal reaches the statement ***Readln(flights[count]);***, it evaluates the expression as ***flights[2]***. Thus, the second input (166) is assigned to the second element in the array. This process continues until 200, 701, and 190 have been read into ***flights[3]***, ***flights[4]***, and ***flights[5]***. At this point, ***count*** is equal to 5. When the **for** loop tries to execute again, ***count*** is set to 6, which is greater than ***arraySize***. Execution will fall through to the next statement, which is another **for** loop.

The second **for** statement's processing is identical to the simpler one above it. For each iteration of the loop, two pieces of information will be printed: the subscript number and the contents of that place in the array. The output generated will look like this:

```
Array slot 1 holds flight number 882
Array slot 2 holds flight number 166
Array slot 3 holds flight number 200
Array slot 4 holds flight number 701
Array slot 5 holds flight number 190
```

Note that while the array subscripts are in increasing numerical order, the contents of each array position are in an arbitrary order — the array subscript, as noted earlier, has no bearing on what is stored in each location.

Let's look at another example. The Fibonacci series is a famous mathematical sequence. The sequence begins with a pair of 1's. The following numbers in the sequence are found by adding the previous two numbers. Thus, the third number is found by adding the first and second numbers (2 = 1 + 1); then the fourth number (3) by adding the second (1) and third (2) numbers; and so on. The beginning of the sequence is:

1 1 2 3 5 8 13 21 34 55...

We can use the computer to calculate and store the numbers in the sequence. The following code fragment uses an array to store the values of the sequence.

```
{ Procedure Fib                                          }
{ This procedure calculates the Fibonacci sequence.      }
```

```
{ The numbers in the sequence are stored in order          }
{ in an array.                                             }

const
   sizeSequence = 20;              { number of elements to calculate      }

procedure Fib;

var
   curNum: integer;                { position in sequence being calculated }
   seq: array[1..sizeSequence] of integer;{ elements in Fibonacci sequence }

begin
{ assign initial values }
   seq[1] := 1;
   seq[2] := 1;

{ calculate remainder of sequence }
   for curNum := 3 to sizeSequence do
      seq[curNum] := seq[curNum-1] + seq[curNum-2]

end; { Fib }
```

When this procedure is executed, ***seq*** begins with 20 garbage values. The first two assignment statements place the value 1 in each of the first two positions in the array.

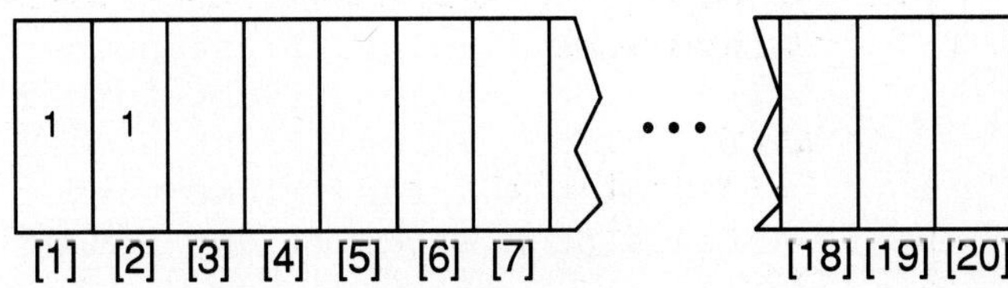

Figure 11.3 Array at beginning of hand simulation

Next, the **for** loop is executed. On the first iteration, ***curNum*** is set to 3. Thus, the assignment statement evaluates to ***seq[3] := seq[2] + seq[1];***. As with all assignment statements, the expression on the right is evaluated first. ***seq[2]*** (the second element in ***seq***) is equal to 1, as is ***seq[1]***. Thus, ***seq[3]*** gets the value 1 + 1, or 2. The array now looks like Figure 11.4.

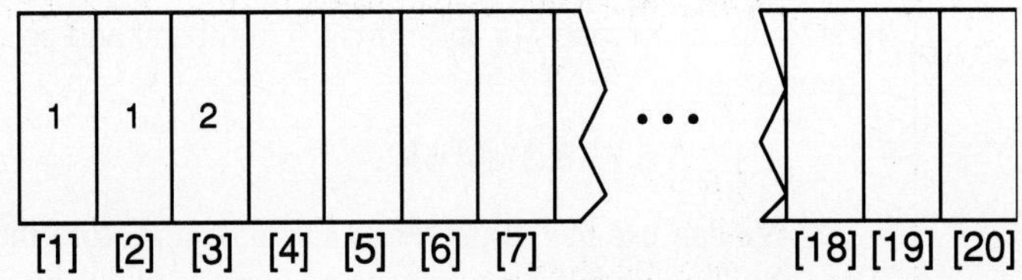

Figure 11.4 Array at end of first iteration

In the next iteration of the loop, ***seq[4]*** receives the value ***seq[2] + seq[3]***. ***seq[3]*** received a value in the previous iteration, so the expression evaluates to

1 + 2, or 3. After that, ***seq[5]*** receives the sum of ***seq[4]*** and ***seq[3]***. The execution continues until ***seq[sizeSequence]*** receives the final value.

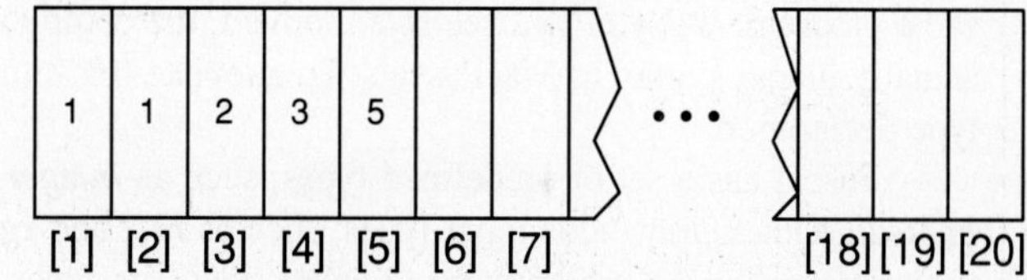

Figure 11.5 Array after ***seq[5]*** receives value

Notice that the array was filled one position at a time. In Figure 11.5, slots 6 through 20 hold garbage values. Still, we can use elements of ***seq*** on the right side of assignment statements, as long as we refer to those that have already received values. If we inadvertently use an index indicating a garbage value, the situation is identical to using any uninitialized atomic variable.

11.4 Defining Types

The array declaration is much longer than simple data type declarations. This makes for quite a bit of typing, because every time an array is passed as a parameter, we have to specify the entire array declaration again. Suppose we declare an array in the mainline and pass it to two different procedures. You might think of using the following declarations:

```
const
    maxWords = 100;                               { total num of words on a page}

var
    paper : array[1..maxWords] of string[20];     { all words on a page          }

{ Illegal data type in parameter declaration }
procedure Initialize(var page: array[1..maxWords] of string[20]);
                                                  { all words on a page          }
    ...

procedure Print(printPage: array[1..maxWords] of string[20]);
                                                  { all words on a page          }
    ...

{ mainline }
begin
    Initialize(paper);
    ...
    Print(paper)
end. { mainline }
```

Because most computer scientists have never been particularly fond of typing, they develop methods of avoiding it whenever possible. The designers of Pascal did not want to have to write out an entire complex declaration so many times in the same program. (As you will see in a moment, the complex declarations above are actually illegal syntax in MacPascal.) To alleviate this situation, they created the type declaration.*

Pascal has a set of predefined types, such as ***integer***, ***real***, ***char***, and ***boolean***. QuickDraw adds more types, such as ***rect*** and ***rgnHandle***. The **type** declaration allows a programmer to create new data types from predeclared types and then use these new data types to create variables in the **var** declarations. Think of a type as a template or rubber stamp defining a data format that can be replicated ("instantiated" in computer science lingo) as needed.

types are like **consts** in that they are defined once and used throughout the entire program. The **type** declarations appear at the beginning of your program right after the **const** declarations. The following is a **type** declaration for a simple variable.

```
type
   countingNumber = integer;
```

The new type appears on the left under the **type** heading and is followed by an equals sign. Any previously defined type then can appear after the equals sign. Notice that an equals sign, not an assignment symbol (**:=**), separates the two parts. The equals sign says that two things are equivalent. The **type** and **const** declarations are similar in that they allow identifiers to be used as notations for certain other values.

With the above declaration, imagine that each occurrence of ***countingNumber*** will be replaced by the word ***integer***. In this program, the variable ***loopCtr*** can be declared as

```
var
   loopCtr: countingNumber;              { current novelization        }
```

rather than

```
var
   loopCtr: integer;                     { current novelization        }
```

Although this example isn't particularly useful (in fact, it causes more typing than it saves), it does demonstrate how a **type** declaration works. Because the **type** declaration provides a shorthand, it's easy to see how **type** declarations can greatly clarify a declaration as complicated as that of an array. Instead of typing out the entire array declaration every time, you can declare a one-word **type** and use it instead. Declaring a **type** is a way of declaring your own special data type, which is temporarily added to the list of legal data types for the duration of the program.

Now a brief excursion into computer science thinking: every identifier in a program has a *lexical scope*, which indicates where the identifer can be used legally. Identifiers declared under the **const** and **type** declarations at the top of a program

---

* We have no idea if this actually happened, but it does make a good story.

have what is known as *global scope*. These identifiers can be used throughout the program without being declared again. Identifiers declared under **var** headings in procedures are *local* to that procedure; thus, their scope is limited to a single procedure. Now you have seen that a **var** heading can also appear at the top of the program. Technically, these variable identifiers can then be used throughout the program, but we prefer to limit their use to the mainline.

At first glance, this seems rather inconsistent — we encourage the use of global constants and types, but discourage the use of global variables. The distinction is that constant and type identifiers cannot change values during the program, while variables can. If a variable can be changed anywhere in the program, debugging is a great deal more difficult. If the variable receives an erroneous value somewhere, you may have to check every line in the program to find the mistaken statement. Keeping variables local promotes the program's *modularity*, that is, independent procedures and functions that can be copied, without alteration, for use in other programs. In particular, a procedure's designer can use specific names for local variables, secure in the knowledge that no other procedure can access those variables, unless information is explicitly passed via parameters.

Global variables do have a proper place in structured programming. For example, if a particularly large data structure is used by nearly every procedure in a program, then it might make sense to make that data structure a global variable rather than passing it around. However, global variables won't be used in the example programs in this book.

Syntax Box 11.2
type

Purpose To declare any number of types

Syntax

```
type
    < type name > = < type format >;
```

where < type name > is the type identifier.

< type format > is any previously defined type or Pascal predefined type.

Usage Any number of types can be declared in the **type** section. The declared type name is now a template of the < type format > and can be used in variable declarations just as the predefined types ***integer*** or ***real*** are used.

Think of the **type** declaration as a declaration of an alias. Each occurrence of < type name > in the program will be replaced with < type format >.

Once you declare a **type**, you can use it immediately. Thus, one **type** declaration can refer to another **type** declaration. Like a procedure, though, a **type** declaration must be defined before it can be used.

The example at the beginning of this section can be rewritten as follows:

```
const
   maxWords = 100;                    { total num of words on a page      }

type
   pageType = array[1..maxWords] of string[20];
                                      { holds a list of words       }

var
   paper : pageType;                  { all words on a page         }

procedure Initialize(var page: pageType);
                                      { all words on a page         }
   ...

procedure Print(printPage: pageType);
                                      { all words on a page         }
   ...

{ mainline }
begin
   Initialize(paper);
   ...
   Print(paper)
end. { mainline }
```

Every time Pascal finds the identifier ***pageType***, it replaces it with **array*[1..maxWords]* of string*[20];***. Thus, this example produces the same results as the code that began this section — it simply requires fewer keystrokes when entering the program.

In MacPascal, parameter types cannot contain more than one word. Since the type **array*[1..maxWords]* of string*[20];*** consists of several words, you *must* use a **type** for any array parameter. You will get a syntax error if you declare a parameter with the full declaration **array*[1..maxWords]* of string*[20];***. The first code examples in this section were presented for illustrative purposes only.

11.5 An Array Example

To explore the concept of an array a little more fully, we are going to develop a short program that uses a simple array structure. The program keeps track of the product inventory for a company warehouse. This particular company produces 30 different pieces of equipment and keeps this equipment stored in its warehouse until it is shipped out. Equipment parts will be numbered from 1 to 30.

The input for this program consists of a set of two integers for each transaction. First, the user types in the part number of the transaction, then the change in inventory. The second number is a positive integer if the warehouse has gained parts and a negative integer if it has sent out parts. For example, if 300 units of part 12 are sent out, the user types in 12 for the part number and –300 for the change in inventory. If any transaction puts the total number of that part below zero, an error message is printed. That is, the warehouse cannot have a negative inventory of parts. An input of zero for the part number is the sentinel. When all transactions have been completed, the total inventory in the warehouse is printed.

Let's pseudocode the example:

```
Initialize array to hold zero values for inventory amounts
Read input and process inventory
Print inventory list
```

We can now refine the pseudocode by specifying each step as a procedure.

```
CALL: Initialize array to hold zero values for inventory amounts
CALL: Read input and process inventory
CALL: Print inventory list

{ Initialize array to hold zero values for inventory amounts }
FOR each array position DO
   Set element to 0

{ Read input and process inventory }
Read part number
WHILE there are still parts to process DO
   BEGIN
      Read inventory change
      Update current inventory
      Print error message for negative inventory counts
      Read part number
   END

{ Print inventory list }
FOR each item in warehouse DO
   Print amount of item in stock
```

This problem assumes that the inventory of each part is stored in the array slot corresponding to its part number; for example, the current inventory of part number 15 is stored in array slot number 15.

The program has one error condition. If the inventory, after the gain or loss of parts, becomes a negative number, the transaction must be incorrect and should produce an error message. This means that we have to update the inventory count only if the result will not be negative.

In addition, we can decide to print just those items that are actually in stock. With this information, we can refine the second part of the pseudocode as follows:

```
CALL: Initialize array to hold zero values for inventory amounts
CALL: Read input and process inventory
CALL: Print inventory list

{ Initialize array to hold zero values for inventory amounts }
FOR each array position DO
   Set element to 0

{ Read input and process inventory }
Read part number
WHILE there are still parts to process DO
   BEGIN
      Read inventory change
      IF change in inventory will result in negative number THEN
         Print error message
      ELSE
         Update current inventory
      Read part number
   END

{ Print inventory list }
FOR each item in warehouse DO
   IF there is at least one of the item in stock THEN
      Print number of items in stock
```

Code 11.1
Program *Inventory*

```
{ D. Niguidula          Program: InventoryChange   October 11         }
{  This program updates the number of parts in stock and reports      }
{ the final tally. The user is asked to input the part number that has }
{ been counted in the inventory, and then the change in the quantity of }
{ that item. The quantity of each part is kept in an array, in the     }
{ position corresponding to the part number. When the sentinel is      }
{ input, the quantities of all the part numbers are printed.           }

program InventoryChange;

  const
    maxParts = 30;                { maximum number of parts           }
    sentinel = 0;                 { marks end of user input           }

  type
    inventory = array[1..maxParts] of integer;
      { holds information on all parts                                 }

{ Mainline variables }
  var
    parts : inventory;            { list of all parts in stock         }
    partNumber : integer;         { item which is being counted        }
```

Code 11.1
(continued)

```
{ Procedure: Init                                                        }
{   This procedure initializes the number of each part in stock to 0.    }
{ Called by : Mainline        Calls: none                                }

  procedure Init (var parts : inventory);       { list of all parts in stock  }

  var
     loop : integer;                            { loop counter                }

  begin

     for loop := 1 to maxParts do
        parts[loop] := 0

  end; {Init }

{ Procedure: Update                                                      }
{  In this procedure, the user is then prompted to enter the change      }
{ in inventory of a given part. The quantity of the part is updated      }
{ unless the change will cause the  total inventory to dip below 0. In   }
{ that case, an error message is printed.                                }
{ Called by : Mainline        Calls: none                                }

  procedure Update (var parts : inventory;      { list of all parts in stock     }
                  partNum : integer);           { part number to update          }

  var
     change : integer;                          { increase/decrease in stock     }
  begin
     Write('Enter net change in inventory: ');
     Readln(change);

     if (parts[partNumber] + change) < 0 then
        Writeln('Change not processed.  Result would be a negative inventory.')
     else
        begin
           parts[partNumber] := parts[partNumber] + change;
           Write(parts[partNumber] : 3, ' items of part number ',
              partNumber : 3);
           Writeln(' are now in stock.')
        end { else }

  end; { Update }

{ Procedure: Print                                                       }
{   This procedure prints the final totals for each of the parts in      }
{ stock. If the inventory is not equal to zero, the total is printed.    }
{ Called by : Mainline        Calls: none                                }
```

Code 11.1 (continued)

```
    procedure Print (parts : inventory);            { list of all parts in stock    }
      var
        loop : integer;                             { loop counter                  }
    begin

      for loop := 1 to maxParts do
        if parts[loop] <> 0 then
          Writeln(parts[loop] : 4, ' items of part number', loop : 3, ' in stock.')

    end; {Print }

  { Procedure: Mainline                                                        }
  {   After the part numbers are initialized, the mainline prompts the         }
  { user to enter the part number to be updated. If that part number           }
  { does not exist, the user is given a chance to try again.                   }
  {   The user changes the inventory of different parts until he enters        }
  { a sentinel to end the processing. Then, the quantities of all the          }
  { parts are printed.                                                         }
  { Calls: Init, Print                                                         }

  begin
    Init(parts);

    Write('Enter the part number that has been counted, or 0 to exit: ');
    Readln(partNumber);

    while (partNumber <> sentinel) do
      begin

        { loop until legal part number }

        while (partNumber < 0) or (partNumber > maxParts) do
          begin
            Writeln('Sorry, you have entered a part number that does not exist.');
            Writeln('The part numbers range from 1 to ', maxParts : 3);
            Writeln;
            Write('Please enter the part number or 0 to exit: ');
            Readln(partNumber)
          end;

      { Change inventory for that part number }
        Update(parts, partNumber);

      { Get next item to process }
        Writeln;
        Write('Please enter the part number or 0 to exit: ');
        Readln(partNumber)

      end; { while }
    Print(parts)

  end. { InventoryChange }
```

```
Enter the part number that has been counted, or 0 to exit: 15
Enter net change in inventory: 100
100 items of part number  15 are now in stock.

Please enter the part number or 0 to exit: 8
Enter net change in inventory: 452
452 items of part number   8 are now in stock.

Please enter the part number or 0 to exit: 15
Enter net change in inventory: -25
 75 items of part number  15 are now in stock.

Please enter the part number or 0 to exit: 23
Enter net change in inventory: -75
Change not processed.  Result would be a negative inventory.

Please enter the part number or 0 to exit: 11
Enter net change in inventory: 273
273 items of part number  11 are now in stock.

Please enter the part number or 0 to exit: 21
Enter net change in inventory: 221
221 items of part number  21 are now in stock.

Please enter the part number or 0 to exit: 1
Enter net change in inventory: 120
120 items of part number   1 are now in stock.

Please enter the part number or 0 to exit: 4
Enter net change in inventory: 405
405 items of part number   4 are now in stock.

Please enter the part number or 0 to exit: 52
Sorry, you have entered a part number that does not exist.
The part numbers range from 1 to  30

Please enter the part number or 0 to exit: 11
Enter net change in inventory: -68
205 items of part number  11 are now in stock.

Please enter the part number or 0 to exit: 15
Enter net change in inventory: -95
Change not processed.  Result would be a negative inventory.

Please enter the part number or 0 to exit: 0
 120 items of part number  1 in stock.
 405 items of part number  4 in stock.
 452 items of part number  8 in stock.
 205 items of part number 11 in stock.
  75 items of part number 15 in stock.
 221 items of part number 21 in stock.
```

Figure 11.6
Output of Program
Inventory

11.6 Array Searches

Sequential access is useful for storing or printing information. Suppose, though, that you want to search for one particular item in the array. You cannot use the same algorithm for searching that you have used for initializing. Since array searches are common in programming, it is worthwhile to look at what happens when you need to find one element in the array.

Let's go back to the flight numbers example. Imagine that the user wants to know if flight number 312 is still running. Assume that the array ***flightNums*** already contains all current flight numbers. However, the numbers are stored in no particular order. If 312 is in the array — anywhere — the flight is currently running. Otherwise, the flight does not exist.

Think about how to find the flight by using a real-world analogy. Suppose you have a list of numbers in random order on a printed page. You're trying to find one specific number in the list, so you start at one end. As you read each number, you instantly determine if you have found the number you want. If you have found your number, you stop. If you haven't found your number, you go on to the next one on the list. This process continues until you either find the number or reach the end of the list.

We can use this same algorithm to search for a particular element in an array. We can set this algorithm up as a function. The function returns TRUE if the *key* (the value we are searching for) is found; otherwise the function returns FALSE. We begin the function by starting at the beginning of the array. If the first element contains the value we want, then we're done. Otherwise, we continue to the next element. Now, if the array has only one element, then the algorithm concludes. Since we searched the entire (one-element) array and did not find the key, the value must not exist. However, if there are still more items, we can compare the key to the value of that next element in the array. This algorithm continues until we either reach the end of the list or find the key.

Let's think about this algorithm now in terms of flow-of-control constructs. We are obviously repeating part of the algorithm, so we want to use a loop. We do not know how many times we will need to move to the next element in the array, so we need to use an indefinite loop. Inside the loop are three possible actions. If we have reached the end of the list, the loop should exit and the function should return FALSE. If we have found the key, the loop should exit and the function should return TRUE. If neither of these conditions holds, we should move to the next element. Put in pseudocode terms, the algorithm follows:

```
WHILE not finished DO
   BEGIN
      IF at end of list THEN
         BEGIN
            Set exit condition to TRUE
            Key is not in list
         END
```

```
        ELSE IF key is in current element THEN
            BEGIN
                Set exit condition to TRUE
                Key is in list
            END
        ELSE
            Increment current element
    END { WHILE }
```

This can be easily coded as a function called ***Find***:

```
const
    maxFlights = 100;                       { maximum number of flights }

type
    flightType = array[1..maxFlights] of integer;
                                            { holds flight numbers       }

function Find(key: integer;                 { value to search for        }
        flightNums: flightType):            { list of all flight nums    }
        boolean;                            { returns TRUE if found      }

var
    curElem: integer;                       { current position in array  }
    done: boolean;                          { indicates loop is finished }
    found: boolean;                         { indicates how loop exits   }

begin
    {initialize values }
    curElem := 1;
    done := FALSE;

    { find key in array }
    while not done do
        begin
            if curElem > maxFlights then { searched to end of list }
                begin
                    done := TRUE;
                    found := FALSE
                end { if }
            else if flightNums[curElem] = key then { key is found }
                begin
                    done := TRUE;
                    found := TRUE
                end { if }
            else
                curElem := curElem +1
        end; { while }

    Find := found { return value to caller }
end; { Find }
```

The order of the conditions in the **if-then-else if** is important in one instance. Imagine that we switched the order of testing the conditions:

```
...
if flightNums[curElem] = key then { key is found }
   begin
      done := TRUE;
      found := TRUE
   end { if }
else if curElem > maxFlights then { off end of list }
   begin
      done := TRUE;
      found := FALSE
   end { if }
else
   curElem := curElem +1;
...
```

Let's hand simulate what happens in the second fragment when the key is not in the array. Let's start where ***curElem*** = 100. Since ***done*** is not TRUE (we have not found the key in the first 99 elements), the loop executes. ***flightNums[100]*** does not equal ***key***, so we move to the **else if** condition. The condition ***curElem* > *100*** is FALSE, so we follow the **else** and increment ***curElem*** to 101.

We again begin execution at the top of the loop. When we try to test the first condition, though, we cause an *out-of-bounds error* because the condition evaluates to ***flightNums[101] = key***, and the index of 101 causes Pascal to try to access a memory location that isn't in the array. In the ***Find*** function we declared first, we do not have this problem. The first condition there is ***curElem* > *100***. This condition is TRUE whenever ***curElem*** threatens to cause an out-of-bounds error. Thus, when the key is not found, the condition ***flightNums[101] = key*** is never reached and therefore cannot cause an error.

11.7 Potential Array Bugs

The most common problem encountered when programming with arrays is the out-of-bounds error. This means that the current index value of the array is not within the range specified in the **type** declaration. For example, if we have an array with a range *[3..20]*, the program should not try to index the element number 21 or element number 2. Should such a thing happen during the program's execution, you will receive an error message similar to **An invalid array index has been found.** To track down this bug, you may want to use the Observe window to print out the index of the subscript that is causing the error.

In some cases, you may also want to test the index in an **if** statement before the array slot is processed. More specifically, you want to ensure that the index is in the valid range for the array. This way, the out-of-bounds error cannot appear. In the above example, we could use the condition:

```
const
    upLim = 20;                          { upper limit of array        }
    lowLim = 3;                          {lower limit of array         }
    ...
begin
    if (current >= lowLim) and(current <= upLim) then
        { process array element }
    else
        Writeln('Subscript ', current:3, 'is out of the legal bounds.')
end; { Procedure }
```

The above code fragment assumes that ***current*** will be used as the index to an array. This code guarantees that an array element is not accessed if it is not within the range ***3..20***.

Another common error with arrays has to do with memory. Since arrays contain many variables, a good deal of memory has to be allocated for each array variable. Then, when an array is passed as a value parameter, the receiving procedure must make another copy of the array's contents. If you pass arrays often as value parameters, you may have many copies of the same values floating around memory. Your program may suddenly halt with the ominous message **There is not enough memory to continue running**.

To combat this problem, first make sure that you really need to pass the entire array. You do not have to pass an entire array if you are going to use only one element. For example, if you have an array of integers declared as a ***flightType*** (see above code fragments), you can send each individual element to a procedure — one at a time — as follows:

```
procedure Receiver(singleNum: integer);
....
procedure Caller(flights: flightType); { all flight numbers }
var
    counter : integer;  { current element in array }
begin
    for counter := 1 to maxFlights do
        Receiver(flights[counter])
end; { Caller }
```

In this fragment, the procedure ***Caller*** calls the procedure ***Receiver***. At each call, ***Caller*** sends an element from the array ***flights***. Since the array's elements are of data type ***integer***, it is legal to send a single element to the procedure ***Receiver***. Both the formal and actual parameters are of the type ***integer***, so the fragment will not cause any mismatches of type.

There are times, however, when you simply must pass the entire array. If passing an array as a value parameter causes you to run out of memory, you may want to pass it as a variable parameter. Whenever you pass a variable parameter, MacPascal does not make a copy of the actual parameter. Instead, any reference to the variable parameter in ***Receiver*** uses the same location in main memory that holds the original variable in ***Caller***. While you may not be changing any values in the array, you may still want to pass it as a variable parameter to make sure that you do not run out of memory. Of course, this is a last resort. Leave all parameters that are not supposed to change as value parameters, since they ensure that any potential changes in the receiving procedure will be eliminated when the data structure is passed back. Do not give up this security unless you absolutely must.

11.8 Parallel Arrays

Not all collections of information reduce simply to one type of data. For example, for every one of Turbulent Airline's flights, there is a flight number, a city of origin, and a city of destination. When creating programs that handle large amounts of data, it is often helpful to use *parallel arrays*. Parallel arrays are two or more correlated arrays that have related information stored at the same index in each array. For example, for each flight we could store the cities in two arrays of **string[3]**: the originating airport codes can be held in an array called ***origins*** and the destination airport codes in an array called ***dests***.

Since these will be parallel arrays, we can set up a correspondence between elements with the same subscript. In other words, if ***origins[47]*** is flight 190's origin, then ***dests[47]*** is flight 190's destination. Similarly, if ***dests[83]*** is the destination of flight 811, then the origin can be found in ***origins[83]***. Thus, in a program constructed with parallel arrays, once we know the subscript, or index value, of one piece of information, we know that elements with the same subscript in the other arrays hold related information.

Parallel arrays need not hold the same data type. Because the arrays are declared separately, an array of **string**s could be parallel to an array of ***integer***s or an array of ***boolean***s. To continue the example, we could use a third array, parallel to the ***origins*** and ***dests*** arrays, to hold the flight numbers. If we call this array ***flightNums***, then ***flightNums[47]*** should hold the integer 190.

Parallel arrays, as their name implies, are structurally identical. That is, they have the same range of elements. For example, we could declare three parallel arrays as follows:

```
const
   maxFlights = 100;                          { max number of airline flights            }
type
   cityType = array[1..maxFlights] of string[3]; { holds a set of airport codes          }

   flightType = array[1..maxFlights] of integer;{ holds a set of flight numbers          }
{ mainline variables }
var
   origins,                                   { airport codes for originating cities     }
   dests: cityType;                           { codes for all destination cities         }
   flights: flightType;                       { all flight numbers                       }
```

The arrays ***flights***, ***origins***, and ***dests*** can be parallel because they each have the same range. Simply having the same range, however, does not mean that the arrays must be logically parallel. If a program establishes a logical correspondence between the arrays, then the arrays will be parallel in usage as well as in structure.

Suppose we have a data file that contains (in order) the origins, destinations, and flight numbers for each flight. The data file could look like this:

```
PVD
LAX
811
BOS
JFK
101
```

We could set up the program to read the first origin code into the first slot of the ***origins*** array, the first destination code into the first slot of the ***dests*** array, and the first flight number into the first slot of the ***flights*** array. Thus, ***origins[1]***, ***dests[1]***, and ***flights[1]*** all hold information about the same flight (see Figure 11.7). The procedure to read in information could be as follows:

```
const
   maxFlights = 100;                     { max number of airline flights     }

type
   cityType = array[1..maxFlights] of string[3];
                                         { holds a set of airport codes      }

   flightType = array[1..maxFlights] of integer;
                                         { holds a set of flight numbers     }

procedure ReadInfo(var origins,          { originating airport codes         }
   dests: cityType;                      { destination airport codes         }
   var flights: flightType;              { all flight records                }
   var flightInfo: text);                { data file of flight info          }

var
   curFlight: integer;                   { loop counter                      }

begin
   Reset(flightInfo, OldFileName('Please choose data file'));
   curFlight := 1;

   while (curFlight <= maxFlights) and not Eof(flightInfo) do
      begin

         { get flight info directly from data file }
         Readln(flightInfo, origins[curFlight] );
         Readln(flightInfo, dests[curFlight]);
```

```
            Readln(flightInfo, flights[curFlight]);

         { increase counter to go to next flight in list }
         curFlight := curFlight + 1

      end { while }
   end; { ReadInfo }
```

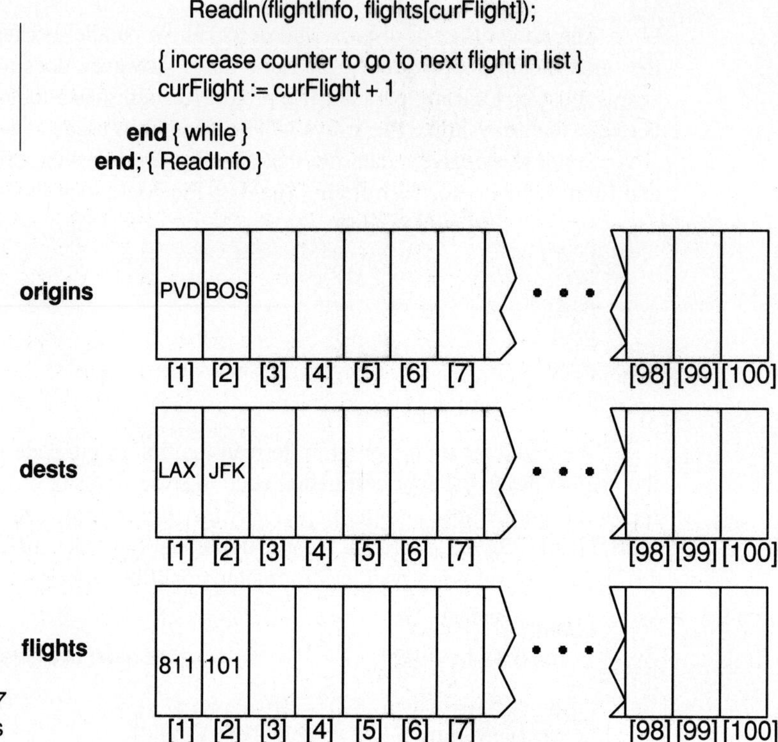

Figure 11.7
Parallel arrays

The following procedure shows another way of using parallel arrays. We can use a **for** loop to print a table of all the origins, destinations, and flight numbers of all the flights in the arrays.

```
procedure Print(origins,              { originating airport codes     }
                dests: cityType;      { destination airport codes     }
                flights: flightType); { all flight numbers            }
var
   current: integer;                  { loop counter                  }

begin
   for current := 1 to maxFlights do
      begin

         Write('Flight number ', flights[current]:4);
         Writeln(' goes from ', origins[current]:4, ' to ', dests[current]:4)

      end { for }
end; { Print }
```

This procedure prints out each flight's number, origin, and destination on the same line. Notice the use of the same subscript (***current***) to print out the same flight's information.

11.9 Multi-Dimensional Arrays

The arrays discussed so far have all been diagrammed as a single horizontal column of storage locations. Such linear representations show why those arrays are known as *one-dimensional* arrays, or *vectors*. Not all collections of data can be represented this way. For example, to show the positions of pieces in a chess game, you would want to use a grid of two dimensions, where every square is denoted by its row and its column. Arrays can be generalized to have two, three, or *n* dimensions. This section discusses two-dimensional arrays, but the ideas can be generalized to arrays of higher dimensions.

Suppose we want to represent in memory the origins and destinations where Turbulent Airlines flies. Specifically, we want to be able to determine quickly if there is a direct flight from Providence (PVD) to Sarasota (SRQ). We could use the parallel arrays from section 11.8, but first we would have to find all the occurrences of the string 'PVD' in the ***origins*** array. Then, for each occurrence, we would have to see if the corresponding element in the ***dest*** array contained the string 'SRQ'. Doing this type of searching is time consuming and unnecessary.

The problem is not the way we search for data; the problem is how we've *stored* the data. With pencil and paper, we might list the flights not in parallel columns but in a grid, as in Figure 11.8.

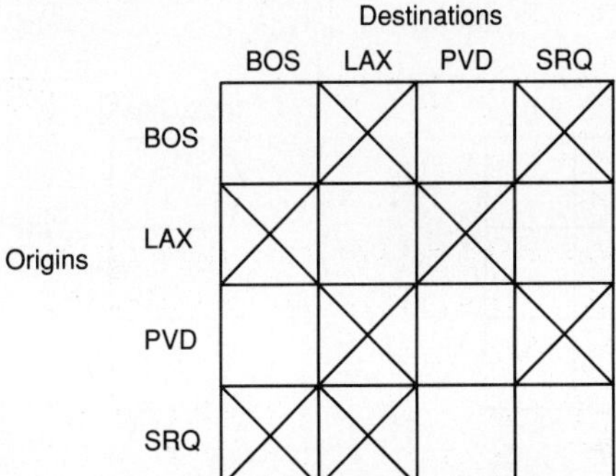

Figure 11.8
Airline flights grid

The columns and rows are the airport codes. The rows represent the origin cities and the columns represent the destination cities. Each X in the grid represents a flight from one city to another. If a square has no X, there is no direct flight between the locations. For example, Figure 11.8 shows that there is a flight from PVD to SRQ, but none from SRQ to PVD.

This grid is easily translated into a two-dimensional array. Each box in the grid is an element in the array. Instead of labeling the rows and columns with airport codes, though, we use numeric subscripts. Like one-dimensional arrays, all of the elements in a multi-dimensional array must have the same type. In the airline example above, each element can be represented as a ***boolean***. The element is TRUE if a direct flight exists; otherwise, the element is FALSE. Thus, in the two-dimensional array in Figure 11.9, the element in row [3], column [4] is TRUE.

Destinations

Origins	[1]	[2]	[3]	[4]
[1]	FALSE	TRUE	FALSE	TRUE
[2]	TRUE	FALSE	TRUE	FALSE
[3]	FALSE	TRUE	FALSE	TRUE
[4]	TRUE	TRUE	FALSE	FALSE

Figure 11.9 Boolean representation of airline flights grid

Therefore, assuming that the rows are the origins and the columns are the destinations, this means a flight exists from city 3 to city 4.

To declare a multi-dimensional array, we need to indicate the range in each dimension. This allows Pascal to reserve enough space in memory for all of the elements. To do this, we simply list the ranges, separated by commas, between the square brackets. For instance, the airline network can be reserved as shown in Figure 11.10.

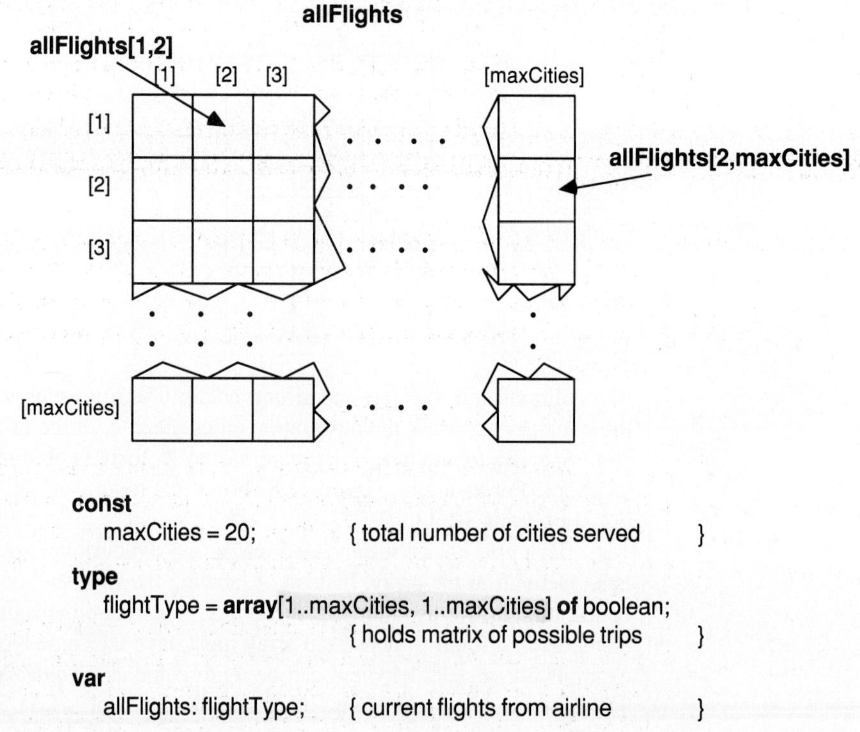

Figure 11.10 Two-dimensional array

```
const
   maxCities = 20;          { total number of cities served       }
type
   flightType = array[1..maxCities, 1..maxCities] of boolean;
                            { holds matrix of possible trips      }
var
   allFlights: flightType;  { current flights from airline        }
```

In the above declarations we have set up a data structure of booleans that will allow us to represent the flights.

Syntax Box 11.3
Declaring multi-dimensional arrays

Purpose To allow usage of arrays of more than one dimension

Syntax **var**

< array var > **: array[** < range 1 >, < range 2 >,... < range *n* > **] of**
< elem type > **;**

where < array var > is any legal variable identifier.

Each of the ranges (< range 1 >, < range 2 >,..., < range *n* >) takes the form < low bounds >**..**< up bounds >. < low bounds > and < up bounds > both must be ordinal type constants. < up bounds > must also be greater than < low bounds >. < low bounds > and < up bounds > represent, respectively, the lower and upper bounds of the particular range.

< elem type > is the data type of each individual element in the array. This type can be any predefined type (see Appendix A) or any type declared in the program's **type** declarations.

Usage The range of the array (< low bounds >**..**< up bounds >) says two things about the array: the number of subdivisions in the array and the legal values of the index to the array.

When referring to arrays, use the form:
< array name > [< index 1 >, < index 2 >,...,< index *n* >].

Each index must be in the range specified in the array declaration. For example, < index 1 > must be in the upper and lower bounds of < range 1 >. If any index is out of bounds, the program will halt.

In a one-dimensional array, we specify the array and a single subscript to reference any element. With a two-dimensional array, we have to specify two subscripts to gain access to an element. These two subscripts are separated by a comma. Thus, if there is a flight from city 3 to city 4, we can use the following assignment:

```
allFlights[3, 4] := TRUE;
```

The order of the indices is crucial. A reference to ***allflights[11,4]*** is not the same as a reference to ***allflights[4,11]***. One statement refers to the 11th row and 4th column of the grid; the other to the 4th row and 11th column. Both statements, however, are perfectly legal since both 4 and 11 are in the legal ranges.

The dimensions of a multi-dimensional array need not be specified with the same range, i.e., the array need not be square. For example, suppose you want to declare a two-dimensional array to represent prices of seats in a theatre. The theatre has 20 rows with 35 seats in every row. The following declaration shows how this can be done:

```
const
   numberRows = 20;          { number of rows in theatre           }
   seatsPerRow = 35;         { number of seats in each row          }

type
   seatsType = array[1..numberRows, 1..seatsPerRow] of real;
                             { holds value for each seat            }

var
   seating: seatsType;       { prices for each seat in theatre      }
```

11.10 Example Program

Using multi-dimensional arrays is similar to using a one-dimensional array. You can use random access or sequential access to manipulate the elements in any array. The following example uses both a two-dimensional and a one-dimensional array.

Consider a reservations clerk for Turbulent Airlines. A travel agent who calls the clerk usually wants to know two things: first, if Turbulent has a direct flight between two given cities, and second, if there is a flight, is there any room left on the plane. If the plane can accommodate the agent's customers, then the office will book the passengers on the plane.

The airline wants us to write a program so that a user can easily find out if a direct flight exists between two cities. If such a flight exists, the user should be able to find out how many passengers are currently booked on the flight. If there is room on the plane, the user should be able to update the current reservations.

For purposes of this example, we assume that the airline flies only one plane between any two points. We also assume that all of Turbulent's aircrafts are the same size — that is, all the planes hold the same number of passengers. Finally, we assume that all of the reservations are being made for the same day. While this example may not be very realistic by itself, it forms a basis for more realistic programs.

To begin the pseudocode, we think about the user interface. What will the user need to enter, and what output will result? First, we have to see if the flight exists at all. Then, if the flight is running, we have to determine how many seats are left. If the flight can fit the customers, then the reservations are updated. These processes are shown in the following pseudocode:

```
Ask user for origin code
WHILE more data to process DO
   BEGIN
      Ask user for destination code

      IF flight goes between origin and destination THEN
         BEGIN
            Ask user to enter number of seats requested
            IF customers can fit on plane THEN
               Add number of seats requested to plane's booking
```

```
                ELSE
                    Tell user that plane is booked full
            END { IF }
        ELSE
            Tell user that no flight exists
        Ask user for origin code
    END { WHILE }
```

We have designed the algorithm. Now, we should consider how to store the data. To do this, we have to figure out what information we actually need in the program. We need to know where Turbulent's flights go and the number of passengers currently booked on each flight. In addition, we need to know the maximum number of passengers that can be booked on any plane. This final piece of information can be represented by an integer constant.

From what we have seen in the last section, it seems reasonable to store the origins and destinations of the airline's flights in a two-dimensional array of booleans. We can then have a parallel two-dimensional array of integers representing the current number of passengers for each flight. Suppose we call the two two-dimensional arrays ***exist*** (for the two-dimensional array that tells where the flights go) and ***bookings*** (for the two-dimensional array that lists the number of passengers). Thus, if there is a flight from city 3 to city 4, we would set ***exist[3,4]*** to TRUE, and ***bookings[3,4]*** would have the number of passengers booked on the flight. Figure 11.11 shows what the arrays look like when they have some arbitrary values.

	[1]	[2]	[3]	[4]
[1]	T	F	F	T
[2]	T	F	F	F
[3]	F	T	T	T
[4]	T	T	T	F

exist

	[1]	[2]	[3]	[4]
[1]	35	0	0	0
[2]	53	0	0	0
[3]	0	61	87	31
[4]	5	18	0	0

booking

Figure 11.11
Data structures for reservation program

This solution does meet all the specifications. However, it is not the most efficient solution. When you are dealing with compound data structures, it is a good idea to reduce the number of storage places as much as possible. Let's see, then, if we can combine the two two-dimensional arrays. We can look at the information in another form by listing the values of the two arrays:

```
exist[1,1] = T          booking[1,1] = 35
exist[1,2] = F          booking[1,2] = 0
exist[1,3] = F          booking[1,3] = 0
exist[1,4] = T          booking[1,4] = 0
exist[2,1] = T          booking[2,1] = 53
...                     ...
```

What we are looking for is some method of combining information. By using this list, we may be able to find patterns in the storage and see if any pattern can be used to combine the arrays. From this list, we notice many zeros in the ***booking*** array. We ask ourselves, does each zero in ***booking*** correspond to a non-existent flight? We look carefully, and find this conjecture is false. Just because a position contains zero, though, we cannot assume that the corresponding position in ***exist*** is FALSE. What happens, though, when we go in the other direction? Is there any correlation between the value in a slot in ***exist*** and the corresponding position in ***booking***? If we look at all positions in ***exist*** that are set to FALSE, we see that the corresponding element in ***booking*** is set to 0.

This brings up the idea that we can just use the ***booking*** matrix. We need a way of differentiating between flights that exist but have no passengers and flights that do not exist at all. Since a flight must have a positive number of passengers, we can use a negative number to indicate where the flights do not exist. Thus, the zeroes in the ***booking*** matrix that correspond to FALSE values in the ***exist*** matrix can be changed to negative numbers. Figure 11.12 shows how to condense the two arrays into one.

	[1]	[2]	[3]	[4]
[1]	35	-1	-1	0
[2]	53	-1	-1	-1
[3]	-1	61	87	31
[4]	5	18	0	-1

booking

Figure 11.12 Revised data structure for reservation program

We can determine if a flight exists by seeing if ***booking[< origin city >, < destination city >]*** is a negative number. To do this, though, we need to specify the origin and destination cities as integers. We could ask the user to keep a list of city codes as follows:

SFO — 1
PVD — 2
SRQ — 3
CLE — 4
JFK — 5
...

Still, this is not the most user-friendly technique. We would like the user to enter the airport code and have the program translate the three-letter code into the subscript reference. Since the above list has a predetermined number of entries numbered consecutively, we can store them in an array. Thus, the user can type the string SFO, instead of 1, for San Francisco. Then the computer can look in an array. If SFO is stored in position 1, we assume that we want to use the subscript 1. This is using an array as a *lookup table.*

Having made these decisions about the data structures, we can revise the algorithm part of the pseudocode as follows:

```
Initialize data structures
Ask user for origin code
WHILE still more reservations to make DO
   BEGIN

      { Get trip requested by user }
      Ask user for destination code
      Translate codes using look up table

      IF flight goes between origin and destination THEN
         BEGIN
            Ask user to enter number of seats requested
            IF customers can fit on plane THEN
               Add number of seats requested to plane's booking
            ELSE
               Tell user that plane is booked full
         END { IF }
      ELSE
         Tell user that no flight exists

      Ask user for next origin code
   END { WHILE }
```

Another error condition may arise in the program. What if the user enters a city code that is not served by the airline? We can tell the user to enter another city code and not process the data unless the user has entered correct codes. By adding another branch to the program, we can complete the pseudocode:

```
Initialize data structures
Ask user for origin code
WHILE still more reservations to make DO
   BEGIN

      { Get trip requested by user }
      Ask user for destination code
      Translate codes using look up table

      IF user has entered legal codes THEN
         BEGIN
            IF flight goes between origin and destination THEN
               BEGIN
                  Ask user to enter number of seats requested
                  IF customers can fit on plane THEN
                     Add number of seats requested to plane's booking
                  ELSE
                     Tell user that plane is booked full
               END { IF }
```

```
            ELSE
                Tell user that no flight exists
         END { IF }
      ELSE
         Tell user that codes are not legal
      Ask user for next origin code
   END { WHILE }
```

To initialize the data structures, we need to know which flights exist. We assume that no flights exist at first, so we can set each element in the ***booking*** array to the negative-number indicator.

Since the airline's flights are unlikely to change, we can specify that the user enter them into a data file. From this file, we can read the number of cities served by the airline, the codes of those cities, and the origin and destination of each flight. For example, the following data file lists 5 cities and 3 flights.

```
5
SEA
MIA
HOU
LAX
DET
SEA
DET
HOU
MIA
LAX
DET
```

This file begins with the number 5, which designates the number of cities currently served by the airline. (We assume that this number will be no larger than 30 when we establish the data structures.) Then comes the list of the cities. We can load this list directly into the lookup table — the first city (SEA) occupies the first slot in the array and so on. Then come the origins and destinations of the flights. In the above file, DET is the last city in the lookup table. The three flights, then, are SEA to DET, HOU to MIA, and LAX to DET. Using this data, we can set the existing flights to 0. We can pseudocode the initialization this way:

```
{ Initialize data structures }
Get rid of garbage values in booking matrix
Open file for reading
Read num of cities
FOR each city DO
   Read code from data file to look up table
WHILE still more flights DO
   Read origin and destination code of each flight
```

The airport codes can be translated to integer subscripts with a variation of the ***Find*** procedure seen earlier. We do not want simply to indicate whether or not we have found an airplane code — we need to know *where* we found it. Thus, instead of returning the boolean value TRUE if the key is found, we return the subscript of its position in the array. If the key is not there, we return the value 0. (Think back to the ***Pos*** function in Chapter 8. The function returns the value where a pattern is found in a string and returns 0 if the pattern does not exist.)

Code 11.2 Program *Reservations*

```
{ Program Reservations      D. Niguidula      October 12                }
{ This program keeps track of the current reservations on               }
{ an airline. First, the number of cities served, the airport          }
{ codes for the airline's cities, and the origins and destinations     }
{ of each of the airline's flights are read from a file.               }
{ The program allows the user to request reservations on               }
{ a flight between any two cities. Assuming that the flight            }
{ exists, the program then determines if there is any room             }
{ left on the flight. The user may enter the number of                 }
{ seats to reserve. If the customer's request can be                   }
{ accommodated, then the reservations are made. The program            }
{ exits when the user enters a sentinel code for the originating city. }

program Reservations;

  const
    sentinel = 'XXX';            { indicates end of user input          }
    maxCities = 20;              { maximum number of cities served      }
    noFlight = -1;               { indicates that a flight does not exist }
    notFound = -1;               { indicates unsuccessful search        }
    maxSeats = 125;              { total number of seats per plane      }

  type
    lookupType = array[1..maxCities] of string[3];
                                 { holds airport codes }

    bookingType = array[1..maxCities, 1..maxCities] of integer;
                                 { holds information for each possible flight }

  var
    lookup : lookupType;              { airport codes for airline's cities   }
    booking : bookingType;            { current reservations for each flight }
    origCode, destCode : string[3];   { airport codes                        }
    origIndex, destIndex,             { numeric representation of airports   }
    numCities : integer;              { number of cities currently served    }

{ Procedure InitFlights                                          }
{ This procedure initializes the data structure that holds the  }
```

Code 11.2 (continued)

```
{ flights. The program  initially assumes that no flights exist.       }
{ Calls: none               Called By: Mainline                        }

   procedure InitFlights (var booking : bookingType);
                                        { current reservations          }

      var
         initOrig, initDest : integer;     { loop counters              }

   begin
      for initOrig := 1 to maxCities do
         for initDest := 1 to maxCities do
            booking[initOrig, initDest] := noFlight
   end; { InitFlights }

{ Function Find     }
{ In the program, each airport code is represented by a unique          }
{ number. This function uses the lookup table to translate any          }
{ airport code to its corresponding number. If the function             }
{ finds the key value in the table, its code (the array subscript)      }
{ is returned. If the key is not found, then the function returns       }
{ a signal value indicating that the airport is not served by the       }
{ airline .                                                              }
{ Returns: the airport code or a signal that the key was not found.     }
{ Calls: none            Called by: ReadData,  Mainline                 }

   function Find (key : string;          { value to find in lookup table      }
         table : lookupType;             { list of all airport codes          }
         numCities : integer) :          { number of cities served            }
      integer;                           { Returned value                     }

      var
         curElem : integer;              { current position in search         }
         done : boolean;                 { indicates end of search            }
         whereFound : integer;           { temp var for returned value        }

   begin
      done := FALSE;
      curElem := 1;

      while not done do
         if curElem > numCities then  { end of list has been reached }
            begin
               done := TRUE;
               whereFound := notFound
            end
         else if table[curElem] = key then  { key has been found }
            begin
               done := TRUE;
```

Code 11.2
(continued)

```
                whereFound := curElem
            end { else }
        else                        { move to next element }
            curElem := curElem + 1;

        Find := whereFound
    end; { Find }

{ Function Ltrim and Function Trim                                    }
{  The following two routines remove blanks from a string.            }
{ Ltrim removes the leading blanks from a string, and Trim            }
{ removes the trailing blanks. The length of the string returned      }
{ by either function is changed ( unless no blanks were removed).     }
{ Called by : Mainline          Calls: none                           }

    function Ltrim (str : string) : string;  { removes leading blanks  }
    begin
        while Pos(' ', str) = 1 do
            str := Omit(str, 1, 1);
        Ltrim := str
    end; { Ltrim }

    function Trim (str : string) : string;        { removes trailing blanks }
    begin
        if str <> '' then
            while (str[Length(str)] = ' ') and (Length(str) > 1)do
                str := Copy(str, 1, Length(str) - 1);
        if str = ' ' then
            Trim :=''
        else
            Trim := str
    end; {  Trim  }

{ Procedure ReadData                                                    }
{  This procedure receives the information from a data file.            }
{ The user is first asked to specify the file. In this file, the        }
{ following format is expected.  The first line should contain the      }
{ current number of cities served by the airline. Then, the next        }
{ lines should contain the codes for each of the cities served.         }
{ Following that list, the rest of the file should contain the flights. }
{ Each flight is represented by two lines, the origin and the destination }
{ airport codes, in that order.  The <eof> marker denotes the end of    }
{ the list of flights.                                                  }
{  If the file contains an origin or destination code that has not      }
{ been specified, the program will print an error message.              }
{ Called by: mainline          Calls: Find                              }

    procedure ReadData (var booking : bookingType; { current reservations    }
            var lookup : lookupType;               { list of airport codes    }
            var numCities : integer);              { number of cities served  }
```

Code 11.2 (continued)

```
    var
        flightData : text;                  { file buffer for input              }
        userFileName : string[80];          { file name specified by user        }
        origCity, destCity : string[3];     { airport codes                      }
        origCode, destCode,                 { numeric representation of airports }
        cityCtr : integer;                  { loop counter                       }

  begin
    repeat { choose file for input }
        userFileName := OldFileName('Please choose the airport file: ');
    until userFileName <> '';
    Reset(flightData, userFileName);

  { input number of cities and airport codes }
    Readln(flightData, numCities);
    for cityCtr := 1 to numCities do
        Readln(flightData, lookup[cityCtr]);

  { get flights }
    while not Eof(flightData) do
        begin
            Readln(flightData, origCity);
            Readln(flightData, destCity);
            origCode := Find(origCity, lookup, numCities);
            destCode := Find(destCity, lookup, numCities);

        { Check if codes are legal }
            if (origCode <> notFound) and (destCode <> notFound) then
                booking[origCode, destCode] := 0

            else { print error message }
                begin
                    Writeln('Error in data file: ');
                    if (origCode = notFound) then
                        Writeln(origCity : 3, ' is not served by the airline.');
                    if (destCode = notFound) then
                        Writeln(destCity : 3, ' is not served by the airline.')
                end { else }

        end; { while }
    Writeln
  end; { ReadData }

{ Procedure Print                                                    }
{  This procedure outputs the current reservations on each of the    }
{ airline's flights. The routine produces output for only those flights }
{ that exist.                                                        }
{ Calls: none    Called By: Mainline                                 }
```

Code 11.2
(continued)

```
procedure Print (lookup : lookupType;             { airport codes          }
    bookings : bookingType;                         { current reservations   }
    numCities : integer);                           { num of cities served   }

    var
        curOrig, curDest : integer;         { current origin and destination   }

begin
    Writeln;
    Writeln('          CURRENT RESERVATIONS    ');
    Writeln;
    for curOrig := 1 to numCities do
        begin

            Writeln('FROM  ', lookup[curOrig], ':');
            for curDest := 1 to numCities do
                if bookings[curOrig, curDest] <> noFlight then
                    Writeln('    TO ', lookup[curDest], ': ',
                        bookings[curOrig, curDest] : 4)

        end { for }
end; { Print }

{ Procedure Reserve                                                    }
{ This procedure allows the user to reserve seats on a flight.         }
{ First, the procedure determines if the flight is full. If it is      }
{ full, then an appropriate message is printed. If it isn't full,      }
{ the program asks the user to enter the number of seats to            }
{ reserve. If the user's request can be accommodated, the              }
{ current reservation list is updated.                                 }
{ Called by: Mainline          Calls: none                             }

procedure Reserve (var curBooking : integer; { reservation on flight        }
        lookup : lookupType);                   { list of airport codes        }

    var
        seatsRequested : integer;           { number of seats requested by user }

begin
    if curBooking = noFlight then
        Writeln(' The airline does not fly this route.')
    else if curBooking = maxSeats then
        Writeln(' The flight is booked full')
    else
        begin
            Writeln(' There are ', maxSeats - curBooking : 3, ' seats left.');
            Write('How many seats would you like to reserve? ');
            Readln(seatsRequested);
            if curBooking + seatsRequested > maxSeats then
                Writeln(' There are not enough seats on the flight.')
```

Code 11.2 (continued)

```
            else
              begin
                Writeln(' ', seatsRequested : 3, ' seats have been reserved.');
                curBooking := curBooking + seatsRequested
              end { else }
          end { else }
      end; { Reserve }

{ Procedure Mainline                                                    }
{  The mainline begins by calling procedures to initialize the data    }
{ structures. Then the user is asked to enter the origin and destination }
{ codes. If the user enters the sentinel for the origin, then the program }
{ halts. Otherwise, the program translates the airport codes into      }
{ numeric codes. If a flight does not exist, an error message is printed. }
{ If the flight does exist, the reservations are made.                 }
{ Calls : Initialize, ReadData, Find, Reserve, Ltrim, Trim, Print      }

begin
  InitFlights(booking);
  ReadData(booking, lookup, numCities);

  Write('Please enter originating city or ', sentinel : 3, ' to exit: ');
  Readln(origCode);
  origCode := Ltrim(Trim(origCode));

  while origCode <> sentinel do
    begin
      Write('Please enter destination city : ');
      Readln(destCode);
      destCode := Ltrim(Trim(destCode));

      origIndex := Find(origCode, lookup, numCities);
      destIndex := Find(destCode, lookup, numCities);

      if (origIndex <> notFound) and (destIndex <> notFound) then
        Reserve(booking[origIndex, destIndex], lookup)
      else
        begin
          if origIndex = notFound then
            Writeln(origCode, ' is not a legal airport code');
          if destIndex = notFound then
            Writeln(destCode, ' is not a legal airport code')
        end; { else }

      Writeln;
      Write('Please enter originating city or ', sentinel : 3, ' to exit: ');
      Readln(origCode);
      origCode := Ltrim(Trim(origCode))
    end; { while }

  Print(lookup, booking, numCities)
end. { Reservations }
```

```
6
BOS
CLE
SRQ
HOU
LAX
SEA
BOS
SEA
MIA
BOS
HOU
LAX
HOU
SEA
LAX
BOS
SEA
CLE
BOS
CLE
CLE
HOU
```

Figure 11.13a
Input to program *Reservations*

```
Error in data file:
MIA is not served by the airline.

Please enter originating city or XXX to exit: BOS
Please enter destination city : CLE
 There are 125 seats left.
How many seats would you like to reserve? 8
   8 seats have been reserved.

Please enter originating city or XXX to exit: CLE
Please enter destination city : SRQ
 The airline does not fly this route.

Please enter originating city or XXX to exit: LAX
Please enter destination city : BOS
 There are 125 seats left.
How many seats would you like to reserve? 3
   3 seats have been reserved.

Please enter originating city or XXX to exit: BOS
Please enter destination city : CLE
 There are 117 seats left.
How many seats would you like to reserve? 117
 117 seats have been reserved.

Please enter originating city or XXX to exit: BOS
Please enter destination city : CLE
 The flight is booked full
```

Figure 11.13b
Output of program Reservations

```
Please enter originating city or XXX to exit: LAX
Please enter destination city : BOS
 There are 122 seats left.
How many seats would you like to reserve? 125
 There are not enough seats on the flight.

Please enter originating city or XXX to exit: SEA
Please enter destination city : CLE
 There are 125 seats left.
How many seats would you like to reserve? 45
  45 seats have been reserved.

Please enter originating city or XXX to exit: XXX

              CURRENT RESERVATIONS

FROM  BOS:
     TO CLE:  125
     TO SEA:    0
FROM  CLE:
     TO HOU:    0
FROM  SRQ:
FROM  HOU:
     TO LAX:    0
     TO SEA:    0
FROM  LAX:
     TO BOS:    3
FROM  SEA:
     TO CLE:   45
```

Figure 11.13b (continued)

11.11 Chapter Summary

This chapter looked at the first of the compound data structures. Arrays are used to handle a list of identical items that have the same purpose. An array can be used when you know the maximum number of elements the array can hold and that all the elements have the same data type. Single elements in an array can be manipulated by identifying the name of the array and its subscript or index. Elements in an array can be manipulated through either random access, where the order of manipulation is arbitrary, or sequential access, where the order of manipulation is consecutive.

type declarations allow you to create a template for a data structure. You can create your own data types from the data types that Pascal has previously defined. You can also declare data types that Pascal would normally recognize (such as an array), but which are cumbersome to repeat. Array types *must* be used to pass arrays as parameters.

Arrays can also be used in parallel. In a set of parallel arrays, the information indicated by a subscript in one array is related to information indicated by the same subscript in another array.

Finally, you can also have multi-dimensional arrays. These are used when each element in the array should have multiple indexes. A common example of the two-dimensional array is a checkerboard, where every square is denoted by its row and its column. Again, these arrays hold identical elements and each element shares a common purpose in the program.

11.12 Exercises

Understanding Concepts

1. Consider the following declarations and mainline variables:

```
type
    figure = integer;
    number = figure;

{ mainline variables }
var
    digit: figure;
    answer: integer;
    first: char;
    operand: number;

procedure Calculate(first: figure;
    second: integer);
begin
...
end; { Calculate }
```

   Which of the following are legal calls to ***Calculate***? What is wrong with the others?

   a. Calculate(digit, answer);
   b. Calculate(digit * answer, operand);
   c. Calculate(answer, digit);
   d. Calculate(first, digit);

2. What, if anything, is wrong with the following declarations?

   a.
```
type
    list = array[5..1] of integer;
```

   b.
```
type
    nums = array[–3..3] of real;
```

   c.
```
procedure Sort( var items: array[1..20] of integer);
```

   d.
```
var
    codes: array['a'..'z'] of integer;
```

   e.
```
const
    size = 8;
type
    board = array[1..size] [1..size] of char;
```

f. ```
function totals(num1, num2, num3: real):
   array[1..3] of boolean;
```

g. ```
const
   left = 15;
   right = 5;
type
   extra = array[left..right] of boolean;
```

h. ```
type
   dozen = array[1..6, 7..12] of integer;
```

3. In the code in Section 11.6, why couldn't you use the condition

   **while** (curElem <= maxFlights) **and** (flightNums[curElem] = key) **do**

   instead of

   **while not** done **do** ?

4. The following procedure performs what is called an *insertion sort*. In general, an insertion sort examines a list of items one at a time. When you are looking at item *n* in the array, you assume that the first *n*–1 items in the array are in sorted order. The algorithm then finds the correct position for item *n*. Item *n* is "inserted" into the array after all numbers that are higher than item *n* are moved one position over. When item *n* is placed in its correct position, the array then contains *n* sorted items. This procedure sorts five items. Note that the array contains a 0 subscript. This element contains a dummy value that is smaller than all the other values to be sorted.

```
const
   maxNums = 5;

type
   list = array[0..maxNums] of integer;

procedure Sort(var numbers: list);   { the list of nums to sort   }

var
   mover,   { number being inserted   }
   position,   { loop counter to check and move nums   }
   counter: integer;   { loop counter for sorting numbers   }

begin
   numbers[0] := -1; { set dummy number to smallest value }
   for counter := 2 to maxNums do
      begin
         mover := numbers[counter];
         position := counter;
```
```

```
            while numbers[position -1] > mover do
              begin
                numbers[position] := numbers[position-1];
                position := position -1
              end; { while }
            numbers[position ] := mover
        end { for }
    end; { Sort }
```

If ***Sort*** is called with the initial array of

[0]	[1]	[2]	[3]	[4]	[5]
-1	44	2	16	9	37

what does ***numbers*** contain at the moment that ***counter*** is assigned the value 4 (i.e., at the top of the **for** loop)? What does ***numbers*** contain when ***counter*** is assigned the value 5?

5. Write a header comment for the following procedure:

```
const
  maxPoints = 30;                    { max number of pts in object  }
type
  relCoords = array[1..maxPoints] of integer;
procedure MakeObject(horizList,
                                     { list of relative horiz coords  }
        vertList: relCoords);        { list of relative vert coords   }

var
    horiz, vert: integer;            { user selected starting point  }
    ctr: integer;                    { loop counter                   }

begin

  repeat
    GetMouse(horiz, vert);
  until Button;

  MoveTo(horiz, vert);
  for ctr := 1 to maxPoints do
    Move(horizList[ctr], vertList[ctr])
end; { MakeObject }
```

6. Given the following arrays:

Mozart	Bach	Beatles	Bartlett	**loves**
4	1	3	2	**order**
[1]	[2]	[3]	[4]	array subscripts

and assuming that ***ctr*** is a variable of type ***integer***, what do the following fragments produce?

a.
```
for ctr := 1 to 4 do
    Writeln(loves[ctr]);
```

b.
```
for ctr := 4 downto 1 do
    Writeln(order[ctr]);
```

c.
```
for ctr := 1 to 4 do
    Writeln(loves[order[ctr]]);
```

7. Document the following program:

```
program Concept7;

var
   most : array[0..9] of integer;
   key: integer;
   ctr: integer;
   dataFile: text;

begin
   Reset(dataFile);
   Readln(dataFile, key);

   while not Eof(dataFile) do
      begin
         if most[key mod 10] > key then
            most[key mod 10] := key;
         Readln(dataFile, key)
      end; { while }

   for ctr := 0 to 9 do
      Writeln(key[ctr])
end. { program }
```

8. The local actors' guild wants to keep track of the number of performers in three categories:

   1. sex: male and female
   2. best talent: drama, comedy, singing, dancing
   3. age: less than 13, 13–17, 18–25, 26–35, 36–45, 46–60, over 60

   Write a declaration for a multi-dimensional array of integers to hold this information. Then, given this declaration, write code that prints the number of

   a. male comedians between 36 and 45
   b. female performers over 25
   c. singers
   d. dancers who are under 18

9. What is wrong with the following code?

```
{ A group of 5 artists take turns hosting a weekly gathering. This        }
{ program prints the host for each of the 12 weeks in the season.        }

program DetermineHosts;
type
    artType = array[1..5] of string[15]; { list of names                   }

var
    artists: artType;                    { list of artists in group        }
    ctr: integer;                        { loop counter                    }

{ Mainline: Initialize array and print host for each of 12 weeks          }
begin
  artist[1] := 'Angela';
  artist[2] := 'Pablo';
  artist[3] := 'Jean-Claude';
  artist[4] := 'Juanita';
  artist[5] := 'Seymour';

  for ctr := 1 to 12 do
    Writeln('Week #', ctr:2, ':', artist[ctr mod 5], ' ''s hangout.')
end. { Program }
```

Coding Exercises

1. Given the declarations:

```
const
    edge = 8;

type
    side = array[1..edge] of integer;
    complete = array[1..edge] of side;
    allIn1 = array[1..edge, 1..edge] of integer;

var
    moves: complete;
    matrix: allIn1;
```

write a procedure that prints out all the values of ***moves***. Write another procedure that prints out all the values of ***matrix***.

2. Write a procedure that multiplies two 3 x 3 matrices. When multiplying matrices *A* and *B*, the element in row *r* and column *c* of the product (*AB*) is found by using the following formula:

$$A_{r1}B_{1c} + A_{r2}B_{2c} + A_{r3}B_{3c} = AB_{rc}$$

The resulting matrix should be returned to the caller.

3. Given an array of six team names, write a procedure that prints all the games in a round-robin tournament (a tournament in which each team plays every other team exactly once).

4. Given two arrays, one of which contains the strings "John," "Paul," "George," and "Ringo," and the other of which contains the strings "Yoko," "Linda," "Krishna," and "Barbara," write a procedure that prints all the possible pairings for square dances. That is, you should print all combinations where each person in one array is paired with someone in the other.

5. Write two procedures: one that allows the user to enter an FM frequency (ranging from 87.9 to 108.1) and see the call letters for that frequency, and another that allows the user to enter the call letters and see the frequency.

6. Write a function that performs the same operation as the string function ***Pos*** but receives parameters that are arrays of characters instead of strings.

7. Write a procedure that receives a parameter ***english3*** of type ***class***. The type ***class*** has been defined as **array*[1..24]* of string*[40]***. In the array, ***english3[1]*** contains the first name in alphabetical order; ***english3[24]*** contains the last name in the order; all the other names are sorted in between. Print the class list in four columns in which the names are in alphabetical order:

Berry, C.	Grant, C.	Nelson, P.	Ridgeway, S.
Day, D.	Holly, B.	Presley, E.	Rydell, B.

8. Write a procedure that creates a connect-the-dots puzzle. The user should first pick a series of points in the Drawing window; as the points are chosen, they are numbered on the screen. After the user picks the last point (by choosing a pixel within two pixels of the first point), the dots should be connected in order.

9. Write a procedure that has the following header:

```
type
    voteType = array[1..15] of integer;        { list of votes      }

{ This function calculates a point total by giving 15 points for     }
{ each first place vote, 14 for each second place vote, etc.         }

function Tally(votes: voteType):    { votes[1] contains num        }
         integer;                   { of first place votes,        }
                                    { votes[2] contains num        }
                                    { of second place votes, etc.  }
```

Programming Problems

1. Revise the spelling correction program (Chapter 9, programming problem 2) by reading the dictionary from the file into parallel arrays. Assume that the dictionary has no more than forty entries.

2. Maintain a top-40 list. Your program should use an input file that lists last week's top 40 songs. Each line of the file contains one song, and the songs are in order from 1 to 40. After the file has been read, the user is asked where each of last week's 40 songs is placed on this week's list. The user either enters a number from 1 to 40, indicating the song's position, or 0, indicating that the song is no longer on the chart. After moving last week's songs, the user should be asked to enter the remaining songs on the chart. Finally, the new top 40 should be stored in a file, including the song name and its position on both this week's and last week's chart. For example, the line

```
1 3 Where's the Beat?
```

indicates that the song "Where's the Beat?" is the number 1 song this week and was the number 3 song last week.

3. Write a program to draw and number a crossword puzzle board. Start with a 12 x 12 grid. Your program should first read the contents of a file. The file contains two integers per line; each line represents the horizontal and vertical coordinates of the black squares in the grid. You should then place a number at the beginning of each word in the puzzle, starting at the first row and moving from left to right. Words begin immediately to the left and immediately below each square. Words also begin at the top and left borders. Thus, a file that begins with:

```
5 1
8 1
12 1
1 2
5 2
4 3
```

defines the top of the following puzzle:

1	2	3	4		5	6		7	8	9	
	10				11		12				13
14				15							

4. Write a program that keeps score in a bowling game. In each of the first nine frames, the user gets two chances to knock down ten pins. If the user strikes (knocks down all ten on the first roll), the score for the frame is 10 plus the pins on the next two rolls. If the user spares (all ten pins in two rolls), the score is 10 plus the pins on the next roll. If the user opens (less than 10 pins in the frame), the score is the number of pins knocked down.

A user who opens the tenth (and last) frame with a strike gets two extra rolls. A user who makes a spare in the tenth gets one extra roll.

Your program should print the score, frame by frame, whenever a frame is completed. A strike is represented by an X; a spare by a /. (The X and / are placeholders and thus are in the output only when the extra rolls have not yet been made.)

For example, if the user starts with a strike in the first two frames, scores an 8-spare in the third, and a 6-3 open in the fourth, the output should look like this:

(Output after frame 1):	X
(Output after frame 2):	X X
(Output after frame 3):	28 48 8/
(Output after frame 4):	28 48 64 73

5. The Post Office wants to know which zip codes are getting the most use. Write a program that compares the usage of 5- and 9-digit zip codes. Your program will read a set of zip codes from a file. The program should determine how many times each zip code appears and should also compute the total number of both types of zip codes. Assume that no more than a total of ten unique zip codes will appear.

6. Write a layout program that allows the user to delete, as well as draw, rectangles and circles. If the user chooses the Delete button, she should then click on the shape to be removed. If the user selects a point where two shapes overlap, the shape that was added more recently should be removed. Also, after the shape is deleted, all the shapes should be redrawn.

7. In the game of Scrabble™, the letters are distributed on the tiles as follows:

A-9	F-2	K-1	P-2	U-4	Z-1
B-2	G-3	L-4	Q-1	V-2	
C-2	H-2	M-2	R-6	W-2	
D-4	I-9	N-6	S-4	X-1	
E-12	J-1	O-8	T-6	Y-2	

(We are ignoring the two blanks in the set.) Write a program where the user can perform two commands:

a. The user can enter a play, which reduces the number of letters in the distribution. For example, if the user enters the play KUMQUAT, the U distribution should be decreased by 2, while the K, M, Q, A and T distributions should each be decreased by 1.

b. The user can ask to see how many tiles of a given letter remain.

8. Write a program that asks a user to enter the monthly guava production for a country over a twelve-month period. Then, depending on the user's choice, show the data as a bar chart or as a line graph.

9. In a popular board game, the object is to answer questions in six different categories. Assume that you have six files of questions and answers (one for each category; the format of the files is up to you). The user first indicates a category and then answers a question that has been read from the appropriate file. The user can ask for categories in any order; the only restriction is that a user who has correctly answered a question in one category may not choose that category again. The program ends when the user decides to quit or correctly answers questions in all the categories.

10. Write a program that prints all possible class schedules in a six-period school day. The input will come from the keyboard; the user should first enter the periods in which each of the six courses (History, English, Math, Science, Lunch, Phys.Ed.) will be offered. Each schedule must contain each of the six classes.

12

Records

We first introduced the idea of storing and manipulating information in Pascal by using atomic variables. Then we found that the composite data type array could be used to store and manipulate many values of the same type. Now we will examine how values of *different* types can be grouped in a single data structure called a *record* and how these new units of storage can be further grouped together.

As you have seen, arrays are used for keeping related information together and providing easy access to that information. Instead of remembering 100 different variable names for 100 pieces of information of the same type, say 100 names in a class, you have to remember only one name for the group. From there, you can refer to any given element by its subscript.

Chapter 11 showed an example of how to store origins, destinations, and flight numbers of airplane flights in three parallel arrays. To print all the information about any particular flight, we had to gain access to three different arrays. Suppose, instead, that we had 30 pieces of information for each flight, including such information as pilot, times of departure and arrival, and type of airplane. We would need thirty parallel arrays to store all the information about every flight. Some of these arrays are illustrated in Figure 12.1.

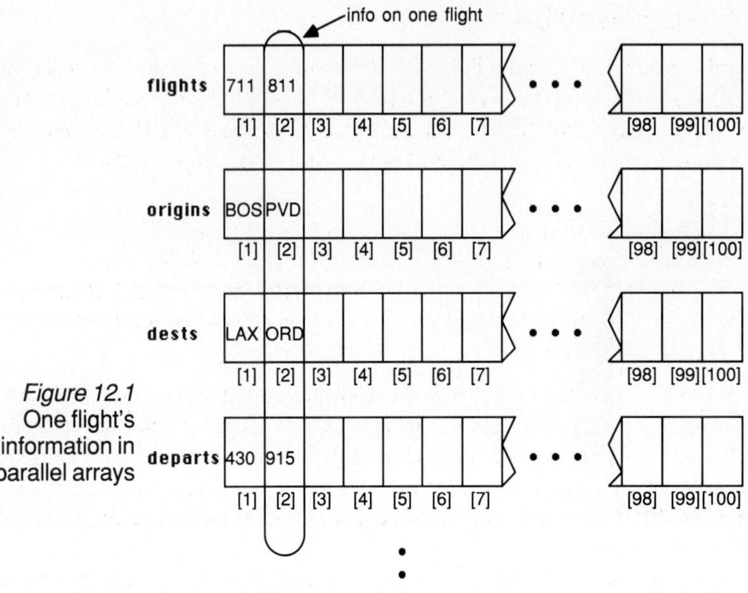

Figure 12.1
One flight's information in parallel arrays

The information about one flight appears at the same subscript in each array. This means that we need to list thirty array elements to refer to any one flight's information. While we can use the same subscript when referring to each array, we still have to name all the arrays.

Pascal provides the record data type to group related information together under one name. Unlike arrays, however, this information need not be of the same type. Thus, the 30 parallel arrays condenses to a single array of records, as shown in Figure 12.2.

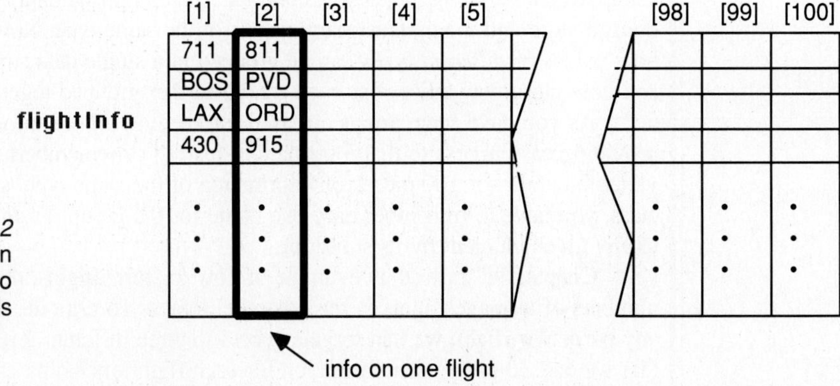

Figure 12.2
Flight information condensed into records

You will see how to create a collection of records later in this chapter. First, though, let's look at how you can work with a single record.

12.1 Record Variables

A record is a block of storage holding a group of disparate elements, called *fields*. Suppose we want to form a record for each of fifty club members. Each record can contain three fields: one for the name, one for the phone number, and one for the membership number. A typical record data type declaration follows:

```
type
   member = record                         { club member                  }
         name: string[40];                 { name of member in club       }
         phone: string[15];                { phone number of club member  }
         membership: integer               { membership num of member     }
      end; { member }
```

We use a **type** declaration for the record in the same way that we use **type**s for arrays. While the type name is used in variable and parameter declarations, the fields specified in the record's **type** declaration can be used in assignment statements and expressions. Notice that the fields are of different types; these types are noted after the field names. The declaration of fields looks very much like the declaration of variables and parameters.

The above **type** declaration creates a template for a record that has three fields. Because the number of fields in a record can vary, Pascal uses the reserved word **end** to indicate the end of the field list. Now that the type ***member*** has been declared, it can be used just like any other data type. For example, we can declare a variable called ***clubMember*** as follows:

```
var
   clubMember : member;                    { information on a single member }
```

The declaration of ***clubMember*** can also be rewritten as:

```
var
   clubMember : record                     { club member info             }
         name: string[40];                 { name of member in club       }
         phone: string[15];                { phone number of club member  }
         membership: integer               { membership num of member     }
      end; { clubMember }
```

Typically, however, record data types are almost always given a type declaration before they are used in variable declarations.

All the information in a record is held under a single variable name. Usually, though, we want to access a single field in a record. For example, if we want to input a string into the ***phone*** field of the record declared above, we use the statements:

```
Write('Please input the member's phone number: ');
Readln(clubMember.phone);
```

We gain access to the field of a record by specifying the record name (in the above example, ***clubMember***), followed by a period (.) and the field name (***phone***), as shown in Figure 12.3.

clubMember	
<string>	**clubMember.name**
<string>	**clubMember.phone**
<integer>	**clubMember.membership**

Figure 12.3 Record ***clubMember***

Using this two-component naming scheme is called specifying the *fully qualified* name. Fully qualified names start with the name of the composite data structure. From there, punctuation indicates which parts of the data structure you want to work with. We saw a similar scheme when we dealt with arrays: the array variable came first, followed by the subscript number.

The < record >.< field > notation is similar to using < last name >, < first name > notation to specify people's names. The < last name > indicates a family; the < first name > indicates a particular member in that family.

Imagine all the people in the world sitting in alphabetical order in a room. (Let's not worry about where we get a room of that size...yet... .) To find 'McCall, Leslie J.', you can begin by going to the part of the room with the people whose last name is McCall. You still have a sizable group who meet this first qualification. Next, out of all those people whose last name is McCall, you find all the Leslies. You have limited the group even further. Then, of all the Leslie McCalls, you find those who have the middle initial J. If the field still isn't narrowed down to one, you can use more qualifiers, such as date of birth or full middle names. Eventually, you can find that one person in the entire universe of people.

This scheme — starting with the largest set of items and breaking it down into smaller subsets — is how we create fully qualified names. We will see, in the next section, how to find a single field in an array of records. No matter how complex the data structures become (e.g., an array of records that have fields containing two-dimensional arrays), we can always find a single component by starting at the highest level of grouping and working down.

In addition to assigning to individual fields in a record, we can assign an entire record at once to another record of the same type. Pascal will automatically copy the individual fields. For example, suppose membership numbers for the club change every year. If we have two variables and field assignment statements written as follows:

```
var
   lastYear, thisYear: member;          { info for two years }
begin
   lastYear.name := 'Carrie Tower';
   lastYear.phone := '555-8315';
   lastYear.membership := 1586;
   ...
```

we can use the assignment statement

```
   thisYear := lastYear;
```

to copy the contents of ***lastYear*** into ***thisYear***. This statement assigns the values 'Carrie Tower', '555-8315', and 1586 to the fields ***thisYear.name***, ***thisYear.phone***, and ***thisYear.membership***, respectively. In effect, ***thisYear*** has become a copy of ***lastYear***. Now, all we have to do to update the membership number is change the contents of the field ***thisYear.membership***:

```
thisYear.membership := 2784;
```

In the same way that we passed an entire array as a parameter, we would like to be able to pass an entire record. For example, using the above declarations, if you wanted to pass a member's name, phone, and membership number as parameters to a procedure, you would need to pass only that member's record.

```
procedure PrintInfo(applicantInfo: member);
begin
   Writeln('Applicant''s name: ', applicantInfo.name);
   Writeln('Membership number: ', applicantInfo.membership:6);
   Writeln('Applicant's phone: ', applicantInfo.phone)
end; { PrintInfo }
```

Syntax Box 12.1
Declaration of records

Purpose To group related information in blocks of storage

Syntax

```
type
   < record type > = record
         < field list 1 > : < type >;
         < field list 2 > : < type >;
         ...
         < field list n > : < type >
      end;

var
   < record name > : < record type >;
```

where < record type > is the type defined for the record structure.

< record name > is any legal Pascal identifier name.

< field list 1 >,< field list 2 >,...,< field list *n* > are lists of the fields within the record. The names of the fields within each list are separated by commas.

< type > is the data type of the field.

Usage The syntax used to refer to the field of a record is:
< record name >.< field name >

Records are used to group non-homogenous pieces of information together. For instance, a record can be used to store two strings, a boolean, and an array of integers under a single name.

The above procedure received only one parameter, but inside the procedure, we could refer to the record parameter's component fields. Notice that the field names ***name***, ***membership***, and ***phone*** *did not* have to be declared in the procedure statement. Since ***applicantInfo*** is a record of type ***member***, it is known to contain a ***name*** field, a ***membership*** field, and a ***phone*** field. The field names in a record are analogous to the subscripts of an array; both refer to elements of a compound variable.

You do not have to pass entire data structures. Just as a single element of the two-dimensional array was passed in Chapter 11's Reservation program (see the Mainline's call to the ***Reserve*** procedure), you can pass any field of a record as a parameter. As usual, the formal parameter type and the actual parameter have to match. Thus, if you want to pass a field of a record, you need to declare the formal parameter as the field's data type. For example, to input the ***name*** field of the ***applicantInfo*** in a procedure, we can write:

```
procedure ReadName(var newName: string); { name read from input }

begin
   Write('What is the member''s name? ');
   Readln(newName)
end; { ReadName }

...
procedure GetInfo(var applicantInfo: member);
   { entire record on applicant }

begin
   ...
   ReadName(applicantInfo.name);
   ...
end; { GetInfo }
```

Notice that in ***GetInfo***, no variables or parameters of type **string** have been declared. However, since the ***name*** field of ***applicantInfo*** is a **string**, it can be passed legally as a parameter to ***ReadName***. When ***ReadName*** is concluded, only the ***name*** field of ***applicantInfo*** is changed. Still, a change to any field of a record is treated as a change to the entire record; thus, if we want the new name to go back to whatever called ***GetInfo***, we need to declare ***applicantInfo*** as a variable parameter.

12.2 Records and Arrays

In addition to grouping records as single units, it is useful to combine array and record structures. For instance, instead of having one record, as we had one variable, we can have an array of records, just as we had arrays of single variables. In the club example in the last section, we need a record for each of the club's 50 members. We don't want to instantiate 50 different variables of type ***member***; therefore, we'd like to use an array of records.

The following example sets up an array numbered from 1 to 50 to store the information for each club member. The array consists of 50 records, each of which has the three fields with the members' names, phone numbers, and membership numbers. When declaring records, we need to set up a template with the **type** statement first, just as we did with arrays. The mailing list for the club could be set up like this:

```
const
   maxMembers = 50;                    { maximum num of members in club      }

type
   member = record                     { club member                         }
         name : string[40];            { name of member in club              }
         phone : string[15];           { phone number of club member         }
         membership : integer          { membership num of club member       }
      end; { member }

   list = array[1..maxMembers] of member; {list of member records            }

var
   club : list;                        { membership list                     }
```

Figure 12.4 shows how the ***club*** array would look.

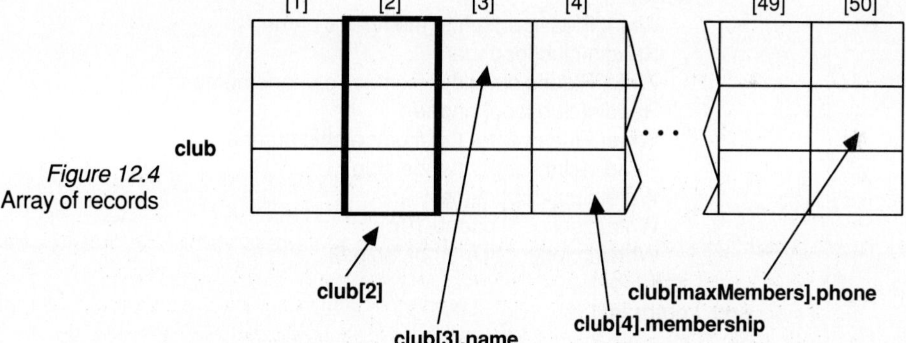

Figure 12.4
Array of records

The ***name*** field in the third record can be initialized by the statement

```
club[3].name := 'Carrie Tower';
```

This can be read as the name field of the third club element. ***club***, according to the **var** declarations, is a variable of type ***list***. Going back to the **type** declarations, we see that ***list*** is an array of ***member*** (record) variables. Therefore, ***club*** is the entire list of members, and ***club[3]*** is the ***member*** in the third array position.

Since ***member*** has been declared as a record type, ***club[3]*** is a specific record. As before, to gain access to a field of a record, we need to place a period and the field name after the record name. ***name*** is a field in the record ***club[3]***. Note that the naming convention gets progressively more specific from left to right. It goes from a whole array to a single element (a record) to a particular field in that element.

If we have set up a data file with the names, phone numbers, and membership numbers of all the club members, we can read that information into our array of records. The following procedure reads and echo-prints the list of club members.

```
program EchoPrint;

const
   maxMembers = 50;                  { maximum members in club          }

type
   member = record                   { club member                      }
         name : string[40];          { name of member in club           }
         phone : string[15];         { phone number of club member      }
         membership : integer        { membership num of club member    }
      end; { member }

   list = array[1..maxMembers] of member; {list of member records       }

var
   club : list;                      { membership list                  }
   loop : integer;                   { loop counter                     }

begin
   for loop := 1 to maxMembers do
      begin
         Write('Please enter the member''s name: ');
         Readln(club[loop].name);
         Write('Please enter the member''s phone number: ');
         Readln(club[loop].phone);
         Write('Please enter the membership number: ');
         Readln(club[loop].membership);
         Write(club[loop].name);
         Write(club[loop].phone:10);
         Writeln(club[loop].membership:6)
      end { for }
end. { program }
```

Figure 12.5 shows the array after the first iteration of the loop body given the following data:

```
Josiah Carberry
123-4567
2031
```

Figure 12.5 shows an array of records. It is also possible to create an array inside a record. We said before that records are used to group information of different types in one place. The example below shows the use of user-defined types in record **type** declarations. The record ***student*** contains a field for the student's name, year, and test scores.

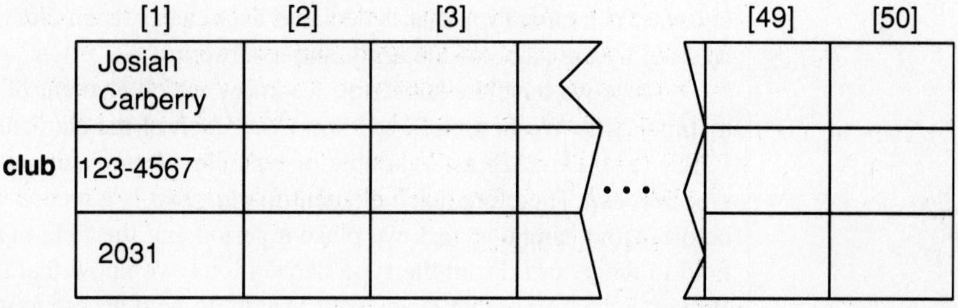

	[1]	[2]	[3]	...	[49]	[50]
	Josiah Carberry					
club	123-4567					
	2031					

Figure 12.5
Array ***club*** after one iteration of loop

```
const
    numTests = 10;                          { number of tests given during term}
type
    scoreList = array[1..numTests] of integer;
                                            { array of scores                   }

    student = record                        { student information               }
            name: string[40];               { student name                      }
            year: integer;                  { student class year                }
            testScores : scoreList          { student's test scores             }
        end; { student }
```

Going a step further, it is possible to combine these structures to group information in many different ways. If we wanted to keep student information of the kind above for every student in the class, we would do the following:

```
const
    numTests = 10;                          { number of tests given during term }
    numStudents = 50;                       { num of students in class          }
type
    scoreList = array[1..numTests] of integer;
                                            { array of scores                   }

    student = record                        { student information               }
            name: string[40];               { student name                      }
            year: integer;                  { student class year                }
            testScores : scoreList          { student's test scores             }
        end; { student }

    classType = array[1..numStudents] of student;
                                            { entire class's info               }
var
    classList: classType;                   { info on all students in class     }
```

The ***classType*** template provides an array of records, or ***student***s. Each record has the student's name, year, and an array of test scores. Figure 12.6 is a representation of the structure in the above code. To get at any given element of the data structure, we have to start "from the outside" and work our way in. Since

classList is a ***classType*** that is declared as an array, each ***classList*** element is denoted by the name of the array and a subscript.

Once we have the subscript, we know which element of the array we are manipulating. We now need to know what each of the elements of the array contains. In this case, ***classList*** as a variable of type ***classType*** is an array of records of type ***student***. Therefore, each element in ***classList*** is a record with three fields. As before with a single record, we place a period and the field name to get to a particular field in the record. From the **type** declarations, we know that records of type ***student*** have a field that is an array. Again, to gain access to a particular item in an array, we need to use a subscript.

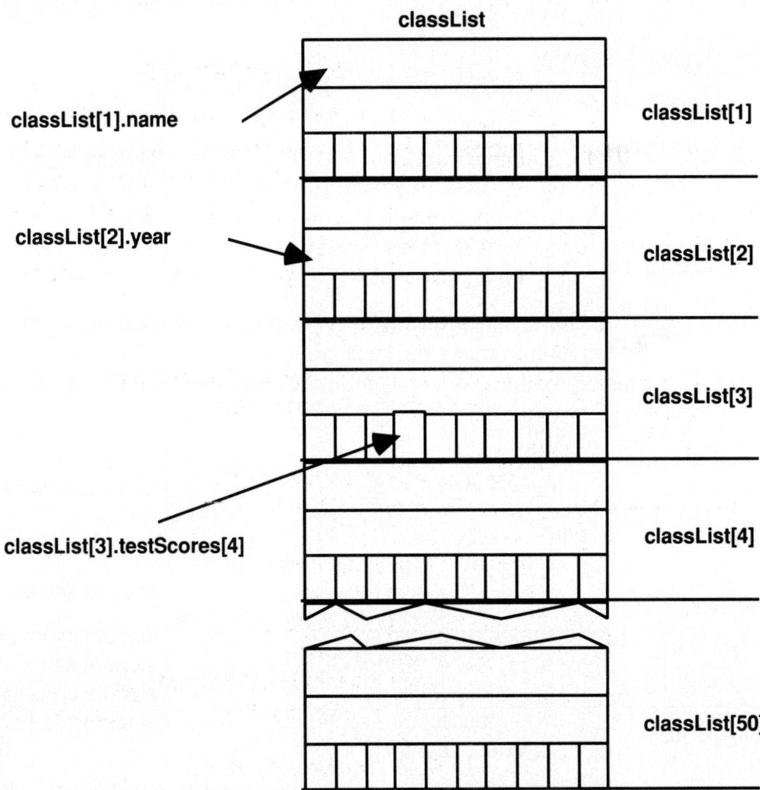

Figure 12.6
Array *classList*, which has records of type *student*

Suppose we want to find out the fourth test score of the third student in the class. We start with the array name (***classList***) and add the subscript ***[3]***. We are now looking at the third record in the ***classList*** array. To get the test score, we need to get to the ***testScores*** field of the record. We thus add a period and the field name ***testScores*** to the statement we are forming. Finally, we append the subscript ***[4]*** to gain access to the fourth test score. The entire sequence is ***classList[3].testScores[4]***.

12.3 with

In the club member example, every time we referred to a field in the record, we had to specify the fully qualified name. But using fully qualified names can be cumbersome. If we tried to use a single ***Writeln*** statement to print the three fields of the ***club*** record, the length of each variable name in the statement would make the list long and too complicated to read easily.

```
Writeln(club[loop].name, club[loop].phone:10, club[loop].membership:6);
```

Pascal provides a statement that makes the manipulation of records easier. The **with** statement lets you specify the record you will refer to repeatedly in the subsequent block of code. The example above can be rewritten as:

```
with club[loop] do
   Writeln(name, phone:10, membership:6);
```

The syntax of a **with** statement resembles that of the flow-of-control constructs we first saw in Chapters 4 and 5. The statement begins with a header: **with** < record name > **do**. The **with** header is then followed by one statement or a **begin/end** block. Unlike the loop and branching constructs, **with** does not affect the flow of control.

An example is in order. A previous section of code can be rewritten using the **with** statement:

```
var
   club: list;              { info on all club members    }
   current : integer;       { loop counter                }

begin
   for loop := 1 to maxMembers do
      with club[current] do
         begin
            Write('Enter name: ');
            Readln(name);
            Write('Enter phone: ');
            Readln(phone);
            Write('Enter membership num: ');
            Readln( membership);
            Writeln;
            Write('Member ', current:3);
            Writeln(name, phone:10, membership:6)
         end { with }
end;
```

In this code, any field referred to in the body of the **with** statement is assumed to be part of the record specified by ***club[current]***. When Pascal finds a variable name, it first checks whether the name is a field of the **with** record. If the name is not part of the record, as the variable ***current*** above is not part of the ***club*** record, then the name is treated as an ordinary variable.

Multiple record names, separated by commas, can be placed in a **with** statement. The resulting **with** statement is equivalent to a series of nested **with** statements. That is, the header

with < record 1 >, < record 2 >, < record 3 > **do**

is equivalent to

with < record 1 > **do**
    with < record 2 > **do**
        with < record 3 > **do**

In each statement in the **with**'s block, Pascal looks for field names. When a field name is found, the interpreter or compiler first tries to append the innermost record name to the field. With the above header, the interpreter or compiler would first determine whether the field was a field of the record < record 3 >. If the field did not exist in that record, then the interpreter or compiler would determine whether the field was declared as part of the record < record 2 >.

Syntax Box 12.2
with

Purpose To provide a shorthand reference to records

Syntax **with** < record name 1 >, < record name 2 >,...,< record name *n* > **do**
    begin
        < statement 1 >;
        < statement 2 >;
        ...
        < statement *n* >
    end;

where < record name 1 >, < record name 2 >,..., < record name *n* > are any legal record names.

< statement >s are any legal Pascal statements.

Usage Pascal considers the **with** statement to be one complete statement and therefore ends it with a semicolon.

The **with** statement allows the programmer to use field names of a record without repeatedly typing the name of the record. When a field name is encountered in the body of the **with** statement, Pascal prefixes the field with < record name >. Identifiers that are not field names in the designated record are not affected by the **with** statement.

with statements can be nested in the same way as loops and conditional statements.

You may have two records with identical field names in the same program. However, some special cases may arise when you use identical field names. If you use, in a **with** statement, two records that contain any identical field names, you must specify the entire record name when referring to one of those fields. Otherwise, Pascal assumes that the field belongs to the record listed last in the **with** statement.

Multiple records are useful in a **with** statement if you have nested records. Suppose you are writing a graphics program to lay out furniture in a classroom. The classroom can contain students' desks, teachers' desks, tables, and personal computers. In this program, we want to allow a user to arrange furniture around the room. The user can pick a piece of furniture and then move it to another location.

To allow the user to choose a piece of furniture and move it, we need to keep track of several items for each object. First, we have to know what type of furniture (student's desk, teacher's desk, table, or computer). Then, we can specify the location of the furniture. Since we need to be able to pick on a piece of furniture, we can use ***rect*** variables for each item; thus, we need to store the ***rect*** variable associated with the furniture. We also need to keep track of the corners of the ***rect*** because they may change when we move the object. Since we will refer to the ***rect*** variable much more often than the top, left, bottom, and right coordinates of the rectangle, we can nest record declarations. The coordinates can be stored in a record that is a field of the furniture record. This means that the furniture record has three fields: the type of furniture (represented as an integer; 1 = student desk, 2 = teacher desk, etc.), the ***rect*** variable used for picking, and the coordinates of the corners of the ***rect***. The coordinates are a record within the record. The following declaration creates one such record.

```
type
   coordType = record
         left: integer;           { lower x coordinate of furniture       }
         top: integer;            { lower y coordinate of furniture       }
         right: integer;          { upper x coordinate of furniture       }
         bottom: integer          { upper y coordinate of furniture       }
      end; { coords }

   furnType = record              { info for each piece of furniture      }
         outline: rect;           { used to pick furniture on screen      }
         itemCode: integer;       { specifies type of furniture           }
         coords: coordType        { coordinates for furniture outline     }
      end; { outerRec }

var
   firstFurn: furnType;           { first piece of furniture drawn        }
```

Given this declaration, we can use the following statements to assign a value to the fields of the record:

```
Writeln('Available types of furniture:');
Writeln(' 1 = teacher desk, 2 = student desk');
Writeln(' 3 = computer, 4 = table');
Write('Please enter the code for the type of furniture: ');
Readln(firstFurn.itemCode);
```

```
Writeln('Please pick the top left corner of the furniture.');
repeat
   GetMouse(firstFurn.coords.left, firstFurn.coords.top);
until Button;

Writeln('Please pick the bottom right corner of the furniture.');
repeat
   GetMouse(firstFurn.coords.right, firstFurn.coords.bottom);
until Button;

SetRect(firstFurn.outline, firstFurn.coords.top, firstFurn.coords.left,
   firstFurn.coords.bottom, firstFurn.coords.right);
...
```

This code can be condensed if we specify the first record using a **with** statement.

```
with firstFurn do
   begin
      Writeln('Available types of furniture:');
      Writeln('1 = teacher desk, 2 = student desk');
      Writeln(' 3 = computer, 4 = table');
      Write('Please enter the code for the type of furniture: ');
      Readln(itemCode);

      Writeln('Please pick the top left corner of the furniture.');
      repeat
         GetMouse(coords.left, coords.top);
      until Button;

      Writeln('Please pick the bottom right corner of the furniture.');
      repeat
         GetMouse(coords.right, coords.bottom);
      until Button;

      SetRect(outline, coords.top, coords.left, coords.bottom,
         coords.right);
      ...
   end; { with }
```

We are still using the inner record quite a bit. We can condense the code even further by adding the record name ***coords*** to the **with** list.

```
with firstFurn, coords do
   begin
      Writeln('Available types of furniture:');
      Writeln(' 1 = teacher desk, 2 = student desk');
      Writeln(' 3 = computer, 4 = table');
      Write('Please enter the code for the type of furniture: ');
      Readln(itemCode);

      Writeln('Please pick the top left corner of the furniture.');
      repeat
```

```
        GetMouse(left, top);
    until Button;

    Writeln('Please pick the bottom right corner of the furniture.');
    repeat
        GetMouse(right, bottom);
    until Button;

    SetRect(outline, top, left, right, bottom);
    ...
end; { with }
```

When MacPascal finds this block, it first appends ***coords*** to each of the fields in that record (each occurrence of ***top***, ***left***, ***bottom***, and ***right***). Then, ***firstFurn*** is added to each occurrence of ***outline***, ***coords***, and ***itemCode***. Thus, the code will be expanded in the reverse order that we contracted it.

12.4 Sample Program

The following program demonstrates how a single record can be manipulated. (Consider how the same program can be modified to handle an array of records.)

Luke Hunk Heartthrob is a soap opera actor with a bubble for a brain. His character on *Days of Our Young and Restless General Guiding Light* is always falling in and out of love, and poor Luke cannot keep track of his affairs. He continually asks the director "Who am I having an affair with now?" His agent, watching her ten percent go up in smoke, sees that this could be a problem. She also sees that keeping track of affairs could be a problem for most of her soap opera clients. To solve this dilemma, she now decides to develop (what else?) a computer program.

First, the agent determines that no soap opera has more than 25 characters of either sex; therefore, a character cannot have more than 25 affairs. She wants her clients to keep track of their past and present lovers, the duration of each affair, the method by which each affair ended, if the character is currently involved in an affair, and, taking nothing for granted, the character's name. To end the program, the agent decides to use the sentinel 'FINIS' (after all, these are theater people).

Her first level of pseudocode for the problem is as follows:

```
Initialize data structure
Prompt user to type the character's name

Prompt user to type first lover's name
WHILE user does not type sentinel DO
    BEGIN
        Prompt user for other information about affair
        Store information in data structure
        Prompt user to type next lover's name
    END
Print out information on all affairs
```

The agent refines the pseudocode by specifying three procedures and adding a line to the initialization.

```
Initialize data structure
Indicate that character is not in an affair

Prompt user to type the character's name

Prompt user to type first lover's name
WHILE user does not type sentinel DO
   BEGIN
      CALL: Prompt user for other information about affair
      CALL: Store information in data structure
      Prompt user to type next lover's name
   END

CALL: Print out information on all affairs

{ Prompt user for other information about affair }
Prompt user for the year the affair began
Prompt user for the year the affair ended
Prompt user for the method of ending the affair

{ Store information in data structure }
Store lover's name
Store length of affair
Store method of ending affair
IF affair has not ended THEN
   Indicate that the character is still involved in an affair

{ Print out information on all affairs }
FOR each affair DO
   BEGIN
      Print lover's name
      Print duration of affair
      Print ending
   END { FOR }
Print message indicating if character is still involved in an affair
```

The above pseudocode makes references to a pseudodata structure. In addition, lines in the pseudocode discuss "storing" without mentioning the type of variable in which the information will be stored. Since all the information the agent wants to store is related, she wants to keep it in one data structure; since all the information will not be represented by the same data type, she needs to use a record. However, the agent does not have to decide on the data structure until she is ready to start coding. Other data structures are certainly possible for this program. The agent might decide to combine the three parallel arrays into a single record and then nest the lovers' names/affair lengths/description of endings record inside the larger record. In either case, the agent is using the minimal amount of storage for the program.

In the highest levels of pseudocode, do not be concerned with the implementation of your data structure; you need decide only whether the data structure will be atomic or compound. The above pseudocode certainly can be translated into a program that uses parallel arrays for the names, durations, and endings, and separate variables to denote the character's name and to indicate if the character is currently in an affair. This method of delaying the choice of data structure is a part of using *data abstraction.*

Previously, we have used flow of control and procedural abstraction. We have used Pascal key words to indicate conditional executions and loops, but we have been deliberately vague about test and exit conditions in the initial levels of pseudocode. We have also referred to not-yet-written procedures to perform some operation (e.g., "Initialize data structure," and, in the Reservation program in Chapter 11, "Find code for airport"). We have assumed that the procedure would do some designated action; we did not figure out exactly *how* that action would be executed until later. Similarly, data abstraction is helpful in that it allows you to concentrate more on the problem solving and less on the computer language. Abstraction involves a great deal more than the explanation we provide here; we will go into slightly more detail in a later chapter. For now, you should concentrate on developing pseudodata structures in parallel with your pseudocode; the pseudodata structure and pseudocode should get progressively more specific at roughly the same rate.

Figure 12.7 shows the data structure for the program. The illustration on the left is the pseudodata structure: the list of items that the agent needs. On the right are several different possibilities for representing this data. All of the implementations of the data are different and require slightly different declarations and code manipulations. All of the implementations, however, contain the same information as the pseudodata structure.

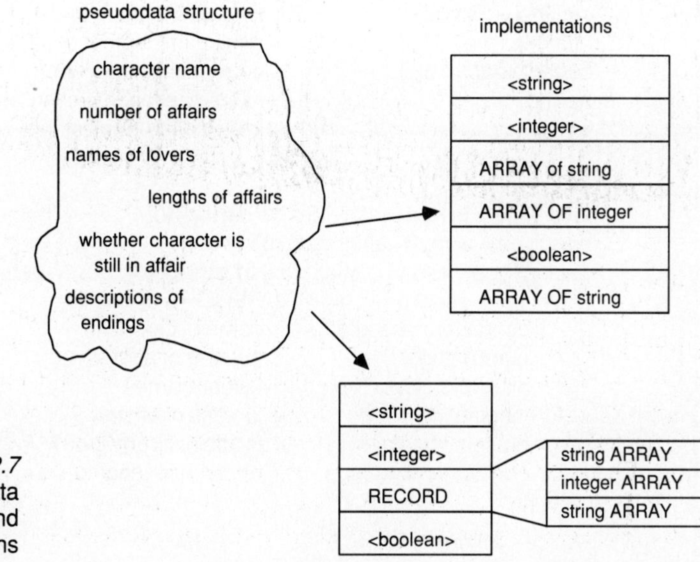

Figure 12.7 Pseudodata structure and implementations

Let's get back to the pseudocode. In the output, the actor's agent wants to print the list of lovers, followed by a message indicating whether the character is currently having an affair. While the array can hold the information on 25 lovers, it is certainly possible that not all of the array slots will be filled. The empty, or garbage, values in the array should not be printed in the final list. To avoid printing these extra values, the agent adds another field to the record. This last field holds an integer to count the number of affairs. Since there is one slot for every lover in the character's life, the counter will indicate how many slots in the output should be printed.

Finally, the agent needs to determine how the program will know if an affair is currently going on. She decides that if the affair has not ended, the user will type in the dummy value "0." With this problem solved, she can code the program as follows (Figure 12.8 shows its output).

Code 12.1
Program *Soap*

```
{ Program: Soap      D. Niguidula        October 15                          }
{   This program helps a soap opera actor or actress keep track of his or    }
{ her character's affairs.                                                   }
{   The program reads in the names of the character's lovers, the dates      }
{ that the relationship began and ended, and a reminder of how the affair    }
{ ended. For purposes of this program, it is assumed that there are no       }
{ more than 25 characters on the show.                                       }
{   The user types in the information from the keyboard.  To let the         }
{ program know when he or she is finished, the user types the sentinel       }
{ 'FINIS'.  The program prints the results in an easy-to-read table.         }

program Soap;

  const
    sentinel = 'FINIS';           { key word to mark end of data             }
    affairMax = 25;               { maximum number of affairs                }
    currentYear = 1987;           { current calendar year                    }
    noEnd = 0;                    { input for affair that hasn't ended       }
    empty = '';                   { initialization blank string              }

  type
    loverType = array[1..affairMax] of string[40];      { names of lovers       }
    timeType = array[1..affairMax] of integer;          { lengths of affairs    }
    endingType = array[1..affairMax] of string[40];     { methods of break-up }
    affairType = record           { RECORD of love life                      }
        character : string[40];   { name of character                        }
        num : integer;            { number of affairs                        }
        allLovers : loverType;    { lovers' names                            }
        lengths : timeType;       { lengths of affairs                       }
        present : boolean;        { is affair still going on?                }
        ending : endingType       { reminder of ending                       }
    end;
```

Code 12.1 (continued)

```
{ Mainline variables }
   var
      affair : affairType;                   { record of love life info      }
      lover : string[40];                    { name of new lover             }
      relationStart,                         { year of affair's start        }
      relationEnd : integer;                 { year of affair's end          }
      methodEnding : string[40];             { method of affair's ending     }

{  Procedure : Initialize                                                     }
{   This procedure is called to set the fields of the record to their         }
{  initial conditions. The number of affairs is set to 0 and the boolean      }
{  that denotes if the actor is having an affair is set to FALSE. The         }
{  information on the lovers' names and methods of termination is set        }
{  to the empty string, while the length of each affair is set to 0.          }
{  Called by : Mainline     Calls: none                                       }

   procedure Initialize (var initAffair : affairType);    { love life info    }

      var
         count : integer;                                  { loop counter      }

   begin

      with initAffair do
         begin

            num := 0;    { no current affairs }
            present := FALSE;

            for count := 1 to affairMax do
               begin
                  allLovers[count] := empty;
                  lengths[count] := 0;
                  ending[count] := empty
               end { for }

         end { with }
   end; { Initialize }

{ Function Ltrim and Function Trim                                            }
{ The following two routines remove blanks from a string.                     }
{ Ltrim removes the leading blanks from a string, and Trim                    }
{ removes the trailing blanks. The length of the string returned              }
{ by either function is changed (unless no blanks were removed).              }
{ Called by : Mainline       Calls: none                                      }

   function Ltrim (str : string) : string; { removes leading blanks           }
```

Code 12.1 (continued)

```
    begin
        while Pos(' ', str) = 1 do
            str := Omit(str, 1, 1);
        Ltrim := str
    end; { Ltrim }

    function Trim (str : string) : string; { removes trailing blanks          }
    begin
        if str <> '' then
            while (str[Length(str)] = ' ') and (Length(str) > 1) do
                str := Copy(str, 1, Length(str) - 1);
        if str = ' ' then
            Trim := ''
        else
            Trim := str
    end; { Trim }

{ Procedure : Add                                                              }
{   This procedure stores the information read in the mainline. The            }
{ procedure is passed all of the relevant information about a single affair.   }
{   First, the counter of the character's affairs is incremented. The          }
{ lover's name, the length of the affair, and the method of ending are then    }
{ added into the arrays in the record. Finally, the procedure determines       }
{ if the character is still having an affair. If the year listed as the        }
{ ending date is the current year, then the program assumes that the           }
{ affair is continuing.                                                        }
{ Called by : Mainline        Calls: none                                      }

    procedure Add (var addAffair : affairType;      { love life info           }
        lover : string;                             { name of new lover        }
        start,                                      { year of affair's start   }
        endYear : integer;                          { year of affair's end     }
        method : string);                           { method used to end affair }

    begin
        with addAffair do
            begin
                num := num + 1;      { add one more lover }
                allLovers[num] := lover;
                if (endYear = noEnd) then  { if affair still exists }
                    begin
                        present := TRUE;
                        lengths[num] := currentYear - start
                    end
                else  { affair has ended }
                    lengths[num] := endYear - start;

                ending[num] := method
            end { with }
  end; { Add }
```

Code 12.1
(continued)

```
{ Procedure : PrintTable                                                    }
{   This procedure is called to print out the information about a character's }
{ affairs. A table of the character's lovers, the duration of each           }
{ affair, and the method of ending is printed. A message indicating if       }
{ the character is still having an affair is also printed.                   }
{ (Note that all of the information can be sent in a single parameter.)      }
{ Called by : Mainline          Calls: none                                  }

  procedure PrintTable (prtAffairs : affairType); { love life info          }

    var
      count : integer;                { loop counter                 }
      fldWidth : integer;             { number of spaces for field   }

  begin

    Writeln; { Print headers of table }
    Writeln('Lovers', 'Length' : 26, 'Ending' : 10);
    Writeln('------', '------' : 26, '------' : 10);
    with prtAffairs do
      begin

  { fill columns of table }

        for count := 1 to num do
          begin
            Write(allLovers[count]);
            fldWidth := 27 – Length(allLovers[count]);
            Write(lengths[count] : fldWidth);
            Writeln(' years   ', ending[count])
          end;

  { print message on character's current status }

        Write(character);
        if (present = TRUE) then
          Writeln(' is still having an affair.')
        else
          Writeln(' is not presently enjoying an affair.')

      end { with }
  end;{ PrintTable }
```

Code 12.1 (continued)

```
{ Mainline                                                            }
{   The Mainline's primary function is to read information about a char- }
{ acter's affairs. After calling a procedure to initialize the data struc- }
{ ture, the user is asked to type in the character's name. Then, the user }
{ is asked to type the lover's name, the years the affair began and ended, }
{ and how the character lost the lover. The user stops the program by  }
{ typing the sentinel value for the lover's name. The Mainline does    }
{ no error checking.                                                   }
{ Calls: Initialize, Add, PrintTable                                   }

begin

    Initialize(affair);
    Write('Please enter the character''s name: ');
    Readln(affair.character);
    Writeln;

    Write('Input the lover''s name or ''FINIS'': ');
    Readln(lover);

    while (Ltrim(Trim(lover)) <> sentinel) and (affair.num < affairMax) do
        begin

            Write('What year did the affair start? ');
            Readln(relationStart);
            Write('What year did the affair end (Enter ', noEnd : 2, ' if not over) ? ');
            Readln(relationEnd);
            Write('How did the affair end? ');
            Readln(methodEnding);

            Add(affair, lover, relationStart, relationEnd, methodEnding);
            Writeln;
            Write('Input the lover''s name or ''FINIS'': ');
            Readln(lover)

        end; { while }

    PrintTable(affair)

end.{ Soap }
```

Figure 12.8 Output of **program *Soap***

```
Please enter the character's name: Luke Hunk Heartthrob

Input the lover's name or 'FINIS': Lauren Jackson
What year did the affair start? 1980
What year did the affair end (Enter  0 if not over) ? 1981
How did the affair end? During an assembly
```

```
Input the lover's name or 'FINIS': Martha Foxboro
What year did the affair start? 1980
What year did the affair end (Enter  0 if not over) ? 1982
How did the affair end? Luke's artificial intelligence

Input the lover's name or 'FINIS': Lee Driftwood
What year did the affair start? 1983
What year did the affair end (Enter  0 if not over) ? 0
How did the affair end? Hasn't yet

Input the lover's name or 'FINIS': Karen Smith
What year did the affair start? 1982
What year did the affair end (Enter  0 if not over) ? 1984
How did the affair end? Incompatible date types

Input the lover's name or 'FINIS': Ellen Robinson
What year did the affair start? 1978
What year did the affair end (Enter  0 if not over) ? 1985
How did the affair end? He didn't want a commitment

Input the lover's name or 'FINIS': FINIS

Lovers                    Length    Ending
------                    ------    ------
Lauren Jackson            1 years   During an assembly
Martha Foxboro            2 years   Luke's artificial intelligence
Lee Driftwood             4 years   Hasn't yet
Karen Smith               2 years   Incompatible date types
Ellen Robinson            7 years   He didn't want a commitment
Luke Hunk Heartthrob is still having an affair.
```

Figure 12.8 (continued)

12.5 Chapter Summary

This chapter looked at the second compound data structure — the record. The difference between arrays and records is that arrays can hold information of only one data type, while records can hold information of different types. Usually, records are declared in the **type** declarations; the new types are then used to declare record variables.

Records and arrays are often combined. Records can contain arrays as one of the fields; arrays can hold a particular number of records. You can create any combination of arrays and records that fits the needs of your particular problem.

Because record and array names tend to become long, Pascal has a shorthand known as the **with** statement. Usually, the **with** statement indicates that a single record is being used in a block of code. (In some cases, you may want to have more than one record in the same **with** statement.) In the block of statements covered by the **with** statement, you can refer to a field of a record without specifying the entire record name.

Finally, we briefly mentioned the idea of data abstraction. At this point, a number of Pascal data structures are available to you. As you write your pseudocode, you should not be concerned with which data structure your program will ultimately use; your main concern in the highest levels of pseudocode is to break the problem down into manageable parts. The actual use of data structures such as arrays and records in the program can be arranged later to fit your solution to the problem. Pseudodata structures are to Pascal data structures as pseudocode is to Pascal code. In general, you should be as abstract in the one as in the other, making them increasingly specific as you complete each level of stepwise refinement.

12.6 Exercises

Understanding Concepts

1. When is a record more appropriate than an array?

2. Tell how you could store each of the following in one data structure:
   a. The names of the owners of boxes 1-300 at the local post office.
   b. The 50 states and their corresponding two-letter abbreviations (e.g., the data structure should contain both 'RHODE ISLAND' and 'RI').
   c. One person's name, street address, city, state, and zip code.
   d. The shows aired by one television station between 7 and 11 p.m.
   e. Same as (d), adding the times that each show goes on the air.
   f. Same as (e), except that the data structure should handle three stations instead of one. The data structure should also hold the channel number of each station.

3. Draw a picture of each of the data structures in Exercise 2.

4. Consider the declarations

```
type
  stuff = record
        word,
        total: string
     end; { stuff }

  equation = record
        total,
        num: real
     end; { equation }

var
  first: stuff;
  second: equation;
```

   Which of the following are legal?

   a. `first.word := 'XYZ';`
   b. `first.total := 7;`
   c. `with first do`
      `total := 'QRS';`

d. **with** equation **do**
```
    total := 7.3;
```
e. **with** first, second **do**
```
    total := 3.7;
```
f. first := second;

g. first.total := second.real;

5. The Computer Science Department's requirements for a bachelor's degree are seven computer science courses, three mathematics courses, and a writing course. Create a data structure that stores the name and the number of each course a student passes and the semester and year in which it is passed.

6. Consider the declarations:

```
type
  houseRec = record
         houseNum: integer;
         street: string
     end;

  aptRec = record
         houseNum: integer;
         street: string;
         aptNum: integer
     end;

var
   jrPlace: houseRec;
   srPlace: aptRec;
```

Which of the following are legal Pascal statements?

a. jrPlace := srPlace;

b. srPlace.houseNum := jrPlace.houseNum;

c. srPlace.aptNum := jrPlace.houseNum;

d. srPlace.aptNum := srPlace.houseNum;

e. jrPlace.street := srPlace.street;

7. Assuming that ***location*** is a variable of type ***locType***, which in turn is defined as:

```
type
  locType = array[1..40] of houseRec; { see previous exercise }
```

which of the following print all of the house numbers and streets in the array?

a. **for** ctr := 1 **to** 40 **do**
```
      Writeln(locType[ctr].houseNum, locType[ctr].street);
```
b. **with** location **do**

```
     for ctr := 1 to 40 do
        Writeln([ctr].houseNum, [ctr].street);
```

c.
```
for ctr := 1 to 40 do
     with location do
        Writeln(houseNum[ctr], street[ctr]);
```

d.
```
with locType[ctr] do
     for ctr := 1 to 40 do
        Writeln(houseNum, street);
```

e.
```
for ctr := 1 to 40 do
     Writeln(houseNum[ctr], street[ctr]);
```

f.
```
for ctr := 1 to 40 do
     with location[ctr] do
        Writeln(houseNum, street);
```

Coding Exercises

Exercises 1 through 6 refer to the following declarations:

```
const
   maxChildren = 10;
   maxFriends = 50;
type
   childInfo = record
         childNames : array[1..maxChildren] of string[30];
         childAges : array[1..maxChildren] of integer
      end; { childInfo }

   friend = record
         name: string[40];
         spouse: string[40];
         children: childInfo
      end; { friend }

   families = array[1..maxFriends] of friend;
var
   giftList: families;
```

1. Write a procedure that prints the contents of all of the information in ***giftList***.

2. Write a procedure that prints all the ***name*** fields that begin with D.

3. Write a procedure that counts how many of your friends have 10-year-old children (i.e., how many ***childAges*** arrays within ***giftList*** contain the value 10).

4. Draw a picture of this data structure and create another possible declaration (in one data structure) for the same data.

5. Write a procedure that sorts the contents of ***childAges*** in each record.

6. Write a procedure that alphabetizes all the records by ***spouse*** fields.

7. Write a procedure that produces a shuffled deck of cards. Each of the 52 cards should appear exactly once in the deck. Use the ***Random*** function to generate a random order.

   Exercises 8 through 10 refer to a simplified version of the way QuickDraw defines ***point*** and ***rect*** variables:

```
type
  rect = record
      top, left, bottom, right: integer
    end; { rect }

  point = record
      v,              { vertical coordinate      }
      h: integer      { horizontal coordinate    }
    end; { point }
```

8. Write a procedure that performs the same function as ***OffsetRect***.

9. Write a procedure that performs the same function as ***SetRect***.

10. Write a function that performs the same function as ***PtInRect***.

11. Write a function called ***PtInArc*** with the following heading:

```
type
  arcRec = record                  { area shaded by a PaintArc command   }
      surround: rect;              { rectangle surrounding oval          }
      start,                       { angle where shading begins          }
      angleLength: integer         { num of degrees in angle             }
    end;

{ This function returns TRUE if the specified point is within the area   }
{ specified by arcArea.                                                  }

function PtInArc(arcArea: arcRec;
  userPt: point): boolean;
```

Programming Problems

1. Write a program that calculates a grade-point average. For each course, the user inputs a grade and a number of credit hours. The grade points are the grade (A = 4, B = 3, ...) multiplied by the credit hours. Calculate a student's GPA for each semester and cumulatively.

2. Revise the newsletter layout program (Chapter 3, programming problem 2) so that the user can place up to three pictures on each of eight pages. Only one page is in the Drawing window at any time.

3. Write a program that reads a team roster from a file — names, uniform numbers, and positions — and prints a list sorted by any of these fields. (Assume the team has no more than 40 players.)

4. Write a program that gives the user a multiple choice test. A question and four possible answers are read from a file and printed in the Drawing window. The user then chooses one of the answers. The program responds by highlighting both the user's choice (in a box) and the correct answer (by inverting). Thus, if the user answers the question correctly, the answer is both inverted and boxed. Continue asking questions until the file contains no more data. (Assume a character in the Drawing window is 8 pixels wide by 16 pixels long.)

5. The four planets closest to the sun move in their orbits at different rates, as shown in the following chart.

Planet	*Days in orbit*	*Distance from sun (millions of kilometers)*
Mercury	88	58
Venus	225	108
Earth	365	150
Mars	687	228

   Write a program in which the user picks the starting position for each planet in its orbit. Then show the position of the planets at 10-day intervals for one Earth-year. (For simplicity's sake, pretend that the planets move in circular orbits.)

6. Write a program that reads ten North American city names and their latitude and longitude coordinates in degrees, minutes, and seconds. (One degree is equal to 60 minutes; one minute to 60 seconds; one second to about 30-2/3 meters.) After reading the information, print a chart showing the distance in meters from each city to every other city in the list.

7. In the game of concentration, fifteen pairs of icons are hidden behind 30 numbered rectangles. The first user sees a grid of areas, numbered from 1 to 30, then picks two of these areas. The icons behind the chosen numbers are revealed after each pick. If the icons match, they are removed; the player gets a point and picks again. Otherwise, the icons are again hidden, and the other user gets to choose. Write a program that allows two players to play this game.

8. Write a program that allows two users to play a game of dots and lines. The game takes place on a board of 64 dots, arranged in 8 rows of evenly spaced dots. Users take turns drawing line segments between dots. (One question you will have to tackle is how users can designate where they want to draw a segment.) If a user's line completes a box (or two), the box is shaded in that player's color (black or gray), and that player gets to draw another segment. The winner is the user with the most boxes when all of the segments have been drawn.

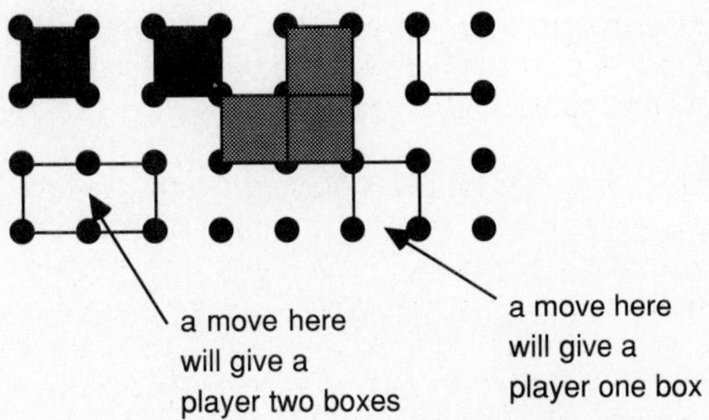
a move here
will give a
player two boxes
a move here
will give a
player one box

9. Write a program that allows two players to play tic-tac-toe. The program should end the game when one player wins or when all of the squares are filled. (Hint: there are eight possible ways to win: three horizontal, three vertical, and two diagonal. You may want to keep track of which ways are still possible for each player. For example, if X takes the middle square, O cannot win on the middle row, the middle column, or either diagonal.)

10. Write a program that simulates the movement of a cat and a mouse in a living room. The room is an 11 x 11 tiled floor and contains furniture and a mousehole. The simulation begins by placing the cat, mouse, and mousehole in the living room according to the user's specifications. Each item occupies one square on the 11 x 11 grid; the user can then position furniture on any number of the remaining squares.

    When the board is set up, the cat and mouse alternate moves, with the mouse going first, according to the following algorithm:

    MOUSE:
    IF the mouse can't see the cat THEN
        It moves one tile closer to the mousehole
    ELSE IF the mouse is closer to the hole than the cat is to the hole THEN
        It moves one tile closer to the mousehole
    ELSE
        It moves one tile farther from the cat

    CAT:
    IF the cat can see the mouse THEN
        It moves one tile closer to the mouse
    ELSE
        It just sits there (not the brightest cat in the world...)

    "Seeing" is determined by a clear path (i.e., no furniture) on the most direct line between the cat and the mouse. A move of "one tile closer" means in any direction — horizontally, vertically, diagonally. (Note: the user may enter some configuration of furniture and creatures that will send your program into an infinite loop. Check for this possiblity before beginning the chase.)

13

More Structured Data Types

The data types examined thus far have two constraints. First, the range of representation of the predefined data type is established somewhere in the depths of the Pascal software. For example, the ***boolean*** type is predefined somewhere to have a range of two values: TRUE and FALSE. Second, variables of any of the atomic data types can hold only one value at a time; even the fields in a record and the elements of an array can each hold just one value. This chapter will examine three data types, two of which allow you to break these constraints.

First, we will look at *enumerated types*. With enumerated types you can create a list of possible values for a variable. That is, you can establish the entire range of representation for a new type.

Then, we will break the second restriction. Instead of having variables that can have only one value, we will look at *set* variables. A set variable, just like the mathematical sets you learned about in elementary school, refers to all of the elements in a collection at once.

Finally, we will examine the *variant record*. Unlike the records of Chapter 12, which have fixed fields, a variant record can have different fields during different executions of the same program.

You can write programs for a long time without using any of these types, because many of the operations on these types can be simulated using other data structures. Still, it's worth examining these types because in certain situations — such as those examined in this chapter — it is easier to store and manipulate the data using these types. Besides, when solving problems, it's always a good idea to have some extra tools at your disposal.

13.1 Enumerated Types

Consider the following pseudocode:

```
Start distance at 0
FOR each day of the week DO
   BEGIN
      Add 200 meters to distance
      Print day of week and distance
   END
```

This pseudocode is for a program that prints how far a jogger should jog during a week. Each day, the jogger wants to go 200 meters farther than the day before. When we code this algorithm, the calculation is easy. However, how should we store the days of the week?

We could create an array of strings and code the program as follows:

```
...
var
   days : array[1..7] of string[3];          {days of week        }
   distance : integer;                       {distance in meters  }
   counter : integer;                        {current day of week }
begin
   days[1] := 'Sun';
   days[2] := 'Mon';
   days[3] := 'Tue';
   days[4] := 'Wed';
   days[5] := 'Thu';
   days[6] := 'Fri';
   days[7] := 'Sat';
   distance := 0;
   for counter := 1 to 7 do
      begin
         distance := distance + 200;
         Writeln(days[counter] : 3, '--', distance)
      end
end.
```

There are two aesthetic problems with this code. First, we have to type an assignment statement for every element of the array. Then, in the **for** loop, we use the code **for** ***counter := 1*** **to** ***7*** **do** to encode the pseudocode "FOR each day of week DO." In short, we have to translate the days to numeric subscripts. It would be easier and more economical to refer to the days *as days* instead of numbers. Whenever we have a list of items that will not change throughout the program, we can use an *enumerated type*.

An enumerated type is defined, naturally enough, in the **type** declarations. In previous type declarations, such as ***list*** **= array*[1..3]* of *integer***, we have combined predefined types (in this case, **array** and ***integer***). With an enumerated type, however, we have to specify the type's range of representation. All the possible values for the type are placed in parentheses. The following example shows how to create a type for the days of the week:

```
type
   day = (Sun, Mon, Tue, Wed, Thu, Fri, Sat);
```

As before, once the type has been defined, we can declare variables of that type. Any variable can contain only one value at a time. For example, if we have a variable called ***current*** of type ***day***, it may have one of the seven values listed in the type definition.

Before discussing how to work with ***day*** or any other enumerated type, let's look at the one enumerated type we have already used extensively. ***boolean*** is a predefined enumerated type, defined as follows:

```
type
   boolean = (FALSE, TRUE);
```

When we have a variable of type ***boolean***, we can assign it one of two values: TRUE or FALSE. Note that apostrophes are not used around the boolean values — TRUE and FALSE are *not* strings. Thus, just as we can make the assignment

```
done := TRUE;
```

for a boolean variable, we can make the assignment

```
current := Tue;
```

for a variable of type ***day***.

Variables of enumerated types can be input and output.* Input of enumerated types is identical to input of integers and character strings. You should, however, ensure that the user enters a valid value. For example, say that ***current*** is of type ***day*** and you have the following code:

```
Write('Please enter the day of the week: ');
Readln(current);
```

The user might mistakenly enter Wednesday or W rather than Wed. An input of an unidentifiable value will result in the error message: **An invalid name was found while attempting to read an enumerated value.** To reduce the chance of this error, we can change the prompt to:

```
Write('Please enter the first 3 letters of the day of the week: ');
Readln(current);
```

* This is a feature of Macintosh Pascal and Lightspeed Pascal. Enumerated type I/O is *not* possible on many other versions of Pascal.

or we can list all of the legal values:

```
Writeln('The days of the week are Sun, Mon, Tue, Wed, Thu, Fri, Sat');
Write('Please enter the day of the week: ');
Readln(current);
```

When an enumerated value is output, it is treated like a character string. The field-width formatting from Chapter 8 also applies to the identifiers in the enumerated type.

Syntax Box 13.1 Declaration of enumerated type

Purpose	To define a type and its range of representation
Syntax	**type** **< type name > = (< val 1 >, < val 2 >,..., < val *n* >);**
where	< type name > is any legal identifier. < val 1 >, < val 2 >,..., < val *n* > are the possible values for the type.
Usage	Variables of the type < type name > can be assigned any of the values listed in < val 1 >,..., < val *n* >. No value can appear in more than one enumerated type in the same program. The values in the list are assigned a sequence number. < val 1 > is given number 0, < val 2 > is given number 1, and so on, up to < val *n* >, which is given number *n-1*. These numbers determine which values are greater or less than others, that is, they induce a lexical ordering like the ASCII sequence.

13.2 Order of Enumerated Types

The values of an enumerated type should be listed in order. This ordering allows us to perform several functions associated with numbers. For example, we can tell if one value is "greater than" or "less than" another. Using the definition of ***day*** from before, we can say that Wednesday > Monday is TRUE.

How is this ordering possible? Think back to the discussion of ***char*** comparisons in Chapter 8, which mentioned that we could compare characters by comparing their ASCII representations. Similarly, enumerated types have a numeric representation. The first value in the list is associated with the number 0, the second with number 1. If the list has *n* items, the last value is associated with the number *n–1*. (This ordering accounts for the name *enumerated type*.) The associated values are called the *ordinal numbers* for the type. Thus, Pascal determines that

Wednesday > Monday because Wednesday is associated with the ordinal number 2 in the definition of ***day***, and Monday is associated with the ordinal number 0.

The ordering does *not* imply that the enumerated values are the same as constants. For example, ***Wednesday + 7*** is not the same as ***2 + 7***. In fact, the expression ***Wednesday + 7*** is not legal. Only integer and real expressions can be used in arithmetic *operations*; enumerated types, however, can be used in arithmetic *comparisons*.

Besides being used in comparisons, enumerated values can also be used as the limits of a **for** loop. Let's return to the jogging example.

```
type
   day = (Sun, Mon, Tue, Wed, Thu, Fri, Sat);

var
   distance : integer;                  { amount jogged              }
   current : day;                       { current day of week        }

begin
   distance := 0;
   for current := Sun to Sat do
      begin
         distance := distance + 200;
         Writeln(current : 3, '--', distance)
      end  { for }
end.  { program }
```

When MacPascal first encounters the **for** loop, it assigns the lower limit value (Sun) to the variable ***current***. The loop body is executed (the line

```
Sun -- 200
```

is output) and flow of control returns to the top. Pascal cannot add 1 to the value of ***current*** since ***current*** is not an integer. ***current*** is a variable of an enumerated type, so it is given the next value from the enumerated type's list. Following Sun is the value Mon. Since Mon is less than the upper limit (Sat), the loop is executed again. This process loops through all of the values of the ***day*** type as they are listed. When ***current*** eventually receives the value Sat, the loop is executed one last time and then exits.

We mentioned earlier that arithmetic operations are not possible with enumerated types. Still, Pascal provides two functions for enumerated types that are similar to addition and subtraction. Both functions depend on the order of items in the range of representation. The ***Succ*** function (for successor) takes as a parameter one value from an enumerated type and returns the next value in the list. The ***Pred*** (for predecessor) function returns the previous value in the list. For example, given the ***day*** type above, ***Succ(Tue)*** returns ***Wed***, and ***Pred(Tue)*** returns ***Mon***. The functions, however, do not "wrap around." If you pass the last value to ***Succ*** or the first value to ***Pred***, an error message such as **The value of a variable or subexpression is out of range for its intended use** appears. Note that this is the same error message that appears when we have an out-of-bounds error in an array.

A third function translates an enumerated type to its associated ordinal number. The ***Ord*** function, like ***Succ*** and ***Pred***, takes a single enumerated value as a parameter. ***Ord*** returns the value's position in the enumerated type. Remember that the numbering of the enumerated type's values starts at 0. Again referring to the ***day*** type, ***Ord(Thu)*** returns 4 and ***Ord(Sun)*** returns 0.

The ***Pred***, ***Succ***, and ***Ord*** functions work on any ordinal type, that is, any type that can be ordered: integers, characters, or enumerated types, including ***boolean***. These functions are also used occasionally with variables of type ***char***, but rarely with integers. Technically, we can use an integer as the parameter to, for example, the ***Pred*** function, but it seems rather pointless; the function simply returns an integer one less than the parameter it receives.

Let's look at a short example. Suppose we had the following enumerated type:

```
type
   spaces = (Go, Mediterranean, ComChest1, Baltic...
                                    { other names go here           }
      ParkPlace, LuxuryTax, Boardwalk);
```

This type represents the spaces in the Monopoly™ board game. Now let's write a procedure that simulates a move on the board. The procedure is given three parameters: the current position on the board, the number of spaces to move, and whether the movement is forward or backward. The procedure should alter the current position with the ***Pred*** and ***Succ*** functions. For example, if we want to move three spaces forward, we can apply the ***Pred*** function three times to the current position. The only boundary condition occurs when the player moves past Boardwalk. The procedure should move the player to Boardwalk and complete the move starting at Go. We use the ***Ord*** function to determine if the player's current position, plus the new movement, will move the player past Boardwalk.

```
type
   spaces = (Go, Mediterranean, ComChest1, Baltic...
                                    { other names go here           }
     ParkPlace, LuxuryTax, Boardwalk); { names of all spaces on board }

procedure MakeMove(var curPos : space;      {player's current position }
      amount : integer;                     {# of spaces to move       }
      forward : boolean);                   {TRUE if moving forward    }
var
   ctr : integer;                           { loop counter             }
begin
   { if moving past Boardwalk... }
   if (Ord(curPos) + amount > Ord(Boardwalk)) and forward then

      begin
         curPos := Go;  { move to Go }
         amount := Ord(Boardwalk) - Ord(curPos)  { adjust movement }
      end;
```

```
        for ctr := 1 to amount do
            begin
                if forward then
                    curPos := Succ(curPos)  { move to next space }
                else
                    curPos := Pred(curPos)  { move back 1 space }
            end { for }
    end; { procedure }
```

Syntax Box 13.2
Ordinal functions

Purpose To provide information about order of ordinal types.

Syntax
Pred(< ord expression >)
Succ(< ord expression >)
Ord(< ord expression >)

where < ord expression > is an expression of an ordinal type (***integer, char, boolean,*** enumerated type).

Returns ***Pred*** and ***Succ*** return a value of the same ordinal type as the parameter (e.g., if < ord expression > is a ***char, Pred*** and ***Succ*** return a ***char***). ***Ord*** returns an integer.

Usage ***Pred*** returns the predecessor of < ord expression >. If < ord expression > is an integer, ***Pred*** returns < ord expression > – 1. If < ord expression > is a ***char, Pred*** returns the preceding character in the collating sequence. If < ord expression > is an enumerated type, ***Pred*** returns the preceding value in the range of representation. If < ord expression > is –32767 (the minimum integer), the null character, or the first value in an enumerated list, ***Pred*** yields an error.

Succ returns the successor of < ord expression >. If < ord expression > is an integer, ***Succ*** returns < ord expression > + 1. If < ord expression > is a ***char, Succ*** returns the next character in the collating sequence. If < ord expression > is an enumerated type, ***Succ*** returns the next value in the list. If < ord expression > is 32767 (the maximum integer) or the last value in an enumerated list, ***Succ*** produces an error.

Ord returns the position of < ord expression > in a list. If < ord expression > is a ***char, Ord*** returns its ASCII value. If < ord expression > is an enumerated type, ***Ord*** returns its position in the list.

Ord can be used on computers that do not use the ASCII collating sequence. In those situations, ***Ord*** returns whatever the decimal equivalent of ***char*** is in that computer's collating sequence.

This sort of code, often used in programs with enumerated types, allows us to find the value that is ***amount*** away from any value in the enumerated type.

13.3 Sets

If you aren't a math major, you probably haven't seen sets since Mr. Farber's fourth-grade arithmetic class. Think back. What you remember about sets in arithmetic may come back to you as we discuss how to use sets in Pascal.

Sets are collections of things. In Pascal, this is what differentiates sets from all other data types—set variables are treated as collections, rather than as a convenient grouping of individual items. Typically, when working with sets, we want to use the entire collection at once, as opposed to looking consecutively at, say, individual elements in an array. For example, an array can hold the value 'a' in position 1, 'b' in position 2, and so on, while a set variable can hold all the characters from 'a' to 'z' simultaneously, and treat them as a collective whole.

Pascal places two restrictions on sets. First, all members of the set must be of the same data type. This data type is known as the set's *base type*. Second, there is an upper limit on the base type's *cardinality*: the number of members in the set's base type. In MacPascal, the maximum cardinality is 65536. Since there are 65536 integers in MacPascal's range of representation, ***integer*** is a legal base type. Characters and enumerated types (with fewer than 65536 members) are also legal base types. ***real*** and **string**, however, are not legal base types since they have more than 65536 possible values.

Declaring set variables is similar to declaring array variables, using the reserved word **set** instead of **array**. We begin by defining a type. The following example defines a type that holds sets of characters.

```
type
    charSet = set of char;  { can hold any number of chars }
```

The type name is ***charSet***. Any variable of that type will hold a collection of ***char*** values. ***charSet*** can next be used as a data type in any parameter or variable list. Thus, the following declaration reserves storage for four sets:

```
var
    letter,                     { set of letters of alphabet          }
    digits,                     { set of numeric digits               }
    punctuation,                { set of punc. used in Pascal         }
    operator : charSet;         { set of arithmetic & relative ops    }
```

As usual, these declarations tell only what data types are involved; actual values must be assigned to the sets by explicit assignment. So, let's look at how we assign values to these sets. Suppose that we want ***punctuation*** to hold some of the punctuation symbols used in Pascal. In mathematical set notation (not Pascal), we could call the set P and use the following equation:

P = {'.', ';', ':', '[', ']', '{', '}', '^', ' " ' }

In Pascal, we can't use the curly brackets since they are used to contain comments. Thus, we need to use some other symbol to delimit the set—square brackets. We can assign all the set members to the set variable using one assignment statement:

```
punctuation := ['.', ';', ':', '[', ']', '{', '}', '^', ' " ']
```

Note that all of the set members are assigned at once.

The ordering of members in the set is irrelevant. This is because members of a set are not used individually, but collectively. The following assignment statements all achieve the same result:

```
operator := ['+', '–', '*', '/', '=', '>', '<'];
operator := ['<', '+', '–', '/', '>', '=', '*'];
operator := ['–', '/', '=', '<', '>', '+', '*'];
```

Also, a set cannot have more than one member of the same value. For example,

```
state := ['M', 'i', 's', 's', 'i', 's', 's', 'i', 'p', 'p', 'i'];
```

is the same as

```
state := ['M', 'i', 's', 'p'];
```

since all multiple values are ignored.

Sometimes it's useful to have a shorthand notation. Consider the following assignment:

```
letter := ['a', 'b', 'c', 'd', 'e', 'f', 'g', 'h', 'i', 'j', 'k', 'l', 'm', 'n', 'o', 'p', 'q', 'r', 's', 't', 'u',
      'v', 'w', 'x', 'y', 'z'];
```

For a series of consecutive values, you can use a *subrange.*

We first saw subranges in the array declaration. A subrange takes the form < lower limit >.. < upper limit >. The limits can be of any ordinal type, as shown in the following examples:

```
6..12
'A'..'z'
Mon..Fri
```

The first subrange is the kind we've seen before; two integers represent the limits. The second subrange holds a list of characters; it consists of all the characters in the collating sequence between the upper and lower limits. Thus, 'A'.. 'z' contains all characters with ASCII values between 65 and 122 — the upper-case letters, the lower-case letters, and the symbols [, \,], ^, _, and ` (see the collating sequence in Appendix F). The third subrange uses values from the enumerated type ***day***. This subrange includes all the values listed in the enumerated type between the designated limits.

Subranges can be used whenever you would use any other ordinal type. That is, any occurrence of the reserved word ***char*** can be replaced by a character subrange. For example, if you know that a particular variable will hold capital letters only, you do not have to use the declaration

```
var
   cap : char;                                { a single capital letter }
```

Instead, you can use the declaration

```
var
   cap : 'A'..'Z';                            { a single capital letter }
```

You can also declare subranges as types. The above declaration can be rewritten as:

```
type
   upperRange= 'A'..'Z';                      { range of capital letters }

var
   cap : upperRange;                          { a single capital letter   }
```

When dealing with sets, subranges are useful in two situations. First, you can use subranges when listing the members of a set. Thus, the assignment for the set variable ***letters*** can be condensed to:

```
letters := ['a'.. 'z'];
```

Subranges need not be the only thing in the set membership list. For example, the following declaration is valid:

```
consonants := ['b', 'c', 'd', 'f'.. 'h', 'j'..'n', 'p'.. 't', 'v'.. 'z'];
```

Subranges can also be used as a base type. For example, the following code fragment creates a set type using the subrange 1..36 as a base type. Then a variable of that type is created and assigned a value.

Syntax Box 13.3
Set declarations

Purpose	To create a set type.
Syntax	**type** < type name > = **set of** < base type >;
where	< type name > is any legal identifier. < base type > is an ordinal type with no more than 65536 possible values.
Usage	The < base type > can be ***char***, ***integer*** any enumerated type with 65536 or fewer values in its range of representation, or a subrange of 65536 or fewer values. Other versions of Pascal may allow a different maximum cardinality.

```
type
   lotteryNums = set of 1.. 36;    { all available lottery numbers        }
var
   winningTicket : lotteryNums;    { winning combination                  }
begin
   winningTicket := [1, 7, 10, 20, 21, 27];
   ...
```

One more thing should be said about set assignments. In set manipulations, the *empty set* is the set with no elements. No matter what its base type, any set variable can be assigned the empty set. The empty set is denoted by two square brackets as follows:

```
var
   myWinningNums : lotteryNums; { winning nums I chose }
begin
   myWinningNums := [ ] ; { empty set }
   ...
```

The empty set is the set that plays the same role in set manipulations as the integer 0 in arithmetic or the null character in string manipulation. Its importance will be shown in the next section.

Syntax Box 13.4
Set constants

Purpose To define members of a set

Syntax [< value 1 >, < value 2 >,..., < value n >]

where < value 1 >, < value 2 >,..., < value *n* > are values in the set's base type.

Usage Any of < value 1 >,..., < value *n* > can be expressions (including constants or variables) that evaluate to the base type.

< value 1 >,..., < value *n* > should be distinct values. The second, third, fourth, etc. occurrences of the same value are ignored.

The constant notation can be used in places where set expressions are needed as on the right side of an assignment symbol or in set operations.

The order of the values is irrelevant.

The empty set is denoted by the symbol [ ].

Subranges can be listed with the values.

13.4 Set Operations

In Pascal, we can combine sets in three ways. We can create a *union* of sets, find the *intersection* of sets, and determine the *difference* between sets. You probably remember something about these operations from your 4th grade class — although you may not be quite sure which operation the $\cap$ stood for.

Imagine that you and your friend Terry have found an apartment, but you need to find a third roommate. How do you determine with whom you should live? You know that you are most compatible with folks born under Aries, Gemini, Virgo, or Pisces. Terry is compatible with sun signs Gemini, Scorpio, Aquarius, and Pisces. Figure 13.1 shows one representation of this information.

This information can also be represented in code, using the enumerated type ***signs***, as follows:

```
type
   signs = (Aries, Taurus, Gemini, Cancer, Leo, Virgo, Libra, Scorpio,
            Sagittarius, Capricorn, Aquarius, Pisces);
                                        { list of zodiac signs       }
   compats = set of signs;              { holds a bunch of signs     }
var
   myList,                         { signs compatible with me        }
   terryList : compats;            { signs compatible with Terry     }
begin
   myList := [Aries, Gemini, Virgo, Pisces];
   terryList := [Gemini, Scorpio, Aquarius, Pisces];
   ...
```

You want to find those signs that are compatible with either of you. This can be found by taking the *union* of the sets ***myList*** and ***terryList***. If you have a ***compats*** variable called ***eitherOne***, you can use the following assignment:

```
eitherOne := myList + terryList;
```

The addition sign, when placed between sets, combines the members of both sets, as shown in Figure 13.2.

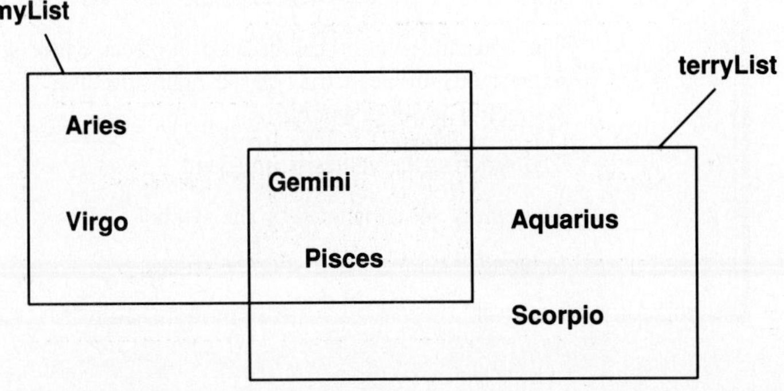

Figure 13.1
Sets ***myList*** and ***terryList***

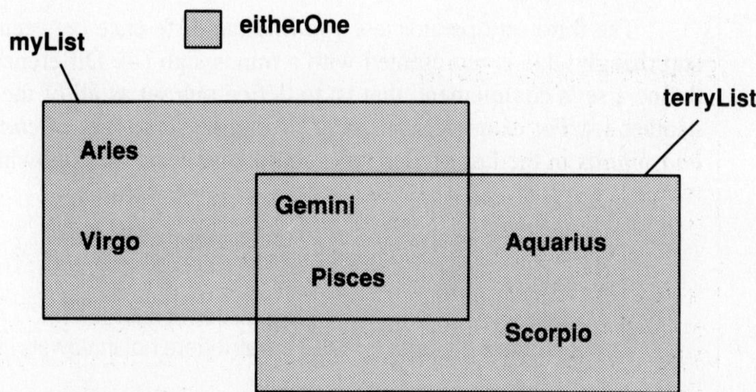

Figure 13.2
Union of sets

Thus, this assignment statement places the set ***[Aries, Gemini, Virgo, Scorpio, Aquarius, Pisces]*** in the variable ***eitherOne***. Gemini and Pisces appear only once in the result, even though they are in both ***myList*** and ***terryList***. In any set, no value can appear more than once.

The union of two sets contains all the members that are in one set *or* the other. You can also determine the intersection of two sets: the members that are in one set *and* the other. In MacPascal, an intersection is represented by the asterisk (*). For example, if you want to find the signs that are compatible with both Terry and yourself, you can create a ***compats*** variable called ***compatWithBoth*** and use the assignment

```
compatWithBoth := myList * terryList;
```

This assignment places the set ***[Gemini, Pisces]*** in ***compatWithBoth***, since Gemini and Pisces are in both ***myList*** and ***terryList***. If the two sets had nothing in common, the empty set would have been assigned to ***compatWithBoth***.

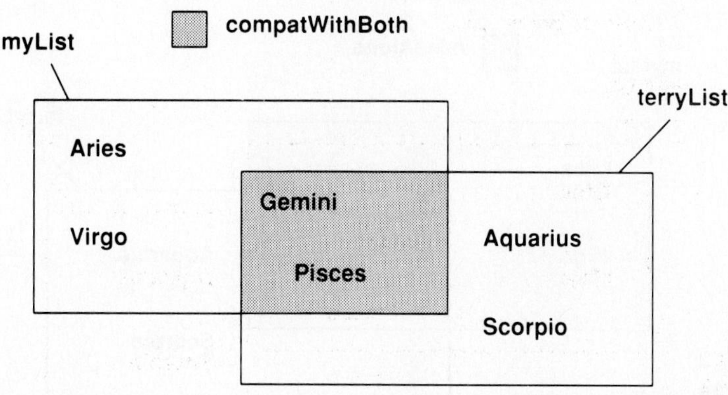

Figure 13.3
Intersection of sets

The third set operator lets you find the difference between two sets. Not surprisingly, this is represented with a minus sign (–). Differences are often used to define a set's complement, that is, to define one set as all of the members *not* in another set. For example, instead of listing the subranges of ***chars*** to define the set ***consonants*** in the last section, you could have used the following fragment:

```
type
   letters : set of char;        { holds many characters          }

var
   vowels,                       { small vowel characters         }
   consonants : letters;         { small letters not in vowels    }

begin
   vowels := ['a', 'e', 'i', 'o', 'u'];
   consonants := ['a'.. 'z'] – vowels;
   ...
```

When Pascal finds the syntax < set 1 > – < set 2 >, it copies all the members of < set 1 > into a temporary variable. Pascal then removes any member of < set 2 > from the temporary variable. The temporary variable is now the result. In the above fragment, ***consonants*** is the set of all letters between 'a' and 'z' that are not in the set ***vowels***.

Not every member of the set on the right of the minus sign (< set 2 >) has to be in the set on the left (< set 1 >). Go back to the horoscope check. Suppose you create a variable ***mineAlone*** of type ***compats*** and enter the statement

```
mineAlone := myList – terryList;
```

When Pascal sees this statement, it begins by assigning ***[Aries, Gemini, Virgo, Pisces]*** to a temporary block of memory. Then, Pascal determines what values in that temporary block are also in ***terryList*: *Gemini*** and ***Pisces***. The values ***Scorpio*** and ***Aquarius*** are ignored since they are not in ***myList***. The common values to both ***myList*** and ***terryList*** are removed, yielding a result of ***[Aries, Virgo]***. As shown in Figure 13.4, this set represents those members of ***myList*** that are not in ***terryList***.

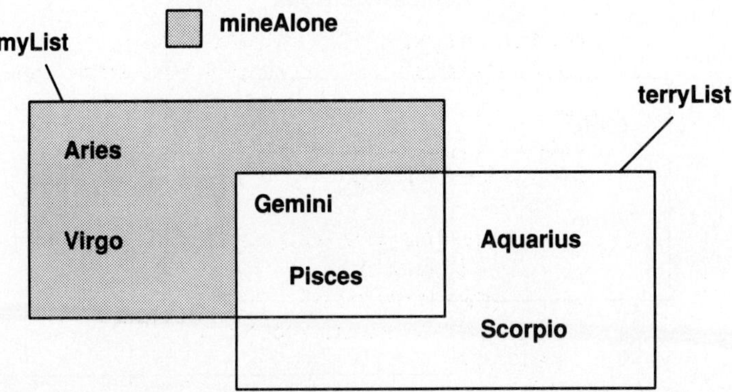

Figure 13.4
Difference of sets

Syntax Box 13.5
Set operations

Operation	Syntax	Result
union	< set 1 > + < set 2 >	Resultant set contains all values that are in either < set 1 > or < set 2 >.
intersection	< set 1 > * < set 2 >	Resultant set contains all values that are in both < set 1 > and < set 2 >.
difference	< set 1 > – < set 2 >	Resultant set contains all values that are in < set 1 > but not in < set 2 >.

Set operations have much in common with the arithmetic operations that use the same symbols. For example, intersection (*) takes precedence over union and difference (+ and –). Operations can be chained together in the same statement, and parentheses can be used to alter the order of operation. However, the operators must have sets on both sides, and the sets must be compatible, that is, have the same base type. For example,

```
myList := myList + Libra;
```

is not a valid statement since the value ***Libra*** is not a set. To add the value ***Libra*** to ***myList***, you need to use set notation:

```
myList := myList + [Libra];
```

Entire sets cannot be input at the keyboard. You can, however, enter individual set members and use the union operator to add them into the set. For example, in the following fragment, the user enters six integers, which are then placed in the set.

```
type
   lotteryNums = set of 1..36;              { all available lottery numbers   }
procedure EnterNums(var userlist : lotteryNums);
                                            { numbers on user's ticket        }
var
   counter : integer;              { loop counter             }
   curNum : integer;               { number entered by user   }
begin
   userList := [ ];                { begin at empty set       }
   for counter := 1 to 6 do
      begin
         Write('Enter choice # ', counter : 1, ': ');
         Readln(curNum);
         { add number to set }
         userList := userList + [curNum]
      end { for }
end; { EnterNums }
```

Note that adding square brackets around the variable ***curNum*** turns an integer into a set with one member. The square brackets are necessary to make the assignment statement legal; ***userList := userList + curNum;*** is not valid because Pascal cannot determine if the + signals addition (because ***curNum*** is an integer) or a union (because ***userList*** is a set).

13.5 Set Relationships

Two set values can be compared, using five different comparison operators. The first two are obvious. You can determine if two sets are equal by using the notation

< set 1 > = < set 2 >.

This is a boolean expression that returns TRUE if every member of < set 1 > is also in < set 2 >. Since order does not matter in sets,

['a', 'e', 'i', 'o'] = ['o', 'a', 'i', 'e']

yields the result TRUE. The not equals operator returns the opposite of the equals operator and is represented (as in the arithmetic and string comparisons) by the symbol <>.

Two other comparison operators determine if one set is a *subset* of another. The notation

< set 1 > <= < set 2 >

is asking whether every member of < set 1 > is also in < set 2 >. The following comparisons all yield TRUE:

1. ['a'] <= ['a'.. 'z']
2. ['a', 'e', 'i', 'o'] <= ['a'..'z']
3. ['k'.. 'n'] <= ['a'..'z']
4. ['a'..'z'] <= ['a'..'z']
5. [ ] <= ['a'..'z']

Comparison 1 is TRUE because the member 'a' is in the range 'a'.. 'z'. In comparisons 2 and 3, multiple members of the range 'a'.. 'z' are listed on the left, but since each member on the left is in the set defined on the right, the comparisons yield TRUE. Comparison 4 shows that a set is a subset of itself. Again, the same criterion is used: each member of the set on the left is contained in the set on the right. Finally, as seen in comparison 5, the empty set is a subset of every set.

The notation < set 1 > >= < set 2 > yields TRUE if < set 1 > is a *superset* of < set 2 >. A superset contains all the members of another set. Put another way, the notation < set 1 > >= < set 2 > asks if < set 2 > is a subset of < set 1 >. The same definition of subsets applies here.

The fifth set-comparison operator does not really compare sets. In fact, it determines if a *member* is in a set. This comparison uses the reserved word **in**. The notation

< member > **in** < set >

returns TRUE if < member > is inside < set >. This comparison is legal only if < member > is a member of < set >'s base type. Thus, you can have the following fragment:

```
type
    letters : set of char;          { all possible characters       }
var
    menuOptions : letters;          { set of all available options            }
    userChoice : char;              { menu choice entered by user             }
begin
    menuOptions := ['D', 'Q', 'C', 'H'];
    ...
    Write('Please enter a menu option');
    Readln(userChoice);
    if userChoice in menuOptions then
        begin
            case userChoice of
            ...
        end { if }
    else
        Writeln(userChoice, 'is not a menu option');
    ...
```

userChoice is a single ***char*** value. In the **if** statement, the code determines if the character input by the user is contained in the set of legal menu options. If it is, the appropriate action is performed; otherwise, an error message is printed.

'D'* in *menuOption is a legal boolean expression, but ***['D']* in *menuOption*** is not, since ***['D']*** is a set, not a member. Also, the member to the left of the **in** must be in the set's *base type*, even though you may not know if the member will be in the set itself.

When the base type is a subrange, a slightly inconsistent set of rules applies. For example, the comparison that follows:

```
type
    lotteryNums = set of 1..36;          { all possible lottery nums    }
var
    winner : lotteryNums;                { set of winning numbers       }
begin
    ...
    if 45 in winner then
        Writeln('Something''s wrong');
    ...
end
```

is legal even though the member 45 is not in the base type of ***winners***. The base type of ***winners***, for purposes of this comparison, is not the subrange 1..36, but the type ***integer***. We won't even try to rationalize this one. However, if you do attempt a comparison that MacPascal interprets as illegal, such as

```
...
if 'L' in winner then
      Writeln('Something''s wrong');
...
```

you will receive an error message such as **An incompatibility between types has been found.** The set-comparison operators are summarized in Syntax Box 13.6.

Syntax Box 13.6
Set comparison

Syntax	Meaning
< set 1 > = < set 2 >	**Equality**: returns TRUE when all members of < set 1 > are in < set 2 > and all members of < set 2 > are in < set 1 >.
< set 1 > <> < set 2 >	**Inequality**: returns TRUE when one set contains a member that is not in the other set.
< set 1 > <= < set 2 >	**Subset**: returns TRUE if all members of < set 1 > are in < set 2 > or if < set 1 > is the empty set.
< set 1 > >= < set 2 >	**Superset**: returns TRUE if all members of < set 2 > are in < set 1 > or if < set 2 > is the empty set.
< member > **in** < set >	**Containment**: returns TRUE if < member > is contained in < set >.

13.6 Variant Records

Consider a layout program that draws rectangles, ovals, arcs, and rounded rectangles. Any of these shapes can be framed, painted, or inverted. Now imagine that we want to keep track of the shapes as they are drawn. For each shape, we need to know the corners of the rectangle that surrounds it and the style in which it was drawn. If the shape is an arc, we need to know its beginning angle and its length. If the shape is a rounded rectangle, we need to know the height and width of the oval corners.

In short, some of the information we need is identical for every shape, and some of the information varies depending on the particular shape. In Pascal, we can create records with varying fields. These data types are known as *variant records.*

A variant record declaration contains three parts. The information needed in every record is stored in *fixed fields*. Then the record contains a *tag field*. Depending on the value of the tag field, the record also contains *variant fields*. Let's look at an example:

```
type
    shapeType = (Rectangle, Oval, RoundRect, Arc);
                                        { all possible shapes           }
    styleType = (Frame, Paint, Invert);
                                        { all possible styles           }
    shapeInfo = record
        top, left,                      { coordinates of surrounding    }
        bottom, right : integer;        { rectangle                     }
        style : styleType;              { fill style of shape           }

        case shape : shapeType of
            Rectangle, Oval : (          { no extra fields               }
            );

            RoundRect : (
                ovalHeight,             { height of rounded corner      }
                ovalWidth : integer     { width of rounded corner       }
            );

            Arc : (
                startAngle,             { angle where arc begins        }
                arcLength : integer     { length of arc                 }
            )

    end; {shapeInfo}
```

The declaration of the fields in the record ***shapeInfo*** begins in the same way as fields were declared in Chapter 12. The fields ***top***, ***left***, ***right***, ***bottom***, and ***style*** are the record's fixed fields. Every variable of type ***shapeInfo*** has these fields.

The next part of the record looks amazingly like a **case** statement. Instead of a selector variable, though, we have a field name and field type between the **case** and **of**. This tag field also appears in every record variable of type ***shapeInfo***.

The remaining part of the declaration is the variant part. Depending on the value of the tag field, some additional fields are also available. As with the **case** flow-of-control statement, the **of** in a variant record is followed by a series of constant values and colons. The constant values are known as *tag values*, since they are the possible values of the tag type. In this instance, since the tag field is of type ***shapeType***, the values to the left of the colons are values of type ***shapeType***. Following the tag values in parentheses are the variant fields. These fields come into existence only when the tag field is given a value.

The syntax for the above fragment can be translated as: "***shapeInfo*** is a record type. Any variable of this type contains the ***integer*** fields ***top***, ***left***, ***bottom***, ***right***, the ***styleType*** field ***style***, and the ***shapeType*** field ***shape***. When the ***shape*** field of a ***shapeInfo*** type variable receives a value, some extra fields may be created. If the ***shape*** field is assigned the value ***RoundRect***, the fields ***ovalHeight*** and ***ovalWidth*** are created. If the ***shape*** field is assigned the value ***Arc***, the fields ***startAngle*** and ***arcLength*** are created. If the ***shape*** field is assigned either the value ***Rectangle*** or ***Oval***, no new fields are created."

The variant fields are similar, but not identical, to the options in a **case** statement. Let's quickly look at the differences:

- In a **case** statement, an ordinal (***integer***, ***char***, ***boolean***, enumerated type or subrange) variable is between the **case** and the **of**. In a variant record, the tag field *and the tag type* are between the **case** and the **of**.
- In a **case** statement, each value is followed by a statement block. The block is delimited by the reserved words **begin** and **end**. In a variant record, each value is followed by a list of field names and field types. The variant fields are delimited by parentheses.
- A **case** statement concludes with its own **end** statement. The **case** in a variant record does not have its own **end**; thus, only one **end** appears in any record declaration.

Note that this is still a *declaration*. The ***shape*** field has not been assigned anything yet. (Actually, no fields have been assigned values.) The tag values ***Rectangle***, ***Oval***, ***RoundRect***, and ***Arc*** are only the potential values for that field. Even though these values appear in the declaration, *no assignments have yet been made*.

13.7 Using Variant Records

When you declare a variable that has a data type of a variant record, the variable contains only the fixed fields and the tag field. The variant fields come into existence only when the tag field is assigned a value. Without looking at the declaration, it is impossible to tell which fields are fixed and which are variant; the notation < record var >.< field name > works for all fields.

Syntax Box 13.7
Variant records

Purpose To declare a record to hold different information depending on the situation.

Syntax

```
type
   < name > = record
         < fixed field list >;
         case < tag field > : < tag type > of
            < tag value 1 > : (
               < variant field list 1 >
            );
            < tag value 2 > : (
               < variant field list 2 >
            );
            ...
            < tag value n > : (
               < variant field list n >
            ) { no semicolon before end }
      end;
```

Syntax Box 13.7
(continued)

where < fixed field list > is a list of fields in the format:

```
< field name 1 > : < field type 1 >;
...
< field name n > : < field type n >;
```

where < field name 1 >,..., < field name *n* > are identifiers for fields, and < field type 1 >,..., < field type *n* > are some previously defined data types.

No field name may be repeated in the record.

The semicolon appears on the last fixed field type but not on the last field type in any set of parentheses.

< tag field > is another field name.

< tag type > is an ordinal type (***integer, char, boolean,*** enumerated type, subrange).

< tag value 1 >,..., < tag value *n* > are constant values of the < tag type >. Multiple values can be separated by commas. Subranges of values can also be placed before the colon.

Each of < variant field list 1 >,..., < variant field list *n* > is a list of fields and types included in the variant. The variant field list usually consists only of fixed fields, but it can also contain nested tag fields and variants.

Only one **end** appears in any record declaration.

Usage When a variable of the designated record type is declared, space for the fixed fields and the tag field is allocated in memory. During execution of the program, the tag field may receive a value. When this happens, the variant field list that corresponds to the tag value comes into existence.

Once a value is assigned to any of a record's variant fields, the tag field cannot be altered.

Only one sequence of variant fields is available at any time.

Nested variant fields can appear in a record. Only one tag field, however, can appear inside any set of parentheses or in the main record body: that is, the record declaration cannot have consecutive **case** constructs.

When we declare a record variable in a procedure's **var** list, all the fields are undefined. Since the tag field is also undefined, none of the variant fields exists. Figure 13.5 shows a diagram of a variable called ***object*** immediately after it has been declared:

```
var
   object : shapeInfo;            { single object on the screen }
```

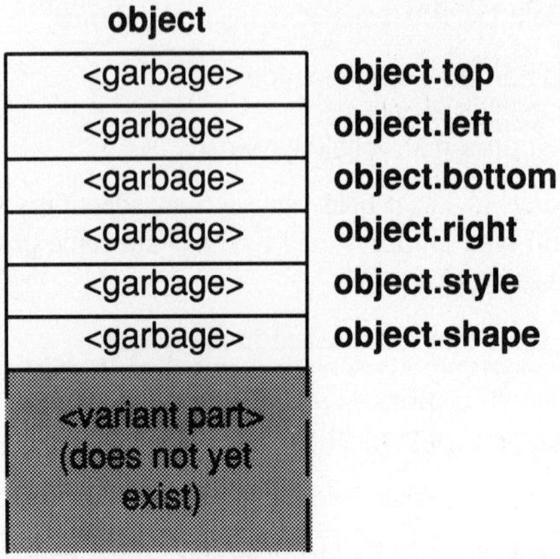

object

<garbage>	**object.top**
<garbage>	**object.left**
<garbage>	**object.bottom**
<garbage>	**object.right**
<garbage>	**object.style**
<garbage>	**object.shape**
<variant part> (does not yet exist)	

Figure 13.5
Initial variant record

Typically, when we assign values to fields of a variant record, the tag field receives a value before any variant field does. When the tag field gets a value, then the variant fields come into existence (see Figure 13.6).

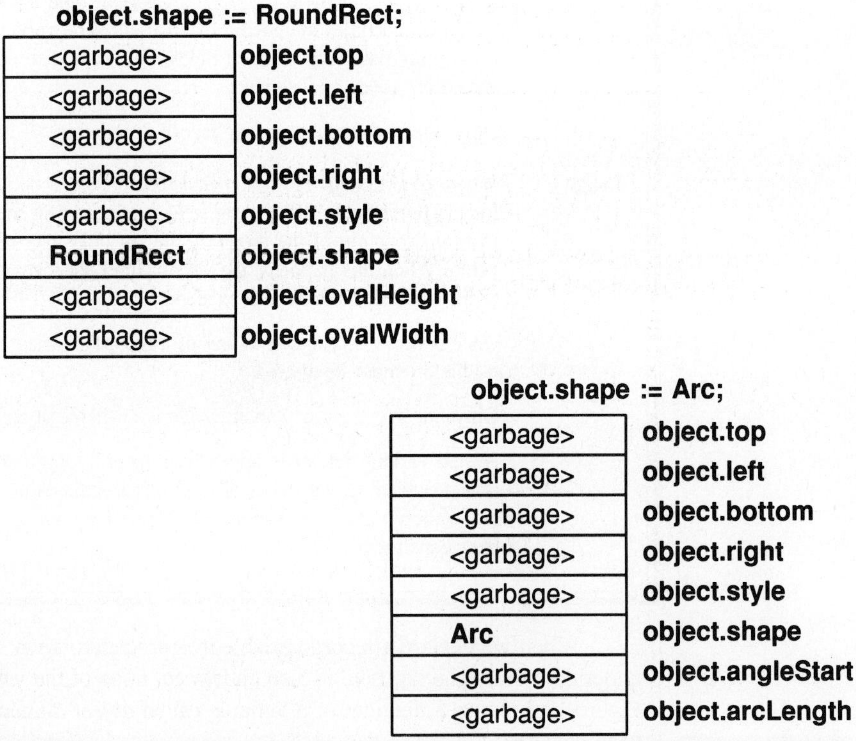

object.shape := RoundRect;

<garbage>	**object.top**
<garbage>	**object.left**
<garbage>	**object.bottom**
<garbage>	**object.right**
<garbage>	**object.style**
RoundRect	**object.shape**
<garbage>	**object.ovalHeight**
<garbage>	**object.ovalWidth**

object.shape := Arc;

<garbage>	**object.top**
<garbage>	**object.left**
<garbage>	**object.bottom**
<garbage>	**object.right**
<garbage>	**object.style**
Arc	**object.shape**
<garbage>	**object.angleStart**
<garbage>	**object.arcLength**

Figure 13.6
Result of tag field assignment

object.shape := Oval;

<garbage>	**object.top**
<garbage>	**object.left**
<garbage>	**object.bottom**
<garbage>	**object.right**
<garbage>	**object.style**
Oval	**object.shape**

Figure 13.6 (continued)

Now that the variant fields have been created, we can complete the rest of the assignments:

```
with object do
   begin
      shape := RoundRect;
      ovalHeight := 3;
      ovalWidth := 8
   end; { with }
```

```
with object do
   begin
      shape := Arc;
      angleStart := 90;
      arcLength := 180
   end; { with }
```

Variant records are often used with **case** statements. For example, the following procedure uses a **case** to assign values to the variant fields.

Code 13.1 Procedure *SaveShape*

```
{ Procedure SaveShape                                                      }
{  This procedure saves information about a given object. The user has     }
{ already selected the shape type and its fill style (framed, painted, or  }
{ inverted). In this procedure, the user specifies the corner of the sur-  }
{ rounding rectangle. Then, if needed, the procedure stores the starting   }
{ position and length of the arc or the height and width of the rounded    }
{ rectangle's oval corners.                                                }

   procedure SaveShape (var object : shapeInfo;      { shape information     }
            curShape : shapeType;                    { type of shape         }
            curStyle : styleType);                   { frame, paint, or invert }

   begin
      with object do
         begin
            style := curStyle;
            shape := curShape;

      { pick corners of surrounding rect }
            Writeln('Please pick top left corner of surrounding rectangle.');
            repeat
               GetMouse(left, top)
            until Button;
```

Code 13.1
(continued)

```
            Writeln('Please pick bottom right corner of surrounding rectangle.');
            repeat
                GetMouse(right, bottom)
            until Button;

        { Assign extra information to variant fields }
            if (shape = Arc) or (shape = RoundRect) then
                case shape of
        { arc is quarter of a circle }
                    Arc :
                        begin
                            startAngle := 180;
                            arcLength := 90
                        end; { Arc }

        { oval corners are 1/8 of rect }
                    RoundRect :
                        begin
                            ovalHeight := (top + bottom) div 8;
                            ovalWidth := (top + bottom) div 8
                        end { RoundRect }

                end{ case }
        end{ with }
    end; { procedure }
```

It's a common error to refer to the wrong variant fields. For example, when the ***shape*** field is assigned the value ***Arc***, it is an error to refer to the ***ovalHeight*** and ***ovalWidth*** fields of the same record. Since those fields do not exist when the tag field has the value ***Arc***, MacPascal cannot assign values to the fields ***ovalHeight*** and ***ovalWidth***. During execution, the following code:

```
object.shape := Arc;
if (object.ovalHeight > 12) or (object.arcLength > 180) then
...
```

will produce an error such as **An attempt has been made to access a field in an inactive variant.**

It is not possible in MacPascal to assign values to variant fields *before* the tag field has a value. For example, the following code:

```
var
    current : shapeInfo;
begin
    current.ovalHeight := 12;
    ...
```

produces the same error message as in the preceding paragraph. Before the ***ovalHeight*** field can receive a value, the ***shape*** field must be set to ***RoundRect***.

To summarize, variant records should be given values in two steps. First, the tag field should be given a value. When this has been done, the list of variant fields comes into existence, and those variant fields can then be given values.

13.8 Chapter Summary

This chapter looked at enumerated types, sets, and variant records.

Enumerated types allow you to create a range of representation for a type name. Enumerated types are declared (naturally) in the **type** section of a program. Unlike other types, though, enumerated types do not use predefined names. Instead, the type name is followed by a list of values you choose, such as the days of the week or the months of the year. Variables of this type can hold any one of the values used in the range of representation.

These creatures are called "enumerated types" because each value is associated with an ordinal number. The first value in the list is associated with the number 0, the second value with 1, and so on. Because the values can be placed in order, you can use values in the list in **for** loops, **case** statements, and other places where other ordinal types (such as integers, characters, and booleans) are expected.

Three functions rely on an ordinal type's sequence. The ***Pred*** function, given an integer, character, or enumerated type, returns the previous value in the sequence. The ***Succ*** function also takes an ordinal value as a parameter and returns the succeeding value. The ***Ord*** function, when applied to a ***char***, returns its ASCII value; this same function, when given an enumerated value, returns its position in the range of representation.

Sets in Pascal are much like sets in mathematics. Although square, rather than curly, brackets enclose their members, sets in Pascal have the same properties as their mathematical counterparts. Set variables are used to hold a collection of values. All of these values must be of the same data type (known as the base type), and no more than 65536 of these values can exist in the base type.

Assignment statements can be used to assign a list of members to a set. You can use subrange notation — < lower limit >.. < upper limit > — as a shorthand for a series of consecutive values. You cannot, however, input or output entire sets. To input a set, you have to input a member, place the member in a set, and use the union operator to join the new set and the result set.

The three set operations are union, intersection, and difference. Pascal also provides five operations for comparing sets. You can determine if one set is equal to another, is not equal to another, is a subset of another, is a superset of another, or contains a particular member.

Variant records are more powerful than fixed records because extra fields can be allocated during the program's execution. They are used to hold information for a class of data items that share a set of fields in common but additionally may have some specialized information, depending on the value of one of the common fields. For example, to keep a list of people in records, you could include a number of common fields, such as each person's name and address, and variant fields, such as spouse's name, which are needed only for certain people (in this case, those people who are married).

There are three types of fields in a variant record. The fixed fields are those fields that are always available. One of the fixed fields is designated as the tag field. This tag field must be of an ordinal type. Then, depending on the value of the tag field, a series of variant fields can come into existence.

Only one series of variant fields can be active at any time. Thus, in practice, you usually assign a value to the tag field first. When the tag field receives its value, the variant fields come into existence and can then be used.

13.9 Exercises

Understanding Concepts

1. What is wrong with the following declaration?

```
type
    cardType = (Ace, 2..10, Jack, Queen, King);
```

2. Why isn't ***real*** an ordinal type?

3. Write a declaration for a data structure that represents a Rubik's Cube™, a 3x3x3 cube of panels, in which each panel is one of the colors Ivory, Orange, Yellow, Blue, Green, or Red.

4. If ***curFrame*** is a variable of an enumerated type, what does ***Pred(Succ(curFrame))*** yield?

5. Given the declarations

```
type
    profs = (Dull, Ok, Exciting);
    dept = set of profs;
var
    introCourseTeachers: dept;
```

   what are the possible values of ***introCourseTeachers***?

6. When does < set 1 > – < set 2 > yield an empty set? What do we know about the maximum size of < set 1 > – < set 2 >?

7. What does the following code do?

```
type
    medals = (Gold, Silver, Bronze);
    winType = array[Gold..Bronze] of string[20];

procedure ListChampions(winners: winType);
```

```
var
   curMedal: medals;
begin
   for curMedal := Gold to Bronze do
      Writeln('The number', Ord(curMedal) +1, ' place finisher is ',
         winners[curMedal])
end; { ListChampions }
```

8. Given the declarations

```
type
   musicians = (Elvis, Platters, Fats, Supremes, Beatles, Stones, Dylan,
      Springsteen, Bangles);
var
   female, allArtists, fifties, solo, sixties, seventies: set of musicians;
```

and assignment statements:

```
female := [Supremes, Bangles];
allArtists := [Elvis..Bangles];
fifties := [Elvis..Fats];
solo := [Elvis, Fats, Dylan, Springsteen];
sixties := [Supremes..Dylan];
seventies := [Stones..Springsteen];
```

what do the following yield?

a. allArtists - female
b. sixties * seventies
c. Elvis **in** (allArtists - fifties)
d. sixties + seventies
e. (female * sixties) + (fifties - solo)
f. (fifties + sixties + seventies) = allArtists
g. Dylan **in** (sixties - seventies)
h. female - solo
i. [ ] <= allArtists
j. [Bangles] **in** female

9. Write a declaration for a record that contains a course name, number, professor, and, if needed, prerequisites.

10. Can a boolean field be used as a tag field? Can a set? a real?

Coding Exercises

1. Write a function called ***Next*** that is similar to ***Succ*** except that if ***Next*** is sent the last value in the enumerated type's list, it returns the first value in the enumerated type.

2. Write a function that performs the inverse of ***Ord***: given a number, the function returns the value associated with that number in the enumerated type. (This function should accept parameters of one specific enumerated type only, unlike ***Ord***, which works with all ordinal types.)

3. Write a ***PtInObject*** function. This is similar to ***PtInRect*** except that the second parameter is of type ***shapeInfo*** (as shown in section 13.6).

4. Chess masters sometimes determine that it is worth sacrificing a piece if one can capture a more powerful piece. The pieces, in ascending order of importance, are: pawn, knight, bishop, rook, queen, king. Write a function that compares a white piece and a black piece and determines which player (if either) gains from the exchange, that is which player captures the more powerful piece.

5. A set's cardinality is the number of elements in the set. Given the declaration:

```
type
   voices = (Soprano, Alto, Tenor, Baritone, Bass);
   chorus = set of voices;
```

   write a function that accepts a variable of type ***chorus*** and returns the set's cardinality.

6. Write a function that creates a set with three random elements from ***voices***.

7. Write a function that accepts a parameter of type ***lowerCase*** (defined as follows):

```
type
   lowerCase = set of 'a'..'z';
```

   and returns the complement. The complement of set A is a set containing all the elements in the base type that are not in A.

8. In chess, each square on the board has two names — one from white's point of view, one from black's (shown in the figure below). Determine a data structure in which one name of any square can be represented. Then write a function that accepts one name of a square and returns the other name.

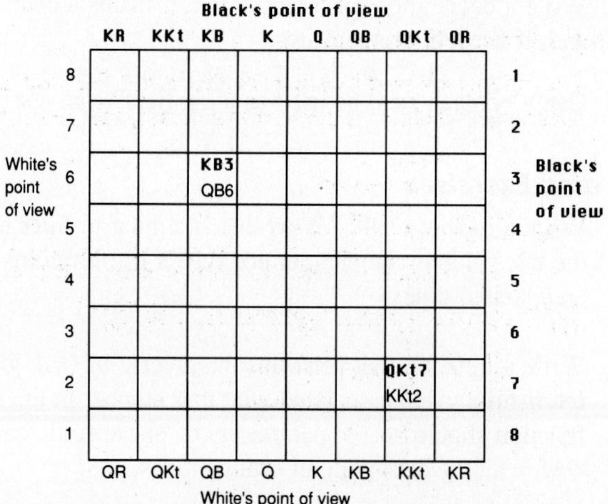

Problems 9 and 10 refer to the following declarations:

```
const
   maxTokens = 19;

type
   opType = (add, sub, mult, divide, eqls);
   eqType = (operator, operand);

   token = record
         case equationPart: eqType of
            operator: (
               op: opType
            );
            operand: (
               num: real
            )
      end; { token }
```

9. Write a procedure that reads an equation as a string and loads it into an array of type ***totalEqn***. (Assume that the input is legal.) For example, the input 6 + 37 * 14 / – 1 = should yield the array shown in the figure below.

totalEqn

operator		add		mult		divide	sub		eqls	...
operand	6		37		14			1		...

10. Write a function that receives a parameter of type ***totalEqn*** and evaluates the equation in the order read in (i.e., without regard to operand priority). The equation should end with an equals sign.

Programming Problems

1. The figure below shows part of the Boston subway system (with some minor alterations). There are four subway lines; the points where the lines intersect are

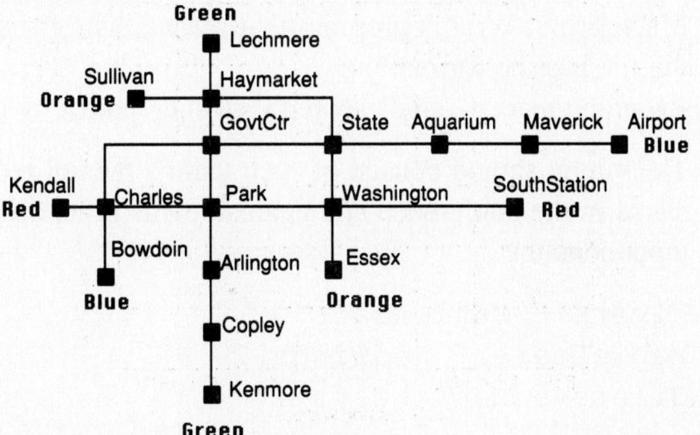

stations where passengers can transfer from one line to another. The names of the lines (Blue, Green, Red, Orange) denote the ends of the lines in the diagram. Write a program that allows a user to choose an origin and a destination and prints directions indicating which lines to take. For example, the program should tell a user who wants to get from Copley to Kendall to take the Green Line from Copley to Park, transfer to the Red Line, and take the Red Line from Park to Kendall.

2. Write a program that allows the user to draw a map, using up to 10 non-overlapping rectangles. Then, paint the rectangles so that no shapes that share a border are shaded with the same pen pattern. (Rectangles that share a corner only may have the same pen pattern.)

3. The game of Master Mind™ involves two players. One creates a code of four pegs, using six colors (black, white, red, yellow, blue, green). The other player then has 12 guesses to determine the code. The guesser presents a possible 4-peg code. The codemaker responds with another code: a filled circle for each peg if the correct color in the correct place, and a framed circle for each peg of the correct color in the wrong place. For example, if the code is Blue-Yellow-Blue-Green, the following are possible guesses and responses:

Yellow-Yellow-Yellow-Yellow	●
Blue-Yellow-Green-Blue	●●○○
Red-Blue-White-Green	●○
Blue-Blue-Red-Black	●○
Black-Blue-White-Red	○

Note that the position of the circle does not correspond to the peg — the black circles are always printed before the white circles.

Write a program in which the user plays the computer. (You can choose which role the computer will play, codemaker or guesser.)

4. In a particular hockey conference, there are ten teams in two divisions: the Northern division consists of the Canucks, Oilers, Flames, Jets, and Kings; the Southern division has the RedWings, NorthStars, Blues, BlackHawks, and MapleLeafs. Write a program that reads a list of scores from a file. Each line of the file has the format:
<winning team> <goals scored> <losing team> <goals scored>

The output should consist of each team's overall record and its record against teams in the conference and against teams in its division. For example, if the input contains:

```
Flyers 8 MapleLeafs 3
MapleLeafs 6 RedWings 2
Oilers 5 MapleLeafs 1
```

then the MapleLeafs have an overall record of 1-2 (1 win and 2 losses), a conference record of 1-1 and a division record of 1-0. Note that the input file can contain names of teams, such as Flyers, that are not in the conference.

5. Write a Layout program for floor plans. Three types of rooms are available: kitchens, bathrooms, and other. In a kitchen, a user should be able to position a sink, an oven, and a refrigerator. In a bathroom, a user should find locations for a sink and a shower or tub. Any room or fixture can be relocated at any time. At the end of the session, the details about the layout should be stored in a file that can be read when the program is opened again.

6. Write a program that keeps track of the cost (for students) of college courses. For each course, the program should retain the number of credit hours, the name, and the department. The tuition fee for a course is $170 per credit hour. Extra fees, such as the cost of books, lab fees, and material costs, should be input for each course. After the information about all of the possible courses is input, the user can enter a desired total tuition figure in dollars and a number of credit hours. The program should output the schedule of courses that comes closest to the user's dollar figure and matches the number of credit hours.

7. Write a program that finds the best housing value. For each house or apartment, input the number of rooms, the area (in square feet or meters), the number of people living in the place, the monthly rent or mortgage payment, and the costs of the various utilities. The program should be able to rank the places by total cost, cost per square foot or meter, and cost per room.

8. You're the host of a variety show. Your program has twelve acts, which change from show to show. Your acts are comics, solo singers, musical groups, and animal acts. You want to store the names of each act (including each member of the groups and the names of the animals) and other information (specifically, the type of music played by the soloist or group — jazz, rhythm & blues, classical, or pop — the instrument played by the soloist or each member of the group, or the type of animals). After receiving all the information, your program should print a schedule of acts. No two consecutive acts should be of the same type — meaning that no two comics, animal acts, or musicians who play the same type of music should appear consecutively.

9. Take a poll of the people in your class. Find out each person's name, astrological sign, shoe size, favorite type of music, and favorite type of fastener (paper clip, staples, glue, etc.). Then determine the most compatible pairs (those with the most things in common and the closest shoe sizes) and the most incompatible pairs.

10. Write a program that stores the graphic components of notes in a music layout

program (earlier seen in the programming problems in Chapter 6, number 6; Chapter 5, number 1; Chapter 4, number 10; and Chapter 3, number 1). That is, allow the user to create several measures of music notation. Then store the lines, dots, and circles of the notation in a file that can be reproduced when the program is restarted.

14

Pointers and Linked Lists

So far, when we have wanted to group a number of identical data items, we have used arrays. There are difficulties inherent in the use of arrays, however, because it is necessary to declare either the exact or the maximum size of the array. What if you don't know how much data to expect? Declaring enough storage to cover the largest amount that could be requested is very wasteful and, in some cases, impossible.

This chapter looks at *pointers* and *linked lists*. Like an array, a linked list holds a set of variables of the same type; typically those variables are records. Unlike an array, the maximum number of variables that the linked list holds can change dynamically; that is, the number of variables can change during a program's execution without being constrained by a predefined upper limit.

14.1 The Problem with Arrays

Suppose you want to write a program to keep a list of all the students in a class. Suppose further that you want to use the same program for every class at Finite State University. The problem is that each course has a varying number of students. According to the registrar's course rosters, Egyptology 184 has 3 students, Computer Science 11 has 250 students, and Engineering 9 has 32,745 students. You could declare an array of 32,745 slots to hold the largest class, but when you ran the program for Egyptology 184, there would be 32,742 unused slots in the array.

The problem is that storage in arrays is *static*, not *dynamic*. In other words, the number of array slots is fixed and cannot change during the execution of your program. When you define your array variable, you tell Pascal how many storage positions you'll need. If your list turns out to be longer than that, you're out of luck.

Moving information around in arrays can also cause problems. Suppose you have kept an array of club members in alphabetical order, and a new member joins the club. To put the new member's name in the array in the correct order, you have to find the right spot to insert the new member and then move every single piece of information in the array after that spot over one slot in the array. Figure 14.1 shows how the information in an array would have to be manipulated.

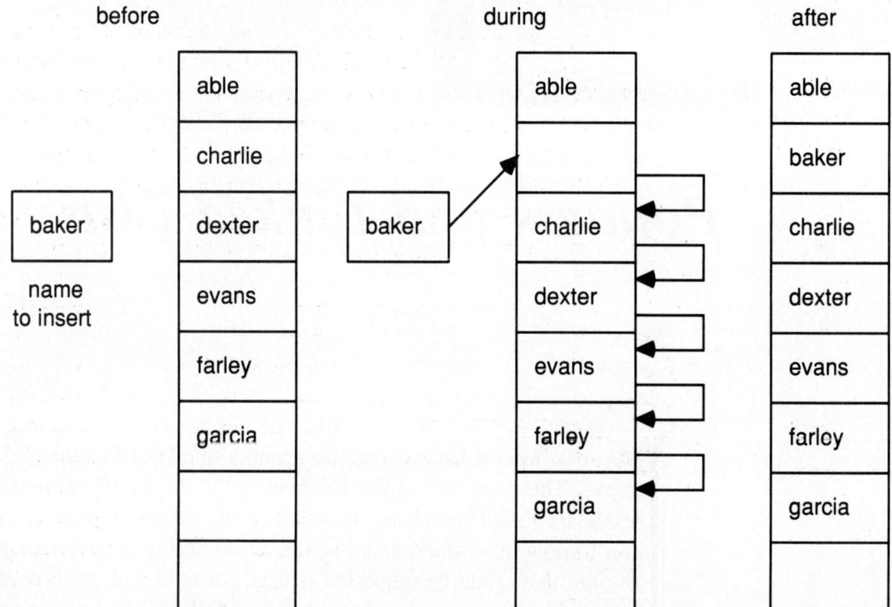

Figure 14.1
Inserting a name into an array in alphabetical order

Deletion from arrays is also a problem. Every time a member leaves the club, you would have to perform the same type of data move that you did with insertion. Otherwise, you'd have to check each slot to see if it contains a "real" value or a deleted value; furthermore, you couldn't recycle the slot where the deleted member's name used to be. With large amounts of data, these consecutive data moves are extremely inefficient and unnecessary.

In general, arrays are most useful when there is a reasonable limit on the amount of information to store and you don't need to move that information around very much. However, not every problem that requires a list of variables conforms to these restrictions. Thus, you need a method of storing information that will enable you to manipulate lists more easily and more dynamically than does the array structure. For this purpose, Pascal provides a feature called *pointer variables*. Pointer variables (or "pointers," as they are most often called) make list insertion and deletion easy and efficient and also allow use of *dynamic storage* — that is, storage that can grow and shrink in size as a program runs.

14.2 Linked Lists

What are pointers used for? We mentioned earlier that the problems we were going to deal with were data manipulation in lists and dynamic storage. There is a specific data structure that simplifies list manipulation. When using arrays of records, we are forced to refer to each record by its subscript. We also must tell the computer exactly how many records to create when we declare the array size. Instead of doing this, we can create a structure known as a *linked list* (see Figure 14.2).

In a linked list, each record, or *node*, contains a field that links, that is, points to, the next node in the list. The number of nodes can increase or decrease during a program's execution. If you wrote a program that kept a linked list of records, one for each student enrolled in a class, the linked list would have 3 nodes for Egyptology 184, 250 nodes for Computer Science 11, and 32,745 nodes for Engineering 9. A linked list makes it possible to create as many nodes as needed. Furthermore, it is possible to reorder the list by changing the way nodes point to one another; it is not necessary to move the nodes themselves around in memory.

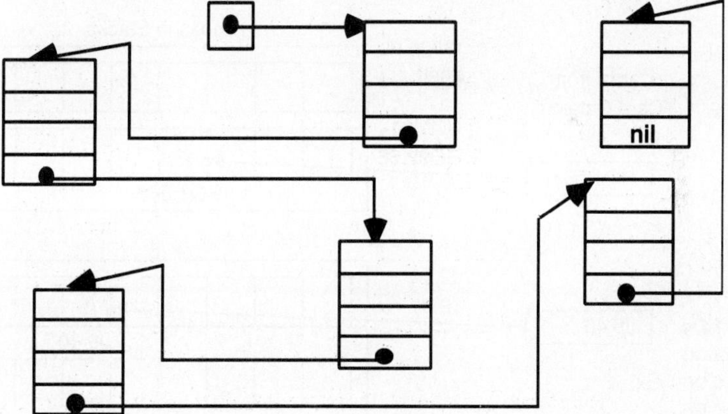

Figure 14.2
A linked list

While the records in an array are found in contiguous blocks of memory, the records in a linked list can be placed at random throughout main memory. Since the records are scattered, links, or pointers, are used to connect the records together. A special pointer called a **nil** pointer designates the end of the list.

Each node in the above list is a record with four fields, in which one has been declared as a pointer variable. It is used to point to another block of information of the same type as the data record. The pointer field does not have to be the last one in the record, but it is standard practice to put the pointer fields either last or first in the record.

Figure 14.2 shows the nodes of a linked list as scattered all over memory. For convenience, however, we usually represent the nodes of a linked list in a row. Figure 14.3 is a typical diagram of a linked list.

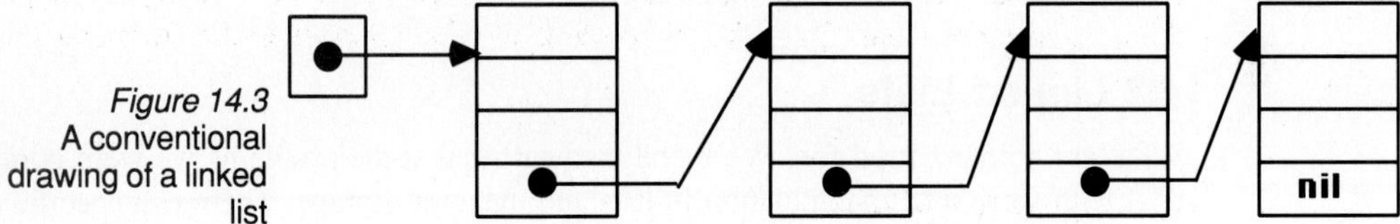

Figure 14.3
A conventional drawing of a linked list

14.3 Pointers in Real Life

We have described, in relatively vague terms, what a pointer does. But what exactly *is* a pointer? A pointer is a variable that contains not a value but rather the *address* of a value that is stored somewhere in the computer's main memory. Thus, it "points" to the value. An example of pointers in real life is the card catalog system in a library. A card does not hold the contents of a book, but it does tell you the book's location (address) in the stacks. Thus, each card can be considered a "pointer" to a certain piece of data. Figure 14.4 illustrates how the cards in a card catalog "point" to books.

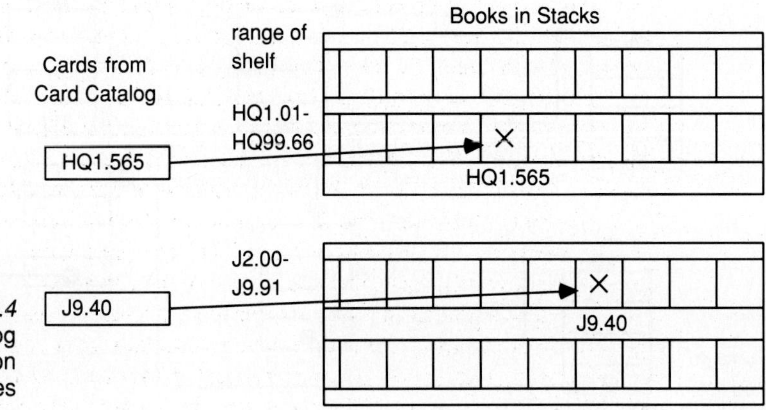

Figure 14.4
Cards in a catalog "pointing" to books on a library's shelves

The advantages that computer scientists derive from their pointers are similar to those that librarians derive from their catalogue systems. Librarians can arrange their cataloguing system by changing the locations of cards in the card catalogue, not the locations of all the books on the shelves. For instance, almost every library has two card catalogues: one organized by author and title and one organized by subject. While it's easy to have two sets of cards organized in different ways, it would be impossible to have two complete sets of books organized in different ways.

If the library receives a collection of rare books as a gift, it might put those books together in one safe place. However, the books would still have to be indexed by author and subject. The cards for the rare books are interleaved with the cards for the other books, even though the two sets of books remain in separate parts of the library. In a similar way, pointers make *data management*, or the ordering of information, a less monumental task. By using pointers, programmers can regroup their data lists without changing the location of the data in main memory. To explore this idea in more detail, let's take a short look at what happens in the computer's memory.

14.4 Main Memory

Main memory is essentially a very large one-dimensional array of storage locations. As mentioned in Chapter 1, each variable is stored in its own memory location; compound variables occupy consecutive memory locations. Each location, you'll remember, contains a *byte*. A byte, defined as eight consecutive bits in memory, is the standard unit of measurement for computer memory. When you are told that you are working with a 512K Macintosh, that means your machine's memory contains 512 kilobytes. (The K is an abbreviation for kilobyte, or 1024 bytes.) Each data type uses a different number of bytes. For example, an integer variable occupies 2 bytes in memory. A character occupies 1 byte; thus, a string of 80 characters occupies 80 bytes.

When Pascal needs to declare a compound data structure, it reserves memory for each field of the record or each element of the array in consecutive bytes in memory. If we have a record with two fields of **string*[80]*** and one field of ***integer***, Pascal reserves 80 + 80 + 2, or 162 consecutive locations in memory. The last byte of the first string immediately precedes the first byte of the second string.

In the same way that every item in a Pascal array has a subscript, every one of these (byte-long) memory locations has a distinct hardware identification number called an *address*. When Pascal reserves memory for a variable, the variable's address is the *first* byte it occupies. If a **string*[3]*** occupies locations 20A5, 20A6 and 20A7, the string's address is the first location, or 20A5. (These addresses are referred to in hexadecimal — base 16 — notation.) Pointers are possible because Pascal internally numbers the bytes and keeps track of the addresses.

To create a pointer to a memory location, we start by declaring a variable. Pascal reserves as many consecutive memory locations as necessary to store the variable. Figure 14.5 shows the memory locations for an integer and a record with three fields. The two memory locations starting at 1A4C have been reserved to hold the integer, and 162 memory locations starting at 20A5 have been reserved to hold the three fields of a record. The addresses of the integer and record variables are 1A4C and 20A5, respectively.

A pointer indicates where in main memory a variable is stored, just as a card in a catalogue indicates where on a library's shelves a book is stored. In Figure 14.6, ***recPtr*** and ***intPtr*** are pointer variables that contain memory addresses of the variables to which they refer: ***intPtr*** points to the single integer; ***recPtr*** points to the record. Note that the pointers indicate where the record starts. The integer begins at location 1A4C, and the rest of the record is in the memory locations immediately following 20A5.

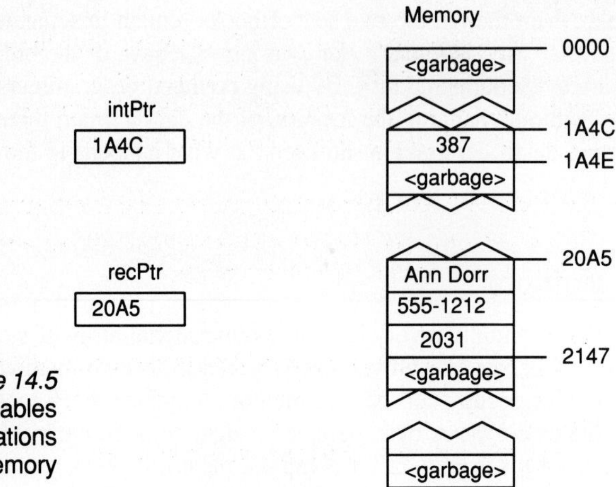

Figure 14.5
Pointer variables pointing to locations in memory

It doesn't matter where in main memory the information is stored. More important, in Pascal you do not need to know that ***intPtr*** points to memory location 1A4C — all you need to know is that ***intPtr*** points to an integer. In this sense, pointers are better than cards in a catalogue. The card can tell you the book's call number, but then you need to find the call number's address in the stacks. With pointers, however, you do not need to know the variable's address. Variables can be kept anywhere in memory, as long as there are pointers to indicate their position. As you work with pointers, you will not actually need to deal with the numeric address of a variable's memory location; Pascal will "fetch the book" from memory for you. Diagrams of pointer variables, then, usually do not show the memory addresses, since we do not have to remember them. Instead, pointers are represented with arrows that begin in some variable and point to a piece of data, as in Figure 14.6.

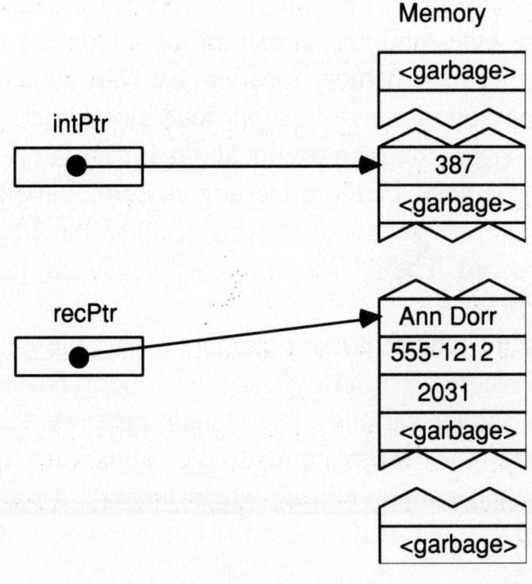

Figure 14.6
Pointer variables using arrow notation

14.5 Declaring Pointers

To use pointers, you must first reserve a space in main memory large enough to hold the data. But how does the computer know what kind of space to reserve? As with other variable types, this is accomplished with a variable declaration at the beginning of your procedures. The first step in doing this is to define the pointer's type.

Syntax Box 14.1
Declaration of pointer types and variables

Purpose The type defines a template for pointer variables; the variable declaration reserves memory for the pointer.

Syntax

```
type
    < pointer-type identifier > = ^< data type to be pointed to >;

var
    < variable name > : < pointer-type identifer >;
```

where < pointer-type identifier > is any legal Pascal identifier.

^ is the caret sign. To print this symbol, press the shift key and the number 6 key.*

< data type to be pointed to > is the type of storage group the pointer will be used to reference. This storage group is defined after the pointer definition.

< variable name > is any legal identifier for a variable.

Usage When you declare a pointer variable, memory is reserved for the pointer itself, not for the data the pointer points to.

Pointer variables can be used to point to any type of variable, but are usually used to point at records.

When you want to refer to a pointer variable in a statement, use < variable name >; when you want to refer to what the pointer variable points to, use < variable name > followed by a caret. Examples of this notation are shown in Section 14.7.

A convention used in glossaries for pointer types and variables is to use two hyphens and a greater-than sign (-->) to indicate the words "points to" and then say what is being pointed to.

---

* Other versions of Pascal use an at-sign (@) or up-arrow (↑) where a caret is used in MacPascal and Lightspeed.

A pointer makes no sense by itself; a pointer needs to point to *something*. Once you've defined the type of pointer, you must declare the type of data it will be pointing at. In the following example ***clubMemPtr*** has been declared to point to a record of type ***member***.

```
type
  memPtr = ^member;                { --> member record               }

  member = record                  { club member record              }
      name : string[40];           { club member name                }
      phone : string[40];          { club member phone number        }
      membership : integer         { club membership number          }
    end; { member }

var
  clubMemPtr: memPtr;              { -- > club member                }
```

In declaring the pointer type, we have not actually set up the space in memory and made it ready for use. As always with **type** declarations, all we have done is give the computer a template that we can build on and fill in during the program's execution.

We now know that the variable ***clubMemPtr*** is a pointer and that it points to a record of type ***member***. It is crucial to keep track of what information a pointer points to; you cannot expect ***clubMemPtr*** to point to a real.

A pointer variable, such as ***clubMemPtr***, lets you keep track of a place in memory, but more important, you know what is stored in that memory. It's as if you have a key to a room with valuable information. The key itself — a three-inch piece of metal — is not important; what is important is that it allows you to gain access to the room. You rarely concern yourself with how the key works inside the lock mechanism; all you are concerned with is that the key gets you into the room. Similarly, you rarely pay attention to *how* pointer variables and addresses work inside Pascal; you are concerned only with the information that the pointer leads you to.

To carry the analogy further, you need to remember which key lets you into which room. Just as keys may all appear to be the same on a key ring, pointers all appear the same to Pascal (i.e., they are all variables that hold addresses). Still, you cannot use your back-door key to enter your front door. Unless you use the right key, you cannot get into the room you want. In the same manner, you need to use a pointer that will lead you to the desired information. Mnemonic naming of variables helps you to keep track of which pointer variable points to which information. For example, ***memPtr*** in the previous example denotes a pointer variable pointing to a member-type record.

14.6 The New Procedure

Pointers enable us to use *dynamic storage*. That means that we can create as much storage as we want and are not limited to an amount declared initially, as we are with arrays. When we use pointers, we create storage for each piece of data as needed, using a predefined procedure that is executed while the program is running. This procedure, ***New***, creates space for the record and sets the pointer variable to point at it. The pointer variable then acts as a "key" to the newly created record, so that we can refer to the record's fields.

Syntax Box 14.2
New

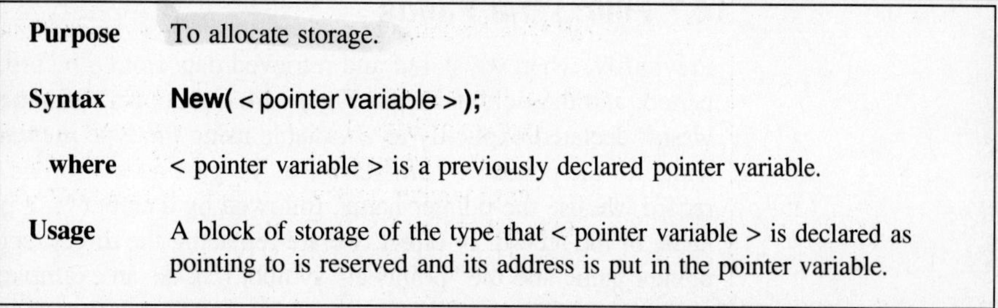

Purpose	To allocate storage.
Syntax	**New(** < pointer variable > **);**
where	< pointer variable > is a previously declared pointer variable.
Usage	A block of storage of the type that < pointer variable > is declared as pointing to is reserved and its address is put in the pointer variable.

Using the pointer type declared in the last section, we write a program with the following declarations and calls to the ***New*** procedure:

```
type
   memPtr = ^member;                         { member record               }

   member = record                           { club member record          }
         name : string[40];                  { club member name            }
         phone : string[40];                 { club member phone number    }
         membership : integer                { club membership number      }
      end; { member }

var
   clubMemPtr : memPtr;                      { -- > club member            }

begin
   New (clubMemPtr);
   ...
end. { Program }
```

This program creates the situation shown in Figure 14.7. The record, of course, is like any other variable before you put information in it. Thus, before the program assigns values to the record's fields, they contain garbage left over from a prior use of that section of memory.

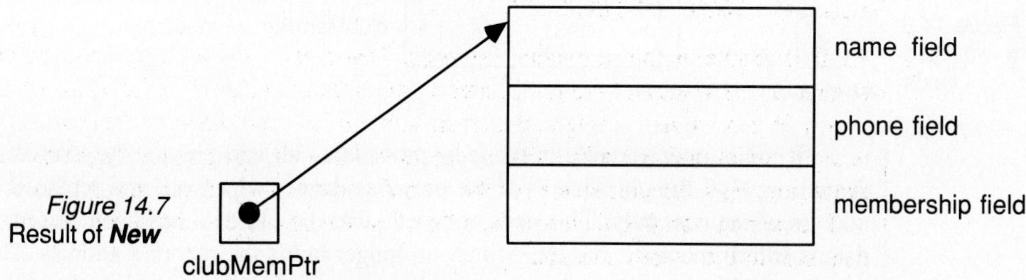

Figure 14.7
Result of ***New***

14.7 Filling the Fields

Previously, when we stored and retrieved data from a record, we used a record name, a period, and the field name. In Figure 14.7, there isn't a name for the record because it wasn't declared explicitly as a variable using the type ***member***. There is, however, a name for the pointer — ***clubMemPtr***. To gain access to one of the fields in the record, we use the pointer name, followed by a caret (^), a period (.), and the field name of the record. In effect, we are replacing the direct record name with the indirect pointer name and the "points at" symbol (^). As an example, let's see what program statements it takes to fill in a record for Ann Dorr after using the ***New*** statement to allocate its storage.

```
New(clubMemPtr);
clubMemPtr^.name := 'Ann Dorr';
clubMemPtr^.phone := '123-4567';
clubMemPtr^.membership := 2031;
```

The second statement can be translated into the following English sentences: "***clubMemPtr*** points at a record. The ***name*** field of that record is assigned the string 'Ann Dorr'." This is clearly quite similar to operations using normal records. In fact, since the notation ***clubMemPtr^*** refers to a record, we can rewrite the above code using a **with** statement as follows:

```
New(clubMemPtr);
with clubMemPtr^ do
  begin
    name := 'Ann Dorr';
    phone := '123-4567';
    membership := 2031
  end; { with }
```

The prefix ***clubMemPtr^*** is appended to each of the fields inside the **with** block. Figure 14.8 shows the result of these assignments.

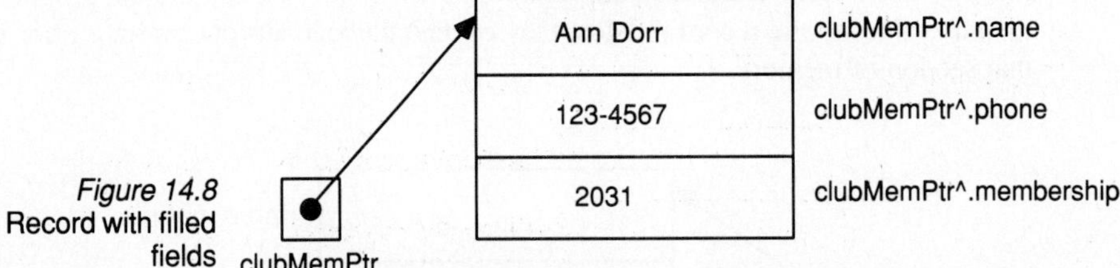

Figure 14.8
Record with filled fields

If the pointer variable in the ***New*** procedure call had previously pointed to something else, the old address of the previous data is wiped out and replaced by the address of the new data. This does not mean that the old data has been erased. The old data is still in memory, but the pointer no longer holds the record's address. Thus, the data is "lost" in memory and unusable.

Say we have the following code to add a new record for a club member after we have filled in the one for Ann Dorr:

```
type
   memPtr = ^member;                         { member record               }

   member = record                           { club member record          }
         name : string[40];                  { club member name            }
         phone : string[40];                 { club member phone number    }
         membership : integer                { club membership number      }
      end; { member }

var
   clubMemPtr : memPtr;                      { --> club member             }

begin
   New (clubMemPtr);
   New(clubMemPtr);
   clubMemPtr^.name := 'Ann Dorr';
   clubMemPtr^.phone := '123-4567';
   clubMemPtr^.membership := 2031;
   New(clubMemPtr);
   ...
end. { Program }
```

Before we fill the fields for the next member, we would have the situation shown in Figure 14.9.

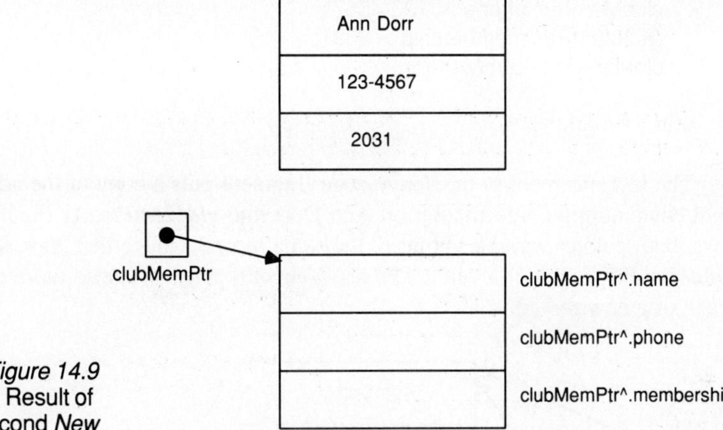

Figure 14.9 Result of second *New*

The information on Ann Dorr is still in memory. However, we did not declare names for club member records, and now there is no pointer to this record. Thus, we can no longer gain access to the information in Ann Dorr's record. We will deal with the problem of recovering the record's information when we discuss linked lists later in this chapter.

14.8 Assignment of Pointers

When we tell MacPascal to assign one record to another, the contents of the first record are copied, one field at a time, to the other record. Often, though, we don't actually need to copy the information; we just need two methods of referring to the record.

If we have a pointer to the record, we can copy the record's pointer into another pointer variable. We are not actually copying the information in the record anywhere; we are just putting the address of the record in another pointer. Thus, we have two pointers to the same information in memory. Say that we use the following declarations and that ***clubMem*** points to the information on member Ann Dorr:

```
type
   memPtr = ^member;                    { member record               }

   member = record                      { club member record          }
         name : string[40];             { club member name            }
         phone : string[40];            { club member phone number    }
         membership : integer           { club membership number      }
      end; { member }

var
   clubMemPtr,                          { -- > club member            }
   oldMemPtr: memPtr;                   { -- > member no longer in club }

begin
   New (clubMemPtr);
   clubMemPtr^.name := 'Ann Dorr';
   clubMemPtr^.phone := '123-4567';
   clubMemPtr^.membership := 2031;
   oldMemPtr := clubMemPtr;
   ...
end. { Program }
```

The last statement in the above code fragment puts a copy of the address of the record containing the information on Ann Dorr into ***oldMemPtr***. As Figure 14.10 shows, both pointer variables point to the same record. Notice that ***New*** wasn't used on ***oldMemPtr*** to give it a value. We use ***New*** only when we need more space for storage of a new record.

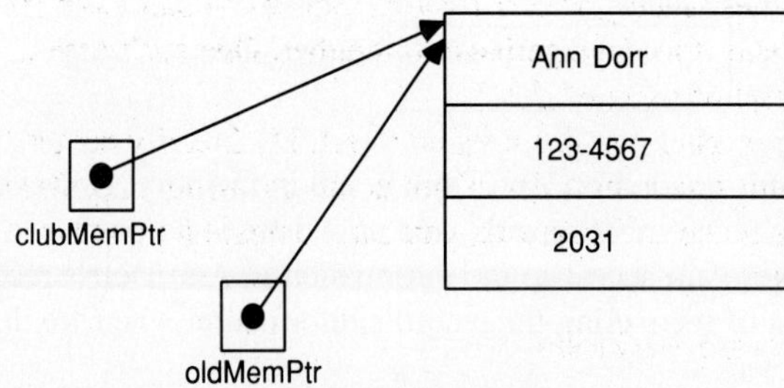

Figure 14.10 Result of pointer assignment

Since both pointers point to the same record, the following two statements have the same effect:

```
clubMemPtr^.membership := 2087;
oldMemPtr^.membership := 2087;
```

This situation means that if we change the value of a field in our record using ***clubMemPtr***, we also notice the change if we refer to that field through the ***oldMemPtr*** pointer.

```
type
   memPtr = ^member;                        { member record                  }

   member = record                          { club member record             }
         name : string[40];                 { club member name               }
         phone : string[40];                { club member phone number       }
         membership : integer               { club membership number         }
      end; { member }

var
   clubMemPtr,                              { -- > club member               }
   oldMemPtr: memPtr;                       { -- > member no longer in club  }

begin
   New (clubMemPtr);
   clubMemPtr^.name := 'Tex Processor';
   clubMemPtr^.phone := '301-7654';
   clubMemPtr^.membership := 1484;
   oldMemPtr := clubMemPtr;
   Write(oldMemPtr^.name);
   Write(oldMemPtr^.phone);
   Writeln(oldMemPtr^.membership);
   ...
end. { Program }
```

The above code fragment prints out:

```
Tex Processor 301-7654 1484
```

14.9 The nil Pointer

There are times when you don't want a pointer to point to a memory location, but you don't want it to have garbage in it either. One such case is when you want to denote the end of a linked list.

You can give pointers a value of **nil**. Nil literally means "nothing," and that's what a pointer given the value of **nil** points to — nothing. Pascal recognizes **nil** as a valid pointer value. Therefore, you can compare a pointer's value to **nil** with the comparison:

```
if < ptr var > = nil then
```

As you will see, this type of test determines whether you've reached the end of a linked list.

If your code attempts to reference data through a pointer set to **nil**, it will generate a runtime error. For example, suppose you have a pointer variable ***endPtr*** that is of type ***memPtr***. If you set the pointer to **nil** with the statement

```
endPtr := nil;
```

then any attempt to use ***endPtr*** as a reference will produce a runtime error. The statement

```
Write(endPtr^.name);
```

produces an error such as **An attempt has been made to dereference a pointer whose value is NIL.** This is because ***endPtr*** contains the value **nil**. Pascal cannot get at a ***name*** field through a **nil** pointer; therefore, Pascal cannot find the information you are looking for.

14.10 Coding Linked Lists

Section 14.2 looked at the structure of a linked list; this section discusses how to build the actual list. The first step is to design templates in the **type** declarations for the typical record and its pointer. Each node, or item, in the linked list is a record with four fields. To create the structures shown in Figure 14.2, one of the fields is declared as a pointer as follows:

```
type
   memPtr = ^member;                     { member record                }

   member = record                       { club member record           }
         name : string[40];              { club member name             }
         phone : string[40];             { club member phone number     }
         membership : integer;           { club membership number       }
         nextMem: memPtr                 { -- > to next member in list  }
      end; { member }
```

The next step is to use the ***New*** procedure to get a storage block for each node. In the example that follows, the user can input members into the club list, one at a time, at the Macintosh.

Two conventions used in the manipulation of linked lists are shown in the example. One is known as a *head pointer*. A head pointer is a pointer at the beginning of the list that never changes its value: it always points to the beginning of the list. Often, the head pointer points not at the first data node but at a dummy node. Without a dummy node, you would have to change the value of the head pointer each time an insertion was made at the front of the list. With a dummy node, however, all insertions to the linked list can be made in the same way. (The method of insertion is explained in further detail in the next sections.)

The second convention involves keeping track of the end of the list. The very last node in the list obviously points to nothing, and so its pointer field will point to **nil**.

In the example, we assume that the records should be kept in the order in which the user types them in. Thus, each node must be placed at the end of the list. Since each new node becomes the last node in the list, we will point the last node's pointer field to the new node, and set the new node's pointer field to **nil**. Let's develop the pseudocode for the example:

```
Start the list
Get number of members in list
For each member, enter info
```

From this start, we can break down the problem:

```
CALL: Start the list
CALL: Get number of members in list
CALL: For each member, enter info

{ Start the list }
Create header node
Point header node's pointer field to NIL
Initialize previous (a pointer variable) to header node (See below)

{ Get number of members in list }
Input number of members in list

{ For each member, enter information }
FOR each member in list
  BEGIN
    Create node
    Point node's pointer field to NIL
    Input name
    Input phone
    Input membership number
    Point previous to new node
  END { FOR }
```

There will be three pointers in this algorithm. The variable ***headPtr*** points to the head (dummy) node of the list, and ***clubMemPtr*** points to the current club member record being inserted. ***previous*** is a pointer variable that aids in the insertion, because it points to the node immediately before the place we want to insert. After we fill the data fields of the new node, we can easily insert it into the list because ***previous*** points to the place before the insertion point in the list.

```
type
   memPtr = ^member;                        { member record                    }
   member = record                          { club member record               }
         name : string[40];                 { club member name                 }
         phone : string[40];                { club member phone number         }
         membership : integer;              { club membership number           }
         nextMem: memPtr                    { -- > next member in list         }
      end; { member }

{ Mainline }
var
   clubMemPtr,                              { -- > current club member         }
   previous,                                { -- > last member added to list   }
   headPtr : memPtr;                        { -- > first member in list        }
   loop,                                    { loop counter                     }
   numMembers : integer;                    { number of members in club        }

begin
   New (headPtr);                           { create first node in list        }

   headPtr^.nextMem := nil;                 { initialize the end of the list   }

   previous := headPtr;                     { initialize previous ptr          }

   Write('Enter number of members: ');
   Readln(numMembers);
   for loop := 1 to numMembers do
      begin
         New(clubMemPtr); { create new node }

      { fill fields of new node }
         clubMem^.nextMem := nil;
         Write('Enter member name: ');
         Readln(clubMemPtr^.name);
         Write('Enter phone number: ');
         Readln(clubMemPtr^.phone);
         Write('Enter membership number: ');
         Readln(clubMemPtr^.membership);
         previous^.nextMem := clubMemPtr; {  insert new code                }
         previous := previous^.nextMem    { move previous up in list        }
      end { for }
 end { Mainline }
```

After the execution of this code, the linked list is filled with the input. If the input is

```
Ann Dorr
123-4567
2101
Tex Processor
301-7654
1033
```

```
Nan D. Gate
502-2003
001
```

the final linked list will be that shown in Figure 14.11.

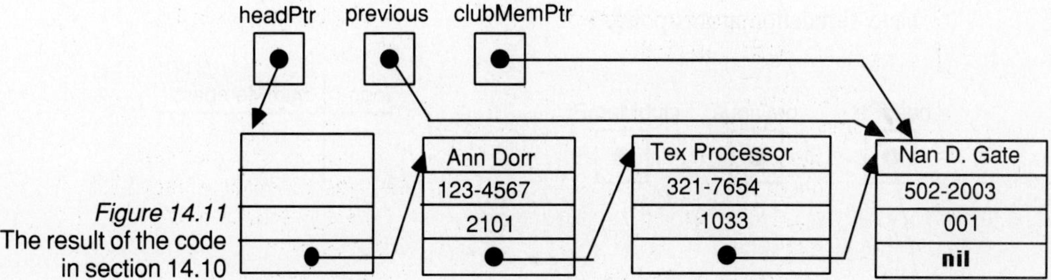

Figure 14.11
The result of the code in section 14.10

14.11 Hand Simulating Linked Lists

To show how the linked list is built, let's hand simulate the code. When we hand simulate programs that use pointers, we represent the pointer as a box with an arrow. However, when the program starts, we don't know where the arrows are pointing. At this point, therefore, the pointer variables are empty boxes. Thus, we start with the variable table shown in Figure 14.12.

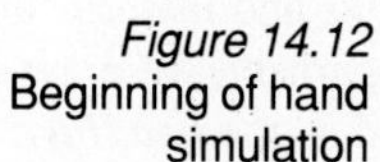

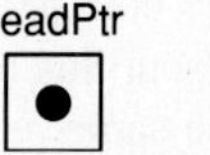

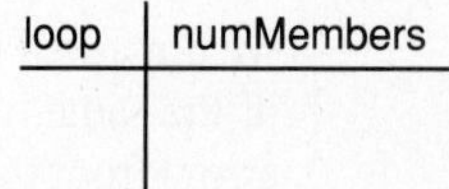

Figure 14.12
Beginning of hand simulation

The code begins with the statement

```
New(headPtr);
```

To represent this in the hand simulation, we draw an arrow from the ***headPtr*** box. From the **var** declarations, we know that ***headPtr*** is a ***memPtr***; from the **type** declarations, we know that variables of type ***memPtr*** point to records of type ***member***. Thus, the arrow coming from ***headPtr*** points to a record with four fields, as shown in Figure 14.13.

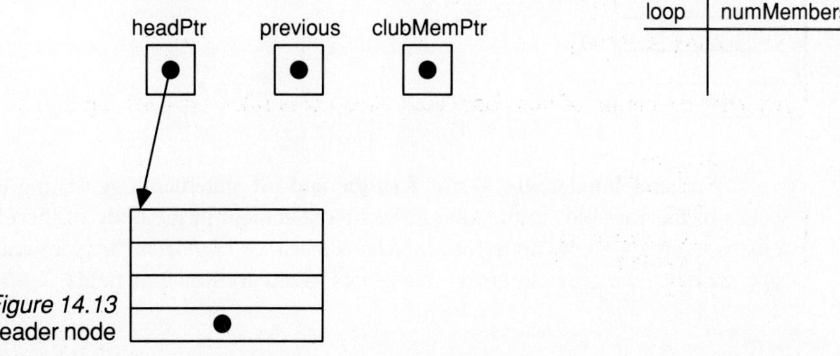

Figure 14.13
Creating header node

The next statement is

```
headPtr^.nextMem := nil;
```

As we have seen before, ***headPtr^*** is the code that means we should look at whatever ***headPtr*** is pointing at. The statement means that the ***nextMem*** field of the record that ***headPtr*** points at should be assigned the **nil** pointer. Figure 14.14 shows the hand simulation at this point.

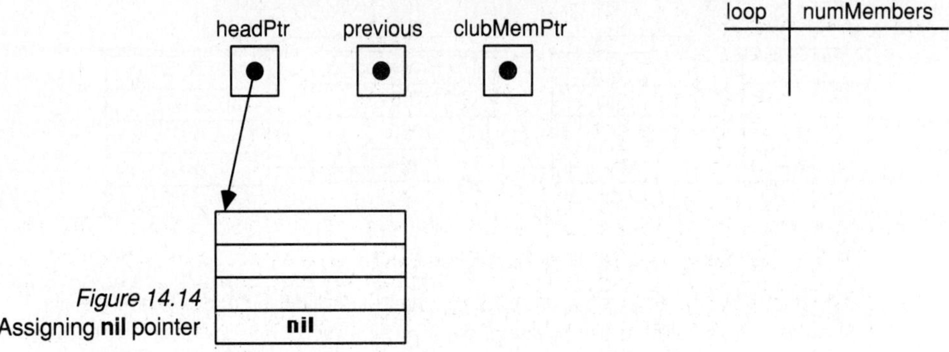

Figure 14.14
Assigning **nil** pointer

In the third statement,

```
previous := headPtr;
```

we are asked to assign one pointer to another. Since both ***previous*** and ***headPtr*** are of the same type, this assignment is legal. To represent this assignment, we draw an arrow from the ***previous*** box. The arrow ends at the same record as the ***headPtr*** arrow, but the ***previous*** and ***headPtr*** arrows are distinct.

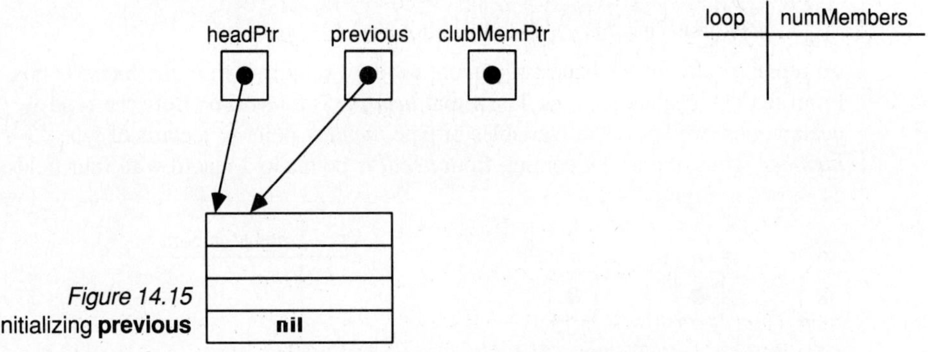

Figure 14.15
Initializing **previous**

We hand simulate the ***Write***, ***Readln***, and **for** statements by writing the values of the variables in the table. The first statement in the body of the **for** loop tells us to create a new node for ***clubMemPtr***. Since ***clubMemPtr*** is a variable of type ***memPtr***, we draw an arrow that points to a record of four fields.

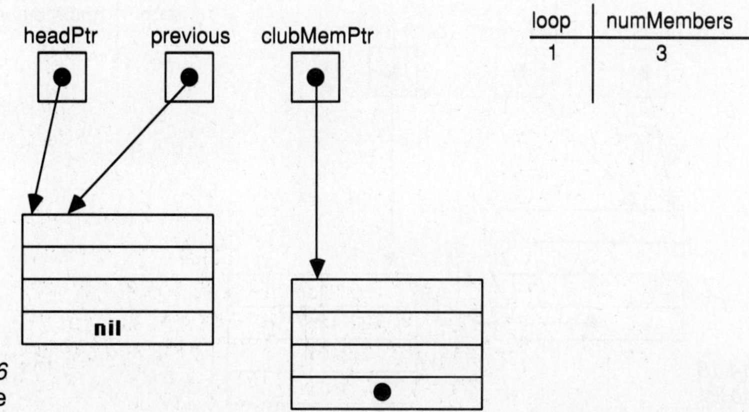

Figure 14.16
Creating new node

The next statements in the loop assign values to the record that ***clubMemPtr*** points to. First, we assign a **nil** pointer to the ***nextMem*** field of the record that ***clubMemPtr*** points to. Then, we accept the record's name, phone, and membership fields from input. At this point, the hand simulation looks like Figure 14.17.

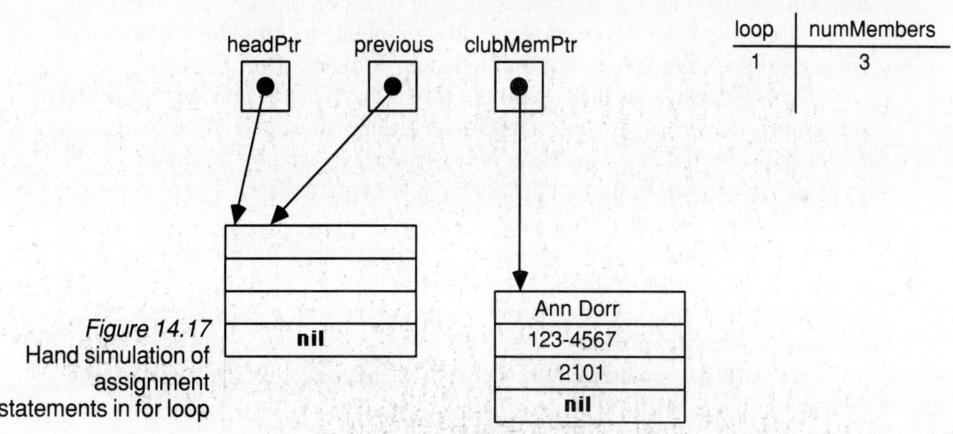

Figure 14.17
Hand simulation of assignment statements in for loop

The next statement in the **for** loop is

```
previous^.nextMem := clubMemPtr;
```

Looking at the **var** and **type** declarations, we see that both ***previous^.nextMem*** and ***clubMemPtr*** are pointers to records of type ***member***. Since the types are compatible, the assignment is legal.

To represent the assignment, we start at the pointer ***previous*** and follow the arrow that comes from the ***previous*** box to a record. The statement asks us to look at the ***nextMem*** field of this record. We draw an arrow from this field to the same place where ***clubMemPtr*** points.

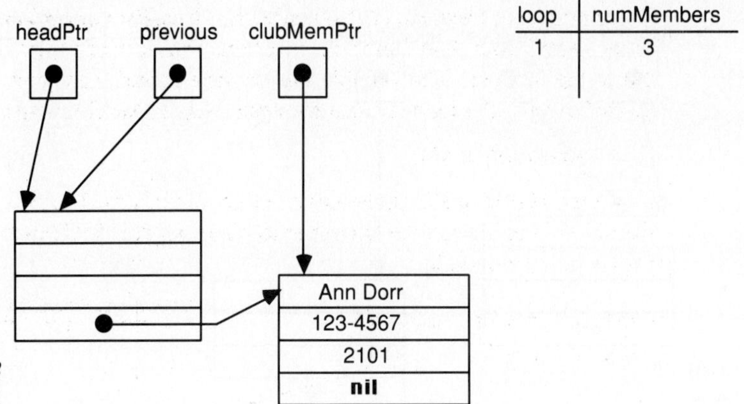

Figure 14.18
Adding node to list

Finally, we reach the last statement in the **for** loop:

```
previous := previous^.nextMem;
```

Again, we are assigning one pointer to another. To draw this assignment, we first evaluate the expression on the right of the :=, namely, the value of ***previous^.nextMem***. We start at the ***previous*** box and follow the arrow to its endpoint. We then look at the ***nextMem*** field of the record we have found. We follow the arrow from the ***nextMem*** field — it points to Ann Dorr's information. Thus, ***previous^.nextMem*** points to the record with Ann Dorr.

The statement says that we should assign the value of ***previous^.nextMem*** to ***previous***. However, ***previous*** already has a value. Since this is an assignment statement, the old value of ***previous*** is erased and replaced by the value of ***previous^.nextMem***. In the example, the old arrow is replaced by an arrow to Ann Dorr's information.

Before the assignment, ***clubMemPtr*** and ***previous^.nextMem*** were pointing at the same node in the list. We could have achieved the same result by replacing the line ***previous := previous^.nextMem;*** with the assignment ***previous := clubMemPtr;***.

We have now completed one iteration of the **for** loop. The hand simulation appears in Figure 14.19.

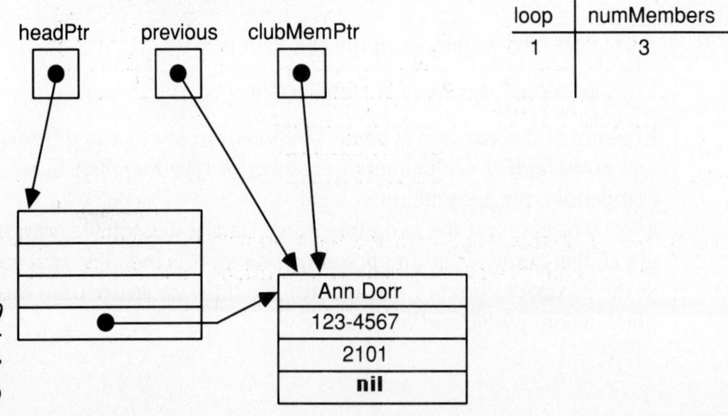

Figure 14.19
Hand simulation after one execution of **for** loop

Three pointers (***previous***, ***clubMemPtr***, and ***headPtr^.nextMem***) are pointing to the record with Ann Dorr's information. The flow of control now goes back to the top of the **for** loop. The variable ***loop*** is incremented, and since ***loop*** is less than ***numMembers***, the loop is executed again. Again, the first statement of the loop is

```
New(clubMemPtr);
```

However, ***clubMemPtr*** is already pointing to a record. The ***New*** procedure erases the old pointer and creates a pointer to a new record. We thus have the situation shown in Figure 14.20.

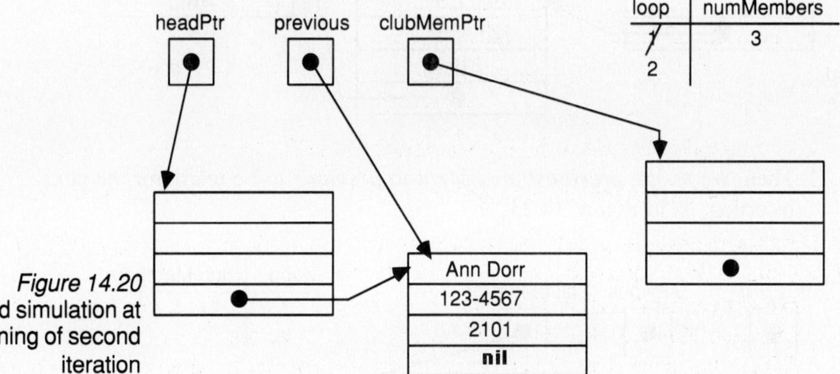

Figure 14.20
Hand simulation at beginning of second iteration

We can still gain access to Ann Dorr's record. ***previous*** still points to that record, even though we changed the value of ***clubMemPtr***. Because of the existence of ***previous***, we have an easy way to access the last node in the list when an even newer record is created.

Again, we fill the fields of the record that ***clubMemPtr*** points to (Figure 14.21).

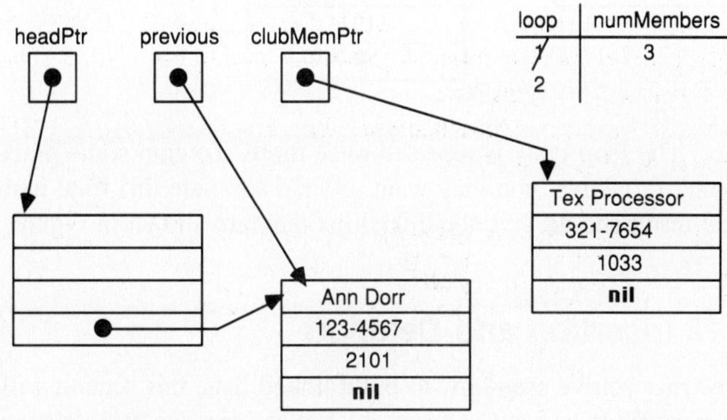

Figure 14.21
Filling in fields

We finish this iteration of the **for** loop with two pointer assignments. First, we assign ***clubMemPtr*** to ***previous^.nextMem***, as in Figure 14.22.

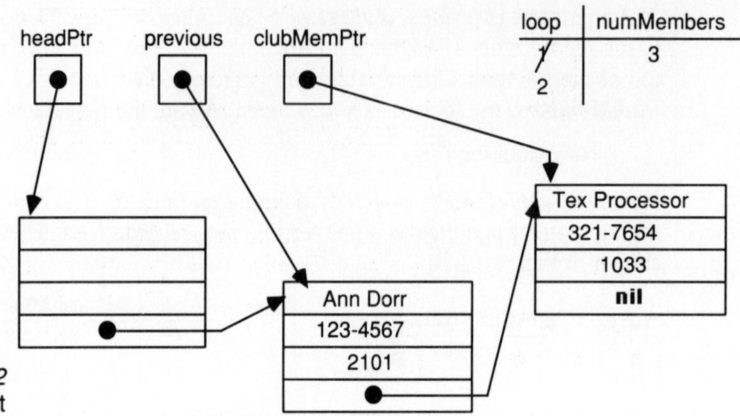

Figure 14.22
Linking node to list

Then, we assign ***previous^.nextMem*** to ***previous*** to be ready for the next insertion, as in Figure 14.23.

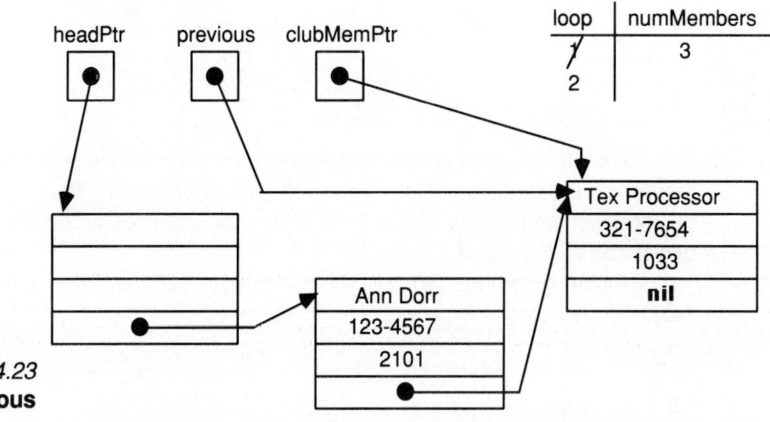

Figure 14.23
Moving **previous**

The loop body is repeated once more. To gain some practice at hand simulating pointer programs, you may want to hand simulate this final iteration yourself. The final result should give the linked list diagram shown in Figure 14.11 on page 525.

14.12 Insertion and Deletion

Now that you've seen how to build linked lists, this section will examine moving information in and out of them, known as *insertion* and *deletion.* Suppose you have a linked list that is in alphabetical order. The list is made up of records with several fields, the first field being a letter in the alphabet. You have the initial structure shown in Figure 14.24.

You want to add a record "F" that would go between E and M. You create a new record with an "F." Then start at the beginning of the list and find the position

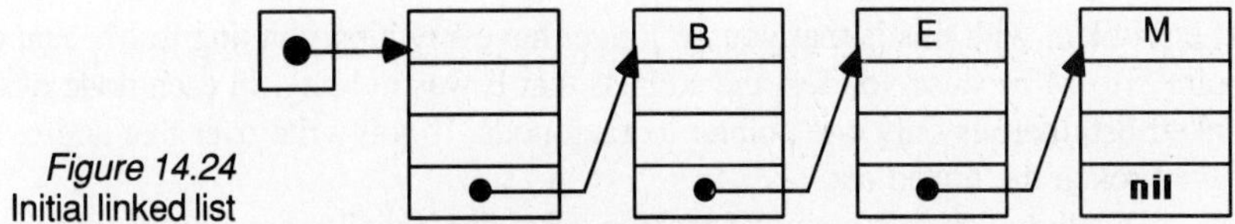

Figure 14.24
Initial linked list

where the new node belongs. Then point that node at M. Now there are two different nodes whose pointer fields both point to M (see Figure 14.25). The second step is to change E from pointing to M to pointing to F (see Figure 14.26).

Why do the insertion in this particular order? Well, look at what would happen if you immediately pointed E at a new "F" node. You would have the structure shown in Figure 14.27.

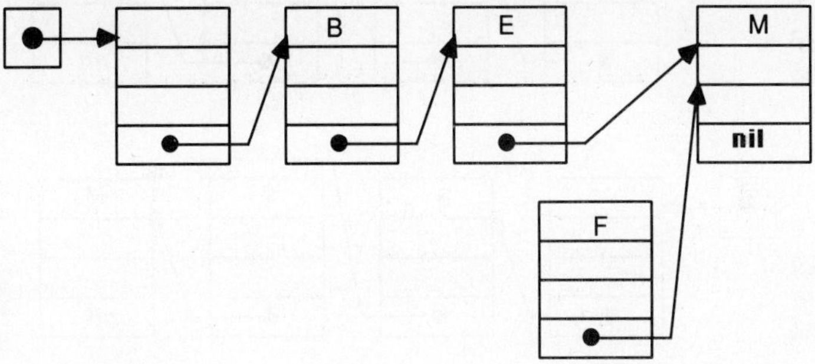

Figure 14.25
First step of inserting new record in linked list

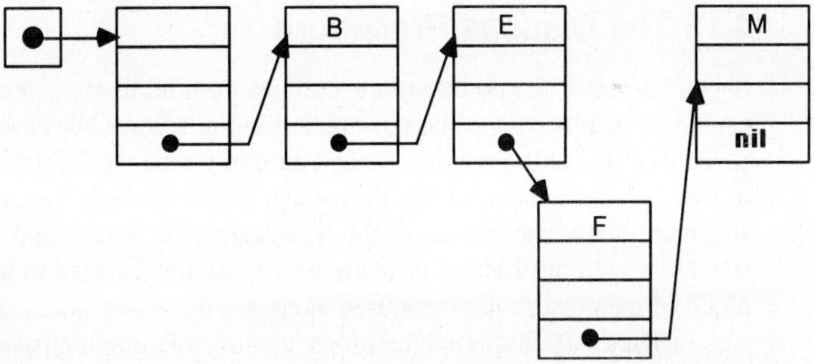

Figure 14.26
Finishing insertion of new record to linked list

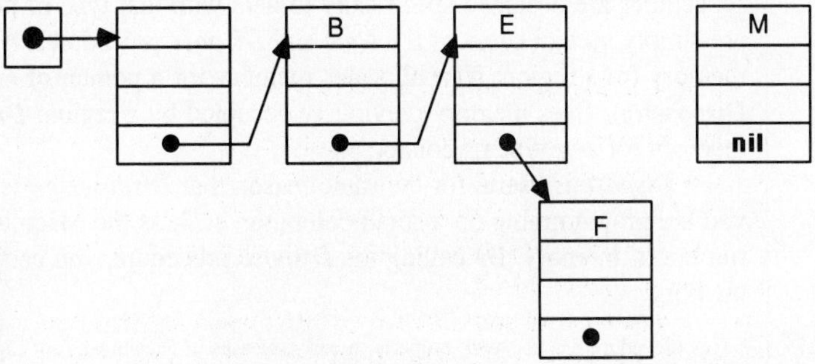

Figure 14.27
Incorrect insertion of new record to linked list

The problem with this is that you no longer have anything pointing to M. You can't point F to M because you lost the address that E was holding. In each node of the linked list, there is only one pointer to each node. If you write over that address, you have broken the linked list.

Deletion works in a similar fashion. You don't really move the record you are going to delete. You simply overwrite the pointer to it. If you go back to the same structure you started with (see Figure 14.28) and you want to delete E, then simply point B to M. You now have no access to the record with E, as shown in Figure 14.29; the record is thus "deleted."

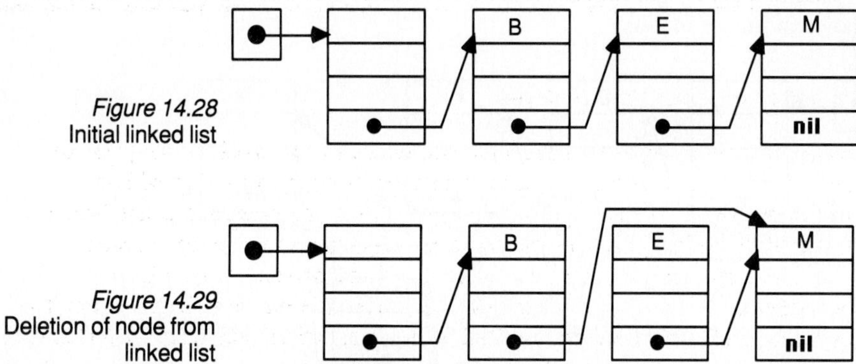

Figure 14.28
Initial linked list

Figure 14.29
Deletion of node from linked list

14.13 The Dispose Procedure

If you get rid of the pointer to a record, as you did to the E record above, not only can't you gain access to the information in the record, but Pascal can't even use the space it occupies in memory. Since you don't need the information, it is a good idea to free up the memory so that Pascal can later recycle it. Pascal has a ***Dispose*** statement that is the inverse of the ***New*** statement. You supply the ***Dispose*** statement with the address of the node you no longer need to use, and it frees up that block of memory so it can be used again.*

Chapter 10 discussed the procedures ***NewRgn*** and ***DisposeRgn***. The type ***rgnHandle*** is a predefined pointer type, and the ***NewRgn*** and ***DisposeRgn*** procedures are designed specifically to deal with that type of pointer. These procedures are simply special cases of the ***New*** and ***Dispose*** procedures. ***NewRgn*** allocates memory for a region; ***New*** allocates memory for a pointer of any type. ***DisposeRgn*** frees memory previously occupied by a region; ***Dispose*** frees memory for any type of pointer.

Dispose is useful for the same reason that ***DisposeRgn*** is helpful. When you are programming on a small computer, such as the Macintosh, it is very easy to run out of memory. By calling the ***Dispose*** procedure, you can recycle some of that memory.

* This procedure did not work properly in early releases of Macintosh (not Lightspeed) Pascal. Thus, even if you use ***Dispose*** correctly, your program may still not recycle the memory.

Syntax Box 14.3
Dispose

Purpose	To free unused storage
Syntax	**Dispose(** < variable pointer > **);**
where	< variable pointer > is a pointer to a node to be discarded.
Usage	The ***Dispose*** procedure is used to release a block of memory. When you are finished with a record that has a pointer, use the ***Dispose*** procedure to tell Pascal that the memory is no longer needed.

14.14 Boundary Conditions

Ideally, whenever you write a program, you would like to check all the possible conditions. This is best done by hand simulation. Section 14.11 showed how a linked list program should be hand simulated. When you insert and delete from a linked list, however, some special conditions may arise that *must* be checked.

These problems usually occur at the beginning and end of your list manipulation. Thus, when you hand simulate your code and pseudocode, check the boundary conditions. First see if the linked list is initialized correctly. Then check what happens when you insert the first node into the list.

Once your program passes the initial test, examine what happens when it tries to delete the last node in the list. You may also want to see what happens when the list has only one node and your program wants to delete it.

Finally, check a typical case. Make a list with three or four nodes and see what happens when you insert a node into the middle of the list. Is the correct spot for insertion found? After the insertion, are all the pointers pointing to nodes in the correct order? What happens if you insert at the end of the list? After answering these questions, you may want to do the same for the code that deletes nodes from your linked list.*

We have suggested this method of checking the first, last, and typical cases earlier, when we were discussing loops. It is then not surprising that one of the common bugs that arises with linked lists is similar to a bug that appears in loops: the off-by-one error. You may use a pointer variable such as ***currentPtr*** when you really want to refer to the next pointer in the list (perhaps denoted as ***currentPtr^.next***) or vice-versa. Such an error should be caught by the careful hand simulation described above.

Linked list manipulation is one of the most powerful and error-prone processes in programming. With the ***New*** and ***Dispose*** procedures, you are actually manipulating a section of memory; usually Pascal handles all memory management for you in the declarations. Since memory is being moved and allocated during the

* This method of hand simulation resembles a mathematical proof by induction. The first boundary condition corresponds to the basis step, and the typical case corresponds to the N+1th, or induction, step.

program's execution, you may find that your program works for simple data, but not for longer or more complex data. In short, you can't be too careful; make sure you consider all possibilities.

14.15 Example Program

Now that you know the Pascal constructs for operating with pointers, let's look at a program example that illustrates their usage a little more extensively. This program again maintains a list of club members. Members can be deleted and inserted into the list, which is maintained in alphabetical order on last names. The list can be printed out at any time.

The pseudocode for this example follows.

```
Initialize the list
WHILE user still wants to execute program DO
   IF command is insert THEN
      Insert new member into list
   ELSE IF command is delete THEN
      Delete a member from the list
   ELSE IF command is print THEN
      Print out current list
   ELSE
      Print error message
```

At this point, the "list" is the pseudodata structure. This program can be implemented using arrays or a linked list. We can even refine the pseudocode one more level with this pseudodata structure.

```
Initialize the list
WHILE user still wants to execute program DO
   IF command is insert THEN
      CALL: Insert new member into list
   ELSE IF command is delete THEN
      CALL: Delete a member from the list
   ELSE IF command is print THEN
      CALL: Print out current list
   ELSE
      Print error message

{ Insert new member into list }
Input name to insert
IF name is not already in list THEN
   BEGIN
      Input phone and membership number
      Add new information to list
   END { IF }
ELSE
   Print error message
```

```
{ Delete a member from the list }
Input name to delete
IF name is in list THEN
   BEGIN
      Confirm that the user wants to delete member
      IF user confirms THEN
         Remove member from list
      ELSE
         Print message that node was not deleted
   END { IF }
ELSE
   Print message that name is not in linked list

{ Print out current list }
Start at first name in list
WHILE not at end of list DO
   BEGIN
      Print information on each member
      Proceed to next member of list
   END { WHILE }
```

We have now added the error conditions. At this point, though, we cannot go any further without determining how the list will be implemented. Since the number of members in the list is likely to vary, we decide to use a linked list. We know that the node will have four fields: the name, phone number, membership number, and a pointer to the next node.

Now that we have the type of data structure, we can refine the pseudocode further. First, we notice that both the ***Insert*** and ***Delete*** procedures depend on finding whether a name is in the linked list. Since both procedures find a node by using the same code, we can create a utility procedure that determines if a name is in the linked list. The ***Find*** procedure is similar to the find procedure we used to search for a key in an array.

```
{ Find name in list }
Initialize previous ptr to beginning of linked list
Initialize current ptr to beginning of linked list
REPEAT
   IF current ptr's name < name to find THEN
      BEGIN
         Move previous ptr to current ptr
         Move current ptr to next node in list
      END { IF }
   ELSE IF current ptr's name is the name to be found THEN
      BEGIN
         Set a flag to TRUE indicating that name has been found
         Set exit condition of loop to TRUE
      END { ELSE IF }
```

```
    ELSE { current ptr's name > name to find }
      BEGIN
        Name has not been found
        Set exit condition of loop to TRUE
      END
  UNTIL at end of linked list OR exit boolean has been set to TRUE
```

This pseudocode means that we have to set the previous node to the beginning of the linked list in the ***Insert*** and ***Delete*** procedures. We can update the pseudocode for those two procedures this way:

```
{ Insert new member into list }
Input name to insert
Initialize previous ptr to head ptr of linked list
CALL: Find name in list
IF name is not already in list THEN
  BEGIN
    Create a new node
    Input fields of node
    Fill in pointer field of new node with current ptr
    Get record that previous ptr is pointing to
    Set previous ptr's record's pointer field to new node
  END { IF }
ELSE
  Print error message

{ Delete a member from the lst }
Input name to delete
Set previous ptr to head ptr of linked list
CALL: Find name in list
IF name is in linked list THEN
  BEGIN
    Confirm that the user wants to delete the node
    IF user confirms THEN
      BEGIN
        Set previous node's pointer field to current node's pointer field
        Dispose current node
      END { IF }
    ELSE
      Print message that node was not deleted
  END { IF }
ELSE
  Print message that name is not in linked list
```

From this, we can write the code for the program. The insertion and deletion code may be easier to understand if you refer to the diagrams in section 14.12.

The code in this program is often found in programs using linked lists. Make sure you understand how nodes are inserted and deleted and how the ***Print*** procedure loops through the entire list. You may find yourself adapting this code in your own programs; however, simply copying someone else's algorithms without understanding them is likely to lead to a monstrous debugging session.

Code 14.1
Program *Club*

```
{ Program: Club        Karen Seiler and David Niguidula                    }
{ This program maintains a linked list of club members, their phone        }
{ numbers and club membership numbers. The list is kept in                 }
{ alphabetical order by name. Names can be added and deleted and           }
{ the list can be printed out. Duplicate names are not allowed and will    }
{ generate an error message. Input is accepted in the form of              }
{ commands. Commands must be entered at the keyboard in capital            }
{ letters.  The 'STOP' command acts as a sentinel and causes the           }
{ the program to exit.                                                     }

program Club;

  const
    insertMember = 'INSERT';                   { insert command            }
    deleteMem = 'DELETE';                      { delete command            }
    printMember = 'PRINT';                     { print command             }
    endProg = 'STOP';                          { exit command              }
    minValue = '';                             { lowest value for string   }

  type
    memPtr = ^member;                          { --> to member record      }
    member = record                            { club member record        }
        name : string[40];                     { club member name          }
        phone : string[40];                    { club member phone         }
        membership : integer;                  { club membership number    }
        nextMem : memPtr                       { --> next record in list   }
      end;                                     { club                      }

  var
    header : memPtr;                           { --> header to linked list }
    command : string[40];                      { command read in           }

{ Function Init                                                            }
{ This function initializes the linked list by creating a header node.     }
{ The header node's fields are initialized to the null string and zero.    }
{ The header points to NIL.                                                }
{ Called by: Mainline          Calls: none                                 }
{ Returns : pointer to head of list                                        }

  function Init : memPtr;
```

Code 14.1 (continued)

```
    var
        ptr : memPtr;                              { --> to head of list         }
  begin
    New(ptr);   { create a new node }
    with ptr^ do
        begin
            nextMem := nil;  {  fill with initial info }
            name := minValue;
            phone := minValue;
            membership := 0
        end; { with }
    Init := ptr     { assign value of function  }
  end; { Init }

{ Function Ltrim and Function Trim                                            }
{ The following two routines remove blanks from a string.                     }
{ Ltrim removes the leading blanks from a string, and Trim                    }
{ removes the trailing blanks. The length of the string returned              }
{ by either function is changed (unless no blanks were removed).              }
{ Called by : Mainline                     Calls: none                        }

  function Ltrim (str : string) : string; { removes leading blanks            }

  begin
    while Pos(' ', str) = 1 do
        str := Omit(str, 1, 1);
    Ltrim := str
  end; { Ltrim }

  function Trim (str : string) : string; { removes trailing blanks            }

  begin
    if str <> '' then
        while str[Length(str)] = ' ' do
            str := Copy(str, 1, Length(str) - 1);
    Trim := str
  end; { Trim }

{  Procedure  Find                                                            }
{  This procedure searches through the linked list until it hits the end      }
{  of the list (denoted by NIL) or it finds the name it is searching for.     }
{  Called by: Insert, DeleteMember       Calls: none                          }

  procedure Find (name : string;              {  key to find                 }
    var previous : memPtr;                    {  prior pointer in list       }
    var curPtr : memPtr;                      {  current node in list        }
    var found : boolean);                     {  indicates name found in list  }
```

Code 14.1
(continued)

```
var
    done : boolean;                         { hit end of list            }

begin
    curPtr := previous;                     { init to beginning of list  }
    found := FALSE;
    done := FALSE;
    repeat
        if name > curPtr^.name then
            begin
                previous := curPtr;         { go to next node in list    }
                curPtr := curPtr^.nextMem
            end
        else if curPtr^.name = name then
            begin
                done := TRUE;    { name found in list  }
                found := TRUE
            end
        else
            done := TRUE;    { name not in list }
    until (done) or (curPtr = nil)

end; { Find }

{ Procedure  Insert                                                    }
{ This procedure inserts a new name into the linked list. If the       }
{ user tries to input a duplicate name an error message will be        }
{ generated. Insert calls a search routine to search through the       }
{ linked list to find the correct place to insert the name in          }
{ alphabetical order.                                                  }
{ Called by: Mainline        Calls: Find                               }

procedure Insert (header : memPtr);          { header to linked list     }

    var
        newName : string[40];                { name to be inserted       }
        previous,                            { --> previous node in list }
        current,                             { --> current node in list  }
        newPtr : memPtr;                     { --> new node in list      }
        found : boolean;                     { name found in list        }

begin
    Write('Enter name to insert: ');  { get info }
    Readln(newName);
    newName := Ltrim(Trim(newName));
    previous := header;
    Find(newName, previous, current, found);
```

Code 14.1
(continued)

```
      if (not found) then
         begin
            New(newPtr);  { create new node }
            with newPtr^ do
               begin
                  name := newName; { fill fields of new node }
                  Write('Enter phone number: ');
                  Readln(phone);
                  Write('Enter membership number:  ');
                  Readln(membership);
                  nextMem := current { insert new node in list }
               end; { with }
            previous^.nextMem := newPtr;
            Writeln;
            Writeln('Member ', newName, ' added to list')
         end { if }
      else
         begin
            Writeln('Name ', newName, ' already exists in list with info:');
            Writeln(current^.phone, ' ', current^.membership)
         end { else }
   end; { Insert }

{  Procedure: DeleteMember                                               }
{  This procedure deletes a name from the linked list. If the name       }
{  does not exist in the list, an error message is generated. If        }
{  the name does exist in the list, its information is printed out      }
{  and the user is asked to verify the deletion. If the user doesn't    }
{  verify, control goes back to the mainline without performing         }
{  the delete.                                                           }
{  Called by: Mainline              Calls: Find                          }

   procedure DeleteMember (header : memPtr); { header to linked list     }

      var
         delName : string[40];              { name to be deleted         }
         delPtr,                            { --> node to be deleted     }
         previous : memPtr;                 { --> previous node in list  }
         found : boolean;                   { name found in list         }
         answer : char;                     { verify answer              }

   begin
      Write('Enter name to be deleted: ');
      Readln(delName);
      delName := Ltrim(Trim(delName));

      previous := header;
      Find(delName, previous, delPtr, found);
```

Code 14.1
(continued)

```
        if found then
            with delPtr^ do
                begin
                    Writeln('Verify deletion of member ', name, ' with info:');
                    Writeln('Phone: ', phone, ' Membership number: ', membership);
                    Write('Delete? (Enter y for yes, n for no): ');
                    Readln(answer);

                    if answer = 'y' then
                        begin{ delete node by moving ptrs }
                            previous^.nextMem := delPtr^.nextMem;
                            Writeln(delPtr^.name, ' has been deleted. ');
                            Dispose(delPtr)
                        end { if }
                    else
                        Writeln('Name not deleted.')

                end { with }
        else
            Writeln('Cannot delete. Name not found.')

    end; { DeleteMember }

{ Procedure Print                                                    }
{ This procedure prints out the current linked list in alphabetical  }
{ order. The records in the list are printed until the NIL pointer   }
{ is encountered.                                                    }
{ Called by: Mainline        Calls: none                             }

    procedure Print (header : memPtr); { header to linked list       }
        var
            curPtr : memPtr;                    { --> current node    }

    begin
        curPtr := header;    { start at head of list                  }
        while (curPtr^.nextMem <> nil) do
            begin
                curPtr := curPtr^.nextMem;    { go to next record in list }
                with curPtr^ do
                    begin
                        Writeln;
                        Writeln('---------------------------------------------');
                        Writeln('MEMBER: ', name);
                        Writeln('PHONE: ', phone, '  MEMBERSHIP NUMBER: ',
                            membership : 8)
                    end { with }
            end { while }
    end; { Print }
```

Code 14.1
(continued)

```
{   Mainline                                                            }
{   This procedure reads in the command from the keyboard. If the       }
{   command is STOP, the program is exited.  Otherwise, the commands    }
{   are executed and when each one finishes, control returns to the    }
{   mainline.  Illegal input will generate an error message that prints }
{   out the acceptable commands                                         }
{   Calls: Init, Insert, DeleteMember, Print                            }

begin
   Writeln('Commands: STOP, INSERT, DELETE, PRINT');
   Writeln('--------------------------------------');
   Writeln;
   header := Init;
   Write('Enter command: ');
   Readln(command);
   command := Ltrim(Trim(command));

   while (command <> endProg) do
      begin

         if command = insertMember then
            Insert(header)
         else if command = deleteMem then
            DeleteMember(header)
         else if command = printMember then
            Print(header)
         else
            begin
               Writeln;
               Writeln(command, ' is not a legal command. Try again.');
               Writeln;
               Writeln('Legal commands: STOP, INSERT, DELETE, PRINT.')
            end; { else }
         Writeln;
         Write('Enter command: ');
         Readln(command);
         command := Ltrim(Trim(command))

      end; { while }

   Writeln('Exit.');
   Writeln

end. { Club }
```

```
Commands: STOP, INSERT, DELETE, PRINT
----------------------------------------

Enter command: PRINT

Enter command: DELETE
Enter name to be deleted: Zonker Harris
Cannot delete. Name not found.

Enter command: INSERT
Enter name to insert: Zonker Harris
Enter phone number: 555-1414
Enter membership number:  1234

Member Zonker Harris added to list

Enter command: INSERT
Enter name to insert:  Joan Caucus
Enter phone number: 124-7777
Enter membership number:  9876

Member Joan Caucus added to list

Enter command: ADD

ADD is not a legal command. Try again.

Legal commands: STOP, INSERT, DELETE, PRINT.

Enter command: INSERT
Enter name to insert: Mike Doonesbury
Enter phone number: 043-8169
Enter membership number:  2356

Member Mike Doonesbury added to list

Enter command: PRINT

------------------------------------------------
MEMBER: Joan Caucus
PHONE: 124-7777  MEMBERSHIP NUMBER:      9876

------------------------------------------------
MEMBER: Mike Doonesbury
PHONE: 043-8169  MEMBERSHIP NUMBER:      2356

------------------------------------------------
MEMBER: Zonker Harris
PHONE: 555-1414  MEMBERSHIP NUMBER:      1234

Enter command: DELETE
Enter name to be deleted: Mike Doonesbury
Verify deletion of member Mike Doonesbury with info:
Phone: 043-8169 Membership number:      2356
Delete? (Enter y for yes, n for no): y
```

Figure 14.30 Output of program *Club*

```
Mike Doonesbury has been deleted.

Enter command: INSERT
Enter name to insert: Zonker Harris
Name Zonker Harris already exists in list with info:
555-1414     1234

Enter command: PRINT

------------------------------------------------
MEMBER: Joan Caucus
PHONE: 124-7777  MEMBERSHIP NUMBER:      9876

------------------------------------------------
MEMBER: Zonker Harris
PHONE: 555-1414  MEMBERSHIP NUMBER:      1234

Enter command: STOP
Exit.
```

Figure 14.30 (continued)

14.16 Chapter Summary

This chapter looked at a method of manipulating lists more powerful than using arrays. Linked lists allow you to create programs that use only as much memory as necessary. Instead of declaring a maximum-size array, you can use linked lists that are as long (or short) as you want.

Linked lists rely on the use of pointers. A pointer is a variable that holds a particular address in memory. When you use pointers, you are concerned not with the actual contents of the pointer variable, but with the data that it points to. That is, you are concerned not with the address held by the pointer variable, but with the fact that the pointer points to a datum of a certain type.

The advantage of a linked list is that it allows you to allocate storage locations dynamically, that is, during the program's execution. A ***New*** procedure call creates a new record by reserving particular storage locations. The pointer passed to the ***New*** procedure is then set to the new record. You can gain access to any field in the new record as long as you keep track of its pointer's name.

Within this new record, you can create another pointer field. This field can hold a pointer that points to the next record in a linked list. The pointer field can also hold a special pointer called **nil** that indicates the end of the linked list.

You can manipulate any individual piece of data in the list as long as you keep track of the pointer to the top of the list. If you know the head pointer's name, you can move from one record to the next. This move is possible if you know that each record contains a field that points to the next field. To get at any particular field, start at the top of the list. With another pointer, move to each node in the list, in order, until you find the desired field or reach the end of the list.

Finally, insertion and deletion are easier in linked lists than in arrays. In an array, you may have to make many data moves to insert or delete an item. With linked lists, you only have to change the values of two pointer fields for either operation. While you do need an extra field to hold a pointer in each node (as opposed to holding the information in an array of records), you save some time in execution because you do not have to make the array's data movements.

14.17 Exercises

Understanding Concepts

1. What are the differences between a linked list and an array in terms of accessing information? Inserting information? Deleting information?

2. Given the declarations:

```
type
    intPtr = ^integer;
var
    ptToInt: intPtr;
```

is the statement ***ptToInt := 750;*** legal? If not, how could you correct it?

3. What is the purpose of a dummy header node?

4. Given the declarations:

```
type
   nodePtr = ^node;
   node = record
            name: string[50];
            next: nodePtr
      end;
var
   current, head: nodePtr;
```

what does the following code yield?

```
New(current);
current^.name := 'Greg';
New(current^.next);
New(current^.next^.next);
current^.next^.next^.name := 'Peter';
current^.next^.name := 'Bobby';
```

5. With the same declarations as Exercise 4, what does the following code fragment yield?

```
New(current);
head := current;
New(current^.next);
current := current^.next;
New(current^.next);
current := current^.next;
```

```
current^.name := 'Marcia';
New(current^.next);
head^.name := 'Jan';
current := head^.next;
current^.name := 'Cindy';
Dispose(current^.next^.next);
```

6. If ***current^.name*** = ***head^.name***, is it necessarily true that ***current*** = ***head***? What about the converse: if ***current*** = ***head***, is it necessarily true that ***current^.name*** = ***head^.name***?

7. Document the following code.

```
type
   numPtr = ^numRec;
   numRec = record
         num: integer;
         next: numPtr
      end;

procedure Question(head: numPtr);

var
   total, thisOne: integer;
   current: numPtr;

begin
   current := head^.next;
   total := 0;
   thisOne := 0;
   while current <> nil do
      begin
         total := total + current^.num;
         thisOne := thisOne + 1;
         current := current^.next
      end; { while }
   Writeln('The result is ', total/thisOne:5:2)
end; { Question }
```

8. Show the hand simulation of the code in Section 14.10 with the following input:

```
3
Bullwinkle J. Moose
555-1212
8163
Rocket J. Squirrel
801-4279
4119
Boris Badenov
911
6728
```

9. Debug the following code without adding any variables to the procedure. Use ***nodePtr*** and ***node*** as defined in Exercises 4 and 5.

```
{ This procedure inserts a name in an alphabetical list. }
procedure Insert(insName: string[50];        { name to add to list      }
    head: nodePtr);                          { --> head of ordered list }

var
    prev,                { --> node prior to place to insert new name }
    newRec: nodePtr;     { --> node to hold new name                  }

begin
    { create new record }
    New(newRec);
    newRec^.name := insName;

    { find name prior to name to insert }
    prev := head;
    while prev^.name < insName do
        prev := prev^.next;

    { insert node }
    prev^.next := newRec;
    newRec^.next := prev^.next

end; { Insert }
```

10. Draw a picture of the data structure defined by the following declaration:

```
const
    maxDiseases = 20;

type
    symPtr = ^symptom;
    symptom = record
            highTemp: boolean;
            incubationTime: integer;
            otherItems: string[30];
            next: symPtr
        end; { symptom }

    diagnosis = record
            disease: string[30];
            symptomHead: symPtr
        end; { diagnosis }

    diagList = array[1..maxDiseases] of diagnosis;
```

Coding Exercises

1. Write a procedure that prints the last element in a linked list.

2. Write a procedure that receives a head of a linked list and an integer ***num*** as parameters. The procedure prints the ***num***th element in the list (assume the

linked list has a dummy header node and use the declaration from Understanding Concepts exercise 4).

Problems 3 through 6 refer to the following declaration. A linked-list representation of a polynomial uses the following type:

```
type
    polyPtr = ^polyNode;            { -- > term of polynomial      }
    polyNode = record               { info on each term            }
          coeff,                    { coefficient of term          }
          power: integer;           { power of x in this term      }
          next: polyPtr             { -- > next term               }
       end; { polyNode }
```

Each polynomial linked list begins with a header node and is ordered by the contents of each node's ***power*** field. For example, the polynomial $3x^7 - 4x^3 + 1$ is represented by the following list:

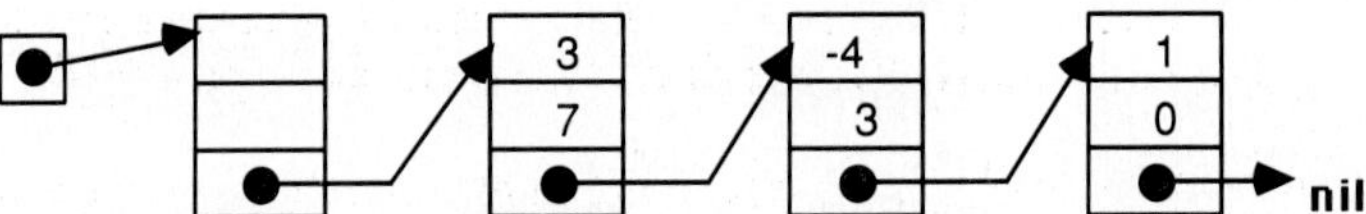

3. Write a procedure (and supporting subprocedures, if needed) that receives a polynomial as an input string (e.g., '3 x 7 – 4 x 3 + 1') and creates the corresponding linked list.

4. Write a procedure that receives the heads of two polynomial linked lists as parameters and prints the sum.

5. Write a procedure that receives the heads of two polynomial linked lists as parameters and prints the product.

6. Write a function that receives a polynomial linked list and a value for x as parameters and evaluates the resulting expression.

Problems 7 through 11 refer to the following declaration. A doubly linked list has pointers that work in both directions. The ***head*** points to the first node in the list; the ***tail*** points to the last. The linked list in the figure below is defined by the following declaration:

```
type
    listPtr = ^node;                { -- > one node in double list    }
    node = record                   { single item in list             }
          name: string[50];         { name of person in list          }
          front,                    { -- > next name in list          }
          back: listPtr             { -- > previous name in list      }
       end; { node }

var
    head, tail: listPtr;            { -- > front and back of list     }
```

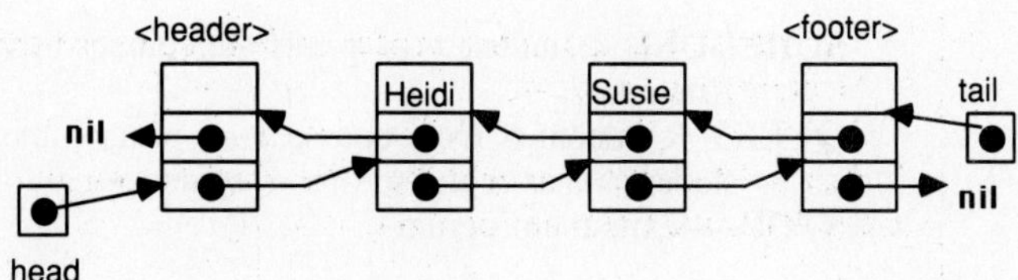

7. Write a procedure that creates the initial doubly linked list, that is, a list with dummy header and footer nodes.

8. Write a procedure that, given the parameters ***head*** and a variable of type **string*[50]***, inserts the string variable into the doubly linked list. The list should remain in alphabetical order, and the chain of pointers in each direction should be maintained.

9. Write a procedure that prints the list in reverse alphabetical order.

10. Write a procedure that determines whether a particular ***name*** field (received as a parameter) is closer to the ***head*** or ***tail*** pointer.

11. Write a procedure that deletes a given name from the list.

Programming Problems

1. A popular one-player peg game is played with 14 pegs arranged in a triangle, with the center hole left empty.

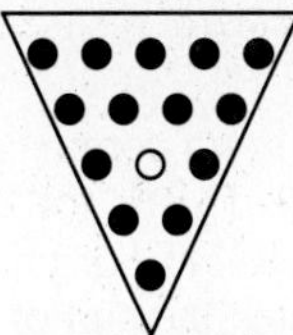

   Pegs are moved by jumping over any one other peg in a straight line. The peg that is jumped is removed. Thus, the first jump in this game must come from the second or fourth hole along the top row. The object of the game is to leave as few pegs as possible.

   Allow the user to simulate this game, using the mouse to choose which pegs to move. As an extension, allow the user to choose which hole will initially be empty.

2. Write a program that maintains a registrar's database. The program should first read a list of courses (no more than 20) from a file. Then the user should enter commands at the keyboard. The user can enter five commands:

   ADD < student > **TO** < course > — adds a specified student to the registration of < course >.
   PRINTCLASS < course > — prints the list of students in a class in alphabetical order.

SCHEDULE < student > — prints the courses in which the student is registered.
QUERY < student > **IN** < course > — prints a message indicating whether < student > has registered for < course >.
STOP — exits the program

Your program should print error messages if the syntax of any command is incorrect. **Variation:** When the user chooses **STOP**, save the contents of the database in a file. Each time the program is restarted, the contents of the file are loaded.

3. Write a program that simulates commands in the language LOGO. In that language, a triangular object (known as a turtle) starts in the center of the screen, facing the top of the screen. The turtle has a current position and direction. The turtle and the screen can then be controlled with the following commands:

FORWARD < x > — moves the turtle < x > pixels in the current direction. If the pen is down, a line is also drawn.
BACK < x > — moves the turtle < x > pixels in the reverse of the current direction. If the pen is down, a line is also drawn.
LEFT < x > and **RIGHT** < x > — changes the turtle's current direction by < x > degrees to the left or right. This occurs whether or not the pen is up.
PEN UP and **PEN DOWN** — When the program begins, the pen is down, meaning that each **FORWARD** and **BACK** command has a visible result on the screen. **PEN UP** (like QuickDraw's ***HidePen***) means that future **FORWARD** and **BACK** commands still change the current position but do not show any visible result. **PEN DOWN**, like QuickDraw's ***ShowPen***, reverses the effect of **PEN UP**.
TO < procedure name >
< statements >
END — Procedures are declared with two commands. The **TO** command both declares and begins the procedure. This is followed by a series of **PEN, FORWARD, BACK, LEFT, RIGHT,** or previously declared procedure statements. **END** denotes the end of the procedure; after this, the < procedure name > can be used simply by stating < procedure name > as a statement.

The figure below shows a sample program and its result. (The turtle's starting position is the lower left corner of the right triangle.) Your program need not check for syntax errors.

```
TO TRIANGLE
FORWARD 50
RIGHT 135
FORWARD 70
RIGHT 135
FORWARD 50
END
TRIANGLE
PEN UP
FORWARD 100
RIGHT 90
PEN DOWN
TRIANGLE
```

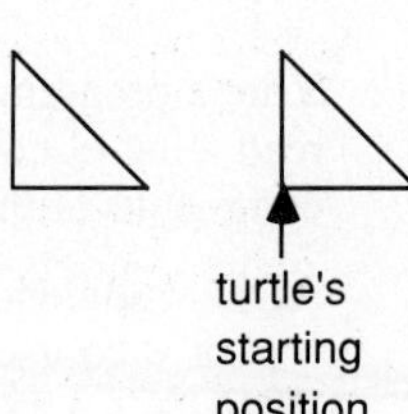

4. Write a layout program with which the user can draw filled rectangles, ovals, or lines, and delete any object on the screen. If an object is deleted, the screen is refreshed, that is, the Drawing window is cleared and all the remaining objects are redrawn in the order in which they were created.

5. Write a layout program that supports *segmentation*, or the grouping of objects. When the user chooses the Start Segment command, all primitives that are drawn are collected until the End Segment command is chosen. Then the segment is treated as a single unit that can be moved or deleted.

6. The airline example of Section 11.9 uses a two-dimensional array to store the origins and destinations of flights. Rewrite this program using an array of linked lists (one linked list for each originating city).

7. Modify the newsletter layout program (last seen as Programming Problem 2 in Chapter 12) so that the user can enter any number of pictures on a page.

8. Write a program to allow two players to play dominoes. A domino set consists of 28 tiles. Each tile has two sides with a number of dots ranging from 0 to 6. Each tile combination (0-0, 0-1, 0-2,..., 0-6, 1-1, 1-2,...) appears exactly once. In this game, each person is given six tiles. The remaining tiles are called the "pool." A random tile from the pool becomes the first piece on the table.

   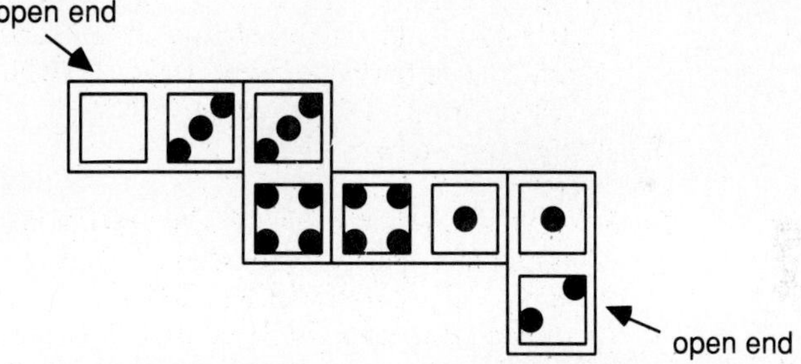

   Each player takes a turn adding a tile to the table. Any tile that is added must match one of the open ends. The figure above shows a domino layout after several plays. Since the open ends have 0 and 2 dots, the next player must place a tile with either 0 or 2 dots.

   A player who cannot place a tile next to one of the open ends must choose a tile from the pool. A player who still cannot make a play (or if there are no tiles left in the pool) loses a turn. The game ends when one player wins by playing all of her tiles or when neither player can lay down any more tiles.

9. Write a program that maintains a list of names and phone numbers. Allow the user to print the list alphabetically or in order of phone number.

10. Allow a user to create a map. The user first sees a pattern of grid lines, as in the figure below. The number of grid lines is up to you.

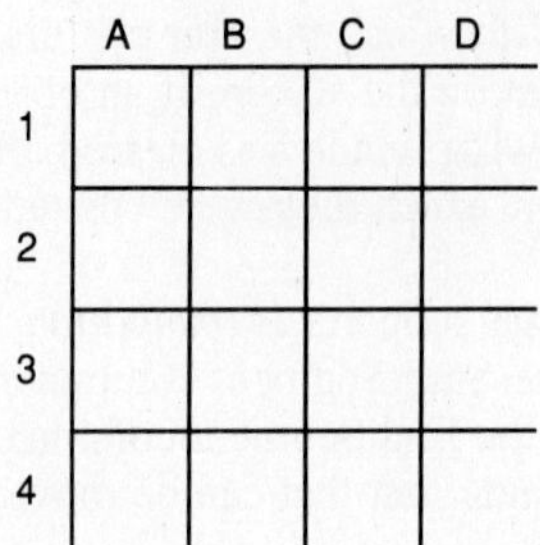

The user can then select the positions of cities and towns. The user chooses a location on the Drawing window and inputs the municipality's name and population. The name and the city symbol then appear on the screen. The symbol indicates the city population (the exact symbols are up to you, but some suggestions are: hollow circles for towns of up to 10,000; filled circles for towns of 10,000 to 50,000; larger filled circles for towns over 50,000).

When the user decides to stop selecting, you should print a legend: an alphabetical list of cities, their populations, and their location on the grid.

Variation: Print the legend alphabetically within each grid location (that is, alphabetically in A-1, then in A-2, and so on).

15

Abstract Data Types: Stacks and Queues

Imagine you are a furniture maker's apprentice. You have been taught how to select wood, how to use nails and tacks, and how to work with saws and hammers. Now that you know the basics, you are assigned the task of building kitchen sets. After building a few chairs and tables, you find yourself spending a great deal of time making legs. You decide to spend some time concentrating on how to create table and chair legs. You do some experimenting and come up with an efficient method of creating legs and attaching them to chairs and tables. Now when you are designing your furniture, you think of the legs as a single entity, not as a particular combination of wood and nails. When creating blueprints for your furniture, you assume that you know how to create and attach legs, so the details about those operations do not go into your plan.

Up to this point in the book, each concept has led to the use of a different construct in the Pascal language. At this point, we have seen all the available constructs. Now we will spend some time examining common methods in which these constructs are combined. Just as examining how a leg is created is helpful in a number of furniture-making situations, examining how particular data structures and algorithms are used can be helpful in solving a number of programming problems. The remainder of the book will discuss common algorithms and abstract data types.

We will spend less time on *how* to code such creatures and more time on judging *when* it is appropriate to use a particular data type or algorithm.

15.1 Abstract Data Types

Abstraction is a term computer scientists use a lot, but is difficult to define out of context. To understand abstraction, let's digress momentarily and discuss large programming projects.

Programs of any size (except class assignments) are usually done by teams of people. The program is divided into parts called *modules* or *units* (groups of procedures and functions) that individuals develop on their own. Presumably, each person knows everything there is to know about her own module. To get the parts to work together, however, each programmer has to know something about what the other people are doing.

Consider the following (fictional) scenario. A team of three people is assigned the task of rewriting the Macintosh Desktop software. In the design stage, the team members are given the tasks of working on the menu manipulation, the icon manipulation, and the window manipulation. Each team member has unique tasks to perform, such as creating pull-down menus, allowing the user to rearrange icons, or determining how a window could be moved. Yet there are tasks that overlap; for example, when the user chooses **Open...** from the **File** menu or double-clicks on a selected disk, a new window with the disk's contents should appear. Thus, each team member's code has to communicate with the other members' modules.

At the same time, the team members want to control their individual environments. That is, no programmer wants her code to be crashed by another team member. To avoid unintentional bombs, each programmer wants to limit the others' access to her module.

Typically, what happens is that each team member determines exactly what information will be public — that is, information that any programmer on the team will have access to — and what information will be private, or hidden. Thus, each team member gets a partial view of what is available in the other modules. This partial view is an abstraction.

The abstraction separates the programming world into two parts: the *implementors*, who work with the hidden as well as the public information, and the *users*, who are everyone else. (The *user*, in this context, is not a person who chooses **Go** on the **Run** menu, but rather a programmer who uses an abstraction.)

The level of abstraction varies with each situation. One thing, however, is constant: the users of the abstraction should have exactly as much information as they need — no more, no less.

This chapter discusses common *abstract data types*. First, we will think of ourselves as users of the abstract type. The information we have about the data type is the data that it holds and the operations we can perform on it. (For example, if we use the abstraction "desktop icon," we know that each icon refers to a file, a disk, or the trash can, and that we can perform the operations of selecting, double-clicking, and dragging on the icon.) The information that is hidden concerns the way in which the data is stored. As users, we don't know how the data types are manipulated in Pascal, and we don't care. Our code should work *no matter how* the abstraction is implemented.

Then, we will look at the abstraction from the other side. As implementors, we will look at different methods of creating concrete representations (e.g., arrays, records, pointers) of the abstractions. We will also determine how to keep unnecessary information completely hidden, and thus protected, from the users.

In a typical programming project, the users and the implementors spend a good deal of time deciding how to create the abstraction. The users may say to the implementors, "We need you to store this information, and we need to be able to retrieve it in some particular fashion. We don't care how you store the data; just let us get at it when we want." The implementors may respond, "We can give you these methods of storing and retrieving information. To gain access to your data, you have to specify the following parameters." Let's look at an analogy in a typical office. The executives may tell the record-keepers to file some papers. The record-keepers file the papers so they can be retrieved later. The executives don't care whether the papers are filed alphabetically or chronologically; when they want information, they tell the record-keepers what they want, and it is up to the record-keepers to find the information. The record-keepers, however, control, *how* the executives may ask for information. The record-keepers may ask, "Do you want that information for the last year? For the last month? For the last three weeks?" The users (the executives) specify the information to store; the implementors (the record-keepers) develop the method for storing. When the users asked to retrieve information, the implementors asked for the retrieval to be specified in a particular way.

Take a more familiar example. In some respects, the predefined Pascal and QuickDraw data types are abstract types. For example, when you use a variable of type **string**, you know that you can store up to 256 characters and perform a specific set of operations on the variable. You don't concern yourself with exactly how a string is manipulated or stored inside MacPascal, as long as you get consistent results. Similarly, you can consider yourself a user of the abstract data types ***rect*** and ***rgnHandle***; the implementations (and their implementors) exist somewhere out there in Apple-land.

In general, abstract data types that we create have more specific purposes and are more complex than the predefined types. Technically, though, predefined types are abstract types because they hide information about their implementation and are associated with a certain set of operations. In short, "abstraction" is a relative term.

15.2 Queues: The User's View

Let's start with an easy abstract data type: the queue. A queue is simply a linear list of items. The items are processed in a first-come, first-served order. To put it another way, queues work on a FIFO (first in, first out) basis.

Imagine a far-fetched example. Suppose your school has more students than computers. When the computer lab gets too crowded, a waitlist is started and maintained by a monitor. When a student arrives and finds that all of the computers are in use, she gives her name to the monitor. The monitor places her name at the bottom of the waitlist. When a student leaves and frees up a computer, the monitor looks at the name at the top of the waitlist, and assigns that person the available computer. The name at the top of the list is then crossed out. This process continues until the computer lab closes.

The waitlist in this example is a queue. The first person to sign her name to the waitlist becomes the first person to get a computer — first in, first out. There are two operations associated with queues: *enqueueing* and *dequeueing* (computer science jargon at its best — these words do not exist in English dictionaries). Enqueueing is the process of adding something to the tail (the back end) of the queue; dequeueing is the process of removing something from the head (the front end) of the queue.

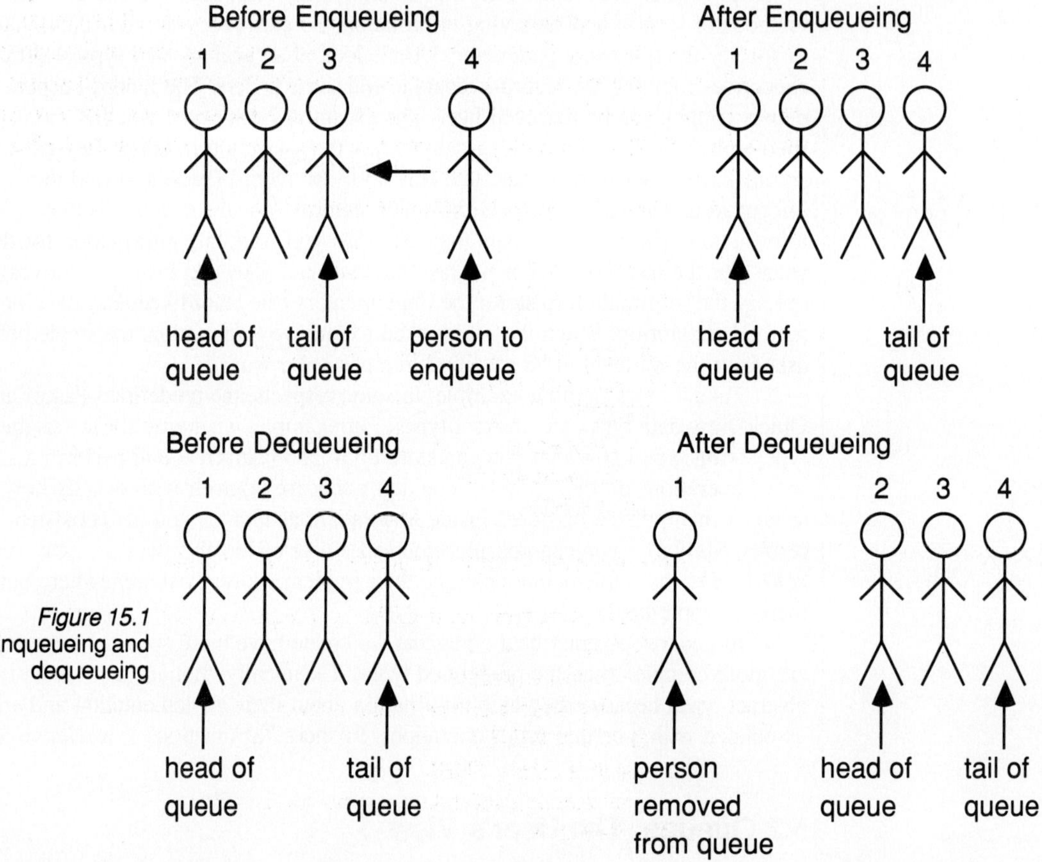

Figure 15.1 Enqueueing and dequeueing

At this point, a queue does not look very different from a linked list. The difference is that the order of a queue is kept constant at all times. Students on the waitlist are always enqueued at the tail of the list and are always dequeued from the front of the list. There is no "cutting" into the middle of the line. (It certainly is possible, however, to implement queues with pointers.)

Suppose you decide to code the waitlist algorithm. You decide to represent each name in the queue as a **string[50]**. The implementor of the queue tells you that four operations are available:

InitQueue(< queue >**);**
< boolean > **:= EmptyQueue(**< queue >**);**
Enqueue(< queue >**,** < element to add >**);**
Dequeue(< queue >**,** < element removed from queue >**);**

The ***InitQueue*** procedure initializes a queue. The notation < queue > indicates a variable of type ***queue*** (which has also been defined by the implementor). The ***EmptyQueue*** function returns the boolean value TRUE if the queue is empty, FALSE otherwise. ***Enqueue*** adds the < element to add > to the tail of the queue specified by < queue >. ***Dequeue*** removes the element at the head of the queue and returns it in < element removed from queue >. Since the queue holds elements that are of type **string[50]**, the second parameters in both ***Enqueue*** and ***Dequeue*** are expressions of type **string[50]**. ***Dequeue*** crashes the program if < queue > has no elements.

The pseudocode for the program looks like this:

```
Initialize queue
WHILE lab is not closed DO
  BEGIN
    Determine how many people have arrived
    FOR each new arrival DO
      BEGIN
        Get student's name
        Enqueue student
      END { FOR }

    Determine how many computers are now available

    WHILE computers are available AND queue is not empty DO
      BEGIN
        Dequeue student
        Tell student that computer is available
      END { WHILE }
    IF queue is empty THEN
      Print message indicating that no one is waiting
  END { WHILE }
```

To determine the number of new arrivals or available computers, you ask the program's user to enter the number. Assume that the lab is closed when the user enters a sentinel for the number of new arrivals. Since the implementor of the queue abstraction has provided you with methods of initializing, enqueuing, and dequeueing, you can code your end of the program. The code appears as follows:

Code 15.1
Waitlist program:
user end

```
{ Program: Waitlist    D. Niguidula         March 3                   }
{ This program maintains a list of students waiting                   }
{ to use one of a number of computers. The user is                    }
{ asked to enter the number and names of people who                   }
{ have arrived. Then, the user is asked how many                      }
{ computers are currently available. For each                         }
{ machine that is available, a name is removed                        }
{ from the waitlist and printed. This process continues               }
{ until the user enters a sentinel value.                             }

program Waitlist;

  const
    sentinel = -1;                    { indicates end of program   }

  type
    name = string[50];                { contains student names     }

{ queue data type will be defined by implementor }

{ Mainline variables }
  var
    wait : queue;                     { waiting list of students              }
    loop,                             { loop counter                          }
    numArrive : integer;              { num of students to add to list        }

{ Abstraction: InitQueue, EmptyQueue, Enqueue,           }
{   Dequeue -- to be implemented by someone              }
{   else at this location.                               }

{ Procedure AddStudents                                  }
{ This procedure receives the names of the students      }
{ to be added to the waitlist. The user is asked to enter }
{ a name for each new arrival. The name is then added    }
{ to the queue.                                          }
{ Called by: Mainline    Calls: Enqueue                  }

  procedure AddStudents (var addQueue : queue;      { waitlist of students      }
    numArrive : integer);                           { number of new arrivals    }

    var
      loop : integer;                 { loop counter              }
      student : name;                 { name of current student   }
```

Code 15.1
(continued)

```
   begin

      for loop := 1 to numArrive do
         begin
            Write('Please enter new student''s name : ');
            Readln(student);
            Enqueue(addQueue, student)  { add student to queue }
         end { for }

   end; { AddStudents }

{ Procedure AssignMachines                                   }
{  This procedure assigns available computers to the         }
{ people on the waitlist.  The user is asked to enter the    }
{ number of machines available. For each machine, a          }
{ name is removed from the waiting list and printed. If no   }
{ names remain on the waitlist, an appropriate message is    }
{ printed and the procedure exits.                           }
{ Called by: Mainline     Calls: Dequeue, EmptyQueue         }

   procedure AssignMachines (var assignQueue : queue);
                                        { waitlist of students             }

      var
         numAvail,                      { number of available machines     }
         loop : integer;                { loop counter                     }
         student : name;                { name of current student          }
         done : boolean;                { indicates end of loop            }

   begin

      Write('How many computers are now available? ');
      Readln(numAvail);
      loop := 1;

      while (loop <= numAvail) and (not EmptyQueue(assignQueue)) do
         begin
            Dequeue(assignQueue, student);
            Writeln('Machine now available for ', student);
            loop := loop + 1
         end; { while }

      if EmptyQueue(assignQueue) then
         Writeln('No students left on waitlist')
   end; { AssignMachines }

{ Mainline                                                   }
{  The Mainline begins by initializing the queue. Then       }
{ it asks the user to enter the number of new arrivals.      }
```

Code 15.1 (continued)

```
{ If the user enters the sentinel value, the program       }
{ exits. Otherwise, the students' names are added to       }
{ the waitlist. Any available machines are assigned        }
{ to students, starting at the top of the waitlist. The    }
{ process continues until the user enters the sentinel.    }
{ Calls: InitQueue, AddStudents, AssignMachines            }
begin
   InitQueue(wait);  { Initialize queue }
   Write('How many people have arrived? (', sentinel : 2, ' to exit): ');
   Readln(numArrive);

   while numArrive <> sentinel do
      begin
         AddStudents(wait, numArrive);
         Writeln;

         AssignMachines(wait);

         Writeln;
         Write('How many people have arrived? (', sentinel : 2, ' to exit): ');
         Readln(numArrive)
      end { while }
end.
```

This code fakes the abstraction with a large hole in the program. If you were actually going to run this code in MacPascal, you would need to combine the user end, above, and the implementor end (pp. 564–566) in the same file. In Lightspeed Pascal, you can run programs where the different modules are stored in separate files. Because of space constraints, we cannot do an adequate job of explaining exactly how you do this; for more information refer to Chapter 8 of the *Lightspeed Pascal User's Guide and Reference Manual.*

The above code is all the user of the data abstraction has to provide. Now we switch roles and become the implementor of the procedures ***Init***, ***EmptyQueue***, ***Enqueue***, and ***Dequeue***. Remember, these are not predefined Pascal procedures; someone has to implement the other end of the program.

15.3 Queues: The Implementor's View

The actual implementation of any abstract data type depends on how it is being used. For example, if we know that a queue needs to hold no more than five items, then we can use an array. We also need to know the type of each element in the queue. In this case, we define the type ***name*** to represent the student names. In the waitlist program, the queue has an indefinite length; thus, we decide to use a linked list.

To enqueue and dequeue elements, we have to be able to gain access to both the head and the tail of the list. The data type ***queue***, therefore, should allow us to keep track of both ends of the queue. We therefore define ***queue*** as a record with two fields, containing the head and tail pointers:

```
queue = record
      head: queuePtr;                          { -- > first element in queue }
      tail: queuePtr                           { -- > last element in queue }
   end; { queue }
```

But what is a ***queuePtr***? This pointer should point to a single element in the list. Each node in the linked list, then, needs two fields: the name of the person on the waitlist and the pointer to the next node:

```
queuePtr = ^element;             { -- > any element in queue               }
element = record                 { info on each person on waitlist         }
      person: name;              { name of individual on list              }
      next: queuePtr             { -- > next name in list                  }
   end; { element }
```

From here, we can define the three procedures. Initially, the queue contains no elements. To represent this, we point both the head and tail pointers at **nil**, as shown in Figure 15.2.

head
nil
nil
tail

Figure 15.2
Initial queue

When one element is enqueued, it becomes both the head and the tail of the list, since it is simultaneously the first and the last element in the queue (Figure 15.3).

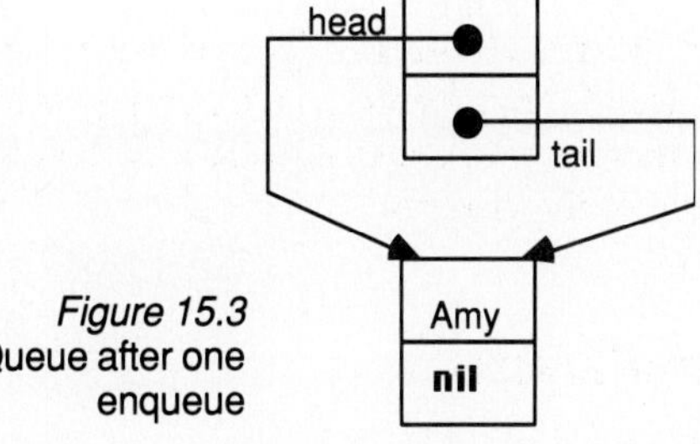

Figure 15.3
Queue after one enqueue

When a second node is added, it goes at the end of the line. The second node belongs between the first node and the **nil** pointer. The head pointer continues to point at the first node, but the tail pointer moves to the second node (Figure 15.4). Enqueueing a third name again moves the tail node but has no effect on the head node (See Figure 15.5).

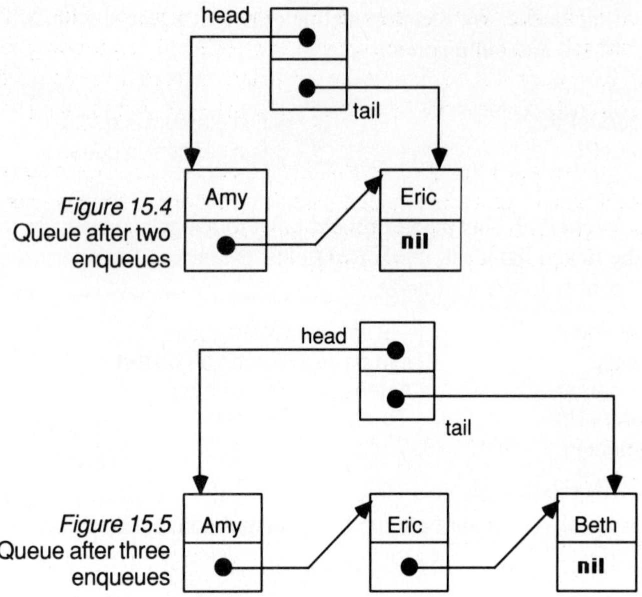

Figure 15.4 Queue after two enqueues

Figure 15.5 Queue after three enqueues

If we now dequeue, we should remove the first name from the list. This affects the value of the head pointer but does not affect the tail node. The information in the top node is sent back to the caller, and the head pointer is moved one position down the linked list (See Figure 15.6).

Dequeueing once more returns us to the special case in which only one node is in the list (Figure 15.7).

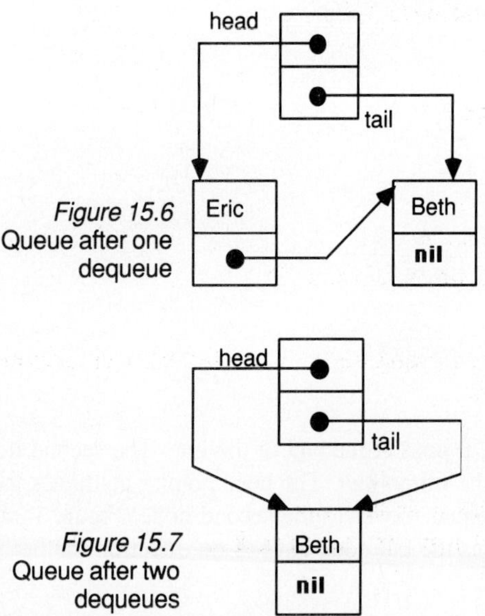

Figure 15.6 Queue after one dequeue

Figure 15.7 Queue after two dequeues

If we dequeue again, the head pointer is again moved down one node, to the **nil** pointer. This time, though, the value of the tail pointer is affected; dequeueing the only element in the list means that the tail no longer points to anything. We need to reset the tail pointer to **nil**. We now are back to the original state, with nothing on the queue.

If we try to dequeue when the queue contains no elements, an error results. We cannot move the head pointer down one node in the list if there are no elements to begin with. We send back a signal to the calling routine by returning the null string.

We can now pseudocode the four operations.

```
{ Init }
   Set head to nil
   Set tail to nil

{ EmptyQueue }
   IF queue is empty THEN
      Return TRUE
   ELSE
      Return FALSE

{ Enqueue }
   Create node
   { Attach node to end of list }
      Set next field of new node to tail^.next
      Point tail at new node
      IF head is nil THEN
         head := tail

{ Dequeue }
   IF head and tail point to same node THEN
      BEGIN
         Return name field of head
         Set head and tail to nil
      END
   ELSE
      BEGIN
         Return name field of head
         Move head pointer down one node in list
      END
```

The two cases in the Dequeue pseudocode are similar. We can regroup the tasks in that procedure as follows:

```
{ Dequeue }
   Return name field of head
   Move head pointer down one node in list
   IF head now is nil THEN { that was the last node }
      Set tail to nil
```

We can now complete the code for the Waitlist program. Again, notice that the two modules (the implementation of the queue and the use of the queue) were created separately but are part of the same program. Neither part can stand completely on its own.

The header for the program, the procedures ***Init***, ***Enqueue***, and ***Dequeue***, and the function ***EmptyQueue*** follow.*

---

* If you implement this as a separate unit in Lightspeed, you should change the names of the ***Enqueue*** and ***Dequeue*** functions, or you will receive an error message such as **Link Error: "DEQUEUE" is multiply defined.**

Code 15.2
Implementation of queue

```
program Waitlist;

{ implementor's section of program }

   const
      sentinel = -1;                        { indicates end of program    }

   type
      name = string[50];                    { contains student names      }

{ definition of queue data type }

      queuePtr = ^element;                  { --> student in queue        }
      element = record
            person : name;                  { name of student             }
            next : queuePtr                 { --> next student in queue   }
         end;

      queue = record
            head : queuePtr;                { --> first student in queue  }
            tail : queuePtr                 { --> last student in queue   }
         end; { queue }

{ Procedures for queue abstraction }

{ Procedure InitQueue                                 }
{ The InitQueue procedure initializes the queue.      }
{ The head and tail pointers are set to nil.          }
{ Called by: Mainline          Calls: none            }

   procedure InitQueue (var initQ : queue); { waitlist }

   begin
      initQ.head := nil;
      initQ.tail := nil
   end; { InitQueue }
```

Code 15.2
(continued)

```
{ Function EmptyQueue                              }
{ The EmptyQueue function returns TRUE if          }
{  the queue is empty, FALSE otherwise.            }
{ Called by: Mainline      Calls: none             }

   function EmptyQueue (checkQueue : queue) { waitlist }
         : boolean;

   begin
      if checkQueue.head = nil then
         EmptyQueue := TRUE
      else
         EmptyQueue := FALSE
   end; { EmptyQueue }

{ Procedure Enqueue                                        }
{  This procedure adds a student to the queue. A new       }
{ node is created and filled. Then the new node is         }
{ attached to the end of the queue. In the special case    }
{ when the queue is receiving its first element, the       }
{ head pointer is set to the new element as well.          }
{ Called by: AddStudents            Calls: none            }

   procedure Enqueue (var addQueue : queue;{ waitlist                  }
      newName : name);                     { student to add to queue   }

      var
         newElement : queuePtr;            { node for new element      }

   begin
      New(newElement);   { create node and fill fields }
      newElement^.person := newName;

      with addQueue do
         begin
         { attach node to end of list }
            newElement^.next := nil;
            if tail <> nil then
               tail^.next := newElement;
            tail := newElement;

      { set head of list if node is first element }
            if head = nil then
               head := tail
         end { with }
   end; { Enqueue }
```

Code 15.2 (continued)

```
{ Procedure Dequeue                                            }
{  This procedure removes a student from the queue. First      }
{ the procedure determines if there are any students           }
{ currently in the queue. If not, a signal is sent back        }
{ to the calling procedure. If so, the name of the student     }
{ is returned to the calling procedure.                        }
{   When a student is removed from the queue, the head         }
{ pointer is moved down one node in the list, and the old      }
{ node is disposed. In the special case when the last          }
{ node in the list is being removed, the tail pointer is       }
{ set to nil, since there is nothing left in the queue.        }
{ Called by : AssignMachines   Calls : none                    }

   procedure Dequeue (var remQueue : queue;         { waitlist                  }
      var remName : name);                          { name removed from queue  }

      var
         newElement : queuePtr;                     { node for new element      }

   begin
      with remQueue do
         begin
            remName := head^.person;

      { move head pointer down one node in queue }
            head := head^.next;

      { if no more names in queue, reset tail pointer }
            if head = nil then
               tail := nil
         end { with }
   end; { Dequeue }
```

15.4 Stacks: The User's View

The stack data structure is another method of storing lists of data. Elements in the stack are processed in LIFO (last in, first out) order. While queues are more common in real life, stacks appear more often in computer science.

The stack data structure works very much like a stack of plates in a cafeteria. Consider a cafeteria line: each person takes the top plate off the stack. As people finish eating and dishes are washed, a kitchen worker comes along and places several clean plates on top of the stack, burying the plate that was on top. If ten new plates are put on the stack, the one that was on top is now the eleventh one taken off.

Two operations are associated with stacks. When a new element is placed on the top of the stack, it has been *pushed* on the stack. Figure 15.8 shows how a plate is pushed on a stack.

Elements can also be lifted off the top of the stack, as shown in Figure 15.9. When an item is removed, it has been *popped* from the stack.

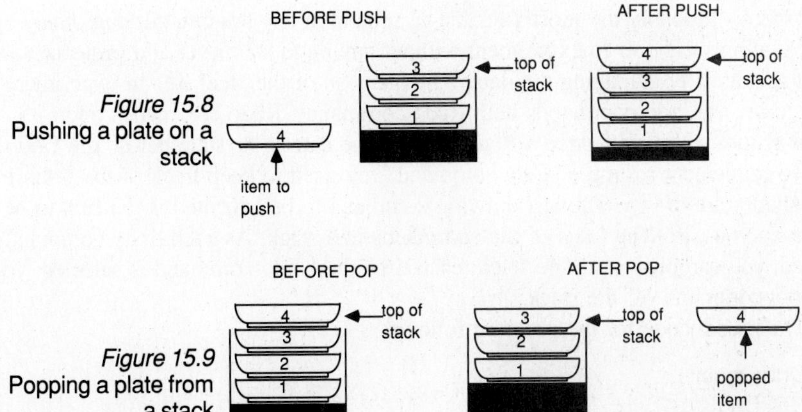

Figure 15.8
Pushing a plate on a stack

Figure 15.9
Popping a plate from a stack

The most important thing to remember about stacks is that you can gain access to only one element at a time. You can pop only the top element off the stack; you can push elements only onto the top of the stack. As with queues, you cannot gain access to any elements in the middle. Unlike queues, you cannot gain access to the bottom of the stack. The processes of pushing and popping are useful when you want to enter elements in one order and access them in reverse order.

Let's write yet another variation of the layout programs seen earlier. This program will have four commands: Draw Rectangle, Draw Oval, Stop, and Undo. These commands are to appear on a menu in the Drawing window.

When the user picks either Draw button, she is instructed to choose the top left and bottom right corners of the shape. A framed shape is then drawn at the specified location. The Stop button signals the end of the program.

The fourth button requires some more explanation. When using a layout program — or any program for that matter — you may find that you've made a mistake. You may accidentally choose the wrong endpoint for a corner or simply decide that you don't want the shape in your drawing. The Undo command allows you to correct mistakes by reversing the effect of the most recent command. Thus, to Undo the drawing of a shape, you can use the Undo command to erase the shape from the screen, as in Figure 15.10.

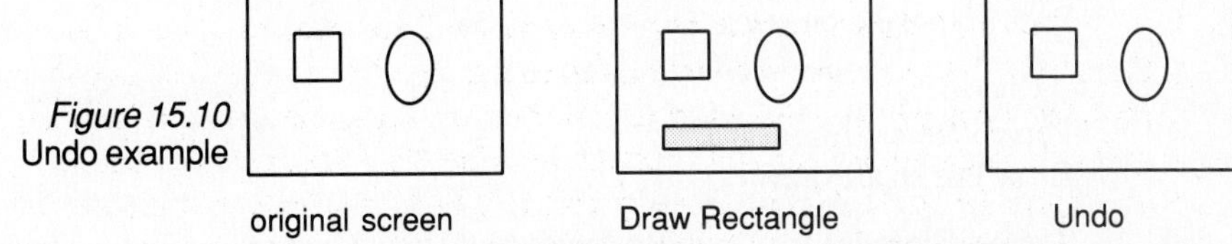

Figure 15.10
Undo example

The Undo button can be selected multiple times. Each Undo reverses one command. By continually selecting Undo, the user can eventually reverse all the commands that have been entered.

Undo is probably the most valuable command in any system. Among other things, it allows the user to experiment without having to start over and protects against accidentally damaging the data. An extension of the "feel free to experiment" idea is to invert Undo commands with Redo commands. Redo commands undo undone actions. In other words, a Redo restores the data to its state before the Undo.

To implement a simple Undo command, you need to keep track of the order in which shapes are drawn. The last drawing command to be executed is the first to be undone, so you can keep track of the commands in a stack. As each draw command is executed, you can push it on the stack; each time the Undo command is selected, you can pop a command off the stack.

The pseudocode for the program follows:

```
Draw menu
REPEAT
   Ask user to pick button
   IF user chooses Draw Rectangle THEN
      CALL: Draw Rectangle
   ELSE IF user chooses Draw Oval THEN
      CALL: Draw Oval
   ELSE IF user chooses Stop THEN
      done := TRUE
   ELSE IF user chooses Undo THEN
      CALL: Undo
   ELSE
      Tell user that pick was not on menu
UNTIL done

{ Draw Rectangle }
Ask user to pick top left corner
Ask user to pick bottom right corner
Frame Rectangle
Push command on stack

{ Draw Oval }
Ask user to pick top left corner
Ask user to pick bottom right corner
Frame Oval
Push command on stack

{ Undo }
Pop command from stack
Erase last shape drawn
```

The pseudocodes for Draw Rectangle and Draw Oval are similar, so you can create a generic procedure to draw a shape as follows:

```
{ Draw Shape }
Ask user to pick top left corner
Ask user to pick bottom right corner
```

```
IF rectangle is being drawn THEN
   Frame Rectangle
ELSE
   Frame Oval
Push command on stack
```

In the stack, you will store the information about each drawing command. You need to store what shape (rectangle or oval) has been drawn and where it has been placed on the screen. A ***rect*** variable can indicate the shape's location on the screen; a ***char*** can designate the shape type.

Thus, you tell the implementor that you need three commands:

```
< boolean > := EmptyStack(< stack >);
Push(< stack >, < shape location >, < shape type >);
Pop(< stack >, < shape location >, < shape type >);
```

< shape location > is a variable of type ***rect***, indicating the location of the shape. < shape type > is a ***char*** indicating whether the shape is a rectangle or an oval. < signal > is a boolean variable. The ***Pop*** procedure causes an error when the stack is empty; thus, you have an ***EmptyStack*** function that returns TRUE when the stack is empty and FALSE otherwise. You don't have to worry about such error conditions coming from ***Push***.*

The pseudocode should be revised for the undo procedure to handle the empty stack condition. If there is nothing to undo, the user should receive a message. If there is something to undo, the < shape type > and < shape location > indicate where to erase.

```
{ Undo }
IF stack is empty THEN
   Tell user there is nothing to undo
ELSE { Erase last shape drawn }
   BEGIN
      Pop command from stack
      IF shape was rectangle THEN
         Erase rectangle
      ELSE
         Erase oval
   END { ELSE }
```

Both ***Push*** and ***Pop*** assume that the stack variable < stack > exists. Therefore, it is probably a good idea to ask the implementor to create an ***InitStack*** procedure to initialize the stack, with the syntax:

```
InitStack(< stack >);
```

Given this information about how to interface with the implementation of the stack, you can code the user's end as follows.

---

* At least not in the stack implemented here. When working with potentially very large stacks, you may need to check for *stack overflow*, which occurs when you try to push an item on the stack, but no memory is left.

Code 15.3
Program that uses stacks as an abstraction

```
{ Program: Layout    D. Niguidula    November 22                }
{ This program allows the user to draw rectangles and            }
{ ovals on the screen. The program is driven by a menu.          }
{ When the user chooses the Draw Rectangle or Draw               }
{ Oval button, the program asks the user to select the           }
{ corners for the shape. When the user chooses the Stop          }
{ button, the program exits. When the user chooses the           }
{ Undo button, the last shape that was drawn is removed          }
{ from the screen.                                               }

program Layout;

   const
      rectangle = 'R';                  { character codes for shapes          }
      oval = 'O';
      maxShapes = 35;                   { max number of shapes on screen      }

{ stack abstraction defined by implementor here }

   var
      rectBtn,                          { button for Draw Rectangle     }
      ovalBtn,                          { button for Draw Oval          }
      undoBtn,                          { button for Undo               }
      stopBtn : rect;                   { button for Stop               }
      userHoriz, userVert : integer;    { coords selected by user       }
      userPt : point;                   { point selected by user        }
      shapeStack : stack;               { stack of drawn shapes         }
      done : boolean;                   { indicates end of program      }

{ Procedures InitStack, EmptyStack, Push, and Pop          }
{  will be defined by implementor in this location.        }

{ Procedure DrawButton                                      }
{  This procedure draws a menu button with text. The        }
{ procedure sets a rect variable for the button, draws it   }
{ and then places text in the middle of the button.         }
{ Called By: DrawMenu      Calls: none                      }

   procedure DrawButton (var btn : rect;     { area of screen for button        }
            left, top,                        { coordinates of one endpoint      }
            right, bottom : integer;          { coords of other endpoint         }
            title : string);                  { text to place in button          }

   begin
      SetRect(btn, left, top, right, bottom);
      FrameRect(btn);
   { draw text in center of button }
      MoveTo(left + 5, (top + bottom) div 2);
      WriteDraw(title)
   end; { DrawButton }
```

Code 15.3
(continued)

```
{ Procedure DrawMenu                                              }
{  This procedure draws the four menu buttons for the             }
{ layout program. It sets the coordinates for each button         }
{ and then calls another procedure to draw the button.            }
{ Called by: Mainline    Calls: DrawButton                        }

   procedure DrawMenu (var rectBtn,     { button for Draw Rect   }
      ovalBtn,                          { button for Draw Oval   }
      undoBtn,                          { button for Undo        }
      stopBtn : rect);                  { button for Stop        }

   begin
      DrawButton(rectBtn, 0, 0, 50, 25, 'RECT');
      DrawButton(ovalBtn, 50, 0, 100, 25, 'OVAL');
      DrawButton(undoBtn, 100, 0, 150, 25, 'UNDO');
      DrawButton(stopBtn, 150, 0, 200, 25, 'STOP')
   end; { DrawMenu }

{ Procedure DrawShape                                             }
{  This procedure draws either a rectangle or an oval on the      }
{ screen. The user is asked to choose the top left and bottom     }
{ right of the rectangle that will circumscribe the shape.        }
{ Using those points, a rect variable is given a value, and the   }
{ shape is drawn. Then information about the shape is pushed      }
{ on the shape stack.                                             }
{ Called By: Mainline     Calls:  Push                            }

   procedure DrawShape (var shapeStack : stack; { stack of shapes          }
      curShape : char);                         { indicates rect or oval   }

      var
         shapeRect : rect;              { area circumscribing shape       }
         top, left,                     { top left corner of shape        }
         bottom, right : integer;       { bottom right corner of shape    }

   begin
   { Get corners of shape }
      Writeln('Please choose the top left corner of the shape');
      repeat
         GetMouse(left, top);
      until Button;

      Writeln('Please choose the bottom right corner of the shape');
      repeat
         GetMouse(right, bottom);
      until Button;
```

Code 15.3 (continued)

```
{ Draw shape }
   SetRect(shapeRect, left, top, right, bottom);
   if curShape = rectangle then
      FrameRect(shapeRect)
   else
      FrameOval(shapeRect);

   Push(shapeStack, shapeRect, curShape)

end; { DrawShape }

{ Procedure Undo                                              }
{ The Undo procedure reverses the last action performed.      }
{ This procedure pops a shape off the stack. If there are     }
{ no commands to be undone, an error message is printed.      }
{ Otherwise, the shape is erased from the screen.             }
{ Called by: Mainline       Calls: Pop, EmptyStack            }

procedure Undo (var shapeStack : stack);        { stack of shapes          }

   var
      loc : rect;                           { location of shape on screen  }
      curShape : char;                      { indicates rectangle or oval  }

begin

   if EmptyStack(shapeStack) then
      Writeln('Nothing left to undo.')
   else
      begin
         Pop(shapeStack, loc, curShape);
         if curShape = oval then
            EraseOval(loc)
         else
            EraseRect(loc)
      end { else }

end; { Undo }

{ Mainline                                                    }
{   The mainline controls the menu selection. First, it calls }
{ on another procedure to draw the menu. Then Mainline        }
{ asks the user to choose a point on the menu. If the user    }
{ misses the menu, an error message is printed. If the user   }
{ chooses the stop button, the program exits. Otherwise,      }
{ the appropriate procedure is called.                        }
{ Calls: DrawMenu, DrawShape, Undo                            }
```

Code 15.3
(continued)

```
begin
{ Initialization }
    InitStack(shapeStack);
    DrawMenu(rectBtn, ovalBtn, undoBtn, stopBtn);
    done := FALSE;

    repeat
    { ask user to choose point }
        Writeln('Please pick a point on the menu.');
        repeat
            GetMouse(userHoriz, userVert);
        until Button;
        SetPt(userPt, userHoriz, userVert);

        if PtInRect(userPt, rectBtn) then
            DrawShape(shapeStack, rectangle)
        else if PtInRect(userPt, ovalBtn) then
            DrawShape(shapeStack, oval)
        else if PtInRect(userPt, undoBtn) then
            Undo(shapeStack)
        else if PtInRect(userPt, stopBtn) then
            done := TRUE
        else
            Writeln('You did not pick a point on the menu.');

        Writeln
    until done

end. { Layout }
```

Figures 15.11 through 15.17 show how the stack and the screen change during one run of the program. When the program begins, the menu is placed on the screen, and the user has four options. Say that she first chooses Draw Rectangle. The program instructs her to choose two endpoints, and the shape then appears on the screen. The program sends information about the rectangle to the procedure ***Push***; there, the rectangle is pushed on the stack. At this point, the screen and stack look like Figure 15.11.

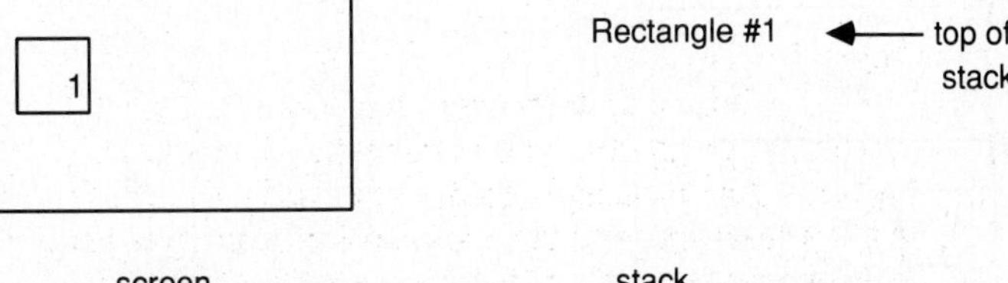

Figure 15.11
Result of drawing shape

(In the diagrams, numbers are in the shapes for illustrative purposes. The code does not place any text on the screen.) Now say that the user decides to drawn an oval, followed by another rectangle. The program asks the user for the endpoints of each shape, draws the shape on the screen, and pushes the information on the stack. There are now three shapes on the screen and three commands in the stack, as shown in Figure 15.12.

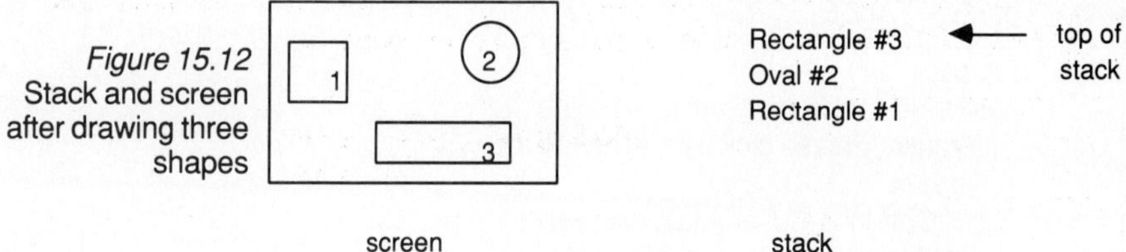

Figure 15.12 Stack and screen after drawing three shapes

Looking at the screen, the user decides that she doesn't really want that last rectangle. To remove it, she chooses the Undo button. When this occurs, the program calls the ***Undo*** procedure. That procedure first calls ***EmptyStack***; the function returns FALSE, indicating that the stack is not empty. You then call ***Pop***, which tells you that the last shape drawn was rectangle 3. That rectangle is erased from the screen, and the result is shown in Figure 15.13.

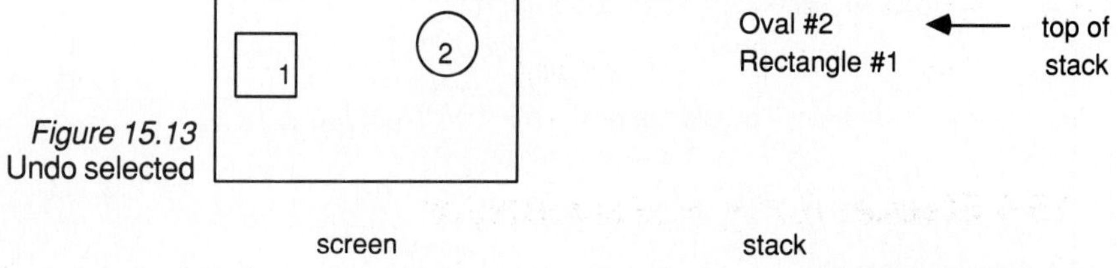

Figure 15.13 Undo selected

The user then decides to draw an oval. As before, she is instructed to select the corners, and the shape is pushed on the stack (Figure 15.14).

Now the user decides to start all over again. The undo button allows her to undo all the shapes to the beginning. When the user first picks Undo, the shape at the top of the stack (oval 4) is popped and erased from the screen (Figure 15.15).

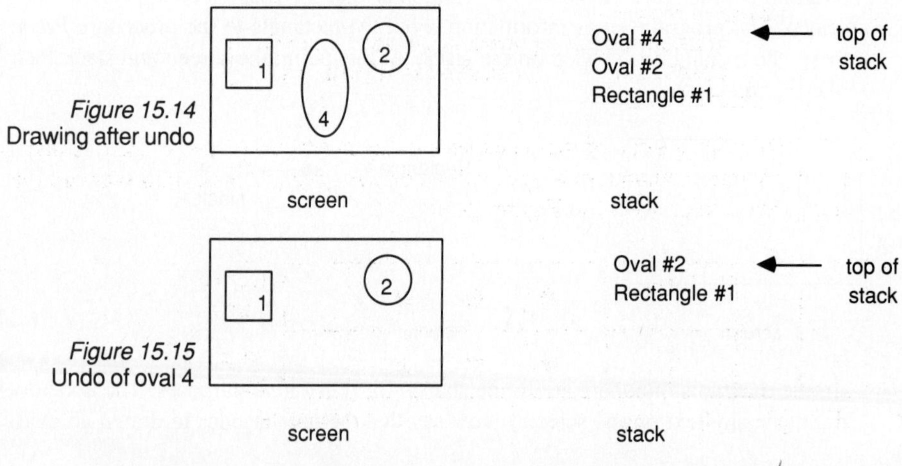

Figure 15.14 Drawing after undo

Figure 15.15 Undo of oval 4

When the user chooses Undo again, the same routine erases oval 2, since that shape has moved to the top of the stack (Figure 15.16). The next Undo removes the remaining shape from the screen (Figure 15.17).

If the user chooses Undo yet again, the ***Undo*** procedure receives the value TRUE from ***EmptyStack***. This means no more shapes remain in the stack. The message "Nothing left to Undo" appears in the text window.

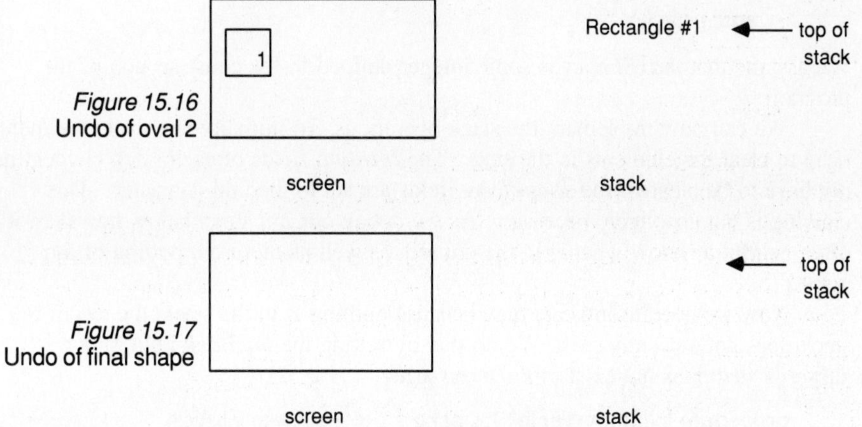

Figure 15.16
Undo of oval 2

Figure 15.17
Undo of final shape

15.5 Stacks: Array Implementation

Like queues, stacks can be implemented with any number of data structures. We shall look at two possible implementations.

First, let's examine how we could use an array for the Undo stack. We know that each element in the stack is represented by two pieces of information: the location and the type of shape. Since we are storing associated information with different data types, we can declare each element as a record:

```
element = record
        location: rect;      { position of shape on screen   }
        shape: char          { indicates rectangle or oval   }
    end; { element }
```

To create a stack of these elements using an array, we have to assume that some maximum number of shapes will be on the screen. We can thus diagram the stack data type as shown in Figure 15.18.

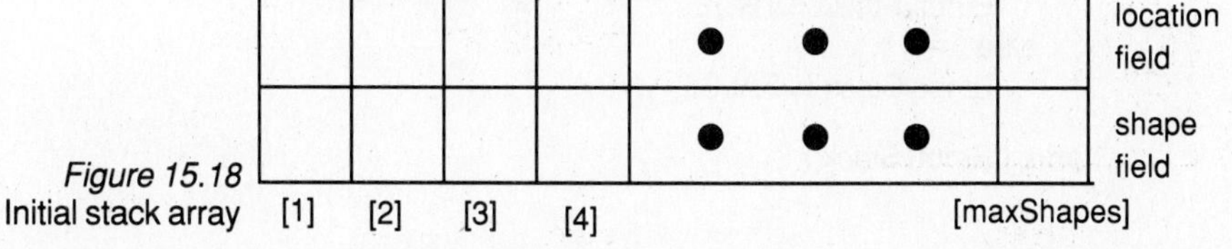

Figure 15.18
Initial stack array

Part of the definition of a stack is that only one element can be accessed at any time. We keep track of this element by denoting which subscript holds the top of the stack. The stack is represented by an array of elements and an integer denoting the stack's top.

```
stack = record
      topStack: integer;                      { subscript of top element        }
      items: array [ 1..maxShapes] of element    { list of all shapes          }
   end; { stack }
```

We assume that ***maxShapes*** is some integer defined in the **const** section of the program.

We can now implement the stack operations. To initialize the stack, we merely need to clear the elements in the stack. The ***location*** fields of each stack element do not have to be cleared; the ***shapeType*** fields are set to the null character. (This clearing is not absolutely necessary. As we debug our implementation, however, it is often helpful to know what is in the unused, as well as the used, portion of the stack.)

Now we need to indicate that, because nothing is in the stack, the top of the stack does not currently exist. We do this by setting the ***topStack*** field to 0, a subscript that does not exist in the ***items*** array.

```
procedure InitStack (var initS: stack);        { stack to initialize      }

var
   loop: integer;                              { loop counter             }

begin

   { clear elements in stack }
   for loop := 1 to maxShapes do
      initS.items[loop].shape := '';

   { set top of stack to 0 element }
   initS.topStack := 0

end; { InitStack }
```

The ***EmptyStack*** function should determine if the stack is empty. From the code for ***InitStack***, we know that the ***topStack*** field of an empty stack is 0. Thus, the function can be written as follows:

```
function EmptyStack (var checkStack: stack); { stack to check }

begin

   if checkStack.topStack = 0 then
      EmptyStack := TRUE
   else
      EmptyStack := FALSE

end; { EmptyStack }
```

The ***Push*** procedure is given the stack and the information for the new shape. When we push an element, we want to place it at the top of the stack. To do this, we can increment the stack counter and then insert the new element in the array.

```
procedure Push(var shapeStack: stack;           { stack of shapes      }
      curLocation: rect;                        { location of shape    }
      curShape: char);                          { type of shape        }

begin
   with shapeStack do
      begin
         topStack := topStack + 1; { increment stack counter }

         { load information about new shape }
         items[topStack].location := curLocation;
         items[topStack].shape := curShape
      end { with }
end; { Push }
```

Popping elements off the stack is the inverse of pushing. The stack counter again tells us where the top of the stack resides. We send back the element to be popped and decrement the stack counter so that the previous element becomes the top of the stack.

```
procedure Pop(var popStack: stack;          { stack of shapes            }
      var popLocation: rect;                { location of popped shape   }
      var popShape: char);                  { type of popped shape       }

begin
   with popStack do
      begin
         { Retrieve information about shape to pop }
         popLocation := items[topStack].location;
         popShape := items[topStack].shape;
         topStack := topStack – 1  { move stack down one }
      end { with }
end; { Pop }
```

Let's return to the Undo example from the last section. We'll pick up the action after three shapes have been drawn on the screen. At this point, the stack record looks like Figure 15.19. In the illustrations, integers represent the ***rect*** variables, and the codes R and O indicate the shape types rectangle and oval, respectively.

Now suppose the user chooses Undo. When we pop an element off the stack, we have the result shown in Figure 15.20.

The only change to the stack data structure is that the stack counter has been decremented. Rectangle 3 still exists in the array, but it can no longer be accessed. The stack and the array are not the same thing; the stack contains only elements 1 through ***topStack***. Since ***topStack*** is currently 2, the shapes in array slots 3, 4, 5, and so on, are not a part of the stack.

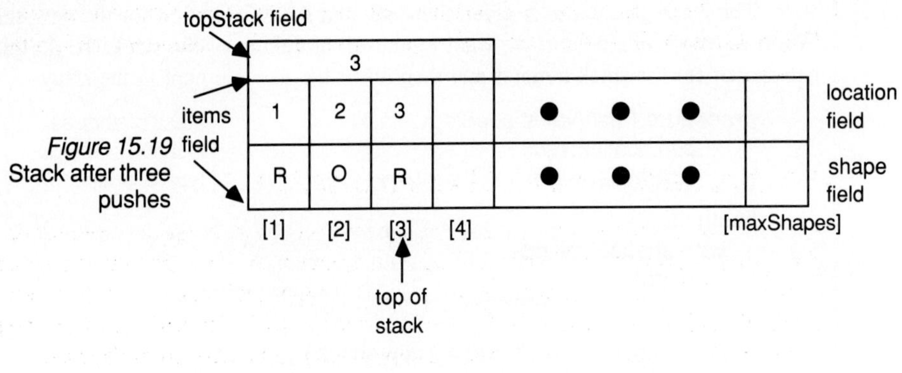

Figure 15.19 Stack after three pushes

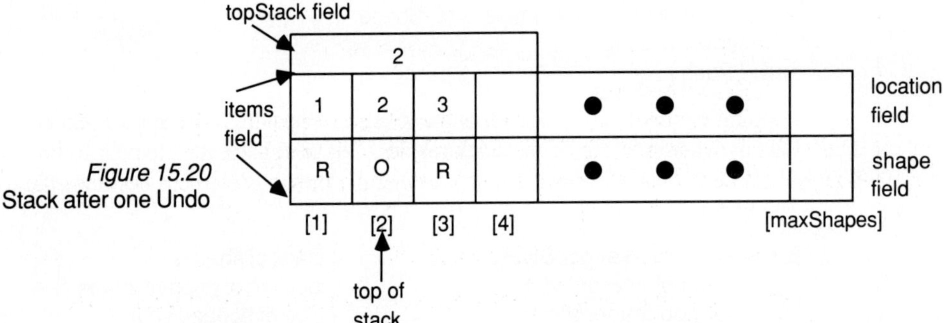

Figure 15.20 Stack after one Undo

In fact, information beyond the end of the stack has no effect on future events. Let's examine what happens when we push another element on the stack. Suppose the user draws oval 4 after undoing rectangle 3. The user chooses the endpoints, and the shape is drawn. When ***Push*** is called, ***topStack*** is incremented; it now contains the value 3. The information about oval 4 is stored in the third slot in the ***items*** array. The stack data structure now looks like Figure 15.21.

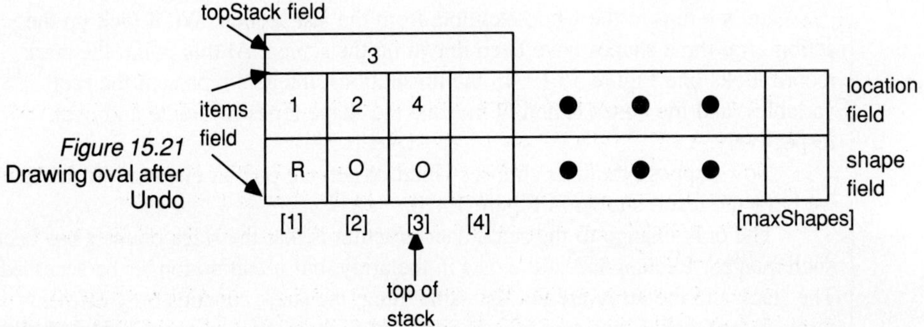

Figure 15.21 Drawing oval after Undo

The old contents have been overwritten, and the stack now contains three shapes: rectangle 1, oval 2, and oval 4.

Our three procedures and one function meet all the specifications for the stack. Combined with the earlier code, this array implementation completes the layout program.

15.6 Stacks: Linked List Implementation

For the undo example, a linked list implementation probably makes more sense. We do not know how many shapes will be on the screen, and any maximum number we choose to define an array will be arbitrary. The major difference between an array and a linked list implementation is that the top of the stack is denoted not by an integer array index but by a pointer. Thus, the type ***stack*** can be defined as follows:

```
type
    nextPtr = ^element;         { --> element in stack           }
    element = record
        location: rect;         { position of shape on screen    }
        shape: char;            { indicates rectangle or oval    }
        next: nextPtr           { --> next element in stack      }
      end; { element }
    stack = nextPtr;            { --> top of stack               }
```

Let's implement the four stack operations (***InitStack***, ***EmptyStack***, ***Push***, and ***Pop***) using this data structure.

When the stack begins, there are no items in it. The entire stack can be represented as a **nil** pointer. The **nil** pointer serves the same purpose as the 0 subscript in the array implementation: to designate the bottom of the stack. Assuming that ***stackTop*** is a variable of type ***stack*** and represents the top of the stack, the ***InitStack*** procedure has the result shown in Figure 15.22.

nil

stackTop

Figure 15.22 Initial stack

Because we have defined our initial stack this way, we can also say that an empty stack is one where the top of the stack is **nil.**

Pushing nodes onto the stack is similar to adding nodes to a standard linked list. First, we have to create a node to push. (In the figures, the pointer ***newNodePtr*** points to the new node.) Then, the ***location*** and ***shapeType*** fields are filled (Figure 15.23).

Now we have to connect the new node to the stack. Since the new node should be at the top of the stack, we should point the new node to the top of the current stack. This means that we assign the value of ***stackTop*** to the pointer field of the new node (Figure 15.24).

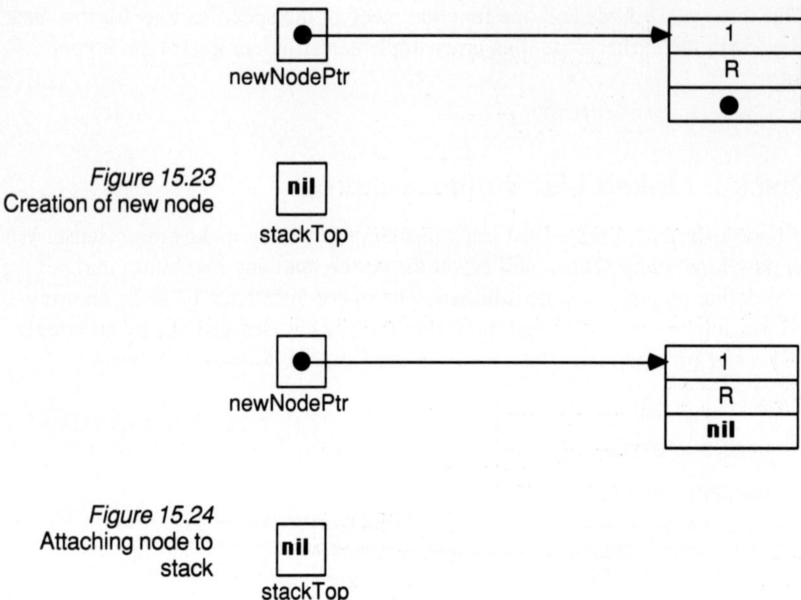

Figure 15.23
Creation of new node

Figure 15.24
Attaching node to stack

To end the push, we reset the stack pointer to the top of the stack (Figure 15.25).

When we push any other element on the stack, we repeat the same procedure. First, we create a node and fill its non-pointer fields (Figure 15.26). Then we assign ***stackTop*** to the pointer field of the new node (Figure 15.27).

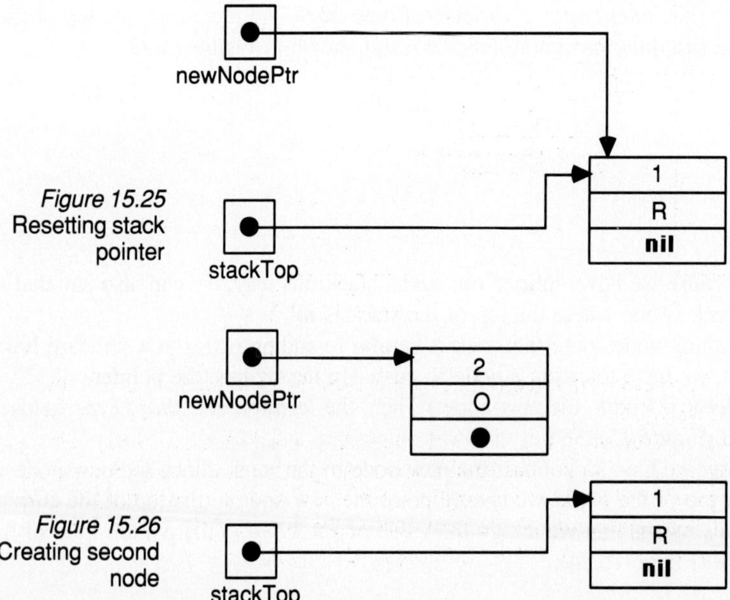

Figure 15.25
Resetting stack pointer

Figure 15.26
Creating second node

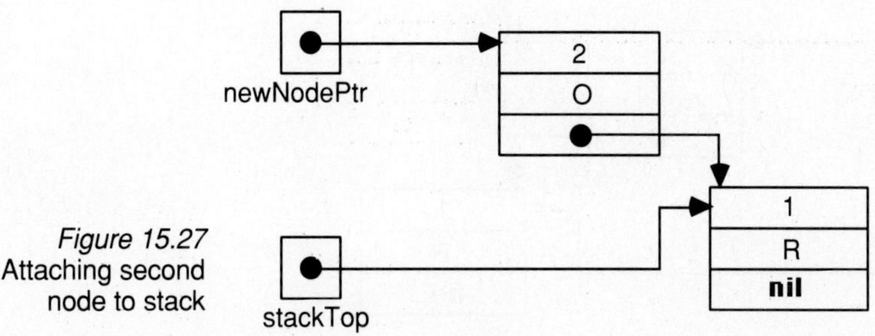

Figure 15.27 Attaching second node to stack

Finally, ***stackTop*** is reset to the top of the stack (Figure 15.28).

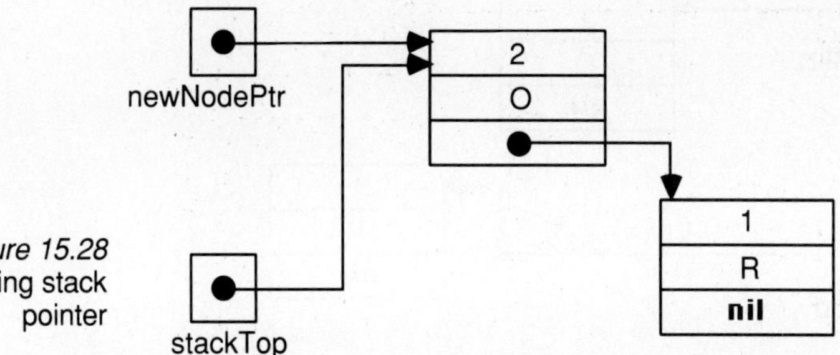

Figure 15.28 Resetting stack pointer

Notice that ***stackTop*** allows us to access only the top of the stack. To pop an element from a linked list stack, we first separate the node to pop from the remainder of the stack. This is accomplished with a new pointer (***poppedPtr*** in the figures) that is set to ***stackTop*** (Figure 15.29). (We assume ***newNodePtr*** was a variable local to the pushing routine, so it no longer exists.)

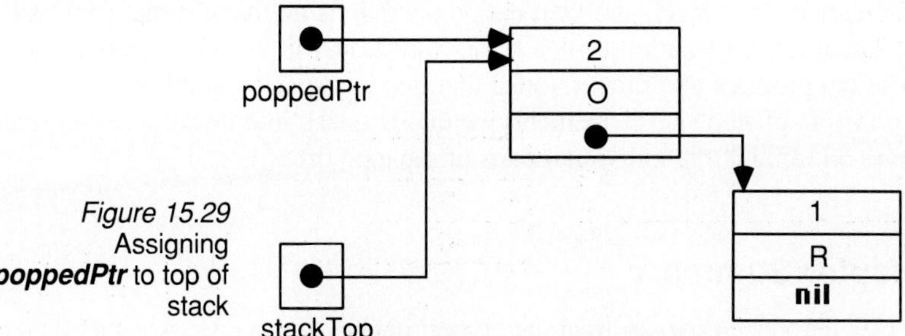

Figure 15.29 Assigning ***poppedPtr*** to top of stack

To disconnect the node, we first move ***stackTop*** to the top of the new stack (Figure 15.30).

Then we set the pointer field of ***poppedPtr*** to **nil** (Figure 15.31). This completes the separation. This final pointer assignment isn't really necessary, since the popped element is no longer in the stack (the path from ***stackTop*** to **nil**). However, separating the element does make our program cleaner. We can now use ***Dispose*** to recycle the node ***poppedPtr*** points to.

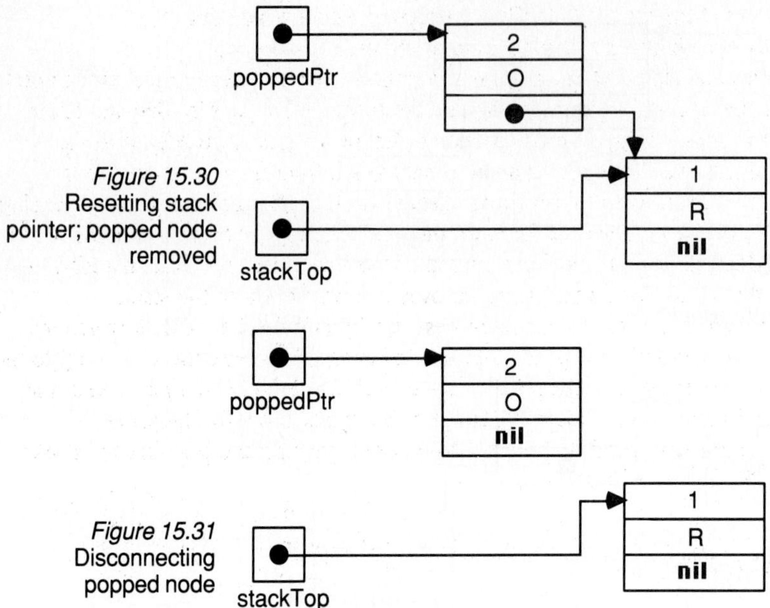

Figure 15.30 Resetting stack pointer; popped node removed

Figure 15.31 Disconnecting popped node

The choice between linked list and array implementations is made by examining the data. If we can determine the approximate number of elements the stack will hold at any time, then an array is appropriate; if we can't, a linked list is a better choice. In either case, we are using the same operations. The code that uses ***Push***, ***Pop***, ***EmptyStack***, and ***InitStack*** works no matter how the type ***stack*** is implemented.

When designing your own programs, you may wish to consider how your data is stored on an abstract level, and then define operations on that abstract data type. Save the actual implementation for later; this way, you will be able to concentrate on one part of the program at a time. (Notice that this is a specific application of the general principle of stepwise refinement: we divide a task into its components and concentrate on refining the individual parts at separate times.)

15.7 Chapter Summary

This chapter introduced two abstract data types: queues and stacks. Abstract data types are typically created by one programmer in one module but used by another programmer in a different module. Abstract data types are characterized by the data they hold and the operations that can be performed on them. The concrete representation of the abstraction is not important to its users.

You can look at abstract types from two points of view: that of the user and that of the implementor. Both the user's and the implementor's code are defined inside a program. The examples in this book show the user's viewpoint, for example, in manipulating regions. When you include the statement **uses**

QuickDraw2; at the top of a MacPascal program, you are including the implementor's code for the manipulation of regions.

Queues and stacks were examined from both perspectives. From a user's point of view, a queue is a line. Items in the line are processed in first-in, first-out order. Two operations can be performed on queues. Enqueueing an item adds it to the bottom of the queue. Dequeueing an item removes it from the top of the queue.

Stacks are also used to implement lists of data. Stacks are useful for processing items in reverse order, since stacks work on a last-in, first-out basis. All items in the stack are added to or removed from the top of the stack. Pushing an item adds it to the top of the stack. Popping an item removes it from the top of the stack.

Both queues and stacks can be represented by any number of data structures. Usually, arrays and linked lists are appropriate concrete representations; it is up to the implementor to decide how the stack or queue will be defined. No matter what the implementation, these very common abstract data types allow for the same operations: enqueueing and dequeueing for queues, pushing and popping for stacks.

15.8 Exercises

Understanding Concepts

1. Suppose you are writing a new Macintosh application program and want to use pull-down menus, just like those in the Finder and MacPascal. Somebody else is the implementor of the menu software. What are some of the operations that you would like to call from the implementor's software (e.g., the procedure that makes the menu appear when you press on the menu name)?

2. Sketch two concrete representations of the abstract data type ***bookShelf***, which is a set of books on shelf in a library. The user can use the following commands:

   BeginRange(< bookShelf >**)** — returns beginning of call numbers on shelf
   EndRange(< bookShelf >**)** — returns end of call numbers on shelf
   Count(< bookShelf >**)** — returns number of books on shelf
   ListTitles(< bookShelf >**)** — prints a list of all book titles on shelf
   QueryAuthor(< bookShelf >, < author >**)** — returns TRUE if any book by < author > is on shelf

3. What are some possible implementations of the QuickDraw data type ***rgnHandle***, given what you know about commands that use regions?

4. Section 15.1 discussed a possible scenario of how software teams might divide the tasks in rewriting the Macintosh Desktop software. What is another possible division of tasks for the same project?

5. If it is possible, show how to enqueue the data 1, 2, 3, 4 (in order) on a queue and dequeue them in the order 2, 3, 1, 4 in a single queue.

6. In the following sequence, the command ***Enqueue*** < x > adds the datum < x > to a queue; the command ***Dequeue*** removes an item from the queue and prints it. What does the sequence output?

   Enqueue A, Dequeue, Enqueue B, Enqueue C, Dequeue, Enqueue D, Dequeue, Dequeue, Enqueue E, Dequeue, Dequeue

7. If it is possible, show how you can push the data 1, 2, 3, 4 (in order) on a stack and pop them in the order 2, 3, 1, 4 in a single stack.

8. Why is it not possible, using the input 1, 2, 3, 4, to manipulate a single stack (with pushes and pops) so that they can be popped in the order 3, 1, 4, 2?

9. In the following sequence, the command ***Push*** < x > adds the datum < x > to a stack; the command ***Pop*** removes an item from the stack and prints it. What does the sequence output?

   Push A, Pop, Push B, Push C, Pop, Push D, Pop, Pop, Push E, Pop, Pop

10. Hand simulate the code in section 15.4 by choosing the following buttons (in order):

    Rectangle, Oval, Undo, Oval, Rectangle, Undo, Oval, Undo, Undo, Undo, Rectangle, Undo

Programming Problems

1. Write a program to shuffle a deck of cards and allow the user to play solitaire. In this game, seven piles of cards are dealt face down (one card in the first pile, two in the second, and so on). The top card on each pile is placed face up. These piles are called the tableaus.

   You can build on the top cards of the tableaus. Cards are placed in descending order and alternating colors. For example, a black queen can be played on a red king. All the face-up cards on one tableau can be moved to build on another tableau. Whenever a face-down card becomes the top of the pile, it is turned over. The cards not initially in the tableau are the hand. Cards are dealt, three at a time, from the hand to a pile called the talon. The card at the top of the talon can be played on any of the tableaus, and the subsequently exposed cards can also be played.

   The top card on the talon or on any of the tableaus can also be placed on one of the four foundations. These are built up, starting with the ace, in ascending order and in suit.

In your program, the user should be able to quit at any time; if the user doesn't quit, the game ends when all of the cards are on the foundation.

2. Write a program to play the card game Crazy Eights. Deal eight cards to the user and eight to the computer. The remaining cards are the stack. The top card of the stack is revealed and becomes the top of the discard pile. The user then discards a card that matches the discard pile's suit or number. For example, if the discard pile is headed by the jack of clubs, the user can discard any jack or any club. The computer should then discard a card matching the suit or number of the card played by the user.

   Eights are wild — they match any number and can be played on any turn. When a player discards an 8, that player gets to announce a new suit, which the other player must match on the next turn.

   A player who cannot make a play must draw cards from the stack until a play is possible. If the stack runs out of cards, all the cards in the discard pile except the top card are shuffled and become the new stack.

   A player wins by running out of cards.

3. Modify the Layout program in this chapter by adding a Delete button. Remember, deletion of a shape can be undone.

4. Modify the Layout program in this chapter by adding a Redo button. This option is an undo of an undo. For example, if the user draws an oval and chooses Undo, the oval disappears. If the user then chooses Redo, the oval reappears.

   Redo can reverse the actions only of the Undo commands following the last action (an action being defined as drawing or deleting). This means that if the user draws four shapes and then chooses Undo three times, Redo can be chosen three times. However, if the user draws four shapes, chooses Undo three times, and then draws another shape, Redo has no effect because there is no Undo following the last action.

5. In music, there are 12 names for notes. In order, these are C, C# (pronounced C-sharp), D, D#, E, F, F#, G, G#, A, A#, and B. Each note in this list is a half-step above the previous note. This list is circular, that is, following B is another C, C#, D, and so on.

   Write a program that accepts a note name as input and outputs the major scale that begins at that note. A major scale consists of 8 tones in the following pattern:

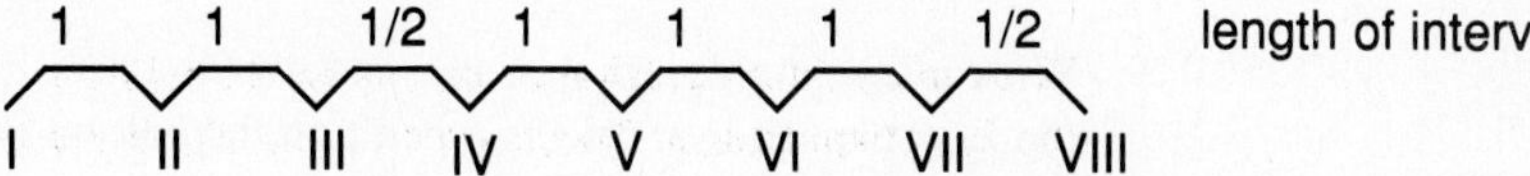

Thus, the major scale that begins at D is: D, E, F#, G, A, B, C#, D.

Variations:

a. If you know music notation, display the scale graphically on a treble staff.
b. Another listing of the notes is C, Db (pronounced D-flat), D, Eb, E, F, Gb, G, Ab, A, Bb, B (in other words, Db and C# are the same note). Use flats if the user enters a flat or the note F, and sharps for any other notation.

6. Modify the Calculator program of Chapter 7 by adding buttons for left and right parentheses. (Hint: keep a stack of running totals. Left and right parentheses should correspond to a push and pop, respectively, on this stack.)

7. Write a program that simulates the activity at a supermarket. At any given moment, there is a 3 in 10 chance that someone will get in any one of the five cashiers' lines. Each customer in line has between 1 and 50 items (your program should determine this by using a random number generator). A cashier takes 10 seconds to ring up each item. Write a program that shows the activity at 1-minute intervals for an hour.

8. Write a program that tests memorization skills. Divide the Drawing window into four rectangular areas. Then randomly choose one of the four areas and highlight it for a few seconds (an empty **for** loop, such as **for** ctr := 1 **to** 1000 **do** ; can freeze the action). The user then has to indicate which area the computer highlighted by clicking on that area.

   If the user is right, the program should highlight the first area, and then highlight a second area, chosen at random. The user should respond by clicking the two areas in order. The program gives the user longer and longer sequences, adding one area each time. Here is a possible sequence of five turns (T = top, B = bottom, L = left, R = right):

   TL
   TL BR
   TL BR TL
   TL BR TL BL
   TL BR TL BL BL

   The process repeats until the user correctly remembers a sequence of 16 areas or makes a mistake. In the latter case, the program should respond with a message and display the correct sequence.

   Extension: Highlight each rectangular area with a different pen pattern. The user must remember both pen pattern and position.

9. Write a layout program that allows a user to draw, delete, and move shapes. To move a shape, a user selects a point on the screen. If the point is in more than

one shape, the program should choose the shape that was created or moved most recently.

10. We all have lists of things to do. Write a program that helps maintain priorities. The program should ask the user to do one of two things: add to the list or do something from the list. If he wants to add something, he should input the task and assign a priority number to it. This priority number is an integer from 1 to 10, where 10 indicates the most urgent task. The program should then list the current things to do in order of urgency.

    If the user says that it is time to do something, the program should tell the user what task should be performed. This task is then removed from the list. The program ends when the user indicates that he wants to quit. (This program does not use a stack or queue in the manner described in this chapter.)

16

Recursion and Binary Trees

Every programmer, with practice, develops a bag of tricks: techniques to manipulate data or execute code more efficiently. When used properly, these techniques lend a certain sophistication to a program. Understanding and developing elegant algorithms and data structures for your own repertoire means that you have advanced beyond the initial level of programming. Just as proper use of metaphors and other rhetorical devices can make your writing more effective, proper use of coding devices can improve your programming.

This chapter will introduce you to a sophisticated technique of repetition called recursion and an abstract data type called a binary tree. As with the other concepts in this book, these devices have specific purposes. These new techniques are variations of concepts you have seen earlier. They are introduced here not only because they are useful but also to encourage you to consider variations on the standard techniques you have already seen. In problem solving, it's important to consider alternate possibilities, not just the first thing that pops into your head.

16.1 Recursive Algorithms

Chapter 1 compared the Mainline and the procedures it calls to a person in charge delegating tasks to subordinates. Procedures and functions are used to divide and conquer work. Unlike a human organization, however, procedures can save work by asking themselves to do work. In effect, procedures can "clone" themselves.

Think back to a classic book from your childhood. In Dr. Seuss's *The Cat In The Hat Comes Back** the cat in the hat needs to clean up a spot. But he decides he can't clean up the spot by himself. So he lifts his hat and out pops Little Cat A, who is a smaller version of the Cat in the Hat. Little Cat A looks at the spot and decides that they need even more help. The smaller cat lifts his hat, and another even smaller cat is there. Little Cat A says,

> "This is Little Cat B.
> And I keep him about,
> And when I need help,
> Then I let him come out."

Each cat has a little replica of himself under his hat — and the littler cats come out to help the bigger cats. Ultimately, Little Cat Z appears and cleans the spot. When the job is finished, the cats, one by one, return to their hats.

A similar process exists in computer programming. An algorithm that repeats itself in this manner — using "smaller" replicas of itself to assist with the larger task — is called a *recursive* algorithm. Recursion is a special type of repetition, one that isn't handled by a loop construct. Recursion is the repetition of a procedure or function from *within* that procedure or function.

Now, before you think about that for too long, let's look at another recursive algorithm. The Towers of Hanoi puzzle involves three poles and a number of disks (the wooden kind, not the kind that fit in a drive), each with a hole in the center. No two disks are the same size. Initially, all the disks are on one pole, in order of size, with the smallest on top. Figure 16.1 shows the initial setup of the puzzle using two disks.

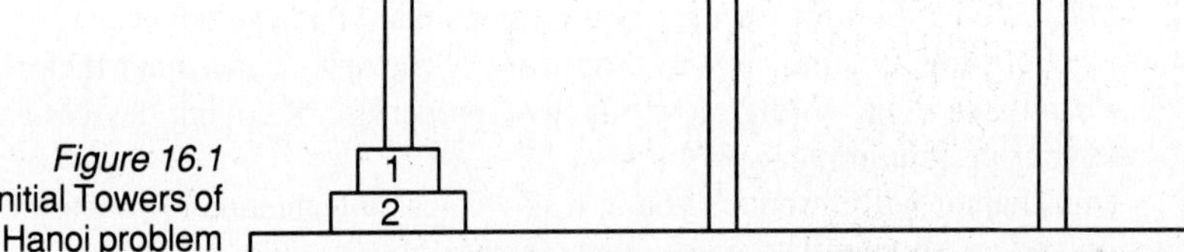

Figure 16.1 Initial Towers of Hanoi problem

The object of the problem is to move all the disks to another pole. Disks are moved according to two rules: 1) only one disk can be moved at a time, and 2) a disk can never be put on top of a smaller disk.

There is a strategy to solving this problem. First, let's consider the case where we have only one disk. The solution in this case is exceedingly simple — we move the disk to another pole and the puzzle is solved. Let's call this algorithm Towers(1) since it solves the problem with one disk.

*New York: Beginner Books, 1958.

Let's now consider moving two disks to the right-hand pole. First, we move the smaller disk to an intermediate pole (Figure 16.2). Then we can move the larger disk to the right-hand pole (Figure 16.3). Finally, we move the smaller disk to the right-hand pole (Figure 16.4).

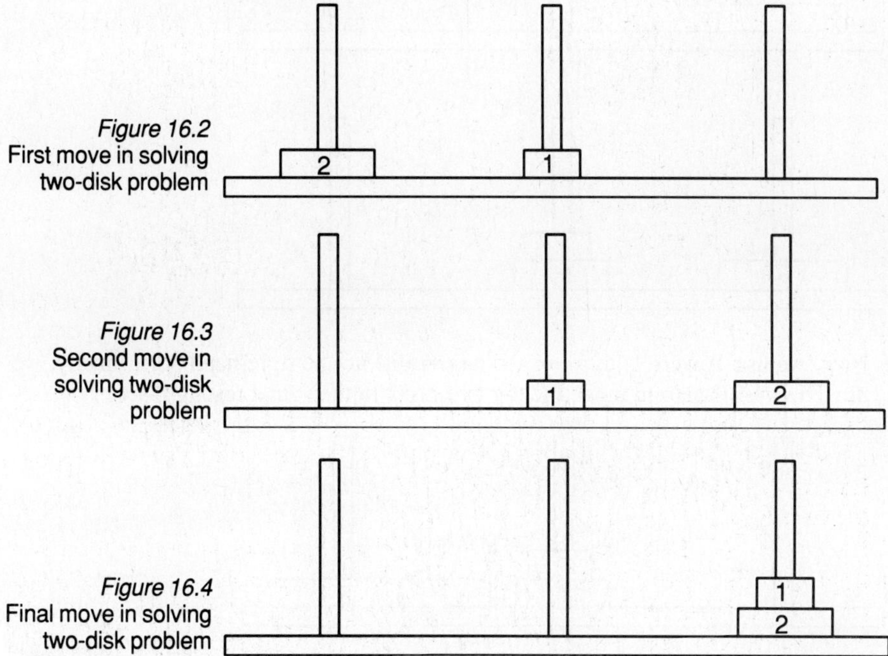

Figure 16.2 First move in solving two-disk problem

Figure 16.3 Second move in solving two-disk problem

Figure 16.4 Final move in solving two-disk problem

Towers(2), the solution with two disks, can be summarized as follows:

Move top disk to intermediate pole
Move bottom disk to final pole
Move top disk to final pole

Each of these moves can be considered to be a use of Towers(1). That is, the algorithm can be rewritten as follows:

Use Towers(1) to move top disk to intermediate pole
Use Towers(1) to move bottom disk to final pole
Use Towers(1) to move top disk to final pole

Let's move on to three disks. Here, the pattern may not be so obvious. If we cheated, we could treat the top two disks as if they were one, park them on the intermediate pole, move the bottom one into place, and then move the two parked disks together to their final resting place. But this really can be done without cheating because we know how to move two disks to any desired pole — we solved that problem as Towers(2). Thus, Towers(3) begins by using Towers(2) for the top two disks.

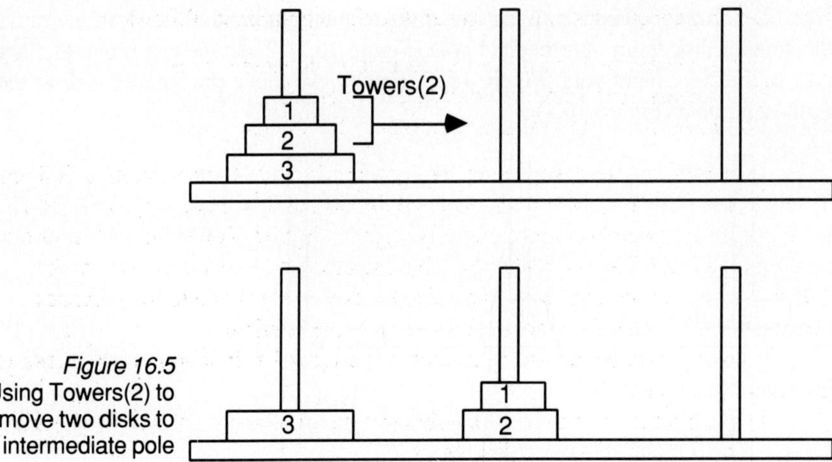

Figure 16.5 Using Towers(2) to move two disks to intermediate pole

Now, we use Towers(1) to move the largest disk to the right-hand pole. Finally, we use Towers(2) again to move the top two disks to their final resting place.

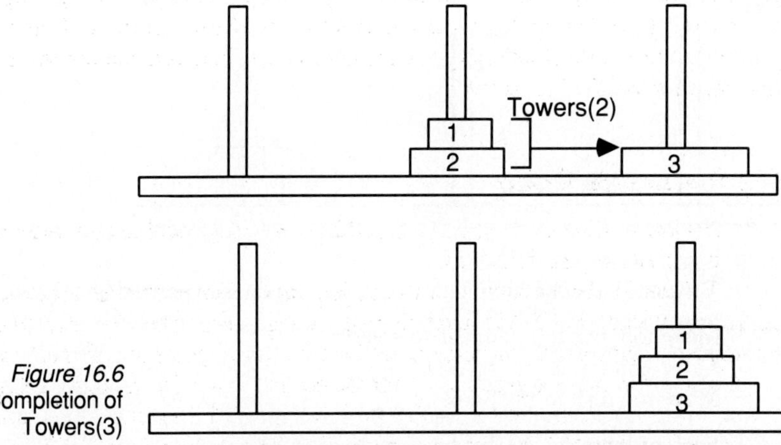

Figure 16.6 Completion of Towers(3)

Towers(3) can be summarized as follows:

Use Towers(2) to move top disks to intermediate pole
Use Towers(1) to move bottom disk to final pole
Use Towers(2) to move top disks to final pole

Now we can use our knowledge of how to move three disks to solve the Towers of Hanoi problem for four disks. We use the following algorithm:

Use Towers(3) to move top disks to intermediate pole
Use Towers(1) to move bottom disk to final pole
Use Towers(3) to move top disks to final pole

It follows that for n disks, we can generalize the algorithm as follows:

Use Towers(n – 1) to move top disks to intermediate pole
Use Towers(1) to move bottom disk to final pole
Use Towers(n – 1) to move top disks to final pole

Towers(n) is a recursive algorithm because it refers to itself in its definition. The definition of Towers(n) refers to the definition of Towers(n – 1). Towers(n – 1) is identical to Towers(n) except that it is slightly simpler. Towers(n – 1) in turn calls on a simpler case, Towers(n – 2), to solve the problem. Eventually, we reach Towers(1), which we can solve immediately. Towers(1) is where the recursion "bottoms out," because no more recursive calls are required.

Formally, two conditions must exist for a recursive function or procedure to be properly constructed:

1. Each recursive call must involve simpler arguments, so that the problem becomes successively simpler, and
2. The problem must eventually get so simple that the recursion bottoms out (sometimes called the *limit case* or the *stopping state*).

Think of recursion as a cloning of the procedure or function; each successive clone does a slightly simpler version of the previous clone's job. Using proper computer science terminology, we talk about *successive invocations* of the same procedure, each with simpler arguments, until in the limit case the lowest-level invocation must yield an answer.

16.2 Recursive Code

Now that we've discussed recursive algorithms, we can examine how recursion is used in procedures and functions.

You are probably familiar with the definition of the mathematical function called n-factorial, or n!. This function arises, for instance, when we wish to calculate how many unique seating arrangements there are for n guests at a dinner table. There are n places for the first guest, n – 1 for the second, n – 2 for the third, and so on. Thus, we have a total of $n * (n - 1) * (n - 2) * ... * 2 * 1$ unique *permutations* of n seating arrangements. The definition of $n!$ is $n * (n - 1) * (n - 2) * ... * 2 * 1$ (the ellipses stand for that well-known mathematical concept "you know what I mean").

The most elegant formulation of $n!$ is derived from saying, in effect: "I could solve $n!$ if I only knew the answer to $(n - 1)!$ because then I would just put $n! = n * (n - 1)!$" This is a circular definition, it seems, since the factorial appears on both sides of the "is defined as" symbol (the equals sign). But notice that the argument of the factorial function on the right is one less than that on the left, so that the two sides aren't strictly the same. By repeating the algorithm, we determine that $(n - 1)! = (n - 1) * (n - 2)!$, $(n - 2)! = (n - 2) * (n - 3)!$, and so on. Eventually, we come to a definition that doesn't require another invocation on the right hand side of the definition: $0! = 1$.

Once we know what 0! is, we can go back and finish off the computation of 1!, which leads to 2!, which leads to 3!, and so on, until we back up all the way to $n!$ as a function of $(n-1)!$. It is essential to note that if we didn't have an explicit definition for 0!, we would keep decrementing the argument and never terminate.

As with the Towers of Hanoi problem, what we are doing is turning a single problem into a collection of nearly equivalent problems. Each is just a little simpler than the previous one in the sequence, and eventually the problem becomes so simple that it can be solved by itself. Until the $n!$ sequence of problems finally terminates with the simplest problem, one that can be solved by inspection, all problems are in a state of suspension until at last the next to be invoked can return with an answer. At this point, the sequence of recursive invocations can be unwound bottom up until we get back to the initial problem that is too hard to solve directly. Thus 0! leads to 1!, which leads to 2!, and so on, all the way back up to $n!$.

Now let's code the factorial function. By definition, we are coding the following algorithm:

```
IF n = 0 THEN
   n! = 1
ELSE
   n! = n * (n – 1)!
```

(If you are familiar with mathematical induction, you may note the similarity between the limit case and the "basis" of an inductive proof and between the general recursive invocation and the inductive step.)

A procedure or function is recursively called the same way that you would call any other routine. Thus, if we translate the notation "$n!$ =" to "function returns value calculated by," we translate the notation "$(n-1)!$" to "call the function that calculates the factorial, and pass the parameter $n-1$." The code for the procedure looks like this:

```
{ Recursive definition of n! }

function Factorial (number: integer) : integer;

begin
   { test to see if recursion has bottomed out }

   if number = 0 then
      Factorial := 1   { Return value of limit case }
   else
      Factorial := number * Factorial(number-1)
end; { Factorial }
```

In more general terms, we can look at the factorial pseudocode as follows:

```
IF this is the limit case THEN
   Solve for this simple case
ELSE
   Make recursive call with slightly simpler case
```

The test ***number = 0*** determines whether we are looking at the limit case, since 0! is the case where we have a simple definition. The answer is returned to the caller. If we are not looking at the limit case, we need to simplify the problem. This means that we call ***Factorial*** again with a smaller argument.

Think of each recursive call as a call to a completely separate procedure. The same things happen when you call a procedure recursively as happen when you call any other procedure. Parameters are passed from the calling to the called procedure. Then the calling procedure is frozen. The called procedure takes control, and space is reserved for its local variables. The called procedure performs its function (including calling other procedures if necessary); when it reaches its **end**, flow of control is passed back to its caller.

Recursive calls give the code an elegance because a complex problem can be solved in a very few lines of code. For example, the code for the Towers of Hanoi algorithm follows.

Code 16.1
Procedure *Towers*

```
program Hanoi;

   type
      pole = (left, middle, right);  { different poles available in puzzle          }

{ This procedure prints the algorithm for solving the Towers of                 }
{ Hanoi puzzle for a given number of disks. The procedure prints,               }
{ in order, how each disk should be moved.                                      }

   procedure Towers (origin, dest, intermed : pole;     {the three poles             }
         numDisks : integer);                            { number of disks to move  }

   begin
      if numDisks > 0 then   { check for bottom-out case }
         begin
         { Move top n-1 disks to intermediate pole }
            Towers(origin, intermed, dest, numDisks - 1);

         { Move bottom disk to destination pole }
            Writeln('Move disk ', numDisks : 2, ' from ', origin, ' to ', dest);

         { Move top n-1 disks from intermediate to destination pole }
            Towers(intermed, dest, origin, numDisks - 1)
         end { if }
   end; { Towers }

{ Mainline (Driver) }
begin
   Towers(left, right, middle, 3) { Sample call to Towers }
end.
```

As it turns out, many recursive algorithms can be rewritten with iterative techniques. We'll look at recursive techniques in more detail toward the end of this chapter, but in the next few sections, we will look at an iterative solution to a particular problem: walking down a binary tree.

16.3 Binary Trees

I'm thinking of a number between 1 and 1000. I want you to guess what that number is. If you don't guess it, I will tell you whether my number is greater or less than your guess. How many guesses do you need to identify my number?

The "trick" to minimizing the number of guesses is realizing that each response of "greater" or "less than" eliminates many of the numbers. For example, if you guess 750, and I say "greater," you've eliminated three quarters of the numbers, but if I say "less than," you've eliminated only one quarter of the possibilities. What you want to do is guarantee that you will eliminate as many numbers as possible. Since my answer will divide the numbers into two parts, you want to guarantee that each response will eliminate half the numbers.

Your first guess should be the halfway point: 500. No matter how I respond, half of the numbers will be eliminated. Let's say I respond with "less than." You know now that the number is between 1 and 499. Again, you choose the halfway point and guess 250. (Similarly, if I say "greater than" to your first guess of 500, your second guess should be 750.) No matter how I respond to your second guess, you will have 250 possiblities left. The third guess should again split the possibilities in half, leaving 125 choices. Continuing in this manner, you can leave, in succession, 63, 32, 16, 8, 4, 2, and 1 possibilities. Thus, you can close in on a single number between 1 and 1000 in 10 guesses. This method of successively dividing the possibilities in half is known as a *binary search.*

The guesses can be diagrammed as shown in Figure 16.7. The response to each guess takes you down one of two paths. In the diagram, the response on the left is the next guess if you receive a "less than," and the response on the right is the next guess if you receive a "greater than." So, if your second guess is 750 and you are told "less than," your third guess should be 625.

In the diagram, each number appears only once. If you follow the diagram, there is only one set of questions that leads to any single answer. However, any number from 1 to 1000 can be found in ten (or fewer) steps.

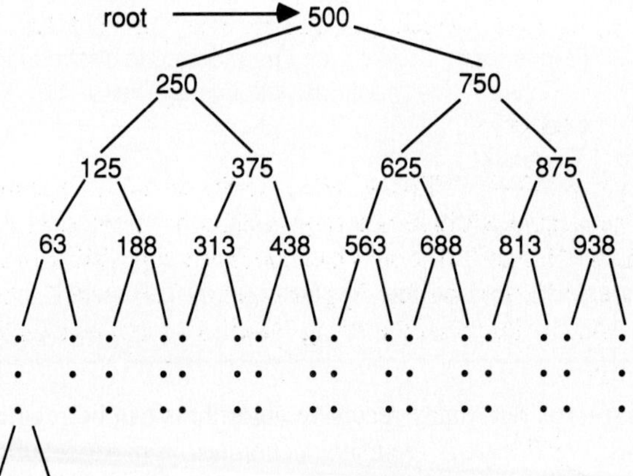

Figure 16.7
Diagram of numeric guesses

The structure shown is an abstract data type called a *binary tree*. (Yes, binary pyramid would be a better name, but we're kind of stuck at this point.) Each element in the tree is called a *node*. The top node in the tree is called the *root*, and any node that is at the bottom of a path is called a *leaf*. The relationship between consecutive nodes is often expressed in familial terms. For example, in our tree, 250 is the *parent* node of 125 and 375; 125 is the *left child* and 375 is the *right child* of 250.

Traditionally, the root node is drawn at the top of the tree. While normal people may wonder about this convention, computer scientists often do things upside-down — such as stay up all night and sleep all day.

Trees are used for storing large sets of data and are particularly useful when we want to randomly access any individual node. Imagine that instead of storing 1000 numbers, we decide to store the names and phone numbers of all the people in the Topeka phone book. Imagine what would happen if we stored them in linear (sequential) order, so that the first element in the data structure held 'Aaron' and the last element held 'Zyman'. We have seen two data structures to solve this problem: arrays and linked lists. When we have to find a particular name in the phone book, the array is clearly the better choice, since by using a subscript, we can access any name in the array instantly. With a linked list, we have to start at the beginning and may have to look at 40000 names (Aaron, Abbott, Abercrombie,...) before finding what we want. On the other hand, if we want to insert a name in the array in alphabetical order, we may have to move thousands of entries; in a linked list, items can be easily inserted by manipulating a few pointers. Computer scientists are a greedy lot; they want to have both speedy access and speedy insertion. The binary tree fills this bill, while both arrays and linked lists fall short.

16.4 Building a Binary Tree

We make one assumption when building a binary tree: no item appears more than once. Given this assumption, we can build a binary tree from the root up — or down, depending on your point of view. Say we decide to keep a list of all of the things in a closet. We'll put them in the tree as we pull them out of the closet.

First, we find a bunch of 'NAILS'. The term 'NAILS' will be the root of our tree.

Figure 16.8
Adding root of tree

```
NAILS
```

Next, we find a 'FISHBOWL'. Additions are always made at the bottom of the tree, so the second addition is always a child of the root. In this case, 'FISHBOWL' is a child of 'NAILS'. But on which side? We will follow the typical convention that places "greater" items on the right and "lesser" ones on the left. Since the string 'FISHBOWL' is less than the string 'NAILS', it belongs on the left, as shown in Figure 16.9.

Figure 16.9
Adding second node to tree

```
          NAILS
          /
   FISHBOWL
```

Going back to the closet, we find a 'KOALA' bear. Again, we have to determine where the new node belongs in the tree. We start at the root. Since 'KOALA' < 'NAILS', we move to the left. We cannot insert 'KOALA' as the left child of 'NAILS', though, because 'FISHBOWL' is already in that location. Since something is in the desired location, we compare what we want to add to what is occupying the space. In this case, we compare 'KOALA' to 'FISHBOWL'. Since 'KOALA' > 'FISHBOWL', we move to the right. Nothing is currently at the right of 'FISHBOWL', so we can insert 'KOALA' in that location, as shown in Figure 16.10.

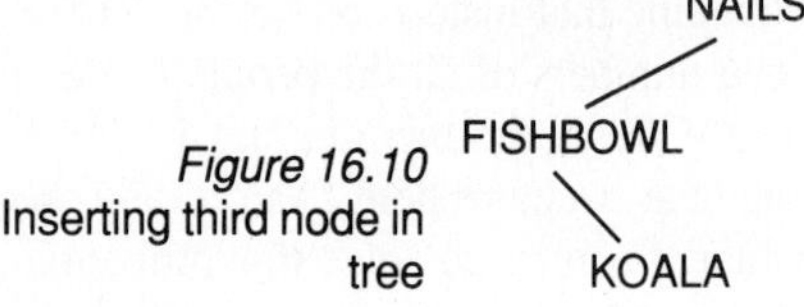

Figure 16.10 Inserting third node in tree

The next item we find is a 'SAXOPHONE'. We've now developed a general strategy. We start at the root and compare the new item to the current node. If the new item is less than the current node, we move to the left; otherwise we move to the right. We see if a node currently exists in that location. If one does, we again move to the left or right. Otherwise, we create a new node and attach it to the bottom of the tree.

Thus, to insert 'SAXOPHONE', we compare the item to 'NAILS'. Since 'SAXOPHONE' > 'NAILS', we move to the right. Nothing is on the right of 'NAILS', so we can insert 'SAXOPHONE' there, as in Figure 16.11.

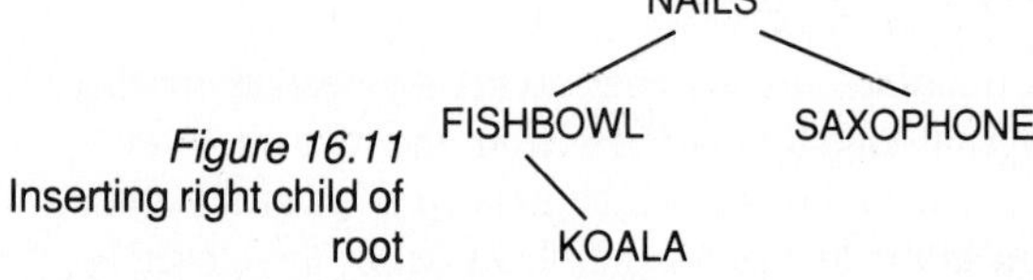

Figure 16.11 Inserting right child of root

We can formalize this algorithm in pseudocode:

```
Current node starts at root
REPEAT
   IF new item > current node THEN
      IF left child exists THEN
         Left child becomes current node
      ELSE
         BEGIN
            Insert node as left child of current node
            Set exit condition of loop to TRUE
         END
   ELSE  { new item < current node }
      IF right child exists THEN
         Right child becomes current node
```

```
    ELSE
      BEGIN
        Insert node as right child of current node
        Set exit condition of loop to TRUE
      END
UNTIL done
```

Notice that, unlike a linear structure, the order of the input determines the shape of the tree. For example, if the input was in the order 'KOALA', 'NAILS', 'SAXOPHONE', 'FISHBOWL', the tree would look like Figure 16.12.

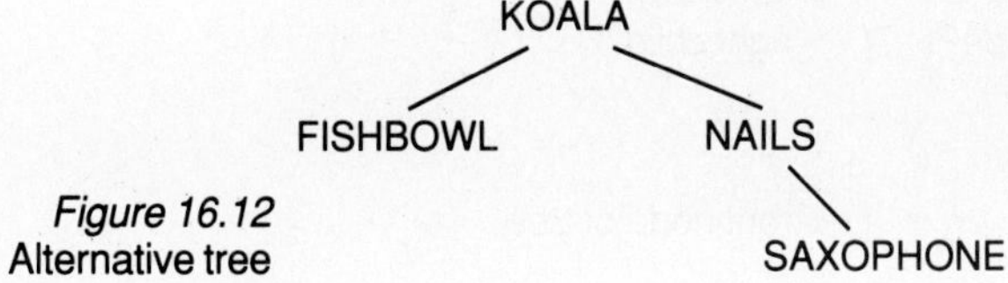

Figure 16.12
Alternative tree

If the input was in the sorted order 'SAXOPHONE', 'NAILS', 'KOALA', 'FISHBOWL', the tree would look like Figure 16.13.

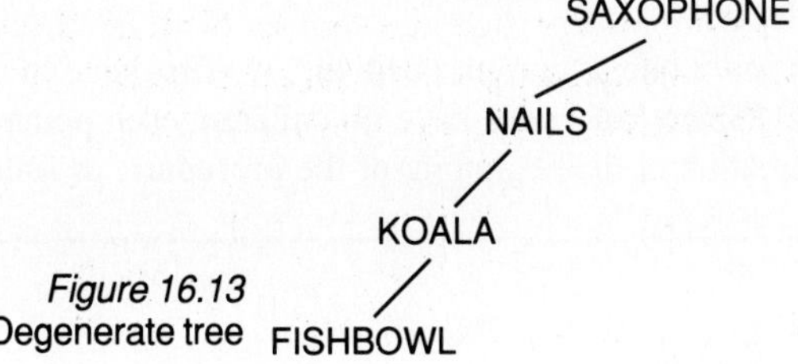

Figure 16.13
Degenerate tree

A structure like that in Figure 16.13 has the unfortunate name of *degenerate tree*. This tree is nothing more than a linked list down the left side of the tree. Because the items came from the input in sorted order, each element was put one to the left of the previous addition. In Figures 16.11 and 16.12, however, the trees have about the same number of nodes on both sides. For this reason, they are called *balanced* trees. The diagram of the 1000 numbers in Figure 16.7 is an example of a perfectly balanced tree; all the leaf nodes are either 9 or 10 moves away from the root. Most binary trees are somewhere between the perfect balance of Figure 16.7 and the degenerate tree of Figure 16.13. If the input appears, for the most part, in random order, the tree will be, for the most part, balanced.

There are algorithms for balancing trees, but they are a bit beyond the scope of this book. For the moment, just concentrate on the fact that a balanced tree is more efficient than a degenerate one, because its maximum *height* — that is, the number of nodes between the root and the furthest leaf — is as low as possible.

16.5 Implementation of a Binary Tree

Let's now consider the implementation of a binary tree. We can represent each node concretely using pointers. We need to have two paths from each node — the left and the right. We can refer to each child by using a pointer.

```
type
   str80 = string[80]      { type for each item from closet      }
   nodePtr = ^node;        { --> any node in tree                }
   node = record
         item: str80;      { item from the closet                }
         left: nodePtr;    { --> left child                      }
         right: nodePtr    { --> right child                     }
      end; { node }

var
   root: node;             { --> root node of tree               }
```

In this tree, each node contains a string to hold the name of the item from the closet.

Let's code the tree-building algorithm from the last section as a procedure. To translate the pseudocode, we code one line at a time. We start by setting the current node to the root. Next we add the **repeat**. Then we try to code "IF right child exists THEN." Since the right child is designated by a pointer, we can determine if the child exists by seeing if the pointer points to anything. The child does not exist if the pointer is **nil**.

To code the line "Insert new node at current position," we first have to create a new node, which will be a leaf. Since leaf nodes have no children, each pointer field is set to **nil**. We will do this creation at the beginning of the procedure, as follows.

Code 16.2
Procedure
AddNode

```
{ AddNode                                                  }
{ This procedure adds a node to a binary tree. The procedure }
{ begins by creating the new node. Then a series of         }
{ comparisons is performed. Each time the new node is       }
{ less than the node being inspected, the procedure moves   }
{ to the left child. Each time the new node is greater,     }
{ the procedure moves to the right child.                   }
{ The procedure assumes that no node is added more than     }
{ once. When the search reaches a leaf node, the new node   }
{ is added at that position.                                }

   procedure AddNode (newItem : str80;       { item to add       }
         root : nodePtr);                    { --> root of tree  }

      var
         current : nodePtr;     { --> node currently being inpsected  }
         newNode : nodePtr;     { --> node to add                     }
         done : boolean;        { indicates end of loop               }
```

Code 16.2
(continued)

```
begin
{ create new node }
   New(newNode);
   newNode^.item := newItem;
{ new node has no children }
   newNode^.left := nil;
   newNode^.right := nil;

   done := FALSE;
   current := root;

   repeat
      if newItem < current^.item then
         begin
            if current^.left <> nil then
               current := current^.left
            else
               begin  { found the place to add }
                  current^.left := newNode;
                  done := TRUE
               end { else }
         end { if }
      else
         begin
            if current^.right <> nil then
               current := current^.right
            else
               begin { found the place to add }
                  current^.right := newNode;
                  done := TRUE
               end { else }
         end { else }
   until done
end; { AddNode }
```

This code will work in every case except one. The code assumes that the root node already exists, and it will therefore bomb when we try to enter the first item in the tree. Specifically, the comparison ***newItem > current^.item*** will fail because ***current*** is **nil**. What we need is a dummy node at the root.

We can initialize the tree by creating a dummy node. But what to put in the dummy node's ***item*** field? Since we are creating a dummy node, that is, a node that is not actually a part of the tree, we want the ***item*** field to be less than all of the "real" nodes in the tree. Thus, we use the null string, since all other strings are greater than null (we also used a null string to create a dummy node in a linked list because it is less than all other strings).

Code 16.3
procedure
InitTree

```
{ InitTree                                                    }
{  This procedure creates the dummy root of the tree.         }
{ Although the procedure creates a new node for the           }
{ pointer variable root, the real root will not be added      }
{ until AddNode is called.                                    }

   procedure InitTree (var root : nodePtr);        { --> root of tree }

   begin
   { create new node }
      New(root);
      root^.item := '';
      root^.left := nil;
      root^.right := nil
   end; { Init }
```

We could use the following mainline to ask the user to enter the elements of the tree.

Code 16.4
Mainline

```
{ Mainline variables }
   const
      sentinel = 'nothing';              { indicates end of data      }

   var
      root : nodePtr;                    { --> top of tree            }
      thing : str80;                     { item from closet           }

{ Mainline                                                            }
{ This mainline accepts input from the user. After the tree           }
{ is initialized, the user is asked to enter an item from the         }
{ closet. The new item is added to the tree. Entries are              }
{ accepted from the user and added to the tree until the user         }
{ enters the sentinel value.                                          }
{ Calls: AddNode, InitTree                                            }

begin
   InitTree(root);
   Write('What did you find in the closet (Enter ', sentinel);
   Write(' to exit) ? ');
   Readln(thing);
   while thing <> sentinel do
      begin
         AddNode(thing, root);
         Write('What did you find in the closet (Enter ', sentinel);
         Write(' to exit) ? ');
         Readln(thing)
      end { while }

end. { Mainline }
```

Let's hand simulate the code, using the same data as in the last section. After ***InitTree*** is called, our tree structure looks like Figure 16.14.

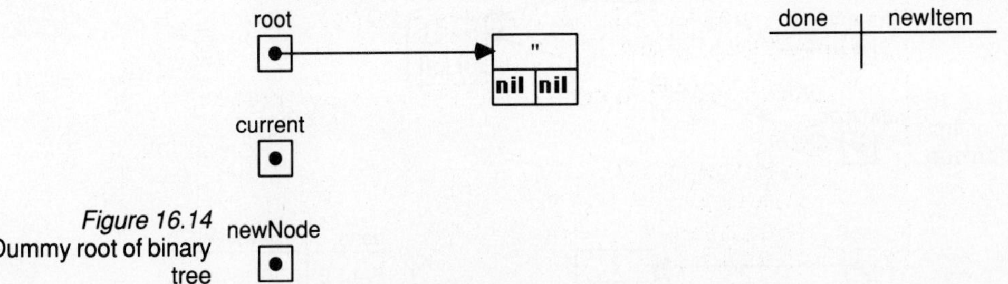

Figure 16.14
Dummy root of binary tree

Now, let's see what happens when we enter 'NAILS' as the first element in the tree. We call the ***AddNode*** procedure with the parameters ***root*** and ***'NAILS'***. At the beginning of the procedure, ***current*** is set to ***root***. The new node is created but is not connected to anything (Figure 16.15).

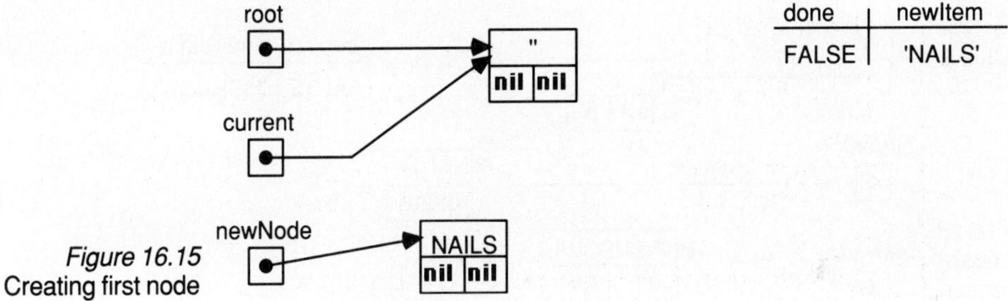

Figure 16.15
Creating first node

We enter the **repeat** loop and immediately compare ***newItem*** ('NAILS') to ***current^.item***. ***current*** is pointing to the dummy node, so ***current^.item*** is the null string. This means that the condition ***newItem > current^.item*** is TRUE, so we perform the associated statements.

The next statement asks us to compare ***current^.right*** to **nil**. ***current*** is pointing to a node with no children, so ***current^.right*** is **nil**. We move to the **else** block and set ***current^.right*** to ***newNode***. In the same block, ***done*** is set to TRUE, so the loop and the procedure are exited (See Figure 16.16).

All remaining entries will be children of 'NAILS'. For example, let's say the second entry is 'FISHBOWL'. When we call ***AddNode*** with the parameters ***root*** and ***'FISHBOWL'***, the new node is created and ***current*** is set to ***root*** (Figure 16.17).

We enter the **repeat** loop and compare ***newItem*** ('FISHBOWL') to ***current^.item*** (the null string). Since ***newItem*** is greater, we perform the statements in the **if** clause. Next, we look at ***current^.right***. Since this pointer is not **nil**, ***current*** moves down one level in the tree (Figure 16.18).

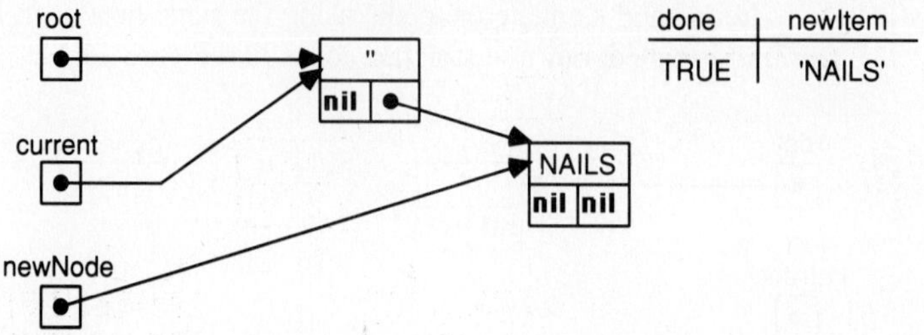

Figure 16.16
Completion of first
AddNode

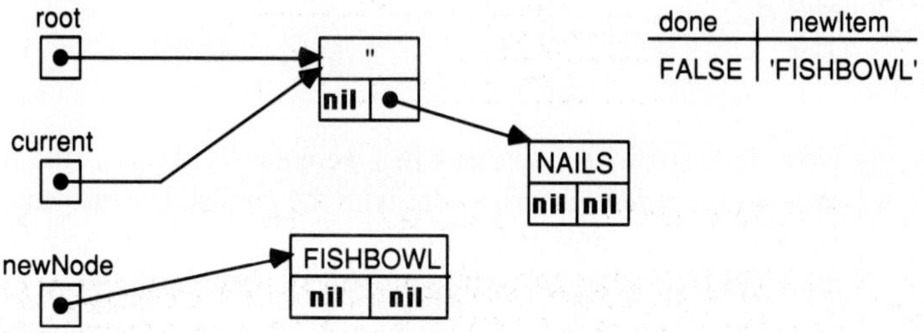

Figure 16.17
Creation of node for
'FISHBOWL'

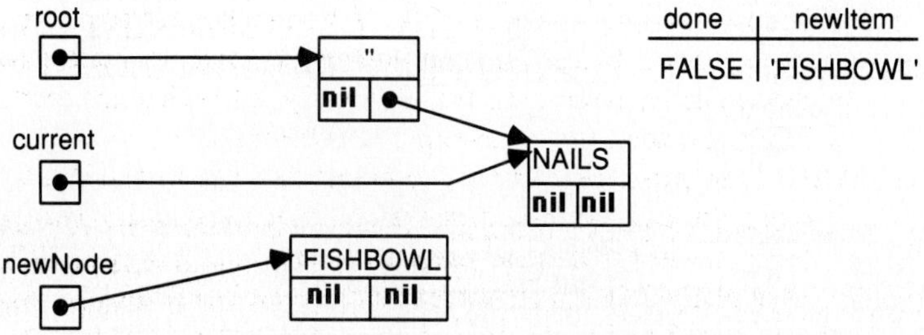

Figure 16.18
Moving ***current***
after first comparison

We return to the top of the loop and compare ***newItem*** ('FISHBOWL') to ***current^.item*** ('NAILS'). ***newItem > current^.item*** is FALSE, so the **else** clause is executed. We look at ***current^.left***, that is, the left child of 'NAILS'. Since this pointer is **nil**, the 'FISHBOWL' node is attached to the left side of the 'NAILS' node (Figure 16.19). We repeat the procedure, adding (in order), 'KOALA', 'SAXOPHONE', and 'BOWLER'. The resulting tree looks like Figure 16.20. The code follows the pseudocode in Section 16.4, except that a dummy node exists above the root.

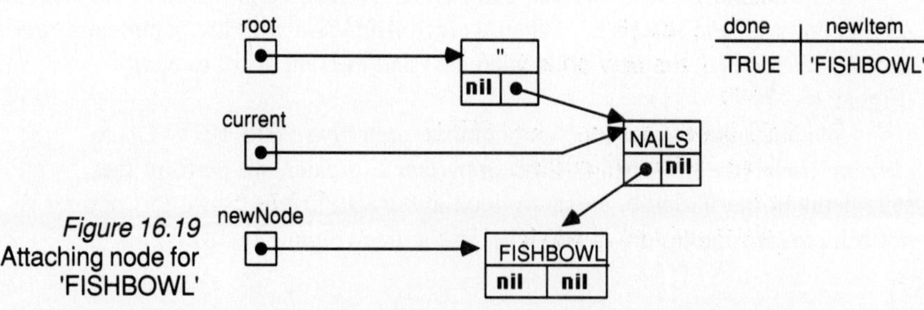

Figure 16.19
Attaching node for
'FISHBOWL'

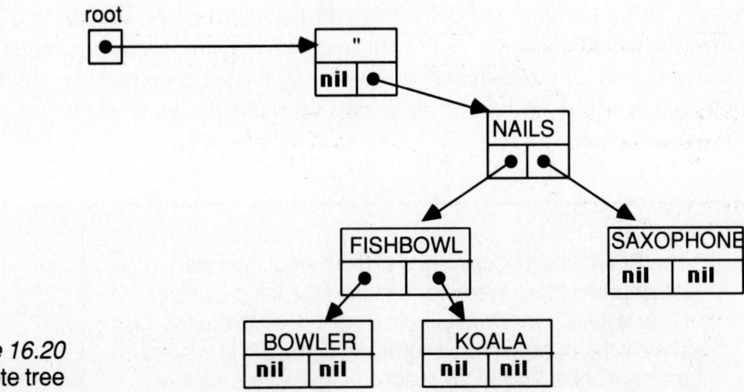

Figure 16.20
Complete tree

16.6 Searching in a Binary Tree

Once we have placed the items in the tree, we need a method of retrieving any single item. When we begin looking for anything in the tree, we have only one piece of information available: the root. If the root happens to contain the item we want (that is, the *key*), we can stop looking. If the root doesn't contain anything, that is, the tree is empty, we can also stop looking. If we have to continue looking, we compare the key to the item at the root. If the key is less than the root's item, we move to the left; if the key is greater, we move to the right.

Suppose we've moved to one of the child nodes. If the node exists, we can look at the item it contains and compare it to the key. If the items are equal, we've found the key, so we can stop searching. Otherwise, we move to the left or right. If we have reached the bottom of the tree, we can't continue searching, so the key must not be in the tree. In pseudocode form, the search algorithm looks like this:

```
Set current node to root
WHILE not done DO
  IF current node is bottom of tree THEN
    BEGIN
      Stop search
      Key is not in tree
    END
  ELSE IF current item = key THEN
    BEGIN
      Stop search
      Key has been found
    END
  ELSE if current item < key THEN
    Make left child current
  ELSE
    Make right child current
```

This algorithm works because, throughout the tree, the left child's item is less than the parent's and the right child's item is greater than the parent's. At each node, we can go in only one direction, even though each node has two children. Of course, the search will work only if the nodes were added correctly. The Pascal code to search the tree follows.

Code 16.5
Procedure *Search*

```
{ Search                                                    }
{ The Search procedure starts at the root of the tree.      }
{ It compares the current node to the key. If the current   }
{ node is less than the key, current is moved to the left   }
{ child; if the current node is greater, current is moved to }
{ the right child. This movement continues until the key is }
{ found or the bottom of the tree is found. The function    }
{ returns a boolean value indicating whether the key has    }
{ been found.                                               }

  function Search (key : str80;           { item to find               }
        root : nodePtr) :                 { --> top of tree            }
    boolean;                              { indicates if key was found }

    var
      found,                              { temporary return value     }
      done : boolean;                     { indicates end of search    }
      current : nodePtr;                  { --> current node in tree   }

  begin
    current := root;
    done := FALSE;

    while not done do
      begin
        if current = nil then
          begin
            found := FALSE;  { key not in tree }
            done := TRUE
          end
        else if (current^.item) = key then
          begin
            found := TRUE;   { key has been found }
            done := TRUE
          end

      { move further down tree }
        else if current^.item > key then
          current := current^.left
        else
          current := current^.right
      end; { while }
    Search := found
  end; { Search }
```

To digress for a moment: the principle behind a binary tree search can also be applied to finding any key in a *sorted* array. We use a divide-and-conquer method to partition the list. We begin the search by examining the midpoint of the array. If the key is less than the midpoint, we look to the left; otherwise, we look to the right. We subdivide the array until we either find the key or have a subdivision with no elements. That is, an unsuccessful search is marked by a subdivision where the left boundary is to the right of the right boundary. In pseudocode form:

```
IF left and right boundaries have crossed THEN
   Search is unsuccessful
ELSE
   BEGIN
      Find midpoint
      IF search key = midpoint value THEN
         Search is successful
      ELSE IF search key < midpoint value THEN
         Recursively call routine on left side of midpoint
      ELSE
         Recursively call routine on right side of midpoint
   END { ELSE }
```

In the code, we designate a successful search by passing back the position in the array where the key resides. An unsuccessful search is denoted by passing back a sentinel value. Assuming that we have the following definitions at the top of the program:

```
const
   notFound = -1;        { designates unsuccessful search        }
   maxNums = 32;         { maximum number of keys                }

type
   listType = array[1..maxNums] of char;  { holds entire list    }
```

we can code the binary search as follows:

```
function Binary(var list: listType;   { list of keys - var used to save space  }
      key: char;                       { value to find                          }
      left, right: integer):           { boundaries of current sublist          }
      integer;                         { returns position of key in list        }
var
   keyPos,                             { position of key in list                }
   midPt: integer;                     { halfway pt in list                     }

begin
   if left > right then                { boundaries have crossed                }
      keyPos := notFound
   else
      begin
         midPt := (left + right) div 2;
```

```
            if key = list[midPt] then { key has been found }
              keyPos := midPt
            else if key < list[midPt] then { look at left side }
              keyPos := Binary(list, key, left, midPt-1)
            else                    { look at right side }
              keyPos := Binary(list, key, midPt+1, right)
        end; { else }
      Binary := keyPos              { return position of key }
   end; { Binary }
```

16.7 Advantages of Tree Searching

How long does a binary tree search take? Well, we do not have to look at all the items in the tree. In fact, the number of items we have to look at depends on the height of the tree. The tree's height is the number of nodes from the root to a leaf, as shown in Figure 16.21. The number of items also depends on how well the tree is balanced. For the moment, assume that we are dealing with trees that are close to being perfectly balanced.

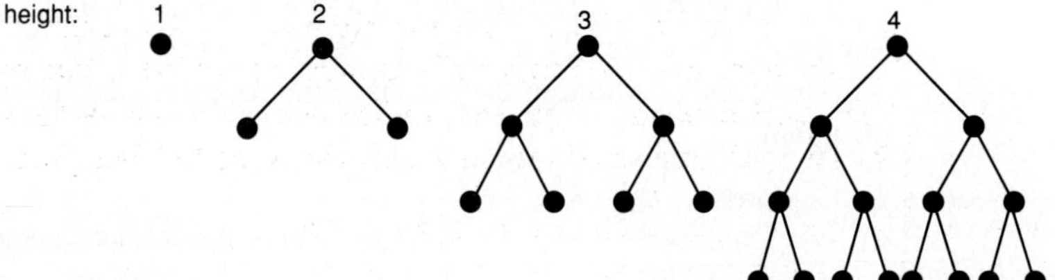

Figure 16.21 Height of balanced trees

The height depends on the number of nodes of the balanced tree. A tree with a height of 1 holds only one node: the root. A tree with a height of 2 can contain, at most, three nodes: the root and its children. A balanced tree with a height of 3 adds the children of the second-level nodes. Since there are two children at the second level and each of them can have two children, four more nodes can be added at level 3. Thus, a tree with a height of 3 can contain, at most, seven nodes. In the same manner, the four nodes at level 3 can be parents to eight children at level 4. A tree with a height of 4 can contain, at most, fifteen nodes.

You may see a pattern developing:

Height	*Number of nodes*
1	1 (1)
2	3 (1 + 2)
3	7 (1 + 2 + 4)
4	15 (1 + 2 + 4 + 8)

At each height, we add twice as many children as we did at the previous height. Since we added 8 nodes at level 4, we will add 16 nodes at level 5, for a total of 31.

This pattern of number of nodes per height can also be described using the mathematical formula $2^n - 1$, where n is the height of the tree. For example, to determine how many nodes are in a balanced tree of height 6, we calculate $2^6 - 1$. The result is 64 – 1, or 63.

We can use $2^n - 1$ to determine the number of nodes in a balanced tree, given the height. But what about the inverse: given the number of nodes, how do we determine the height? We use the inverse of the exponentiation function. The notation $\log_2 x$ means " find the number of times we have to multiply 2 by itself to get x." Thus, $\log_2 32$ is 5.

Of course, because not all numbers are powers of 2, $\log_2 x$ does not return an integer for all values of x (for example, $\log_2 18$ is a little more than 4). What the log does tell us, though, is the approximate number of searches required to find any item. If we have 18 nodes in a balanced tree, we will need to look at (on the average) about four nodes.

Now, let's compare that to the average search time for a linear list in sequential order. Say we have seven items in a linked list in alphabetical order. To find any item, we have to start at the beginning and look at each element until we find the desired key. To find the first item, we have to look at just one item in the list. On the other hand, to find the last item we would have to examine all seven. Let's compute the average number of comparisons needed to find any item. We add all of the possible searches (one item for the first node, two for the second, etc.) and divide by the total number of searches. This yields the following equation:

$$\frac{1 + 2 + 3 + 4 + 5 + 6 + 7}{7} = \frac{28}{7} = 4$$

Thus, in a list of 7 items, we have to look at an average of 4 items during any search. In general, for a list of n items, the average is calculated as follows:

$$\frac{1 + 2 + ... + (n\text{-}2) + (n\text{-}1) + n}{n} = \frac{n + 1}{2}$$

We approximate $(n + 1)/2$ to $n/2$.

Thus, for a linear list, an average search requires looking at about $n/2$ items, while for a binary tree, a search requires looking at an average of approximately $\log_2 n$. For small sets of data, the difference is minimal. For example, if we have eight items, a linear list search requires looking at 8/2, or 4 items, while a binary tree search requires looking at $\log_2 8$, or 3 items. When data sets are large, though, the difference is substantial. For example, if we have 128 items, a linear search requires looking at about 128/2, or 64 items, while a binary search requires looking at $\log_2 128$, or 7 items. Because of this difference, a binary search is more *efficient* than a linear search. The binary algorithm is faster for the average case, although in the worst case (where the binary tree is degenerate), the binary tree algorithm and the linear algorithm are equal.

Now, the binary search algorithm for arrays at the end of the last section is about equivalent to the binary tree search algorithm. However, we have to sort the array before we can use it. The binary tree is an improvement over the array because we do not have to move any data within the tree. We also do not have to move any data in a linked list, but, as we have just seen, a search in a linear structure is much slower than a search in a binary structure.

All of this serves as a very brief introduction to the field of *analysis of algorithms*. In this branch of computer science, algorithms are compared mathematically and analysts determine which algorithms are most appropriate for which situations.

16.8 Printing Trees

We have seen how to add a node and find a node in a tree. Each operation has dealt with a random access of a single item. Now we consider how to access each node sequentially.

Although they may not appear that way at first glance, the tree's nodes are in alphabetical order. Every move to the left is a move toward the beginning of the order. Thus, if we start at the root and go as far to the left as we can, we will find the item that is first alphabetically. Similarly, the node all the way at the right is the item at the bottom of the list.

But what of the nodes in between? Let's consider the simple tree with three nodes shown in Figure 16.22.

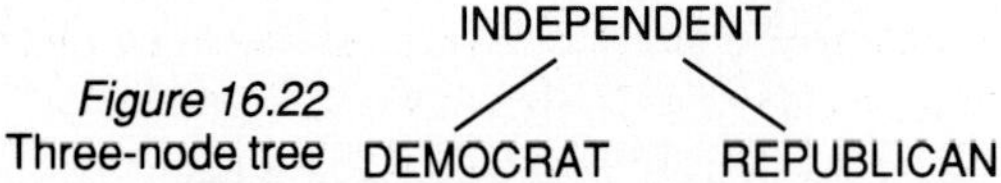

Figure 16.22
Three-node tree

To print this tree in alphabetical order, we first print the root's left child, followed by the root, followed by the root's right child.

Let's move to the slightly more complex tree shown in Figure 16.23.

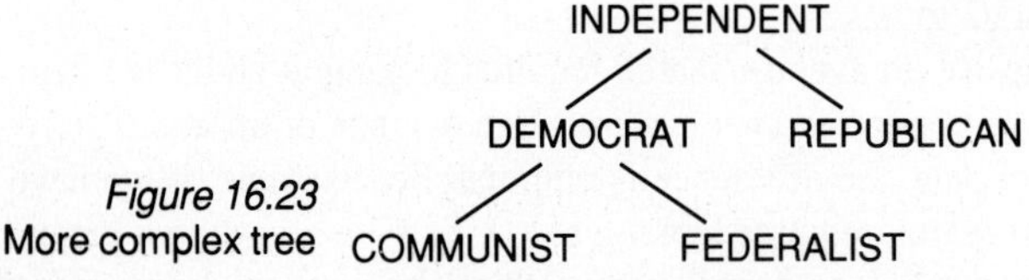

Figure 16.23
More complex tree

Again, we want to print what's to the left of the root, followed by the root itself, followed by what's to the right of the root. But what is to the left of the root? The answer: another three-node tree. We saw in Figure 16.22 how to print a parent and its children. We use that algorithm to print this subtree. First, we print

'COMMUNIST' (the left child) followed by 'DEMOCRAT' (the node itself) followed by 'FEDERALIST'. Since we've now printed everything to the left of the root, we can continue and print 'INDEPENDENT' (the contents of the root itself) and 'REPUBLICAN' (the contents of the root's right child). To summarize, we use the following algorithm to print the tree:

Print what's to the left of the root's left child
Print the contents of the root's left child
Print what's to the right of the root's left child

To break down the first line, we use the following algorithm:

Print what's to the left of the root
Print the contents of the root
Print what's to the right of the root

Look familiar? Yes, it's the same algorithm used to print the tree starting at the root. It is used here to print the subtree starting at the root's left child. What we have is a recursive definition. (There are iterative solutions to this problem, but they are much more complex than this recursive solution.)

To use recursion properly, we have to answer two questions. First, does each recursive call work on a simpler problem? In this case, we begin with the problem of printing the entire tree. The first recursive calls print a subtree starting with either the left or right child on level 2. Further recursive calls print smaller and smaller subtrees. Since each recursive call begins on a node farther down the tree, we are indeed making simpler problems.

Second, where does the recursion bottom out? Since we are dealing with smaller and smaller subtrees, it makes sense to stop making recursive calls when we reach a leaf node. In the type definition of ***node*** used here, a leaf node has children that point to **nil**. Thus, the printing procedure looks like this:

Code 16.6
procedure *Print*

```
{ Print                                                  }
{   The Print procedure begins by printing everything to        }
{ the left of the current node; then the contents of the    }
{ current node; and finally, everything to the right of     }
{ the current node.                                      }

  procedure Print (current : nodePtr);    { --> node to print       }

  begin

    if current <> nil then             { check for bottom-out case            }
      begin
        Print(current^.left);          { print stuff on left           }
        Writeln(current^.item);        { print current node            }
        Print(current^.right)          { print stuff on right          }
      end { if }

  end; { Print }
```

This may be clearer if we hand simulate the printing of a simple tree:

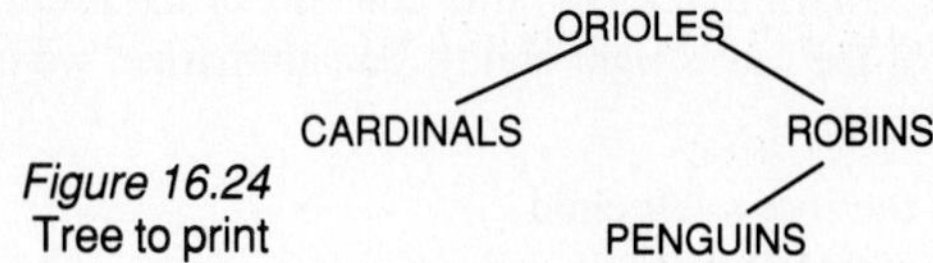
ORIOLES
CARDINALS
ROBINS
PENGUINS

Figure 16.24
Tree to print

The diagrams that follow show the recursive calls by overlapping copies of the procedure ***Print***. Each procedure will have a number; the procedure that has the highest number is the procedure that is active. Also, with each recursive call, another ***current*** pointer comes into existence. The numbers of the ***current*** pointers correspond to the call of the procedure.

Initially, we call the ***Print*** procedure with the statement

```
Print(root^.right);
```

because we do not want to print the dummy root node (not shown in the diagrams). Figure 16.25 shows the situation when ***Print*** is first called.

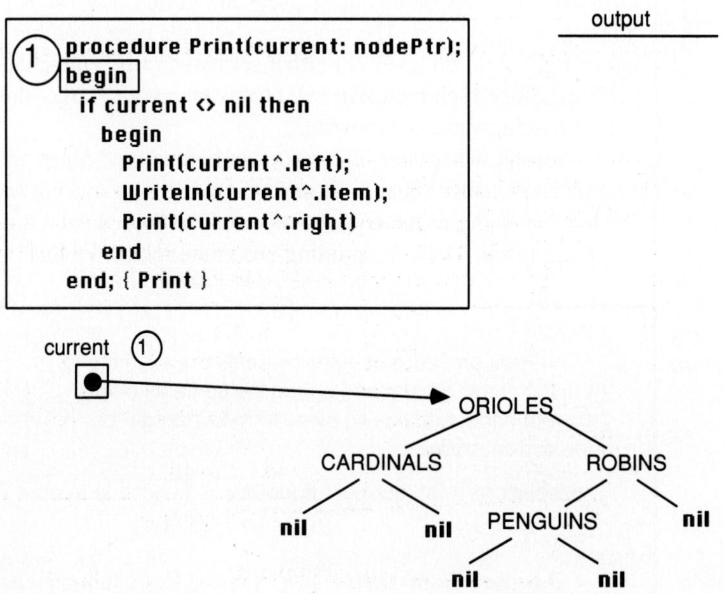
1
procedure Print(current: nodePtr);
begin
if current <> nil then
begin
Print(current^.left);
Writeln(current^.item);
Print(current^.right)
end
end; { Print }
output
current 1
ORIOLES
CARDINALS
ROBINS
nil
nil
PENGUINS
nil
nil
nil

Figure 16.25
Beginning of *Print* 1

(In these diagrams, a box highlights the line in each procedure that is currently being executed.)

We begin the procedure by comparing ***current*** to **nil**. Since ***current*** is not **nil**, ***Print*** is called again. ***current***'s left child becomes current in the second call.

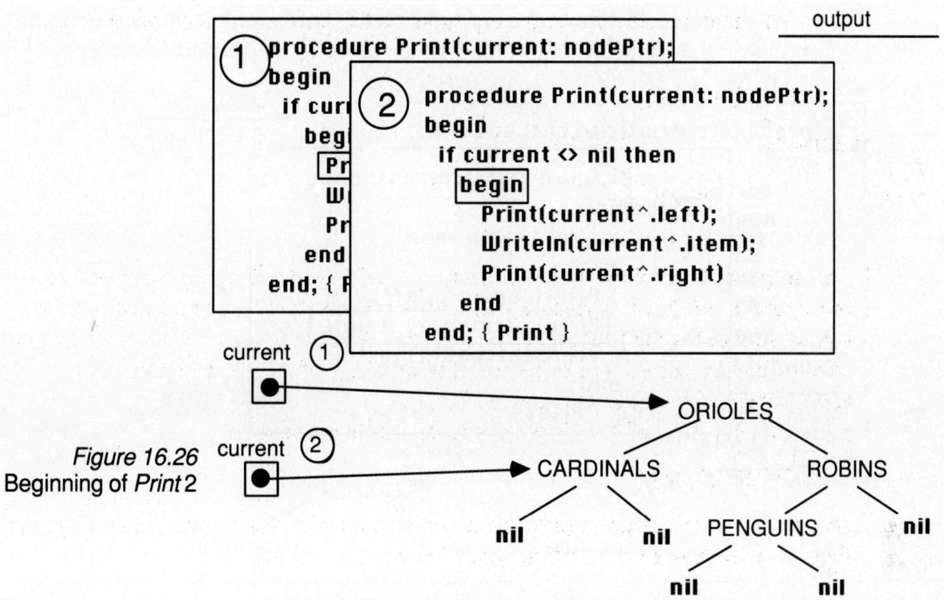
output
1
procedure Print(current: nodePtr);
begin
2
procedure Print(current: nodePtr);
begin
if current <> nil then
begin
Print(current^.left);
Writeln(current^.item);
Print(current^.right)
end
end; { Print }
current 1
current 2
ORIOLES
CARDINALS
ROBINS
nil
nil
PENGUINS
nil
nil
nil

Figure 16.26
Beginning of *Print* 2

Now, we begin ***Print*** 2. Again, we see that ***current*** is not **nil**. Thus, we call ***Print*** a third time.

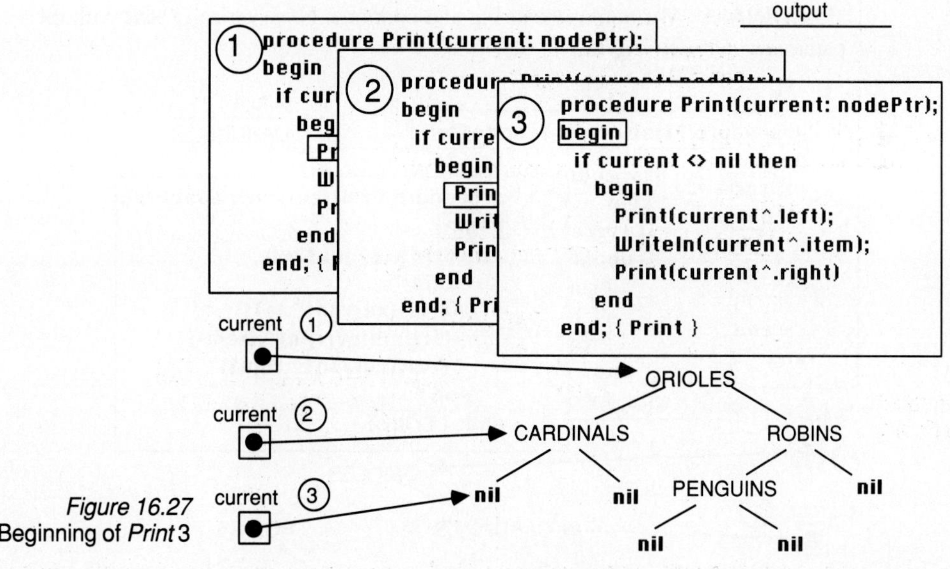
output
1
procedure Print(current: nodePtr);
begin
2
begin
3
procedure Print(current: nodePtr);
begin
if current <> nil then
begin
Print(current^.left);
Writeln(current^.item);
Print(current^.right)
end
end; { Print }
current 1
current 2
current 3
ORIOLES
CARDINALS
ROBINS
nil
nil
PENGUINS
nil
nil
nil

Figure 16.27
Beginning of *Print* 3

We see this time that ***current*** is equal to **nil**. We thus exit the procedure and return to the caller, which was ***Print*** 2.

As Figure 16.28 shows, we pick up ***Print*** 2 where we left off. Since we are finished with the recursive call to the left, we move to the ***Writeln*** statement.

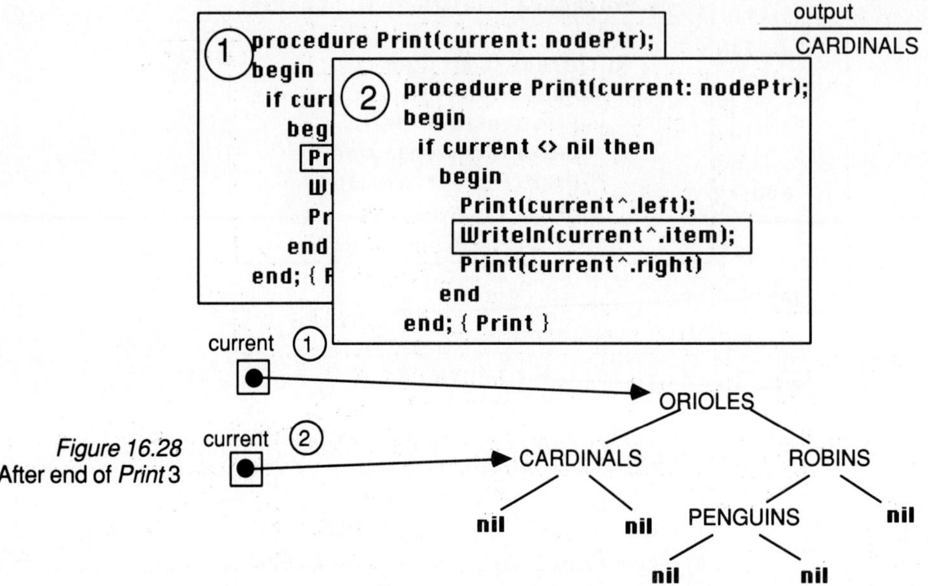

Figure 16.28
After end of *Print* 3

current 2 is the active version of that variable, so ***current^.item*** is 'CARDINALS'. We output the string and continue. Now we call ***Print*** with the parameter ***current^.right***.

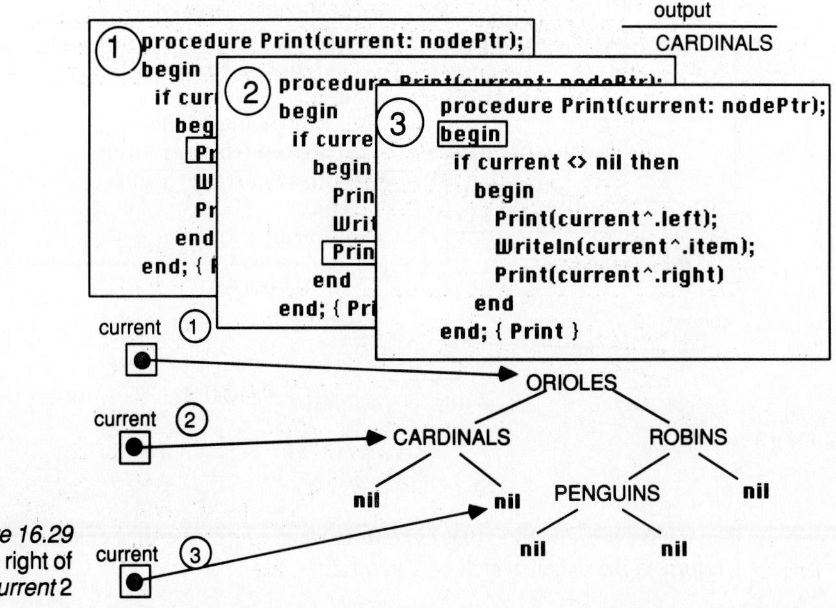

Figure 16.29
Printing to right of *current* 2

This invocation ends immediately after the first comparison, because the new value of ***current*** is **nil**. We then go back to ***Print*** 2.

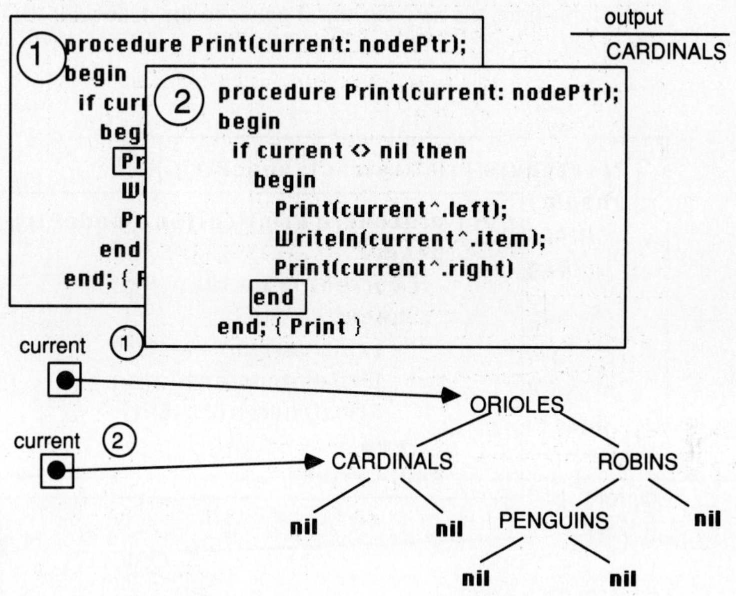
output
CARDINALS
1
procedure Print(current: nodePtr);
begin
if curr
beg
Pr
Wr
Pr
end
end; { P
2
procedure Print(current: nodePtr);
begin
if current <> nil then
begin
Print(current^.left);
Writeln(current^.item);
Print(current^.right)
end
end; { Print }
current 1
current 2
ORIOLES
CARDINALS
ROBINS
nil
nil
PENGUINS
nil
nil
nil

Figure 16.30
Returning at end of *Print* 3

We have reached the final **end** of ***Print*** 2, so flow of control moves back to ***Print*** 1.

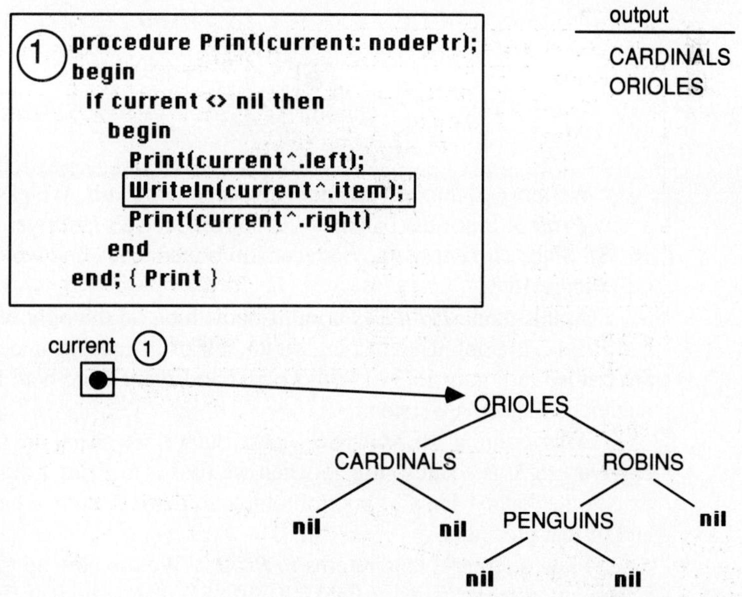
output
CARDINALS
ORIOLES
1
procedure Print(current: nodePtr);
begin
if current <> nil then
begin
Print(current^.left);
Writeln(current^.item);
Print(current^.right)
end
end; { Print }
current 1
ORIOLES
CARDINALS
ROBINS
nil
nil
PENGUINS
nil
nil
nil

Figure 16.31
After end of *Print* 2

We've now printed everything to the left of ***current*** 1. We continue by printing the contents of ***current*** 1's node (Figure 16.32). Then to print everything on the right of ***current*** 1, we pass ***current^.right*** to ***Print*** again. When ***Print*** is called this time, the new ***current*** 2 points to the node with 'ROBINS'.

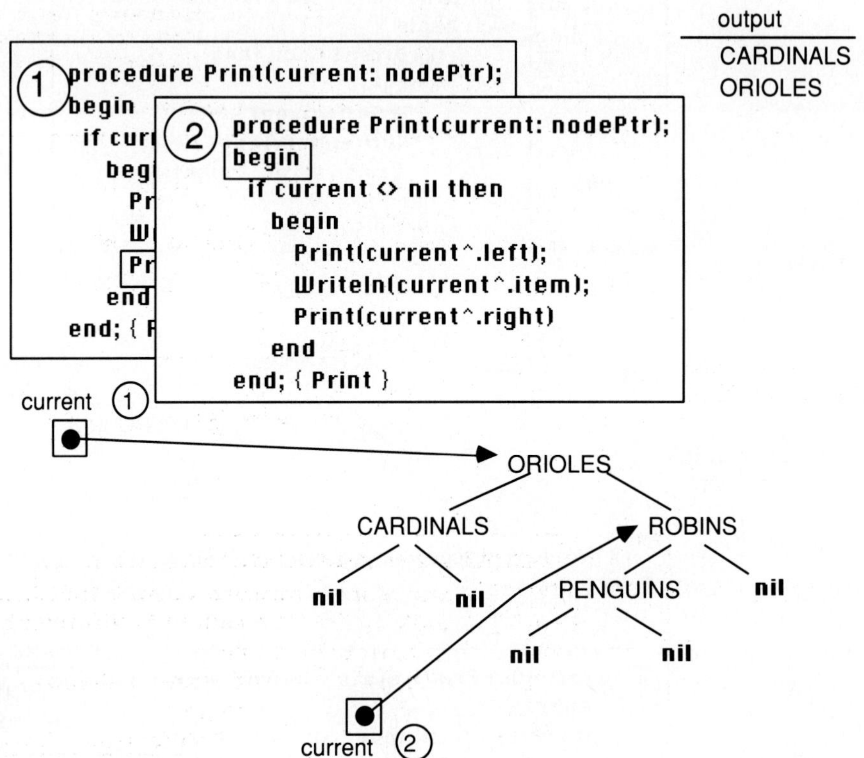
output
CARDINALS
ORIOLES
1
procedure Print(current: nodePtr);
begin
if cur
beg
Pr
W
Pr
end
end; { P
2
procedure Print(current: nodePtr);
begin
if current <> nil then
begin
Print(current^.left);
Writeln(current^.item);
Print(current^.right)
end
end; { Print }
current 1
ORIOLES
CARDINALS
ROBINS
nil
nil
PENGUINS
nil
nil
nil
current 2

Figure 16.32 Beginning of recursive call to print right subtree

We proceed through this new invocation of ***Print***. We pass ***current^.left*** to a new ***Print*** 3. Since the parameter is not **nil**, we call ***Print*** yet again (Figure 16.33). Since ***current*** is **nil**, the recursion bottoms out, and we return to ***Print*** 3 (see Figure 16.34).

At this point, ***Print*** 1 is printing something on the right of its ***current*** node and ***Print*** 2 is printing something on the left of its ***current*** node. (Note which lines are framed in Figure 16.34.) Still, ***Print*** 1 and ***Print*** 2 are both frozen. All that matters is the active version.

After printing 'PENGUINS' in the output, we check the right side. ***current^.right*** is equal to **nil**, so when we pass it to ***Print*** 4 the new procedure exits immediately. Flow of control returns to ***Print*** 3, but we have also reached the end of that procedure.

Flow of control then returns to ***Print*** 2. We are now up to the ***Writeln*** statement: ***current*** 2's ***items*** field ('ROBINS') is now printed (Figure 16.35).

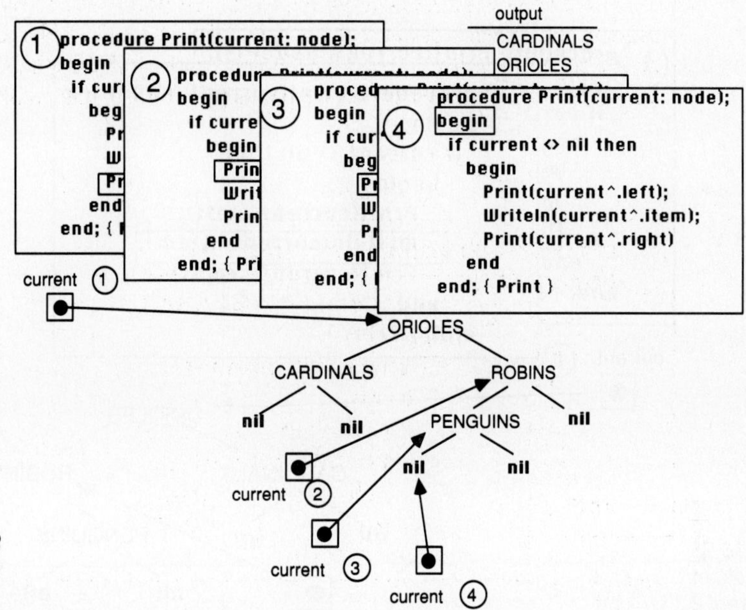
output
CARDINALS
ORIOLES
procedure Print(current: node);
begin
if current <> nil then
begin
Print(current^.left);
Writeln(current^.item);
Print(current^.right)
end
end; { Print }
current
ORIOLES
CARDINALS
ROBINS
nil
nil
PENGUINS
nil
nil
nil
current
current
current

Figure 16.33
Beginning of *Print* 4

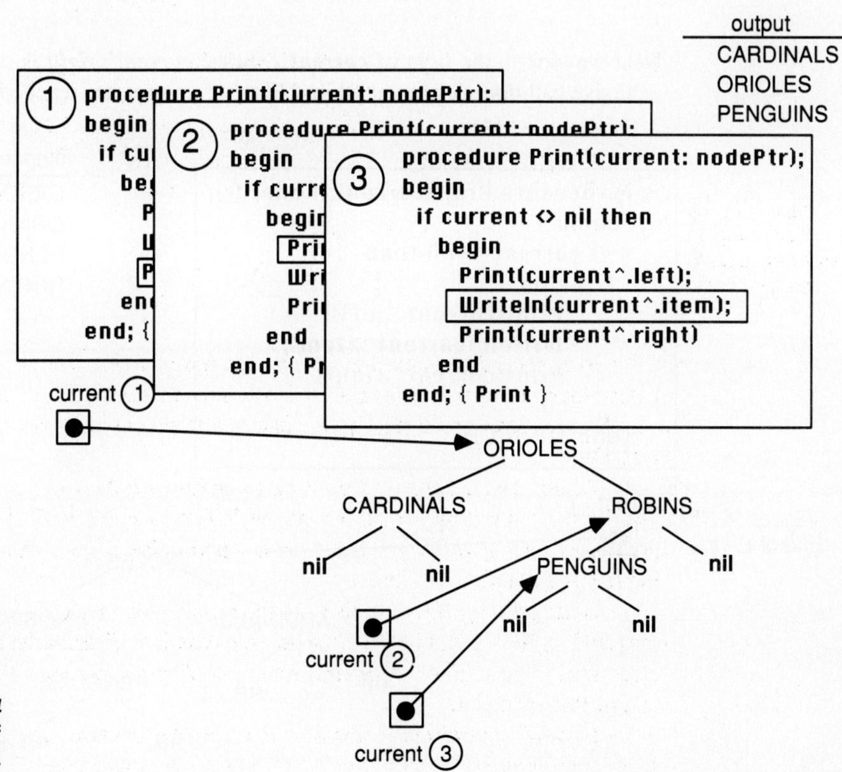
output
CARDINALS
ORIOLES
PENGUINS
procedure Print(current: nodePtr);
begin
if current <> nil then
begin
Print(current^.left);
Writeln(current^.item);
Print(current^.right)
end
end; { Print }
current
ORIOLES
CARDINALS
ROBINS
nil
nil
PENGUINS
nil
nil
nil
current
current

Figure 16.34
After completion of *Print* 4

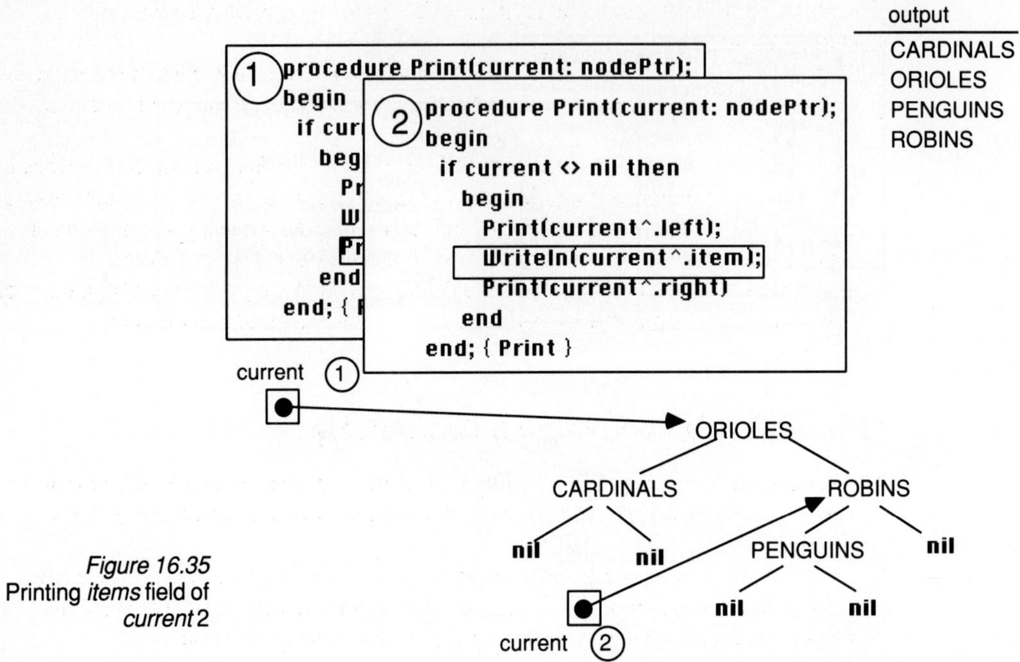
output
CARDINALS
ORIOLES
PENGUINS
ROBINS
procedure Print(current: nodePtr);
begin
if current <> nil then
begin
Print(current^.left);
Writeln(current^.item);
Print(current^.right)
end
end; { Print }
current
ORIOLES
CARDINALS
ROBINS
nil
nil
PENGUINS
nil
nil
nil
current

Figure 16.35
Printing *items* field of *current* 2

Next we look to the right of ***current*** 2. Since ***current^.right*** is equal to **nil**, the recursive call doesn't print anything. Flow of control has reached the **end** of ***Print*** 2.

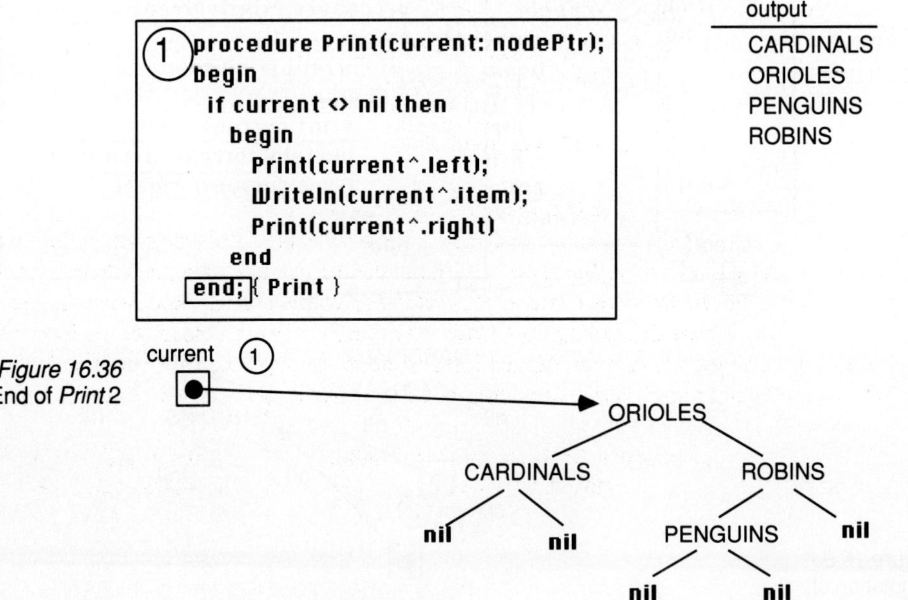
output
CARDINALS
ORIOLES
PENGUINS
ROBINS
procedure Print(current: nodePtr);
begin
if current <> nil then
begin
Print(current^.left);
Writeln(current^.item);
Print(current^.right)
end
end; { Print }
current
ORIOLES
CARDINALS
ROBINS
nil
nil
PENGUINS
nil
nil
nil

Figure 16.36
End of *Print* 2

We have completed printing everything to the right of ***current*** 2, so we exit ***Print*** 2 and return to its caller.

We have finished printing everything at ***current*** 1's right. Since the second recursive call has returned, we are at ***Print*** 1's **end** statement, and ***Print*** is exited altogether.

You can think of the recursive calls as a stack. The last version to be entered is the first to be exited. At any time, though, only one invocation of the procedure is active. All of the other invocations — and their variables and parameters — are in suspended animation until the current version passes back flow of control. Furthermore, the depth of the stack equals the maximum height of the tree: a copy of each procedure is executed for each node to the leaf furthest from the root.

16.9 Adding and Searching Recursively

The recursive algorithm used to print the tree can also be used to add and search for keys. We can replace the ***AddNode*** and ***Search*** procedures from earlier sections with shorter, recursive fragments.

First, we pseudocode the algorithms to break the problem down into smaller, similar parts. In its simple form, the ***AddNode*** algorithm can be pseudocoded as follows, assuming we start by pointing the current node at the root:

```
IF current node is a leaf THEN
   BEGIN
      Create node
      Add node to tree
   END
ELSE IF current node < key to add THEN
   CALL: AddNode(left child)
ELSE
   CALL: AddNode(right child)
```

Again, we assume that there are no duplications.

The statements "AddNode(left child)" and "AddNode(right child)" represent recursive calls to the same routine. In the earlier ***AddNode*** procedure, each move down the tree was handled by an iteration of the **repeat** loop. Since the recursion will repeat the adding on a smaller subtree, we have no need for the loop structure. (The recursion is an implicit kind of indefinite loop; the exit condition is the "bottom out" case.) Thus, the code for the recursive ***AddNode*** is simpler:

```
procedure AddNode( newItem: str80;          { item to add      }
         var current: node);                { current node     }
```

```
begin
    { if at leaf, add node }
    if current = nil then
        begin
            New(current);
            with current do
                begin
                    current^.item := newItem;
                    current^.left := nil;
                    current^.right := nil
                end {with}
        end

    {else, move further down tree }
    else if newItem < current^.item then
        AddNode(newItem, current^.left)
    else
        AddNode(newItem, current^.right)
end; { AddNode }
```

At first glance, it might appear that ***current*** is not attached to anything. Notice, though, that ***current*** is a variable parameter. The new value of ***current*** is sent back to the procedure that called it. In this case, the call is recursive; after ***current*** receives a value, it is passed back to the previous invocation of the same procedure. The new value is sent back and is assigned to ***current^.left*** or ***current^.right*** from the previous call.

The ***Search*** function can also be changed from an iterative to a recursive algorithm. To do this, we simply remove the **while** loop and replace the assignment statements ***current := current^.left;*** and ***current := current^.right;*** with recursive calls:

```
function Search( key: str80;             { item to find              }
        current: node):                  { --> current node on tree  }
        boolean;                         { indicates if key was found }
var
    found: boolean;                      { temporary return value    }
begin
    if current = nil then
        found := FALSE                   { key not in tree           }
    else if current^.item = key then
        found := TRUE                    { key has been found        }

    else if key < current^.item then     { move further down tree    }
        found := Search(current^.left)
    else
        found := Search(current^.right);

    Search := found                      { return value to caller    }
end; { Search }
```

In this code, the function traverses the tree until the key is found or the bottom is reached. At that point, the value TRUE or FALSE is returned to the caller and the recursion begins to unravel. Eventually, the final value is returned all the way to the original (non-recursive) caller.

The code for the recursive ***AddNode*** and ***Search*** procedures is shorter than the iterative algorithms seen earlier in the chapter. Still, the recursive solutions require more procedure calls; after all, recursion means that a problem is solved by having a procedure call itself. Recursion is not better than iteration or vice versa. You should be aware that while recursion usually means you can type in fewer lines, you may not necessarily be making your programs faster. At the same time, you should know that many recursive algorithms are considered to be quite efficient.

16.10 Chapter Summary

Have you ever felt overwhelmed by work? Have you ever said to yourself, "I wish there were three of me, so that I could get everything done?" If there were three of you, you could give each of your selves some part of your work load and thus simplify your problem.

Recursion works on this same principle. A recursive procedure or function calls itself to simplify its work. Each recursive call causes the routine to clone itself — the procedure or function is invoked and executed. The simplification arises, however, because the recursive call works with a slightly simpler case than the original procedure. For example, if the first invocation of a procedure is supposed to determine 6 factorial, the second invocation deals with a simpler case, 5 factorial.

The simplification of the cases takes place systematically. That is, each case is simplified by some constant amount. Eventually, the case is simplified to the point that no more recursion is needed. At this point, the recursion is said to "bottom out." The procedure determines the answer to the limit case, and the recursion unwinds. When you use recursion, ask yourself two questions. First, how does the case get simpler for the recursive call? Second, where does the recursion bottom out? Because of the amount of memory required for each recursive call, a recursive call that does not bottom out will quickly occupy all the memory your Mac can spare. While recursion can often be used to simplify iterative code, the recursion comes at the added cost of extra procedure calls.

The binary tree is an abstract data type that is used to store large amounts of data. Items in the tree are not stored in sequential order but are placed in the tree in the order in which they are entered. Thus, the order in which elements are input affects the way the tree is built.

Items are always added at the bottom of the tree. You find the place to add by starting at the root and comparing the item to add to the root's contents. If the item to add is less than the contents of the root, move to the left child. Otherwise, move to the right child. Then, compare the item to add to the child's contents. Again, depending on the comparison, move to the left or the right. Eventually this path will take you to a leaf of the tree, where you can add the item.

Searching for a key item follows the same algorithm as adding items. Start at the root and move to the left or right, depending on how the contents of the current node compare to the key.

Searches in balanced binary trees are more efficient than searches in linear lists. For a list of n items, a search in a binary tree requires looking at approximately $\log_2 n$ items, while a search in a linear list requires looking at approximately $n/2$ items. A degenerate tree, however, requires just as much time as a linear list.

Finally, you can use recursion to work with the items in a tree in order. For example, when you print the entire tree, first print everything to the left of the root, then the root itself, and then everything to the right of the root. This same algorithm can be used recursively to print each subtree. Recursion can also be used to add or find nodes within a tree.

16.11 Exercises

Understanding Concepts

Problems 1 through 3 refer to the following function.

```
{ Calculates balance and interest for a certain number of days.      }
{ Interest is compounded daily.                                      }

function Compound(balance,          { balance in the account          }
    intRate: real;                  { annual interest rate            }
    days: integer):                 { num of days $$ is in bank       }
    real;                           { balance for today               }

var
    newBal: real;                   { balance for today               }

begin
    if days = 0 then
        Compound := balance
    else
        begin
            { Calculate balance by adding a portion of the yearly interest }
            newBal := balance * (1 + intRate/365);
            Compound := Compound(newBal, intRate, days-1)
        end { else }
end; { Compound }
```

1. What does the function call ***Compound(100, 0.075, 4)*** return? (This is the new balance on $100 stored in the bank for 4 days at 7.5% interest.)

2. What is the bottom-out condition of the recursion?

3. Rewrite this code using iteration instead of recursion.

4. The following is a recursive implementation of a common Pascal function. What does it do?

```
{ Restriction: num1 >= num2 }

function LongWay(num1, num2: integer): integer;

begin
   if num1 < num2 then
      LongWay := 0
   else
      LongWay := LongWay(num1 – num2, num2) + 1
end; { LongWay }
```

5. Hand simulate the following code with the call ***Fibonacci(5)***.

```
function Fibonacci( position: integer): integer;

begin
   if position < 3 then
      Fibonacci := 1
   else
      Fibonacci := Fibonacci(position – 1) + Fibonacci(position – 2)
end; { Fibonacci }
```

6. Hand simulate the following procedure with the tree from Figure 16.25. (The initial call is ***Print(root^.right, 0);*** where ***root^.right*** points at the node containing 'ORIOLES'.) If needed, how would you debug this code?

```
procedure Print( current: nodePtr;          { --> node to print         }
      var level: integer);                  { level of node in tree     }
begin
   if current^.left <> nil then
      Print(current^.left, level + 1);

   Writeln(current^.item, ' is at level ', level:3, ' in the tree.');

   if current^.right <> nil then
      Print(current^.right, level + 1)

end; { Print }
```

7. What are the two conditions that mark a successful use of recursion?

8. Draw the binary tree that results when the following names are added in the given order to an empty tree:

```
chicken, alligator, cat, cow, bee, cattle
```

Show the same tree when these names are entered in reverse order.

9. If a linear list has 35 items, what is the worst case for a search, that is, what is the maximum number of comparisons you would have to do before finding a particular key in the list? What is the average case? What are the worst and average cases for 35 items in a balanced binary tree?

10. Reread the opening section of Chapter 1.

Coding Exercises

1. Write a recursive procedure that prints the contents of a linked list in reverse.

   Consider the following for problems 2 through 5. In certain geometric algorithms, points are stored in a two-dimensional tree. This is similar to a binary tree, except that the criterion for moving left and right alternates from level to level. If the point to be found has a smaller vertical coordinate than the point at the root, move left; otherwise, move right. At the next level, use the horizontal coordinate. At the third level go back to the vertical coordinate, and alternate on down the tree.

2. Modify the ***AddNode*** procedure from section 16.5 to add a point to a two-dimensional tree.

3. Modify the ***Print*** procedure for the two-dimensional tree and connect the points in the order in which they are printed.

4. Modify the ***Search*** procedure so that the user clicks a point on the screen, and the procedure finds the point in the two-dimensional tree that is closest to the selected point.

5. Modify the ***Print*** procedure for the two-dimensional tree in the following way: for each point on an even-numbered level, draw a horizontal line through the point from border to border in the Drawing window. For each point on an odd-numbered level, draw a vertical line through the point from top to bottom. (The root is level number 0.)

6. The greatest common denominator (GCD) of two positive integers ***num1*** and ***num2*** is defined by the following pseudocode. Implement the pseudocode as a procedure:

   IF ***num2*** = 0 THEN
       GCD = ***num1***
   ELSE
       GCD = greatest common denominator of ***num2*** and ***(num1* mod *num2)***

7. Write a procedure that prints the contents of a binary tree in reverse alphabetical order.

8. Write a recursive function that raises a number to an integer power.

9. Write a procedure to delete a node from a binary tree. The process is illustrated in the figure below. To delete a node, you first have to find the node in the tree — call this ***delNode***. To retain the tree's structure, you have to replace ***delNode*** with one of the leaf nodes. To determine which leaf, start at ***delNode*** and search for the node to delete. Of course, this second search will be unsuccessful, but it will lead to a leaf node. This leaf is the one that should replace ***delNode***.

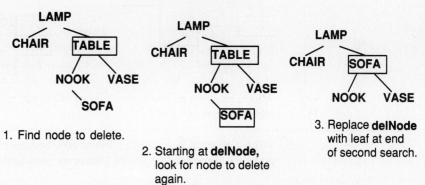

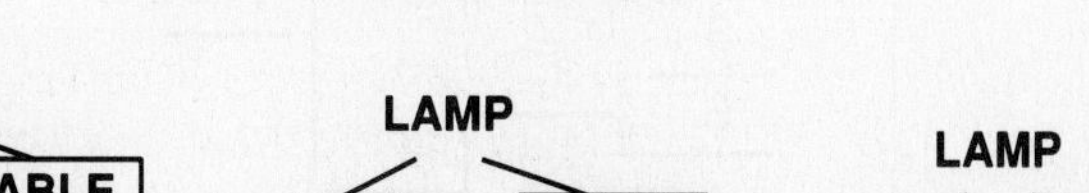

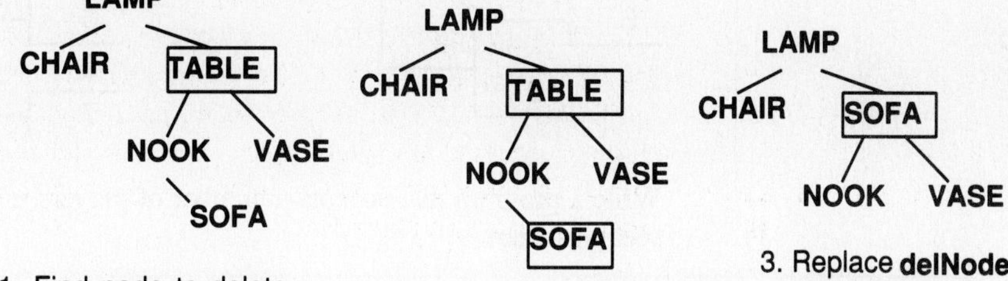

1. Find node to delete.

2. Starting at **delNode,** look for node to delete again.

3. Replace **delNode** with leaf at end of second search.

10. Implement the following multiplication algorithm using recursion: Start with two numbers a and b, where $a > b$. Create pairs of numbers, halving a (ignore fractional parts) while doubling b. Continue this operating until the halving yields 1.

    To find the product $a * b$, add all the doubled numbers that correspond to odd numbers in the halving operation. For example, 18 times 51 is calculated as follows:

51	25	12	6	3	1
18	36	72	144	288	576

    The product is: 18 + 36 + 288 + 576 = 918.

Programming Problems

1. In a tennis tournament, all players are seeded, that is, ranked by ability. In the first round, the top-seeded player plays the lowest-seeded player; the second-seeded player plays the second-lowest, and so on. The remaining rounds are based on the assumption that the higher-ranked player will win each match; the top-ranked player is supposed to play the lowest-seeded player among those who survived the first round. If the number of players in the tournament is not a

power of 2, the top seeds get byes, that is, they do not have to play a match in the first round. In the first example shown in the figure below, the top two seeds get byes directly into the second round. The figure also shows a tournament seeding for an 8-player tournament.

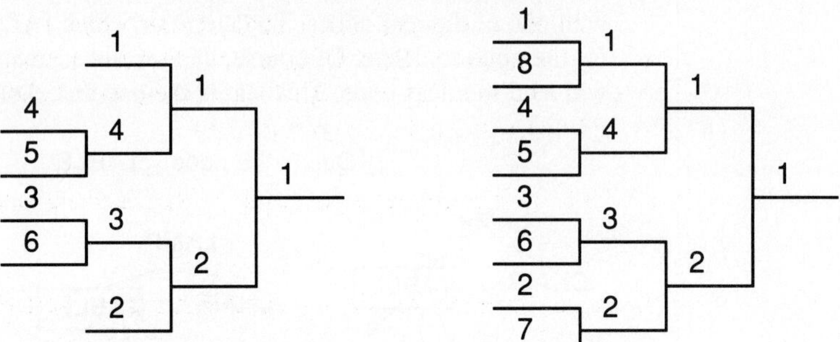

Write a program that accepts a number of players in a tournament and prints a seedings chart.

2. Write a program that accepts a Morse code sequence of dots and dashes and prints the corresponding letters. Letters are separated by spaces.

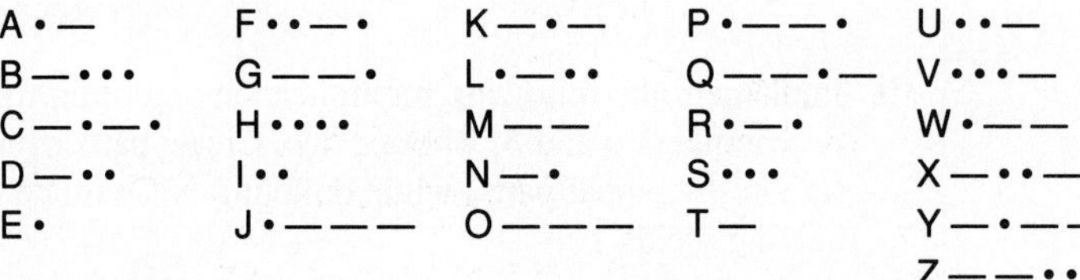

A •—	F ••—•	K —•—	P •——•	U ••—
B —•••	G ——•	L •—••	Q ——•—	V •••—
C —•—•	H ••••	M ——	R •—•	W •——
D —••	I ••	N —•	S •••	X —••—
E •	J •———	O ———	T —	Y —•——
				Z ——••

3. Pascal's triangle (which has nothing to do with the language Pascal, except that they were named after the same person) looks like this:

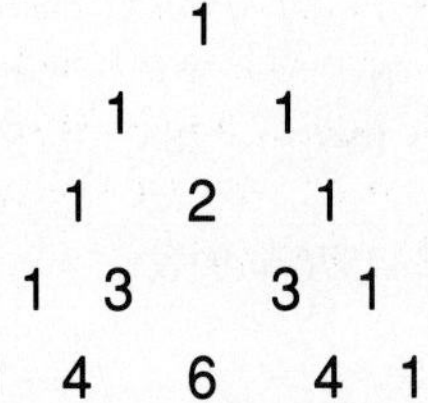

Each value in the triangle is found by adding the two values above it in the triangle. (Note that this triangle differs from a binary tree because many nodes share children.) Write a program that accepts a number from 1 to 10 and outputs that row in Pascal's triangle.

4. Programming problem 9 in Chapter 12 asked you to write a tic-tac-toe program for two users. Now, write a program where the computer plays tic-tac-toe with

the user. Before making a move, the program should consider the user's three next possible moves and choose for itself the move that has the best chance of yielding a win. (This algorithm uses a tree, but not necessarily a binary one.)

5. Implement the binary tree algorithms from this chapter using an array. The root is stored in array position 1, the root's left child is in slot 2, and the root's right child is in slot 3. The left child's children are in positions 4 and 5, and the right child's children are in 6 and 7. In general, slot x's left child is in position $2x$, and the right child is in position $2x + 1$.

6. Write a program that determines the length of the longest path from the root to a leaf.

7. Write a program to print every other name in a sorted list stored in a binary tree.

8. Create a taxonomy of things in the universe using a binary tree. Each non-leaf node contains a yes or no question; the leaf nodes contain things in the universe.

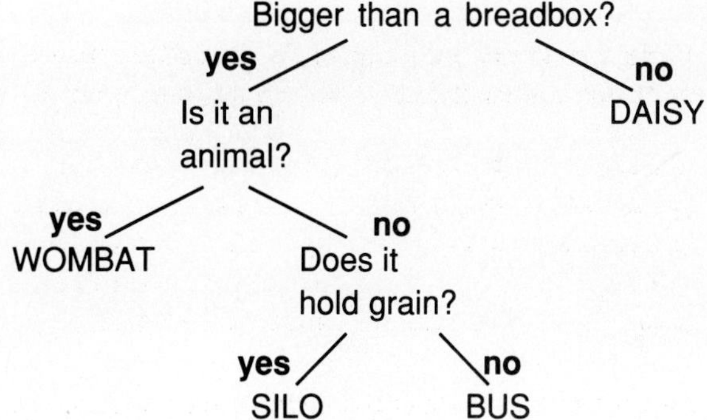

Allow the user to insert items in the taxonomy. For each new item, the user should answer yes or no to the questions in the path. When the program reaches a leaf, the user should enter a new question that differentiates the new item from the leaf. For example, the following user-program dialogue inserts the item HARMONICA in the tree. (User's input is in bold.)

What is the item to insert?
HARMONICA
Is it bigger than a breadbox?
no
You have described a DAISY.
What question differentiates a DAISY from a HARMONICA?
Does it play music?
Is HARMONICA a YES or NO response to this question?
yes

The resulting tree is shown in the figure below. Note that the addition to the tree is not strictly at the leaf.

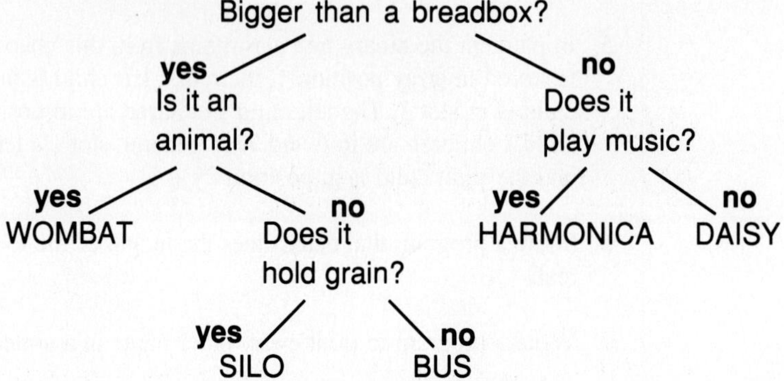

Appendix A: Reserved Words

Pascal, like any programming language, has a set of words that are reserved for particular purposes. This appendix summarizes these words by category. In all categories, case is irrelevant; upper- and lower-case characters in the word produce the same result (e.g., ***integer*** is equivalent to ***INTEGER*** and ***Integer***).

Word Symbols

The words in the following list appear in **boldface** when formatted by pretty printing. Under no circumstances can these words be used as your variable, constant, procedure, or function identifiers.

(Note: the word symbols **otherwise**, **string**, and **uses** are specific to MacPascal; the remaining symbols are part of the "ANSI Standard" Pascal.)

and	**array**	**begin**	**case**	**const**	**div**
do	**downto**	**else**	**end**	**file**	**for**
function	**goto**	**if**	**in**	**label**	**mod**
nil	**not**	**of**	**or**	**otherwise**	**packed**
procedure	**program**	**record**	**repeat**	**set**	**string**
then	**to**	**type**	**until**	**uses**	**var**
while	**with**				

Lightspeed Pascal includes all of the above, plus the following symbols:

inline	**interface**	**implementation**	**unit**

Predefined Type Identifiers

The following words are predefined atomic data types. (MacPascal considers **string** to be a special case, so it is listed as a word symbol.) These words can be used on the right side of colons in variable or parameter declarations.

boolean	char	computational
double	extended	integer
longint	real	text

Standard Procedure and Function Identifiers

The following words are names of predefined procedures and functions in MacPascal and QuickDraw. These words *can* be used as identifiers, although you should avoid doing so whenever possible. If you redefine a standard procedure or function name, the MacPascal interpreter or Lightspeed compiler will use your definition rather than the predefined definition. Thus, if you create a procedure called ***Writeln***, any call in your program to ***Writeln*** will call your procedure rather than the predefined procedure.

The Standard Pascal procedures and functions are defined in the ANSI standard and thus are available in all versions of Pascal. The MacPascal procedures and functions are specific to THINK Technologies' Macintosh Pascal and Lightspeed Pascal software, but functions similar to these are available in many versions of Pascal. The MacPascal list also includes extensions to the operating system software. The QuickDraw procedures and functions are found in Macintosh's read-only memory; thus, similar procedures and functions should exist in all languages available on the Macintosh. In MacPascal (not Lightspeed), the QuickDraw2 procedures and functions are available only when the statement **uses** ***QuickDraw2;*** follows the program declaration.

By convention, each word in a procedure or function name is capitalized.

Standard Pascal Procedures and Functions

Abs	Arctan	Chr	Close	Cos
Dispose	Eoln	Eof	Exp	FilePos
Get	Ln	New	Odd	Ord
Ord4	Open	Pack	Page	Pointer
Pred	Put	Read	Readln	Reset
Rewrite	Round	Seek	Sin	Sqr
Sqrt	Succ	Trunc	Unpack	Write
Writeln				

MacPascal Procedures and Functions

Button	BlockMove	Concat	Copy
Delete	DisposeHandle	DrawLine	EventAvail
GetDrawingRect	GetTextRect	GetHandleSize	GetMouse
GetNextEvent	GetSoundVol	HideAll	Include
Insert	InvertCircle	Length	NewFileName
NewHandle	Note	OldFileName	Omit
PaintCircle	Pos	ReadString	SaveDrawing
SetDrawingRect	SetSoundVol	SetTextRect	ShowDrawing

ShowText	SizeOf	SoundDone	StartSound
StillDown	StopSound	StringOf	Synch
SysBeep	TickCount	WaitMouseUp	WriteDraw

QuickDraw Procedures and Functions

AddPt	CharWidth	DrawChar	DrawString
DrawText	EmptyRect	EqualPt	EqualRect
EraseArc	EraseOval	EraseRect	EraseRoundRect
FillArc	FillOval	FillRect	FillRoundRect
FrameArc	FrameOval	FrameRect	FrameRoundRect
GetFontInfo	GetPen	GetPenState	GetPixel
GlobalToLocal	HideCursor	HidePen	InitCursor
InsetRect	InvertArc	InvertOval	InvertRect
InvertRoundRect	Line	LineTo	LocalToGlobal
MapPt	MapRect	Move	MoveTo
ObscureCursor	OffsetRect	PaintArc	PaintOval
PaintRect	PaintRoundRect	PenMode	PenNormal
PenPat	PenSize	Pt2Rect	PtInRect
PtToAngle	Random	ScalePt	SectRect
SetCursor	SetOrigin	SetPenState	SetPt
SetRect	ShowCursor	ShowPen	SpaceExtra
StringWidth	StuffHex	SubPt	TextFace
TextFont	TextMode	TextSize	TextWidth
UnionRect			

QuickDraw2 Procedures and Functions

BackColor	ClosePicture	ClosePoly	ClosePort
CloseRgn	ColorBit	CopyBits	CopyRgn
DiffRgn	DisposeRgn	DrawPicture	EmptyRgn
EqualRgn	ErasePoly	EraseRgn	FillPoly
FillRgn	ForeColor	FramePoly	FrameRgn
GetClip	GetPort	GrafDevice	InitGraf
InitPort	InsetRgn	InvertPoly	InvertRgn
KillPicture	KillPoly	MapPoly	MapRgn
MovePortTo	NewRgn	OffsetPoly	OffsetRgn
OpenPicture	OpenPoly	OpenPort	OpenRgn
PaintPoly	PaintRgn	PicComment	PortSize
PtInRgn	RectInRgn	RectRgn	ScrollRect
SectRgn	SetClip	SetEmptyRgn	SetPort
SetPortBits	SetRectRgn	SetStdProcs	StdArc
StdBits	StdComment	StdGetPic	StdLine
StdOval	StdPoly	StdPutPic	StdRect
StdRgn	StdRRect	StdText	StdTxMeas
UnionRgn	XorRgn		

Appendix B: Standard Functions

This appendix lists the predefined functions and their purposes. For each function, the following notation is used:

< result type > **:=** < function name >**(**< parameter list — type >**);**

This does *not* imply that functions must be used in assignment statements; functions can be nested inside expressions or passed as parameters.

The < result type > and parameter types use the following codes:

i	integer
r	real
n	numeric (integer or real)
s	string
c	character
b	boolean
o	ordinal type (integer, character, boolean, or enumerated type)
p	pointer variable

Thus, the first notation below means that the function ***Abs*** takes a parameter of type ***integer*** and returns a value of type ***integer***.

Arithmetic Functions

i := **Abs**(i);
r := **Abs**(r); { absolute value }

b := **Odd**(i); { returns TRUE if i is odd }

i := **Sqr**(i);
r := **Sqr**(r); { square of a number }

r := **Sqrt**(n); { square root of a number }

r := **Sin(** < radians — n > **);** { returns sine of angle n }

r := **Cos(** < radians — n > **);** { returns cosine of angle n }

```
r := Arctan( < radians — n > );          { returns arctangent of angle n }

r := Exp(n);                             { returns e to the nth power }

r := Ln(n);                              { returns natural log of n }

i := Random;                             { returns random integer between –32767 and 32768}
```

Ordinal Functions

```
i := Ord(o);                             { returns ordinality of o }
                                         { if o is a character, Ord returns ASCII value }

c := Chr(i);                             { returns character with ASCII value of i }
                                         { i should be between 0 and 255 }

o := Succ(o);                            { returns successor of value }
                                         { result is same type as parameter }

o := Pred(o);                            { returns predecessor of value }
                                         { result is same type as parameter }
```

String Functions

```
i := Length(s);                          { returns length of string }

i := Pos(< pattern — s >, < source — s >);
                                         { returns position of < pattern > in < source > }

s := Concat(< str1 — s >, < str2 — s >,..., < str n — s >);
                                         { concatenates strings }

s := Copy(< source — s >, < start — i >, < numChars — i >);
                                         { returns substring starting at < start > }

s := Omit(< source — s >, < start — i >, < numChars — i >);
                                         { returns everything except specified substring }

s := Include(< source — s >, < includeStr — s >, < pos — i >);
                                         { inserts < includeStr > in < source > at < pos > }
```

Memory Manipulation

```
{ Ok, ok, so they aren't functions, but they had to go somewhere... }

New(< pointer variable >);               { allocates memory for pointer   }

Dispose(< pointer variable >);           { frees memory from pointer      }
```

Appendix C: Input/Output Procedures and Functions

Textual Input

```
Read(< var1 >, < var2 >,... < var n >);
                    { reads input from keyboard                        }

Readln(< var1 >, < var2 >,... < var n >);
                    { reads input from keyboard                        }

Read(< text var >, < var1 >, < var2 >,... < var n >);
                    { reads input from file                            }

Readln(< text var >, < var1 >, < var2 >,... < var n >);
                    { reads input from file; moves file pos to next line }
```

Textual Output

```
{ In the following statements, < exp > denotes an expression —        }
{ i.e., a constant, variable, function, or combination thereof.        }
{ Each expression can be followed by formatting as follows:            }
{     < exp > : < field width >                                        }
{ Real expressions can be formatted as follows:                        }
{     < exp > : < field width > : < precision >                        }

Write(< exp 1 >, < exp 2 >,..., < exp n >); { writes output to Text window      }
Writeln(< exp 1 >, < exp 2 >,..., < exp n >);
                  { writes output to Text window and skips to next line         }

Write(< text var >, < exp 1 >, < exp 2 >,..., < exp n >); { writes output to file }
Writeln(< text var >, < exp 1 >, < exp 2 >,..., < exp n >);
                  { writes output to file and skips to next line     }
```

Graphic Input

```
b := Button;                  { returns TRUE when button has been pressed    }
GetMouse(< horiz >, < vert >); { gets position over which mouse is placed }
```

Graphic Variables Manipulation

```
{ set rectangle and point variables }
SetRect(< rect var >, < left >, < top >, < right >, < bottom >);
SetPt(< point var >, < horiz >, < vert >);

b := PtInRect(< point Var >, < rect Var >);
                        { returns TRUE if < point Var > is in < rect Var > }

{ work with regions }
< rgnHandle variable > := NewRgn;       { allocate memory for region }
OpenRgn;                                { begin defining region }
CloseRgn(< rgnHandle >);                { end of definition }
DisposeRgn(< rgnHandle >);              { free memory from region }

{ moving and resizing objects }
OffsetRect( < rect var >, < diffHoriz >, < diffVert > );
OffsetRgn( < rgnHandle >, < diffHoriz >, < diffVert > );
InsetRect( < rect var >, < diffHoriz >, < diffVert > );
InsetRgn( < rgnHandle >, < diffHoriz >, < diffVert > );
```

Graphic Output

```
HidePen;        { takes ink out of pen }
ShowPen;        { places ink in pen }
PenPat(< black, white, dkGray, gray, ltGray >);
                                  { changes color of pen                 }

MoveTo(< horiz >, < vert >);      { moves CP to designated position      }
Move(< horizDiff >, < vertDiff >); { moves CP using relative coords      }
LineTo(< horiz >, < vert >);
                { draws line to designated pos; moves CP                 }
Line(< horizDiff >, < vertDiff >);
                { draws line using relative coords; moves CP             }
DrawLine(< horiz1 >, < vert1 >, < horiz2 >, < vert2 >);
        { draws line from (< horiz1 >,< vert1 >) to (< horiz2 >, < vert2 >)   }

WriteDraw(< exp 1 >, < exp 2 >,... < exp n >);
                { writes output to Drawing window at current position    }
```

```
{ A reference to < rect > in the following procedure calls          }
{  can be replaced by < top >, < left >, < bottom >, < right >      }

{ draw outline of shapes }
FrameRect(< rect >);
FrameOval(< rect >);
FrameArc(< rect >, < startAngle >, < numDegrees >);
FrameRoundRect(< rect >, < ovalWidth >, < ovalHeight >);
    { < ovalWidth > and < ovalHeight > determine roundness of corners }
FrameRgn(< rgnHandle >);

{ draw shapes filled in current pen pattern }
PaintRect(< rect >);
PaintOval(< rect >);
PaintArc(< rect >, < startAngle >, < numDegrees >);
PaintRoundRect(< rect >, < ovalWidth >, < ovalHeight >);
PaintRgn(< rgnHandle >);
PaintCircle(< centerHoriz >, < centerVert >, < radius >);

{ draw shapes in background color }
EraseRect(< rect >);
EraseOval(< rect >);
EraseArc(< rect >, < startAngle >, < numDegrees >);
EraseRoundRect(< rect >, < ovalWidth >, < ovalHeight >);
EraseRgn(< rgnHandle >);

{ change pixels in shape from black to white or vice versa }
InvertRect(< rect >);
InvertOval(< rect >);
InvertArc(< rect >, < startAngle >, < numDegrees >);
InvertRoundRect(< rect >, < ovalWidth >, < ovalHeight >);
InvertRgn(< rgnHandle >);
InvertCircle(< centerHoriz >, < centerVert >, < radius >);
```

Appendix D: Menu Summary

Macintosh Pascal Menus

File

File
New ⌘N
Open... ⌘O
Close
Save
Save As...
Revert
Page Setup...
Print...
Quit ⌘Q

New: Creates a new program window.

Open...: Brings up a dialog box from which you can choose a file to work with.

Close: Closes the current window but does not leave MacPascal. Asks if you want to save changes since the last **Save**.

Save: Saves the current version of the file. If the file has not been titled, **Save** has the same effect as **Save As....**

Save As...: Saves the current version of the file and asks you to name the file. A dialog box asks you to give the file a title, indicate which disk should contain the file, and whether you want to save the file as text, as an application, or as an object. (Typically, you want to save the file as text.)

Revert: Restores the file to its state at the last **Save**.

Page Setup: Allows you to make any changes necessary for printing.

Print...: Prints the contents of the program window on whatever printer is connected to the Mac.

Quit: Performs the same function as **Close** and then returns control of the screen to the Finder.

Edit

Cut: Removes the selected text from the program window and places it in the clipboard.

Copy: Copies the selected text from the program window to the clipboard.

Paste: Inserts the contents of the clipboard at the insertion point.

Clear: Removes the selected text from the program window.

Select All: Selects the entire contents of the program window.

Search
Find ⌘F
Replace ⌘R
Everywhere ⌘E
What to find... ⌘W

Search

Find: Finds the next occurrence of the text in the **Search for** box (from **What to find**) within the program window.

Replace: Replaces the selected text with the contents of the **Replace with** (from **What to find**) box.

Everywhere: Repeats the **Find-Replace** sequence continually until the end of the program is reached.

What to find: Allows you to designate the text to **Search for**, the text to **Replace with**, whether you want to find all occurrences or only whole-word occurrences of the **Search for** text, and whether case matters.

Run
Check ⌘K
Reset
Go ⌘G
Go-Go
Step ⌘S
Step-Step
Stops In

Run

Check: Checks your program for syntax errors. This will not catch all errors, particularly those that involve communication between two statements, but it will indicate many.

Reset: Resets all windows to their state before the program was executed.

Go: Runs your program until execution reaches the mainline's **end** or until a stop sign is found.

Go-Go: Runs your program from start to finish, pausing at each stop sign just long enough to update the Observe window.

Step: Executes the next statement in the program.

Step-Step: Executes one statement at a time, stopping when a stop sign is reached.

Stops In: Inserts a gutter for stop signs. If the gutter is already there, the option is **Stops Out**.

Windows
Untitled
Instant
Observe
Text
Drawing
Clipboard
Font Control...
Preferences...

Windows

Program, **Instant**, **Observe**, **Text**, **Drawing**, **Clipboard**: Makes the designated window current. If the window is not currently visible, choosing its name in the **Windows** menu makes it appear on the screen.

Font Control...: Brings up a dialog box that lets you change the fonts in the Program windows (the Program, Observe, and Instant windows) or the Text window.

Preferences...: Allows you to change the size of the indentation, tab stops, and the number of characters saved in the Text window. Also allows you to echo-print the contents of the Text window to a printer or file.

Lightspeed Pascal Menus

Many of the menu options in Lightspeed Pascal perform the same function as an option in Macintosh Pascal. When appropriate, we point you to the equivalent function in the lists on the previous pages.

File
New ⌘N
Open... ⌘O
Close
Save
Save As...
Save a Copy As...
Revert
Page Setup...
Print...
Delete...
Transfer...
Quit ⌘Q

File

New, **Open...**, **Close**, **Save**, : See the same commands in Macintosh Pascal's **File** menu.

Save As...: Saves the current version of the file being edited and asks you to name (or rename) the file. A dialog box asks you to give the file a title, indicate which disk should contain the file, and whether you want to save the text only or the entire document (which includes stop signs).

Save a Copy As...: Make a backup copy of the file being edited. A dialog box asks you to name the backup file. When the copy has been created and saved, you will still be editing the original file.

Revert, **Page Setup...**, **Print...**: See the same commands in Macintosh Pascal's **File** menu.

Delete...: Deletes a file from the file system. A dialog box appears asking you to choose the file to delete. After you choose the file, you will be asked to confirm the deletion.

Transfer...: Quits Lightspeed Pascal and then sends you to another available application (such as a word processor or spreadsheet program).

Quit: Performs the same function as **Close** on all open files and then returns control of the screen to the Finder.

Edit
Undo ⌘Z
Cut ⌘X
Copy ⌘C
Paste ⌘V
Clear
Select All
Show Selection
Show Error
Find ⌘F
Replace ⌘R
Everywhere ⌘E
Find What... ⌘W

Edit

Undo: Allows you to reverse the effect of the last editing action. You can only undo the previous action; that is, you cannot undo all the way back to the beginning.

Cut, **Copy**, **Paste**, **Clear**, **Select All**: See the same commands in Macintosh Pascal's **Edit** menu.

Show Selection: If you have selected text that is no longer visible in the active window, this option scrolls to a place in the window where it becomes visible.

Show Error: If your program's execution or compilation halts because of an error, and the thumbs down icon is no longer visible, this option scrolls to a place in the appropriate program window where the thumb icon is visible.

Find, Replace, Everywhere, Find What...: See the same commands in Macintosh Pascal's **Search** menu. Note that the **Find What...** option in Lightspeed and the **What to find...** option in Macintosh Pascal are identical.

Project
New Project...
Open Project...
Close Project
Add Window
Add File...
Remove
Build & Save As...
View Options...
Run Options...
Source Options...

Project

Note: Projects in Lightspeed can contain multiple program files. Only one project can be open at a time.

New Project...: Creates a new project.

Open Project...: Opens an existing project.

Close Project: Closes the current project.

Add Window: Adds the file currently being edited to the project. If the file being edited is untitled, you will be asked to save the file first.

Add File...: Performs the same function as Add Window but allows you to choose files other than those that are currently open. You will see the same dialog box from the **Open...** or **Open Project...** option. This dialog box reappears after each addition until you choose the **Cancel** button.

Remove: Before choosing this option, you should double-click on a file listed in the project window. When you choose this option, the highlighted file will be removed from the project.

Build & Save As...: Compiles the project and saves the compiled code as an application, library, or compressed project.

View Options...: Brings up a dialog box which lets you alter the format of the project window.

Run Options...: Allows you to change the number of characters saved in the Text window and to echo the Text window output to the printer or to a file. Also allows you to work with resource files and application stack and zone sizes, but you won't need to do that here.

Source Options...: Allows you to specify the font, length of indentation, and width of tab stops in the editing windows.

Run
Check ⌘K
Build ⌘B
Check Link
Reset
Go ⌘G
Go-Go
Step ⌘S
Trace ⌘T
Auto-Save
• Confirm Saves
Don't Save

Run

Check: See **Check** in Macintosh Pascal's **Run** menu.

Build: Compiles the project code.

Check Link: If you are writing a program using multiple files, this option allows you to see if the links between the compiled files are ok.

Reset, **Go**, **Go-Go**, **Step**, **Trace**: See the same commands in Macintosh Pascal's **Run** menu. Note that the **Trace** option in Lightspeed and the **step-step** option in Macintosh Pascal are identical.

Auto-Save, **Confirm Saves**, **Don't Save**: Only one of these three options is active at any given time. **Auto-Save** automatically does a **Save** on all changed files before the program is run. **Confirm Saves** asks if you want to save changes made to your files before the program is run. **Don't Save** means you don't want to save changes before the program is run.

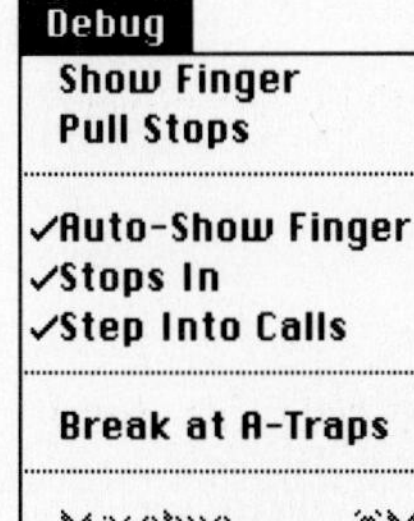

changes made to your files before the program is run. **Don't Save** means you don't want to save changes before the program is run.

Debug

Show Finger: No, this option does not perform an obscene gesture. Rather, it makes visible the finger-pointing icon indicating the next line to be executed. If the file containing the program is not open, the finger points to the file name in the project window.

Pull Stops: All stop signs are removed from the active file window. The stop sign gutter remains.

Note: When any of the next three options are enabled, a check mark appears next to the option in the menu. Choosing an enabled option will disable it.

Auto-Show Finger: (See also: Obscene gestures made while driving.) Useful for programs with code in multiple files. When the program is run with **Go-Go**, **Step**, or **Trace**, the window containing the line of code being executed becomes the current window so that the finger-pointing icon is always visible.

Stops In: Inserts the stop sign gutter.

Step Into Calls: When you run a program with **Go-Go**, **Step**, or **Trace** while this option is enabled, the finger-pointing icon will step through each procedure and function call. When disabled, the finger-pointing icon will only step through the mainline.

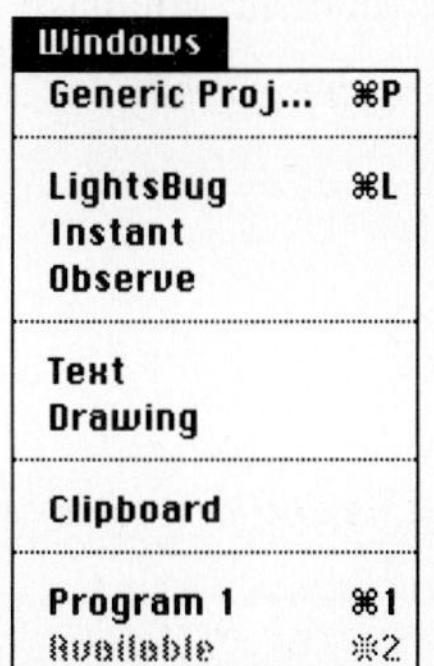

Break at A-Traps, **Macsbug**: Low-level debugging tools.

Windows

Project, LightsBug, Instant, Observe, Text, Drawing, Clipboard, Program: Choosing any option on this menu makes that window active. A diamond to the left of a program window name indicates that changes have been made since the last **Save**. (LightsBug is another low-level debugging tool.)

Appendix E: Editing Time-Savers

Macintosh Pascal and Lightspeed Pascal contain many features that help you enter, edit, and execute programs. All you must have to use MacPascal and Lightspeed is explained in section 1.3, but a number of other features can make your online time more efficient. Two features that are particularly useful for debugging — the Observe and the Instant windows — are explained in Chapters 2 and 7, respectively. Some other features are discussed here. You should read the Primer and Chapter 1 before using this appendix.

This **hands-on** section discusses a program that prints two addresses. Suppose you want to use your Macintosh to create mailing labels. At the moment, you have only two addresses to print:

Al Gorithm
Box 1248
Finite State Univ.
College Town, MA 02912
555-5555

Dee Morgan
Box 101
Finite State Univ.
College Town, MA 02912
555-0011

The first obvious breakdown of the problem is: print one address, followed by the other:

Print Al's address
Print Dee's address

You notice that the two addresses contain two identical lines. You decide to make these lines into a separate procedure. The pseudocode can be refined as follows:

{ Print Al's address }
Print Al's name and box number
Call procedure to print college, state, zip
Print phone number

{ Print Dee's address }
Print Dee's name and box number
Call procedure to print college, state, zip
Print phone number

If you make each address a separate procedure, you can translate the pseudocode into the following Pascal program. (Do not type this program in yet; you will be given instructions on what to do later.)

Code E.1
program *Mailing*

```
{ This program prints two mailing labels.             }

program Mailing;

{ This procedure prints the college and city lines of  }
{ the addresses.                                       }
{ Called by: Al and Dee        Calls: none            }

  procedure CollegeState;

  begin
    Writeln('Finite State Univ');
    Writeln('College Town, MA 02912')
  end; { CollegeState }

{ This procedure prints Al's address.      }
{ Called by: Mainline       Calls: none    }

  procedure Al;

  begin
    Writeln('Al Gorithm');
    Writeln('Box 1248');
    CollegeState;
    Writeln('555-5555')
  end; { Al }

{ This procedure prints Dee's address.     }
{ Called by: Mainline       Calls: none    }

  procedure Dee;

  begin
    Writeln('Dee Morgan');
    Writeln('Box 101');
    CollegeState;
    Writeln('555-0011')
  end; { Dee }
```

Code E.1
(continued)

```
{ The mainline formats the mailing labels. First Al's          }
{ address is printed. Then three blank lines are inserted      }
{ so that Dee's address will begin on the next label.          }
{ Calls: Al, Dee                                               }

begin
  Al;
  Writeln;
  Writeln;
  Writeln;
  Dee
end. { Mailing }
```

Editing Tricks

If you are using Macintosh Pascal,

- Open MacPascal.

If you are using Lightspeed,

- Duplicate **Generic Project**.
- Rename the copy as **Mailing**.
- Open **Mailing**.

For both MacPascal and Lightspeed,

- Enter the program header and procedures ***CollegeState*** and ***Al***.

You may notice that the procedures ***Al*** and ***Dee*** are similar. (If you cannot see the entire lines, you may want to resize the Untitled window.) At this point, you realize that it would be easier to edit a second copy of ***Al*** to create ***Dee*** instead of retyping all of the similar statements. To avoid this repetition, you can use a technique called *copying* and *pasting*.

- Select the ***Al*** procedure, including the header comment.

The selected text, as usual, will be highlighted; your program window should look like Figure E.1.

- Choose the **Copy** option from the **Edit** menu.

This option makes a copy of the selected text and puts it on the Macintosh Clipboard. If you choose **Clipboard** from the **Windows** menu at this point, you will see another copy of the procedure ***Al***. (Again, you may have to resize the window to view the entire contents.)

Now, you need to insert this copy into the program.

- Move the insertion point to the place where the procedure ***Dee*** should go.
- Choose **Paste** from the **Edit** menu.

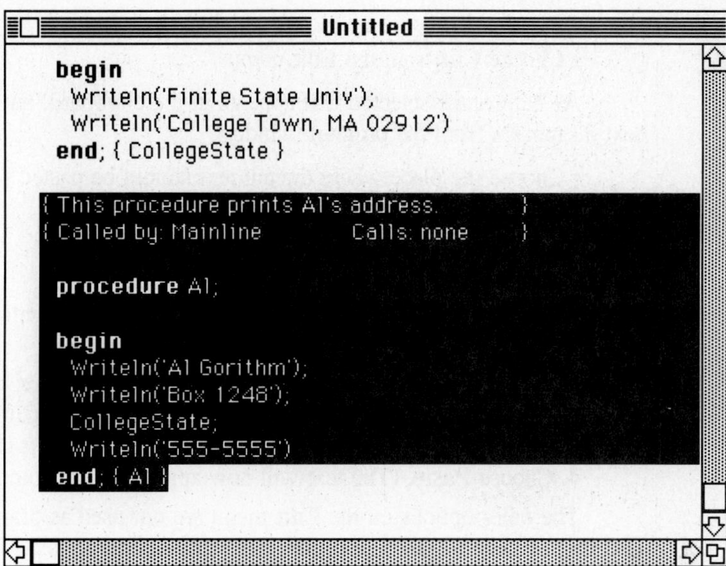

Figure E.1
Highlighted text

You now have two copies of the procedure ***Al***, as shown in Figure E.2.

- Modify the second copy of the procedure ***Al*** to create the procedure ***Dee***.

Suppose you decide to switch the order of the procedures ***Al*** and ***Dee***. As long as these procedures are between the procedure ***CollegeState*** and the mainline, it doesn't matter if ***Al*** comes before ***Dee***, or vice versa.

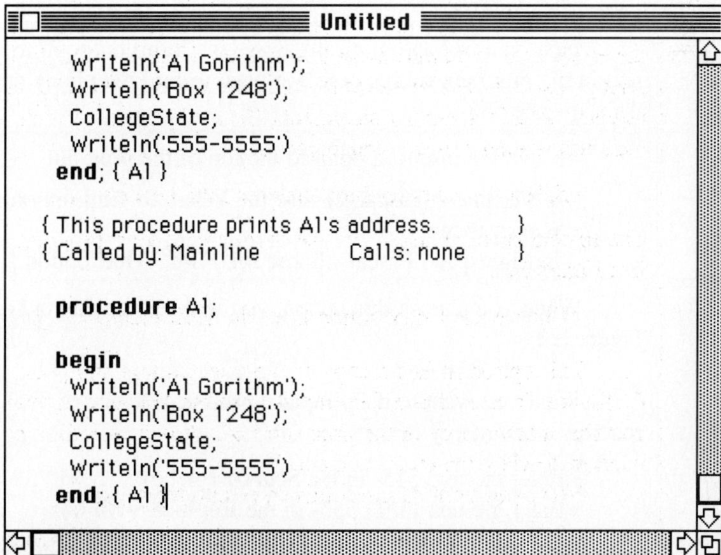

Figure E.2
Result of **Paste**

• Select the text to move (procedure ***Dee***).
• Choose **Cut** from the **Edit** menu.

As before, the selected text appears in the clipboard, but unlike **Copy**, the cut text disappears from the program window.

• Choose the place where the cut text should be pasted by moving the insertion point.
• Select **Paste**.

The text from the clipboard is added at the insertion point.

The cutting/copying and pasting techniques can be summarized as follows:

1. Select the text to move.
2. Choose **Cut** or **Copy** from the **Edit** menu. (The text will disappear from the program but will be visible if you look at the Clipboard.)
3. Move the insertion point to the place where the text should go.
4. Choose **Paste**. (The text will now appear at that point.)

The other options on the **Edit** menu are not used as often as cutting, copying, and pasting. The **Clear** option, like **Cut**, removes any selected text from the program. Unlike **Cut**, though, the selected text does not appear in the Clipboard and thus cannot be pasted. The **Select All** menu simply allows you to select everything in the current window.

• Complete the rest of the program by entering the mainline.

Finding and Replacing

Suppose you decide to change the phone numbers printed on the labels by adding the area code (351). There are two ways to change the phone numbers using menu options. We'll look at each in turn.

First, you can automatically move the insertion point to a desired section of text in the program. In this case, we want to find the phone numbers that begin with the sequence 555-.

• Move the insertion point to the top of the program.

–In Macintosh Pascal, choose the **What to find** option from the **Search** menu.

– In Lightspeed Pascal, choose the **Find What** option from the **Edit** menu.

When you choose this option, you will see the dialog box illustrated in Figure E.3.

What you want to do is replace each occurrence of 555- with (351) 555- . This requires a few steps.

• Enter the text 555- in the **Search for** box.
• Enter the text (351) 555- in the **Replace with** box.

Search for			
Replace with			
◉ Separate Words	◉ Case Is Irrelevant		OK
○ All Occurrences	○ Cases Must Match		Cancel

Figure E.3 **What to find/ Find What** dialog box

You now need to address the two options at the bottom of the box. On the left, you can choose to find **Separate Words** or **All Occurrences**. A "word" in this context is any set of characters surrounded by blanks. Since the 555- is not surrounded by blanks, you need to:

- Choose the **All Occurrences** option.

The other option asks if **Case Is Irrelevant** or if **Cases Must Match**. The **Case is Irrelevant** option means that the words ***First***, ***first***, ***FIRST***, and ***fIrSt*** are taken to match the text ***First***. The **Cases Must Match** option will not match words if the case of the letters (upper or lower) is different. Since case doesn't matter here,

- Choose the **Case Is Irrelevant** option.

This option may already be filled. MacPascal typically assumes that you are looking for separate words and that case is irrelevant.

Now that you have filled in all of the information, you can go on.

- Choose the **OK** button.

The dialog box goes away, but otherwise the screen does not change. The **What to find/Find What** option is useful only as a preparation for the **Find, Replace**, and **Everywhere** options. (These options are on the **Search** menu in MacPascal and on the **Edit** menu in Lightspeed.) You can now change the first phone number.

- Move the insertion point to the top of the program.
- Choose **Find** from the **Search** or **Edit** menu.

The first occurrence of the text listed in the **Search for** box, in this case, the text 555-, is found. The search starts at the insertion point, which is why you moved the insertion point to the top of the program. The text sequence is highlighted, as shown in Figure E.4.

Now you can replace the text.

- Choose the **Replace** option from the **Search** or **Edit** menu.

The text in the **Replace with** box of the **What to find/Find What** dialog box replaces the selected text, as shown in Figure E.5.

- Change the other phone number by choosing **Find** and **Replace**.

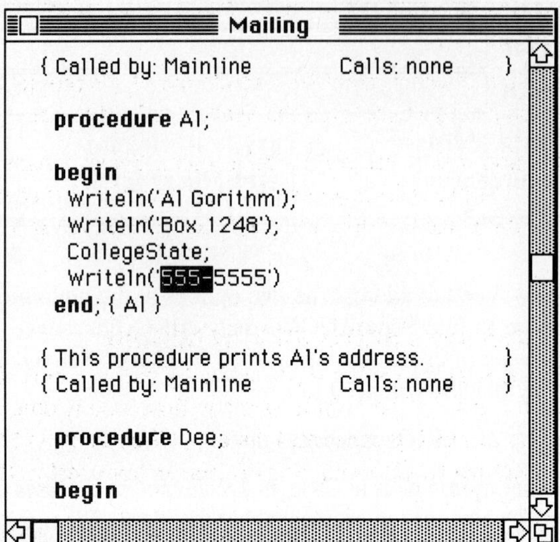

Figure E.4
Result of **Find**

Using a **Find** and **Replace** is fine when you have to make only a few isolated changes. You may, however, have a change that occurs many times in a program. Then you can perform what is called a *global replacement*. This means that you can change every occurrence of the **Search for** text to the **Replace with** text with one action.

Suppose you have the area code wrong — it is actually 357 instead of 351.

- Choose the **What to find** or **Find What** option.
- Indicate that you want to **Search for** 351 and **Replace with** 357.

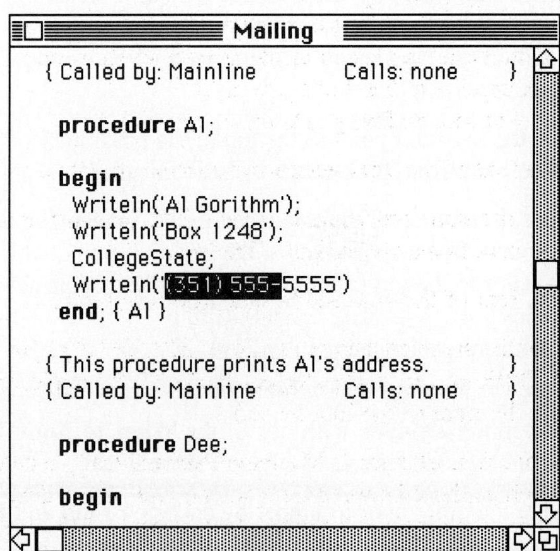

Figure E.5
Result of **Replace**

Notice that selection works in the dialog boxes in the same way that it does in the program window.

- Move the insertion point back to the top of the program.
- Choose **Everywhere** from the **Search** or **Edit** menu.

This option makes the global replacement. Because such changes can be far-reaching, a dialog box asks if you really want to make this change. If you choose **Yes**, the global change is made, and the final replacement is highlighted.

Making Windows Active and Readable

Any MacPascal window can be made active by clicking in it. There is another way to make a window active. The **Windows** menu lists, among other things, the program file name, **Text**, **Drawing**, **Instant**, **Observe**, **Clipboard**, and (in Lightspeed only) the project name. Choosing any of these options makes that window the active window.

The style in which characters appear on the screen is called the *font*. All of the windows, except the Text window, use the same font. You can change the font or the size of the characters using menu options.

To change the font of the windows (except the Text window) in Macintosh Pascal:

- Choose **Font Control** from the **Windows** menu.
- Click on the button next to the words **Program Windows.**
- Click on the **Next** and **Prev** buttons to view the different fonts. (A sample appears on the left side of the box.)
- When you see the font you want, choose **OK.**

To change the font of the windows (except the Text window) in Lightspeed:

- Choose **Source Options...** from the **Project** menu.
- Click on the left and right arrow buttons to view the different fonts. (A sample appears in the box at the top.)
- When you see the font you want, choose **OK.**

To change the font of the Text window in Macintosh Pascal:

- Follow the same procedure as above, EXCEPT that you should click on the button next to the words **Text Window.**

To change the font of the Text window in Lightspeed Pascal:

- Follow the same procedure as above, EXCEPT that you should choose the **Run Options...** from the **Project** menu. (The sample will appear in the box to the right of the font name.)

As we noted in Chapter 1, MacPascal automatically indents subordinate statements, such as those between a **begin** and **end**. The indent width is the length of the indentation, in pixels. (The entire Mac screen is 512 pixels wide.) You can change the length of indentation simply by entering a different number in the corresponding box.

The same dialog box that lets you change the length of indentation also allows you to change the number of pixels in each tab. The tab stops are just like the tabs on a typewriter and can be used to line up comments.

To change the length of indentation or tab stops:

- In Macintosh Pascal, choose the **Preferences...** option from the **Windows** menu.
- In Lightspeed Pascal, choose **Source Options...** from the **Project** menu.
- Click in the box that you want to change (**Indent Width** or **Tab Stops every** in MacPascal; **Indent:** or **Tab Stops:** in Lightspeed).
- Enter the new number of pixels.

Textual Output

When you output characters to the Text window, they are printed from left to right, starting at the top of the window. If there is more text than fits in the window, you can scroll through the output with the scroll bars. However, MacPascal and Lightspeed both have an upper limit on how many characters they can hold in the Text window. The **Preferences...** dialog box in MacPascal and the **Run Options...** dialog box in Lightspeed ask you to set the upper limit for characters. Usually the default setting of 5000 is sufficient; however, you can set an upper limit as high as 32767 characters.

To change the number of characters saved in the Text Window:

- In MacPascal, choose the **Preferences...** option from the **Windows** menu.
- In Lightspeed, choose **Run Options...** from the **Project** menu.
- Then click in the box to the right of the words **Text Window saves.**
- Enter the new number of characters (up to 32767).

The **Print...** option on the **Run** menu prints only the code. Often, it is helpful to get a hard copy of your program's output as well.

To send Text window output to the printer in Macintosh Pascal:

- Choose the **Preferences...** option from the **Windows** menu.
- Click on the box next to the line **Output also to Printer.**
- Choose the **OK** button.

To send Text window output to the printer in Lightspeed Pascal:

- Choose the **Run Options...** option from the **Project** menu.
- Click on the box next to the line **Echo to the printer.**
- Choose the **OK** button.

If you run a program with an X next to the **Output also to Printer** or **Echo to the printer** option, everything that appears in the Text window is "echo-printed" on the printer connected to your Macintosh.

Finally, you can save the contents of the Text window in a file.

To send Text window output to a file in Macintosh Pascal:

- Choose the **Preferences...** option from the **Windows** menu.
- Click on the box next to the line **Output also to a File:**
- Another dialog box will appear. Enter the name of the file in this dialog box and choose **Save.**
- When you return to the original dialog box, choose the **OK** button.

To send Text window output to a file in Lightspeed Pascal:

- Choose the **Run Options...** option from the **Project** menu.
- Click on the box next to the line **Echo to the file.**
- Another dialog box will appear. Enter the name of the file in this dialog box and choose **Save.**
- When you return to the original dialog box, choose the **OK** button.

Final Shortcuts

Many of the frequently used menu options can be performed with key sequences. For example, the **Go** option on the **Run** menu can also be specified by simultaneously pressing the cloverleaf key and the **G** key. The equivalent key sequences are listed on the menus.

Mouse actions can also be used for shortcuts. If you want to select a word, double-click on it. If you want to select an entire line, triple-click on it.

Finally, there are four shortcuts that are useful in all Macintosh applications. Each of these require pressing the cloverleaf, shift, and a number key at the same time.

Command	**Action**
Cloverleaf-Shift-1	Ejects the disk in the internal drive
Cloverleaf-Shift-2	Ejects the disk in the external drive
Cloverleaf-Shift-3	Saves the contents of the screen in a MacPaint file
Cloverleaf-Shift-4	Prints the contents of the screen if the printer is on

Appendix F: The Macintosh Character Set

	0	16	32	48	64	80	96	112	128	144	160	176	192	208	224	240
0	NUL	DLE	SP	0	@	P	`	p	Ä	ê	†	∞	¿	–	‡	
1	SOH	DC1	!	1	A	Q	a	q	Å	ë	°	±	¡	—	·	Ò
2	STX	DC2	"	2	B	R	b	r	Ç	í	¢	≤	¬	"	,	Ú
3	EXT	DC3	#	3	C	S	c	s	É	ì	£	≥	√	"	„	Û
4	EOT	DC4	$	4	D	T	d	t	Ñ	î	§	¥	*f*	'	‰	Ù
5	ENQ	NAK	%	5	E	U	e	u	Ö	ï	•	µ	≈	'	Â	ı
6	ACK	SYN	&	6	F	V	f	v	Ü	ñ	¶	∂	∆	÷	Ê	ˆ
7	BEL	ETB	'	7	G	W	g	w	á	ó	ß	∑	«	◊	À	˜
8	BS	CAN	(	8	H	X	h	x	à	ò	®	∏	»	ÿ	Ë	¯
9	HT	EM	)	9	I	Y	i	y	â	ô	©	π	…	Ÿ	È	˘
10	LF	SUB	*	:	J	Z	j	z	ä	ö	™	∫		/	Í	˙
11	VT	ESC	+	;	K	[	k	{	ã	õ	´	ª	Á	¤	Î	˚
12	FF	FS	,	<	L	\	l	|	å	ú	¨	º	Ã	‹	Ï	
13	CR	GS	-	=	M	]	m	}	ç	ù	≠	Ω	Õ	›	Ì	
14	SO	RS	.	>	N	^	n	~	é	û	Æ	æ	Œ	ﬁ	Ó	
15	SI	US	/	?	O	_	o	DEL	è	ü	Ø	ø	œ	ﬂ	Ô	

The decimal representation of any character is found by adding the row and the column numbers (e.g., the representation of G is 64 + 7, or 71).

NUL stands for the null character (represented by 0); SP stands for the space character (represented by 32).

Characters 0 through 31 and the DEL character (represented by 127) are nonprinting "control codes," which are used by the computer and display to perform various functions, but which are of no concern for our string comparisons.

Appendix G: Syntax Summary

Punctuation

Elements In Compound Data Structures

< recordName >.< field >
< arrayVar >[< subscript >] { element in 1-dimensional array }
< arrayVar >[< sub1 >,...,< sub *n* >] { element in *n*-dimensional array }
[< element1 >,..., < element *n* >] { set of elements }
< pointerToRecord >^.< field >

Arithmetic Symbols

+ { addition, union of sets }
– { subtraction, negation, difference of sets }
* { multiplication, intersection of sets }
/ { division of real numbers }
= { equal to }
< { less than }
> { greater than }
<= { less than or equal to, subset of }
>= { greater than or equal to, superset of }
<> { not equal to }

Other Symbols

:= { assignment }
{ } { comments }
.. { subrange, as in an array }
: { separates variables and functions from types }
, { separates items in a list }
; { statement separator }
' { delimits a character or string }
(* *) { alternative comment symbols }
(..) { alternative array subscript symbols }
$ { indicates a hexadecimal number }
in { containment in a set }

Program Order

```
{ header comment }

program < program name >;

   uses < library >;

const
   < name > = < value >;                                          { glossary }
type
   < typeName > = < predefined type >;                            { glossary }
{ Mainline variables }
var
   < varName > : < type >;                                        { glossary }

{ block comment                                    }
{ function that receives one value parameter      }
function < FunctionName > (< parameter name >:< parameter type >) : { glossary }
   < returned value type >;
{ local variables }
var
   < varName > : < type >;                                        { glossary }
begin
   < statement 1 >;
   < statement 2 >;
      ...
   < statement n >;
   < FunctionName > := < returned value >  { returning value to caller }
end; { FunctionName }
```

```
{ block comment                                                     }
{ procedure that receives one value and one variable parameter      }

procedure < ProcName > (< parameter name >: < parameter type >;   { glossary }
    var < parameter name >: < parameter type >);                  { glossary }

{ local variables }
var
    < varName > : < type >;                                        { glossary }

begin
    < statement 1 >;
        ...
    < statement n >
end; { ProcName }

{ Mainline block comment }

begin
    < statement 1 >;
        ...
    < ProcName >(< parameter 1 >, < parameter 2 >);     { Call procedure    }
    < variable > := < FunctionName >(< parameter 1 >);  { Call function     }
        ...
    < statement n >
end. { Program }
```

Control Structure

case < selector > **of**
< integer, char, or enumerated constant > : < statement >;
< integer, char, or enumerated constant > : < statement >;
otherwise
< statement >
end; { case }

for < integer variable > := < bounds > < **to**, **downto** > < bounds > **do**
< statement >;

if < boolean expression > **then**
< statement >
else if < boolean expression > **then**
< statement >
else
< statement >;

while < boolean expression > **do**
< statement >;

repeat
< statement >;
until < boolean expression >;

with < record1 >,... < record *n* > **do**
< statement >;

NOTE: Any occurrence of < statement > can be replaced with multiple statements using the structure:

begin
< statement 1 >;
< statement 2 >;
...
< statement *n* >
end;

The **begin/end** brackets are necessary to separate multiple statements within each control construct except **repeat-until**.

Declaring Compound Types

```
type                                              { some examples                  }

   grades = array[1..10] of class;                { 1-d array of defined type      }

   colorCount = array[1..10, 4..25] of integer;   { 2-d array                      }

   class = record                                 { record with 2 fields           }
      name : string[15];                          { glossary                       }
      grade : integer                             { glossary                       }
    end; { class }

wordPtr = ^sentence;                   { pointer of node in linked list                }
sentence = record                      { single node in linked list                    }
      currentWord: string[10];         { field of node                                 }
      next: wordPtr                    { -- > next word in sentence                    }
    end; { sentence }

   classes = (Frosh, Soph, Jr, Sr);    { enumerated type }

   charSet = set of char;              { set; base type must have < 65536 values  }

   student = record                    { record with fixed and variant parts           }
      idNum: integer;                  { fixed field                                   }
      case year: classes of            { tag field                                     }
                                       { variant fields                                }
            Frosh: (                   { no extra fields when year=Frosh               }
            );
            Soph, Jr: (
               major: string[10];             { variant when year=Soph or      }
               onLeave: boolean               {  when year=Jr                  }
            );

            Sr: (
               futurePlans: string[80]  { variant when year=Sr                         }
            )
    end; { end for both case and record }
```

Answers to Exercises: Selected Concepts

Chapter 1

1. The input of the computer process is similar to getting materials for a laboratory experiment; the processing of data is similar to performing the experiment; the output of the computer process is similar to the results of the experiment.
2. Items *a, b, c, g,* and *i* are hardware; the remaining are software.
3. A high-level language is closer to English than a low-level language; high-level languages are thus easier for the user to understand.
4. The text appears in outline form; a bug box appears on the screen.
5. To divide and conquer a problem is to break it into smaller parts and then to solve (conquer) the smaller parts.
6. ***Writeln*** outputs a carriage return; ***Write*** does not.
7. *a.* comment brackets — to be ignored by translator; *b.* apostrophes — surround a literal string (in ***Writeln***, indicates text to print); *c.* semicolon — separates statements; *d.* **boldface** — reserved word
8. The **end** is not a statement in itself; with **begin**, it forms a set of brackets or parentheses.
9. *a* and *c* are legal; *b* is illegal (cannot begin an identifier with a number).
10. Comments make the program easier for programmers to read while debugging and for other programmers who want to understand or modify the code later.

12. Get eggs, milk, bread, orange juice from refrigerator; get frying pan, spatula, measuring cup, plate, glass from cabinet; get cooking oil; put bread in toaster; press button to start toaster; pour 1/4 cup milk in cup; crack eggs in cup; stir eggs and milk with fork; place frying pan on stove; pour a little oil into the pan; turn on stove to medium heat; wait about 60 seconds; pour eggs and milk into pan; wait about 60 seconds; with spatula, turn eggs in pan; wait another 60 seconds; turn off stove; with spatula, place eggs on plate; when toast is done, place toast on plate; pour orange juice in glass.

13. *a.* ***Third, First, Second,*** mainline
    b. output:

```
Number 3
Number 1
Number 3
Number 2
Number 3
Number 1
```

14. *a.* check for missing apostrophes (syntax is incorrect); *b.* check for semicolon on line next to thumb — if not there, check lines above thumb; *c.* make sure procedures are in correct order in file; look for ***ChangeCredit*** in file.

Chapter 2

1. *a.* 52; *b.* 2; *c.* 5; *d.* 13.5; *e.* 47.12385 (rounded)
2. The algebraic expression makes no sense, since it says that i is equal to i + 1; the assignment statement makes sense, since it says to add 1 to the value of the variable ***i*** and to store the result back in ***i***.
3. If the left of an assignment statement is an ***integer*** variable, the right side can have ***real*** variables, as long as the final result is an integer (which can be done with the ***Trunc*** and ***Round*** functions); if the left is ***real***, the right side can contain both ***integer*** and ***real*** variables.
4. ***pi*** is a predefined constant; ***area*** must be a variable; ***radius*** may be either a variable or constant.
5. The CP ends up at (100, 100).

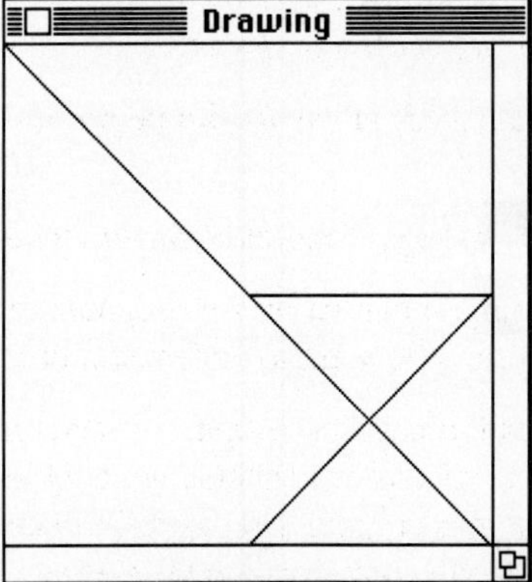

6. *a.* ***numPeople*** gets 5; *b.* ***totalBill*** gets 24.75; *c.* ***totalBill*** gets 25.99; *d.* ***onePersonPart*** gets 5.19.

7. *b* and *d* are legitimate inputs.
8. ***Writeln('$', (numChocs/Price):5:2);***

Chapter 3

1. (50, 150)
2. 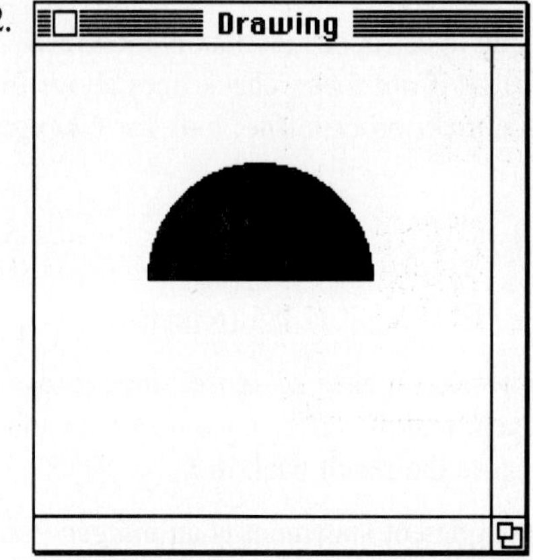

3. PaintArc(50, 50, 150, 150, 270, 180);
4. Code produces the lower right quarter-circle (a 90° arc) of a circle centered at 0, 0. The user's point specifies how large the quarter-circle is.
5. PaintRect(50, 50, 150, 150); or InvertRect(50, 50, 150, 150);
6. 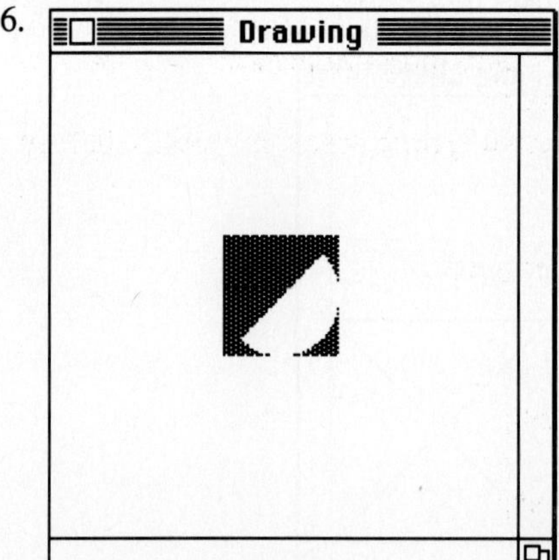

7. The result is a circle; the example will draw the same circle as ***FrameOval(60, 60, 70, 70);***

8. The area stays gray, although different individual pixels will be lit.

9. Draws a line segment from (100, 100) to the user's point.

10. 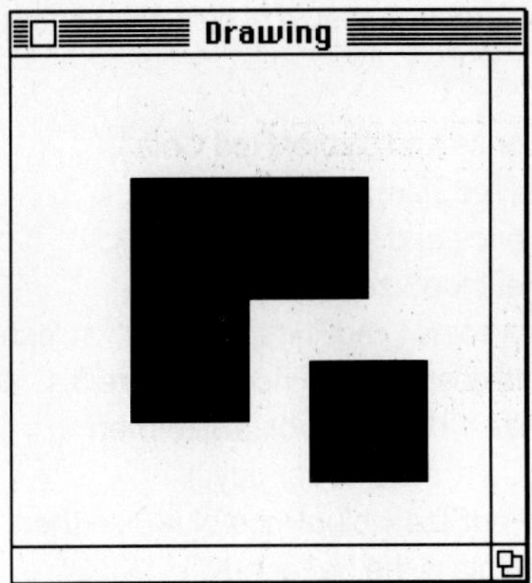

Chapter 4

1. multiples of 4 *not* divisible by 400

2. ***balance*** = 20, output is "You have a surplus of cash"; ***balance*** = 0, output is "You have a surplus of cash"; ***balance***= –15, output is three lines: "You owe money," "Balance has been reset to 0.," "You have a surplus of cash." To change, eliminate the semicolon after the **end**, and replace **if** ***balance*** **>= *0* then** to **else**.

3.
```
if (playerNum = 7) and (playerNum mod 7 = 0) then
   Writeln('fizz-fuzz')
else if (playerNum = 7) or (playerNum mod 7 = 0) then
   Writeln('fizz')
else
   Writeln(playerNum);
```

4.
```
case place of
   1:
      Writeln('1st');
   2:
      Writeln('2nd');
   3:
      Writeln('3rd');
   otherwise
      Writeln(place:1, 'th')
end; { case }
```

5. A real expression cannot be used as the selector to a **case** statement. To fix, change the selector line to **case** ***Trunc(coin * 100)*** **of** and change the selector values to 100, 50, 25, 10, 5, and 1.

6.
```
var
    redPrice, bluePrice,          { price of colas                          }
    redSize, blueSize: real;      { size of cola cointainers, in ounces     }

begin
    Write('Enter the price and size of Red Cola');
    Readln(redPrice, redSize);
    Write('Enter the price and size of Blue Cola');
    Readln(bluePrice, blueSize);
    Writeln('Red Cola costs ', redPrice/redSize:3:1, 'cents per ounce');
    Writeln('Blue Cola costs ', bluePrice/blueSize:3:1, 'cents per ounce');
    if redPrice/redSize > bluePrice/blueSize then
        Writeln('Red Cola is the better buy.')
    else if redPrice/redSize < bluePrice/blueSize then
        Writeln('Blue Cola is the better buy.')
    else
        Writeln('Neither cola is a better buy.')
end; { procedure }
```

7.
```
if distance >= 0 then
    Writeln(distance)
else
    Writeln(distance * -1)
```

8. **begin** and **end** brackets needed around two assignment statements following **if**.

9.
```
if geneLikes and rogerLikes then
    Writeln('Two thumbs up')
else  if geneLikes or rogerLikes then
    Writeln('Split decision')
else
    Writeln('Two thumbs down');
```

10. Currently, any value of ***numToBuy*** over 10 will yield a 10% discount; to fix, change the conditions so ***numToBuy*** is compared to 30 first, followed by a comparison to 20, and finally a compairson to 10.

Chapter 5

1.
```
*
**
***
****
*****
```

2. initialization: lower limit; method of changing: automatically adds 1 to counter; exit condition: comparison of counter to upper limit.

3. 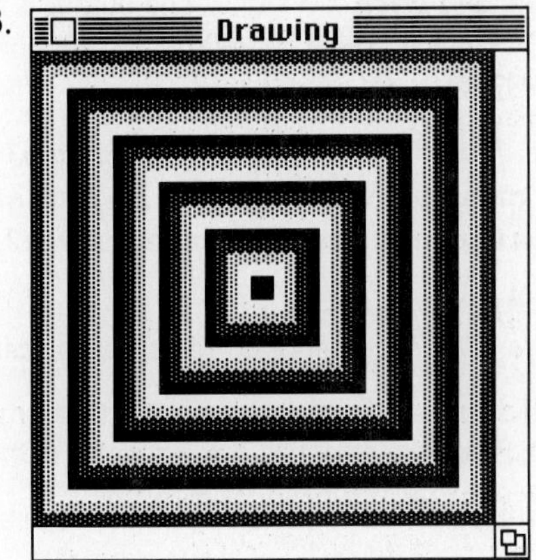

4. *a.* lists the even numbers from 2 to 98; *b.* will print the value 2 infinitely.

5. Currently, the code is an infinite loop; **begin** and **end** brackets should surround the three lines after the **while**. Also, ***total*** must be set to 0.

6. The **for** loop executes one too many times; to fix, change the lower limit from 1 to 2 or change first assignment statement to ***result := 1***.

7. Exits when ***winnings*** is greater than 5000 or ***winnings < losses***.

8. The code establishes one point when the user clicks the mouse button; then, it interactively draws a line from that first point to the mouse's current position until the user clicks the button again. (This technique is known as "rubberbanding.")

9. The first **repeat** can be changed to **while not *Button* do** — the first **until *Button;*** can be eliminated — the second **repeat** can be changed to **while not *Button* do** and **begin** — the second **until *Button*;** can be changed to **end;**.

10. It will be executed 1 + 2 + 3 + ... (***numPlayers*** – 1) + ***numPlayers*** times.

Chapter 6

1. No, because they act the same way within the **begin** and **end** brackets.

2. A value cannot be passed *back* to an expression.

3. A constant or an expression can be sent only to a value parameter; a variable can be sent to either a value or variable parameter.

4. A variable parameter is used when the value that you send might change and the sending procedure needs to know about that change.

5. A function is appropriate when you want to return a single value.

6. *a.* ***percent*** = 10.0 and ***price*** = 35.0; *b.* ***percent*** = 10.0 and ***price*** = 33.39; *c.* ***discount*** = 10.0 and ***price*** = 35.0; *d.* The output is the three lines "The sale price is $31.50," "The sale price is 10.00% off the normal price," and "With tax, the total price is 33.39."

7. *a.* both are value; *b.* ***num1, num2*** are variable, ***num3*** is value; *c.* ***num1*** is variable, ***num2, num3*** are value; *d.* ***num1*** is value, ***num2, num3*** are variable; *e.* ***num1, num3, num4*** are variable, ***num2, num5*** are value.

8. formal: ***SalePrice(percent, price);***
   actual: **procedure** ***SalePrice(percent: real;*** **var** ***price: real);***

9.
```
{ This function asks the user to choose a point with the mouse. When the user     }
{ chooses a point, PickPoint returns the coordinates of the point.                }

function PickPoint: point;          { returns point chosen by user   }

var
   horiz, vert: integer;            { coordinates of user's point    }
   userPoint: point;                { name of user's point           }
```

10. formal:
    procedure ***Init(*****var** ***count, total: integer;*** **var** ***average: real);***
    procedure ***Update(*****var** ***count, total, integer; newValue: integer; curAverage: real);***
    actual:
    Init(count, total, average);
    Update(count, total, number, average);

Chapter 7

11. Add declarations for local variables ***horizMid*** and ***vertMid***; put parentheses around ***left + right*** in first statement and ***top + bottom*** in second statement.

12. Change procedure body to:

```
begin
   done := FALSE;
   repeat
      Write('please enter a shoe size or ', sentinel : 2, ' to exit:');
      Readln(shoeSize);
      if (shoeSize <> sentinel) then
         CheckInventory(shoeSize, curStock);

      if curStock <= 0 then
         begin
            Writeln('no shoes left');
```

```
            done := TRUE
        end
    until done or (shoeSize = sentinel);
end; { ProcessShoeOrders }
```

13. Move ***arrange := 1;*** between **begin** of **while** loop and **for** statement.

Chapter 8

1. ***char*** is more appropriate when you need an ordinal type, such as the selector of a **case** statement.

2. **const**

```
       pop = '''';
```

3. The first statement is legal if ***start*** is declared as a boolean; the second statement is legal if ***start*** is declared as a **string.**

4. ***Length*** and ***Pos*** and ***Include*** return integers; ***Concat***, ***Copy***, ***Include*** and ***Omit*** return strings.

5. All are false except b.

6. *a*. 'A'; *b*. 'BCDEF'; *c*. run-time error caused

7. *a*. 5; *b*. 3; *c*. 'pizzapizza'; *d*. 'zz'; *e*. 4; *f*. 1; *g*. 3; *h*. 'za'; *i*. 0; *j*. 'zzpped'; *k*. 'zapped'

Chapter 9

1. ***Open*** opens a read-write file; ***Reset*** opens a read-only file; ***Rewrite*** opens a write-only file.

2. If treated as integers, there are 4 components; if treated as **string[8]**, there are 2 components.

3. If read as integers, component 0 is 555; if read as **string[8]**, component 0 is '5551212'.

4. The code prompts for an excuse which it reads from the keyboard and then writes to the file ***Excuses***. The prompting, reading, and writing continues until the user enters the sentinel string ***'NO MORE'***.

5. The ***Writeln*** statement cannot write to a read-only file.

6. The file contains the string ***'The second line'***.

7. *a*. at the first < eoln > marker; *b*. at the < eof > marker; *c*. at the top (component 0) of the file ***Something***.

8.
```
{ This program copies the contents of one file into another.          }
{ One line at a time is read from the first file and written into     }
{ the other. This stops when the end of the first file is reached.    }

program Exercise8;

  var
    inLine: string[40];                    { line to copy            }
    file1,                                 { original file           }
    file2: text;                           { file to become copy     }
```

Chapter 10

1. *a.* (Note that ***FrameArc*** does not affect a region definition) ;

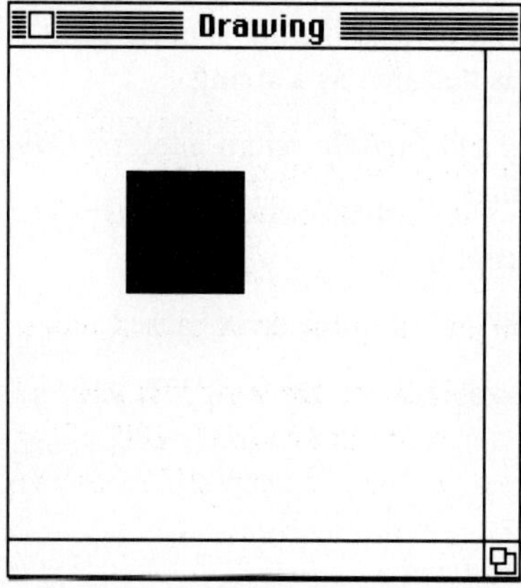

b.

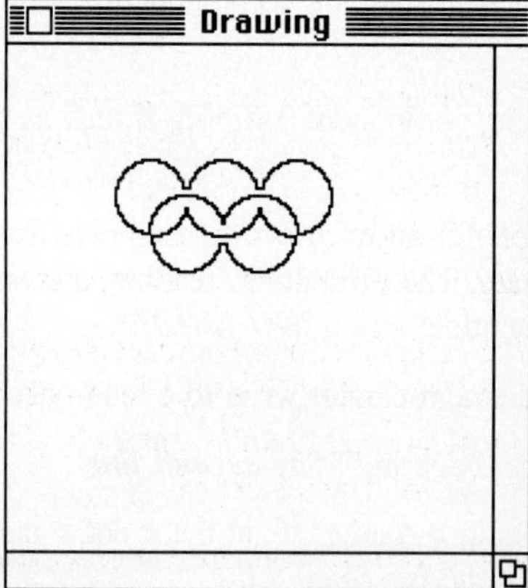

c., *d.* (*c* and *d* produce the same output)

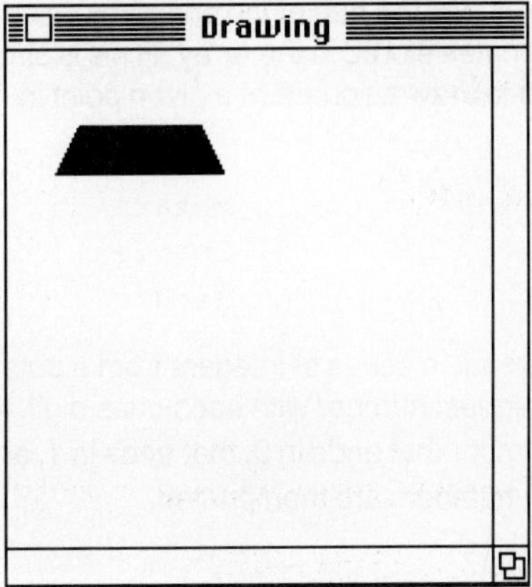

4. Among other things, writing external documentation before writing code helps to catch conceptual errors because it forces you to think out data structure and algorithm issues early on. It is easier to make design changes before the code is written than after.

5. Negative coordinates are possible in both coordinate systems.

6. The point (–70, – 40) in the Drawing window is the same as (242, 90) in the screen coordinate system; Drawing's (–100, 60) is screen's (212, 190); Drawing's (53, 82) is screen's (365, 212); Drawing's (15, – 45) is (327, 85).

Chapter 11

1. *a, b,* and *c* are legal since ***figure*** and ***number*** can both be used in place of ***integer*** in this code; *d* is illegal since ***digit*** is a ***char***.

2. *a.* illegal because elements must be increasing; *b.* legal; *c.* illegal because **array** declarations cannot be used in parameter lists (**type**s must be used instead); *d.* legal; *e.* illegal — to have a 2-dimensional array, the ranges should be rewritten as ***[1..size, 1..size]***; *f.* illegal for same reason as *c* ; *g.* illegal for same reason as *a* ; *h.* legal 2-dimensional array type declaration.

3. If ***key*** is not in the array, the loop will execute until ***curElem*** receives the value ***maxFlights*** + 1. At that point, when the loop condition is checked, both sides of the **and** will be evaluated, and the condition ***(flightNums[curElem] = key)*** will cause an out-of-bounds error.

4. When ***counter*** is 4, ***numbers*** contains (in order from 0 to 5) –1, 2, 16, 44, 9, 37. When ***counter*** is 5, ***numbers*** contains –1, 2, 9, 16, 44, 37.

5.
```
{ This procedure draws an object of up to 30 points. The          }
{ coordinates of the first point are chosen by the user. Then,    }
{ the procedure draws the rest of the shape by using the          }
{ relative coordinates stored in the array. (This is similar to   }
{ the code used to draw a square at a given point in Chapter 2)   }
```

6. *a.*
```
Mozart
Bach
Beatles
Bartlett
```
b.
```
2
3
1
4
```
c.
```
Bartlett
Mozart
Beatles
Bach
```

7.
```
{ This program reads a series of integers from a data file. It       }
{ picks out the highest number with each ones digit, that is,        }
{ the highest number that ends in 0, that ends in 1, and so on.      }
{ These highest numbers are then printed.                            }

program Concept7;

var
   most: array[0..9] of integer;            { highest with each digit   }
   key: integer;                            { current item from file    }
   ctr: integer;                            { loop counter              }
   dataFile: text;                          { file of numbers           }
```

8.
```
const
   male = 1;                                { codes for attributes      }
   female = 2;
   drama = 1;
   comedy = 2;
   singing = 3;
   dancing = 4;
   ageLess13 = 1;
   age13_17 = 2;
   age18_25 = 3;
   age26_35 = 4;
   age36_45 = 5;
   age46_60 = 6;
   ageOver60 = 7;

type
   performers = array[male..female, drama..dancing, ageLess13..ageOver60]
      of integer;

var
   guild: performers;
```

a.
```
   Writeln(guild[male, comedy, age36_45]);
```

b.

```
answer := 0;
for talent := drama to dancing do
    for age := age26_35 to ageOver60 do
        answer := answer + guild[female, talent, age];
Writeln(answer);
```

c.

```
answer := 0;
for sex:= male to female do
    for age := ageLess13 to ageOver60 do
        answer := answer + guild[sex, singing, age];
Writeln(answer);
```

d.

```
answer := 0;
for sex:= male to female do
    for age := ageLess13 to age18_25 do
        answer := answer + guild[sex, dancing, age];
Writeln(answer);
```

9. Subscript in ***Writeln*** should be ***[(ctr* mod *5) + 1]***.

Chapter 12

1. A record is more appropriate than an array when you want to store more than one type of data in the same compound variable.
2. Several answers are possible; note that not all need records.
4. *a.* legal; *b.* illegal (expects a string); *c.* legal; *d.* illegal (variable name, not type, should be in **with** statement); *e.* illegal (***total*** is a **string** in ***second***); *f.* illegal (records are of different types); *g.* illegal (***real*** is not a field name).
6. *a.* illegal (cannot assign records of different types); *b* through *e* are all legal.
7. *a.* incorrect (***locType*** should be ***location***); *b.* correct; *c.* incorrect (***houseNum*** is not an array, so it cannot take an index; ***street[ctr]*** will print an individual character); *d.* incorrect (***locType*** should be ***location***); *e.* incorrect (record names missing; also same problem as *c*); *f.* correct.

Chapter 13

1. **type**

```
    colors = (Ivory, Orange, Yellow, Blue, Green, Red);
    rubik = array[1..3, 1..3, 1..3] of colors;
```

2. Integers (2..10) cannot be used in enumerated type.
3. The original value of ***curFrame***.

4. Real numbers are treated as if there was no definite interval between them. Thus, we do not have "consecutive" real numbers.

5. [ ], [Dull], [Ok], [Exciting], [Dull, Ok], [Dull, Exciting], [Ok, Exciting], [Dull, Ok, Exciting]

6. < set 1 > – <set 2 > yields an empty set when < set 1> is equal to < set 2 >; the maximum size of the difference is the size of < set 1 >.

7. Prints output as follows:

```
The number       1 place finisher is < winner[Gold] >
The number       2 place finisher is < winner[Silver] >
The number       3 place finisher is < winner[Bronze] >
```

8. *a.* [Elvis, Platters, Fats, Beatles, Stones, Dylan, Springsteen]; *b.* [Stones, Dylan]; *c.* FALSE; *d.* [Supremes, Beatles, Stones, Dylan, Springsteen]; *e.* [Supremes, Platters]; *f.* FALSE; *g.* FALSE; *h.* [Supremes, Bangles]; *i.* TRUE; *j.* TRUE

10. A boolean can be used as a tag field because it is an enumerated type and is thus ordinal; a set and a real cannot be used as a tag field because they are not ordinal types.

Chapter 14

1. Any element in an array can be accessed immediately (if you know the subscript); elements in linked lists must be accessed sequentially. When inserting information into an array, you are limited by the size of an array; a linked list can have any number of nodes. If the information is being kept in sorted order, you have to move a number of items in an array when you insert or delete any element; in a linked list, the only elements that are affected by insertion or deletion are the node's neighbors.

2. The statement is not legal because ***ptToInt*** is a pointer not an integer. To correct it, we can use the statement ***ptToInt^ := 750;***.

3. A dummy header node makes insertion into a sorted linked list easier because the same algorithm can be used to add all elements. Without a dummy header, a different algorithm would have to be used to add the first node in a list.

4. 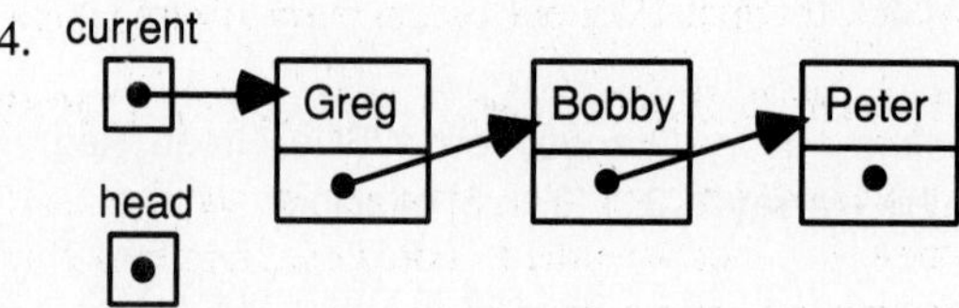

5. 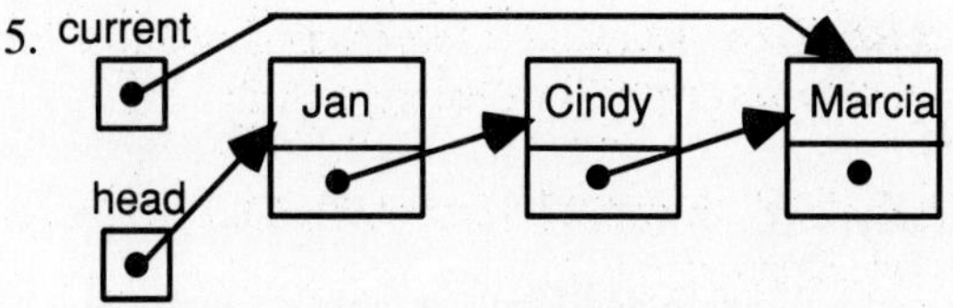

6. If ***current^.name* = *head^.name***, it is not necessarily true that ***current* = *head***. (The two pointers could be pointing at different nodes with one equal field.) The converse, however, is true.

9. Change ***prev^.name*** to ***prev^.next^.name*** in **while** condition; switch last two assignment statements.

10. 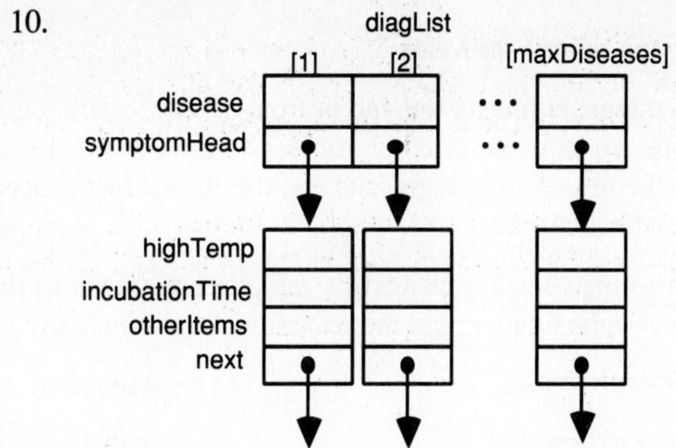

Chapter 15

1. Some procedures that would be useful to call: the procedure that returns the menu option selected by the user; the procedure that makes some options turn gray; the procedure that highlights the option when selected.

2. Two possible representations (others are possible): an array of records, where each record contains the title, author, and call number for a book, or a linked list of records, where each record contains the title, author, and call number, plus a pointer to the next book in the list.

5. Not possible; if 1 is first in, it must be first out.

6. A, B, C, D, E (final Dequeue causes error message, since no elements are left)

7. **Push 1, Push 2, Pop 2, Push 3, Pop 3, Pop 1, Push 4, Pop 4**

8. The 2 is pushed on top of the 1; therefore, the 2 must be popped before the 1 can be popped. It is not possible to pop something buried in the stack until everything above it has been popped.

9. A, C, D, B, E (final Pop causes error message, since no elements are left)

Chapter 16

1. 100.08

2. When ***days***= 0.

3. (Uses same function and local variable declarations.)

```
begin
    newBal := balance;
    for ctr := 1 to days do
        newBal := newBal * (1+intRate/365)
end; { Compound }
```

4. **div**

5. Function returns the value 5.

6. Two things: eliminate the **var** in front of the declaration of ***level*** and, so the routine works even for empty trees, add the condition **if *current* <> nil then** after the procedure's **begin** and enclose the current procedure body inside **begin/end** brackets.

7. Each recursive call must involve simpler arguments so that the problem becomes successively simpler, and the recursion must eventually bottom out.

8. 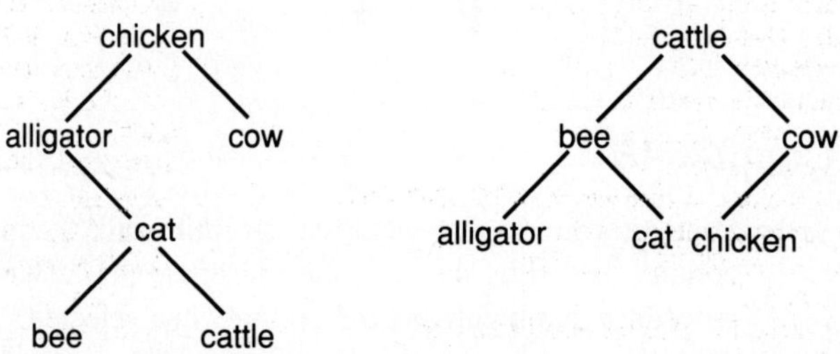

9. In a linear list, the worst case is looking at 35 items; the average case is looking at 35/2 or 17.5 items. In a balanced binary tree, the worst case is looking at 6 items; the average case is looking at $\log_2 35$, or 5.1 items.

10. And in the end, we find the beginning.

Index